Classic Readings in Philosophy

Stan Baronett

Alinea Learning

Boston

Alinea Learning

Boston, Massachusetts

Published in the United States by Alinea Learning, an imprint and division of Alinea Knowledge, LLC, Boston.

Visit our website at **www.alinealearning.com.**

Library of Congress Cataloging-in-Publication Data is available on file.

Print book ISBN: 979-8-9878531-0-8

eBook ISBN: 979-8-9878531-1-5

Table of Contents

Part One: The Role of Philosophy **1**

Part Two: The Value of Philosophy **5**

Bertrand Russell

THE VALUE OF PHILOSOPHY 7

Part Three: Reality **11**

Plato

THE DIVIDED LINE, AND THE CAVE 13

Aristotle

FIRST PRINCIPLES 19

Margaret Cavendish

OBSERVATIONS 25

John Locke

PRIMARY AND SECONDARY QUALITIES 29

Gottfried Leibniz

THE BUILDING BLOCKS OF REALITY 33

George Berkeley

TO BE IS TO BE PERCEIVED 43

David Hume

COMMIT IT TO THE FLAMES` 49

Mary Shepherd

IDEAS 55

Immanuel Kant

REGARDING AN EXTERNAL WORLD 63

Part Four: Knowledge **67**

Plato

KNOWLEDGE IS RECOLLECTION 69

Aristotle

A WRITING TABLET 77

Augustine

THE POSSIBILITY OF DECEPTION 79

René Descartes

DOUBT AND CERTAINTY 81

John Locke

KNOWLEDGE DERIVES FROM EXPERIENCE 89

Gottfried Leibniz

DEEP INSIDE 95

Mary Astell

DEGREES OF CLEARNESS 97

David Hume

MATTERS OF FACT AND RELATIONS OF IDEAS 101

Immanuel Kant

THE POSSIBILITY OF EXPERIENCE 107

Charles S. Peirce

THE FIXATION OF BELIEF 113

Part Five: God 119

5A. Can God's Existence Be Proved Based on Experience? 121

Plato

THE BEGINNING OF EVERYTHING 123

Thomas Aquinas

THE FIVE WAYS 125

Gottfried Leibniz

SUFFICIENT REASON 127

George Berkeley

THE AUTHOR OF NATURE 129

William Paley

THE WATCHMAKER ARGUMENT 133

David Hume

AGAINST THE WATCHMAKER ARGUMENT 137

5B. Can God's Existence Be Proved Independent of Experience? 143

Anselm of Canterbury

THE EXISTENCE OF GOD 145

René Descartes
THE IDEA OF GOD 147
Anne Conway
ON GOD 151
David Hume
WHY IS THERE SOMETHING RATHER THAN NOTHING? 155
5C. Why Do Suffering and Evil Exist? 157
Gottfried Leibniz
THE EXISTENCE OF EVIL AND SUFFERING 159
George Hayward Joyce
THE PROBLEM OF EVIL 169
David Hume
SUFFERING AND EVIL 173
5D. Belief 185
Blaise Pascal
THE WAGER 187
Damaris Cudworth Masham
A NATURAL INSCRIPTION 191
Friedrich Nietzsche
THE END OF AN IDEA 195
William K. Clifford
THE ETHICS OF BELIEF 197
William James
THE WILL TO BELIEVE 203
Part Six: Mind and Body 209
René Descartes
MIND AND BODY 213
Margaret Cavendish
A DOUBLE PERCEPTION 215
Anne Conway
ONE AND THE SAME THING 219
William James
DOES CONSCIOUSNESS EXIST? 223

John Locke

IDENTITY AND DIVERSITY 231

David Hume

I AM A BUNDLE OF PERCEPTIONS 237

Part Seven: Free Will 239

John Locke

FREE AGENTS 241

Baruch Spinoza

EVERYTHING HAPPENS OUT OF NECESSITY 247

David Hume

OF LIBERTY AND NECESSITY 249

Immanuel Kant

FREEDOM OF THE WILL 259

Paul-Henri d'Holbach

A SERIES OF NECESSARY MOMENTS 267

Part Eight: Morality 273

Plato

WHY SHOULD WE BE GOOD? 275

Aristotle

VIRTUES 283

David Hume

MORALITY IS DETERMINED BY SENTIMENT 289

Immanuel Kant

DUTY 295

John Stuart Mill

THE PRINCIPLE OF UTILITY 299

Friedrich Nietzsche

A FREE SPIRIT 309

Thomas H. Huxley

EVOLUTION AND ETHICS 315

Part Nine: Political and Social Philosophy 321

Plato

APOLOGY 323

Plato

SHOULD I OBEY THE LAWS? 339

Aristotle

A POLITICAL ANIMAL 349

Thomas Hobbes

SOLITARY, POOR, NASTY, BRUTISH, AND SHORT 351

John Locke

FOR THE GOOD OF THE PEOPLE 357

Catharine Macaulay

OBSERVATIONS ON REVOLUTION 361

John Stuart Mill

LIBERTY 365

Karl Marx and Friedrich Engels

WORKERS OF THE WORLD, UNITE! 373

Mary Wollstonecraft

A VINDICATION OF THE RIGHTS OF WOMAN 381

Part Ten: Art and Aesthetics 385

Aristotle

TRAGEDY 387

Henri Bergson

AN ANIMAL WHICH LAUGHS, AND IS LAUGHED AT 391

George Santayana

A PLEDGE OF THE POSSIBLE 397

Arthur Schopenhauer

ART TAKES AWAY THE MIST 399

Part Eleven: Does Life Have Meaning? 403

Epicurus

IN WAKING OR IN DREAM 405

Arthur Schopenhauer

THE VANITY OF EXISTENCE 409

William James

IS LIFE WORTH LIVING? 413

Bertrand Russell
FATE IS SUBDUED BY THE MIND 423

Preface

The overriding rationale behind this book is the desire to enrich the lives of college students by introducing them to philosophical thinking in an accessible and engaging manner. The classic selections were chosen to provide personal moments of reflection as students embark upon a journey into philosophy.

The opening section, "The Role of Philosophy," provides a general introduction to philosophy. It uses real-life examples to illustrate how philosophical thinking touches all aspects of our lives, and how it is connected to other academic disciplines. Thereafter, each philosophical area, such as the nature of reality, knowledge, God, free will, and morality, has its own introduction offering further framework and context. These features allow students to connect with the content in an intuitive, natural manner. The surrounding narrative is designed to be conversational and comprehensible. The intent is to furnish a clear path through the material that enables readers to get started in understanding each philosopher's ideas and arguments. The table of contents presents each instructor with the opportunity to choose a set of readings that matches the individual needs of each class.

The goal of any introduction to philosophy anthology should be a selection of readings that stimulate us. Since there are thousands of possible readings that one can choose from, every anthology must make choices. The editing process for this anthology was driven by the need to include material that is challenging, yet accessible. The emphasis on classical readings reveals the rich and varied history of philosophy, and it provides a foundation for understanding modern philosophers' ideas and writings. The readings are long enough to develop important philosophical issues, yet short enough to concentrate on a few topics. The readings are meant to stimulate immediate reflection and offer a platform for discussion.

Part One: The Role of Philosophy

Lively conversations often jump from one topic to another. You probably have experienced being part of a spirited discussion where, at some point, you wondered how the conversation wound up talking about something that seemed to have no connection to where the discussion started. On another occasion, perhaps you were looking for one thing on the Internet and, after several links, you found yourself reading something that seemed far away from where you began. This common occurrence points to the interrelatedness of knowledge.

Philosophy has been defined in many ways, such as "the quest for knowledge," "the love of wisdom," "the search for truth," or "the asking of ultimate questions." Since philosophers do ask questions and propose answers, in a general sense they are similar to scientists, physicians, lawyers, engineers, economists, psychologists, and those in many other professions. Since each of those fields developed its own methods and criteria for acquiring knowledge, in one sense the knowledge of one field is independent of the others. However, even though each field has its particular area of questions and phenomena that it studies, ultimately all knowledge is connected. In fact, interdisciplinary studies attempt to build bridges between different academic fields by recognizing that research in one area can often provide what is missing in another area, or shine a new light on the outstanding questions, or even open up completely new avenues of research.

Philosophy plays an important role in all aspects of intellectual activity. In fact, every major scientific discipline was once part of philosophy. Physics, chemistry, biology, and astronomy are studied by those we now call "scientists," but they were originally called "natural philosophers" (meaning that they studied the *nature* of the physical universe). While many people may imagine Albert Einstein working in a laboratory or gazing through a telescope, his theory of relativity was born from a "thought experiment" that was inspired when he envisioned flying through space at the speed of light.

After graduating from college, Einstein worked as a clerk in the Swiss government patent office. One day, while he was riding home on a streetcar, Einstein noticed the time on a large clock tower. He knew that the information he received from the clock—let's say the time was 6:05—travelled to his eyes by light rays. From this simple everyday event, Einstein made a leap of imagination. He wondered what would happen if he "jumped on the light ray" that carried the time information. He realized immediately that, for him, the time on the clock tower would always be 6:05, because no other light rays could catch up to him. But even more remarkable, Einstein knew that the time on his pocket-watch would keep running as normal. Against the prevailing view of the concept of time, Einstein's radical new idea was that *time* is not absolute; it is relative to our perspective.

Philosophy also played an important part in the development of many of the most recent social science disciplines. For example, philosophers' writings have been the source of psychology, sociology, political science, and economics, to name just a few subjects. Given this, it is not surprising that philosophical questions still echo throughout most modern academic fields.

It is not difficult to see the interrelatedness of knowledge. Let's look at just one example—the problem of crime. Imagine that your brother was rushed to a hospital after collapsing at home. At the hospital you are informed that he has died, and an autopsy is going to be performed in order to find the physical cause of death. The results of the autopsy can be used to help answer your question, "Why did my brother die?"

Scientific advances in forensics, human pathology, chemical analysis, and many other fields allow medical examiners to often pinpoint a precise cause of death. Now suppose that you are told that a lethal dose of an illegal drug was found to be the cause of your brother's death. Your initial reaction might be one of astonishment, especially if you had no knowledge of any drug use by your brother. Perhaps you would need more assurance that there was not some mistake made by the medical examiners, or with the lab results.

When you ask how the physical cause of death has been determined, you are asking questions about knowledge. The area of philosophy that investigates these kinds of questions is called "epistemology." The root word "episteme" means "to know," and the suffix "-logy" means "the study of," so *epistemology* is simply the *study of knowledge*. This branch of philosophy has developed a close relationship with science because scientific advances have become the hallmark of knowledge of the physical world. Therefore, questioning how we know the cause of death would get at the scientific reliability and validity of forensic science, which in this case determines the physical cause of death.

We ask epistemological questions whenever we ask questions such as these:

- How do you know that he died of a drug overdose?
- How do you know that the plane crash was caused by pilot error?
- How do you know that cigarettes can cause lung cancer?
- How do you know that increasing literacy and education reduces racism?
- How do you know that massive doses of Vitamin C have no effect on the common cold?

The epistemological foundation of scientific knowledge of the physical world is also part of the next stage in our investigation—to determine how the drug entered your brother's bloodstream. At this point, law enforcement will get involved in the investigation in order to determine whether the drug was self-administered or whether your brother was the victim of a murder. If the police suspect foul play, then evidence is sought that might lead to the perpetrator. Centuries ago, proving murder was quite difficult. If there were no eyewitnesses to a crime, then objective evidence was hard to gather. And even eyewitness accounts are often unreliable evidence.

In the late 1800s, an interesting hypothesis was developed to help in crime detection. It was known that the eye acts like the lens of a camera; in fact, cameras and film were developed to mimic the way our eyes work. When our eyelids are raised, light strikes the outer part of our eyes and signals are sent to the brain. In a camera, when the shutter opens, light strikes the lens and is projected onto film, which records the picture. It was conjectured that since our eyes act like cameras, then they might "record" the last image seen by a murder victim. The murderer's image should be recorded somewhere in the victim's eye. The problem was how to "develop" the image. Various techniques were developed, none of which worked. Although the hypothesis proved to be unfounded, the idea has been used in novels and was given a humorous depiction in the movie *Wild, Wild West.*

Over the course of the last one hundred years, advancements in crime detection were developed. Fingerprint evidence was one of the first tools used successfully in criminology. Scientific methods for determining blood type proved valuable, and recently, DNA analysis has been introduced. Of course, all these inventions had to be validated as being reliable objective evidence. If a method does not pass scrutiny in the scientific community, it will probably not be admissible in a court of law. For example, lie detector results are typically not admitted as evidence because the process has not been proven to be a reliable source of objective evidence.

Now suppose that after a thorough investigation, it has been determined that your brother was murdered, and someone is arrested. The next step is the murder trial, the legal aspect of the crime. Criminal trials rely on both the physical evidence (the epistemological questions) and the *logical* arguments of the prosecution and the defense. Here we can see the difference between the concept of *proof* and that of *beyond a reasonable doubt.* Criminal trials do not offer proof in the mathematical and logical sense of valid arguments, which are defined as arguments where the conclusion *follows with necessity* from premises. Instead, the prosecution must establish guilt "beyond a reasonable doubt," a concept that has within it the idea of uncertainty. In fact, the concept is not precisely defined by judges when they give directions to juries. Jurors are told to use their consciences when deliberating. (In contrast, civil trials rely on a weaker standard, referred to as "the preponderance of evidence," which is based on the probable truth or accuracy of the evidence.) The jury must decide the strengths and weaknesses of both the defense and prosecutor's arguments. This is both an *epistemological issue* (e.g., the physical evidence and expert testimony) and a *logical issue* (e.g., deciding which is stronger—the prosecution's argument or the defense's argument). In other words, the amount of doubt that exists in the minds of the jurors.

If the trial ends with a guilty verdict, then it enters the punishment phase. Here the philosophical questions concern the areas of *ethics* and *political philosophy*. Any determination of punishment must be grounded in morality, and, since this is a legal case, philosophical questions regarding laws and governments play a big part as well.

There is a fictional story that cleverly illustrates some of these related issues. A man has been found guilty of a crime and is about to be sentenced. The judge asks the defendant if he has anything to say before she announces the sentence. The man says the following:

> I admit that I committed the crime. However, I took an introduction to philosophy course and we studied the issue of free will. If humans have free will, then they have ethical choices for which they are responsible. So, if I freely chose to commit the crime, then my punishment can be justified. But, if humans have no free will, if our behavior is completely determined, like everything else in the physical universe, then we do not choose to commit crimes—we cannot help ourselves. If that is so, then we should not be punished for doing something we were predetermined to do. I have come to believe that we do not have free will. Therefore, judge, you should not punish me.

Upon hearing this, the judge says the following:

> I also took an introduction to philosophy course, and I have thought about the same issues. In fact, I even came to the same conclusion as you—I believe

> that we do not have free will. Therefore, I am sentencing you to life in prison—but I am *not choosing to do it*, my decision has been completely determined.

The story also introduces another area of philosophy—*metaphysics*. This branch of philosophy deals with what are often called "the ultimate questions of reality." These include questions regarding the nature of reality, the existence of God, whether or not humans have free will, and whether mind and matter exist.

There are other types of philosophical questions that are connected to this case. For example, suppose after your brother's death, you go to your religious leader and ask the same question you asked in the hospital—"Why did my brother die?" If your religious leader responds by saying that your brother died from a lethal dose of an illegal drug, you would be surprised. Even though the question is the same, you are *not* seeking a *physical cause answer*, you already have that. Rather, you are now seeking some guidance regarding the *reason* or *purpose* of your brother's death; you need to make some sense of the *meaning* of his death. You might even begin asking yourself some important questions: Does life have any meaning, or is it absurd? Would a good God allow suffering and evil to exist? As you can see, these questions are quite different from those we have been considering.

Philosophy touches on all aspects of life. Our hypothetical example, about a death and a crime, illustrates the philosophical aspects of *epistemology, science, law, logic, ethics, politics, government, metaphysics, and the meaning of life*. On any given day you will find many additional examples of philosophical issues at work in your local and global community. To understand the interrelated aspects of the important questions of life requires contemplating the philosophical questions that lie at the heart of all human understanding. This contemplation involves challenging personal assumptions and conventional wisdom—very powerful skills. The ancient Athenian government found them so powerful and threatening that it condemned Socrates to death by drinking a cup of hemlock. There is no hemlock in the following chapters, just nourishing food for thought that is valuable for all career paths and other worldly pursuits.

Part Two: The Value of Philosophy

The goal of this book is to lay the groundwork for appreciating philosophy and its ideas. To help us, Bertrand Russell's "The Value of Philosophy," provides a clear and useful way to understand philosophy's value. Although Russell placed this piece at the end of his short book, *The Problems of Philosophy*, we will use it to begin understanding how philosophy is intimately connected to everything we do and experience throughout our lives. In that sense, Russell addresses our futures.

The problems of philosophy are timeless. They touch all our lives. In the hustle and congestion of life—especially in the information age in which we live—the profound philosophical questions can get lost amidst the torrent of data immediately available every instant. But sooner or later quiet introspection reaches all of us. It may be triggered by a tragedy, or by a sense of loneliness; it can even happen in moments of happiness and bliss. At those times, having an intimate connection to the important ideas that have been thought about, wrestled with, and argued over for centuries, provides a way of appreciating the complexity of life and the incredible human capacity for understanding.

Bertrand Russell

THE VALUE OF PHILOSOPHY

It will be well to consider what is the value of philosophy and why it ought to be studied. It is the more necessary to consider this question, in view of the fact that many men, under the influence of science or of practical affairs, are inclined to doubt whether philosophy is anything better than innocent but useless trifling, hair-splitting distinctions, and controversies on matters concerning which knowledge is impossible.

This view of philosophy appears to result, partly from a wrong conception of the ends of life, partly from a wrong conception of the kind of goods which philosophy strives to achieve. Physical science, through the medium of inventions, is useful to innumerable people who are wholly ignorant of it; thus the study of physical science is to be recommended, not only, or primarily, because of the effect on the student, but rather because of the effect on mankind in general. This utility does not belong to philosophy. If the study of philosophy has any value at all for others than students of philosophy, it must be only indirectly, through its effects upon the lives of those who study it. It is in these effects, therefore, if anywhere, that the value of philosophy must be primarily sought.

But further, if we are not to fail in our endeavor to determine the value of philosophy, we must first free our minds from the prejudices of what are wrongly called "practical" men. The "practical" man, as this word is often used, is one who recognizes only material needs, who realizes that men must have food for the body, but is oblivious of the necessity of providing food for the mind. If all men were well off, if poverty and disease had been reduced to their lowest possible point, there would still remain much to be done to produce a valuable society; and even in the existing world the goods of the mind are at least as important as the goods of the body. It is exclusively among the goods of the mind that the value of philosophy is to be found; and only those who are not indifferent to these goods can be persuaded that the study of philosophy is not a waste of time.

Philosophy, like all other studies, aims primarily at knowledge. The knowledge it aims at is the kind of knowledge which gives unity and system to the body of the sciences, and the kind which results from a critical examination of the grounds of our convictions, prejudices, and beliefs. But it cannot be maintained that philosophy has had any very great measure of success in its attempts to provide definite answers to its questions. If you ask a mathematician, a mineralogist, a historian, or any other man of learning, what definite body of truths has been ascertained by his science, his answer will last as long as you are willing to listen. But if you put the same question to a philosopher, he will, if he is candid, have to confess that his study has not achieved positive results such as have been achieved by other sciences. It is true that this is partly accounted for by the fact that, as soon as definite knowledge concerning any subject becomes possible, this subject ceases to be called philosophy, and becomes a separate science. The whole study of the heavens, which now belongs to astronomy, was once included in philosophy; Newton's great work was called "the mathematical principles of natural philosophy." Similarly, the study of the human mind, which was a part of philosophy, has now been separated from philosophy and has become the science of psychology. Thus, to a great extent, the uncertainty of philosophy is more apparent than real: those questions which are already capable of definite answers are placed in the sciences, while

Edited from *The Problems of Philosophy,* 1912, Chapter XV which is now in the public domain.

those only to which, at present, no definite answer can be given, remain to form the residue which is called philosophy.

This is, however, only a part of the truth concerning the uncertainty of philosophy. There are many questions—and among them those that are of the profoundest interest to our spiritual life—which, so far as we can see, must remain insoluble to the human intellect unless its powers become of quite a different order from what they are now. Has the universe any unity of plan or purpose, or is it a fortuitous concourse of atoms? Is consciousness a permanent part of the universe, giving hope of indefinite growth in wisdom, or is it a transitory accident on a small planet on which life must ultimately become impossible? Are good and evil of importance to the universe or only to man? Such questions are asked by philosophy, and variously answered by various philosophers. But it would seem that, whether answers be otherwise discoverable or not, the answers suggested by philosophy are none of them demonstrably true. Yet, however slight may be the hope of discovering an answer, it is part of the business of philosophy to continue the consideration of such questions, to make us aware of their importance, to examine all the approaches to them, and to keep alive that speculative interest in the universe which is apt to be killed by confining ourselves to definitely ascertainable knowledge.

Many philosophers, it is true, have held that philosophy could establish the truth of certain answers to such fundamental questions. They have supposed that what is of most importance in religious beliefs could be proved by strict demonstration to be true. In order to judge of such attempts, it is necessary to take a survey of human knowledge, and to form an opinion as to its methods and its limitations. On such a subject it would be unwise to pronounce dogmatically; but if the investigations of our previous chapters have not led us astray, we shall be compelled to renounce the hope of finding philosophical proofs of religious beliefs. We cannot, therefore, include as part of the value of philosophy any definite set of answers to such questions. Hence, once more, the value of philosophy must not depend upon any supposed body of definitely ascertainable knowledge to be acquired by those who study it.

The value of philosophy is, in fact, to be sought largely in its very uncertainty. The man who has no tincture of philosophy goes through life imprisoned in the prejudices derived from common sense, from the habitual beliefs of his age or his nation, and from convictions which have grown up in his mind without the co-operation or consent of his deliberate reason. To such a man the world tends to become definite, finite, obvious; common objects rouse no questions, and unfamiliar possibilities are contemptuously rejected. As soon as we begin to philosophize, on the contrary, we find, as we saw in our opening chapters, that even the most everyday things lead to problems to which only very incomplete answers can be given. Philosophy, though unable to tell us with certainty what is the true answer to the doubts which it raises, is able to suggest many possibilities which enlarge our thoughts and free them from the tyranny of custom. Thus, while diminishing our feeling of certainty as to what things are, it greatly increases our knowledge as to what they may be; it removes the somewhat arrogant dogmatism of those who have never travelled into the region of liberating doubt, and it keeps alive our sense of wonder by showing familiar things in an unfamiliar aspect.

Apart from its utility in showing unsuspected possibilities, philosophy has a value—perhaps its chief value—through the greatness of the objects which it contemplates, and the freedom from narrow and personal aims resulting from this contemplation. The life of the instinctive man is shut up within the circle of his private interests: family and friends may be included, but the outer world is not regarded except as it may help or hinder what comes within the circle of instinctive wishes. In such a life there is something feverish and confined, in comparison with which the philosophic life is calm and free. The private world of instinctive interests is a small one, set in the midst of a great and powerful world which must, sooner or later, lay our private world in ruins. Unless we can so enlarge our interests as to include the whole outer world, we remain like a garrison in a beleaguered fortress, knowing that the enemy prevents escape and that ultimate surrender is inevitable. In such a life there is no peace, but a constant strife between the insistence of desire and the powerlessness of will. In one way or another, if our life is to be great and free, we must escape this prison and this strife.

One way of escape is by philosophic contemplation. Philosophic contemplation does not, in its widest survey, divide the universe into two hostile camps—friends and foes, helpful and hostile, good and bad—it views the whole impartially. Philosophic contemplation, when it is unalloyed, does not aim at proving that the rest of the universe is akin to man. All acquisition of knowledge is an enlargement of the Self, but this enlargement is best attained when it is not directly sought. It is obtained when the desire for knowledge is alone operative, by a study which does not wish in advance that its objects should have this or that character, but adapts the Self to the characters which it finds in its objects. This enlargement of Self is not obtained when, taking the Self as it is, we try to show that the world is so similar to this Self that knowledge of it is possible without any admission of what seems alien. The desire to prove this is a form of self-assertion and, like all self-assertion, it is an obstacle to the growth of Self which it desires, and of which the Self knows that it is capable. Self-assertion, in philosophic speculation as elsewhere, views the world as a means to its own ends; thus it makes the world of less account than Self, and the Self sets bounds to the greatness of its goods. In contemplation, on the contrary, we start from the not-Self, and through its greatness the boundaries of Self are enlarged; through the infinity of the universe the mind which contemplates it achieves some share in infinity.

For this reason greatness of soul is not fostered by those philosophies which assimilate the universe to Man. Knowledge is a form of union of Self and not-Self; like all union, it is impaired by dominion, and therefore by any attempt to force the universe into conformity with what we find in ourselves. There is a widespread philosophical tendency towards the view which tells us that Man is the measure of all things, that truth is man-made, that space and time and the world of universals are properties of the mind, and that, if there be anything not created by the mind, it is unknowable and of no account for us. This view, if our previous discussions were correct, is untrue; but in addition to being untrue, it has the effect of robbing philosophic contemplation of all that gives it value, since it fetters contemplation to Self. What it calls knowledge is not a union with the not-Self, but a set of prejudices, habits, and desires, making an impenetrable veil between us and the world beyond. The man who finds pleasure in such a theory of knowledge is like the man who never leaves the domestic circle for fear his word might not be law.

The true philosophic contemplation, on the contrary, finds its satisfaction in every enlargement of the not-Self, in everything that magnifies the objects contemplated, and thereby the subject contemplating. Everything, in contemplation, that is personal or private, everything that depends upon habit, self-interest, or desire, distorts the object, and hence impairs the union which the intellect seeks. By thus making a barrier between subject and object, such personal and private things become a prison to the intellect. The free intellect will see as God might see, without a here and now, without hopes and fears, without the trammels of customary beliefs and traditional prejudices, calmly, dispassionately, in the sole and exclusive desire of knowledge—knowledge as impersonal, as purely contemplative, as it is possible for man to attain. Hence also the free intellect will value more the abstract and universal knowledge into which the accidents of private history do not enter, than the knowledge brought by the senses, and dependent, as such knowledge must be, upon an exclusive and personal point of view and a body whose sense-organs distort as much as they reveal.

The mind which has become accustomed to the freedom and impartiality of philosophic contemplation will preserve something of the same freedom and impartiality in the world of action and emotion. It will view its purposes and desires as parts of the whole, with the absence of insistence that results from seeing them as infinitesimal fragments in a world of which all the rest is unaffected by any one man's deeds. The impartiality which, in contemplation, is the unalloyed desire for truth, is the very same quality of mind which, in action, is justice, and in emotion is that universal love which can be given to all, and not only to those who are judged useful or admirable. Thus contemplation enlarges not only the objects of our thoughts, but also the objects of our actions and our affections: it makes us citizens of the universe, not only of one walled city at war with all the rest. In this citizenship of the universe consists man's true freedom, and his liberation from the thraldom of narrow hopes and fears.

Thus, to sum up our discussion of the value of philosophy: Philosophy is to be studied, not for the sake of any definite answers to its questions, since no definite answers can, as a rule, be known to be true, but rather for the sake of the questions themselves; because these questions enlarge our conception of what is possible, enrich our intellectual imagination and diminish the dogmatic assurance which closes the mind against speculation; but above all because, through the greatness of the universe which philosophy contemplates, the mind also is rendered great, and becomes capable of that union with the universe which constitutes its highest good.

Part Three: Reality

Introduction

As you might expect, each area of philosophy has developed ways of talking about the questions and issues that fall under its domain. Yet in this respect, philosophy is no different from any other attempt to understand the world. All academic disciplines, businesses, and nearly every kind human endeavor or enterprise has its own set of technical terms. For thousands of years, philosophers have asked important questions: *What is reality? Is reality one thing or many things?* These are general questions about the nature of reality.

For most nonphilosophers, reality comes in two flavors: *matter* and *mind*. In other words, most people would say they have both a *brain* (physical; composed of matter), and a *mind* (nonphysical). One person might believe that her mind can exist independently of her brain, while another person might hold that his mind dies along with his brain. Some people are partial to the mental world (thoughts and ideas), while others prefer the physical world (sensations and motion).

We might ask, "Can reality be conceived or understood directly through reason (the mind)?" On the other hand, we may ask, "Can reality be perceived or experienced through our five senses (matter)?" Some people have even asked, "Are we even capable of understanding reality?"

In many ways, these questions and concerns are the most fundamental of all. After all, if we cannot determine the nature of reality, then how can we ever understand how knowledge is possible? In other words, if we cannot grasp reality, then our knowledge is about—*what?* For example, if your are a *materialist* (someone who believes that reality consists of physical objects), then you probably believe that some truths about reality can be known through experience (through the five senses). On the other hand, if you are a *rationalist*, then you probably believe that some truths about reality can be understood through reason alone (independent of sense experience).

Even at an early age, humans seem inclined to these questions. Although a child's questions may be simple (especially the all-encompassing "Why?"), they affirm Aristotle's opening sentence of his book, *Metaphysics*: "All men by nature desire to know."

One of the things philosophers have tried to answer is the long-standing question of the status of *abstract concepts* (also referred to as the *problem of universals*). Abstract concepts are contrasted with individuals. For example, you are a *particular individual* human being, and so are your parents, friends, and each person you happen to meet. So we can say that individual humans exist. But what about "humanity"? Does that universal abstract concept refer to anything that exists, or is it just a mental construct? Similarly, you can draw a picture of an individual triangle, or recognize one when you see it. But does the universal abstract concept "triangularity" refer to anything that exists? Similar questions can be asked of the concepts "goodness," "beauty," and "honesty." David Hume denied that abstract entities exist because our immediate experience gives us particulars, not universals. For example, I perceive this particular blue object, and some other particular blue object—but I never perceive "blueness." Therefore, reality consists of the particulars of immediate experience.

Plato held that abstract terms refer to the world of Ideas or Forms, which are eternal and changeless, and which can only be grasped by reason. For Plato, only the Ideas truly exist, while everything given through sense perception—the world of experience—is an illusion. Opposed to this idea are *nominalists*—philosophers who deny the existence of abstract entities. *Nominalism* holds that abstract concepts are merely terms that we use for convenience sake, by which we group together things with similar characteristics.

A *realist* holds that reality exists independent of our perceptions. There are different versions of realism. *Platonic realism* argues for the existence of universals (abstract entities). But another type of realism argues for the independent existence of a physical world outside us. A third type, called *Aristotelian realism* argues that, although universals exist, they are subject to (depend on) our experience of particular entities; that is, they arise from our ability to generalize. On the other hand, *idealism* holds that reality consists of *mind* and its *ideas*. For example, George Berkeley argued that all objects of perception are ideas in a mind.

Finally, there are several specific areas each with its own name and its own set of questions and concerns. For example, *ontology* is the study of what there is (sometimes whimsically referred to as "the furniture of the universe"). An ontological theory might describe the basic and fundamental categories of existence (the furniture), and the relations between those categories. Another area is *cosmology*, the study of the origin of the universe and its evolution. We will encounter these concepts, along with philosophers' theories and answers to the most fundamental questions of all.

Plato

THE DIVIDED LINE, AND THE CAVE

In the following passages, Plato creates two vivid pictures. The first passage, "The Divided Line," shows how we are capable of going beyond the physical world of opinions and beliefs, so we can reach the realm of knowledge and reason. The objects of the visible physical world are fleeting and forever changing; thus, they are subject to error and doubt. Our minds are also capable of understanding the world of Forms, an eternal and unchanging world which we are able to grasp through reason.

Plato offers a different presentation of his thoughts in the second passage, "The Cave." Here Plato weaves a fantastic story that indirectly reveals the thought that our sensations delude us about the true nature of reality. Thus, we must use reason and contemplation to gain a true understanding of ultimate reality.

The Divided Line

There are many different things in the world we call "beautiful" and many we call "good." The reason we can bring all the various instances under one term is that they can be captured under a single Idea, which is the essence of each. Further, things in the physical world are seen but not known, whereas the Ideas are known but not seen. It is by means of sight we see the visible things, and with hearing we hear, and with the other senses perceive the other objects of sense. Do you agree, Glaucon?

I agree, Socrates.

But without the addition of some other nature there is no seeing or being seen.

How do you mean?

Unless there is a third nature specially adapted to the purpose, the owner of the eyes will see nothing and the colors will be invisible.

Of what nature are you speaking?

Of that which we call "light." Light enables the eye to see and the visible to appear.

You mean the Sun?

The sun is not sight, but the author of sight. Now just as the Sun is related to things in the visible world, the Good in the intelligible world is related to the mind.

Will you be a little more explicit, Socrates?

Edited from *Republic,* Books VI-VII. Translated by Benjamin Jowett, 1892 which is now in the public domain.

The eyes see dimly when a person directs them toward objects on which the light of day is no longer shining, when seen at night; they seem to have no clearness of vision in them. But when they are directed towards objects on which the sun shines, they see clearly.

Certainly.

And the soul is like the eye; when resting upon that on which truth and being shine, the soul understands and is radiant with intelligence. That which imparts truth to the known and the power of knowing to the knower is what I call the "Idea of Good." This is the foundation of truth in so far as it becomes the subject of knowledge. Light and sight may be said to be like the sun, and yet not to be the sun, so in this other sphere, truth may be said to be like the Good, but not the Good; the Good has a place of higher honor. Would you say that the sun is not only the author of visibility in all visible things, but of generation and nourishment and growth?

Yes.

Similarly, the Good may be said to be not only the author of knowledge to all things known, but of their being and essence, and yet the Good is not essence, but far exceeds essence in dignity and power. You have to imagine, then, that there are two ruling powers, and that one of them is set over the intelligible world, the other over the visible world. May I suppose that you have this distinction of the visible and intelligible fixed in your mind?

I have.

Now take a line which has been cut into two unequal parts, and divide each of them again in the same proportion. One of the main divisions refers the visible realm, and the other to the intelligible realm. Compare the two subdivisions of each main division in respect of their clarity or lack of clarity, and you will find that the first section in the sphere of the visible consists of images. And by images I mean shadows, and reflections in water and on smooth surfaces. Do you understand?

Yes.

Imagine, now, the other subsection in the visible realm to include physical objects—animals and everything that grows or is made.

I understand.

Both sections of this main division provide different kinds of information to our senses. The image is a copy of the physical, so it is a kind of illusion. The physical is the source of belief.

Can you explain that.

An image, such as a shadow, doesn't provide knowledge of the physical object that is the source of the shadow. Physical objects provide more information to us regarding the visible realm, but since those objects are always changing, there is no permanence in the physical world. Thus, we have only beliefs about this realm.

I understand.

We can now consider the subdivisions in the intelligible realm. Those who study geometry and arithmetic assume odd and even numbers, and different kinds of angles. They write numerals, and they draw lines and squares and triangles; these exist in the visible realm. But when we do this we are not thinking of these drawings; we are thinking of the Ideas which they resemble; numbers, and absolute squares and triangles which can be understood only with the mind. The drawings and numerals are only a means to think about and understand the things we draw. For example, in geometry we can deduce certain things about the angles of a triangle, or calculate the area of a square. We can talk about the nature of triangularity, not just the simple line drawing.

That is true.

And when I speak of the other subdivision of the intelligible, I mean the kind of knowledge that only reason itself can attain—what are called Ideas, or Forms if that term is easier for you to grasp.

I understand you, perhaps not perfectly, for you seem to me to be describing a task which is really tremendous. You say that the Ideas or Forms are contemplated only through reason.

You have understood my meaning. And now, corresponding to these four divisions, let there be four faculties in the soul—reason answering to the highest, understanding to the second, belief to the third, and opinion of shadows to the last. And let there be a scale of them, and let us suppose that the several faculties have clearness in the same degree that their objects have truth.

The Cave

Let me show in a story how far our nature is either enlightened or unenlightened. Imagine human beings living in an underground cave where they have been from childhood. They have their legs and necks chained so they cannot move. They are prevented by the chains from turning round their heads; thus, they can see only a wall directly in front of them.

There is a wide walkway above and behind the chained people where a fire is kept blazing. Along this walkway other people walk between the fire and the prisoners chained below. As the people above walk back and forth, they cast shadows on the wall in front of the chained people, like the screen which marionette players have in front of them, over which they show the puppets.

Imagine, Glaucon, that the people walking in front of the fire carry all sorts of objects, statues and figures of animals made of wood and stone, which appear as shadows on the wall in front of the prisoners. And some of the people who are carrying objects are talking, others silent.

You have shown me a strange image, Socrates, and they are strange prisoners.

Like ourselves, Glaucon. And when the prisoners converse with one another, wouldn't they suppose they were naming what was actually before them, having learned the words from those speaking above and behind them?

Yes, they would, Socrates.

And would the prisoners think that when one of the passers-by spoke that the voice which they heard came from the shadow instead?

No question.

To the prisoners, the truth would be literally nothing but the shadows of the images.

That is certain.

And now imagine what will naturally follow if the prisoners are released. At first, when any of them is liberated and compelled suddenly to stand up and turn his neck round and walk toward the light outside the cave, he will suffer sharp pains. The glare will distress him, and he will be unable to recognize the reality of physical objects which in his former state he had seen only as shadows. And then imagine someone saying to him that what he saw before was an illusion, but that now that his vision is turned toward real existence, he has a clearer vision—what will be his reply? And you may further imagine that his instructor is pointing to the objects as they pass and requiring him to name them—will he not be perplexed? Will he not fancy that the shadows which he formerly saw are truer than the objects which are now shown to him?

Far truer.

And if he is compelled to look straight at the light, he will experience pain in his eyes which will make him turn away. And perhaps he will focus instead on the shadows that the objects cast, which were to him real existence.

True.

And suppose that he is reluctantly dragged up a steep and rugged ascent, and held fast until he is forced into the presence of the sun himself, is he not likely to be pained and irritated? When he approaches the light his eyes will be dazzled, and he will not be able to see anything at all of what are now called realities. It will take time to grow accustomed to the sight of the upper world. And first he will see the shadows best, next the reflections of men and other objects in the water, and then the objects themselves. Then he will gaze upon the light of the Moon and the stars and the spangled heaven; and he will see the sky and the stars by night better than the Sun or the light of the Sun by day. But eventually he will be able to see the Sun, and not mere reflections of it in the water; he will see it in its own proper place, and he will contemplate it as it is.

Certainly.

He will then be able to understand that this is what gives the season and the years, and is the guardian of all that is in the visible world, and in a certain way the cause of all things which he can now behold.

Yes, he would first see the Sun and then think about its role in vision.

And when he remembered his old place in the cave, and the wisdom of the cave and his fellow-prisoners, do you not suppose that he would pity them?

Certainly, he would.

And if they were in the habit of conferring honors among themselves on those who were quickest to observe the passing shadows and to remark which of them went before, and which followed after, and which were together; and who were therefore best able to draw conclusions as to the future, do you think that he would care for such honors and glories, or envy the possessors of them?

I think that he would rather suffer anything than entertain these false notions and live again in that miserable manner.

Imagine once more, such a person coming suddenly out of the Sun and replaced in his old situation; would he not be certain to have his eyes full of darkness?

To be sure.

And if there were a contest, and he had to compete in talking about the shadows with the prisoners who had never moved out of the cave, would he not seem ridiculous? Others would say of him that up he went up and beyond and came back without his eyes; and that it was better not even to think of ascending; and if any one tried to free another and lead him up to the light, let them only catch the offender, and they would put him to death.

No question.

This story illustrates an important argument. The prison-house is the world of sight, the light of the fire is the sun, and you will grasp my meaning if you interpret the journey upwards to be the ascent of the soul into the intelligible world. But, whether true or false, my opinion is that in the world of knowledge the Idea of Good appears last of all, and is seen only with a great effort. And when seen, is also inferred to be the universal author of all things beautiful and right, parent of light and of the lord of light in this visible world, and the immediate source of reason and truth in the intelligible; this is the power upon which he who would act rationally either in public or private life must have his eye fixed.

I agree.

Moreover, you must not think that those who attain this great understanding are unwilling to descend to human affairs. As long as they exist in human form, they are drawn back to the world of sensations. Nevertheless, they continue to use reason whenever they can to ascend into the upper world. This desire of is very natural, if our allegory may be trusted.

Yes, very natural.

And is there anything surprising in one who passes from divine contemplations to the evil state of man, misbehaving himself in a ridiculous manner, if, while his eyes are blinking and before he has become accustomed to the surrounding darkness, he is compelled to fight in courts of law, or in other places, about the images or the shadows of images of justice, and is endeavoring to meet the conceptions of those who have never yet seen absolute Justice?

Anything but surprising.

And one who has common sense will remember that the bewilderments of the eyes are of two kinds, and arise from two causes: either from coming out of the light or from going into the light, which is true of the mind's eye, quite as much as of the bodily eye. And he who remembers this when he sees anyone whose vision is perplexed and weak, will not be too ready to laugh; he will first ask whether that soul of man has come out of the brighter life, and is unable to see because unaccustomed to the dark, or having turned from darkness to the day is dazzled by excess of light.

Our argument shows that the power and capacity of learning exists in the soul already. And that just as the eye was unable to turn from darkness to light without the whole body, so too the instrument of knowledge can only by the movement of the soul be turned from the world of becoming into that of being, and learn by degrees to endure the sight of being, and of the brightest and best being—the Good.

Aristotle

FIRST PRINCIPLES

All men by nature desire to know. An indication of this is the delight we take in our senses. By nature animals are born with the faculty of sensation, and from sensation memory is produced. Experience is knowledge of individual things, art is knowledge of universals, and actions are all concerned with the individual. A physician does not cure *man*, he cures Socrates or some other particular man. Yet we think that *knowledge* and *understanding* belong to art rather than to experience. For men of experience know that a thing is so-and so, but do not know *why*, while the others know the *why* and the cause. And in general it is a sign of the man who knows and of the man who does not know, that the former can teach. Again, we do not regard any of the senses as Wisdom; yet surely these give the most authoritative knowledge of particulars. But they do not tell us the *why* of anything—e.g., *why* fire is hot; they only say *that* it is hot.

The point of our present discussion is this: that all men suppose what is called Wisdom to deal with the *first causes* and the principles of things. Since we are seeking this knowledge, we must inquire of what kind are the causes and the principles, the knowledge of which is Wisdom. Now of these characteristics, that of knowing all things must belong to him who has in the highest degree universal knowledge; for he knows in a sense all the instances that fall under the universal. And these things, the most universal, are on the whole the hardest for men to know; for they are farthest from the senses.

We have to acquire knowledge of the original causes (for we say we know each thing only when we think we recognize its first cause), and causes are spoken of in four senses. In one of these we mean the *substance*, i.e., the essence; in another the *matter* or substratum; in a third the *source of the change*; and in a fourth, the *purpose*.

It is right that philosophy should be called knowledge of the truth, for the end of theoretical knowledge is truth, while that of practical knowledge is action. Now we do not know a truth without its cause. Hence the principles of eternal things must be always most true (for they are not merely sometimes true, nor is there any cause of their being, but they themselves are the cause of the being of other things), so that as each thing is in respect of being, so is it in respect of truth.

But evidently there *is* a first principle, and the causes of things are neither an infinite series nor infinitely various in kind. For neither can one thing proceed from another, air from matter, *ad infinitum*; for example, flesh from earth, earth from air, air from fire, and so on without stopping; nor can the sources of movement form an endless series. Similarly the final causes cannot go on *ad infinitum*. But if the *kinds* of causes had been infinite in number, then knowledge would have been impossible; for we think we know only when we have ascertained the causes, but that which is infinite cannot be gone through in a finite time.

The subject of our inquiry is *substance*; for the principles and the causes we are seeking are those of substances. For if the universe is of the nature of a whole, substance is its first part. Sensible substance is changeable, and as change proceeds, there must be something underlying the change; something persists, namely, the *matter*. And since that which "is" has two senses, we must say that everything changes from that which is *potentially* to that which is *actually*, e.g., from potentially white to actually white.

Everything that changes is something, and is changed by something and into something. That by which it is changed is the *immediate mover*; that which is changed, the *matter*; that into which it is changed, the *form*. Some things can exist apart and some cannot, and it is the former that are *substances*. And therefore all things have the same causes, because, without substances, modifications and movements do not exist.

There is a science which investigates being *as* being and the attributes which belong to this in virtue of its own nature. Now this is not the same as any of the so-called special sciences; for none of these others treats universally of being *qua* [as] being. They cut off a part of being and investigate the attribute of this part; this is what the mathematical sciences, for instance, do. Now since we are seeking the first principles and the highest causes, clearly there must be some thing to which these belong in virtue of its own nature. Therefore it is of being *as* being that we also must grasp the first causes.

There are many senses in which a thing may be said to "be," but all that "is" is related to one central point, one definite kind of thing, and is not said to "be" by a mere ambiguity. Everything which is *healthy* is related to *health*, one thing in the sense that it preserves health, another in the sense that it produces it, another in the sense that it is a symptom of health, another because it is capable of it.

So, too, there are many senses in which a thing is said *to be,* but all refer to one starting-point. Some things are said to be because they are substances, others because they are affections of substance, others because they are a process towards substance. It is clear then that it is the work of one science also to study the things that are, *qua* being. But everywhere science deals chiefly with that which is primary, and on which the other things depend, and in virtue of which they get their names. If, then, this is *substance*, it will be of substances that the philosopher must grasp the principles and the causes.

It is evident, then, that it belongs to one science to be able to give an account of these concepts as well as of substance (this was one of the questions in our book of problems), and that it is the function of the philosopher to be able to investigate all things.

And those who study these properties err not by leaving the sphere of philosophy, but by forgetting that *substance* is prior to these other things. So too there are certain properties peculiar to being as such, and it is about these that the philosopher has to investigate the truth.

It is the work of one science to examine being *qua* being, and the attributes which belong to it *qua* being, and the same science will examine not only substances but also their attributes. But since there is one kind of thinker who is above even the natural philosopher (for nature is only one particular genus of being), the discussion of these truths also will belong to him whose inquiry is universal and deals with primary substance.

A principle which everyone must have who understands anything that is, is not a hypothesis; and that which every one must know who knows anything. Such a principle is the most certain of all. It is this: That the same attribute cannot at the same time *belong* and *not belong* to the same subject and in the same respect. This, then, is the most certain of all principles, since it answers to the definition given above. For it is impossible for anyone to believe the same thing *to be* and *not to be.* It is impossible that there should be demonstration [a proof] of absolutely everything (there would be an infinite regress, so that there would still be no demonstration); but if there are things of which one should not demand demonstration, these persons could not say what principle they maintain to be more self-evident than the present one.

There are some who raise a difficulty by asking, who is to be the judge of the healthy man, and in general who is likely to judge rightly on each class of questions. But such inquiries are like puzzling over the question whether we are now asleep or awake. And all such questions have the same meaning. These people demand that a reason shall be given for everything; for they seek a starting-point, and they seek to get this by demonstration, while it is obvious from their actions that they have no conviction. But their mistake is what we have stated it to be; they seek a reason for things for which no reason can be given; *for the starting-point of demonstration is not demonstration.*

To say of what *is* that it *is not*, or of what *is not* that it *is*, is *false*, while to say of what *is* that it *is*, and of what *is not* that it *is not*, is *true*; so that he who says of anything that it is, or that it is not, will say either what is true or what is false; but neither what is nor what is not is said to be or not to be. It must be that which *is* that changes; for change is from something to something. But again it is not the case that all things are at rest or in motion; for there is something which always moves the things that are in motion, and the *first mover* is itself unmoved.

There are several senses in which a thing may be said to "be," for in one sense "being" means "what a thing is" or a "this," and in another sense it means a quality or quantity. While "being" has all these senses, obviously that which "is" primarily is the "what," which indicates the *substance* of the thing. For when we say of what *quality* a thing is, we say that it is good or bad, but when we say *what* it is, we do not say "white" or "hot," but "a man" or a "god." And so one might even raise the question whether the words "to walk," "to be healthy," "to sit" imply that each of these things is existent, and similarly in any other case of this sort; for none of them is either self-subsistent or capable of being separated from substance, but rather, if anything, it is that which walks or sits or is healthy that is an existent thing. Now these are seen to be more real because there is something definite which underlies them (i.e., the substance or individual). Therefore that which is primarily, i.e., not in a qualified sense but without qualification, must be substance.

The question which was raised of old and is raised now, and is always the subject of doubt, namely, what being is, is just the question, *what is substance?* That which underlies a thing is thought to be in the truest sense its substance. We must inquire whether each thing and its essence are the same or different. This is of some use for the inquiry concerning substance; for each thing is thought to be not different from its substance, and the essence is said to be the substance of each thing. Each thing itself, then, and its essence are one and the same in no merely accidental way, and because to know each thing, at least, is just to know its essence. Clearly, then, each primary and self-subsistent thing is one and the same as its essence.

Another question is naturally raised, namely, what sort of parts belong to the *form* and what sort not to the form, but to the concrete thing. In the case of things which are found to occur in specifically different materials, as a circle may exist in bronze or stone or wood, it seems plain that these, the bronze or the stone, are no part of the essence of the circle, since it is found apart from them. The form of man is always found in flesh and bones; are these then also parts of the form? No, they are matter; but because man is not found also in other kinds of matter we are unable to perform the abstraction.

Since this is thought to be possible, but it is not clear when it is the case, some people already raise the question even in the case of the circle and the triangle, thinking that it is not right to define these by reference to lines and to the continuous, but that all these are to the circle or the triangle as flesh and bones are to man, and bronze or stone to the statue. And so to reduce all things thus to Forms and to eliminate the matter is useless labor; for some things surely are a particular form in a particular matter, or particular things in a particular state. It is an error to suppose that man can possibly exist without his parts. For an animal is something perceptible, and it is not possible to define it without reference to movement, nor, therefore, without reference to the parts being in a certain state. It is clear also that the soul is the primary substance and the body is matter, and man or animal is the compound of both. If "Socrates" means simply this particular soul and this particular body, the individual is analogous to the universal in its composition.

Let us return to the subject of our inquiry, which is substance. As the substratum and the essence and the compound of these are called substance, so also is the universal. About two of these we have spoken; both about the essence and about the substratum, of which we have said that it underlies in two senses, either being a "this," which is the way in which an animal underlies its attributes, or as the matter underlies the complete reality. The universal also is thought by some to be in the fullest sense a cause, and a principle; therefore let us attack the discussion of this point also. For it seems impossible that any universal term should be the name of a substance. For firstly the substance of each thing is that which is peculiar to it, which does not belong to anything else; but the universal is common, since that is called universal which is such as to belong to more than one thing. Of which individual then will this be the substance? Either of all or of none; but it cannot be the substance of all. And if it is to be the substance of one, this one will be the others also; for things whose substance is one and whose essence is one are themselves also one.

Further, substance means that which is not predicable of a subject, but the universal is predicable of some subject always. But perhaps the universal, while it cannot be substance in the way in which the essence is so, can be present in this; e.g., "animal" can be present in "man" and "horse." Then clearly it is a formula of the essence. And it makes no difference even if it is not a formula of everything that is in the substance; for nonetheless the universal will be the substance of something, as "man" is the substance of the individual man in whom it is present, so that the same result will follow once more; for the universal, e.g., "animal" will be the substance of that in which it is present as something peculiar to it. And further it is impossible and absurd that the "this," i.e., the substance, if it consists of parts, should not consist of substances nor of what is a "this," but of quality; for that which is not substance, i.e., the quality, will then be prior to substance and to the "this." Which is impossible; for neither in formula nor in time nor in coming to be can the modifications be prior to the substance; for then they will also be separable from it. And in general it follows, if man and such things are substance, that none of the elements in their formulae is the substance of anything, nor does it exist apart from the species or in anything else; I mean, for instance, that no "animal" exists apart from the particular kinds of animal, nor does any other of the elements present in formulae exist apart.

If, then, we view the matter from these standpoints, it is plain that no universal attribute is a substance, and this is plain also from the fact that no common predicate indicates a "this," but rather a "such." Since substance is of two kinds, the concrete thing and the formula, substances in the former sense are capable of destruction (for they are capable also of generation), but there is no destruction of the formula in the sense that it is ever in course of being destroyed (for there is no generation of it either; the being of *house* is not generated, but only the being of *this house*), but without generation and destruction formulae are and are not; for it has been shown that no one begets nor makes these. For this reason, also, there is neither definition of nor demonstration about sensible individual substances, because they have matter whose nature is such that they are capable both of being and of not being; for which reason all the individual instances of them are destructible.

Since substance is a principle and a cause, let us pursue it from this starting point. To inquire "why a thing is itself" is a meaningless inquiry because in order to give meaning to the question "why," the fact or the existence of the thing must already be evident. But we can inquire why man is an animal of such and such a nature. This, then, is plain, that we are not inquiring why he who is a man is a man. We are inquiring, then, why something is predicable of something (that it is predicable must be clear; for if not, the inquiry is an inquiry into nothing); e.g., why does it thunder? This is the same as "why is sound produced in the clouds?" Thus the inquiry is about the predication of one thing of another. The object of the inquiry is most easily overlooked where one term is not expressly predicated of another (e.g., when we inquire "what man is"), because we do not distinguish and do not say definitely that certain elements make up a certain whole. But we must articulate our meaning before we begin to inquire; if not, the inquiry is on the border-line between being a search for something and a search for nothing. Since we must have the existence of the thing as something given, clearly the question is why the matter is some definite thing; e.g., why are these materials a house? Because that which was the essence of a house is present. And why is this individual thing, or this body having this form, a man? Therefore what we seek is the cause, i.e., the form, by reason of which the matter is some definite thing; and this is the substance of the thing. Evidently, then, in the case of simple terms no inquiry nor teaching is possible; our attitude towards such things is other than that of inquiry.

Margaret Cavendish

OBSERVATIONS

Before I deliver my observations upon that part of philosophy which is called "experimental," I thought it necessary to premise some discourse concerning the perception of human sense. It is known that man has five exterior senses, and every sense is ignorant of each other; the nose knows not what the eyes see, the eyes not what the ears hear, neither do the ears know what the tongue tastes; and as for touch, although it is a general sense, yet every specific part of the body has a specific touch, and each part is ignorant of each other's touch: And thus there is a general ignorance of all the parts, and yet a perfect knowledge in each part; for the eye is as knowing as the ear, and the ear as knowing as the nose, and the nose as knowing as the tongue, and one particular touch knows as much as another, at least is capable thereof. Not only is every specific touch, taste, smell, sound or sight, a specific knowledge by itself, but each of them has as many particular kinds of knowledge or perceptions as there are objects presented to them.

Now if there is such variety of several kinds of knowledge, not only in one creature, but in one sort of sense, namely, the exterior senses of one human creature, then what may there be in all the parts of nature? It is true that there are some objects which are not at all perceptible by any of our exterior senses; as for example, rarified air, and the like. But although they are not subject to our exterior sense perception, yet they are subject to our *rational perception*, which is much purer and subtler then the sensitive; so pure and subtle a knowledge that many believe it to be immaterial, as if it were some God, when as it is only a pure, fine and subtle figurative motion or perception; it is so active and subtle, as it is the best informer and reformer of all sense perception; for the rational matter is the most prudent and wisest part of nature, as being the designer of all production, and the most pious and devout part, having the perfect notions of God, I mean, so much as nature can possibly know of God.

But mistake me not: by *rational perception* and knowledge, I mean regular reason, not irregular; where I do also exclude art, which is apt to delude sense, and cannot inform so well as reason does, for reason reforms and instructs sense in all its actions.

Every creature has a double perception, *rational* and *sensitive*, yet each creature or part has *not* an infinite perception. Although each particular creature or part of nature may have some conception of the infinite parts of nature, yet it cannot know the truth of those infinite parts, being but a finite part itself causes errors in perceptions. Thus, it is well said that when they confess themselves, the uncertainty and mistakes of human actions proceed either from the narrowness and wandering of our senses, or from the slipperiness or delusion of our memory, or from the confinement or rashness of our understanding. But, say they, it is no wonder that our power over natural causes and effects is so slowly improved, seeing that we are not only to contend with the obscurity and difficulty of the things on which we work and think, but even the forces of our minds conspire to betray us: And these being the dangers in the process of human reason, the remedies can only proceed from the real, the mechanical, the experimental philosophy, which has this advantage over the philosophy of discourse and disputation: That whereas that chiefly aims at the subtlety of its deductions and conclusions, without much regard to the first groundwork, which ought to be well laid on the sense and memory, so this intends the right ordering of them all, and making them serviceable to each other.

Edited from *Observations Upon Experimental Philosophy,* 1666, Sections 1-2, 16, and 20, which is now in the public domain.

Sense, which is more apt to be deluded than reason, cannot be the ground of reason, no more than art can be the ground of nature. How can a wise man trust his senses, if either the objects are not truly presented according to their natural figure and shape, or if the senses are defective, either through age, sickness, or other accidents, which do alter the natural motions proper to each sense? Hence I conclude that experimental and mechanical philosophy cannot be above the speculative part, by reason most experiments rise from the speculative, so that the artist or mechanic is but a servant to the student.

Nature has knowledge and wisdom, so she has sense and reason; and if sense and reason, then she has self-motion; and if nature has self-motion, then none of her parts can be called inanimate or soul-less, because motion is the life and soul of nature, and of all her parts; and if the body is animate, the parts must be so too, there being no part of the animate body of nature that can be dead, or without motion; an instance might be given of animal bodies, whose parts have all animal life, as well as the body itself. Thus, those who allow a soul, or an informing, actuating and animating form or faculty in nature and her parts, and yet call some parts inanimate or soul-less, do absolutely contradict themselves. And those who say all the varieties of nature are produced, not by self-motion, but that one part moves another, must at last come to something that moves itself: besides, it is not probable, that one part moving another, should produce all things so orderly and wisely as they are in nature. But those that say motion is no substance, and consequently not material, and yet allow generation and annihilation of motion, speak, in my opinion, nonsense: for first, how can self-motion, the author and producer of all things, work all the varieties that are in nature, and be nothing itself?

Next, how can that which is nothing (for all that is not material is nothing in nature, or no part of nature) be generated and annihilated? If motion is material, as surely it is, yet there can neither be a new generation, nor an annihilation of any particular motion in nature because all that is material in nature has its being in and from infinite matter, which is from eternity, it being impossible that any other new matter should be created besides this infinite matter out of which all natural things consist, or that any part of this matter should be lost or annihilated. But perhaps those that believe new generations and annihilations of particular motions, may say, that their opinion is not as if those particular motions were generated out of some new matter, but that the matter of such motions is the same with the matter of all other natural creatures, and that their perishing or annihilation is not an utter destruction or loss of their being out of nature, but only of being such or such a motion, like some vegetables and elements are generated and perish in one night: truly, if that is their meaning, then it were better to name it an alteration or change of motion, rather than a new generation, and a perishing or annihilation. But my intention is not to plead for other men's opinions, but rather to clear my own, which is, that motion is material; for figure, motion and matter are but one thing; and that no particular motion is or can be lost in nature, nor created anew.

And at all this we need not wonder, if we do but consider that nature is full of sense and reason, that is, of sensitive and rational perception, which is the cause that oftentimes the disturbance of one part causes all other parts of a composed figure to take an alarm; for, as we may observe, it is so in all other composed bodies. Neither is it more to be admired, that one color should be within another, then one figurative part is within another; for colors are figurative parts; and as there are several creatures, so there are also several colors; for the color of a creature is as well corporeal as the creature itself; and color is as much a body as place and magnitude, which are but one thing with body. Thus, when the body, or any corporeal part varies, whether solid or rare; place, magnitude, color, and the like, must of necessity change or vary also; which change is no annihilation or perishing, for as no particle of matter can be lost in nature, nor no particular motion, so neither can color.

Therefore the opinion of those who say that when flax or silk is divided into very small threads, or fine parts, those parts lose their colors, and being twisted, regain their colors, seems not conformable to truth; for the division of their parts does not destroy their colors, nor the composing of those parts regain them; but they being divided into such small and fine parts, it makes their colors, which are the finest of their exterior parts, not to be subject to our optic perception; for what is very small or rare, is not subject to the human optic sense. Thus, there are these following conditions required to the optic perception of an exterior object: First, the object must not be too subtle, rare, or little, but of a certain degree of magnitude. Next, it must not be too far distant, or without the reach of our sight; then the medium must not be obstructed, so as to hinder our perception. And lastly, our optic sensorium must be perfect, and the sensitive motions regular; of which conditions, if any are lacking, then there is either no perception at all, or it is an imperfect perception; for the perception of seeing an exterior object, is nothing else but a patterning out of the figure of that same object by the sensitive figurative and perceptive motions; but there are infinite parts that are beyond our human perception, and it would be but a folly for us to deny that which we cannot see or perceive; and if the perceptive motions are not regular in our optic sense, we may see different colors in one object; the corporeal figurative motions in the eye may make several figurative colors, even without the patterns of outward objects; and as there are several colors, so there are also several corporeal figurative motions that make several colors in several parts; and the more solid the parts are, the more fixed are their inherent natural colors.

But superficial colors are more various, though not so various as they would be, if made by dusty atoms, flying about as flies in Sunshine; for if this opinion were true, all colors, and other creatures would be composed or made by chance, rather than by reason, and chance being so ignorantly inconstant, not any two parts would be of the like color, nor any kind or species would be preserved; but wise nature, although she is full of variety, yet she is also full of reason, which is knowledge; for there is no part of nature that has not sense and reason, which is life and knowledge; and if all the infinite parts have life and knowledge, infinite nature cannot be a fool or insensible: But mistake me not, for I do not mean that her parts in particular are infinitely knowing, but I say infinite nature has an infinite knowledge; and by reason nature is material, she is divisible as well as composable, which is the cause that there is an obscurity in her parts, in particular, but not in general. That is, in nature herself, if there were not an obscurity in the particulars, men would not endeavor to prove inherent and natural figures by superficial phenomena.

In my opinion, it is as impossible to imagine a body without color, as it is impossible for the mind to conceive a natural immaterial substance; and if so pure a body as the mind cannot be colorless, much less are grosser bodies. But put the case all bodies that are not subject to exterior light were black as night, yet they would be of a color, for black is as much a color as green, or blue, or yellow, or the like; but if all the interior parts of nature are black, then, in my opinion, nature is a very sad and melancholy lady; and those which are of such an opinion, surely their minds are more dark than the interior parts of nature; I will not hope that clouds of dusty atoms have obscured them. But if not any creature can have imagination without figure and color, much less can the optic sensitive parts; for the exterior sensitive parts are more gross then the rational, and therefore they cannot be without color, no more than without figure: and although the exterior parts of animals are subject to our touch, yet the countenances of those exterior parts are no more perceptible by our touch, than several colors are.

To sum up, I will briefly repeat what I have said before, namely, that there are natural and inherent colors which are fixed and constant, and superficial colors, which are changeable and inconstant, as also artificial colors made by painters and dyers, and that it is impossible that any constant color should be made by inconstant atoms and various lights. It is true that there are streams of dust or dusty atoms which seem to move variously, upon which the Sun or light makes several reflections and refractions; but yet I do not see, nor can I believe, that those dusty particles and light are the cause of fixed and inherent colors; and therefore if experimental philosophers have no firmer grounds and principles than their colors have, and if their opinions be as changeable as inconstant atoms and variable lights, then their experiments will be of no great benefit and use to the world.

John Locke

PRIMARY AND SECONDARY QUALITIES

There are two very different things to be distinguished; it being one thing to perceive and know the idea of white or black, and quite another to examine what kind of particles they must be to make any object appear white or black.

To discover the nature of our *ideas* the better, and to discourse of them intelligibly, it will be convenient to distinguish them *as they are ideas or perceptions in our minds*; and *as they are modifications of matter in the bodies that cause such perceptions in us*: that so we may not think (as perhaps usually is done) that they are exactly the images and resemblances of something inherent in the subject; most of those of sensation being in the mind no more the likeness of something existing without us, than the names that stand for them are the likeness of our ideas, which yet upon hearing they are apt to excite in us.

Whatsoever the mind perceives *in itself*, or is the immediate object of perception, thought, or understanding, that I call *idea*; and the power to produce any idea in our mind, I call *quality* of the subject wherein that power is. Thus a snowball having the power to produce in us the ideas of white, cold, and round, the power to produce those ideas in us, as they are in the snowball, I call *qualities*; and as they are sensations or perceptions in our understandings, I call them *ideas*; which *ideas*; if I speak of sometimes as in the things themselves, I would be understood to mean those qualities in the objects which produce them in us.

Qualities thus considered in bodies are: *First*, such as are utterly inseparable from the body, in what state so ever it be; and such as in all the alterations and changes it suffers, all the force can be acted upon it, it constantly keeps. For example, take a grain of wheat, divide it into two parts; each part has still *solidity, extension, figure,* and *mobility*: divide it again, and it retains still the same qualities; and so divide it on, till the parts become insensible; they must retain still each of them all those qualities. For division, in reducing it to insensible parts, can never take away either solidity, extension, figure, or mobility from any body. These I call *original* or *primary qualities* of body, which I think we may observe to produce simple ideas in us: solidity, extension, figure, motion or rest, and number.

Secondly, such qualities which in truth are nothing in the objects themselves but powers to produce various sensations in us, such as colors, sounds, tastes, etc., these I call *secondary qualities.*

If external objects be not united to our minds when they produce ideas, and yet we perceive these *original* qualities in such of them as singly fall under our senses, it is evident that some motion must be thence continued by our nerves to the brain to produce in our minds the particular ideas we have of them. And since the extension, figure, number, and motion of bodies may be perceived at a distance by sight, it is evident some singly imperceptible bodies must come from them to the eyes, and thereby convey to the brain some motion which produces these ideas which we have of them in us.

After the same manner that the ideas of these original qualities are produced in us, we may conceive that the ideas of *secondary* qualities are also produced, namely by the operation of insensible particles on our senses. Let us suppose that the different motions and figures of such particles, affecting our senses, produce in us those different sensations which we have from the colors and smells of bodies to be produced in our minds.

Edited from *An Essay Concerning Human Understanding,* 1690, Book II, Chapters VIII-IX, which is now in the public domain.

What I have said concerning colors and smells may be understood also of tastes and sounds, and other sensible qualities; which, whatever reality we by mistake attribute to them, are in truth *nothing in the objects themselves*, but powers to produce various sensations in us; and depend on the primary qualities.

I think it easy to draw this observation: that the ideas of primary qualities of bodies are resemblances of them, and their patterns do really exist in the bodies themselves, but the ideas produced in us by these secondary qualities have no resemblance of them at all. Nothing like the ideas produced in us by these secondary qualities exist in the bodies themselves.

The particular bulk, number, figure, and motion of the parts of, for example, fire or snow, are really in them, whether anyone's senses perceive them or not; therefore they may be called *real* qualities, because they really exist in those bodies. But light, heat, whiteness, or coldness, are no more really in them than sickness or pain is in bread. Take away the sensation of them; let not the eyes see light or colors, nor the ears hear sounds; let the palate not taste, nor the nose smell, and all colors, tastes, odors, and sounds, *as they are such particular ideas*, vanish and cease, and are reduced to their causes—bulk, figure, and motion of parts.

Let us consider the red and white colors in porphyry [a type of rock with large crystals]. Hinder light from striking on it, and its colors vanish; it no longer produces any such ideas in us: upon the return of light it produces these appearances on us again. Can anyone think any real alterations are made in the porphyry by the presence or absence of light; and that those ideas of whiteness and redness are really in porphyry in the light, when it is plain *it has no color in the dark*? It has, indeed, such a configuration of particles, both night and day, as are apt, by the rays of light rebounding from some parts of that hard stone, to produce in us the idea of redness, and from others the idea of whiteness; but whiteness or redness are not in it at any time, but such a texture that hath the power to produce such a sensation in us.

Perception, as it is the first faculty of the mind exercised about our ideas; so it is the first and simplest idea we have from reflection, and is by some called thinking in general. For in bare naked perception, the mind is, for the most part, only passive; and what it perceives, it cannot avoid perceiving.

What perception is, every one will know better by reflecting on what he does himself, when he sees, hears, feels, etc., or thinks, than by any discourse of mine. Whoever reflects on what passes in his own mind cannot miss it. And if he does not reflect, all the words in the world cannot make him have any notion of it.

How often may a man observe in himself, that whilst his mind is intently employed in the contemplation of some objects, it takes no notice of impressions of sounds upon the organ of hearing?

I do not doubt that children, by the exercise of their senses about objects that affect them in the womb, receive some few ideas before they are born, as the unavoidable effects, either of the bodies that environ them, or else of those wants or diseases they suffer; amongst which (if one may conjecture concerning things not very capable of examination). I think the ideas of hunger and warmth are two: which probably are some of the first that children have, and which they scarce ever part with again.

But though it be reasonable to imagine that children receive some ideas before they come into the world, yet these simple ideas are far from those *innate principles* which some contend for, and we have rejected. These here mentioned, being the effects of sensation, are only from some affections of the body, which happen to them there, and so depend on something *exterior* to the mind; no otherwise differing in their manner of production from other ideas derived from sense, but only in the precedency of time. Whereas those innate principles are supposed to be quite of another nature; not coming into the mind by any accidental alterations in, or operations on the body; but, as it were, original characters impressed upon it, in the very first moment of its being and constitution.

As there are some ideas which we may reasonably suppose may be introduced into the minds of children in the womb, subservient to the necessities of their life and being there: so, after they are born, those ideas are the earliest imprinted which happen to be the sensible qualities which first occur to them; amongst which light is not the least considerable, nor of the weakest efficacy. And how covetous the mind is to be furnished with all such ideas as have no pain accompanying them, may be a little guessed by what is observable in children new-born; who always turn their eyes to that part from whence the light comes, lay them how you please. But the ideas that are most familiar at first, being various according to the diverse circumstances of children's first entertainment in the world, the order wherein the several ideas come at first into the mind is very various and uncertain.

Perception then being the *first* step and degree towards knowledge, and the inlet of all the materials of it; the fewer senses any man, as well as any other creature, hath; and the fewer and duller the impressions are that are made by them; and the duller the faculties are that are employed about them, the more remote are they from that knowledge which is to be found in some men. It suffices me only to have remarked here, that perception is the first operation of all our intellectual faculties, and the inlet of all knowledge in our minds.

Gottfried Leibniz

THE BUILDING BLOCKS OF REALITY

1. The Monad, of which we shall here speak, is nothing but a *simple* substance, which enters into compounds. By 'simple' is meant 'without parts.'

2. And there must be simple substances, since there are compounds; for a compound is nothing but a collection of simple things.

3. Now where there are no parts, there can be neither extension nor form [*figure*] nor divisibility. These Monads are the real atoms of nature and, in a word, the elements of things.

4. No dissolution of these elements need be feared, and there is no conceivable way in which a simple substance can be destroyed by natural means.

5. For the same reason there is no conceivable way in which a simple substance can come into being by natural means, since it cannot be formed by the combination of parts [*composition*].

6. Thus it may be said that a Monad can only come into being or come to an end all at once; that is to say, it can come into being only by creation and come to an end only by annihilation, while that which is compound comes into being or comes to an end by parts.

7. Further, there is no way of explaining how a Monad can be altered in quality or internally changed by any other created thing; since it is impossible to change the place of anything in it or to conceive in it any internal motion which could be produced, directed, increased or diminished therein, although all this is possible in the case of compounds, in which there are changes among the parts. The Monads have no windows, through which anything could come in or go out. Accidents cannot separate themselves from substances nor go about outside of them, as the 'sensible species' of the Scholastics used to do. Thus neither substance nor accident can come into a Monad from outside.

8. Yet the Monads must have some qualities, otherwise they would not even be existing things. And if simple substances did not differ in quality, there would be absolutely no means of perceiving any change in things. For what is in the compound can come only from the simple elements it contains, and the Monads, if they had no qualities, would be indistinguishable from one another, since they do not differ in quantity. Consequently, space being a *plenum*, each part of space would always receive, in any motion, exactly the equivalent of what it already had, and no one state of things would be discernible from another.

9. Indeed, each Monad must be different from every other. For in nature there are never two beings which are perfectly alike and in which it is not possible to find an internal difference, or at least a difference founded upon an intrinsic quality [*denomination*].

10. I assume also as admitted that every created being, and consequently the created Monad, is subject to change, and further that this change is continuous in each.

11. It follows from what has just been said, that the natural changes of the Monads come from an internal principle, since an external cause can have no influence upon their inner being.

12. But, besides the principle of the change, there must be a particular series of changes, which constitutes, so to speak, the specific nature and variety of the simple substances.

13. This particular series of changes should involve a multiplicity in the unit or in that which is simple. For, as every natural change takes place gradually, something changes and something

Edited from *The Monadology*. Translated by Robert Latta, 1898, which is now in the public domain.

remains unchanged; and consequently a simple substance must be affected and related in many ways, although it has no parts.

14. The passing condition, which involves and represents a multiplicity in the unit or in the simple substance, is nothing but what is called Perception, which is to be distinguished from Consciousness. In this matter the Cartesian view is extremely defective, for it treats as non-existent those perceptions of which we are not consciously aware. This has also led them to believe that minds alone are Monads, and that there are no souls of animals. Thus, like the crowd, they have failed to distinguish between a prolonged unconsciousness and absolute death, which has made them fall again into the Scholastic prejudice of souls entirely separate [from bodies], and has even confirmed ill-balanced minds in the opinion that souls are mortal.

15. The activity of the internal principle which produces change or passage from one perception to another may be called Appetition. It is true that desire cannot always fully attain to the whole perception at which it aims, but it always obtains some of it and attains to new perceptions.

16. We have in ourselves experience of a multiplicity in simple substance, when we find that the least thought of which we are conscious involves variety in its object. Thus all those who admit that the soul is a simple substance should admit this multiplicity in the Monad; and M. Bayle ought not to have found any difficulty in this, as he has done in his Dictionary article 'Rorarius.'

17. Moreover, it must be confessed that perception and that which depends upon it are inexplicable on mechanical grounds, that is to say, by means of figures and motions. And supposing there were a machine, so constructed as to think, feel, and have perception, it might be conceived as increased in size, while keeping the same proportions, so that one might go into it as into a mill. That being so, we should, on examining its interior, find only parts which work one upon another, and never anything by which to explain a perception. Thus it is in a simple substance, and not in a compound or in a machine, that perception must be sought for. Further, nothing but this (namely, perceptions and their changes) can be found in a simple substance. It is also in this alone that all the internal activities of simple substances can consist.

18. All simple substances or created Monads might be called Entelechies, for they have in them a certain perfection; they have a certain self-sufficiency which makes them the sources of their internal activities and, so to speak, incorporeal automata.

19. If we are to give the name of Soul to everything which has perceptions and desires in the general sense which I have explained, then all simple substances or created Monads might be called souls; but as feeling is something more than a bare perception, I think it right that the general name of Monads or Entelechies should suffice for simple substances which have perception only, and that the name of Souls should be given only to those in which perception is more distinct, and is accompanied by memory.

20. For we experience in ourselves a condition in which we remember nothing and have no distinguishable perception; as when we fall into a swoon or when we are overcome with a profound dreamless sleep. In this state the soul does not perceptibly differ from a bare Monad; but as this state is not lasting, and the soul comes out of it, the soul is something more than a bare Monad.

21. And it does not follow that in this state the simple substance is without any perception. That, indeed, cannot be, for the reasons already given; for it cannot perish, and it cannot continue to exist without being affected in some way, and this affection is nothing but its perception. But when there is a great multitude of little perceptions, in which there is nothing distinct, one is stunned; as when one turns continuously round in the same way several times in succession, whence comes a giddiness which may make us swoon, and which keeps us from distinguishing anything. Death can for a time put animals into this condition.

22. And as every present state of a simple substance is naturally a consequence of its preceding state, in such a way that its present is big with its future.

23. And as, on waking from stupor, we are conscious of our perceptions, we must have had perceptions immediately before we awoke, although we were not at all conscious of them; for one perception can in a natural way come only from another perception, as a motion can in a natural way come only from a motion.

24. It thus appears that if we had in our perceptions nothing marked and, so to speak, striking and highly-flavored, we should always be in a state of stupor. And this is the state in which the bare Monads are.

25. We see also that nature has given heightened perceptions to animals, from the care she has taken to provide them with organs, which collect numerous rays of light, or numerous undulations of the air, in order, by uniting them, to make them have greater effect. Something similar to this takes place in smell, in taste and in touch, and perhaps in a number of other senses, which are unknown to us. And I will explain presently how that which takes place in the soul represents what happens in the bodily organs.

26. Memory provides the soul with a kind of consecutiveness, which resembles reason, but which is to be distinguished from it. Thus we see that when animals have a perception of something which strikes them and of which they have formerly had a similar perception, they are led, by means of representation in their memory, to expect what was combined with the thing in this previous perception, and they come to have feelings similar to those they had on the former occasion. For instance, when a stick is shown to dogs, they remember the pain it has caused them, and howl and run away.

27. And the strength of the mental image which impresses and moves them comes either from the magnitude or the number of the preceding perceptions. For often a strong impression produces all at once the same effect as a long-formed habit, or as many and oft-repeated ordinary perceptions.

28. In so far as the concatenation of their perceptions is due to the principle of memory alone, men act like the lower animals, resembling the empirical physicians, whose methods are those of mere practice without theory. Indeed, in three-fourths of our actions we are nothing but empirics. For instance, when we expect that there will be daylight tomorrow, we do so empirically, because it has always so happened until now. It is only the astronomer who thinks it on rational grounds.

29. But it is the knowledge of necessary and eternal truths that distinguishes us from the mere animals and gives us Reason and the sciences, raising us to the knowledge of ourselves and of God. And it is this in us that is called the rational soul or mind.

30. It is also through the knowledge of necessary truths, and through their abstract expression, that we rise to acts of reflection, which make us think of what is called I, and observe that this or that is within us: and thus, thinking of ourselves, we think of being, of substance, of the simple and the compound, of the immaterial, and of God Himself, conceiving that what is limited in us is in Him without limits. And these acts of reflection furnish the chief objects of our reasonings.

31. Our reasonings are grounded upon two great principles, that of contradiction, in virtue of which we judge false that which involves a contradiction, and true that which is opposed or contradictory to the false.

32. And that of sufficient reason, in virtue of which we hold that there can be no fact real or existing, no statement true, unless there be a sufficient reason, why it should be so and not otherwise, although these reasons usually cannot be known by us.

33. There are also two kinds of truths, those of reasoning and those of fact. Truths of reasoning are necessary and their opposite is impossible: truths of fact are contingent and their

opposite is possible. When a truth is necessary, its reason can be found by analysis, resolving it into more simple ideas and truths, until we come to those which are primary.

34. It is thus that in Mathematics speculative Theorems and practical Canons are reduced by analysis to Definitions, Axioms and Postulates.

35. In short, there are simple ideas, of which no definition can be given; there are also axioms and postulates, in a word, primary principles, which cannot be proved, and indeed have no need of proof; and these are identical propositions, whose opposite involves an express contradiction.

36. But there must also be a sufficient reason for contingent truths or truths of fact, that is to say, for the sequence or connection of the things which are dispersed throughout the universe of created beings, in which the analyzing into particular reasons might go on into endless detail, because of the immense variety of things in nature and the infinite division of bodies. There is an infinity of present and past forms and motions which go to make up the efficient cause of my present writing; and there is an infinity of minute tendencies and dispositions of my soul, which go to make its final cause.

37. And as all this detail again involves other prior or more detailed contingent things, each of which still needs a similar analysis to yield its reason, we are no further forward: and the sufficient or final reason must be outside of the sequence or series of particular contingent things, however infinite this series may be.

38. Thus the final reason of things must be in a necessary substance, in which the variety of particular changes exists only eminently, as in its source; and this substance we call God.

39. Now as this substance is a sufficient reason of all this variety of particulars, which are also connected together throughout; there is only one God, and this God is sufficient.

40. We may also hold that this supreme substance, which is unique, universal and necessary, nothing outside of it being independent of it; this substance, which is a pure sequence of possible being, must be illimitable and must contain as much reality as is possible.

41. Whence it follows that God is absolutely perfect; for perfection is nothing but amount of positive reality, in the strict sense, leaving out of account the limits or bounds in things which are limited. And where there are no bounds, that is to say in God, perfection is absolutely infinite.

42. It follows also that created beings derive their perfections from the influence of God, but that their imperfections come from their own nature, which is incapable of being without limits. For it is in this that they differ from God. An instance of this original imperfection of created beings may be seen in the natural inertia of bodies.

43. It is farther true that in God there is not only the source of existences but also that of essences, in so far as they are real, that is to say, the source of what is real in the possible. For the understanding of God is the region of eternal truths or of the ideas on which they depend, and without Him there would be nothing real in the possibilities of things, and not only would there be nothing in existence, but nothing would even be possible.

44. For if there is a reality in essences or possibilities, or rather in eternal truths, this reality must needs be founded in something existing and actual, and consequently in the existence of the necessary Being, in whom essence involves existence, or in whom to be possible is to be actual.

45. Thus God alone (or the necessary Being) has this prerogative that He must necessarily exist, if He is possible. And as nothing can interfere with the possibility of that which involves no limits, no negation and consequently no contradiction, this [His possibility] is sufficient of itself to make known the existence of God *a priori*. We have thus proved it, through the reality of eternal truths. But a little while ago we proved it also a posteriori, since there exist contingent beings, which can have their final or sufficient reason only in the necessary Being, which has the reason of its existence in itself.

46. We must not, however, imagine, as some do, that eternal truths, being dependent on God, are arbitrary and depend on His will, as Descartes, and afterwards M. Poiret, appear to have held. That is true only of contingent truths, of which the principle is fitness or choice of the best, whereas necessary truths depend solely on His understanding and are its inner object.

47. Thus God alone is the primary unity or original simple substance, of which all created or derivative Monads are products and have their birth, so to speak, through continual fulgurations of the Divinity from moment to moment, limited by the receptivity of the created being, of whose essence it is to have limits.

48. In God there is Power, which is the source of all, also Knowledge, whose content is the variety of the ideas, and finally Will, which makes changes or products according to the principle of the best. These characteristics correspond to what in the created Monads forms the ground or basis, to the faculty of Perception and to the faculty of Appetition. But in God these attributes are absolutely infinite or perfect; and in the created Monads or the Entelechies there are only imitations of these attributes, according to the degree of perfection of the Monad.

49. A created thing is said to act outwardly in so far as it has perfection, and to suffer [or be passive] in relation to another, in so far as it is imperfect. Thus activity [action] is attributed to a Monad, in so far as it has distinct perceptions, and passivity [passion] in so far as its perceptions are confused.

50. And one created thing is more perfect than another, in this, that there is found in the more perfect that which serves to explain *a priori* what takes place in the less perfect, and it is on this account that the former is said to act upon the latter.

51. But in simple substances the influence of one Monad upon another is only ideal, and it can have its effect only through the mediation of God, in so far as in the ideas of God any Monad rightly claims that God, in regulating the others from the beginning of things, should have regard to it. For since one created Monad cannot have any physical influence upon the inner being of another, it is only by this means that the one can be dependent upon the other.

52. Accordingly, among created things, activities and passivities are mutual. For God, comparing two simple substances, finds in each reasons which oblige Him to adapt the other to it, and consequently what is active in certain respects is passive from another point of view; active in so far as what we distinctly know in it serves to explain what takes place in another, and passive in so far as the explanation of what takes place in it is to be found in that which is distinctly known in another.

53. Now, as in the Ideas of God there is an infinite number of possible universes, and as only one of them can be actual, there must be a sufficient reason for the choice of God, which leads Him to decide upon one rather than another.

54. And this reason can be found only in the fitness, or in the degrees of perfection, that these worlds possess, since each possible thing has the right to aspire to existence in proportion to the amount of perfection it contains in germ.

55. Thus the actual existence of the best that wisdom makes known to God is due to this, that His goodness makes Him choose it, and His power makes Him produce it.

56. Now this connection or adaptation of all created things to each and of each to all, means that each simple substance has relations which express all the others, and, consequently, that it is a perpetual living mirror of the universe

57. And as the same town, looked at from various sides, appears quite different and becomes as it were numerous in aspects; even so, as a result of the infinite number of simple substances, it is as if there were so many different universes, which, nevertheless are nothing but aspects [perspectives] of a single universe, according to the special point of view of each Monad.

58. And by this means there is obtained as great variety as possible, along with the greatest possible order; that is to say, it is the way to get as much perfection as possible.

59. Besides, no hypothesis but this (which I venture to call proved) fittingly exalts the greatness of God; and this Monsieur Bayle recognized when, in his Dictionary, he raised objections to it, in which indeed he was inclined to think that I was attributing too much to God, more than it is possible to attribute. But he was unable to give any reason which could show the impossibility of this universal harmony, according to which every substance exactly expresses all others through the relations it has with them.

60. Further, in what I have just said there may be seen the reasons *a priori* why things could not be otherwise than they are. For God in regulating the whole has had regard to each part, and in particular to each Monad, whose nature being to represent, nothing can confine it to the representing of only one part of things; though it is true that this representation is merely confused as regards the variety of particular things in the whole universe, and can be distinct only as regards a small part of things, namely, those which are either nearest or greatest in relation to each of the Monads; otherwise each Monad would be a deity. It is not as regards their object, but as regards the different ways in which they have knowledge of their object, that the Monads are limited. In a confused way they all strive after the infinite, the whole; but they are limited and differentiated through the degrees of their distinct perceptions.

61. And compounds are in this respect analogous with simple substances. For all is a plenum (and thus all matter is connected together) and in the plenum every motion has an effect upon distant bodies in proportion to their distance, so that each body not only is affected by those which are in contact with it and in some way feels the effect of everything that happens to them, but also is mediately affected by bodies adjoining those with which it itself is in immediate contact. Wherefore it follows that this inter-communication of things extends to any distance, however great. And consequently every body feels the effect of all that takes place in the universe, so that he who sees all might read in each what is happening everywhere, and even what has happened or shall happen, observing in the present that which is far off as well in time as in place. But a soul can read in itself only that which is there represented distinctly; it cannot all at once unroll everything that is enfolded in it, for its complexity is infinite.

62. Thus, although each created Monad represents the whole universe, it represents more distinctly the body which specially pertains to it, and of which it is the entelechy; and as this body expresses the whole universe through the connection of all matter in the plenum, the soul also represents the whole universe in representing this body, which belongs to it in a special way.

63. The body belonging to a Monad (which is its entelechy or its soul) constitutes along with the entelechy what may be called a living being, and along with the soul what is called an animal. Now this body of living being or of an animal is always organic; for, as every Monad is, in its own way, a mirror of the universe, and as the universe is ruled according to a perfect order, there must also be order in that which represents it, i.e., in the perceptions of the soul, and consequently there must be order in the body, through which the universe is represented in the soul.

64. Thus the organic body of each living being is a kind of divine machine or natural automaton, which infinitely surpasses all artificial automata. For a machine made by the skill of man is not a machine in each of its parts. For instance, the tooth of a brass wheel has parts or fragments which for us are not artificial products, and which do not have the special characteristics of the machine, for they give no indication of the use for which the wheel was intended. But the machines of nature, namely, living bodies, are still machines in their smallest parts ad infinitum. It is this that constitutes the difference between nature and art, that is to say, between the divine art and ours.

65. And the Author of nature has been able to employ this divine and infinitely wonderful power of art, because each portion of matter is not only infinitely divisible, as the ancients observed, but is also actually subdivided without end, each part into further parts, of which each has some motion of its own; otherwise it would be impossible for each portion of matter to express the whole universe.

66. Whence it appears that in the smallest particle of matter there is a world of creatures, living beings, animals, entelechies, souls.

67. Each portion of matter may be conceived as like a garden full of plants and like a pond full of fishes. But each branch of every plant, each member of every animal, each drop of its liquid parts is also some such garden or pond.

68. And though the earth and the air which are between the plants of the garden, or the water which is between the fish of the pond, be neither plant nor fish; yet they also contain plants and fishes, but mostly so minute as to be imperceptible to us.

69. Thus there is nothing fallow, nothing sterile, nothing dead in the universe, no chaos, no confusion save in appearance, somewhat as it might appear to be in a pond at a distance, in which one would see a confused movement and, as it were, a swarming of fish in the pond, without separately distinguishing the fish themselves.

70. Hence it appears that each living body has a dominant entelechy, which in an animal is the soul; but the members of this living body are full of other living beings, plants, animals, each of which has also its dominant entelechy or soul.

71. But it must not be imagined, as has been done by some who have misunderstood my thought, that each soul has a quantity or portion of matter belonging exclusively to itself or attached to it for ever, and that it consequently owns other inferior living beings, which are devoted for ever to its service. For all bodies are in a perpetual flux like rivers, and parts are entering into them and passing out of them continually.

72. Thus the soul changes its body only by degrees, little by little, so that it is never all at once deprived of all its organs; and there is often metamorphosis in animals, but never metempsychosis or transmigration of souls; nor are there souls entirely separate [from bodies] nor unembodied spirits. God alone is completely without body.

73. It also follows from this that there never is absolute birth [generation] nor complete death, in the strict sense, consisting in the separation of the soul from the body. What we call births [generations] are developments and growths, while what we call deaths are envelopments and diminutions.

74. Philosophers have been much perplexed about the origin of forms, entelechies, or souls; but nowadays it has become known, through careful studies of plants, insects, and animals, that the organic bodies of nature are never products of chaos or putrefaction, but always come from seeds, in which there was undoubtedly some preformation; and it is held that not only the organic body was already there before conception, but also a soul in this body, and, in short, the animal itself; and that by means of conception this animal has merely been prepared for the great transformation involved in its becoming an animal of another kind. Something like this is indeed seen apart from birth [generation], as when worms become flies and caterpillars become butterflies.

75. The animals, of which some are raised by means of conception to the rank of larger animals, may be called spermatic, but those among them which are not so raised but remain in their own kind (that is, the majority) are born, multiply, and are destroyed like the large animals, and it is only a few chosen ones that pass to a greater theatre.

76. But this is only half of the truth, and accordingly I hold that if an animal never comes into being by natural means, no more does it come to an end by natural means; and that not only will

there be no birth [generation], but also no complete destruction or death in the strict sense. And these reasonings, made *a posteriori* and drawn from experience are in perfect agreement with my principles deduced *a priori*, as above.

77. Thus it may be said that not only the soul (mirror of an indestructible universe) is indestructible, but also the animal itself, though its mechanism [machine] may often perish in part and take off or put on an organic slough.

78. These principles have given me a way of explaining naturally the union or rather the mutual agreement of the soul and the organic body. The soul follows its own laws, and the body likewise follows its own laws; and they agree with each other in virtue of the pre-established harmony between all substances, since they are all representations of one and the same universe.

79. Souls act according to the laws of final causes through appetitions, ends, and means. Bodies act according to the laws of efficient causes or motions. And the two realms, that of efficient causes and that of final causes, are in harmony with one another.

80. Descartes recognized that souls cannot impart any force to bodies, because there is always the same quantity of force in matter. Nevertheless he was of opinion that the soul could change the direction of bodies. But that is because in his time it was not known that there is a law of nature which affirms also the conservation of the same total direction in matter. Had Descartes noticed this he would have come upon my system of pre-established harmony.

81. According to this system bodies act as if (to suppose the impossible) there were no souls, and souls act as if there were no bodies, and both act as if each influenced the other.

82. As regards minds or rational souls, though I find that what I have just been saying is true of all living beings and animals (namely that animals and souls come into being when the world begins and no more come to an end that the world does), yet there is this peculiarity in rational animals, that their spermatic animalcules, so long as they are only spermatic, have merely ordinary or sensuous [sensitive] souls; but when those which are chosen, so to speak, attain to human nature through an actual conception, their sensuous souls are raised to the rank of reason and to the prerogative of minds.

83. Among other differences which exist between ordinary souls and minds, some of which differences I have already noted, there is also this: that souls in general are living mirrors or images of the universe of created things, but that minds are also images of the Deity or Author of nature Himself, capable of knowing the system of the universe, and to some extent of imitating it through architectonic ensamples, each mind being like a small divinity in its own sphere.

84. It is this that enables spirits [or minds] to enter into a kind of fellowship with God, and brings it about that in relation to them. He is not only what an inventor is to his machine (which is the relation of God to other created things), but also what a prince is to his subjects, and, indeed, what a father is to his children.

85. Whence it is easy to conclude that the totality of all spirits must compose the City of God, that is to say, the most perfect State that is possible, under the most perfect of Monarchs.

86. This City of God, this truly universal monarchy, is a moral world in the natural world, and is the most exalted and most divine among the works of God; and it is in it that the glory of God really consists, for He would have no glory were not His greatness and His goodness known and admired by spirits. It is also in relation to this divine City that God specially has goodness, while His wisdom and His power are manifested everywhere.

87. As we have shown above that there is a perfect harmony between the two realms in nature, one of efficient, and the other of final causes, we should here notice also another harmony between the physical realm of nature and the moral realm of grace, that is to say, between God, considered

as Architect of the mechanism [machine] of the universe and God considered as Monarch of the divine City of spirits.

88. A result of this harmony is that things lead to grace by the very ways of nature, and that this globe, for instance, must be destroyed and renewed by natural means at the very time when the government of spirits requires it, for the punishment of some and the reward of others.

89. It may also be said that God as Architect satisfies in all respects God as Lawgiver, and thus that sins must bear their penalty with them, through the order of nature, and even in virtue of the mechanical structure of things; and similarly that noble actions will attain their rewards by ways which, on the bodily side, are mechanical, although this cannot and ought not always to happen immediately.

90. Finally, under this perfect government no good action would be unrewarded and no bad one unpunished, and all should issue in the well-being of the good, that is to say, of those who are not malcontents in this great state, but who trust in Providence, after having done their duty, and who love and imitate, as is meet, the Author of all good, finding pleasure in the contemplation of His perfections, as is the way of genuine 'pure love', which takes pleasure in the happiness of the beloved. This it is which leads wise and virtuous people to devote their energies to everything which appears in harmony with the presumptive or antecedent will of God, and yet makes them content with what God actually brings to pass by His secret, consequent and positive [decisive] will, recognizing that if we could sufficiently understand the order of the universe, we should find that it exceeds all the desires of the wisest men, and that it is impossible to make it better than it is, not only as a whole and in general but also for ourselves in particular, if we are attached, as we ought to be, to the Author of all, not only as to the architect and efficient cause of our being, but as to our master and to the final cause, which ought to be the whole aim of our will, and which can alone make our happiness.

George Berkeley

TO BE IS TO BE PERCEIVED

It is evident to any one who takes a survey of the objects of human knowledge, that they are either ideas actually imprinted on the senses; or else such as are perceived by attending to the passions and operations of the mind; or lastly, ideas formed by help of memory and imagination—either compounding, dividing, or barely representing those originally perceived in the aforesaid ways. By sight I have the ideas of light and colors, with their several degrees and variations. By touch I perceive hard and soft, heat and cold, motion and resistance, and of all these more and less either as to quantity or degree. Smelling furnishes me with odors; the palate with tastes; and hearing conveys sounds to the mind in all their variety of tone and composition. And as several of these are observed to accompany each other, they come to be marked by one name, and so to be reputed as one thing. Thus, for example a certain color, taste, smell, figure and consistence having been observed to go together, are accounted one distinct thing, signified by the name apple; other collections of ideas constitute a stone, a tree, a book, and the like sensible things—which as they are pleasing or disagreeable excite the passions of love, hatred, joy, grief, and so forth.

But, besides all that endless variety of ideas or objects of knowledge, there is likewise something which knows or perceives them, and exercises diverse operations, as willing, imagining, remembering, about them. This perceiving, active being is what I call *mind, spirit, soul,* or *myself.* By which words I do not denote any one of my ideas, but a thing entirely distinct from them, wherein, they exist, or, which is the same thing, whereby they are perceived—for the existence of an idea consists in being perceived.

That neither our thoughts, nor passions, nor ideas formed by the imagination, exist without the mind, is what everybody will allow. And it seems no less evident that the various sensations or ideas imprinted on the sense, however blended or combined together (that is, whatever objects they compose), cannot exist otherwise than in a mind perceiving them. I think an intuitive knowledge may be obtained of this by any one that shall attend to what is meant by the term *exists,* when applied to sensible things. The table I write on I say exists, that is, I see and feel it; and if I were out of my study I should say it existed—meaning thereby that if I was in my study I might perceive it, or that some other spirit actually does perceive it. There was an odor, that is, it was smelt; there was a sound, that is, it was heard; a color or figure, and it was perceived by sight or touch. This is all that I can understand by these and the like expressions. For as to what is said of the absolute existence of unthinking things without any relation to their being perceived, that seems perfectly unintelligible. Their *esse est percepi* [to be is to be perceived], nor is it possible they should have any existence out of the minds or thinking things which perceive them.

It is indeed an opinion strangely prevailing amongst men, that houses, mountains, rivers, and in a word all sensible objects, have an existence, natural or real, distinct from their being perceived by the understanding. But, with how great an assurance and acquiescence so ever this principle may be entertained in the world, yet whoever shall find in his heart to call it in question may, if I mistake not, perceive it to involve a manifest contradiction. For, what are the fore-mentioned objects but the things we perceive by sense? And what do we perceive besides our own ideas or sensations? And is it not plainly repugnant that any one of these, or any combination of them, should exist unperceived?

Edited from *A Treatise Concerning the Principles of Human Knowledge,* 1710, Sections 1-41, , which is now in the public domain.

If we thoroughly examine this tenet it will, perhaps, be found at bottom to depend on the doctrine of *abstract ideas*. For can there be a nicer strain of abstraction than to distinguish the existence of sensible objects from their being perceived, so as to conceive them existing unperceived? Light and colors, heat and cold, extension and figures—in a word the things we see and feel—what are they but so many sensations, notions, ideas, or impressions on the sense? And is it possible to separate, even in thought, any of these from perception? For my part, I might as easily divide a thing from itself. I may, indeed, divide in my thoughts, or conceive apart from each other, those things which, perhaps I never perceived by sense so divided. Thus, I imagine the trunk of a human body without the limbs, or conceive the smell of a rose without thinking of the rose itself. So far, I will not deny, I can abstract—if that may properly be called *abstraction* which extends only to the conceiving separately such objects as it is possible may really exist or be actually perceived asunder. But my conceiving or imagining power does not extend beyond the possibility of real existence or perception. Hence, as it is impossible for me to see or feel anything without an actual sensation of that thing, so is it impossible for me to conceive in my thoughts any sensible thing or object distinct from the sensation or perception of it.

Some truths there are so near and obvious to the mind that a man need only open his eyes to see them. Such I take this important one to be, namely, that all the choir of heaven and furniture of the earth, in a word all those bodies which compose the mighty frame of the world, have not any subsistence without a mind, that their *being* is to be perceived or known; that consequently so long as they are not actually perceived by me, or do not exist in my mind or that of any other created spirit, they must either have no existence at all, or else subsist in the mind of some Eternal Spirit—it being perfectly unintelligible, and involving all the absurdity of abstraction, to attribute to any single part of them an existence independent of a spirit. To be convinced of which, the reader need only reflect, and try to separate in his own thoughts the *being* of a sensible thing from its *being perceived*.

From what has been said it follows there is not any other Substance than *Spirit*, or *that which perceives*. But, for the fuller proof of this point, let it be considered the sensible qualities are color, figure, motion, smell, taste, etc., i.e., the ideas perceived by sense. Now, for an idea to exist in an unperceiving thing is a manifest contradiction, for to have an idea is all one as to perceive; that therefore wherein color, figure, and the like qualities exist must perceive them; hence it is clear there can be no unthinking substance or *substratum* of those ideas.

But, say you, though the ideas themselves do not exist without the mind, yet there may be things like them, whereof they are copies or resemblances, which things exist without the mind in an unthinking substance. I answer, an idea can be like nothing but an idea; a color or figure can be like nothing but another color or figure. If we look but never so little into our thoughts, we shall find it impossible for us to conceive a likeness except only between our ideas. Again, I ask whether those supposed originals or external things, of which our ideas are the pictures or representations, be themselves perceivable or no? If they are, then they are ideas and we have gained our point; but if you say they are not, I appeal to any one whether it be sense to assert a color is like something which is invisible; hard or soft, like something which is intangible; and so of the rest.

Some there are who make a distinction between *primary* and *secondary* qualities. By the former they mean extension, figure, motion, rest, solidity or impenetrability, and number; by the latter they denote all other sensible qualities, as colors, sounds, tastes, and so forth. The ideas we have of these they acknowledge not to be the resemblances of anything existing without the mind, or unperceived, but they will have our ideas of the primary qualities to be patterns or images of things which exist without the mind, in an unthinking substance which they call Matter. By Matter, therefore, we are to understand an inert, senseless substance, in which extension, figure, and motion do actually subsist. But it is evident from what we have already shown, that extension, figure, and motion are only ideas existing in the mind, and that an idea can be like nothing but another idea, and that consequently neither they nor their archetypes can exist in an unperceiving substance. Hence, it is plain that that the very notion of what is called *Matter* or *corporeal substance* involves a contradiction in it.

They who assert that figure, motion, and the rest of the primary or original qualities do exist without the mind in unthinking substances, do at the same time acknowledge that colors, sounds, heat, cold, and suchlike secondary qualities, do not—which they tell us are sensations existing in the mind alone, that depend on and are occasioned by the different size, texture, and motion of the minute particles of matter. This they take for an undoubted truth, which they can demonstrate beyond all exception. Now, if it be certain that those original qualities are inseparably united with the other sensible qualities, and not, even in thought, capable of being abstracted from them, it plainly follows that they exist only in the mind. But I desire any one to reflect and try whether he can, by any abstraction of thought, conceive the extension and motion of a body without all other sensible qualities. For my own part, I see evidently that it is not in my power to frame an idea of a body extended and moving, but I must withal give it some color or other sensible quality which is acknowledged to exist only in the mind. In short, extension, figure, and motion, abstracted from all other qualities, are inconceivable. Where therefore the other sensible qualities are, there must these be also, to wit, in the mind and nowhere else.

It is said extension is a mode or accident of Matter, and that Matter is the *substratum* that supports it. Now I desire that you would explain to me what is meant by Matter's *supporting* extension. Say you, I have no idea of Matter and therefore cannot explain it. I answer, though you have no positive, yet, if you have any meaning at all, you must at least have a relative idea of Matter; though you know not what it is, yet you must be supposed to know what relation it bears to accidents, and what is meant by its supporting them. It is evident "support" cannot here be taken in its usual or literal sense—as when we say that pillars support a building; in what sense therefore must it be taken?

If we inquire into what the most accurate philosophers declare themselves to mean by *material substance*, we shall find them acknowledge they have no other meaning annexed to those sounds but the idea of Being in general, together with the relative notion of its supporting accidents. The general idea of Being appears to me the most abstract and incomprehensible of all other; and as for its supporting accidents, this, as we have just now observed, cannot be understood in the common sense of those words; it must therefore be taken in some other sense, but what that is they do not explain. So that when I consider the two parts or branches which make the signification of the words *material substance*, I am convinced there is no distinct meaning annexed to them.

But, though it were possible that solid, figured, movable substances may exist without the mind, corresponding to the ideas we have of bodies, yet how is it possible for us to know this? Either we must know it by sense or by reason. As for our senses, by them we have the knowledge only of our sensations, ideas, or those things that are immediately perceived by sense, call them what you will: but they do not inform us that things exist without the mind, or unperceived, like to those which are perceived. This the materialists themselves acknowledge. It remains therefore that if we have any knowledge at all of external things, it must be by reason, inferring their existence from what is immediately perceived by sense. But what reason can induce us to believe the existence of bodies without the mind, from what we perceive, since the very patrons of Matter themselves do not pretend there is any necessary connection between them and our ideas? I say it is granted that it is possible we might be affected with all the ideas we have now, though there were no bodies existing without resembling them. Hence, it is evident the supposition of external bodies is not necessary for the producing our ideas; since it is granted they are produced sometimes, and might possibly be produced always in the same order, we see them in at present, without their concurrence.

But, say you, surely there is nothing easier than for me to imagine trees, for instance, in a park, or books existing in a closet, and nobody by to perceive them. I answer, you may so, there is no difficulty in it; but what is all this, I beseech you, more than framing in your mind certain *ideas* which you call books and trees, and the same time omitting to frame the idea of any one that may perceive them? But do not you yourself perceive or think of them all the while? This therefore is nothing to the purpose; it only shows you have the power of imagining or forming ideas in your mind: but it does not show that you can conceive it possible the objects of your thought may exist without the mind. To make out this, it is necessary that you conceive them existing unconceived or unthought of, which is a manifest repugnancy. When we do our utmost to conceive the existence of external bodies, we are all the while only contemplating our own ideas. But the mind taking no notice of itself, is deluded to think it can and does conceive bodies existing unthought of or without the mind, though at the same time they are apprehended by or exist in itself.

We perceive a continual succession of ideas, some are anew excited, others are changed or totally disappear. There is therefore some cause of these ideas, whereon they depend, and which produces and changes them. I must therefore be a substance; but it has been shown that there is no corporeal or material substance: it remains therefore that the cause of ideas is an incorporeal active substance or Spirit.

A spirit is one simple, undivided, active being—as it perceives ideas it is called the *understanding*, and as it produces or otherwise operates about them it is called the *will*. Hence there can be no *idea* formed of a soul or spirit; for all ideas whatever, being passive and inert, they cannot represent unto us, by way of image or likeness, that which acts. Such is the nature of *spirit*, or that which acts, that it cannot be of itself perceived, but only by the effects which it produces. So far as I can see, the words *will*, *soul*, *spirit*, do not stand for different ideas, or, in truth, for any idea at all, but for something which is very different from ideas, and which, being an agent, cannot be like, or represented by, any idea whatsoever.

But, whatever power I may have over my own thoughts, I find the ideas actually perceived by Sense have not a like dependence on my will. When in broad daylight I open my eyes, it is not in my power to choose whether I shall see or no, or to determine what particular objects shall present themselves to my view; and so likewise as to the hearing and other senses; the ideas imprinted on them are not creatures of my will. There is therefore some *other* Will or Spirit that produces them.

The ideas of Sense are more strong, lively, and distinct than those of the imagination; they have likewise a steadiness, order, and coherence, and are not excited at random, as those which are the effects of human wills often are, but in a regular train or series, the admirable connection whereof sufficiently testifies the wisdom and benevolence of its Author. Now the set rules or established methods wherein the Mind we depend on excites in us the ideas of sense, are called the *laws of nature*; and these we learn by experience, which teaches us that such and such ideas are attended with such and such other ideas, in the ordinary course of things.

This gives us a sort of foresight which enables us to regulate our actions for the benefit of life. And without this we should be eternally at a loss; we could not know how to act anything that might procure us the least pleasure, or remove the least pain of sense. That food nourishes, sleep refreshes, and fire warms us; that to sow in the seed-time is the way to reap in the harvest; and in general that to obtain such or such ends, such or such means are conducive—all this we know, not by discovering any necessary connection between our ideas, but only by the observation of the settled laws of nature, without which we should be all in uncertainty and confusion, and a grown man no more know how to manage himself in the affairs of life than an infant just born.

And yet this consistent uniform working, which so evidently displays the goodness and wisdom of that Governing Spirit whose Will constitutes the laws of nature, is so far from leading our thoughts to Him, that it rather sends them wandering after second causes. For, when we perceive certain ideas of Sense constantly followed by other ideas and we know this is not of our own doing, we forthwith attribute power and agency to the ideas themselves, and make one the cause of another, than which nothing can be more absurd and unintelligible. Thus, for example, having observed that when we perceive by sight a certain round luminous figure we at the same time perceive by touch the idea or sensation called heat, we do from thence conclude the sun to be the cause of heat. And in like manner perceiving the motion and collision of bodies to be attended with sound, we are inclined to think the latter the effect of the former.

The ideas imprinted on the Senses by the Author of nature are called *real things*; and those excited in the imagination being less regular, vivid, and constant, are more properly termed *ideas*, or *images of things*, which they copy and represent. But then our sensations, be they never so vivid and distinct, are nevertheless ideas, that is, they exist in the mind, or are perceived by it, as truly as the ideas of its own framing. The ideas of Sense are allowed to have more reality in them, that is, to be more strong, orderly, and coherent than the creatures of the mind; but this is no argument that they exist without the mind. They are also less dependent on the spirit, or thinking substance which perceives them, in that they are excited by the will of another and more powerful spirit; yet still they are *ideas*, and certainly no idea, whether faint or strong, can exist otherwise than in a mind perceiving it.

It will be objected that by the foregoing principles all that is real and substantial in nature is banished out of the world, and instead thereof a chimerical scheme of *ideas* takes place. All things that exist, exist only in the mind, that is. What therefore becomes of the sun, moon and stars? What must we think of houses, rivers, mountains, trees, stones; nay, even of our own bodies? Are all these but so many illusions? To which I answer, that by the principles premised we are not deprived of any one thing in nature. Whatever we see, feel, hear, or anywise conceive or understand remains as secure as ever, and is as real as ever.

But after all, say you, it sounds very harsh to say we eat and drink ideas, and are clothed with ideas. I acknowledge it does so—the word *idea* not being used in common discourse to signify the several combinations of sensible qualities which are called *things*; and it is certain that any expression which varies from the familiar use of language will seem harsh and ridiculous. But this doth not concern the truth of the proposition, which in other words is no more than to say, we are fed and clothed with those things which we perceive immediately by our senses. The hardness or softness, the color, taste, warmth, figure, or suchlike qualities, have been shown to exist only in the mind that perceives them; and this is all that is meant by calling them *ideas*; which word if it was as ordinarily used as *thing*, would sound no harsher nor more ridiculous than it. I am not for disputing about the propriety, but the truth of the expression. If therefore you agree with me that we eat and drink and are clad with the immediate objects of sense, which cannot exist unperceived or without the mind, I shall readily grant it is more proper or conformable to custom that they should be called things rather than ideas.

If it be demanded why I make use of the word *idea*, and do not rather in compliance with custom call them *things*; I answer, I do it for two reasons: first, because the term *thing* in contradistinction to *idea*, is generally supposed to denote somewhat existing without the mind; secondly, because *thing* hath a more comprehensive signification than *idea*, including spirit or thinking things as well as ideas. Since therefore the objects of sense exist only in the mind, I chose to mark them by the word *idea*, which implies those properties.

It will be objected that there is a great difference between real fire and the idea of fire, between dreaming or imagining oneself burnt, and actually being so: if you suspect it to be only the idea of fire which you see, do but put your hand into it and you will be convinced with a witness. This and the like may be urged in opposition to our tenets. To all which the answer is evident from what hath been already said; and I shall only add in this place, that if real fire be very different from the idea of fire, so also is the real pain that it occasions very different from the idea of the same pain, and yet nobody will pretend that real pain either is, or can possibly be, in an unperceiving thing, or without the mind, any more than its idea.

David Hume

COMMIT IT TO THE FLAMES

There is a species of skepticism, antecedent to all study and philosophy, which is much inculcated by Descartes and others, as a sovereign preservative against error and precipitate judgment. It recommends an universal doubt, not only of all our former opinions and principles, but also of our very faculties; of whose veracity, say they, we must assure ourselves, by a chain of reasoning, deduced from some original principle, which cannot possibly be fallacious or deceitful. But neither is there any such original principle, which has a prerogative above others, that are self-evident and convincing: or if there were, could we advance a step beyond it, but by the use of those very faculties, of which we are supposed to be already diffident. The Cartesian doubt, therefore, were it ever possible to be attained by any human creature (as it plainly is not) would be entirely incurable; and no reasoning could ever bring us to a state of assurance and conviction upon any subject.

It must, however, be confessed, that this species of skepticism, when more moderate, may be understood in a very reasonable sense, and is a necessary preparative to the study of philosophy, by preserving a proper impartiality in our judgments, and weaning our mind from all those prejudices, which we may have imbibed from education or rash opinion. To begin with clear and self-evident principles, to advance by timorous and sure steps, to review frequently our conclusions, and examine accurately all their consequences; though by these means we shall make both a slow and a short progress in our systems; are the only methods, by which we can ever hope to reach truth, and attain a proper stability and certainty in our determinations.

There is another species of skepticism, *consequent* to science and enquiry, when men are supposed to have discovered, either the absolute fallaciousness of their mental faculties, or their unfitness to reach any fixed determination in all those curious subjects of speculation, about which they are commonly employed. Even our very senses are brought into dispute, by a certain species of philosophers; and the maxims of common life are subjected to the same doubt as the most profound principles or conclusions of metaphysics and theology. As these paradoxical tenets (if they may be called tenets) are to be met with in some philosophers, and the refutation of them in several, they naturally excite our curiosity, and make us enquire into the arguments, on which they may be founded.

I need not insist upon the more trite topics, employed by the skeptics in all ages, against the evidence of *sense*; such as those which are derived from the imperfection and fallaciousness of our organs, on numberless occasions; the crooked appearance of an oar in water; the various aspects of objects, according to their different distances; the double images which arise from the pressing one eye; with many other appearances of a like nature. These skeptical topics, indeed, are only sufficient to prove, that the senses alone are not implicitly to be depended on; but that we must correct their evidence by reason, and by considerations, derived from the nature of the medium, the distance of the object, and the disposition of the organ, in order to render them, within their sphere, the proper *criteria* of truth and falsehood. There are other more profound arguments against the senses, which admit not of so easy a solution.

It seems evident, that men are carried, by a natural instinct or prepossession, to repose faith in their senses; and that, without any reasoning, or even almost before the use of reason, we always

Edited from *An Enquiry Concerning Human Understanding,* 1748, Section XII, Parts 1 and III, , which is now in the public domain.

suppose an external universe, which depends not on our perception, but would exist, though we and every sensible creature were absent or annihilated.

It seems also evident, that, when men follow this blind and powerful instinct of nature, they always suppose the very images, presented by the senses, to be the external objects, and never entertain any suspicion, that the one are nothing but representations of the other. This very table, which we see white, and which we feel hard, is believed to exist, independent of our perception, and to be something external to our mind, which perceives it. Our presence bestows not being on it: our absence does not annihilate it. It preserves its existence uniform and entire, independent of the situation of intelligent beings, who perceive or contemplate it.

But this universal and primary opinion of all men is soon destroyed by the slightest philosophy, which teaches us, that nothing can ever be present to the mind but an image or perception, and that the senses are only the inlets, through which these images are conveyed, without being able to produce any immediate intercourse between the mind and the object. The table, which we see, seems to diminish, as we remove farther from it: but the real table, which exists independent of us, suffers no alteration: it was, therefore, nothing but its image, which was present to the mind. These are the obvious dictates of reason; and no man, who reflects, ever doubted, that the existences, which we consider, when we say, *this house* and *that tree*, are nothing but perceptions in the mind, and fleeting copies or representations of other existences, which remain uniform and independent.

So far, then, are we necessitated by reasoning to contradict or depart from the primary instincts of nature, and to embrace a new system with regard to the evidence of our senses. But here philosophy finds herself extremely embarrassed, when she would justify this new system, and obviate the cavils and objections of the skeptics. She can no longer plead the infallible and irresistible instinct of nature: for that led us to a quite different system, which is acknowledged fallible and even erroneous. And to justify this pretended philosophical system, by a chain of clear and convincing argument, or even any appearance of argument, exceeds the power of all human capacity.

By what argument can it be proved, that the perceptions of the mind must be caused by external objects, entirely different from them, though resembling them (if that be possible) and could not arise either from the energy of the mind itself, or from the suggestion of some invisible and unknown spirit, or from some other cause still more unknown to us? It is acknowledged, that, in fact, many of these perceptions arise not from anything external, as in dreams, madness, and other diseases. And nothing can be more inexplicable than the manner, in which body should so operate upon mind as ever to convey an image of itself to a substance, supposed of so different, and even contrary a nature.

It is a question of fact, whether the perceptions of the senses be produced by external objects, resembling them: how shall this question be determined? By experience surely; as all other questions of a like nature. But here experience is, and must be entirely silent. The mind has never anything present to it but the perceptions, and cannot possibly reach any experience of their connection with objects. The supposition of such a connection is, therefore, without any foundation in reasoning.

To have recourse to the veracity of the Supreme Being, in order to prove the veracity of our senses, is surely making a very unexpected circuit. If his veracity were at all concerned in this matter, our senses would be entirely infallible; because it is not possible that he can ever deceive. Not to mention, that, if the external world be once called in question, we shall be at a loss to find arguments, by which we may prove the existence of that Being or any of his attributes.

This is a topic, therefore, in which the profounder and more philosophical skeptics will always triumph, when they endeavor to introduce an universal doubt into all subjects of human knowledge and enquiry. Do you follow the instincts and propensities of nature, may they say, in assenting to the veracity of sense? But these lead you to believe that the very perception or sensible image is the external object. Do you disclaim this principle, in order to embrace a more rational opinion, that the perceptions are only representations of something external? You here depart from your natural propensities and more obvious sentiments; and yet are not able to satisfy your reason, which can never find any convincing argument from experience to prove, that the perceptions are connected with any external objects.

There is another skeptical topic of a like nature, derived from the most profound philosophy; which might merit our attention, were it requisite to dive so deep, in order to discover arguments and reasonings, which can so little serve to any serious purpose. It is universally allowed by modern enquirers, that all the sensible qualities of objects, such as hard, soft, hot, cold, white, black, etc., are merely secondary, and exist not in the objects themselves, but are perceptions of the mind, without any external archetype or model, which they represent. If this be allowed, with regard to secondary qualities, it must also follow, with regard to the supposed primary qualities of extension and solidity; nor can the latter be any more entitled to that denomination than the former. The idea of extension is entirely acquired from the senses of sight and feeling; and if all the qualities, perceived by the senses, be in the mind, not in the object, the same conclusion must reach the idea of extension, which is wholly dependent on the sensible ideas or the ideas of secondary qualities. Nothing can save us from this conclusion, but the asserting, that the ideas of those primary qualities are attained by *abstraction*, an opinion, which, if we examine it accurately, we shall find to be unintelligible, and even absurd. An extension, that is neither tangible nor visible, cannot possibly be conceived: and a tangible or visible extension, which is neither hard nor soft, black nor white, is equally beyond the reach of human conception. Let any man try to conceive a triangle in general, which is neither *isosceles* nor *scalene*, nor has any particular length or proportion of sides; and he will soon perceive the absurdity of all the scholastic notions with regard to abstraction and general ideas.

Thus the first philosophical objection to the evidence of sense or to the opinion of external existence consists in this, that such an opinion, if rested on natural instinct, is contrary to reason, and if referred to reason, is contrary to natural instinct, and at the same time carries no rational evidence with it, to convince an impartial enquirer. The second objection goes farther, and represents this opinion as contrary to reason: at least, if it be a principle of reason, that all sensible qualities are in the mind, not in the object.

Bereave matter of all its intelligible qualities, both primary and secondary, you in a manner annihilate it, and leave only a certain unknown, inexplicable *something*, as the cause of our perceptions; a notion so imperfect, that no skeptic will think it worth while to contend against it.

The greater part of mankind are naturally apt to be affirmative and dogmatical in their opinions; and while they see objects only on one side, and have no idea of any counterpoising argument, they throw themselves precipitately into the principles, to which they are inclined; nor have they any indulgence for those who entertain opposite sentiments. To hesitate or balance perplexes their understanding, checks their passion, and suspends their action. They are, therefore, impatient till they escape from a state, which to them is so uneasy: and they think, that they could never remove themselves far enough from it, by the violence of their affirmations and obstinacy of their belief. But could such dogmatical reasoners become sensible of the strange infirmities of human understanding, even in its most perfect state, and when most accurate and cautious in its determinations; such a reflection would naturally inspire them with more modesty and reserve, and diminish their fond opinion of themselves, and their prejudice against antagonists. The illiterate may reflect on the disposition of the learned, who, amidst all the advantages of study and reflection, are commonly still diffident in their determinations: and if any of the learned be inclined, from their natural temper, to haughtiness and obstinacy, a small tincture of Pyrrhonism might abate their pride, by showing them, that the few advantages, which they may have attained over their fellows, are but inconsiderable, if compared with the universal perplexity and confusion, which is inherent in human nature. In general, there is a degree of doubt, and caution, and modesty, which, in all kinds of scrutiny and decision, ought for ever to accompany a just reasoner.

The *imagination* of man is naturally sublime, delighted with whatever is remote and extraordinary, and running, without control, into the most distant parts of space and time in order to avoid the objects, which custom has rendered too familiar to it. Those who have a propensity to philosophy, will still continue their researches; because they reflect, that, besides the immediate pleasure attending such an occupation, philosophical decisions are nothing but the reflections of common life, methodized and corrected. But they will never be tempted to go beyond common life, so long as they consider the imperfection of those faculties which they employ, their narrow reach, and their inaccurate operations. While we cannot give a satisfactory reason, why we believe, after a thousand experiments, that a stone will fall, or fire burn; can we ever satisfy ourselves concerning any determination, which we may form, with regard to the origin of worlds, and the situation of nature, from, and to eternity?

This narrow limitation, indeed, of our enquiries, is, in every respect, so reasonable, that it suffices to make the slightest examination into the natural powers of the human mind and to compare them with their objects, in order to recommend it to us. We shall then find what are the proper subjects of science and enquiry.

It seems to me, that the only objects of the abstract science or of demonstration are quantity and number, and that all attempts to extend this more perfect species of knowledge beyond these bounds are mere sophistry and illusion. As the component parts of quantity and number are entirely similar, their relations become intricate and involved; and nothing can be more curious, as well as useful, than to trace, by a variety of mediums, their equality or inequality, through their different appearances. But as all other ideas are clearly distinct and different from each other, we can never advance farther, by our utmost scrutiny, than to observe this diversity, and, by an obvious reflection, pronounce one thing not to be another. Or if there be any difficulty in these decisions, it proceeds entirely from the undeterminate meaning of words, which is corrected by more just definitions. That *the square of the hypotenuse is equal to the squares of the other two sides*, cannot be known, let the terms be ever so exactly defined, without a train of reasoning and enquiry. But to convince us of this proposition, *that where there is no property, there can be no injustice*, it is only necessary to define the terms, and explain injustice to be a violation of property. This proposition is, indeed, nothing but a more imperfect definition. It is the same case with all those pretended syllogistical reasonings, which may be found in every other branch of learning, except the sciences of quantity and number; and these may safely, I think, be pronounced the only proper objects of knowledge and demonstration.

All other enquiries of men regard only *matter of fact* and existence; and these are evidently incapable of demonstration. Whatever *is* may *not be*. No negation of a fact can involve a contradiction. The non-existence of any being, without exception, is as clear and distinct an idea as its existence. The proposition, which affirms it not to be, however false, is no less conceivable and intelligible, than that which affirms it to be. The case is different with the sciences, properly so called. Every proposition, which is not true, is there confused and unintelligible. That the cube root of 64 is equal to the half of 10, is a false proposition, and can never be distinctly conceived.

But that Caesar, or the angel Gabriel, or any being never existed, may be a false proposition, but still is perfectly conceivable, and implies no contradiction.

The existence, therefore, of any being can only be proved by arguments from its cause or its effect; and these arguments are founded entirely on experience. If we reason *a priori*, anything may appear able to produce anything. The falling of a pebble may, for aught we know, extinguish the sun; or the wish of a man control the planets in their orbits. It is only experience, which teaches us the nature and bounds of cause and effect, and enables us to infer the existence of one object from that of another.

When we run over libraries, persuaded of these principles, what havoc must we make? If we take in our hand any volume; of divinity or school metaphysics, for instance; let us ask, *Does it contain any abstract reasoning concerning quantity or number?* No. *Does it contain any experimental reasoning concerning matter of fact and existence?* No. Commit it then to the flames: for it can contain nothing but sophistry and illusion.

Mary Shepherd

IDEAS

The questions intended to be investigated in the following pages are stated in David Hume's Treatise Upon Human Nature: "Why we attribute a continued existence to objects even when they are not present to the senses?" and "Why we suppose them to have an existence distinct from the mind; i.e., external in their position, and independent in their existence and operation?" Mr. Hume argues at great length, that it is not by means either of the "senses, or of reason" that "we are induced to believe in the existence of body," but that we gain the notion entirely by an operation of the "imagination" which has "a propensity to pretend the continued existence of all sensible objects, and as this propensity arises from some lively impressions on the memory, it bestows a vivacity on that fiction, or in other words, makes us believe the continued existence of body." It is not my intention to analyze Mr. Hume's reasoning on this subject, which I conceive to be altogether erroneous, and which it would be very tedious to examine. I prefer, therefore, answering the question as it stands, according to my own views of it, setting down what experience and reflection suggest to my mind as the operations of nature in this matter; and I shall endeavor to point out what complication of objects, and what arrangement of them is necessary towards that result which appears to us from its familiarity and constancy of appearance, perfectly simple and easy to be understood. But first, I shall shortly observe, that Mr. Hume's error in general is similar to that in the essay on "necessary connection," namely of substituting "imagination" and "vivacity of thought," as a ground of belief, instead of "reason."

"An idea," says Mr. Hume, "acquires a vivacity by its relation to some present impression," and this at once, according to him, forms the whole ground upon which our "belief" rests, of the necessity there is, that *similar effects should flow from similar causes*, and that objects should continue to exist unperceived. It is my intention to show here, as upon a former occasion, that as the very act of reasoning consists in drawing out to observation the relations of things as they are included in their juxtaposition to each other; so upon this question, concerning our "knowledge of the existence of body," it is reason, which taking notice of the whole of our perceptions, and of their mutual relations, affords those proofs "of body" which first generate, and after examination will substantiate, the belief of its existence.

The question proposed in the treatise is thus: "By what argument can it be proved, that the perceptions of the mind must be caused by external objects?" It is also held that "Reason does not have it in her power to find any convincing argument to prove, that the perceptions are connected with any external objects," but that on the contrary, "the slightest philosophy teaches us, that the senses are not able to produce any immediate intercourse between the mind and the object; for that the table which we see seems to diminish as we remove further from it, but that the real table which exists independent of us suffers no alteration."

It will be seen by any intelligent reader, accustomed to discussions of this sort, that the consideration of the question, as stated in Mr. Hume's *Treatise,* and the notions I have deduced will contain a doctrine capable of answering any errors of Dr. Berkeley's on the same subject, whose opinions, which originally had been intended as the foundation of the most secure belief in Deity by Mr. Hume has endeavored to convert, by an enlarged application of them (by an induction of the non-existence of mind as well as matter) into a source of universal skepticism.

In the discussion of this subject as to our knowledge of the existence of body, I mean to follow the example of Dr. Berkeley in the use of the word "sensation" chiefly, instead of "perception" because it is a generic term, comprehensible to every consciousness whatever. Dr. Reid is most unphilosophical in supposing perception to be a power of the mind independent of sensation, and that it can be contradistinguished from it; whereas, although every sensation may not be the perception of an exterior object, acting on either of the five organs of sense, yet there can be no perception of such objects without that inward act of consciousness, which, as a consciousness, is in truth a sensation of the mind. When it is apprehended that all we know must be by means of consciousness or sensations, then will be the time to analyze their various classes, to examine their relations, to notice their peculiarities, in order to discover by what means it is we come to the belief of non-sentient existences. I know, indeed, that it is usual to apply the term sensation to those perceptions only which are unaccompanied with the notion of their inhering in an outward object, as the pain arising from the incision of a sharp instrument is a sensation, which is not in the instrument. But in reality every thought, notion, idea, feeling, and perception, which distinguishes a sentient nature from unconscious existence, may be considered generally as sensation. Whereas perception, as used by some authors, begs the question under debate; i.e., of the existence of objects or masses of external qualities already perceived. For under any illusion of the senses, a person would say (as of sight, for instance), "I thought there had been a bird in this room, until I perceived it was only a painting," meaning that he made use of the whole knowledge relating to the subject, then in the mind, as an instrument, an inward eye, to correct the impressions at first received.

When the doctrine I propose becomes unfolded, the following is the conclusion to which I wish it may lead: The relations of various sensations generate conclusions, which become new sensations or perceptions, and which, as so many inward objects of sense, afford an evidence of the existence of the exterior objects to which they refer, equal to the evidence there is for any existing sensation whatever, in the mere consciousness of its presence.

Mr. Hume uses the word "perception" in the sense I do—that of sensation, i.e., for any consciousness whatever. But on account of the ambiguity to which that word is exposed, I prefer the latter term. However, when I occasionally use the word "perception," I use it in the sense of a "consciousness of sensation," a sensation *taken notice of by the mind*, and this is the sense in which Mr. Locke defines the word.

Having said thus much for the sake of clearness, I proceed to state the question proposed, with some slight variation of expression, thus: Why is it, that many of the sensations with which we are acquainted are considered as objects continuous in their existence, outward from, and independent of our own, when it is obvious they are still upon the same footing as those are allowed to be, which are considered as interrupted, inward, and dependent beings; being all of them equally perceptions, or feelings of a mind, which when not perceiving, or feeling, cannot take notice of any existence whatever?

I answer that we do not conceive our sensations so to exist, but by habit associate them with the notion of some sort of corresponding continuous existences. We gain the knowledge that there must be some continuous and independent existences—beings that are not sensations—by the means of reasoning, which reasoning itself consists of other and super-induced sensations arising from the comparison of the relations of simple sensations among themselves, thus testifying the existence of the external objects it represents, as much as the experience of simple sensations, (of color, sound, etc.) testifies the existence of their respective internal objects. Although we are only conscious of our sensations, yet our whole combined sensations include in their relations the necessity, that there should be, and the proof that there are, other existences than the mere sensations themselves.

In dreams and madness the mind is not in a state to perceive and examine these relations for several reasons: First, there is no remembrance of the place the percipient is in; therefore, the relation of place in regard to all those vivacious images which are moving in the fancy is wanting, which, did it exist, would show they were merely parcels of sensible qualities, independent of the action of the senses on external objects, and thus render the mind conscious that it was in a delirium; a very peculiar state of mind no doubt, but one which experience proves may take place, and which at once renders futile that notion of Hume and Berkeley, that the reality of things consists only in the superior vivacity of their impressions.

Secondly, the mind is not in a fit state to perceive that these masses of sensible qualities are not such as can return upon the sense when called for; and so are wanting in that proof of continuous existence.

Thirdly, the mind is not in a state to combine with these observations the knowledge that these masses of sensible qualities cannot owe their existence to those methods of formation which in nature determine objects, independent of each man's sense in particular, and, therefore, wholly different.

In order to discover what these relations are, from which this result is deduced, let us inquire, first, by what means it is we acquire the notion of continuous existences, in opposition to the interrupted sensations by which they appear to the mind?

Secondly, examine the foundations for considering such objects external to, instead of a part of, or included in the perceiving mind.

Thirdly, consider where the notion originates, that such objects are entirely independent of our own existence, although we can only know them by our sensations, *which themselves depend upon our existence*?

In the consideration of these three branches of the question, I shall take notice, how far the method nature takes to generate the notions of independent existence, proves it, and cursorily observe all the errors of Mr. Hume and Bishop Berkeley on these points.

First, I observe, that the method in which what are called "external objects" introduce themselves to the mind, occasions it to judge that the cause of each sensation in particular is different from the cause of sensation in general, and may continue to exist when unperceived. For by a general sensation present to the mind, it always possesses the notion of the possibility of the existence of unperceived objects; and from the facts which take place, it can only explain the appearance of objects, by the supposition that they actually do exist when unperceived or unfelt. For the mind perceives that unless they are created purposely, ready to appear, upon each irregular call of the senses, they must *continue to exist*, ready to appear to them upon such calls.

Also, the mind knows there must necessarily be some sort of continually existing beings which are not perceptions, on account of their successively vanishing; for there must continue sufficient objects to cause a renewal of them, otherwise they would each in their turn begin their own existences. Such is the latent reasoning silently generated in the minds of all men, from infancy; by returning on their steps men can again recover the image of the house or the tree they have just passed. Do these objects continue to exist in them? And is the eye put in action? And does motion take place in relation only to the mind, or more indefinitely to the object called *self* (an individual capacity for sensation in general)? No, in vain would sights and motion attempt to call up these images, unless as objects different from the mind, or object termed self, or simple capacity for general sensation, they were ready to appear in relation to those appropriate methods for their introduction, namely, motion and the use of the eye, which cannot gain any appearance of them by only applying such methods as call upon the inward sentient principle, termed *mind.* The readiness to appear when called for by the use of the organs of sense, mixed with the reasoning that the organs of sense and mind being the same, a third set of objects is needed in order to determine those perceptions in particular which are neither the organs of sense nor mind in general, forms together the familiar reason which yields to all the notion of the continual existence of objects unperceived.

Interrupted sensations of mind, when the organs of sense are not used, are not ready to appear upon any irregular call of any power we are possessed of. But the mind is conscious of the interruptions of its sensations; therefore, the ultimate causes which exist ready and capable to renew them, must be *uninterrupted causes*, otherwise they would "begin their own existences," a proposition which has at large been proved to be impossible for any being to be capable of.

The more refined kinds of reasoning, I grant, lie not in the compass of thinking, of which ordinary minds are capable; and as this essay is intended to explain the popular notion of all men, and to show exactly what it is, and how far philosophy will support it, and how far dissent from it, so I shall chiefly dwell upon the method nature takes with all men. And, therefore, I repeat, that men take notice from their earliest infancy, that the call of the organs of sense, and the use of motion, are related to things constantly ready to appear in relation to them, and that the action of the organs of sense and motion have nothing to do with, and can gain nothing by applying themselves, to that object they consider their minds.

But this may easily be translated into philosophical language, and resolves itself into the consideration, that that class of sensations, called the use of the senses and motion, will by application however irregular to some sort of existences, introduce the notice of them to the mind, and that these existences, being always ready to appear upon these irregular calls of the senses and motion, must continue to exist when not called upon, in order to be thus ready to appear. But the sensations in which they appear to the mind, are by consciousness known to be interrupted; therefore, the existences which are uninterrupted and continue to exist, and which are in relation to the senses and motion, do not continue to exist perceived by the mind, but continue to exist unperceived by the mind. Moreover, the capacity for sensation in general being given with the use of any particular organ of sense, certain perceptions belonging to that sense do not arise; therefore, when these remain the same, and the perceptions in question do arise, they must be occasioned by unperceived causes affecting it, the existence of which causes is known, and is proved by these their effects.

These observations and reasonings when compounded together, give evidence for the continued and unperceived existences which are in relation to the senses, as much as the exhibition of any simple sensation whatever, affords an evidence of the existence of that new being in the universe in which the sensation consists. For color, sound, etc., may be considered as so many beings; and every variety of them, as so many various beings, whose existence cannot be disputed, after a consciousness of their appearance to the mind. In like manner, the relations of the simple sensations are equally true in their existence.

Now all that is wanted for the argument is to show, that reason, or the observation of the relation of our simple sensations, does as a new sensation of the mind, give evidence of unperceived existence, and therefore affords a solution to the difficulty which appears to be in the question: How can we know of any continued existence when we can immediately know nothing but our sensations, which are obviously only interrupted existences?

It arises that it is owing to the intimate union and association of the sensible impressions with the ideas of their causes, that these causes or objects can never be contemplated except under the forms of those unions, by which it comes to pass that the whole union is considered in a popular way as existing unperceived: and it requires a philosophical examination to separate that natural junction of thought. This explains, I think, by an easier as well as truer method, than that of the "feigned imagination" to which Mr. Hume has recourse, where it is that color, sound, etc., as well as extension and solidity (all our perceptions of primary and secondary qualities), are thought to exist unperceived, when yet perception certainly cannot exist unperceived, nor a sensation unfelt. It also explains why even philosophy does not readily give up the notion of the separate existence of primary sensible qualities unperceived, because first, it is too great a stress for the imagination to separate all sensible images from the ideas of their causes; that which is left seems like nothing; and the mind cannot bear that vacuity of thought. Secondly, a number of arguments are lost, as men think, for creation, for deity, etc., which is really not the case; and if with minds equally removed from unfounded fears on the one hand, and insidious intentions on the other, men would pursue logical deductions, and rise above the weakness of keeping up a false philosophy in order to avoid the consequences of truth, they would come to clearer notions of all important truths, and establish them more firmly than they possibly can do, by the retention of any popular prejudice, however it appears to favor them.

Popular prejudice, it is true, leads frequently to a belief in those results, which reason, by different steps, may assure us to be correct. But the vicious mixture of philosophical analysis, with some erroneous notions, only gives birth to monstrous opinions; the old and common habits of thought are disturbed by it; the road, which before seemed so plain and direct, assumes a different appearance under the partial lights of a temporizing philosophy, which are only sufficient to disclose the dangers through which we managed before to walk, blindly indeed, but with sufficient security for every ordinary purpose of life.

From what has been said, we can see the error of Bishop Berkeley, who perceiving that the sensations of qualities (commonly termed *sensible qualities*), could not exist unfelt, concluded that "nothing material could exist unfelt," so that all the "furniture of heaven and earth were nothing without a mind"; and as his followers conceive after him when they say, "Time is nothing; extension nothing; solidity and space equally nothing." That such propositions are professed is not a fancy, for I have heard the notions maintained in the conversations of the day, especially with regard to time, which as it was concluded to be only a quality in reference to a perception of mind, so it could not be a measure, adequate to the allotment of any peculiar portion of existence, as necessary to the attainment of certain ends; such as the possibility of the events of a long life taking place in the short space of a moment, of that twinkling of an eye. In other words, time is a mere succession of ideas in a mind.

It may be seen where in dreams we mistake the qualities which present themselves for the qualities belonging to the continuously existing objects of sense, it is because they are combined in the same forms in which they appear in our waking state. But on account of our ignorance of remaining in the same place during the time of the dream, the relation of place is wanting to enable us to correct the false inferences from these vivacious imaginations, and view them in their true character. They are considered therefore as owing their existences to causes which will respond to every future call of the senses. A waking moment shows that on account of our being in the same place during the time of the dream, these objects will not be able to fill their whole definitions; i.e., be ready to appear upon the irregular call of the senses, or be taken notice of by more minds than one; and therefore the same objects which thus appear are not the objects of sense, but of the imagination. The circumstance of objects fulfilling their definitions, or not, is what renders them real, or the contrary. It is not on account of the superior order, variety, and force in which they appear to the mind, as Berkeley and Hume contend to be the case; for a real object is that which comprehends all the qualities for which its name stands. And dreams do not present real things, because they cannot answer all the qualities expected of them after waking.

Now because we perceive, when awake, that sensible qualities are no more than one set of the conjoined effects flowing from exterior objects, which when meeting with various other circumstances, are known to be capable of determining the remainder of their qualities. We therefore refer them to such compound objects as their causes, and as capable of their further effects; and this reasoning is the step the mind takes in arguing from the present sensible qualities of things to their future properties, and that which Hume eagerly enquires after denying the possibility of finding it.

It is not, as Mr. Hume says, in the nature of bread, that the sensible qualities of its color and consistency lead us immediately to expect nourishment. Sensible qualities are effects, and are always considered as such. In dreams and insanities, this reference is made by the mind; for the sensible appearing qualities, the vivacious images of things, are considered to be what they usually are, in a waking state; i.e., one set of the effects which are determined by compound objects, equal to fulfilling the remainder of their definitions, and therefore real, or usual objects, for which certain names first stood. At the moment of waking, the understanding regains its ascendency; and perceiving that during the time of the dream the mind had only been in one place, it justly concludes, that therefore the vivacious perceptions of sensible qualities could not be similar effects from similar objects or causes, but partial effects from partial causes: therefore must necessarily be mere delusions. When new sets of sensible qualities, which rush in upon the mind, are also justly considered to be the true effects from continually existing things, which now shall be capable of fulfilling their whole definitions; for they do not appear to lie open to any objection to the contrary, while also the superior accuracy of the whole sensations, when compared with the former ones, gives the mind immediate security. And if in any other state of being than this, all our knowledge of outward and independent things could be proved to have arisen only from an action of the brain, and so this life should be shown to have been but a waking dream, still whatever should renew the memory of past life with the then present sense, would continue the notion of our own continuous existence, although we might require further proof than what we had enjoyed for the assurance of the existence of other beings than ourselves. But I can conceive no method possible of conveying the assurances of other existences besides ourselves, than such as is analogous to what we enjoy; for such assurances must come through some means, some notions in the soul, some reasonings, some probabilities. And if we will always say the notions are the things, and the things separate from the notions are not proved, it appears to me to exclude the possibility of proof upon the subject; for I hardly can conceive how the Deity himself, in granting proofs to us finite creatures, can go beyond affording us such sensations, and such relations of sensations, as are capable of the inference, that "in order to support the phenomena there must be other continuous existences than ourselves," and that there must necessarily be continually existing causes for every variety of sensation which continues either to exist or to appear.

It may therefore be concluded, in contradiction to the idealists, that by our sensations we do have the notions of existences of objects which are unperceived or unfelt. We can have notions of things which have it not in their capacity to yield a sensation, such as of sound sleep and death, neither of which was ever felt by anyone; yet the meaning of which we perfectly understand, by the negative ideas which stand as their signs, and the words which stand as the signs of those ideas. And although it be true that "nothing can be like a sensation but sensation," yet by perceiving that objects unperceived cannot be like perceived objects by that very notion we do predicate something concerning unperceived objects and concerning our knowledge of them in their unperceived state, namely, that they are not similar to our perceptions. And this knowledge arises from a reflection, which is itself a sensation; and thus it may be seen that the whole of our sensations includes our knowledge of *continuous existences*, which are unperceived.

Immanuel Kant

REGARDING AN EXTERNAL WORLD

Human reason, in one sphere of its cognition, is called upon to consider questions, which it cannot decline, as they are presented by its own nature, but which it cannot answer, as they transcend every faculty of the mind.

It falls into this difficulty without any fault of its own. It begins with principles, which cannot be dispensed with in the field of experience, and the truth and sufficiency of which are, at the same time, insured by experience. With these principles it rises, in obedience to the laws of its own nature, to ever higher and more remote conditions. But it quickly discovers that, in this way, its labors must remain ever incomplete, because new questions never cease to present themselves; and thus it finds itself compelled to have recourse to principles which transcend the region of experience, while they are regarded by common sense without distrust. It thus falls into confusion and contradictions, from which it conjectures the presence of latent errors, which, however, it is unable to discover, because the principles it employs, transcending the limits of experience, cannot be tested by that criterion. The arena of these endless contests is called *Metaphysics*.

In recent times the hope dawned upon us of seeing those disputes settled, and the legitimacy of her claims established by a kind of *physiology* of the human understanding—that of the celebrated Locke. But it was found that—although it was affirmed that this so-called queen could not refer her descent to any higher source than that of common experience, a circumstance which necessarily brought suspicion on her claims—as this *genealogy* was incorrect, she persisted in the advancement of her claims to sovereignty. Thus metaphysics necessarily fell back into the antiquated and rotten constitution of *dogmatism*, and again became obnoxious to the contempt from which efforts had been made to save it. At present, as all methods, according to the general persuasion, have been tried in vain, there reigns none but weariness and complete *indifferentism*—the mother of chaos and night in the scientific world, but at the same time the source of, or at least the prelude to, the re-creation and reinstallation of a science, when it has fallen into confusion, obscurity, and disuse from ill-directed effort.

We very often hear complaints of the shallowness of the present age, and of the decay of profound science. But I do not think that those which rest upon a secure foundation, such as mathematics, physical science, etc., in the least deserve this reproach, but that they rather maintain their ancient fame, and in the latter case, indeed, far surpass it. The same would be the case with the other kinds of cognition, if their principles were but firmly established. In the absence of this security, indifference, doubt, and finally, severe criticism are rather signs of a profound habit of thought. Our age is the age of criticism, to which everything must be subjected. The sacredness of religion, and the authority of legislation, are by many regarded as grounds of exemption from the examination of this tribunal. But, if they on they are exempted, they become the subjects of just suspicion, and cannot lay claim to sincere respect, which reason accords only to that which has stood the test of a free and public examination.

It is, in fact, a call to reason, again to undertake the most laborious of all tasks—that of self-examination, and to establish a tribunal, which may secure it in its well-grounded claims, while it pronounces against all baseless assumptions and pretensions, not in an arbitrary manner, but

Edited from *Critique of Pure Reason,* Preface; Second Division, Book II, Chapter 1. Translated by J. M. D. Meiklejohn, 1900, which is now in the public domain.

according to its own eternal and unchangeable laws. This tribunal is nothing less than the *critical investigation of pure reason.*

I do not mean by this a criticism of books and systems, but a critical inquiry into the faculty of reason, with reference to the cognitions to which it strives to attain *without the aid of experience*; in other words, the solution of the question regarding the possibility or impossibility of metaphysics, and the determination of the origin, as well as of the extent and limits of this science. All this must be done on the basis of principles.

This path—the only one now remaining—has been entered upon by me; and I flatter myself that I have, in this way, discovered the cause of—and consequently the mode of removing—all the errors which have hitherto set reason at variance with itself, in the sphere of non-empirical thought. I have not returned an evasive answer to the questions of reason, by alleging the inability and limitation of the faculties of the mind; I have, on the contrary, examined them completely in the light of principles, and, after having discovered the cause of the doubts and contradictions into which reason fell, have solved them to its perfect satisfaction. It is true, these questions have not been solved as dogmatism, in its vain fancies and desires, had expected; for it can only be satisfied by the exercise of magical arts, and of these I have no knowledge. But neither do these come within the compass of our mental powers; and it was the duty of philosophy to destroy the illusions which had their origin in misconceptions, whatever darling hopes and valued expectations may be ruined by its explanations. My chief aim in this work has been thoroughness; and I make bold to say that there is not a single metaphysical problem that does not find its solution, or at least the key to its solution, here. Pure reason is a perfect unity; and therefore, if the principle presented by it prove to be insufficient for the solution of even a single one of those questions to which the very nature of reason gives birth, we must reject it, as we could not be perfectly certain of its sufficiency in the case of the others.

While I say this, I think I see upon the countenance of the reader signs of dissatisfaction mingled with contempt, when he hears declarations which sound so boastful and extravagant; and yet they are beyond comparison more moderate than those advanced by the commonest author of the commonest philosophical program, in which the dogmatist professes to demonstrate the simple nature of the soul, or the necessity of a primal being. Such a dogmatist promises to extend human knowledge beyond the limits of possible experience; while I humbly confess that this is completely beyond my power. Instead of any such attempt, I confine myself to the examination of reason alone and its pure thought; and I do not need to seek far for the sum-total of its cognition, because it has its seat in my own mind. Besides, common logic presents me with a complete and systematic catalogue of all the simple operations of reason; and it is my task to answer the question how far reason can go, without the material presented and the aid furnished by experience.

So much for the completeness and thoroughness necessary in the execution of the present task. The aims set before us are not arbitrarily proposed, but are imposed upon us by the nature of cognition itself.

However harmless idealism may be considered—although in reality it is not so—in regard to the essential ends of metaphysics, it must still remain a scandal to philosophy and to the general human reason to be obliged to assume, as an article of mere belief, the existence of things external to ourselves (from which, yet, we derive the whole material of cognition for the internal sense), and not to be able to oppose a satisfactory proof to any one who may call it in question.

Fourth Paralogism [illogical or fallacious reasoning]: *That the existence of which can only be inferred as a cause of given perceptions, has a merely doubtful existence.*

All outer appearances are of such a nature that their existence is not immediately perceived, and that we can only *infer* them as the cause of given perceptions. Therefore, the existence of all objects of the outer senses is doubtful. This uncertainty I entitle the *ideality of outer appearances*, and the doctrine of this ideality is called *idealism*, as distinguished from the counter-assertion of a possible certainty in regard to objects of outer sense, which is called *dualism*.

Critique of the Fourth Paralogism: Let us first examine the premises. We are justified, it is argued, in maintaining that only what is in ourselves can be perceived immediately, and that my own existence is the sole object of a mere perception. The existence, therefore, of an actual object outside me (if this word 'me' be taken in the intellectual, not in the empirical, sense) is never given directly in perception. Perception is a modification of inner sense, and the existence of the outer object can be added to it only in thought, as being its outer cause, and accordingly as being inferred. For the same reason, Descartes was justified in limiting all perception, in the narrowest sense of that term, to the proposition, 'I, as a thinking being, exist.' Obviously, since what is without is not in me, I cannot encounter it in my apperception, nor therefore in any perception, which, properly regarded, is merely the determination of apperception.

I am not, therefore, in a position to *perceive* external things, but can only infer their existence from my inner perception, taking the inner perception as the effect of which something external is the proximate cause. Now the inference from a given effect to a determinate cause is always uncertain, since the effect may be due to more than one cause. Accordingly, as regards the relation of the perception to its cause, it always remains doubtful whether the cause be internal or external; whether, that is to say, all the so-called outer perceptions are not a mere play of our inner sense, or whether they stand in relation to actual external objects as their cause. At all events, the existence of the latter is only inferred, and is open to all the dangers of inference, whereas the object of inner sense (I myself with all my representations) is immediately perceived, and its existence does not allow of being doubted.

The term '*idealist*' is not, therefore, to be understood as applying to those who deny the existence of external objects of the senses, but only to those who do not admit that their existence is known through immediate perception, and who therefore conclude that we can never, by way of any possible experience, be completely certain as to their reality.

Before exhibiting our paralogism in all its deceptive illusoriness, I have first to remark that we must necessarily distinguish two types of idealism, the transcendental and the empirical. By *transcendental idealism* I mean the doctrine that appearances are to be regarded as being, one and all, representations only, not things in themselves, and that time and space are therefore only sensible forms of our intuition, not determinations given as existing by themselves, nor conditions of objects viewed as things in themselves. To this idealism there is opposed a *transcendental realism* which regards time and space as something given in themselves, independently of our sensibility. The transcendental realist thus interprets outer appearances (their reality being taken as granted) as things-in-themselves, which exist independently of us and of our sensibility, and which are therefore outside us—the phrase 'outside us' being interpreted in conformity with pure concepts of understanding. It is, in fact, this transcendental realist who afterwards plays the part of empirical idealist. After wrongly supposing that objects of the senses, if they are to be external, must have an existence by themselves, and independently of the senses, he finds that, judged from this point of view, all our sensuous representations are inadequate to establish their reality.

The transcendental idealist, on the other hand, may be an empirical realist or, as he is called, a *dualist*; that is, he may admit the existence of matter without going outside his mere self-consciousness, or assuming anything more than the certainty of his representations, that is, the *cogito, ergo sum* [I think, therefore I am]. For he considers this matter and even its inner possibility to be appearance merely, and appearance, if separated from our sensibility, is nothing. Matter is with him, therefore, only a species of representations (intuition), which are called external, not as standing in relation to objects *in themselves external*, but because they relate perceptions to the space in which all things are external to one another, while yet the space itself is in us.

From the start, we have declared ourselves in favor of this transcendental idealism; and our doctrine thus removes all difficulty in the way of accepting the existence of matter on the unaided testimony of our mere self-consciousness, or of declaring it to be thereby proved in the same manner as the existence of myself as a thinking being is proved. There can be no question that I am conscious of my representations; these representations and I myself, who have the representations, therefore exist. External objects (bodies), however, are mere appearances, and are therefore nothing but a species of my representations, the objects of which are something only through these representations. Apart from them they are nothing. Thus external things exist as well as I myself, and both indeed, upon the immediate witness of my self-consciousness. The only difference is that the representation of myself, as the thinking subject, belongs to inner sense only, while the representations which mark extended beings belong also to outer sense. In order to arrive at the reality of outer objects I have just as little need to resort to inference as I have in regard to the reality of the object of my inner sense, that is, in regard to the reality of my thoughts. For in both cases alike the objects are nothing but representations, the immediate perception (consciousness) of which is at the same time a sufficient proof of their reality.

The transcendental idealist is, therefore, an empirical realist, and allows to matter, as appearance, a reality which does not permit of being inferred, but is immediately perceived. Transcendental realism, on the other hand, inevitably falls into difficulties, and finds itself obliged to give way to empirical idealism, in that it regards the objects of outer sense as something distinct from the senses themselves, treating mere appearances as self-subsistent beings, existing outside us. On such a view as this, however clearly we may be conscious of our representation of these things, it is still far from certain that, if the representation exists, there exists also the object corresponding to it. In our system, on the other hand, these external things, namely matter, are in all their configurations and alterations nothing but mere appearances, that is, representations in us, of the reality of which we are immediately conscious.

Part Four: Knowledge

Introduction

Most people have doubts about something. For example, some people in relationships have doubts about the loyalty of their partners. They might even doubt whether the relationship will last. In a different situation, someone might doubt the sincerity of a co-worker, or wonder whether the co-worker was undermining that person in order to get ahead. Even something as simple as getting a car repaired might lead you to doubt the high cost of the repair, or even whether it is necessary to do everything the mechanic recommends. Some people have doubts about the fairness of elections; some people have cultural doubts about the pressure of following old traditions; some people have religious doubts; others have doubts about their government's foreign or domestic policies; some people have doubts about the guilt or innocence of a person on trial; and many people doubt the claims made in advertisements.

Consider for a moment recent doubts that you have felt in your personal life. Have you doubted the truth of something you have heard or read? If the economy fails to improve substantially, then do you have doubts about securing a well-paying job, or being able to enter a career that you will enjoy? But is it possible to doubt everything? What would that mean? Could you doubt even that your life is real, that perhaps it is just a dream? Can you seriously doubt every belief you have?

As you will soon discover, some philosophers have searched for a method for arriving at knowledge. The search has driven many philosophers' quests to find the *foundations of knowledge*, the *role of doubt*, and the *possibility of certainty*. The nature of knowledge is studied by the area of philosophy called *epistemology*.

Twenty-five hundred years ago, Plato explored the problem of doubt regarding the world of *appearance* (given though our sensations), which is fleeting and always changing. From this, Plato concluded that knowledge is *not* available in the world of appearance. Therefore, knowledge must be of a realm of unchanging *being*—what Plato called the realm of *Ideas*—to which humans have an *innate* association. However, we do not have direct access to knowledge when we are born. For Plato, knowledge is not learned or gained through experience, but it can be *recalled* (recollected) through the mind's capacity to *reason*.

Plato's student, Aristotle, disagreed with Plato about innate ideas. Aristotle argued that we are *not* born with any innate ideas. Our minds are initially like a clean, blank piece of paper on which experience writes all that we come to know.

Philosophers such as Plato, who argue that we arrive at knowledge through reason, are called *rationalists*. Philosophers such as Aristotle, who argue that we arrive at knowledge through experience, are called *empiricists*. We will meet both kinds in this section.

Plato's arguments for innate ideas as the source of knowledge, and Aristotle's arguments for experience as the source of knowledge, became the dominant positions regarding knowledge for over two thousand years. How about you—do you identify with Plato or Aristotle? Are you a rationalist, an empiricist, or a little of both at this point? Don't worry if you can't answer the question just yet. The readings to follow will provide you the opportunity to think clearly and deeply about these issues, as you come to understand the arguments and discussions of many of the great philosophers.

You will see how later thinkers such as René Descartes, John Locke, Gottfried Leibniz, Mary Astell, and others, extended the arguments of Plato and Aristotle. In fact, the problems associated with *doubt*, *knowledge*, and *certainty* are still being discussed today.

There is a long and rich history of discussion regarding what constitutes knowledge. The readings in this section will provide ample opportunity for you to think about the important issues regarding knowledge. The differing viewpoints are revealed in each philosopher's response to the question, "What do we know, and how do we know it?"

Plato

KNOWLEDGE IS RECOLLECTION

How will you inquire, Socrates, into that which you do not know? And if you find what you want, how will you ever know that this is the thing which you did not know?

I understand, Meno, what you mean. You argue that man cannot inquire either about that which he knows, or about that which he does not know; for if he knows, he has no need to inquire; and if not, he cannot; for he does not know the very subject about which he is to inquire.

Well, Socrates, is not the argument sound?

I think not.

Why not?

I have heard from certain wise persons who spoke of a glorious truth. They say that the soul of man is immortal, and at one time has an end, which is dying, and at another time is born again, but is never destroyed. The soul, then, being immortal, and having been born again many times, and having seen all things that exist, whether in this world or in the next, has knowledge of them all. And it is no wonder that she should be able to remember all that she ever knew about virtue, and about everything else, for as all nature is alike, and the soul has learned all things, there is no difficulty in her eliciting, or as men say learning, out of a single recollection all the rest, if a man is strenuous and does not faint. All enquiry and all learning are but recollection. Therefore we ought not to listen to this sophistical argument about the impossibility of enquiry, for it will make us idle; and it is sweet only to the sluggard; but the other saying will make us active and inquisitive.

Yes, Socrates; but what do you mean by saying that we do not learn, and that what we call learning is only a process of recollection? Can you teach me how this is?

Meno, you are a rogue. You ask whether I can teach you, after I already said that there is no teaching, but only recollection; and thus you imagine that you will involve me in a contradiction.

I had no such intention. I only asked the question from habit; but if you can prove to me that what you say is true, I wish that you would.

It will be no easy matter. Suppose that you call one of your attendants, that I may demonstrate on him.

Certainly. I will call a young lad who works for me.

Does he speak Greek?

Edited from *Meno*. Translated by Benjamin Jowett, 1892, which is now in the public domain.

Yes, indeed.

Pay attention to the questions that I ask him, and observe whether he learns from me or only remembers.

I will.

Tell me lad, do you know that a figure like this is a square?

I do.

And you know that a square figure has four sides equal?

Certainly.

And these lines which I have drawn through the middle of the square are also equal?

Yes.

A square may be of any size?

I think so.

And if one side of the figure is two feet, and the other side is two feet, then how much will the whole be? If in one direction the space was two feet, and in other direction one foot, the whole would be of two feet taken once?

Yes.

But since this side is also two feet, there are twice two feet?

There are.

Then the square is twice two feet?

Yes.

And how many are twice two feet? Count and tell me.

Four, Socrates.

And might there not be another square twice as large as this, and having the lines equal?

Yes.

And how many feet will that be?

Eight feet.

And now try to tell me the length of the line which forms the side of that double square. This one is two feet—but what will that one be?

It will be double.

Do you observe, Meno, that I am not teaching the lad anything, but only asking him questions. And now he think's that he knows how long a line is necessary in order to produce a figure of eight square feet—does he not?

Yes.

But does he really know?

No, he does not.

He only guesses that because the square is double, the line is double.

Yes.

Observe him while he recalls the steps in regular order. Tell me lad, do you assert that a double space comes from a double line? Remember that I am not speaking of an oblong, but of a square figure equal every way, and twice the size of this—that is to say, of eight feet; and I want to know whether you still say that a double square comes from a double line?

I think so.

Does this line become doubled if we add another such line here?

Yes, it does.

And four such lines will make a space containing eight feet?

Yes.

Let us draw such a figure. Now, would you say that this is the figure of eight feet?

Yes.

And are there not these four divisions in the figure, each of which is equal to the figure of four feet?

Yes.

And is not that four times four?

It is.

And four times is not double?

No, it is not.

How much, then?

Four times as much.

Therefore, the double line has given a space, not twice, but four times as much.

Yes.

Four times four are sixteen—are they not?

Yes.

At this point we know that a space of four feet is made from the side of our original square. Now we know that doubling the original side creates a space of sixteen feet. So, can we say that a space of eight feet is twice the original square but half the new square?

Yes.

Such a space, then, will be made out of a side greater than the first one but less than the second one?

It will.

Very good. I like to hear you say what you think. Then the line that forms the side of eight feet must be more than the line of two feet, but less than the other of four feet?

It must be.

See if you can tell me how much it will be.

Three feet.

Then if we add a half to this line of two, that will be the line of three. Here are two and there is one; and on the other side, here are two also and there is one: and that makes the figure of which you speak?

That is the figure.

But if there are three feet this way and three feet that way, then the whole space will be three times three feet, will it not?

It will.

And how much are three times three feet?

Nine.

And how much is the double of four?

Eight.

Then the figure of eight is not made out of a line of three.

No.

We know, now, that the figure of eight feet, which is what we want, is not made out of a side of three. Based on what we have done, can you now see the correct answer?

No, Socrates, I have no idea.

Do you see, Meno, what advances he has made in his power of recollection? He did not know at first, and he does not know now, what is the side of a figure of eight feet. But then he thought that he knew, and answered confidently as if he knew, and had no difficulty. Now he has a difficulty, and neither knows nor thinks that he knows.

True, Socrates.

Is he not better off in knowing his ignorance?

I think that he is.

If we have made him doubt, then have we done him any harm?

No.

We have assisted him in some degree to the discovery of the truth. And now he will wish to remedy his ignorance.

True.

But do you suppose that he would ever have inquired into or learned what he thought that he knew—though he was really ignorant of it—until he had fallen into doubt, but now has the desire to know?

I think not, Socrates.

I shall only ask him, and not teach him, and he shall share the enquiry with me. Watch and see if you find me teaching anything to him, instead of eliciting his opinion. Tell me, lad, is not this a square of four feet which I have drawn?

It is the same as our original square, Socrates.

And now I add another square equal to the former one. And a third, which is equal to either of them. An we can now fill up the vacant corner. Here are four equal spaces, do you agree?

I agree.

And we know from earlier that this large space made up of the four equal spaces is four times the original one?

Yes, I remember that.

But we need it to be twice as large as the original one, not four times?

Yes.

Now I want you to look carefully at the four new lines I have drawn. Notice that each of these new lines go from corner to corner of each of the four spaces, so they cut each of those four spaces in half.

I can see that.

Look closely at the new four equal lines, do they create a new space?

Yes, they do.

And each of the four new lines cut in half the space in each of the four sections?

Yes, they cut each in half.

How big is the new space created by the four new lines?

I don't know.

Do you remember when you said that the four new lines cut each of the four spaces in half?

Yes.

And how many spaces were there in the large area?

Sixteen.

If the four new lines cut each space in half, then how big is the new area?

Eight feet. Now I understand.

And is this what we wanted?

Yes, it is.

I can now give a name to the new lines: "the diagonal." As we have shown, the double space that we were looking for resulted from a square made of the four diagonals. What do you say of him, Meno? Were not all these answers given out of his own head?

Yes, they were all his own, Socrates.

And yet, at the beginning of our enquiry he did not know.

True.

But he must have had in him certain true ideas that he did not yet recollect.

It seems that way.

And these ideas have just been stirred up in him, as in a dream. But if he were frequently asked the same questions, in different forms, he would know as well as any one at last.

I agree.

Without any one teaching him he will recover his knowledge for himself, if he is asked the right questions.

It appears so.

And this spontaneous recovery of knowledge in him is recollection?

That seems to be true.

And this knowledge which he now has, must he not either have acquired or always possessed?

Yes.

But if he always possessed this knowledge he would always have known; or if he has acquired the knowledge he could not have acquired it in this life, unless he has been taught geometry; for he may be made to do the same with all geometry and every other branch of knowledge. Now, has any one ever taught him all this? You must know about him.

I am certain that no one ever did teach him.

And yet he has the knowledge?

It seems so.

But if he did not acquire the knowledge in this life, then he must have had it at some other time?

Clearly, he must.

Which must have been the time when he was not yet born?

Yes.

And if there have always been true thoughts in him, both at the time when he was and was not a man, and which only need to be awakened into knowledge by putting questions to him, his soul must have always possessed this knowledge, for he either was or was not a man.

Obviously.

And if the truth of all things always existed in the soul, then the soul is immortal. Therefore, we should always try to recollect what we do not now know, or rather what we do not remember. I must admit, Meno, that I am not altogether confident in some of things I have said. Nevertheless, we will be better, braver, and less helpless if we think that we ought to enquire, than we would be if we indulged in the idle fancy that there was no knowing and no use in seeking to know what we do not know. That is a theme upon which I am ready to fight, in word and deed, to the utmost of my power.

Aristotle

A WRITING TABLET

As to the part of the soul that knows and understands—whether such part is separable or not separable spatially, but only in thought—we have to consider what is its distinctive character, and how thinking comes about. If thinking is analogous to perceiving, then it will consist in a being acted upon by the object of thought. This part of the soul must be receptive of the form of the object, and potentially like this form, though not identical with it. As the faculty of sense is to sensible objects [objects of sense perception], so must intellect be related to intelligible objects.

The mind, since it thinks all things, must be unlike anything it can know; hence it *can have no nature of its own, other than that of having a certain capacity*. Thus, the part of the soul which we call intellect (and by *intellect* I mean that whereby the soul thinks and conceives) is nothing at all actually before it thinks. Thus, we cannot conceive it to be mixed with the body, for in that case it would acquire some particular quality—cold or heat—or would even have some organ, as the sense faculties have. But it has none. Therefore, the soul is a place of forms or ideas, except that this is not true of the whole soul, but only of the part of soul which can think, and again that the forms are there not in actuality, but potentially.

The faculties of sense are different from that of intellect. For example, a sense loses its power to perceive, if the sensible object has been too intense; thus it cannot hear sound after very loud noises; and after too powerful colors or odors it can neither see nor smell. In contrast, the intellect, when it has been thinking of an object of intense thought, is not less, but even more capable of thinking of other objects. In other words, the faculties of sense are not independent of the body, whereas intellect is independent.

The question might arise: Assuming that the mind is something simple and impassive, and has nothing in common with anything else, how will it think, if to think is to be acted upon? Can mind itself be its own object? The mind is in a manner potentially all objects of thought, but is actually none of them until it thinks, *in the same sense as in a tablet which has nothing actually written upon it—the writing exists potentially*. This is exactly the case with the mind. Moreover, the mind itself is included among the objects which can be thought. For where the objects are abstract, that which thinks and that which is thought are identical. On the other hand, in things containing matter, each of the objects of thought is present potentially. Consequently, material [physical] objects will not have mind in them, for the mind is the power of becoming such objects without their matter; whereas the mind will have the attribute of being its own object.

Edited from *De Anima,* Book III, Part 4. Translated by R. D. Hicks, 1907, which is now in the public domain.

Augustine

THE POSSIBILITY OF DECEPTION

We both are, and know that we are, and delight in our being, and our knowledge of it. Moreover, in these three things no true-seeming illusion disturbs us; for we do not come into contact with these by some bodily sense, as we perceive the things outside of us—colors by seeing, sounds by hearing, smells by smelling, tastes by tasting, hard and soft objects by touching—of all which sensible objects it is the images resembling them, but not themselves which we perceive in the mind and hold in the memory, and which excite us to desire the objects. But, without any delusive representation of images or phantasms, *I am most certain that I am,* and that I know and delight in this.

In respect of these truths, I am not at all afraid of the arguments of the Academicians [skeptics], who say, "What if you are deceived?" *For if I am deceived, I am.* For he who is not, cannot be deceived; and if I am deceived, by this same token I am. And since I am if I am deceived, how am I deceived in believing that I am? For it is certain that I am, if I am deceived. Since, therefore, I, the person deceived, should be, even if I were deceived, certainly I am not deceived in this knowledge that I am. And, consequently, neither am I deceived in knowing that I know. For, as I know that I am, so I know this also, that I know.

Edited from *City of God,* Book XI, Chapter 26. Translated by Rev. Marcus Dods,1866, which is now in the public domain.

René Descartes

DOUBT AND CERTAINTY

Meditation I

Several years have now elapsed since I first became aware that I had accepted, even from my youth, many false opinions for true, and that consequently what I afterwards based on such principles was highly doubtful; and from that time I was convinced of the necessity of undertaking once in my life to rid myself of all the opinions I had adopted, and of commencing anew the work of building from the foundation, if I desired to establish a firm and abiding superstructure in the sciences.

But as this enterprise appeared to me to be one of great magnitude, I waited until I had attained an age so mature as to leave me no hope that at any stage of life more advanced I should be better able to execute my design. On this account, I have delayed so long that I should henceforth consider I was doing wrong were I still to consume in deliberation any of the time that now remains for action. Today, then, since I have opportunely freed my mind from all cares (and am happily disturbed by no passions), and since I am in the secure possession of leisure in a peaceable retirement, I will at length apply myself earnestly and freely to the general overthrow of all my former opinions.

But, to this end, it will *not* be necessary for me to show that the whole of these are false—a point, perhaps, which I shall never reach; but as even now my reason convinces me that I ought not the less carefully to withhold belief from what is not entirely certain and indubitable, than from what is manifestly false, it will be sufficient to justify the rejection of the whole if I shall find in each some ground for doubt. Nor for this purpose will it be necessary even to deal with each belief individually, which would be truly an endless labor; but, as the removal from below of the foundation necessarily involves the downfall of the whole edifice, I will at once approach the criticism of the *principles* on which all my former beliefs rested.

All that I have, up to this moment, accepted as possessed of the highest truth and certainty, I received either from or through the *senses*. I observed, however, that these sometimes misled us; and it is the part of prudence not to place absolute confidence in that by which we have even once been deceived.

But it may be said, perhaps, that, although the senses occasionally mislead us respecting minute objects, and such as are so far removed from us as to be beyond the reach of close observation, there are yet many other of their presentations, of the truth of which it is manifestly impossible to doubt; as for example, that I am in this place, seated by the fire, clothed in a winter dressing gown, that I hold in my hands this piece of paper, with other intimations of the same nature. But how could I deny that I possess these hands and this body, and still escape being classed with persons in a state of insanity, whose brains are so disordered and clouded by dark bilious vapors as to cause them to assert that they are monarchs when they are in the greatest poverty; or clothed in gold and purple when destitute of any covering; or that their head is made of clay, their body of glass, or that they are gourds? I should certainly be not less insane than they, were I to regulate my procedure according to examples so extravagant.

Edited from *Meditations on First Philosophy,* Meditations I and II. Translated by John Veitch, 1901, which is now in the public domain.

Though this is true, I must nevertheless here consider that I am a man, and that, consequently, I am in the habit of sleeping, and representing to myself in dreams those same things, or even sometimes others less probable, which the insane think are presented to them in their waking moments. How often have I dreamt that I was in these familiar circumstances—that I was dressed, and occupied this place by the fire, when I was lying undressed in bed? At the present moment, however, I certainly look upon this paper with eyes wide awake; the head which I now move is not asleep; I extend this hand consciously and with express purpose, and I perceive it; the occurrences in sleep are not so distinct as all this. But I cannot forget that, at other times, I have been deceived in sleep by similar illusions; and, attentively considering those cases, I perceive so clearly that there exist no certain marks by which the state of waking can ever be distinguished from sleep, that I feel greatly astonished; and in amazement I almost persuade myself that I am now dreaming.

Let us suppose, then, that we are dreaming, and that all these particulars—namely, the opening of the eyes, the motion of the head, the forth-putting of the hands—are merely illusions; and even that we really possess neither an entire body nor hands such as we see. Nevertheless it must be admitted at least that the objects which appear to us in sleep are, as it were, painted representations which could not have been formed unless in the likeness of realities; and, therefore, that those general objects, at all events—namely, eyes, a head, hands, and an entire body—are not simply imaginary, but really existent. For, in truth, painters themselves, even when they study to represent sirens and satyrs by forms the most fantastic and extraordinary, cannot bestow upon them natures absolutely new, but can only make a certain medley of the members of different animals; or if they chance to imagine something so novel that nothing at all similar has ever been seen before, and such as is, therefore, purely fictitious and absolutely false, it is at least certain that the colors of which this is composed are real.

And on the same principle, although these general objects, namely, a body, eyes, a head, hands, and the like, are imaginary, we are nevertheless absolutely necessitated to admit the reality at least of some other objects still more simple and universal than these, of which, just as of certain real colors, all those images of things, whether true and real, or false and fantastic, that are found in our consciousness are formed.

To this class of objects seem to belong physical nature in general and its extension; the figure of extended things, their quantity or magnitude, and their number, as also the place in, and the time during, which they exist, and other things of the same sort. We will not, therefore, perhaps reason illegitimately if we conclude from this that physics, astronomy, medicine, and all the other sciences that have for their end the consideration of composite objects, are indeed of a doubtful character; but that arithmetic, geometry, and the other sciences of the same class, which regard merely the simplest and most general objects, and scarcely inquire whether or not these are really existent, contain somewhat that is certain and indubitable: for whether I am awake or dreaming, it remains true that two and three make five, and that a square has but four sides; nor does it seem possible that truths so apparent can ever fall under a suspicion of falsity or uncertainty.

Nevertheless, the belief that there is a God who is all powerful, and who created me, such as I am, has for a long time, obtained steady possession of my mind. How, then, do I know that he has not arranged that there should be neither earth, nor sky, nor any extended thing, nor figure, nor magnitude, nor place, providing at the same time, however, for the perceptions of all these objects, and the persuasion that these do not exist otherwise than as I perceive them? And further, as I sometimes think that others are in error respecting matters of which they believe themselves to possess a perfect knowledge, how do I know that I am not also deceived each time I add together two and three, or number the sides of a square, or form some judgment still more simple, if more simple indeed can be imagined? But perhaps God has not been willing that I should be thus deceived, for He is said to be supremely good. If, however, it were repugnant to the goodness of God to have created me subject to constant deception, it would seem likewise to be contrary to his goodness to allow me to be occasionally deceived; and yet it is clear that this is permitted. Some, indeed, might perhaps be found who would be disposed rather to deny the existence of a being so powerful than to believe that there is nothing certain. But let us for the present refrain from opposing this opinion, and grant that all which is here said of God is a fable. Nevertheless, in whatever way it be supposed that I reach the state in which I exist, whether by fate, or chance, or by an endless series of antecedents and consequents, or by any other means, it is clear (since to be deceived and to err is a certain defect) that the probability of my being so imperfect as to be the constant victim of deception, will be increased exactly in proportion as the power possessed by the cause, to which they assign my origin, is lessened. To this line of reasoning, I have assuredly nothing to reply, but am constrained at last to confess *that there is nothing of all that I formerly believed to be true of which it is impossible to doubt*, and that not through thoughtlessness or levity, but from cogent and maturely considered reasons; so that henceforward, *if I desire to discover anything certain*, I ought to refrain from assenting to those same opinions than to what might be shown to be manifestly false.

But it is not sufficient to have made these observations; care must be taken likewise to keep them in memory. For those old and customary opinions perpetually recur—long and familiar usage giving them the right of occupying my mind, even almost against my will, and subduing my belief. Nor will I lose the habit of deferring to them and confiding in them so long as I shall consider them to be what in truth they are, namely, opinions to some extent doubtful, as I have already shown, but still highly probable, and such as it is much more reasonable to believe than deny. It is for this reason I am persuaded that I shall not be doing wrong, if, taking an opposite judgment of deliberate design, I become my own deceiver, by supposing, for a time, that all those opinions are entirely false and imaginary, until at length, having thus balanced my old by my new prejudices, my judgment shall no longer be turned aside by perverted usage from the path that may conduct to the perception of truth. For I am assured that, meanwhile, there will arise neither peril nor error from this course, and that I cannot for the present yield too much to distrust, since the end I now seek is not action but knowledge.

I will suppose, then, not that God, who is supremely good and the fountain of truth, but that some malignant demon, who is at once exceedingly potent and deceitful, has employed all his artifice to deceive me. I will suppose that the sky, the air, the earth, colors, figures, sounds, and all external things, are nothing better than the illusions of dreams, by means of which this being has laid snares for my credulity. I will consider myself as without hands, eyes, flesh, blood, or any of the senses, and as falsely believing that I am possessed of these. I will continue resolutely fixed in this belief, and if indeed by this means it be not in my power to arrive at the knowledge of truth, I shall at least do what is in my power, namely, withhold judgment and guard with settled purpose against giving my assent to what is false, and being imposed upon by this deceiver, whatever be his power and artifice.

But this undertaking is arduous, and a certain indolence insensibly leads me back to my ordinary course of life. And just as a prisoner, who, perhaps was enjoying in his dreams an imaginary liberty, when he begins to suspect that it is but a vision, dreads awakening, and conspires with the agreeable illusions that the deception may be prolonged, so I, of my own accord, fall back into the train of my former beliefs, and fear to arouse myself from my slumber, so that the time of laborious wakefulness that would succeed this quiet rest, in place of bringing any light of day, should prove inadequate to dispel the darkness that will arise from the difficulties that have now been raised.

Meditation II

The Meditation of yesterday has filled my mind with so many doubts, that it is no longer in my power to forget them. Nor do I see, meanwhile, any principle on which they can be resolved; and, just as if I had fallen all of a sudden into very deep water, I am so greatly disconcerted as to be unable either to plant my feet firmly on the bottom or sustain myself by swimming on the surface. I will, nevertheless, make an effort, and try anew the same path on which I had entered yesterday, that is, proceed by casting aside all that admits of the slightest doubt, not less than if I had discovered it to be absolutely false; and I will continue always in this track until I shall find something that is *certain*, or at least, if I can do nothing more, until I shall know with certainty that there is nothing certain. Archimedes, that he might transport the entire globe from the place it occupied to another, demanded only a point that was firm and immovable; so also, I shall be entitled to entertain the highest expectations, *if I am fortunate enough to discover only one thing that is certain and indubitable.*

I suppose, accordingly, that all the things which I see are false; I believe that none of those objects which my fallacious memory represents ever existed; I suppose that I possess no senses; I believe that body, figure, extension, motion, and place are merely fictions of my mind. What is there, then, that can be esteemed true? Perhaps this only, that there is absolutely nothing certain.

But how do I know that there is not something different altogether from the objects I have now enumerated, of which it is impossible to entertain the slightest doubt? Is there not a God, or some being, by whatever name I may designate him, who causes these thoughts to arise in my mind? But why suppose such a being, for it may be I myself am capable of producing them? Am I, then, at least not something? But I before denied that I possessed senses or a body; I hesitate, however, for what follows from that? Am I so dependent on the body and the senses that without these I cannot exist? But I had the persuasion that there was absolutely nothing in the world, that there was no sky and no earth, neither minds nor bodies; was I not, therefore, at the same time, persuaded that I did not exist? Far from it; I assuredly existed, since I was persuaded. But there is I know not what being, who is possessed at once of the highest power and the deepest cunning, who is constantly employing all his ingenuity in deceiving me. Doubtless, then, I exist, since I am deceived; and, let him deceive me as he may, he can never bring it about that I am nothing, so long as I shall be conscious that I am something. So that it must be maintained, all things being maturely and carefully considered, that this proposition—*I am, I exist*—is *necessarily true* each time it is expressed by me, or conceived in my mind. This alone is inseparable from me. *I am—I exist:* this is *certain*; but how often? As often as I think; for perhaps it would even happen, if I should wholly cease to think, that I should at the same time altogether cease to be. I now admit nothing that is not necessarily true; I am therefore, precisely speaking, only a thinking thing, that is, a mind understanding, or reason—terms whose signification was before unknown to me. I am, however, a real thing, and really existent; but what thing? The answer was, *a thinking thing*, necessarily true each time it is expressed by me, or conceived in my mind.

But I do not yet know with sufficient clearness what I am, though assured that I am; and hence, in the next place, I must take care, in case I inconsiderately substitute some other object for what is properly myself, and thus wander from truth, even in that knowledge which I hold to be of all others the most certain and evident. For this reason, I will now consider anew what I formerly believed myself to be, before I entered on the present train of thought; and of my previous opinion I will retrench all that can in the least be invalidated by the grounds of doubt I have adduced, in order that there may at length remain nothing but what is certain and indubitable.

What then did I formerly think I was? Undoubtedly I judged that I was a man. But what is a man? Shall I say a rational animal? Assuredly not; for then it would be necessary to inquire into what is meant by *animal*, and what by *rational*, and thus, from a single question, I should insensibly glide into others, and these more difficult than the first; nor do I now possess enough leisure to warrant me in wasting my time amid subtleties of this sort. I prefer here to attend to the thoughts that sprung up of themselves in my mind, and were inspired by my own nature alone, when I applied myself to the consideration of what I was. In the first place, then, I thought that I possessed hands, arms, and all the fabric of members that appears in a corpse, and which I called by the name of *body*. It further occurred to me that I was nourished, that I walked, perceived, and thought, and all those actions I referred to the *soul*; but what the soul itself was I either did not stay to consider, or, if I did, I imagined that it was something extremely rare and subtle, like wind, or flame, or ether, spread through my grosser parts. As regarded the body, I did not even doubt of its nature, but thought I distinctly knew it, and if I had wished to describe it according to the notions I then entertained, I should have explained myself in this manner: By body I understand all that can be terminated by a certain figure; that can be comprised in a certain place, and so fill a certain space that excludes every other body; that can be perceived either by touch, sight, hearing, taste, or smell; that can be moved in different ways, not indeed of itself, but by something foreign to it by which it is touched or perceived; for the power of self-motion, as likewise that of perceiving and thinking, I held as by no means pertaining to the nature of body; on the contrary, I was somewhat astonished to find such faculties existing in some bodies.

But as for myself, what can I now say that I am, since I suppose there exists an extremely powerful, and, if I may so speak, malignant being, whose whole endeavors are directed toward deceiving me? Can I affirm that I possess any one of all those attributes of which I have lately spoken as belonging to the nature of body? After attentively considering them in my own mind, I find none of them that can properly be said to belong to myself.

But it is true, perhaps, that those very things which I suppose to be nonexistent, because they are unknown to me, are not in truth different from myself whom I know. This is a point I cannot determine, and do not now enter into any dispute regarding it. I can only judge of things that are known to me: I am conscious that I exist, and I who know that I exist inquire into what I am. It is, however, perfectly certain that the knowledge of my existence, thus precisely taken, is not dependent on things, the existence of which is as yet unknown to me: and consequently it is not dependent on any of the things I can imagine. But I already know that I exist, and that it is possible at the same time that all those images, and in general all that relates to the nature of body, are merely dreams or fantasies.

But what, then, am I? A thinking thing, it has been said. But what is a thinking thing? It is a thing that doubts, understands, conceives, affirms, denies, wills, refuses, imagines, and perceives. Assuredly it is not little, if all these properties belong to my nature. But why should they not belong to it? Am I not that very being who now doubts of almost everything; who, for all that, understands and conceives certain things; who affirms one alone as true, and denies the others; who desires to know more of them, and does not wish to be deceived; who imagines many things, sometimes even despite his will; and is likewise percipient of many, as if through the medium of the senses. Is there nothing of all this as true as that I am, even although I should be always dreaming, and although he who gave me being employed all his ingenuity to deceive me? Is there also any one of these attributes that can be properly distinguished from my thought, or that can be said to be separate from myself? For it is of itself so evident that it is I who doubt, I who understands, and I who desire, that it is here unnecessary to add anything by way of rendering it more clear. And I am as certainly the same being who imagines; for although it may be that nothing I imagine is true, still the power of imagination does not cease really to exist in me and to form part of my thought. I am the same being who perceives, that is, who apprehends certain objects as by the organs of sense, since, in truth, I see light, hear a noise, and feel heat. But it will be said that these presentations are false, and that I am dreaming. Let it be so. At all events it is certain that I seem to see light, hear a noise, and feel heat; this cannot be false, and this is what in me is properly called perceiving, which is nothing else than thinking. From this I begin to know what I am with somewhat greater clearness and distinctness than before.

But, nevertheless, it still seems to me, and I cannot help believing, that corporeal [physical] things, whose images are formed by thought by way of the senses, and are examined by the same, are known with much greater distinctness than that I know not what part of myself which is not imaginable; although, in truth, it may seem strange to say that I know and comprehend with greater distinctness things whose existence appears to me doubtful, that are unknown, and do not belong to me, than others of whose reality I am persuaded, that are known to me, and pertain to my proper nature; in a word, than myself. But I see clearly what is the state of the case. My mind is apt to wander, and will not yet submit to be restrained within the limits of truth. Let us therefore leave the mind to itself once more, and, according to it every kind of liberty to consider the objects that appear to it from without, in order that, having afterward withdrawn it from these gently and opportunely, it may then be the more easily controlled.

Let us now accordingly consider the objects that are commonly thought to be the most distinctly known, namely, the bodies we touch and see; not, indeed, bodies in general, for these general notions are usually somewhat more confused, but one body in particular. Take, for example, this piece of wax; it is quite fresh, having been but recently taken from the beehive; it has not yet lost the sweetness of the honey it contained; it still retains somewhat of the odor of the flowers from which it was gathered; its color, figure, size, are apparent; it is hard, cold, easily handled; and sounds when struck upon with the finger. In short, all that contributes to make a body as distinctly known as possible is found in the one before us. But, while I am speaking, let it be placed near the fire—what remained of the taste exhales, the smell evaporates, the color changes, its figure is destroyed, its size increases, it becomes liquid, it grows hot, it can hardly be handled, and, although struck upon, it emits no sound. *Does the same wax still remain after this change?* It must be admitted that it does remain; no one doubts it, or judges otherwise. What, then, was it I knew with so much distinctness in the piece of wax? Assuredly, it could be nothing of all that I observed by means of the senses, since all the things that fell under taste, smell, sight, touch, and hearing are changed, and yet the same wax remains. It was perhaps what I now think, namely, that this wax was neither the sweetness of honey, the pleasant odor of flowers, the whiteness, the figure, nor the sound, but only a body that a little before appeared to me conspicuous under these forms, and which is now perceived under others. But, to speak precisely, what is it that I imagine when I think of it in this way? Let it be attentively considered, and, retrenching all that does not belong to the wax, let us see what remains. There certainly remains nothing, except something extended, flexible, and movable. But what is meant by flexible and movable? Is it not that I imagine that the piece of wax, being round, is capable of becoming square, or of passing from a square into a triangular figure? Assuredly such is not the case, because I conceive that it admits of an infinity of similar changes; and I am, moreover, unable to compass this infinity by imagination, and consequently this conception which I have of the wax is not the product of the faculty of imagination. But what now is this extension? Is it not also unknown? for it becomes greater when the wax is melted, greater when it is boiled, and greater still when the heat increases; and I should not conceive according to truth, the wax as it is, if I did not suppose that the piece we are considering admitted even of a wider variety of extension than I ever imagined. I must, therefore, admit that I cannot even comprehend by imagination what the piece of wax is, and that it is the mind alone which perceives it.

I speak of one piece in particular; for, as to wax in general, this is still more evident. But what is the piece of wax that can be perceived only by the mind? It is certainly the same which I see, touch, imagine; and it is the same which, from the beginning, I believed it to be. But the perception of it is neither an act of sight, of touch, nor of imagination, and never was either of these, though it might formerly seem so, but is simply an intuition of the mind, which may be imperfect and confused, as it formerly was, or very clear and distinct, as it is at present, according as the attention is more or less directed to the elements which it contains, and of which it is composed.

But, meanwhile, I feel greatly astonished when I observe how prone my mind is to error. For although, without at all giving expression to what I think, I consider all this in my own mind, words yet occasionally impede my progress, and I am almost led into error by the terms of ordinary language. We say, for example, that we see the same wax when it is before us, and not that we judge it to be the same from its retaining the same color and figure: from which I should be disposed to conclude that the wax is known by the act of sight, and not by the intuition of the mind alone, were it not for the analogous instance of human beings passing on in the street below, as observed from a window. In this case I do not fail to say that I see the men themselves, just as I say that I see the wax; and yet what do I see from the window beyond hats and cloaks that might cover artificial machines, whose motions might be determined by springs? But I judge that there are human beings from these appearances, and thus I comprehend, by the faculty of judgment alone which is in the mind, what I believed I saw with my eyes.

The man who makes it his aim to rise to knowledge superior to the common, ought to be ashamed to seek occasions of doubting from the vulgar forms of speech: instead, therefore, of doing this, I shall proceed with the matter in hand, and inquire whether I had a clearer and more perfect perception of the piece of wax when I first saw it, and when I thought I knew it by means of the external sense itself, or, at all events, by the common sense, as it is called, that is, by the imaginative faculty; or whether I rather apprehend it more clearly at present, after having examined with greater care, both what it is, and in what way it can be known. I would certainly be ridiculous to entertain any doubt on this point. For what, in that first perception, was there distinct? What did I perceive which any animal might not have perceived? But when I distinguish the wax from its exterior forms, and when, as if I had stripped it of its vestments, I consider it quite naked, it is certain, although some error may still be found in my judgment, that I cannot, nevertheless, thus apprehend it without possessing a human mind.

But, finally, what shall I say of the mind itself, that is, of myself? for as yet I do not admit that I am anything but mind. What, then! I who seem to possess so distinct an apprehension of the piece of wax—do I not know myself, both, with greater truth and certitude, and also much more distinctly and clearly? For if I judge that the wax exists because I see it, it assuredly follows, much more evidently, that I myself am or exist, for the same reason: for it is possible that what I see may not in truth be wax, and that I do not even possess eyes with which to see anything; but it cannot be that when I see, or, which comes to the same thing, when I think I see, I myself who think am nothing. So likewise, if I judge that the wax exists because I touch it, it will still also follow that I am; and if I determine that my imagination, or any other cause, whatever it be, persuades me of the existence of the wax, I will still draw the same conclusion. And what is here remarked of the piece of wax is applicable to all the other things that are external to me. And further, if the perception of wax appeared to me more precise and distinct, after that not only sight and touch, but many other causes besides, rendered it manifest to my apprehension, with how much greater distinctness must I now know myself, since all the reasons that contribute to the knowledge of the nature of wax, or of any body whatever, manifest still better the nature of my mind? And there are besides so many other things in the mind itself that contribute to the illustration of its nature, that those dependent on the body, to which I have here referred, scarcely merit to be taken into account.

But, in conclusion, I find I have insensibly reverted to the point I desired; for, since it is now manifest to me that bodies themselves are not properly perceived by the senses nor by the faculty of imagination, but by the intellect alone; and since they are not perceived because they are seen and touched, but only because they are understood by thought, I readily discover that there is nothing more easily or clearly apprehended than my own mind. But because it is difficult to rid one's self so promptly of an opinion to which one has been long accustomed, it will be desirable to tarry for some time at this stage, that, by long continued meditation, I may more deeply impress upon my memory this new knowledge.

John Locke

KNOWLEDGE DERIVES FROM EXPERIENCE

Since it is the understanding that sets man above the rest of sensible beings, and gives him all the advantage and dominion which he has over them; it is certainly a subject, even for its nobleness, worth our labor to inquire into. The understanding, like the eye, while it makes us see and perceive all other things, takes no notice of itself; and it requires an art and pains to set it at a distance and make it its own object. But whatever are the difficulties that lie in the way of this inquiry; whatever it is that keeps us so much in the dark to ourselves; sure I am that all the light we can let in upon our minds, all the acquaintance we can make with our own understandings, will not only be very pleasant, but bring us great advantage, in directing our thoughts in the search of other things.

This, therefore, being my purpose—to inquire into the original, certainty, and extent of *human knowledge*, together with the grounds and degrees of *belief*, *opinion*, and *assent*. I shall not at present meddle with the physical consideration of the mind, or trouble myself to examine in what its essence consists; or by what motions of our spirits or alterations of our bodies we come to have any *sensation* by our organs, or any *ideas* in our understandings; and whether those ideas do in their formation, any or all of them, depend on matter or not. These are speculations which, however curious and entertaining, I shall decline, as lying out of my way in the design I am now upon. It shall suffice to my present purpose, to consider the discerning faculties of a man, as they are employed about the objects which they have to do with.

It is therefore worth while to search out the bounds between *opinion* and *knowledge*; and examine by what measures, in things whereof we have no certain knowledge, we ought to regulate our assent and moderate our persuasion. Therefore, I shall pursue the following method: First, I shall inquire into the original of those *ideas*, notions, or whatever else you please to call them, which a man observes, and is conscious to himself he has in his mind; and the ways whereby the understanding comes to be furnished with them.

Second, I shall endeavor to show what *knowledge* the understanding has by those ideas; and the certainty, evidence, and extent of it.

Third, I shall make some inquiry into the nature and grounds of *faith* or *opinion*: whereby I mean that assent which we give to any proposition as true, of whose truth yet we have no certain knowledge. And here we shall have occasion to examine the reasons and degrees of *assent*.

If by this inquiry into the nature of the understanding, I can discover the powers thereof, how far they reach, to what things they are in any degree proportionate, and where they fail us, then I suppose it may be of use to prevail with the busy mind of man to be more cautious in meddling with things exceeding its comprehension; to stop when it is at the utmost extent of its tether, and to sit down in a quiet ignorance of those things which, upon examination, are found to be beyond the reach of our capacities. We should not then perhaps be so forward, out of an affectation of an universal knowledge, to raise questions, and perplex ourselves and others with disputes about things to which our understandings are not suited; and of which we cannot frame in our minds any clear or distinct perceptions, or whereof (as it has perhaps too often happened) we have not any notions at all. If we can find out how far the understanding can extend its view; how far it has faculties to attain certainty; and in what cases it can only judge and guess, we may learn to content ourselves with what is attainable by us in this state.

Edited from *An Essay Concerning Human Understanding,* 1690, Introduction, and Book I, Chapter I.

But, before I proceed on to what I have thought on this subject, I must here in the entrance beg pardon of my reader for the frequent use of the word *idea*, which he will find in the following treatise. It being that term which, I think, serves best to stand for whatsoever is the *object* of the understanding when a man thinks, I have used it to express whatever is meant by *phantasm*, *notion*, *species*, or *whatever it is which the mind can be employed about in thinking*; and I could not avoid frequently using it.

I presume it will be easily granted me, that there are such *ideas* in men's minds: every one is conscious of them in himself; and men's words and actions will satisfy him that they are in others. Our first inquiry then shall be—how they come into the mind.

It is an established opinion among some men, that there are in the understanding certain *innate principles*; some primary notions, characters, as it were stamped upon the mind of man which the soul receives in its very first being, and brings into the world with it. It would be sufficient to convince unprejudiced readers of the falseness of this supposition, if I should only show (as I hope I shall in the following parts of this discourse) how men, barely by the use of their natural faculties, may attain to all the knowledge they have, without the help of any innate impressions; and may arrive at certainty, without any such original notions or principles.

There is nothing more commonly taken for granted than that there are certain *principles*, both *speculative* and *practical*, (for they speak of both), universally agreed upon by all mankind: which therefore, they argue, must be the constant impressions which the souls of men receive in their first beings, and which they bring into the world with them, as necessarily and really as they do any of their inherent faculties.

This argument, drawn from universal consent, has this misfortune in it, that if it were true in matter of fact, that there were certain truths wherein all mankind agreed, it would not prove them innate, if there can be any other way shown how men may come to that universal agreement, in the things they do consent in, which I presume may be done.

But, which is worse, this argument of universal consent, which is made use of to prove innate principles, seems to me a demonstration that there are none such: because there are none to which all mankind give an universal assent. I shall begin with the speculative, an instance in those magnified principles of demonstration, "Whatsoever is, is," and "It is impossible for the same thing to be and not to be"; which, of all others, I think have the most allowed title to innate. These have so settled a reputation of maxims universally received, that it will no doubt be thought strange if any one should seem to question it. But yet I take liberty to say, that these propositions are so far from having an universal assent, that there are a great part of mankind to whom they are not so much as known.

To avoid this, it is usually answered, that all men know and assent to them, *when they come to the use of reason*; and this is enough to prove them innate. For, to apply this answer with any tolerable sense to our present purpose, it must signify one of these two things: either that as soon as men come to the use of reason these supposed native inscriptions come to be known and observed by them; or else, that the use and exercise of men's reason, assists them in the discovery of these principles, and certainly makes them known to them.

If they mean, that by the use of reason men may discover these principles, and that this is sufficient to prove them innate; their way of arguing will stand thus, namely that whatever truths reason can certainly discover to us, and make us firmly assent to, those are all naturally imprinted on the mind; since that universal assent, which is made the mark of them, amounts to no more but this—that by the use of reason we are capable to come to a certain knowledge of and assent to them; and, by this means, there will be no difference between the maxims of the mathematicians, and theorems they deduce from them: all must be equally allowed innate; they being all discoveries made by the use of reason, and truths that a rational creature may certainly come to know, if he apply his thoughts rightly that way.

But how can these men think the use of reason necessary to discover principles that are supposed innate, when reason (if we may believe them) is nothing else but the faculty of deducing unknown truths from principles or propositions that are already known? That certainly can never be thought innate which we have need of reason to discover; unless, as I have said, we will have all the certain truths that reason ever teaches us, to be innate. We may as well think the use of reason necessary to make our eyes discover visible objects, as that there should be need of reason, or the exercise thereof, to make the understanding see what is originally engraved on it, and cannot be in the understanding before it be perceived by it. So that to make reason discover those truths thus imprinted, is to say, that the use of reason discovers to a man what he knew before: and if men have those innate impressed truths originally, and before the use of reason, and yet are always ignorant of them till they come to the use of reason, it is in effect to say, that men know and know them not at the same time.

Those who will take the pains to reflect with a little attention on the operations of the understanding, will find that this ready assent of the mind to some truths, depends not either on native inscription or the use of reason, but on a faculty of the mind quite distinct from both of them, as we shall see hereafter. Reason, therefore, having nothing to do in procuring our assent to these maxims, if by saying, that "men know and assent to them, when they come to the use of reason," is meant that the use of reason assists us in the knowledge of these maxims, it is utterly false; and were it true, would prove them not to be innate.

The senses at first let in *particular* ideas, and furnish the yet empty cabinet, and the mind by degrees growing familiar with some of them, they are lodged in the memory, and names got to them. Afterwards, the mind proceeding further, abstracts them, and by degrees learns the use of general names. In this manner the mind comes to be furnished with ideas and language, the *materials* about which to exercise its discursive faculty. And the use of reason becomes daily more visible, as these materials that give it employment increase. But though the having of general ideas and the use of general words and reason usually grow together, yet I see not how this any way proves them innate. The knowledge of some truths, I confess, is very early in the mind; but in a way that shows them not to be innate. For, if we will observe, we shall find it still to be about ideas, not innate, but acquired; it being about those first which are imprinted by external things, with which infants have earliest to do, which make the most frequent impressions on their senses. In ideas thus got, the mind discovers that some agree and others differ, probably as soon as it has any use of memory; as soon as it is able to retain and perceive distinct ideas. But whether it be then or not, this is certain, it does so long before it has the use of words; or comes to that which we commonly call "the use of reason." For a child knows as certainly before it can speak the difference between the ideas of sweet and bitter (i.e., that sweet is not bitter), as it knows afterwards (when it comes to speak) that wormwood and sugarplums are not the same thing.

Child knows not that three and four are equal to seven, till he comes to be able to count seven, and has got the name and idea of equality; and then, upon explaining those words, he presently assents to, or rather perceives the truth of that proposition. But neither does he then readily assent because it is an innate truth, nor was his assent wanting till then because he wanted the use of reason; but the truth of it appears to him as soon as he has settled in his mind the clear and distinct ideas that these names stand for. And then he knows the truth of that proposition upon the same ground and by the same means, that he knew before that a rod and a cherry are not the same thing; and upon the same grounds also that he may come to know afterwards "That it is impossible for the same thing to be and not to be," as shall be more fully shown hereafter. So that the later it is before any one comes to have those general ideas about which those maxims are; or to know the signification of those general terms that stand for them; or to put together in his mind the ideas they stand for; the later also will it be before he comes to assent to those maxims; whose terms, with the ideas they stand for, being no more innate than those of a cat or a weasel, he must stay till time and observation have acquainted him with them; and then he will be in a capacity to know the truth of these maxims, upon the first occasion that shall make him put together those ideas in his mind, and observe whether they agree or disagree, according as is expressed in those propositions. And therefore it is that a man knows that eighteen and nineteen are equal to thirty-seven, by the same self-evidence that he knows one and two to be equal to three: yet a child knows this not so soon as the other; not for want of the use of reason, but because the ideas the words *eighteen*, *nineteen*, and *thirty-seven* stand for, are not so soon got, as those which are signified by *one*, *two*, and *three*.

If it is said that the understanding has an *implicit* knowledge of these principles, but not an *explicit*, before this first hearing (as they must who will say "that they are in the understanding before they are known") it will be hard to conceive what is meant by a principle imprinted on the understanding implicitly, unless it is this: that the mind is capable of understanding and assenting firmly to such propositions. And thus all mathematical demonstrations, as well as first principles, must be received as native impressions on the mind; which I fear they will scarce allow them to be, who find it harder to demonstrate a proposition than assent to it when demonstrated. And few mathematicians will be forward to believe, that all the diagrams they have drawn were but copies of those innate characters which nature had engraved upon their minds.

There is, I fear, this further weakness in the foregoing argument, which would persuade us that therefore those maxims are to be thought innate, which men admit at first hearing; because they assent to propositions which they are not taught, nor do receive from the force of any argument or demonstration, but a bare explication or understanding of the terms. Under which there seems to me to lie this fallacy—that men are supposed not to be taught nor to learn anything *de novo* [new, or from the beginning]; when, in truth, they are taught, and do learn something they were ignorant of before. For, first, it is evident that they have learned the terms, and their signification; neither of which was born with them. But this is not all the acquired knowledge in the case: the ideas themselves, about which the proposition is, are not born with them, no more than their names, but got afterwards. So that in all propositions that are assented to at first hearing, the terms of the proposition, their standing for such ideas, and the ideas themselves that they stand for, being neither of them innate, I would like to know what there is remaining in such propositions that is innate. For I would gladly have any one name that proposition whose terms or ideas were either of them innate. We *by degrees* get ideas and names, and *learn* their appropriated connection one with another; and then to propositions made in such terms, whose signification we have learnt, and wherein the agreement or disagreement we can perceive in our ideas when put together is expressed, we at first hearing assent; though to other propositions, in themselves as certain and evident, but which are concerning ideas not so soon or so easily got, we are at the same time no way capable of assenting. For, though a child quickly assents to this proposition, "That an apple is not fire," when by familiar acquaintance he has got the ideas of those two different things distinctly imprinted on his mind, and has learned that the names *apple* and *fire* stand for them; yet it will be some years after, perhaps, before the same child will assent to this proposition, "That it is impossible for the same thing to be and not to be"; because that, though perhaps the words are as easy to be learned, yet the signification of them being more large, comprehensive, and abstract than of the names annexed to those sensible things the child has to do with, it is longer before he learns their precise meaning, and it requires more time plainly to form in his mind those general ideas they stand for. Until that is done, you will in vain endeavor to make any child assent to a proposition made up of such general terms; but as soon as ever he has got those ideas, and learned their names, he forwardly closes with the one as well as the other of the aforementioned propositions: and with both for the same reason; namely because he finds the ideas he has in his mind to agree or disagree, according as the words standing for them are affirmed or denied one of another in the proposition. But if propositions are brought to him in words which stand for ideas he has not yet in his mind, to such propositions, however evidently true or false in themselves, he affords neither assent nor dissent, but is ignorant. For words being but empty sounds, any further than they are signs of our ideas, we cannot but assent to them as they correspond to those ideas we have, but no further than that. But the showing by what steps and ways knowledge comes into our minds; and the grounds of several degrees of assent, being the business of the following discourse, it may suffice to have only touched on it here, as one reason that made me doubt of those innate principles.

Gottfried Leibniz

DEEP INSIDE

The question is to know whether the soul in itself is entirely empty, like the tablet on which nothing has yet been written (tabula rasa) according to Aristotle and the author of the Essay [Locke], and whether all that is traced thereon comes solely from the senses and from experience; or whether the soul contains originally the principles of several notions and doctrines which external objects merely awaken on occasions, as I believe, with Plato. Whence there arises another question, whether all truths depend on experience, that is to say, on induction and examples, or whether there are some which have still another basis.

The senses, although *necessary* for all our actual knowledge, are not *sufficient* to give to us the whole of it, since the senses never give anything except examples, that is to say, particular or individual truths. Now all the examples which confirm a general truth, however numerous they be, do not suffice to establish the universal necessity of this same truth; for it does not follow that what *has* happened *will* happen in the same way. Hence, it would seem that *necessary truths*, such as are found in pure mathematics and especially in arithmetic and in geometry, must have principles, the proof of which does not depend on examples, nor, consequently, on the testimony of the senses, although without the senses we would never take it into our heads to think of them. It is true that we must not imagine that these eternal laws of the reason can be read in the soul as an open book, without difficulty and without research; but it is enough that they can be discovered in us by force of attention, for which occasions are furnished by the senses.

It is true that even reason counsels us to expect ordinarily to see that happen in the future which is conformed to a long past experience, but this is not for this reason a necessary and infallible truth, and success may cease when we expect it least, if the reasons which have sustained it change.

This being so, can it be denied that there is much that is innate in our minds, since we are innate, so to say, to ourselves, and since there is in ourselves being, unity, substance, duration, change, action, perception, pleasure, and a thousand other objects of our intellectual ideas? And these objects, being immediate to our understanding and always present (although they cannot be always perceived on account of our distractions and wants), why be astonished that we say that these ideas, with all which depends on them, are innate in us? It is thus that ideas and truths are innate in us, as inclinations, dispositions, habits, or natural capacities, and not as actions; although these capacities are always *accompanied by some* actions, often insensible, which correspond to them.

In addition to this, I say, *why is it necessary that all be* acquired by us through perceptions of external things, and that nothing can be unearthed in ourselves? Is our soul then such a blank that, besides the images imprinted from without, it is nothing? This is not an opinion (I am sure) which our judicious author can approve. And where are there found tablets which are not somewhat varied in themselves? For we never see a surface perfectly even and uniform. Why, then, could we not furnish also to ourselves some object of thought from our own depths, if we should dig therein?

Edited from *New Essays on Human Understanding*. Translated by Alfred Gideox Langley, 1896, which is now in the public domain.

Mary Astell

DEGREES OF CLEARNESS

Truth in general is the object of the understanding, but all truths are not equally evident, because of the limitation of the human mind, which though it can gradually take in many truths, yet cannot any more than our sight attend to many things at once. Likewise, because God has not thought fit to communicate such ideas to us, as are necessary to the disquisition [a long discussion or examination] of some particular truths. For knowing nothing without us but by the idea we have of it, and judging only according to the relation we find between two or more ideas, when we cannot discover the truth we search after by intuition or the immediate comparison of two ideas, it is necessary that we should have a third by which to compare them. But if this middle idea is wanting, though we have sufficient evidence of those two which we would compare, because we have a clear and distinct conception of them, yet we are ignorant of those truths which would arise from their comparison, because we want a third by which to compare them.

Although the human intellect has a large extent, yet being limited as we have already said, this limitation is the cause of those different modes of thinking, which for distinction's sake we call faith, science, and opinion. For in this present and imperfect state in which we know not anything by intuition, or immediate view, except a few *first principles* which we call *self-evident*, most of our knowledge is acquired by reasoning and deduction. These three modes of understanding, faith, science, and opinion, are not otherwise distinguished, than by the different degrees of clearness and evidence in the premises from which the conclusion is drawn.

Knowledge in a proper and restricted sense, and as appropriated to science, signifies that clear perception which is followed by a firm assent to conclusions rightly drawn from premises of which we have clear and distinct ideas. Those premises or principles must be so clear and evident, that supposing us to be reasonable creatures, and free from prejudices and passions (which for the time they predominate as good as deprive us of our reason), we cannot withhold our assent from them without manifest violence to our reason.

But if the nature of the thing is such as that it admits of no undoubted premises to argue from, or at least we don't at present know of any, or that the conclusion does not necessarily follow as to give a perfect satisfaction to the mind and free it from all hesitation, that which we think of it is then called *opinion.*

If the medium we make use of to prove the proposition is *authority*, then the conclusion which we draw from it is said to be *believed*; this is what we call *faith*; and when the authority is God, this is what we call *divine faith.*

Moral certainty is a species of knowledge whose proofs are of a compound nature, in part resembling those which belong to science, and partly those of faith. We do not make the whole process ourselves, but depend on another for the *immediate* proof, but we ourselves deduce the *mediate* from circumstances and principles as certain and almost as evident as those of science, and which lead us to the immediate proofs and make it unreasonable to doubt them. Indeed, we often deceive ourselves in this matter by inclining alternately to both extremes. Sometimes we reject truths which are morally certain as being conjectural and only probable because they do not have a physical and mathematical certainty, which they are incapable of. At another time, we embrace the slightest conjectures, and anything that looks with probability as moral certainties and real

Edited from *A Serious Proposal to the Ladies,* 1697, Chapter III, which is now in the public domain.

truths, if fancy, passion or interest recommend them; so ready are we to be determined by these rather than by solid reason.

In this enumeration of the several ways of knowing, I have not reckoned the senses, because we are more properly said to be *conscious* of them than to *know* such things as we perceive by sensation. And also because that light which we suppose to be let into our ideas by our senses is indeed very dim and fallacious, and not to be relied on till it has passed the test of reason, neither do I think there is any mode of knowledge which may not be reduced to those already mentioned.

Now although there is a great difference between opinion and science, true science being immutable, but opinion variable and uncertain, yet there is not such a difference between faith and science as is usually supposed. The difference consists not in the certainty but in the way of proof; the objects of faith are as rationally and as firmly proved as the objects of science, though by another way. As science demonstrates things that are *seen*, so faith is the evidence of such as are *not seen*. And he who rejects the evidence of faith in such things as belong to its cognizance is as unreasonable as he who denies propositions in geometry that are proved with Mathematical exactness.

There is nothing true which is not in itself demonstrable, or which we should not pronounce to be true had we a clear and intuitive view of it. But as was said above, we see very few things by intuition, nor are we furnished with mediums to make the process ourselves in demonstrating all truths, and therefore there are some truths which we must either be totally ignorant of, or else receive them on the testimony of another person, to whose understanding they are clear and manifest, though not to ours. And if this person is one who can neither be deceived nor deceive, we are as certain of those conclusions which we prove by his authority, as we are of those we demonstrate by our own reason; in fact, more certain, by how much his reason is more comprehensive and infallible than our own.

Science is the following the process ourselves upon clear and evident principles; faith is a dependence on the credit of another, in such matters as are out of our view. And when we have very good reason to submit to the testimony of the person we believe, faith is as firm, and those truths it discovers to us as truly intelligible, and as strongly proved in their kind as science.

In a word, as every sense, so every capacity of the understanding has its proper object. The objects of science are things within our view, of which we may have clear and distinct ideas, and nothing should be determined here without clearness and evidence. To be able to repeat any person's dogma without forming a distinct idea of it ourselves, is *not to know* but *to remember*; and to have a confused indeterminate idea is to *conjecture, not to understand.*

But as it is a fault to believe in matters of science, where we may expect demonstration and evidence, so it is a reproach to our understanding and a proof of our disingenuity to require that sort of process peculiar to science, for the confirmation of such truths as are not the proper objects of it. It is as ridiculous as to reject music because we cannot taste or smell it, or to deny there is such a thing as beauty because we do not hear it. But men of dry reason and a moderate genius, I suppose will think nature has done very well in allotting to each sense its proper employment.

Whoever has not seen Paris has nothing but human authority to assure him there is such a place, and yet he would be laughed at as ridiculous who should call it in question, though he may as well in this as in another case pretend that his informers have designs to serve, intend to impose on him and mock his credulity. How many of us daily make that a matter of faith which indeed belongs to science, by adhering blindly to the dictates of some famous philosopher in physical truths, the principles of which we have as much right to examine, and to make deductions from them as he had?

To sum up: We may know enough for all the purposes of life, enough to busy this active faculty of thinking, to employ and entertain the spare intervals of time, and to keep us from rust and idleness, but we must not pretend to fathom all depths with our short line, we should be wise unto sobriety, and reckon that we know very little if we go about to make our own reason the standard of all truth. It is very certain that nothing is true but what is conformable to reason, that is to the divine reason of which ours is but a short faint ray, and it is as certain that there are many truths which human reason cannot comprehend. Therefore, to be thoroughly sensible of the capacity of the mind, to discern precisely its bounds and limits and to direct our studies and inquiries accordingly, to know what is to be known, and to believe what is to be believed is the property of a wise person. To be content with too little knowledge, or to aspire to over-much is equally a fault, to make that use of our understanding which God has fitted and designed them for is the medium which we ought to take. For the difference between a plow man and a doctor does not seem to me to consist in this: That the business of the one is to search after knowledge, and that the other has nothing to do with it. No, whoever has a rational soul ought surely to employ it about some truth or other, to procure for it right ideas, that its judgments may be true though its knowledge is not very extensive. But herein lies the difference: That though truth is the object of every individual understanding, yet all are not equally enlarged, nor able to comprehend so much; and those whose capacities and circumstances of living do not fit them for it, lie not under that obligation of extending their view which persons of a larger reach and greater leisure do.

David Hume

MATTERS OF FACT AND RELATIONS OF IDEAS

Every one will readily allow that there is a considerable difference between the perceptions of the mind, when a man feels the pain of excessive heat, or the pleasure of moderate warmth, and when he afterwards recalls to his memory this sensation, or anticipates it by his imagination. These faculties may mimic or copy the perceptions of the senses; but they never can entirely reach the force and vivacity [liveliness] of the original sentiment.

We may divide all the perceptions of the mind into two classes or species, which are distinguished by their different degrees of force and vivacity. The less forcible and lively are commonly denominated *thoughts* or *ideas*. The other species want a name in our language. Let us, therefore, use a little freedom, and call them *impressions*; employing that word in a sense somewhat different from the usual. By the term *impression*, then, I mean all our more lively perceptions, when we hear, or see, or feel, or love, or hate, or desire, or will. And impressions are distinguished from ideas, which are the less lively perceptions, of which we are conscious, when we reflect on any of those sensations or movements above mentioned.

When we think of a golden mountain, we only join two consistent ideas, *gold*, and *mountain*, with which we were formerly acquainted. In short, all the materials of thinking are derived either from our outward or inward sentiment. Or, to express myself in philosophical language, *all our ideas are copies of our impressions*.

All ideas, especially abstract ones, are naturally faint and obscure: the mind has but a slender hold of them: and when we have often employed any term, though without a distinct meaning, we are apt to imagine it has a determinate idea annexed to it. On the contrary, all impressions, that is, all sensations, either outward or inward, are strong and vivid: the limits between them are more exactly determined: nor is it easy to fall into any error or mistake with regard to them. When we entertain, therefore, any suspicion that a philosophical term is employed without any meaning or idea (as is but too frequent), we need but enquire, *from what impression is that supposed idea derived*? And if it be impossible to assign any, this will serve to confirm our suspicion. By bringing ideas into so clear a light we may reasonably hope to remove all dispute, which may arise, concerning their nature and reality.

All the objects of human reason or enquiry may naturally be divided into two kinds, *relations of ideas*, and *matters of fact*. Of the first kind are the sciences of geometry, algebra, and arithmetic; and every affirmation which is either intuitively or demonstratively certain. Propositions of this kind are discoverable by the mere operation of thought, without dependence on what is anywhere existent in the universe. Though there never were a circle or triangle in nature, the truths demonstrated by Euclid would forever retain their certainty and evidence.

Matters of fact, which are the second objects of human reason, are not ascertained in the same manner; nor is our evidence of their truth, however great, of a like nature with the foregoing. The contrary of every matter of fact is still possible; because it can never imply a contradiction, and is conceived by the mind with the same facility and distinctness, as if ever so conformable to reality. *That the sun will not rise tomorrow* is no less intelligible a proposition, and implies no more contradiction than the affirmation, *that it will rise*. We should in vain, therefore, attempt to

Edited from *An Enquiry Concerning Human Understanding,* 1748, Sections II, IV-V, which is now in the public domain.

demonstrate its falsehood. Were it demonstratively false, it would imply a contradiction, and could never be distinctly conceived by the mind.

All reasonings concerning matter of fact seem to be founded on the relation of *cause and effect.* By means of that relation alone we can go beyond the evidence of our memory and senses. If you were to ask a man why he believes any matter of fact, which is absent, for instance, that his friend is in the country, or in France, he would give you a reason, and this reason would be some other fact, as a letter received from him, or the knowledge of his former resolutions and promises. A man finding a watch or any other machine in a desert island, would conclude that there had once been men in that island. All our reasonings concerning fact are of the same nature. And here it is constantly supposed that there is a connection between the present fact and that which is inferred from it. Were there nothing to bind them together, the inference would be entirely precarious. If we would satisfy ourselves, therefore, concerning the nature of that evidence, which assures us of matters of fact, we must enquire how we arrive at the knowledge of cause and effect.

I shall venture to affirm, as a general proposition, which admits of no exception, that the knowledge of this relation is not, in any instance, attained by reasonings *a priori* [independent of experience], but arises entirely from experience, when we find that any particular objects are constantly conjoined with each other. Let an object be presented to a man of ever so strong natural reason and abilities; if that object is entirely new to him, he will not be able, by the most accurate examination of its sensible qualities, to discover any of its causes or effects. Adam, though his rational faculties be supposed, at the very first, entirely perfect, could not have inferred from the fluidity and transparency of water that it would suffocate him, or from the light and warmth of fire that it would consume him. No object ever discovers, by the qualities which appear to the senses, either the causes which produced it, or the effects which will arise from it; nor can our reason, unassisted by experience, ever draw any inference concerning real existence and matter of fact.

This proposition, *that causes and effects are discoverable, not by reason but by experience,* will readily be admitted with regard to such objects, as we remember to have once been altogether unknown to us. We fancy, that were we brought on a sudden into this world, we could at first have inferred that one billiard-ball would communicate motion to another upon impulse, and that we needed not to have waited for the event, in order to pronounce with certainty concerning it. Such is the influence of custom, that, where it is strongest, it not only covers our natural ignorance, but even conceals itself, and seems not to take place, merely because it is found in the highest degree.

But to convince us that all the laws of nature, and all the operations of bodies without exception, are known only by experience, the following reflections may, perhaps, suffice. Were any object presented to us, and were we required to pronounce concerning the effect, which will result from it, without consulting past observation, after what manner must the mind proceed in this operation? It must invent or imagine some event, which it ascribes to the object as its effect; and it is plain that this invention must be entirely arbitrary. The mind can never possibly find the effect in the supposed cause, by the most accurate scrutiny and examination. For the effect is totally different from the cause, and consequently can never be discovered in it. Motion in the second billiard-ball is a quite distinct event from motion in the first; nor is there anything in the one to suggest the smallest hint of the other. A stone or piece of metal raised into the air, and left without any support, immediately falls: but to consider the matter *a priori*, is there anything we discover in this situation which can beget the idea of a downward, rather than an upward, or any other motion, in the stone or metal?

When I see, for instance, a billiard-ball moving in a straight line towards another, even suppose motion in the second ball should by accident be suggested to me, as the result of their contact or impulse, may I not conceive that a hundred different events might as well follow from that cause? May not both these balls remain at absolute rest? May not the first ball return in a straight line, or leap off from the second in any line or direction? All these suppositions are consistent and conceivable. Why then should we give the preference to one, which is no more consistent or conceivable than the rest? All our reasonings *a priori* will never be able to show us any foundation for this preference.

In a word, then, every effect is a distinct event from its cause. It could not, therefore, be discovered in the cause, and the first invention or conception of it, *a priori*, must be entirely arbitrary. In vain, therefore, should we pretend to determine any single event, or infer any cause or effect, without the assistance of observation and experience.

When it is asked, *What is the nature of all our reasonings concerning matter of fact?* the proper answer seems to be, that they are founded on the relation of cause and effect. When again it is asked, *What is the foundation of all our reasonings and conclusions concerning that relation?* it may be replied in one word, *Experience*. But if we still carry on and ask, *What is the foundation of all conclusions from experience?* this implies a new question, which may be of more difficult solution and explication. I shall content myself, in this section, with an easy task, and shall pretend only to give a negative answer to the question here proposed. I say then, that, even after we have experience of the operations of cause and effect, our conclusions from that experience are *not* founded on reasoning, or any process of the understanding. This answer we must endeavor both to explain and to defend.

Our senses inform us of the color, weight, and consistence of bread; but neither sense nor reason can ever inform us of those qualities which fit it for the nourishment and support of a human body. But notwithstanding this ignorance of natural powers and principles, we always *presume*, when we see like sensible qualities, that they have like secret powers, and expect that effects, similar to those which we have experienced, will follow from them. As to *past experience*, it can be allowed to give *direct* and *certain* information of those precise objects only, and that precise period of time, which fell under its cognizance: but why this experience should be extended to future times, and to other objects, which for aught we know, may be only in appearance similar, this is the main question on which I would insist. The bread, which I formerly eat, nourished me, but does it follow that other bread must also nourish me at another time. The consequence seems nowise necessary.

These two propositions are far from being the same: *I have found that such an object has always been attended with such an effect,* and *I foresee, that other objects, which are, in appearance, similar, will be attended with similar effects.* I shall allow, if you please, that the one proposition may justly be inferred from the other: I know, in fact, that it always is inferred. But if you insist that the inference is made by a chain of reasoning, I desire you to produce that reasoning.

All reasonings may be divided into two kinds, namely, demonstrative reasoning, or that concerning relations of ideas, and moral reasoning, or that concerning matter of fact and existence. That there are no demonstrative arguments in the case seems evident, since it implies no contradiction that the course of nature may change, and that an object, seemingly like those which we have experienced, may be attended with different or contrary effects. May I not clearly and distinctly conceive that a body, falling from the clouds, and which, in all other respects, resembles snow, has yet the taste of salt or feeling of fire? Now whatever is intelligible, and can be distinctly conceived, implies no contradiction, and can never be proved false by any demonstrative argument or abstract reasoning *a priori*.

If we be, therefore, engaged by arguments to put trust in past experience, and make it the standard of our future judgment, these arguments must be probable only, or such as regard matter of fact and real existence, according to the division above mentioned. We have said that all arguments concerning existence are founded on the relation of cause and effect; that our knowledge of that relation is derived entirely from experience; and that all our experimental conclusions proceed upon the supposition that the future will be conformable to the past. To endeavor, therefore, the proof of this last supposition by probable arguments, or arguments regarding existence, must be evidently going in a circle, and taking that for granted, which is the very point in question.

In reality, all arguments from experience are founded on the similarity which we discover among natural objects, and by which we are induced to expect effects similar to those which we have found to follow from such objects. From causes which appear *similar* we expect similar effects. This is the sum of all our experimental conclusions. Now it seems evident that, if this conclusion were formed by reason, it would be as perfect at first, and upon one instance, as after ever so long a course of experience. But the case is far otherwise. It is only after a long course of uniform experiments in any kind, that we attain a firm reliance and security with regard to a particular event. Now where is that process of reasoning which, from one instance, draws a conclusion, so different from that which it infers from a hundred instances that are nowise different from that single one? I cannot find, I cannot imagine, any such reasoning.

Should it be said that, from a number of uniform experiments, we *infer* a connection between the sensible qualities and the secret powers; this, I must confess, seems the same difficulty, couched in different terms. The question still recurs, on what process of argument this *inference* is founded? Where is the medium, the interposing ideas, which join propositions so very wide of each other? It is confessed that the color, consistence, and other sensible qualities of bread appear not, of themselves, to have any connection with the secret powers of nourishment and support. For otherwise we could infer these secret powers from the first appearance of these sensible qualities, without the aid of experience. Here, then, is our natural state of ignorance with regard to the powers and influence of all objects.

When a man says, *I have found, in all past instances, such sensible qualities conjoined with such secret powers;* And when he says, *Similar sensible qualities will always be conjoined with similar secret powers*, he is not guilty of a tautology [a statement that is necessarily true], nor are these propositions in any respect the same. You say that the one proposition is an inference from the other. But you must confess that the inference is not intuitive; neither is it demonstrative. Of what nature is it, then? To say it is experimental, is begging the question. *For all inferences from experience suppose, as their foundation, that the future will resemble the past*, and that similar powers will be conjoined with similar sensible qualities. If there is any suspicion that the course of nature may change, and that the past may be no rule for the future, all experience becomes useless, and can give rise to no inference or conclusion. It is impossible, therefore, that any arguments from experience can prove this resemblance of the past to the future; *since all these arguments are founded on the supposition of that resemblance.* Let the course of things be allowed hitherto ever so regular; that alone, without some new argument or inference, proves not that, for the future, it will continue so. In vain do you pretend to have learned the nature of bodies from your past experience. Their secret nature, and consequently all their effects and influence, may change, without any change in their sensible qualities. This happens sometimes, and with regard to some objects: Why may it not happen always, and with regard to all objects? What logic, what process or argument secures you against this supposition? My practice, you say, refutes my doubts. But you mistake the purport of my question. As an agent, I am quite satisfied in the point; but as a philosopher, who has some share of curiosity—I will not say skepticism—I want to learn the foundation of this inference.

When a child has felt the sensation of pain from touching the flame of a candle, he will be careful not to put his hand near any candle; but will expect a similar effect from a cause which is similar in its sensible qualities and appearance. If you assert, therefore, that the understanding of the child is led into this conclusion by any process of argument or ratiocination [logical reasoning], I may justly require you to produce that argument; nor have you any pretense to refuse so equitable a demand. You cannot say that the argument is abstruse, and may possibly escape your enquiry, since you confess that it is obvious to the capacity of a mere infant. If you hesitate, therefore, a moment, or if, after reflection, you produce any intricate or profound argument, you, in a manner, give up the question, and confess that it is not reasoning which engages us to suppose the past resembling the future, and to expect similar effects from causes which are, to appearance, similar. If I am right, I pretend not to have made any mighty discovery. And if I am wrong, I must acknowledge myself to be indeed a very backward scholar, since I cannot now discover an argument which, it seems, was perfectly familiar to me long before I was out of my cradle.

Suppose a person, though endowed with the strongest faculties of reason and reflection, to be brought on a sudden into this world; he would, indeed, immediately observe a continual succession of objects, and one event following another; but he would not be able to discover anything farther. He would not, at first, by any reasoning, be able to reach the idea of cause and effect; since the particular powers, by which all natural operations are performed, never appear to the senses; nor is it reasonable to conclude, merely because one event, in one instance, precedes another, that therefore the one is the cause, the other the effect. Their conjunction may be arbitrary and casual. There may be no reason to infer the existence of one from the appearance of the other. And in a word, such a person, without more experience, could never employ his conjecture or reasoning concerning any matter of fact, or be assured of anything beyond what was immediately present to his memory and senses.

Suppose, again, that he has acquired more experience, and has lived so long in the world as to have observed familiar objects or events to be constantly conjoined together; what is the consequence of this experience? He immediately infers the existence of one object from the appearance of the other. Yet he has not, by all his experience, acquired any idea or knowledge of the secret power by which the one object produces the other; nor is it, by any process of reasoning, he is engaged to draw this inference. But still he finds himself determined to draw it. And though he should be convinced that his understanding has no part in the operation, he would nevertheless continue in the same course of thinking. There is some other principle which determines him to form such a conclusion.

This principle is *custom* or *habit*. For wherever the repetition of any particular act or operation produces a propensity to renew the same act or operation, without being impelled by any reasoning or process of the understanding, we always say, that this propensity is the effect of *custom*. By employing that word, we pretend not to have given the ultimate reason of such a propensity. We only point out a principle of human nature, which is universally acknowledged, and which is well known by its effects. Perhaps we can push our enquiries no farther, or pretend to give the cause of this cause; but must rest contented with it as the ultimate principle, which we can assign, of all our conclusions from experience. It is sufficient satisfaction, that we can go so far, without repining at the narrowness of our faculties because they will carry us no farther. And it is certain we here advance a very intelligible proposition at least, if not a true one, when we assert that, after the constant conjunction of two objects, heat and flame, for instance, weight and solidity, we are determined by custom alone to expect the one from the appearance of the other. This hypothesis seems even the only one which explains the difficulty, why we draw, from a thousand instances, an inference which we are not able to draw from one instance, that is, in no respect, different from them. Reason is incapable of any such variation. The conclusions which it draws from considering one circle are the same which it would form upon surveying all the circles in the universe. But no man, having seen only one body move after being impelled by another, could infer that every other body will move after a like impulse. All inferences from experience, therefore, are effects of custom, not of reasoning.

Custom, then, is the great guide of human life. It is that principle alone which renders our experience useful to us, and makes us expect, for the future, a similar train of events with those which have appeared in the past. Without the influence of custom, we should be entirely ignorant of every matter of fact beyond what is immediately present to the memory and senses. We should never know how to adjust means to ends, or to employ our natural powers in the production of any effect. There would be an end at once of all action, as well as of the chief part of speculation.

But here it may be proper to remark, that though our conclusions from experience carry us beyond our memory and senses, and assure us of matters of fact which happened in the most distant places and most remote ages, yet some fact must always be present to the senses or memory, from which we may first proceed in drawing these conclusions. A man, who should find in a desert country the remains of pompous buildings, would conclude that the country had, in ancient times, been cultivated by civilized inhabitants; but did nothing of this nature occur to him, he could never form such an inference. We learn the events of former ages from history; but then we must peruse the volumes in which this instruction is contained, and then carry up our inferences from one testimony to another, till we arrive at the eyewitnesses and spectators of these distant events. In a word, if we proceed not upon some fact, present to the memory or senses, our reasonings would be merely hypothetical; and however the particular links might be connected with each other, the whole chain of inferences would have nothing to support it, nor could we ever, by its means, arrive at the knowledge of any real existence. If I ask why you believe any particular matter of fact, which you relate, you must tell me some reason, and this reason will be some other fact, connected with it. But as you cannot proceed after this manner, *in infinitum* [indefinitely], you must at last terminate in some fact, which is present to your memory or senses, or must allow that your belief is entirely without foundation.

What, then, is the conclusion of the whole matter? A simple one, though, it must be confessed, pretty remote from the common theories of philosophy. All belief of matter of fact or real existence is derived merely from some object, present to the memory or senses, and a customary conjunction between that and some other object. Or in other words, having found, in many instances, that any two kinds of objects, flame and heat, snow and cold, have always been conjoined together, if flame or snow is presented anew to the senses, the mind is carried by custom to expect heat or cold, and to *believe* that such a quality does exist, and will discover itself upon a nearer approach. This belief is the necessary result of placing the mind in such circumstances. All these operations are a species of natural instincts, which no reasoning or process of the thought and understanding is able either to produce or to prevent.

Immanuel Kant

THE POSSIBILITY OF EXPERIENCE

That all our knowledge begins with experience there can be no doubt. For how is it possible that the faculty of cognition should be awakened into exercise otherwise than by means of objects which affect our senses, and partly of themselves produce representations, partly rouse our powers of understanding into activity, to compare, to connect, or to separate these, and so to convert the raw material of our sensuous impressions into a knowledge of objects, which is called *experience*? In respect of time, therefore, no knowledge of ours is antecedent to experience, but begins with it.

But, though all our knowledge begins with experience, it by no means follows that all arises out of experience. For, on the contrary, it is quite possible that our empirical knowledge is a compound of that which we receive through impressions, and that which the faculty of cognition supplies from itself (sensuous impressions giving merely the *occasion*), an addition which we cannot distinguish from the original element given by sense, till long practice has made us attentive to, and skillful in separating it. It is, therefore, a question which requires close investigation, and not to be answered at first sight—whether there exists a knowledge altogether *independent of experience*, and even of all sensuous impressions? Knowledge of this kind is called *a priori*, in contradistinction to *empirical knowledge*, which has its sources *a posteriori*, that is, in experience.

But the expression, "*a priori*," is not as yet definite enough adequately to indicate the whole meaning of the question above started. For, in speaking of knowledge which has its sources in experience, we are wont to say, that this or that may be known *a priori*, because we do not derive this knowledge immediately from experience, but from a general rule, which, however, we have itself borrowed from experience. Thus, if a man undermined his house, we say, "he might know *a priori* that it would have fallen"; that is, he needed not to have waited for the experience that it did actually fall. But still, *a priori*, he could not know even this much. For, that bodies are heavy, and, consequently, that they fall when their supports are taken away, must have been known to him previously, by means of experience.

By the term "knowledge *a priori*," therefore, we shall understand, not such as is independent of this or that kind of experience, but such as is absolutely so of *all* experience. Opposed to this is empirical knowledge, or that which is possible only *a posteriori*, that is, through experience. Knowledge *a priori* is either pure or impure. Pure knowledge *a priori* is that with which no empirical element is mixed up. For example, the proposition, "Every change has a cause," is a proposition *a priori*, but impure, because change is a conception which can only be derived from experience.

The question now is as to a *criterion*, by which we may securely distinguish a pure from an empirical cognition. Experience no doubt teaches us that this or that object is constituted in such and such a manner, but not that it could not possibly exist otherwise. Now, in the first place, if we have a proposition which contains the idea of necessity in its very conception, it is a judgment *a priori*; if, moreover, it is not derived from any other proposition, unless from one equally involving the idea of necessity, it is absolutely *a priori*. Secondly, an empirical judgment never exhibits strict and absolute, but only assumed and comparative universality (by induction); therefore, the most we can say is—so far as we have hitherto observed, there is no exception to this or that rule. If,

Edited from *Critique of Pure Reason*. Introduction. Translated by J. M. D. Meiklejohn, 1900, which is now in the public domain.

on the other hand, a judgment carries with it strict and absolute universality, that is, admits of no possible exception, it is not derived from experience, but is valid absolutely *a priori*.

Empirical universality is, therefore, only an arbitrary extension of validity, from that which may be predicated of a proposition valid in most cases, to that which is asserted of a proposition which holds good in all; as, for example, in the affirmation, "all bodies are heavy." When, on the contrary, strict universality characterizes a judgment, it necessarily indicates another peculiar source of knowledge, namely, a faculty of cognition *a priori*. Necessity and strict universality, therefore, are infallible tests for distinguishing pure from empirical knowledge, and are inseparably connected with each other. But as in the use of these criteria the empirical limitation is sometimes more easily detected than the contingency of the judgment, or the unlimited universality which we attach to a judgment is often a more convincing proof than its necessity, it may be advisable to use the criteria separately, each being by itself infallible.

Now, that in the sphere of human cognition, we have judgments which are necessary, and in the strictest sense universal, consequently pure *a priori*, it will be an easy matter to show. If we desire an example from the sciences, we need only take any proposition in mathematics. If we cast our eyes upon the commonest operations of the understanding, the proposition, "every change must have a cause," will amply serve our purpose. In the latter case, indeed, the conception of a cause so plainly involves the conception of a necessity of connection with an effect, and of a strict universality of the law, that the very notion of a cause would entirely disappear, were we to derive it, like Hume, from a frequent association of what happens with that which precedes, and the habit then originating of connecting representations—the necessity inherent in the judgment being therefore merely subjective. Besides, without seeking for such examples of principles existing *a priori* in cognition, we might easily show that such principles are the *indispensable basis of the possibility of experience itself*, and consequently prove their existence *a priori*. For where could our experience itself acquire certainty, if all the rules on which it depends were themselves empirical, and consequently fortuitous? No one, therefore, can admit the validity of the use of such rules as first principles. But, for the present, we may content ourselves with having established the fact, that we do possess and exercise a faculty of pure *a priori* cognition; and, secondly, with having pointed out the proper tests of such cognition, namely, *universality* and *necessity*.

Not only in judgments, however, but even in conceptions, is an *a priori* origin manifest. For example, if we take away by degrees from our conceptions of a body all that can be referred to mere sensuous experience—color, hardness or softness, weight, even impenetrability—the body will then vanish; but the space which it occupied still remains, and this it is utterly impossible to annihilate in thought. Again, if we take away, in like manner, from our empirical conception of any object, corporeal or incorporeal, all properties which mere experience has taught us to connect with it, still we cannot think away those through which we cogitate it as substance, or adhering to substance, although our conception of substance is more determined than that of an object. Compelled, therefore, by that necessity with which the conception of substance forces itself upon us, we must confess that it has its seat in our faculty of cognition *a priori*.

Of far more importance than all that has been above said, is the consideration that certain of our cognitions rise completely above the sphere of all possible experience, and by means of conceptions, to which there exists in the whole extent of experience no corresponding object, seem to extend the range of our judgments beyond its bounds. And just in this transcendental or supersensible sphere, where experience affords us neither instruction nor guidance, lie the investigations of *Reason*, which, on account of their importance, we consider far preferable to, and as having a far more elevated aim than, all that the understanding can achieve within the sphere of sensuous phenomena. So high a value do we set upon these investigations, that even at the risk of error, we persist in following them out, and permit neither doubt nor disregard nor indifference to restrain us from the pursuit. These unavoidable problems of mere *pure reason* are God, Freedom of the Will, and Immortality. The science which, with all its preliminaries, has for its especial object the solution of these problems is named *metaphysics*—a science which is at the very outset dogmatical, that is, it confidently takes upon itself the execution of this task without any previous investigation of the ability or inability of reason for such an understanding.

Now the safe ground of experience being thus abandoned, it seems nevertheless natural that we should hesitate to erect a building with the cognitions we possess, without knowing whence they come, and on the strength of principles, the origin of which is undiscovered. Instead of thus trying to build without a foundation, it is rather to be expected that we should long ago have put the question, how the understanding can arrive at these *a priori* cognitions, and what is the extent, validity, and worth which they may possess? We say, this is natural enough, meaning by the word natural that which is consistent with a just and reasonable way of thinking; but if we understand by the term, that which usually happens, nothing indeed could be more natural and more comprehensible than that this investigation should be left long unattempted. For one part of our pure knowledge, the science of mathematics, has been long firmly established, and thus leads us to form flattering expectations with regard to others, though these may be of quite a different nature. Besides, when we get beyond the bounds of experience, we are of course safe from opposition in that quarter; and the charm of widening the range of our knowledge is so great, that unless we are brought to a standstill by some evident contradiction, we hurry on undoubtingly in our course. This, however, may be avoided, if we are sufficiently cautious in the construction of our fictions, which are not the less fictions on that account.

Mathematical science affords us a brilliant example, how far, independently of all experience, we may carry our *a priori* knowledge. It is true that the mathematician occupies himself with objects and cognitions only in so far as they can be represented by means of intuition. But this circumstance is easily overlooked, because the said intuition can itself be given *a priori*, and therefore is hardly to be distinguished from a mere pure conception. Deceived by such a proof of the power of reason, we can perceive no limits to the extension of our knowledge. Just in the same way did Plato, abandoning the world of sense because of the narrow limits it sets to the understanding, venture upon the wings of ideas beyond it, into the void space of pure intellect. He did not reflect that he made no real progress by all his efforts; for he met with no resistance which might serve him for a support, as it were, whereon to rest, and on which he might apply his powers, in order to let the intellect acquire momentum for its progress. But as this process does furnish real *a priori* knowledge, which has a sure progress and useful results, reason, deceived by this, slips in, without being itself aware of it, assertions of a quite different kind; in which, to given conceptions it adds others, *a priori* indeed, but entirely foreign to them, without our knowing how it arrives at these, and, indeed, without such a question ever suggesting itself. I shall therefore at once proceed to examine the difference between these two modes of knowledge.

In all judgments where the relation of a subject to the predicate is cogitated (I mention affirmative judgments only here; the application to negative will be very easy), this relation is possible in two different ways. Either the predicate B belongs to the subject A, as somewhat which is contained (though covertly) in the conception A; or the predicate B lies completely out of the conception A, although it stands in connection with it. In the first instance, I term the judgment *analytic*, in the second, *synthetic*. Analytic judgments (affirmative) are therefore those in which the connection of the predicate with the subject is cogitated through identity; those in which this connection is cogitated without identity, are called synthetic judgments. The former may be called *explicative*, the latter *augmentative* judgments; because the former add in the predicate nothing to the conception of the subject, but only analyze it into its constituent conceptions, which were thought already in the subject, although in a confused manner; the latter add to our conceptions of the subject a predicate which was not contained in it, and which no analysis could ever have discovered therein. For example, when I say, "all bodies are extended," this is an *analytic* judgment. For I need not go beyond the conception of *body* in order to find extension connected with it, but merely analyze the conception, that is, become conscious of the manifold properties which I think in that conception, in order to discover this predicate in it: it is therefore an analytic judgment. On the other hand, when I say, "all bodies are heavy," the predicate is something totally different from that which I think in the mere conception of a body. By the addition of such a predicate, therefore, it becomes a *synthetic* judgment.

Judgments of experience, as such, are always *synthetic*. For it would be absurd to think of grounding an analytic judgment on experience, because in forming such a judgment I need not go out of the sphere of my conceptions, and therefore recourse to the testimony of experience is quite unnecessary. That "bodies are extended" is not an empirical judgment, but a proposition which stands firm *a priori*. For before addressing myself to experience, I already have in my conception all the requisite conditions for the judgment, and I have only to extract the predicate from the conception, according to the principle of contradiction, and thereby at the same time become conscious of the necessity of the judgment, a necessity which I could never learn from experience. On the other hand, though at first I do not at all include the predicate of weight in my conception of body in general, that conception still indicates an object of experience, a part of the totality of experience, to which I can still add other parts; and this I do when I recognize by observation that bodies are heavy. I can cognize beforehand by analysis the conception of body through the characteristics of extension, impenetrability, shape, etc., all which are cogitated in this conception. But now I *extend* my knowledge, and looking back on experience from which I had derived this conception of body, I find weight at all times connected with the above characteristics, and therefore I *synthetically* add to my conceptions this as a predicate, and say, "all bodies are heavy." Thus it is experience upon which rests the possibility of the synthesis of the predicate of weight with the conception of body, because both conceptions, although the one is not contained in the other, still belong to one another (only contingently, however), as parts of a whole, namely, of experience, which is itself a synthesis of intuitions.

But to synthetic judgments *a priori*, such aid is entirely wanting. If I go out of and beyond the conception A, in order to recognize another B as connected with it, what foundation have I to rest on, whereby to render the synthesis possible? I have here no longer the advantage of looking out in the sphere of experience for what I want. Let us take, for example, the proposition, "everything that happens has a cause." In the conception of *something that happens*, I indeed think an existence which a certain time antecedes, and from this I can derive analytic judgments. But the conception of a cause lies quite out of the above conception, and indicates something entirely different from "that which happens," and is consequently not contained in that conception. How then am I able to assert concerning the general conception—"that which happens"—something entirely different from that conception, and to recognize the conception of cause although not contained in it, yet as belonging to it, and even necessarily? What is here the unknown = X, upon which the understanding rests when it believes it has found, out of the conception A, a foreign predicate B, which it nevertheless considers to be connected with it? It cannot be experience, because the principle adduced annexes the two representations, cause and effect, to the representation existence, not only with universality, which experience cannot give, but also with the expression of necessity, therefore completely *a priori* and from pure conceptions. Upon such synthetic, that is augmentative propositions, depends the whole aim of our speculative knowledge *a priori*; for although analytic judgments are indeed highly important and necessary, they are so, only to arrive at that clearness of conceptions which is requisite for a sure and extended synthesis, and this alone is a real acquisition.

Mathematical judgments are always synthetical: This fact, though incontestably true and very important in its consequences, seems to have escaped the analysts of the human mind, in fact, to be in complete opposition to all their conjectures. For as it was found that mathematical conclusions all proceed according to the principle of contradiction, which the nature of every apodictic [clearly established; beyond dispute] certainty requires, people became persuaded that the fundamental principles of the science also were recognized and admitted in the same way. But the notion is fallacious; for although a synthetic proposition can certainly be discerned by means of the principle of contradiction, this is possible only when another synthetic proposition precedes, from which the latter is deduced, but never of itself.

Proper mathematical propositions are always judgments *a priori*, and not empirical, because they carry along with them the conception of necessity, which cannot be given by experience. If this be demurred to, it matters not; I will then limit my assertion to *pure* mathematics, the very conception of which implies that it consists of knowledge altogether non-empirical and *a priori*.

We might, indeed, at first suppose that the proposition 7 + 5 = 12 is a merely analytic proposition, following (according to the principle of contradiction) from the conception of a sum of seven and five. But if we regard it more narrowly, we find that our conception of the sum of seven and five contains nothing more than the uniting of both sums into one, whereby it cannot at all be cogitated what this single number is which embraces both. The conception of twelve is by no means obtained by merely cogitating the union of seven and five; and we may analyze our conception of such a possible sum as long as we will, still we shall never discover in it the notion of twelve. We must go beyond these conceptions, and have recourse to an intuition which corresponds to one of the two—our five fingers, for example, and so by degrees, add the units contained in the five given in the intuition, to the conception of seven. For I first take the number 7, and, for the conception of 5 calling in the aid of the fingers of my hand as objects of intuition, I add the units, which I before took together to make up the number 5, gradually now by means of the material image my hand, to the number 7, and by this process, I at length see the number 12 arise. That 7 should be added to 5, I have certainly cogitated in my conception of a sum = 7 + 5, but not that this sum was equal to 12. Arithmetical propositions are therefore always synthetic, of which we may become more clearly convinced by trying large numbers. For it will thus become quite evident, that, turn and twist our conceptions as we may, it is impossible, without having recourse to intuition, to arrive at the sum total or product by means of the mere analysis of our conceptions. Just as little is any principle of pure geometry analytic. "A straight line between two points is the shortest," is a synthetic proposition. For my conception of *straight* contains no notion of *quantity*, but is merely *qualitative*. The conception of the *shortest* is therefore wholly an addition, and by no analysis can it be extracted from our conception of a straight line. Intuition must therefore here lend its aid, by means of which, and thus only, our synthesis is possible.

Some few principles posited by geometricians are, indeed, really analytic, and depend on the principle of contradiction. They serve, however, like identical propositions, as links in the chain of method, not as principles; for example, $a = a$, the whole is equal to itself, or $(a + b) > a$, the whole is greater than its part. And yet even these principles themselves, though they derive their validity from pure conceptions, are only admitted in mathematics because they can be presented in intuition. What causes us here commonly to believe that the predicate of such apodictic judgments is already contained in our conception, and that the judgment is therefore analytic, is merely the equivocal nature of the expression. We must join in thought a certain predicate to a given conception, and this necessity cleaves already to the conception. But the question is, not what we must join in thought to the given conception, but what we really think therein, though only obscurely, and then it becomes manifest that the predicate pertains to these conceptions, necessarily indeed, yet not as thought in the conception itself, but by virtue of an intuition, which must be added to the conception.

The science of Natural Philosophy (Physics) contains in itself synthetic judgments a priori, as principles: I shall adduce two propositions. For instance, the proposition, "in all changes of the material world, the quantity of matter remains unchanged"; or, that, "in all communication of motion, action and reaction must always be equal." In both of these, not only is the necessity, and therefore their origin *a priori* clear, but also that they are synthetic propositions. For in the conception of matter, I do not cogitate its permanency, but merely its presence in space, which it fills. I therefore really go out of and beyond the conception of matter, in order to think on to it something *a priori*, which I did not think in it. The proposition is therefore not analytic, but synthetic, and nevertheless conceived *a priori*; and so it is with regard to the other propositions of the pure part of natural philosophy.

Charles S. Peirce

THE FIXATION OF BELIEF

Few persons care to study logic, because everybody conceives himself to be proficient enough in the art of reasoning already. But I observe that this satisfaction is limited to one's own ratiocination, and does not extend to that of other men. We come to the full possession of our power of drawing inferences the last of all our faculties, for it is not so much a natural gift as a long and difficult art.

The object of reasoning is to find out, from the consideration of what we already know, something else which we do not know. Consequently, reasoning is good if it be such as to give a true conclusion from true premises, and not otherwise. It is not in the least the question whether, when the premises are accepted by the mind, we feel an impulse to accept the conclusion also. The true conclusion would remain true if we had no impulse to accept it; and the false one would remain false, though we could not resist the tendency to believe in it.

We generally know when we wish to ask a question and when we wish to pronounce a judgment, for there is a dissimilarity between the sensation of doubting and that of believing. But this is not all which distinguishes doubt from belief. There is a practical difference. Our beliefs guide our desires and shape our actions. The Assassins, or followers of the Old Man of the Mountain, used to rush into death at his least command, because they believed that obedience to him would insure everlasting felicity. Had they doubted this, they would not have acted as they did. So it is with every belief, according to its degree. The feeling of believing is a more or less sure indication of there being established in our nature some habit which will determine our actions. Doubt never has such an effect.

Nor must we overlook a third point of difference. Doubt is an uneasy and dissatisfied state from which we struggle to free ourselves and pass into a state of belief; while the latter is a calm and satisfactory state which we do not wish to avoid, or to change to a belief in anything else. On the contrary, we cling tenaciously, not merely to believing, but to believing just what we do believe.

Thus, both doubt and belief have positive effects upon us, though very different ones. Belief does not make us act at once, but puts us into such a condition that we shall behave in some certain way, when the occasion arises. Doubt has not the least effect of this sort, but stimulates us to action until it is destroyed. The irritation of doubt causes a struggle to attain a state of belief. I shall term this struggle *inquiry*.

The irritation of doubt is the only immediate motive for the struggle to attain belief. It is certainly best for us that our beliefs should be such as may truly guide our actions so as to satisfy our desires; and this reflection will make us reject every belief which does not seem to have been so formed as to insure this result. But it will only do so by creating a doubt in the place of that belief. With the doubt, therefore, the struggle begins, and with the cessation of doubt it ends. Hence, the sole object of inquiry is the settlement of opinion. We may fancy that this is not enough for us, and that we seek not merely an opinion, but a true opinion. But put this fancy to the test and it proves groundless; for as soon as a firm belief is reached we are entirely satisfied, whether the belief be true or false. The most that can be maintained is that we seek for a belief that we shall *think* to be true. But we think each one of our beliefs to be true, and, indeed, it is mere tautology to say so.

Edited from *Popular Science Monthly* 12, November, 1877, which is now in the public domain.

That the settlement of opinion is the sole end of inquiry is a very important proposition. It sweeps away, at once, various vague and erroneous conceptions of proof. A few of these may be noticed here.

1. Some philosophers have imagined that to start an inquiry it was only necessary to utter a question or set it down on paper, and have even recommended us to begin our studies with questioning everything! But the mere putting of a proposition into the interrogative form does not stimulate the mind to any struggle after belief. There must be a real and living doubt, and without this, all discussion is idle.

2. It is a very common idea that a demonstration must rest on some ultimate and absolutely indubitable propositions. These, according to one school, are first principles of a general nature; according to another, are first sensations. But, in point of fact, an inquiry, to have that completely satisfactory result called demonstration, has only to start with propositions perfectly free from all actual doubt. If the premises are not in fact doubted at all, they cannot be more satisfactory than they are.

3. Some people seem to love to argue a point after all the world is fully convinced of it. But no further advance can be made. When doubt ceases, mental action on the subject comes to an end; and, if it did go on, it would be without a purpose.

If the settlement of opinion is the sole object of inquiry, and if belief is of the nature of a habit, why should we not attain the desired end, by taking any answer to a question, which we may fancy, and constantly reiterating it to ourselves, dwelling on all which may conduce to that belief, and learning to turn with contempt and hatred from anything that might disturb it? This simple and direct method is really pursued by many men. I remember once being entreated not to read a certain newspaper lest it might change my opinion upon free trade. "Lest I might be entrapped by its fallacies and misstatements," was the form of expression. "You are not," my friend said, "a special student of political economy. You might, therefore, easily be deceived by fallacious arguments upon the subject. You might, then, if you read this paper, be led to believe in protection. But you admit that free trade is the true doctrine; and you do not wish to believe what is not true." I have often known this system to be deliberately adopted. Still oftener, the instinctive dislike of an undecided state of mind, exaggerated into a vague dread of doubt, makes men cling spasmodically to the views they already take. The man feels that if he only holds to his belief without wavering, it will be entirely satisfactory. Nor can it be denied that a steady and immovable faith yields great peace of mind. It may, indeed, give rise to inconveniences, as if a man should resolutely continue to believe that fire would not burn him. Thus, if it be true that death is annihilation, then the man who believes that he will certainly go straight to heaven when he dies, provided he have fulfilled certain simple observances in this life, has a cheap pleasure which will not be followed by the least disappointment. A similar consideration seems to have weight with many persons in religious topics, for we frequently hear it said, "Oh, I could not believe so-and-so, because I should be wretched if I did." When an ostrich buries its head in the sand as danger approaches, it very likely takes the happiest course. It hides the danger, and then calmly says there is no danger; and, if it feels perfectly sure there is none, why should it raise its head to see? A man may go through life, systematically keeping out of view all that might cause a change in his opinions, and if he only succeeds—basing his method, as he does, on two fundamental psychological laws—I do not see what can be said against his doing so. It would be an egotistical impertinence to object that his procedure is irrational, for that only amounts to saying that his method of settling belief is not ours. He does not propose to himself to be rational, and, indeed, will often talk with scorn of man's weak and illusive reason. So let him think as he pleases.

But this method of fixing belief, which may be called the *method of tenacity*, will be unable to hold its ground in practice. The social impulse is against it. The man who adopts it will find that other men think differently from him, and it will be apt to occur to him in some saner moment that their opinions are quite as good as his own, and this will shake his confidence in his belief. This conception, that another man's thought or sentiment may be equivalent to one's own, is a distinctly new step, and a highly important one. It arises from an impulse too strong in man to be suppressed, without danger of destroying the human species. Unless we make ourselves hermits, we shall necessarily influence each other's opinions; so that the problem becomes how to fix belief, not in the individual merely, but in the community.

Let the will of the state act, then, instead of that of the individual. Let an institution be created which shall have for its object to keep correct doctrines before the attention of the people, to reiterate them perpetually, and to teach them to the young; having at the same time power to prevent contrary doctrines from being taught, advocated, or expressed. Let all possible causes of a change of mind be removed from men's apprehensions. Let them be kept ignorant, lest they should learn of some reason to think otherwise than they do. Let their passions be enlisted, so that they may regard private and unusual opinions with hatred and horror. Then, let all men who reject the established belief be terrified into silence. Let the people turn out and tar and feather such men, or let inquisitions be made into the manner of thinking of suspected persons, and, when they are found guilty of forbidden beliefs, let them be subjected to some signal punishment. When complete agreement could not otherwise be reached, a general massacre of all who have not thought in a certain way has proved a very effective means of settling opinion in a country. If the power to do this be wanting, let a list of opinions be drawn up, to which no man of the least independence of thought can assent, and let the faithful be required to accept all these propositions, in order to segregate them as radically as possible from the influence of the rest of the world.

This method has, from the earliest times, been one of the chief means of upholding correct theological and political doctrines. But wherever there is a priesthood—and no religion has been without one—this method has been more or less made use of. Wherever there is an aristocracy, or a guild, or any association of a class of men whose interests depend or are supposed to depend on certain propositions, there will be inevitably found some traces of this natural product of social feeling. Cruelties always accompany this system; and when it is consistently carried out, they become atrocities of the most horrible kind in the eyes of any rational man. Nor should this occasion surprise, for the officer of a society does not feel justified in surrendering the interests of that society for the sake of mercy, as he might his own private interests. It is natural, therefore, that sympathy and fellowship should thus produce a most ruthless power.

In judging this method of fixing belief, which may be called the *method of authority*, we must, in the first place, allow its immeasurable mental and moral superiority to the method of tenacity. Its success is proportionately greater; and in fact it has over and over again worked the most majestic results. The mere structures of stone which it has caused to be put together have many of them a sublimity hardly more than rivaled by the greatest works of nature. And, except the geological epochs, there are no periods of time so vast as those which are measured by some of these organized faiths. If we scrutinize the matter closely, we shall find that there has not been one of their creeds which has remained always the same; yet the change is so slow as to be imperceptible during one person's life, so that individual belief remains sensibly fixed. For the mass of mankind, then, there is perhaps no better method than this. If it is their highest impulse to be intellectual slaves, then slaves they ought to remain.

But no institution can undertake to regulate opinions upon every subject. Only the most important ones can be attended to, and on the rest men's minds must be left to the action of natural causes. This imperfection will be no source of weakness so long as men are in such a state of culture that one opinion does not influence another—that is, so long as they cannot put two and two together. But in the most priest-ridden states some individuals will be found who are raised above that condition. These men possess a wider sort of social feeling; they see that men in other countries and in other ages have held to very different doctrines from those which they themselves have been brought up to believe; and they cannot help seeing that it is the mere accident of their having been taught as they have, and of their having been surrounded with the manners and associations they have, that has caused them to believe as they do and not far differently. And their candor cannot resist the reflection that there is no reason to rate their own views at a higher value than those of other nations and other centuries; thus giving rise to doubts in their minds.

They will further perceive that such doubts as these must exist in their minds with reference to every belief which seems to be determined by the caprice either of themselves or of those who originated the popular opinions. The willful adherence to a belief, and the arbitrary forcing of it upon others, must, therefore, both be given up and a new method of settling opinions must be adopted.

Now there are some people, among whom I must suppose that my reader is to be found, who, when they see that any belief of theirs is determined by any circumstance extraneous to the facts, will from that moment not merely admit in words that that belief is doubtful but will experience a real doubt of it, so that it ceases in some degree at least be a belief.

To satisfy our doubts, therefore, it is necessary that a method should be found by which our beliefs may be caused by nothing human, but by some external permanency—by something upon which our thinking has no effect. Our external permanency would not be external, in our sense, if it was restricted in its influence to one individual. It must be something which affects, or might affect, every man. And, though these affections are necessarily as various as are individual conditions, yet the method must be such that the ultimate conclusion of every man shall be the same, or would be the same if inquiry were sufficiently persisted in. Such is the *method of science*. Its fundamental hypothesis, restated in more familiar language, is this: There are real things, whose characters are entirely independent of our opinions about them; those realities affect our senses according to regular laws, and, though our sensations are as different as are our relations to the objects, yet, by taking advantage of the laws of perception, we can ascertain by reasoning how things really and truly are, and any man, if he have sufficient experience and reason enough about it, will be led to the one true conclusion. The new conception here involved is that of *reality*. It may be asked how I know that there are any realities. If this hypothesis is the sole support of my method of inquiry, my method of inquiry must not be used to support my hypothesis. The reply is this:

1. If investigation cannot be regarded as proving that there are real things, it at least does not lead to a contrary conclusion; but the method and the conception on which it is based remain ever in harmony. No doubts of the method, therefore, necessarily arise from its practice, as is the case with all the others.

2. The feeling which gives rise to any method of fixing belief is a dissatisfaction at two repugnant propositions. But here already is a vague concession that there is some *one* thing to which a proposition should conform. Nobody, therefore, can really doubt that there are realities,

or, if he did, doubt would not be a source of dissatisfaction. The hypothesis, therefore, is one which every mind admits. So that the social impulse does not cause men to doubt it.

3. Everybody uses the scientific method about a great many things, and only ceases to use it when he does not know how to apply it.

4. Experience of the method has not led us to doubt it, but, on the contrary, scientific investigation has had the most wonderful triumphs in the way of settling opinion. These afford the explanation of my not doubting the method or the hypothesis which it supposes; and not having any doubt, nor believing that anybody else whom I could influence has, it would be the merest babble for me to say more about it. If there be anybody with a living doubt upon the subject, let him consider it.

But with the scientific method the case is different. I may start with known and observed facts to proceed to the unknown; and yet the rules which I follow in doing so may not be such as investigation would approve. The test of whether I am truly following the method is not an immediate appeal to my feelings and purposes, but, on the contrary, itself involves the application of the method. Hence it is that bad reasoning as well as good reasoning is possible; and this fact is the foundation of the practical side of logic.

The force of habit will sometimes cause a man to hold on to old beliefs after he is in a condition to see that they have no sound basis. But reflection upon the state of the case will overcome these habits, and he ought to allow reflection full weight. People sometimes shrink from doing this, having an idea that beliefs are wholesome which they cannot help feeling rest on nothing. But let such persons suppose an analogous though different case from their own. Would they not say that these persons ought to consider the matter fully, and clearly understand the new doctrine, and then ought to embrace it in its entirety? But, above all, let it be considered that what is more wholesome than any particular belief is integrity of belief; and that to avoid looking into the support of any belief from a fear that it may turn out rotten is quite as immoral as it is disadvantageous. The person who confesses that there is such a thing as truth, which is distinguished from falsehood simply by this, that if acted on it should, on full consideration, carry us to the point we aim at and not astray, and then, though convinced of this, dares not know the truth and seeks to avoid it, is in a sorry state of mind indeed.

Part Five: God

Introduction

For many people, whether God exists is the ultimate question of human existence. For many others, though, questions concerning God and religion are irrelevant. It is certainly possible to live a full, interesting, and moral life with religious beliefs, and it is equally possible to live such a life without any religious beliefs.

There is no doubt that the question of God's existence has played a profound role in human history. Attempts to prove God's existence have captured the imagination of thinkers for thousands of years. And for every argument that has been developed, someone has constructed a counterargument.

There are many issues involved in trying to prove God exists. In fact, since the concept of "proof" requires logical and rational argumentation, there has often been a tension between *faith* and *reason*. For example, some have held that the concept of God is *infinitely incomprehensible* to mere mortals. However, this has not deterred many thinkers from attempting to prove that God exists. For purposes of simple classification, we will present two types of proofs for God's existence. Section 5A presents arguments that rely on *evidence from experience*; these are called *a posteriori* arguments. Section 5B presents arguments that *do not* rely on evidence from experience; these are called *a priori* arguments. Section 5C explores an important question: "Why is there suffering and evil in the world?" In other words, if God is eternal, perfect, all-knowing, all-powerful, and all-good, then how can God allow suffering or evil to exist? Finally, section 5D looks at some underlying questions concerning the role of belief.

5A. Can God's Existence Be Proved Based on Experience?

Introduction

We will look at several versions of the *cosmological proof* (also known as the *cosmological argument*) for the existence of God. Cosmological proofs have a common core of assumptions. First, something exists—the universe. Second, everything that exists must have a cause. Therefore, something had to cause the universe to exist, namely God.

Two versions of the cosmological argument are presented through passages from Thomas Aquinas and Gottfried Leibniz. Although these thinkers pursue the same questions, it is quite remarkable how they are each able to put their own individual stamp on the discussion, thereby allowing us to view a single topic from multiple angles—like seeing the different facets of a diamond as it turns.

Since one of the assumptions of cosmological proofs is that *every effect has a cause*, something is needed to avoid an *infinite regress* (a series that never ends). The description of God as the *first cause* (or *prime mover*) is used to solve that problem. This idea relies on characteristics typically attributed to God—*omnipotent* (all-powerful), *omniscient* (all-knowing), perfectly *benevolent* (all-good), and *eternal*—thus, God is the first cause.

Other readings in this section concentrate on *a posteriori* arguments. For example, the passage from Plato addresses the questions underlying the cosmological proof. Plato agrees that in order to avoid an infinite regress an eternal and unchanging creator must exist as the explanation for the existence of the universe.

George Berkeley argues for the metaphysical position called "idealism," which holds that everything that exists is *in a mind* and *relies on a mind for its existence*. Given this, Berkeley argues that matter does not exist. Although Berkeley denies that physical reality exists, he does not fall into skepticism. Instead, he argues that sensations exist as ideas in our minds; moreover, mind is the only reality. From this, he argues that ideas exist even when you, or I, or anyone else no longer exists. In other words, Berkeley argues that there is an "*omnipresent eternal Mind,* which knows and comprehends all things." Berkeley's position can be captured by the phrase "to be is to be perceived."

The passage from William Paley provides a clear example of a special type of *a posteriori* argument for the existence of God—the *argument by analogy*. This type of argument, often called the *design argument,* claims that since the universe exhibits *design* (order, purpose, and intelligence), then it must have a *designer*. The supreme designer of an intelligent universe is God. The design argument rests on an analogical principle: things that share some obvious similar characteristics probably share other characteristics as well. In other words, because things that have a design and purpose—for example, a watch—must have been created (designed) by someone, and because the universe reveals design and purpose, it, too, must have been created by a supreme designer—God.

Can God's Existence Be Proved Based on Experience?

Of course, the design arguments have been criticized. For example, the reading by David Hume offers counterarguments to several *a posteriori arguments* for the existence of God.

Plato

THE BEGINNING OF EVERYTHING

Everything that becomes or is created must of necessity be created by some cause, for without a cause nothing can be created. Was the heaven or the world always in existence and without beginning, or created, and had it a beginning? Created, I reply, being visible and tangible and having a body, and therefore sensible; and all sensible things are apprehended by opinion and sense and are in a process of creation and created.

Now that which is created must, as we affirm, of necessity be created by a cause. But the father and maker of all this universe is past finding out; and even if we found him, to tell of him to all men would be impossible. And there is still a question to be asked about him: Which of the patterns had the artificer in view when he made the world, the pattern of the unchangeable, or of that which is created? If the world be indeed fair and the artificer good, it is manifest that he must have looked to that which is eternal. Every one will see that he must have looked to the eternal, for the world is the fairest of creations and he is the best of causes. And having been created in this way, the world has been framed in the likeness of that which is apprehended by reason and mind and is unchangeable, and must therefore of necessity, if this is admitted, be a copy of something.

As being is to becoming, so is truth to belief. If then, amid the many opinions about the gods and the generation of the universe, we are not able to give notions which are altogether and in every respect exact and consistent with one another, do not be surprised. Enough, if we adduce probabilities as likely as any others; for we must remember that I who am the speaker, and you who are the judges, are only mortal men, and we ought to accept the tale which is probable and enquire no further.

Thomas Aquinas

THE FIVE WAYS

The existence of God can be proved in five ways:

The *first way* is the argument from motion. It is certain, and evident to our senses, that in the world some things are in motion. Now whatever is in motion is put in motion by something else. For instance, that which is *actually* hot, fire, makes wood, which is *potentially* hot, to be actually hot, and thereby changes it. Now it is not possible that the same thing should be at once actually and potentially at the same time. For what is actually hot cannot simultaneously be potentially hot, but it can be potentially cold. It is therefore impossible that a thing can be both mover and moved, that is, that it should move itself. Therefore, whatever is moved must be moved by another. If that by which it is moved be itself moved, then this also must be moved by another, and that by another again. But this cannot go on to infinity, because then there would be no first mover, and, consequently, no other mover; seeing that subsequent movers move only because as they are moved by the first mover. Therefore it is necessary to arrive at a first mover which is moved by no other. And this everyone understands to be God.

The *second way* is from the nature of causation. In the world of sense we find there is an order of causes. There is no case known (nor indeed, is it possible) in which a thing is found to be the cause of itself, because in that case it would be prior to itself, which is impossible. Now in causation it is not possible to go on to infinity, because in all causes following in order, the first is the cause of the intermediate cause, and the intermediate is the cause of the ultimate cause, whether the intermediate cause be several, or only one. Now to take away the cause is to take away the effect. Therefore, if there is no first cause, there will be no ultimate, nor any intermediate cause. But if it is possible to go on to infinity, then there will be no first cause, neither will there be an ultimate effect—all of which is plainly false. Therefore it is necessary to admit a first cause, to which everyone gives the name of God.

The *third way* is taken from possibility and necessity, and runs thus. We find in nature things that are possible to be and not to be, since they are found to be generated, and to be corrupted, and consequently they are possible to be and not to be. But it is impossible for these always to exist, for that which is possible not to be at some time is not. Therefore, if everything is possible not to be, then at one time there could have been nothing in existence. Now if this were true, even now there would be nothing in existence, because that which does not exist only begins to exist by something already existing. Therefore, if at one time nothing was in existence, it would have been impossible for anything to have begun to exist; and thus even now nothing would be in existence—which is clearly false. Therefore, not all beings are merely possible, but there must exist something the existence of which is necessary. But every necessary thing either has its necessity caused by another, or not. Now it is impossible to go on to infinity in necessary things which have their necessity caused by another. Therefore we must admit the existence of some being having of itself its own necessity, and not receiving it from another, but rather causing in others their necessity. This all men speak of as God.

The *fourth way* is taken from the gradation that is found in things. Among beings there are some more and some less good, true, noble and the like. But "more" and "less" are predicated of different things, according as they resemble in their different ways something which is the

Edited from *Summa Theologica*: First Part, Question 2, Article 3. Translated by Fathers of the English Dominican Province, 1911, which is now in the public domain.

maximum, as a thing is said to be hotter according as it more nearly resembles that which is hottest. There is, then, something which is truest, something best, and something noblest; therefore there must also be something which is to all beings the cause of their being, goodness, and every other perfection. And this we call God.

The *fifth way* is taken from the governance of things. We see that things which lack awareness, such as mere physical objects, act always, or nearly always, in the same way. Hence it is plain that they achieve this, not by chance, but by design. Now whatever lacks awareness cannot move towards a goal, unless it be directed by some being endowed with awareness and intelligence; as the arrow is directed by the archer. Therefore some intelligent being exists by whom all natural things are directed to their end; and this being we call God.

Gottfried Leibniz

SUFFICIENT REASON

It is the knowledge of necessary and eternal truths that distinguishes us from the mere animals and gives us *Reason* and the sciences, raising us to the knowledge of ourselves and of God. And it is this in us that is called the rational soul or mind.

It is also through the knowledge of necessary truths, and through their abstract expression, that we rise to *acts of reflection*, which make us think of what is called *I*, and observe that this or that is within us: and thus, thinking of ourselves, we think of being, of substance, of the simple and the compound, of the immaterial, and of God Himself, conceiving that what is limited in us is in Him without limits. And these acts of reflection furnish the chief objects of our reasonings.

Our reasonings are grounded upon two great principles: (1) that of *contradiction*, in virtue of which we judge false that which involves a contradiction, and true that which is opposed to the false, and (2) that of *sufficient reason*, in virtue of which we hold that there can be no fact unless there be a sufficient reason, why it should be so and not otherwise, although these reasons are not always known by us.

There are also two kinds of truths: those of *reasoning* and those of *fact*. Truths of reasoning are necessary and their opposite is impossible: truths of fact are contingent and their opposite is possible. When a truth is necessary, its reason can be found by analysis, resolving it into more simple ideas and truths, until we come to those which are primary.

But there must also be a *sufficient reason* for contingent truths or truths of fact, that is to say, for the sequence or connection of the things which are dispersed throughout the universe of created beings, in which the analyzing into particular reasons might go on into endless detail, because of the immense variety of things in nature and the infinite division of bodies. There is an infinity of present and past forms and motions which go to make up the cause of my present writing. And since all this detail involves other prior or more detailed contingent things, each of which still needs a similar analysis to yield its reason, we are no further forward: and the sufficient or final reason must be outside of the sequence or *series* of particular contingent things, however infinite this series may be.

Thus the final reason of things must be in a necessary substance, and this substance we call *God*. Now as this substance is a sufficient reason of all that exists, there is only one God, and this God is sufficient.

Edited from *The Monadology*: Sections 29-36. Translated by Robert Latta, 1898, which is now in the public domain.

George Berkeley

THE AUTHOR OF NATURE

Whatever power I may have over my own thoughts, I find the ideas actually perceived by Sense have not a like dependence on my will. When in broad daylight I open my eyes, it is not in my power to choose whether I shall see or no, or to determine what particular objects shall present themselves to my view; and so likewise as to the hearing and other senses; the ideas imprinted on them are not creatures of my will. There is therefore some other Will or Spirit that produces them.

The ideas of Sense are more strong, lively, and distinct than those of the imagination; they have likewise a steadiness, order, and coherence, and are not excited at random, as those which are the effects of human wills often are, but in a regular train or series, the admirable connection whereof sufficiently testifies the wisdom and benevolence of its Author. Now the set rules or established methods wherein the Mind we depend on excites in us the ideas of sense, are called the laws of nature; and these we learn by experience, which teaches us that such and such ideas are attended with such and such other ideas, in the ordinary course of things.

This gives us a sort of foresight which enables us to regulate our actions for the benefit of life. And without this we should be eternally at a loss; we could not know how to act anything that might procure us the least pleasure, or remove the least pain of sense. That food nourishes, sleep refreshes, and fire warms us; that to sow in the seed-time is the way to reap in the harvest; and in general that to obtain such or such ends, such or such means are conducive—all this we know, not by discovering any necessary connection between our ideas, but only by the observation of the settled laws of nature, without which we should be all in uncertainty and confusion, and a grown man no more know how to manage himself in the affairs of life than an infant just born.

And yet this consistent uniform working, which so evidently displays the goodness and wisdom of that Governing Spirit whose Will constitutes the laws of nature, is so far from leading our thoughts to Him, that it rather sends them wandering after second causes. For, when we perceive certain ideas of Sense constantly followed by other ideas and we know this is not of our own doing, we forthwith attribute power and agency to the ideas themselves, and make one the cause of another, than which nothing can be more absurd and unintelligible. Thus, for example, having observed that when we perceive by sight a certain round luminous figure we at the same time perceive by touch the idea or sensation called heat, we do from thence conclude the sun to be the cause of heat. And in like manner perceiving the motion and collision of bodies to be attended with sound, we are inclined to think the latter the effect of the former.

The ideas imprinted on the Senses by the Author of nature are called real things; and those excited in the imagination being less regular, vivid, and constant, are more properly termed ideas, or images of things, which they copy and represent. But then our sensations, be they never so vivid and distinct, are nevertheless ideas, that is, they exist in the mind, or are perceived by it, as truly as the ideas of its own framing. The ideas of Sense are allowed to have more reality in them, that is, to be more strong, orderly, and coherent than the creatures of the mind; but this is no argument that they exist without the mind. They are also less dependent on the spirit, or thinking substance which perceives them, in that they are excited by the will of another and more powerful spirit; yet still they are ideas, and certainly no idea, whether faint or strong, can exist otherwise than in a mind perceiving it.

It is evident to everyone that those things which are called the Works of Nature, that is, the far greater part of the ideas or sensations perceived by us, are not produced by, or dependent on, the wills of men. There is therefore some other Spirit that causes them; since it is repugnant that they should subsist by themselves. But, if we attentively consider the constant regularity, order, and concatenation of natural things, the surprising magnificence, beauty, and perfection of the larger, and the exquisite contrivance of the smaller parts of creation, together with the exact harmony and correspondence of the whole, but above all the never-enough-admired laws of pain and pleasure, and the instincts or natural inclinations, appetites, and passions of animals; I say if we consider all these things, and at the same time attend to the meaning and import of the attributes One, Eternal, Infinitely Wise, Good, and Perfect, we shall clearly perceive that they belong to the aforesaid Spirit.

Hence, it is evident that God is known as certainly and immediately as any other mind or spirit whatsoever distinct from ourselves. We may even assert that the existence of God is far more evidently perceived than the existence of men; because the effects of nature are infinitely more numerous and considerable than those ascribed to human agents. There is not any one mark that denotes a man, or effect produced by him, which does not more strongly evince the being of that Spirit who is the Author of Nature. For, it is evident that in affecting other persons the will of man has no other object than barely the motion of the limbs of his body; but that such a motion should be attended by, or excite any idea in the mind of another, depends wholly on the will of the Creator. He alone it is who, "upholding all things by the word of His power," maintains that intercourse between spirits whereby they are able to perceive the existence of each other. And yet this pure and clear light which enlightens every one is itself invisible.

It seems to be a general pretense of the unthinking herd that they cannot see God. Could we but see Him, say they, as we see a man, we should believe that He is, and believing obey His commands. But alas, we need only open our eyes to see the Sovereign Lord of all things, with a more full and clear view than we do any one of our fellow-creatures. Not that I imagine we see God (as some will have it) by a direct and immediate view; or see corporeal things, not by themselves, but by seeing that which represents them in the essence of God, which doctrine is, I must confess, to me incomprehensible. But I shall explain my meaning; A human spirit or person is not perceived by sense, as not being an idea; when therefore we see the color, size, figure, and motions of a man, we perceive only certain sensations or ideas excited in our own minds; and these being exhibited to our view in sundry distinct collections, serve to mark out unto us the existence of finite and created spirits like ourselves. Hence it is plain we do not see a man—if by man is meant that which lives, moves, perceives, and thinks as we do—but only such a certain collection of ideas as directs us to think there is a distinct principle of thought and motion, like to ourselves, accompanying and represented by it. And after the same manner we see God; all the difference is that, whereas some one finite and narrow assemblage of ideas denotes a particular human mind, whithersoever we direct our view, we do at all times and in all places perceive manifest tokens of the Divinity: everything we see, hear, feel, or anywise perceive by sense, being a sign or effect of the power of God; as is our perception of those very motions which are produced by men.

It is therefore plain that nothing can be more evident to any one that is capable of the least reflection than the existence of God, or a Spirit who is intimately present to our minds, producing in them all that variety of ideas or sensations which continually affect us, on whom we have an absolute and entire dependence, in short "in whom we live, and move, and have our being." That the discovery of this great truth, which lies so near and obvious to the mind, should be attained to by the reason of so very few, is a sad instance of the stupidity and inattention of men, who, though they are surrounded with such clear manifestations of the Deity, are yet so little affected by them that they seem, as it were, blinded with excess of light.

But you will say, Hath Nature no share in the production of natural things, and must they be all ascribed to the immediate and sole operation of God? I answer, if by Nature is meant only the visible series of effects or sensations imprinted on our minds, according to certain fixed and general laws, then it is plain that Nature, taken in this sense, cannot produce anything at all. But, if by Nature is meant some being distinct from God, as well as from the laws of nature, and things perceived by sense, I must confess that word is to me an empty sound without any intelligible meaning annexed to it.

William Paley

THE WATCHMAKER ARGUMENT

In crossing a heath, suppose I pitched my foot against a *stone*, and were asked how the stone came to be there; I might possibly answer, that, for any thing I knew to the contrary, it had lain there for ever: nor would it perhaps be very easy to show the absurdity of this answer. But suppose I had found a *watch* upon the ground, and it should be inquired how the watch happened to be in that place; I should hardly think the answer which I had given before, that the watch might have always been there.

Yet why should not this answer serve for the watch as well as for the stone? Why is it not as admissible in the second case, as in the first? For this reason, and for no other, namely that, when we come to inspect the watch, we perceive (what we could not discover in the stone) that its parts are framed and put together for a purpose, e g., that they are so formed and adjusted as to produce motion, and that motion so regulated as to point out the hour of the day; that, if the different parts had been differently shaped from what they are, of a different size from what they are, or placed after any other manner, or in any other order, than that in which they are placed, either no motion at all would have been carried on in the machine, or none which would have answered the use that is now served by it. We see a cylindrical box containing a coiled elastic spring, which, by its endeavor to relax itself, turns round the box. We next observe a flexible chain communicating the action of the spring from the box to the fusee [a part that acts as an equalizing force on the unwinding of the mainspring]. We then find a series of wheels, the teeth of which catch in, and apply to, each other, conducting the motion from the fusee to the balance, and from the balance to the pointer; and at the same time, by the size and shape of those wheels, so regulating that motion, as to terminate in causing an index, by an equable and measured progression, to pass over a given space in a given time. We take notice that the wheels are made of brass in order to keep them from rust; the springs of steel, no other metal being so elastic; that over the face of the watch there is placed a glass, a material employed in no other part of the work, but in the room of which, if there had been any other than a transparent substance, the hour could not be seen without opening the case. This mechanism being observed (it requires indeed an examination of the instrument, and perhaps some previous knowledge of the subject, to perceive and understand it; but being once, as we have said, observed and understood), the inference, we think, is inevitable: that *the watch must have had a maker*: that there must have existed, at some time, and at some place or other, an artificer or artificers who formed it for the purpose which we find it actually to answer; who comprehended its construction, and designed its use.

Nor would it, I apprehend, weaken the conclusion, that we had never seen a watch made; that we had never known an artist capable of making one; that we were altogether incapable of executing such a piece of workmanship ourselves, or of understanding in what manner it was performed; all this being no more than what is true of some exquisite remains of ancient art, of some lost arts, and, to the generality of mankind, of the more curious productions of modern manufacture. Does one man in a million know how oval frames are turned? Ignorance of this kind exalts our opinion of the unseen and unknown artist's skill, if he be unseen and unknown, but raises no doubt in our minds of the existence and agency of such an artist, at some former time, and in some place or other. Nor can I perceive that it varies at all the inference, whether the

Edited from *Natural Theology,* 1802, which is now in the public domain.

question arise concerning a human agent, or concerning an agent of a different species, or an agent possessing, in some respects, a different nature.

Neither, secondly, would it invalidate our conclusion, that the watch sometimes went wrong, or that it seldom went exactly right. The purpose of the machinery, the design, and the designer, might be evident, and in the case supposed would be evident, in whatever way we accounted for the irregularity of the movement, or whether we could account for it or not. It is not necessary that a machine be perfect, in order to show with what design it was made: still less necessary, where the only question is, whether it were made with any design at all.

Nor, thirdly, would it bring any uncertainty into the argument, if there were a few parts of the watch, concerning which we could not discover, or had not yet discovered, in what manner they conduced to the general effect; or even some parts, concerning which we could not ascertain, whether they conduced to that effect in any manner whatever. For, as to the first branch of the case; if by the loss, or disorder, or decay of the parts in question, the movement of the watch were found in fact to be stopped, or disturbed, or retarded, no doubt would remain in our minds as to the utility or intention of these parts, although we should be unable to investigate the manner according to which, or the connection by which, the ultimate effect depended upon their action or assistance; and the more complex is the machine, the more likely is this obscurity to arise. Then, as to the second thing supposed, namely, that there were parts which might be spared, without prejudice to the movement of the watch, and that we had proved this by experiment, these superfluous parts, even if we were completely assured that they were such, would not vacate the reasoning which we had instituted concerning other parts. The indication of contrivance remained, with respect to them, nearly as it was before.

Nor, fourthly, would any man in his senses think the existence of the watch, with its various machinery, accounted for, by being told that it was one out of possible combinations of material forms; that whatever he had found in the place where he found the watch, must have contained some internal configuration or other; and that this configuration might be the structure now exhibited, namely, of the works of a watch, as well as a different structure.

Nor, fifthly, would it yield his inquiry more satisfaction to be answered, that there existed in things a principle of order, which had disposed the parts of the watch into their present form and situation. He never knew a watch made by the principle of order; nor can he even form to himself an idea of what is meant by a principle of order, distinct from the intelligence of the watch-maker.

Sixthly, he would be surprised to hear that the mechanism of the watch was no proof of contrivance, only a motive to induce the mind to think so. And not less surprised to be informed, that the watch in his hand was nothing more than the result of the laws of *metallic* nature. It is a perversion of language to assign any law, as the efficient, operative cause of any thing. A law presupposes an agent; for it is only the mode, according to which an agent proceeds: it implies a power; for it is the order, according to which that power acts. Without this agent, without this power, which are both distinct from itself, the law does nothing; is nothing. The expression, the law of metallic nature, may sound strange and harsh to a philosophic ear; but it seems quite as justifiable as some others which are more familiar to him, such as the law of vegetable nature, the law of animal nature, or indeed as the law of nature in general, when assigned as the cause of phenomena, in exclusion of agency and power; or when it is substituted into the place of these.

Neither, lastly, would our observer be driven out of his conclusion, or from his confidence in its truth, by being told that he knew nothing at all about the matter. He knows enough for his argument: he knows the utility of the end: he knows the subserviency and adaptation of the means to the end. These points being known, his ignorance of other points, his doubts concerning other points, affect not the certainty of his reasoning. The consciousness of knowing little, need not beget a distrust of that which he does know.

Every indication of contrivance, every manifestation of design, which existed in the watch, exists in the works of nature; with the difference, on the side of nature, of being greater and more, and that in a degree which exceeds all computation. *There cannot be design without a designer.*

David Hume

AGAINST THE WATCHMAKER ARGUMENT

Philo: Our ideas reach no further than our experience: We have no experience of divine attributes and operations. I need not conclude my syllogism: You can draw the inference yourself.

Cleanthes: Look round the world: Contemplate the whole and every part of it: You will find it to be nothing but one great machine, subdivided into an infinite number of lesser machines, which again admit of subdivisions, to a degree beyond what human senses and faculties can trace and explain. All these various machines, and even their most minute parts, are adjusted to each other with an accuracy, which ravishes into admiration all men, who have ever contemplated them. The curious adapting of means to ends, throughout all nature, resembles exactly, though it much exceeds, the productions of human contrivance; of human design, thought, wisdom, and intelligence. Since therefore the effects resemble each other, we are led to infer, by all the rules of analogy, that the causes also resemble; and that the author of nature is somewhat similar to the mind of man, though possessed of much larger faculties, proportioned to the grandeur of the work which he has executed. By this argument *a posteriori*, and by this argument alone, do we prove at once the existence of a deity, and his similarity to human mind and intelligence.

Demea: What! No demonstration of the being of a God! No abstract arguments! No proofs *a priori*! Are these, which have hitherto been so much insisted on by philosophers all fallacy, all sophism? Can we reach no further in this subject than experience and probability? I will not say, that this is betraying the cause of a deity: But surely, by this affected candor, you give advantages to atheists, which they never could obtain by the mere dint of argument and reasoning.

Philo: What I chiefly scruple in this subject, is not so much that all religious arguments are by Cleanthes reduced to experience, as that they appear not to be even the most certain and irrefragable of that inferior kind. That a stone will fall, that fire will burn, that the earth has solidity, we have observed a thousand and a thousand times; and when any new instance of this nature is presented, we draw without hesitation the accustomed inference. The exact similarity of the cases gives us a perfect assurance of a similar event; and a stronger evidence is never desired nor sought after. But wherever you depart, in the least, from the similarity of the cases, you diminish proportionably the evidence; and may at last bring it to a very weak *analogy*, which is confessedly liable to error and uncertainty.

If we see a house, Cleanthes, we conclude, with the greatest certainty, that it had an architect or builder, because this is precisely that species of effect, which we have experienced to proceed from that species of cause. But surely you will not affirm, that the universe bears such a resemblance to a house, that we can with the same certainty infer a similar cause, or that the analogy is here entire and perfect. The dissimilitude is so striking, that the utmost you can here pretend to is a guess, a conjecture, a presumption concerning a similar cause; and how that pretension will be received in the world, I leave you to consider.

Cleanthes: It would surely be very ill received, and I should be deservedly blamed and detested, did I allow, that the proofs of a deity amounted to no more than a guess or conjecture. But is the whole adjustment of means to ends in a house and in the universe so slight a resemblance? The economy of final causes? The order, proportion, and arrangement of every part? Steps of a stair are plainly contrived, that human legs may use them in mounting; and this inference

Edited from *Dialogues Concerning Natural Religion,* 1779, Parts 2 and 5, which is now in the public domain.

is certain and infallible. Human legs are also contrived for walking and mounting; and this inference, I allow, is not altogether so certain, because of the dissimilarity which you remark; but does it, therefore, deserve the name only of presumption or conjecture?

Philo: I argue with Cleanthes in his own way; and by showing him the dangerous consequences of his tenets. Now, however much I may dissent, in other respects, from the dangerous principle of Cleanthes, I must allow that he has fairly represented that argument.

Were a man to abstract from everything which he knows or has seen, he would be altogether incapable, merely from his own ideas, to determine what kind of scene the universe must be, or to give the preference to one state or situation of things above another. For as nothing which he clearly conceives could be esteemed impossible or implying a contradiction, every chimera of his fancy would be upon an equal footing; nor could he assign any just reason, why he adheres to one idea or system, and rejects the others, which are equally possible.

Again; after he opens his eyes, and contemplates the world as it really is, it would be impossible for him, at first, to assign the cause of any one event, much less, of the whole of things or of the universe. He might set his fancy a rambling; and she might bring him in an infinite variety of reports and representations. These would all be possible; but being all equally possible, he would never, of himself, give a satisfactory account for his preferring one of them to the rest. Experience alone can point out to him the true cause of any phenomenon.

Now, according to this method of reasoning, it follows, (and is, indeed, tacitly allowed by Cleanthes himself) that order, arrangement, or the adjustment of final causes is not, of itself, any proof of design; but only so far as it has been experienced to proceed from that principle. For all we can know *a priori*, matter may contain the source or spring of order originally within itself, as well as mind does; and there is no more difficulty in conceiving, that the several elements, from an internal unknown cause, may fall into the most exquisite arrangement, than to conceive that their ideas, in the great universal mind, from a like internal unknown cause, fall into that arrangement. The equal possibility of both these suppositions is allowed. But by experience we find (according to Cleanthes), that there is a difference between them. Throw several pieces of steel together, without shape or form; they will never arrange themselves so as to compose a watch: Stone, and mortar, and wood, without an architect, never erect a house. But the ideas in a human mind, we see, by an unknown, inexplicable economy, arrange themselves so as to form the plan of a watch or house. Experience, therefore, proves, that there is an original principle of order in mind, not in matter. From similar effects we infer similar causes. The adjustment of means to ends is alike in the universe, as in a machine of human contrivance. The causes, therefore, must be resembling.

I was from the beginning scandalized, I must own, with this resemblance, which is asserted, between the deity and human creatures; and must conceive it to imply such a degradation of the supreme being as no sound theist could endure. With your assistance, therefore, Demea, I shall endeavor to defend what you justly call the adorable mysteriousness of the divine nature, and shall refute this reasoning of Cleanthes; provided he allows that I have made a fair representation of it.

Cleanthes: I agree.

Philo: That all inferences concerning fact are founded on experience; and all experimental reasonings are founded on the supposition that similar causes prove similar effects, and similar effects similar causes, I shall not, at present much dispute with you. But observe, I entreat you, with what extreme caution all just reasoners proceed in the transferring of experiments to similar cases. Unless the cases be exactly similar, they repose no perfect confidence in applying their past observation to any particular phenomenon. Every alteration of circumstances occasions a doubt concerning the event; and it requires new experiments to prove certainly, that the new circumstances are of no moment or importance. A change in bulk, situation, arrangement, age, disposition of the air, or surrounding bodies; any of these particulars may be attended with the most unexpected consequences: And unless the objects be quite familiar to us, it is the highest temerity to expect with assurance, after any of these changes, an event similar to that which before fell under our observation. The slow and deliberate steps of philosophers here, if anywhere, are distinguished from the precipitate march of the vulgar, who, hurried on by the smallest similitude, are incapable of all discernment or consideration.

But can you think, Cleanthes, that your usual philosophy has been preserved in so wide a step as you have taken, when you compared to the universe, houses, ships, furniture, machines, and, from their similarity in some circumstances, inferred a similarity in their causes? Thought, design, intelligence, such as we discover in men and other animals, is no more than one of the springs and principles of the universe, as well as heat or cold, attraction or repulsion, and a hundred others, which fall under daily observation. It is an active cause, by which some particular parts of nature, we find, produce alterations on other parts. But can a conclusion, with any propriety, be transferred from parts to the whole? Does not the great disproportion bar all comparison and inference? From observing the growth of a hair, can we learn anything concerning the generation of a man? Would the manner of a leaf's blowing, even though perfectly known, afford us any instruction concerning the vegetation of a tree?

But allowing that we were to take the *operations* of one part of nature upon another for the foundation of our judgment concerning the *origin* of the whole (which never can be admitted) yet why select so minute, so weak, so bounded a principle as the reason and design of animals is found to be upon this planet? What peculiar privilege has this little agitation of the brain which we call thought, that we must thus make it the model of the whole universe? Our partiality in our own favor does indeed present it on all occasions: but sound philosophy ought carefully to guard against so natural an illusion.

So far from admitting that the operations of a part can afford us any just conclusion concerning the origin of the whole, I will not allow any one part to form a rule for another part, if the latter be very remote from the former. Is there any reasonable ground to conclude, that the inhabitants of other planets possess thought, intelligence, reason, or anything similar to these faculties in men? When nature has so extremely diversified her manner of operation in this small globe; can we imagine that she incessantly copies herself throughout so immense a universe? And if thought, as we may well suppose, be confined merely to this narrow corner, and has even there so limited a sphere of action, with what propriety can we assign it for the original cause of all things? The narrow views of a peasant, who makes his domestic economy the rule for the government of kingdoms, is in comparison a pardonable sophism.

But were we ever so much assured, that a thought and reason, resembling the human, were to be found throughout the whole universe, and were its activity elsewhere vastly greater and more commanding than it appears in this globe. Yet I cannot see why the operations of a world, constituted, arranged, adjusted, can with any propriety be extended to a world, which is in its embryo-state, and is advancing towards that constitution and arrangement. By observation, we know somewhat of the economy, action, and nourishment of a finished animal; but we must transfer with great caution that observation to the growth of a fetus in the womb, and still more, to the formation of an animalcule in the loins of its male-parent. Nature, we find, even from our limited experience, possesses an infinite number of springs and principles, which incessantly discover themselves on every change of her position and situation. And what new and unknown principles would actuate her in so new and unknown a situation, as that of the formation of a universe, we cannot, without the utmost temerity, pretend to determine. A very small part of this great system, during a very short time, is very imperfectly discovered to us: And do we thence pronounce decisively concerning the origin of the whole?

Stone, wood, brick, iron, brass, have not, at this time, in this minute globe of earth, an order or arrangement without human art and contrivance: Therefore the universe could not originally attain its order and arrangement, without something similar to human art. But is a part of nature a rule for another part very wide of the former? Is it a rule for the whole? Is a very small part a rule for the universe? Is nature in one situation, a certain rule for nature in another situation, vastly different from the former?

And can you blame me, Cleanthes, if I had answered at first, *that I did not know*, and was sensible that this subject lay vastly beyond the reach of my faculties? You might cry out "skeptic" as much as you pleased. But having found, in so many other subjects, much more familiar, the imperfections and even contradictions of human reason, I never should expect any success from its feeble conjectures, in a subject, so sublime, and so remote from the sphere of our observation. When two *species* of objects have always been observed to be conjoined together, I can *infer*, by custom, the existence of one wherever I *see* the existence of the other: And this I call an argument from experience. But how this argument can have place, where the objects, as in the present case, are single, individual, without parallel, or specific resemblance, may be difficult to explain. And will any man tell me with a serious countenance, that an orderly universe must arise from some thought and art, like the human; because we have experience of it? To ascertain this reasoning, it were requisite, that we had experience of the origin of worlds; and it is not sufficient surely, that we have seen ships and cities arise from human art and contrivance.

***Cleanthes*:** To prove by experience the origin of the universe from mind is not more contrary to common speech than to prove the motion of the earth from the same principle. And someone might raise all the same objections to the *Copernican* system, which you have urged against my reasonings. Have you other earths, might he say, which you have seen to move?

***Philo*:** Yes! We have other earths. Is not the moon another earth, which we see to turn round its center? Is not Venus another earth, where we observe the same phenomenon? Are not the revolutions of the sun also a confirmation, from analogy, of the same theory? All the planets, are they not earths, which revolve about the sun? Are not the satellites moons, which move round Jupiter and Saturn, and along with these primary planets, round the sun? These analogies and resemblances, with others which I have not mentioned, are the sole proofs of the *Copernican* system: And to you it belongs to consider, whether you have any analogies of the same kind to support your theory.

In reality, Cleanthes, the modern system of astronomy is now so much received by all inquirers, and has become so essential a part even of our earliest education, that we are not commonly very scrupulous in examining the reasons, upon which it is founded. In this cautious proceeding of the astronomers, you may read your own condemnation, or rather may see, that the subject in which you are engaged exceeds all human reason and inquiry. Can you pretend to show any such similarity between the fabric of a house, and the generation of a universe? Have you ever seen nature in any such situation as resembles the first arrangement of the elements? Have worlds ever been formed under your eye? And have you had leisure to observe the whole progress of the phenomenon, from the first appearance of order to its final consummation? If you have, then cite your experience, and deliver your theory.

But were this world ever so perfect a production, it must still remain uncertain, whether all the excellences of the work can justly be ascribed to the workman. If we survey a ship, what an exalted idea must we form of the ingenuity of the carpenter who framed so complicated, useful, and beautiful a machine? And what surprise must we feel, when we find him a stupid mechanic, who imitated others, and copied an art, which, through a long succession of ages, after multiplied trials, mistakes, corrections, deliberations, and controversies, had been gradually improving? Many worlds might have been botched and bungled, throughout an eternity, ere this system was struck out; much labor lost, many fruitless trials made; and a slow, but continued improvement carried on during infinite ages in the art of world-making. In such subjects, who can determine, where the truth; nay, who can conjecture where the probability lies, amidst a great number of hypotheses which may be proposed, and a still greater which may be imagined?

And what shadow of an argument can you produce, from your hypothesis, to prove the unity of the Deity? A great number of men join in building a house or ship, in rearing a city, in framing a commonwealth; why may not several deities combine in contriving and framing a world? This is only so much greater similarity to human affairs. By sharing the work among several, we may so much further limit the attributes of each, and get rid of that extensive power and knowledge, which must be supposed in one deity, and which, according to you, can only serve to weaken the proof of his existence. And if such foolish, such vicious creatures as man, can yet often unite in framing and executing one plan, how much more those deities or demons, whom we may suppose several degrees more perfect!

To multiply causes without necessity, is indeed contrary to true philosophy: but this principle applies not to the present case. Were one deity antecedently proved by your theory, who were possessed of every attribute requisite to the production of the universe; it would be needless, I own, (though not absurd,) to suppose any other deity existent. But while it is still a question, whether all these attributes are united in one subject, or dispersed among several independent beings, by what phenomena in nature can we pretend to decide the controversy? Where we see a body raised in a scale, we are sure that there is in the opposite scale, however concealed from sight, some counterpoising weight equal to it; but it is still allowed to doubt, whether that weight be an aggregate of several distinct bodies, or one uniform united mass. And if the weight requisite very much exceeds anything which we have ever seen conjoined in any single body, the former supposition becomes still more probable and natural. An intelligent being of such vast power and capacity as is necessary to produce the universe, or, to speak in the language of ancient philosophy, so prodigious an animal exceeds all analogy, and even comprehension.

But further: men are mortal, and renew their species by generation; and this is common to all living creatures. The two great sexes of male and female, says Milton, animate the world. Why must this circumstance, so universal, so essential, be excluded from those numerous and limited deities?

And why not become a perfect anthropomorphite? Why not assert the deity or deities to be corporeal, and to have eyes, a nose, mouth, ears, etc.? Epicurus maintained that no man had ever seen reason but in a human figure; therefore the gods must have a human figure. And this argument, which is deservedly so much ridiculed by Cicero, becomes, according to you, solid and philosophical.

In a word, Cleanthes, a man who follows your hypothesis is able perhaps to assert, or conjecture, that the universe, sometime, arose from something like design: but beyond that position he cannot ascertain one single circumstance; and is left afterwards to fix every point of his theology by the utmost license of fancy and hypothesis. This world, for aught he knows, is very faulty and imperfect, compared to a superior standard; and was only the first rude essay of some infant deity, who afterwards abandoned it, ashamed of his lame performance: it is the work only of some dependent, inferior deity; and is the object of derision to his superiors: it is the production of old age and dotage in some superannuated deity; and ever since his death, has run on at adventures, from the first impulse and active force which it received from him.

5B. Can God's Existence Be Proved Independent of Experience?

Introduction

In the first reading of this section, Anselm of Canterbury offers a version of the *ontological proof* (or *ontological argument*) for the existence of God. Ontological proofs are *a priori*—arguments that are *independent of experience*. Being *a priori*, they are considered formal proofs—proofs that rely on the *structure* of an argument. In fact, some versions of the ontological proof rely on the argument technique called *reductio ad absurdum* ("reduction to an absurdity"). The idea is this: Start by assuming *the opposite* of what you wish to prove. Next, try to derive a contradiction from your initial assumption. If you are able to derive a contradiction, then you have shown that your *initial assumption must be false*. (It should now be clear why the technique is called *reductio ad absurdum*; an assumption is refuted by proving that it leads to a contradiction—an absurdity.)

A classic version of the ontological argument is presented in the reading from Anselm. In concise form, Anselm asks us to think about the idea of a being than which nothing greater can be conceived, while, at the same time, imagine that being not existing in reality as well. Anselm argues that it is logically impossible to do so.

René Descartes's version of the ontological argument relies on his criteria of *clear and distinct ideas*. An idea is *clear* when it is directly accessible to the mind, and it is *distinct* when it is not confused with any other idea. Since we can easily fall into error, Descartes stresses the importance of subjecting all our ideas to intense scrutiny. Only then can we attain knowledge of the truth.

The reading by Ann Conway invokes the concepts of *time* and *eternity* into the discussion of God. Conway agrees that God is perfect and all-powerful, but she emphasizes the idea that in God there is neither time nor change because God is eternal. In an interesting twist, Conway argues that since times are infinite, an eternal God has probably created an infinity of worlds.

In a passage from David Hume's *Dialogues*, one of the characters proposes an *a priori* argument to show that God's existence is *necessary*. The argument is criticized by pointing out that is impossible to prove a matter of *fact* by an *a priori* argument. As one of the characters remarks, "Whatever we conceive as existent, we can also conceive as non-existent. There is no being, therefore, whose non-existence implies a contradiction."

Anselm of Canterbury

THE EXISTENCE OF GOD

I began to ask myself whether there might be found a single argument which would require no other for its proof than itself alone; and alone would suffice to demonstrate that God truly exists, and that there is a supreme good requiring nothing else, which all other things require for their existence and well-being; and whatever we believe regarding the divine Being.

Although I often and earnestly directed my thought to this end, and at some times that which I sought seemed to be just within my reach, while again it wholly evaded my mental vision, at last in despair I was about to cease, as if from the search for a thing which could not be found. But when I wished to exclude this thought altogether, lest, by busying my mind to no purpose, it should keep me from other thoughts, in which I might be successful; then more and more, though I was unwilling and shunned it, it began to force itself upon me, with a kind of importunity. So, one day, when I was exceedingly wearied with resisting its importunity, in the very conflict of my thoughts, the proof of which I had despaired offered itself, so that I eagerly embraced the thoughts which I was strenuously repelling.

I do not seek to understand that I may believe, but I believe in order to understand. For this also I believe—that unless I believed, I should not understand. And, indeed, we believe that thou art a being than which nothing greater can be conceived. Or is there no such nature, since the fool hath said in his heart, there is no God? (Psalms xiv. 1). But, at any rate, this very fool, when he hears of this being of which I speak—a being than which nothing greater can be conceived—understands what he hears, and what he understands is in his understanding; although he does not understand it to exist.

For, it is one thing for an object to be in the understanding, and another to understand that the object exists. When a painter first conceives of what he will afterwards perform, he has it in his understanding, but he does not yet understand it to be, because he has not yet performed it. But after he has made the painting, he both has it in his understanding, and he understands that it exists, because he has made it.

Hence, even the fool is convinced that something exists in the understanding, at least, than which nothing greater can be conceived. For, when he hears of this, he understands it. And whatever is understood, exists in the understanding. And assuredly that, than which nothing greater can be conceived, cannot exist in the understanding alone. For, suppose it exists in the understanding alone: then it can be conceived to exist in reality; which is greater.

Therefore, if that, than which nothing greater can be conceived, exists in the understanding alone, the very being, than which nothing greater can be conceived, is one, than which a greater can be conceived. But obviously this is impossible. Hence, there is no doubt that there exists a being, than which nothing greater can be conceived, and it exists both in the understanding and in reality.

God cannot be conceived not to exist. God is that, than which nothing greater can be conceived. That which can be conceived not to exist is not God. And it assuredly exists so truly, that it cannot be conceived not to exist. For, it is possible to conceive of a being which cannot be conceived not to exist; and this is greater than one which can be conceived not to exist. Hence, if that, than which nothing greater can be conceived, can be conceived not to exist, it is not that,

Edited from *Proslogion,* Preface, Chapter II-V. Translated by Sidney N. Deane, 1903.

than which nothing greater can be conceived. But this is an irreconcilable contradiction. There is, then, so truly a being than which nothing greater can be conceived to exist, that it cannot even be conceived not to exist; and this being thou art, O Lord, our God.

So truly, therefore, dost thou exist, O Lord, my God, that thou canst not be conceived not to exist; and rightly. For, if a mind could conceive of a being better than thee, the creature would rise above the Creator; and this is most absurd. And, indeed, whatever else there is, except thee alone, can be conceived not to exist. To thee alone, therefore, it belongs to exist more truly than all other beings, and hence in a higher degree than all others.

A thing may be conceived in two ways: (1) when the word signifying it is conceived; (2) when the thing itself is understood. As far as the word goes, God can be conceived not to exist; in reality he cannot. For, in one sense, an object is conceived, when the word signifying it is conceived; and in another, when the very entity, which the object is, is understood. In the former sense, then, God can be conceived not to exist; but in the latter, not at all. For no one who understands what fire and water are can conceive fire to be water, in accordance with the nature of the facts themselves, although this is possible according to the words. So, then, no one who understands what God is can conceive that God does not exist. For, God is that than which a greater cannot be conceived. And he who thoroughly understands this, assuredly understands that this being so truly exists, that not even in concept can it be non-existent. Therefore, he who understands that God so exists, cannot conceive that he does not exist. God is whatever it is better to be than not to be; and he, as the only self-existent being, creates all things from nothing.

René Descartes

THE IDEA OF GOD

I discover in my mind innumerable ideas of certain objects, although perhaps they possess no reality beyond my thought, possess true and immutable natures of their own. As, for example, when I imagine a triangle, although there is not perhaps and never was in any place in the universe apart from my thought one such figure, it remains true nevertheless that this figure possesses a certain determinate nature, form, or essence, which is immutable and eternal, and not in any degree dependent on my thought, e.g., that its three angles are equal to two right angles, and the like, which, I now clearly discern to belong to it, and which accordingly cannot be said to have been invented by me. I can demonstrate diverse properties of the triangle, all of which are assuredly true since I clearly conceive them: and they are therefore something; and I have already fully shown the truth of the principle, that *whatever is clearly and distinctly known is true.*

But now if because I can draw from my thought the idea of an object, it follows that all I clearly and distinctly apprehend to pertain to this object, does in truth belong to it, may I not from this derive an argument for the existence of God? It is certain that I no less find the idea of a God in my consciousness, that is the idea of a being supremely perfect, than that of any figure or number whatever: and I know with not less clearness and distinctness that an eternal existence pertains to his nature than that all which is demonstrable of any figure or number really belongs to the nature of that figure or number; and, therefore, although all the conclusions of the preceding Meditations were false, the existence of God would pass with me for a truth at least as certain as I ever judged any truth of mathematics to be, although indeed such a doctrine may at first sight appear to contain more sophistry than truth. For, as I have been accustomed in every other matter to distinguish between existence and essence, I easily believe that the existence can be separated from the essence of God, and that thus God may be conceived as not actually existing. But, nevertheless, when I think of it more attentively, it appears that the existence can no more be separated from the essence of God, than the idea of a mountain from that of a valley, or the equality of its three angles to two right angles, so that it is not less impossible to conceive a God, that is, a being supremely perfect, to whom existence is wanting, or who is devoid of a certain perfection, than to conceive a mountain without a valley.

But though, in truth, I cannot conceive a God unless as existing, any more than I can a mountain without a valley, yet, just as it does not follow that there is any mountain in the world merely because I conceive a mountain with a valley, so likewise, though I conceive God as existing, it does not seem to follow on that account that God exists; for my thought imposes no necessity on things; and as I may imagine a winged horse, though there be none such, so I could perhaps attribute existence to God, though no God existed. But the cases are not analogous, and a fallacy lurks under the semblance of this objection: for because I cannot conceive a mountain without a valley, it does not follow that there is any mountain or valley in existence, but simply that the mountain or valley, whether they do or do not exist, are inseparable from each other; whereas, on the other hand, because I cannot conceive God unless as existing, it follows that existence is inseparable from him, and therefore that he really exists: not that this is brought about by my thought, or that it imposes any necessity on things, but, on the contrary, the necessity which lies in the thing itself, that is, the necessity of the existence of God, determines me to think in this way:

Edited from *Meditations on First Philosophy,* Meditation V. Translated by John Veitch, 1901, which is now in the public domain.

for it is not in my power to conceive a God without existence, that is a being supremely perfect, and yet devoid of an absolute perfection, as I am free to imagine a horse with or without wings.

Nor must it be alleged here as an objection, that it is in truth necessary to admit that God exists, after having supposed him to possess all perfections, since existence is one of them, but that my original supposition was not necessary. This objection is, I say, incompetent; for although it may not be necessary that I shall at any time entertain the notion of Deity, yet each time I happen to think of a first and sovereign being, and to draw, so to speak, the idea of him from the storehouse of the mind, I am necessitated to attribute to him all kinds of perfections, though I may not then enumerate them all, nor think of each of them in particular. And this necessity is sufficient, as soon as I discover that existence is a perfection, to cause me to infer the existence of this first and sovereign being. So long as I shall be unwilling to accept in thought aught that I do not clearly and distinctly conceive; and consequently there is a vast difference between false suppositions, as is the one in question, and the true ideas that were born with me, the first and chief of which is the idea of God. For indeed I discern on many grounds that this idea is not factitious depending simply on my thought, but that it is the representation of a true and immutable nature: in the first place, because I can conceive no other being, except God, to whose essence existence necessarily pertains; in the second, because it is impossible to conceive two or more gods of this kind; and it being supposed that one such God exists, I clearly see that he must have existed from all eternity, and will exist to all eternity; and finally, because I apprehend many other properties in God, none of which I can either diminish or change.

And, with respect to God, if I were not preoccupied by prejudices, and my thought beset on all sides by the continual presence of the images of sensible objects, I should know nothing sooner or more easily then the fact of his being. For is there any truth more clear than the existence of a Supreme Being, or of God, seeing it is to his essence alone that existence pertains? And although the right conception of this truth has cost me much close thinking, nevertheless at present I feel not only as assured of it as of what I deem most certain, but I remark further that the certitude of all other truths is so absolutely dependent on it that without this knowledge it is impossible ever to know anything perfectly.

For although I am of such a nature as to be unable, while I possess a very clear and distinct apprehension of a matter, to resist the conviction of its truth, yet because my constitution is also such as to incapacitate me from keeping my mind continually fixed on the same object, and as I frequently recollect a past judgment without at the same time being able to recall the grounds of it, it may happen meanwhile that other reasons are presented to me which would readily cause me to change my opinion, if I did not know that God existed; and thus I should possess not true and certain knowledge, but merely vague and vacillating opinions. But after I have discovered that God exists, seeing I also at the same time observed that all things depend on him, and that he is no deceiver, and thence inferred that all which I clearly and distinctly perceive is of necessity true: although I no longer attend to the grounds of a judgment, no opposite reason can be alleged sufficient to lead me to doubt of its truth, provided only I remember that I once possessed a clear and distinct comprehension of it. My knowledge of it thus becomes true and certain. And this same knowledge extends likewise to whatever I remember to have formerly demonstrated, as the truths of geometry and the like: for what can be alleged against them to lead me to doubt of them? Will it be that my nature is such that I may be frequently deceived? But I already know that I cannot be deceived in judgments of the grounds of which I possess a clear knowledge. Will it be that I formerly deemed things to be true and certain which I afterward discovered to be false? But I had no clear and distinct knowledge of any of those things, and, being as yet ignorant of the rule by which I am assured of the truth of a judgment, I was led to give my assent to them on grounds which I afterwards discovered were less strong than at the time I imagined them to be. What further objection, then, is there? Will it be said that perhaps I am dreaming (an objection I lately myself raised), or that all the thoughts of which I am now conscious have no more truth than the reveries of my dreams? But although, in truth, I should be dreaming, the rule still holds that all which is clearly presented to my intellect is indisputably true.

And thus I very clearly see that the certitude and truth of all science depends on the knowledge alone of the true God, *insomuch that, before I knew him, I could have no perfect knowledge of any other thing.*

Anne Conway

ON GOD

God is a spirit, light, and life, infinitely wise, good, just, mighty, omniscient, omnipresent, omnipotent, creator and maker of all things visible and invisible. In God there is neither time nor change, nor composition, nor division of parts: He is wholly and universally one in himself, and of himself, without any manner of variety or mixture: He has no manner of darkness, or corporality in him, and so consequently no kind of form or figure whatsoever.

He is also in a proper and real sense, a substance or essence distinct from his creatures, although he is not divided, or separated from them; but most strictly and in the highest degree intimately present in them all; yet so as they are not parts of him, nor can be changed into him, nor he into them. He is also in a true and proper sense a creator of all things, who does not only give them their form and figure, but also being, life, body, and whatever else of good they have.

Seeing then that in him there is no time, nor any mutability, hence it is that in him there can exist no new knowledge or Will, but his knowledge and Will are eternal, and without or above time. Likewise, in God there can exist no passion, which to speak properly comes from his creatures: For every passion is something temporal, and has its beginning, and end with time.

In God is an *Idea*, which is the image of himself, or a Word existing within him; which in substance or essence is one and same with him, by which he knows not only himself, but all other things, and according to which, by which *Idea* or Word, all things were made and created.

Similarly, Reason in God is a spirit or Will which proceeds from him, and yet as to substance or essence is something one with him, by which creatures receive their being and activity: for creatures have their being and existence simply and alone from him, because God would have them to be, whose Will is according to knowledge most infinite. And thus wisdom and Will in God, are not a certain substance or being distinct from him; but only distinct manners or properties of one and the same substance. All would easily agree in this point: that God has wisdom, and an essential *Idea*, and such a Word in himself by which he knows all things; and when they grant he gives all things their being, they will be necessarily forced to acknowledge that there is a Will in him, by which he can accomplish and bring that into act which was hid in the *Idea*, that is, can produce it, and from it make a distinct essential substance; and this alone is to create, namely, the essence of a creature. Nevertheless, the *Idea* alone does not give being to the creature, but the Will joined with the *Idea*, as when a master-builder conceives in his mind the *Idea* of an house, he does not build that house by the *Idea* alone, but the Will is joined with the *Idea*, and cooperates with it.

For as much as all creatures are, and do exist simply, or alone from him; because God willed them to be, whose Will is infinitely powerful, and whose commandment, without any instrument or instrumental cause, is the only efficient to give being unto his creatures, hence it necessarily follows, seeing the Will of God is eternal, or from eternity, that creation must immediately follow the Will, without any interposition of time. And though it cannot be said that creatures considered in themselves, are co-eternal with God, because after this rate eternity and time would be confounded together; yet nevertheless the creatures, and that Will which created them, are so mutually present, and so immediately happen one after another, that nothing can be said to come in between; even as if two circles should immediately touch each other. Neither can we assign any other beginning to creatures, but God himself, and his eternal Will, which is according to his eternal

Edited from *The Principles of the Most Ancient and Modern Philosophy,* 1692, Chapters I-III, which is now in the public domain.

Idea or wisdom. Hence it follows by natural consequence, that times from the creation are infinite, and without all number, which no created intellect can conceive. How then can this be finite or measured, which had no other beginning but eternity itself?

But if anyone will say that times are finite, then let us suppose the measure of them from the beginning, to be about 6,000 years (even as some do think that the whole age of this world, from the beginning, is of no greater extent) or with others (who think that before this world, there was another invisible world, from which this visible world proceeded), let us suppose the duration of this world to be 600,000 years, or any other number of years, as great as can be by any reason conceived. Now, I demand whether it could be that the world was created before this time? If they deny it, they limit the power of God to a certain number of years; if they affirm it, they allow time to be before all time, which is a manifest contradiction.

These things being premised, it will be easy to answer to that question where numbers have been so exceedingly perplexed: Whether creation was made or could be made, from eternity, or from everlasting? If by eternity, and everlasting, they mean an infinite number of times; in this sense creation was made from everlasting. But if they mean such an eternity, as God himself has, so as to say, creatures are equal or co-eternal with God, and have no beginning in time, this is false, for both creatures and times (which are nothing else but successive motions and operations of created beings) had a beginning, which is God or the eternal Will of God. And why should it seem strange to anyone that times in their whole collection or universality, may be said to be infinite, when the least part of time that can be conceived, contains in itself a kind of infinity? For as there is no time so great that a greater cannot be conceived; so there is no time so small that there may be less; for the sixtieth part of a minute may be divided into sixty other parts, and these again into others, and so *ad infinitum*.

Since time is nothing else but the successive motion or operation of creatures; which motion or operation, if it should cease, time would also cease, and the creatures themselves would cease with time. Therefore, such is the nature of every creature that it is in motion, or has a certain motion, by means of which it advances forward, and grows to a farther perfection. And seeing in God there is no successive motion or operation to a farther perfection, because he is most absolutely perfect, hence there are no times in God or his eternity. Moreover, because there are no parts in God, there are also no times in Him; for all times have their parts, and are indeed infinitely divisible, as before was said.

If the aforementioned attributes of God are duly considered, and especially these two—his wisdom and goodness—the *indifference of Will*, which the Schoolmen [certain theologians of the Middle Ages] and philosophers falsely so called, have imagined to be in God, will be utterly refuted, which also they have improperly called free-will; for although the will of God is most free, so that whatsoever he does in the behalf of his creatures, he does freely without any external violence, compulsion, or any cause coming from them. Whatever he does, he does of his own accord. Yet that indifference of acting, or not acting, can by no means be said to be in God; because this were an imperfection, and would make God like corruptible creatures; for this indifference of Will is the foundation of all change and corruptibility in creatures; so that there would be no evil in creatures if they were not changeable. Therefore, if the same should be supposed to be in God, then He must be supposed to be changeable, and so would be like corruptible man, who often does a thing out of his mere pleasure, not out of a true and solid reason, or the guidance of wisdom, in which he is like those cruel tyrants which are in the world, who act many things out of their mere Will or pleasure, relying on their power, so that they can render no other reason for what they do, than that it is their mere pleasure; whereas any good man of them that acts, or is about to act, can render a suitable reason for it; and that because he knows and understands that true goodness and wisdom has required him to do it, wherefore he wills that it be effected, because it is just, so that if he should not do it he would neglect his duty.

True justice or goodness has in itself no latitude or indifference; hence it is manifest that this indifference of Will has no place in God, by reason it is an imperfection; who though He is the most free agent, yet He is also, above all, the most necessary agent; so that it is impossible that He should not do whatever he does in or for his creatures. Seeing His infinite wisdom, goodness, and justice, is a law unto him, which He cannot transgress. Therefore, it evidently follows, that it was not indifferent to God, whether He would give being to his creatures or not; but He made them out of a certain internal impulse of his divine wisdom and goodness, and so he created the world or creatures as soon as He could, for this is the nature of a necessary agent, to do whatever it can; therefore, seeing he could create the world or creatures in infinite times, before 6,000 years, or before 60,000, or 600,000, etc., it follows He has done it; For God can entirely do that which implies no contradiction; but this does not imply a contradiction, if the worlds or creatures are said to have been or existed in infinite times, before this moment; even as they are infinite times after this moment: If there is no contradiction in the latter, there is also no contradiction in the former.

These attributes duly considered, it follows, that creatures were created in infinite numbers, or that there is an infinity of worlds or creatures made of God: For seeing God is infinitely powerful, there can be no number of creatures so great that He cannot always make more. And because, as is already proved, he does whatever he can do; certainly his Will, goodness, and bounty is as large and extensive as His power; thus, it manifestly follows that creatures are infinite, and created in infinite manners; so that they cannot be limited or bounded with any number or measure. For example; let us suppose the whole universality of creatures to be a circle, whose semi-diameter shall contain so many diameters of the Earth, as there are grains of dust, or sand, in the whole globe of the Earth; and if the same should be divided into atoms, so small that 100,000 of them could be contained in one grain of poppy-seed. Now, who can deny, but the infinite power of God could have made this number greater, and yet still greater, even to an infinite multiplication? Seeing it is more easy to this infinite power, to multiply the real beings of creatures, than for a skillful arithmetician to make any number greater and greater, which can never be so great, but that it may be increased *ad infinitum*. And farther, seeing it is already demonstrated, that God is a necessary agent, and does whatever He can do, it must be that He does multiply, and yet still continues to multiply and augment the essences of creatures, *ad infinitum*.

David Hume

WHY IS THERE SOMETHING RATHER THAN NOTHING?

***Demea*:** If so many difficulties attend the argument *a posteriori*, had we not better adhere to that simple and sublime argument *a priori*, which, by offering to us infallible demonstration, cuts off at once all doubt and difficulty? By this argument, too, we may prove the infinity of the Divine attributes, which, I am afraid, can never be ascertained with certainty from any other topic. For how can an effect, which either is finite, or, for aught we know, may be so; how can such an effect, I say, prove an infinite cause? The unity too of the Divine Nature, it is very difficult, if not absolutely impossible, to deduce merely from contemplating the works of nature; nor will the uniformity alone of the plan, even were it allowed, give us any assurance of that attribute. Whereas the argument *a priori* . . .

***Cleanthes*:** You seem to reason, *Demea*, as if those advantages and conveniences in the abstract argument were full proofs of its solidity. But it is first proper, in my opinion, to determine what argument of this nature you choose to insist on; and we shall afterwards, from itself, better than from its useful consequences, endeavor to determine what value we ought to put upon it.

***Demea*:** The argument, which I would insist on, is the common one. Whatever exists must have a cause or reason of its existence; it being absolutely impossible for any thing to produce itself, or be the cause of its own existence. In mounting up, therefore, from effects to causes, we must either go on in tracing an infinite succession, without any ultimate cause at all; or must at last have recourse to some ultimate cause, that is necessarily existent: Now, that the first supposition is absurd, may be thus proved. In the infinite chain or succession of causes and effects, each single effect is determined to exist by the power and efficacy of that cause which immediately preceded; but the whole eternal chain or succession, taken together, is not determined or caused by any thing; and yet it is evident that it requires a cause or reason, as much as any particular object which begins to exist in time. The question is still reasonable, why this particular succession of causes existed from eternity, and not any other succession, or no succession at all. If there be no necessarily existent being, any supposition which can be formed is equally possible; nor is there any more absurdity in Nothing's having existed from eternity, than there is in that succession of causes which constitutes the universe. What was it, then, which determined Something to exist rather than Nothing, and bestowed being on a particular possibility, exclusive of the rest? External causes, there are supposed to be none. Chance is a word without a meaning. Was it Nothing? But that can never produce any thing. We must, therefore, have recourse to a *necessarily existent* Being, who carries the reason of his existence in himself, and *who cannot be supposed not to exist, without an express contradiction.* There is, consequently, such a Being; that is, there is a Deity.

***Cleanthes*:** I shall not leave it to Philo, though I know that the starting of objections is his chief delight, to point out the weakness of this metaphysical reasoning. It seems to me so obviously ill-grounded, and at the same time of so little consequence to the cause of true piety and religion, that I shall myself venture to show the fallacy of it.

I shall begin with observing, that there is an evident absurdity in pretending to demonstrate a matter of fact, or to prove it by any arguments *a priori.* Nothing is demonstrable, unless the contrary implies a contradiction. Nothing, that is distinctly conceivable, implies a contradiction. Whatever we conceive as existent, we can also conceive as non-existent. There is no being,

Edited from *Dialogues Concerning Natural Religion,* 1779, Part 9, which is now in the public domain.

therefore, whose non-existence implies a contradiction. Consequently there is no being, whose existence is demonstrable. I propose this argument as entirely decisive, and am willing to rest the whole controversy upon it.

It is pretended that the Deity is a necessarily existent being; and this necessity of his existence is attempted to be explained by asserting, that if we knew his whole essence or nature, we should perceive it to be as impossible for him not to exist, as for twice two not to be four. But it is evident that this can never happen, while our faculties remain the same as at present. It will still be possible for us, at any time, to conceive the non-existence of what we formerly conceived to exist; nor can the mind ever lie under a necessity of supposing any object to remain always in being; in the same manner as we lie under a necessity of always conceiving twice two to be four. Therefore, the words "necessary existence" have no meaning; or, which is the same thing, none that is consistent.

5C. Why Do Suffering and Evil Exist?

Introduction

The fact that suffering and evil exist poses a challenge to those who wish to argue for the existence of God. This challenge can be formulated as an argument:

If God exists, then he is omniscient, omnipotent, and morally perfect. Being omniscient, God knows that suffering and evil exist; being omnipotent, God has the power to stop suffering and evil from existing; being morally perfect, God would not want suffering and evil to exist. Since suffering and evil do exist, then either God is not omniscient, or not omnipotent, or not morally perfect. Therefore, God does not exist.

In the first reading in this section, Gottfried Leibniz *does not deny* that evil and suffering exist. However, his explanation for the existence of these things requires a complex argument whose conclusion is that this is *the best of all possible worlds*. Leibniz argues that since God is omnipotent, omniscient, and morally perfect, these characteristics must result in God having created the best possible world. Of course, Leibniz acknowledged that his position has many critics, so in the reading that follows, Leibniz addresses several of those criticisms.

In the reading by George Hayward Joyce, the author agrees that the amount of suffering which the human race endures is immense; nevertheless, he claims that on balance the amount of happiness far outweighs the amount of suffering and evil. However, we still need to know why God allows *any* suffering or evil. Joyce's response is that since God gave us the *gift of freedom*, life is, therefore, a kind of *probation*. It follows that God does not interfere with the course of nature because we must prove ourselves to be moral beings. In order to have any value, salvation has to be earned.

Through a lively dialogue between three characters in the final reading in this section, David Hume shows that those arguing for God's existence in the face of suffering and evil cannot reconcile God's attributes (omnipotent, omniscient, and morally perfect) with the world as we experience it. But, Hume points out, it should be easy for God to prevent these things. Hume argues that although there may be good reasons for why God does not prevent evil and suffering, those reasons are completely unknown to us.

Gottfried Leibniz

THE EXISTENCE OF EVIL AND SUFFERING

"An infinite goodness having guided the Creator in the production of the world, all the characteristics of knowledge, skill, power and greatness that are displayed in his work are destined for the happiness of intelligent creatures. He wished to show forth his perfections only to the end that creatures of this kind should find their felicity in the knowledge, the admiration and the love of the Supreme Being."

This maxim appears to me not sufficiently exact. I grant that the happiness of intelligent creatures is the principal part of God's design, for they are most like him; but nevertheless I do not see how one can prove that to be his sole aim. It is true that the realm of nature must serve the realm of grace: but, since all is connected in God's great design, we must believe that the realm of grace is also in some way adapted to that of nature, so that nature preserves the utmost order and beauty, to render the combination of the two the most perfect that can be. And there is no reason to suppose that God, for the sake of some lessening of moral evil, would reverse the whole order of nature. Each perfection or imperfection in the creature has its value, but there is none that has an infinite value. Thus the moral or physical good and evil of rational creatures does not infinitely exceed the good and evil which is simply metaphysical, namely that which lies in the perfection of the other creatures; and yet one would be bound to say this if the present maxim were strictly true. When God justified to the Prophet Jonah the pardon that he had granted to the inhabitants of Nineveh, he even touched upon the interest of the beasts who would have been involved in the ruin of this great city. No substance is absolutely contemptible or absolutely precious before God. And the abuse or the exaggerated extension of the present maxim appears to be in part the source of the difficulties that M. Bayle puts forward. It is certain that God sets greater store by a man than a lion; nevertheless it can hardly be said with certainty that God prefers a single man in all respects to the whole of lion-kind. Even should that be so, it would by no means follow that the interest of a certain number of men would prevail over the consideration of a general disorder diffused through an infinite number of creatures. This opinion would be a remnant of the old and somewhat discredited maxim, that all is made solely for man.

"The benefits he imparts to the creatures that are capable of felicity tend only to their happiness. He therefore does not permit that these should serve to make them unhappy, and, if the wrong use that they made of them were capable of destroying them, he would give them sure means of always using them well. Otherwise they would not be true benefits, and his goodness would be smaller than that we can conceive of in another benefactor. (I mean, in a Cause that united with its gifts the sure skill to make good use of them.)"

There already is the abuse or the ill effect of the preceding maxim. It is not strictly true (though it appear plausible) that the benefits God imparts to the creatures who are capable of felicity tend solely to their happiness. All is connected in Nature; and if a skilled artisan, an engineer, an architect, a wise politician often makes one and the same thing serve several ends, if he makes a double hit with a single throw, when that can be done conveniently, one may say that God, whose wisdom and power are perfect, does so always. That is husbanding the ground, the time, the place, the material, which make up as it were his outlay. Thus God has more than one purpose in his projects. The felicity of all rational creatures is one of the aims he has in view; but it is not his

Edited from *Theodicy*. Translated by E.M. Huggard, 1890, which is now in the public domain.

whole aim, nor even his final aim. Therefore it happens that the unhappiness of some of these creatures may come about by concomitance, and as a result of other greater goods: this I have already explained, and M. Bayle has to some extent acknowledged it. The goods as such, considered in themselves, are the object of the antecedent will of God. God will produce as much reason and knowledge in the universe as his plan can admit. One can conceive of a mean between an antecedent will altogether pure and primitive, and a consequent and final will. The *primitive antecedent will* has as its object each good and each evil in itself, detached from all combination, and tends to advance the good and prevent the evil. The *mediate will* relates to combinations, as when one attaches a good to an evil: then the will will have some tendency towards this combination when the good exceeds the evil therein. But the *final and decisive will* results from consideration of all the goods and all the evils that enter into our deliberation, it results from a total combination. This shows that a mediate will, although it may in a sense pass as consequent in relation to a pure and primitive antecedent will, must be considered antecedent in relation to the final and decretory will. God gives reason to the human race; misfortunes arise thence by concomitance. His pure antecedent will tends towards giving reason, as a great good, and preventing the evils in question. But when it is a question of the evils that accompany this gift which God has made to us of reason, the compound, made up of the combination of reason and of these evils, will be the object of a mediate will of God, which will tend towards producing or preventing this compound, according as the good or the evil prevails therein. But even though it should prove that reason did more harm than good to men (which, however, I do not admit), whereupon the mediate will of God would discard it with all its concomitants, it might still be the case that it was more in accordance with the perfection of the universe to give reason to men, notwithstanding all the evil consequences which it might have with reference to them. Consequently, the final will or the decree of God, resulting from all the considerations he can have, would be to give it to them. And, far from being subject to blame for this, he would be blameworthy if he did not so. Thus the evil, or the mixture of goods and evils wherein the evil prevails, happens only *by concomitance*, because it is connected with greater goods that are outside this mixture. This mixture, therefore, or this compound, is not to be conceived as a grace or as a gift from God to us; but the good that is found mingled therein will nevertheless be good. Such is God's gift of reason to those who make ill use thereof. It is always a good in itself; but the combination of this good with the evils that proceed from its abuse is not a good with regard to those who in consequence thereof become unhappy. Yet it comes to be by concomitance, because it serves a greater good in relation to the universe. And it is doubtless that which prompted God to give reason to those who have made it an instrument of their unhappiness. Or, to put it more precisely, in accordance with my system God, having found among the possible beings some rational creatures who misuse their reason, gave existence to those who are included in the best possible plan of the universe. Thus nothing prevents us from admitting that God grants goods which turn into evil by the fault of men, this often happening to men in just punishment of the misuse they had made of God's grace.

But to say that God should not give a good which he knows an evil will will abuse, when the general plan of things demands that he give it; or again to say that he should give certain means for preventing it, contrary to this same general order: that is to wish (as I have observed already) that God himself become blameworthy in order to prevent man from being so. To object, as people do here, that the goodness of God would be smaller than that of another benefactor who would give a more useful gift, is to overlook the fact that the goodness of a benefactor is not measured by a single benefit. It may well be that a gift from a private person is greater than one from a prince, but the gifts of this private person all taken together will be much inferior to the prince's gifts all together. Thus one can esteem fittingly the good things done by God only when one considers their whole extent by relating them to the entire universe. Moreover, one may say that the gifts given in the expectation that they will harm are the gifts of an enemy.

But that applies to when there is malice or guilt in him who gives them, as there was in that Eutrapelus of whom Horace speaks, who did good to people in order to give them the means of destroying themselves. His design was evil, but God's design cannot be better than it is. Must God spoil his system, must there be less beauty, perfection and reason in the universe, because there are people who misuse reason?

"A maleficent being is very capable of heaping magnificent gifts upon his enemies, when he knows that they will make thereof a use that will destroy them. It therefore does not beseem the infinitely good Being to give to creatures a free will, whereof, as he knows for certain, they would make a use that would render them unhappy. Therefore if he gives them free will he combines with it the art of using it always opportunely, and permits not that they neglect the practice of this art in any conjuncture; and if there were no sure means of determining the good use of this free will, he would rather take from them this faculty, than allow it to be the cause of their unhappiness. That is the more manifest, as free will is a grace which he has given them of his own choice and without their asking for it; so that he would be more answerable for the unhappiness it would bring upon them than if he had only granted it in response to their importunate prayers."

What was said at the end of the remark on the preceding maxim ought to be repeated here, and is sufficient to counter the present maxim. Moreover, the author is still presupposing that false maxim advanced as the third, stating that the happiness of rational creatures is the sole aim of God. If that were so, perhaps neither sin nor unhappiness would ever occur, even by concomitance. God would have chosen a sequence of possibilities where all these evils would be excluded. But God would fail in what is due to the universe, that is, in what he owes to himself. If there were only spirits they would be without the required connection, without the order of time and place. This order demands matter, movement and its laws; to adjust these to spirits in the best possible way means to return to our world. When one looks at things only in the mass, one imagines to be practicable a thousand things that cannot properly take place. To wish that God should not give free will to rational creatures is to wish that there be none of these creatures; and to wish that God should prevent them from misusing it is to wish that there be none but these creatures alone, together with what was made for them only. If God had none but these creatures in view, he would doubtless prevent them from destroying themselves. One may say in a sense, however, that God has given to these creatures the art of always making good use of their free will, for the natural light of reason is this art. But it would be necessary always to have the will to do good, and often creatures lack the means of giving themselves the will they ought to have; often they even lack the will to use those means which indirectly give a good will. Of this I have already spoken more than once. This fault must be admitted, and one must even acknowledge that God would perhaps have been able to exempt creatures from that fault, since there is nothing to prevent, so it seems, the existence of some whose nature it would be always to have good will. But I reply that it is not necessary, and that it was not feasible for all rational creatures to have so great a perfection, and such as would bring them so close to the Divinity. It may even be that that can only be made possible by a special divine grace. But in this case, would it be proper for God to grant it to all, that is, always to act miraculously in respect of all rational creatures? Nothing would be less rational than these perpetual miracles. There are degrees among creatures: the general order requires it. And it appears quite consistent with the order of divine government that the great privilege of strengthening in the good should be granted more easily to those who had a good will when they were in a more imperfect state, in the state of struggle and of pilgrimage. The good angels themselves were not created incapable of sin. Nevertheless I would not dare to assert that there are no blessed creatures born, or such as are sinless and holy by their nature. There are perhaps people who give this privilege to the Blessed Virgin, since, moreover, the Roman Church to-day places her above the angels. But it suffices us that the universe is very great and very varied: to wish to limit it is to have little knowledge thereof.

"But God has given free will to creatures capable of sinning, without their having asked him for this grace. And he who gave such a gift would be more answerable for the unhappiness that it brought upon those who made use of it, than if he had granted it only in response to their importunate prayers."

But importunity in prayers makes no difference to God; he knows better than we what we need, and he only grants what serves the interest of the whole. It seems that M. Bayle here makes free will consist in the faculty for sinning; yet he acknowledges elsewhere that God and the Saints are free, without having this faculty. However that may be, I have already shown fully that God, doing what his wisdom and his goodness combined ordain, is not answerable for the evil that he permits. Even men, when they do their duty, are not answerable for consequences, whether they foresee them or not.

"It is as sure a means of taking a man's life to give him a silk cord that one knows certainly he will make use of freely to strangle himself, as to plant a few dagger thrusts in his body. One desires his death not less when one makes use of the first way, than when one employs the second: it even seems as though one desires it with a more malicious intention, since one tends to leave to him the whole trouble and the whole blame of his destruction."

Those who write treatises on Duties as, for instance, Cicero, St. Ambrose, Grotius, Opalenius, Sharrok, Rachelius, Pufendorf, as well as the Casuists, teach that there are cases where one is not obliged to return to its owner a thing deposited: for example, one will not give back a dagger when one knows that he who has deposited it is about to stab someone. Let us pretend that I have in my hands the fatal draught that Meleager's mother will make use of to kill him; the magic javelin that Cephalus will unwittingly employ to kill his Procris; the horses of Theseus that will tear to pieces Hippolytus, his son: these things are demanded back from me, and I am right in refusing them, knowing the use that will be made of them. But how will it be if a competent judge orders me to restore them, when I cannot prove to him what I know of the evil consequences that restitution will have, Apollo perchance having given to me, as to Cassandra, the gift of prophecy under the condition that I shall not be believed? I should then be compelled to make restitution, having no alternative other than my own destruction: thus I cannot escape from contributing towards the evil.

One would gladly draw back after the request was made, making vain remonstrances; but they press you, they say to you: *"Do you make oaths that you will not keep?"* The law of the Styx is inviolable, one must needs submit to it; if one has erred in making the oath, one would err more in not keeping it; the promise must be fulfilled, however harmful it may be to him who exacts it. It would be ruinous to you if you did not fulfil it. It seems as though the moral of these fables implies that a supreme necessity may constrain one to comply with evil. God, in truth, knows no other judge that can compel him to give what may turn to evil, he is not like Jupiter who fears the Styx. But his own wisdom is the greatest judge that he can find, there is no appeal from its judgements: they are the decrees of destiny. The eternal verities, objects of his wisdom, are more inviolable than the Styx. These laws and this judge do not constrain: they are stronger, for they persuade. Wisdom only shows God the best possible exercise of his goodness: after that, the evil that occurs is an inevitable result of the best. I will add something stronger: To permit the evil, as God permits it, is the greatest goodness.

One would need to have a bent towards perversity to say after this that it is more malicious to leave to someone the whole trouble and the whole blame of his destruction. When God does leave it to a man, it has belonged to him since before his existence; it was already in the idea of him as still merely possible, before the decree of God which makes him to exist. Can one, then, leave it or give it to another? There is the whole matter.

"A true benefactor gives promptly, and does not wait to give until those he loves have suffered long miseries from the privation of what he could have imparted to them at first very easily, and without causing any inconvenience to himself. If the limitation of his forces does not permit him to do good without inflicting pain or some other inconvenience, he acquiesces in this, but only regretfully, and he never employs this way of rendering service when he can render it without mingling any kind of evil in his favors. If the profit one could derive from the evils he inflicted could spring as easily from an unalloyed good as from those evils, he would take the straight road of unalloyed good, and not the indirect road that would lead from the evil to the good. If he showers riches and honors, it is not to the end that those who have enjoyed them, when they come to lose them, should be all the more deeply afflicted in proportion to their previous experience of pleasure, and that thus they should become more unhappy than the persons who have always been deprived of these advantages. A malicious being would shower good things at such a price upon the people for whom he had the most hatred."

All these objections depend almost on the same sophism; they change and mutilate the fact, they only half record things: God has care for men, he loves the human race, he wishes it well, nothing so true. Yet he allows men to fall, he often allows them to perish, he gives them goods that tend towards their destruction; and when he makes someone happy, it is after many sufferings: where is his affection, where is his goodness or again where is his power? Vain objections, which suppress the main point, which ignore the fact that it is of God one speaks. It is as though one were speaking of a mother, a guardian, a tutor, whose well-nigh only care is concerned with the upbringing, the preservation, the happiness of the person in question, and who neglect their duty. God takes care of the universe, he neglects nothing, he chooses what is best on the whole. If in spite of all that someone is wicked and unhappy, it behoved him to be so. God (so they say) could have given happiness to all, he could have given it promptly and easily, and without causing himself any inconvenience, for he can do all. But should he? Since he does not so, it is a sign that he had to act altogether differently. If we infer from this either that God only regretfully, and owing to lack of power, fails to make men happy and to give the good first of all and without admixture of evil, or else that he lacks the good will to give it unreservedly and for good and all, then we are comparing our true God with the God of Herodotus, full of envy, or with the demon of the poet whose iambics Aristotle quotes, who gives good things in order that he may cause more affliction by taking them away. That would be trifling with God in perpetual anthropomorphisms, representing him as a man who must give himself up completely to one particular business, whose goodness must be chiefly exercised upon those objects alone which are known to us, and who lacks either aptitude or good will. God is not lacking therein, he could do the good that we would desire; he even wishes it, taking it separately, but he must not do it in preference to other greater goods which are opposed to it. Moreover, one has no cause to complain of the fact that usually one attains salvation only through many sufferings, and by bearing the cross of Jesus Christ. These evils serve to make the elect imitators of their master, and to increase their happiness.

"The greatest and the most substantial glory that he who is the master of others can gain is to maintain amongst them virtue, order, peace, contentment of mind. The glory that he would derive from their unhappiness can be nothing but a false glory."

If we knew the city of God just as it is, we should see that it is the most perfect state which can be devised; that virtue and happiness reign there, as far as is possible, in accordance with the laws of the best; that sin and unhappiness (whose entire exclusion from the nature of things reasons of the supreme order did not permit), are well-nigh nothing there in comparison with the good, and even are of service for greater good. Now since these evils were to exist, there must needs be some appointed to be subject to them, and we are those people. If it were others, would there not be the same appearance of evil? Or rather, would not these others be those known as We? When God derives some glory from the evil through having made it serve a greater good, it was proper that he should derive that glory. It is not therefore a false glory, as would be that of a prince who overthrew his state in order to have the honor of setting it up again.

"The way whereby that master can give proof of greatest love for virtue is to cause it, if he can, to be always practiced without any mixture of vice. If it is easy for him to procure for his subjects this advantage, and nevertheless he permits vice to raise its head, save that he punishes it finally after having long tolerated it, his affection for virtue is not the greatest one can conceive; it is therefore not infinite."

I am not yet half way through the nineteen maxims, and already I am weary of refuting, and making the same answer always. M. Bayle multiplies unnecessarily his so-called maxims in opposition to my dogmas. If things connected together may be separated, the parts from their whole, the human kind from the universe, God's attributes the one from the other, power from wisdom, it may be said that God *can cause* virtue to be in the world without any mixture of vice, and even that he can do so *easily*. But, since he has permitted vice, it must be that that order of the universe which was found preferable to every other plan required it. One must believe that it is not permitted to do otherwise, since it is not possible to do better. It is a hypothetical necessity, a moral necessity, which, far from being contrary to freedom, is the effect of its choice.

The objection is made here, that God's affection for virtue is therefore not the greatest which can be conceived, that it is not *infinite*. To that an answer has already been given on the second maxim, in the assertion that God's affection for any created thing whatsoever is proportionate to the value of the thing. Virtue is the noblest quality of created things, but it is not the only good quality of creatures. There are innumerable others which attract the inclination of God: from all these inclinations there results the most possible good, and it turns out that if there were only virtue, if there were only rational creatures, there would be less good. Midas proved to be less rich when he had only gold. And besides, wisdom must vary. To multiply one and the same thing only would be superfluity, and poverty too. To have a thousand well-bound Virgils in one's library, always to sing the airs from the opera of Cadmus and Hermione, to break all the china in order only to have cups of gold, to have only diamond buttons, to eat nothing but partridges, to drink only Hungarian or Shiraz wine—would one call that reason? Nature had need of animals, plants, inanimate bodies; there are in these creatures, devoid of reason, marvels which serve for exercise of the reason. What would an intelligent creature do if there were no unintelligent things? What would it think of, if there were neither movement, nor matter, nor sense? If it had only distinct thoughts it would be a God, its wisdom would be without bounds: that is one of the results of my meditations. As soon as there is a mixture of confused thoughts, there is sense, there is matter. For these confused thoughts come from the relation of all things one to the other by way of duration and extent. Thus it is that in my philosophy there is no rational creature without some organic body, and there is no created spirit entirely detached from matter. But these organic bodies vary no less in perfection than the spirits to which they belong. Therefore, since God's wisdom must have a world of bodies, a world of substances capable of perception and incapable of reason; since, in short, it was necessary to choose from all the things possible what produced the best effect together, and since vice entered in by this door, God would not have been altogether good, altogether wise if he had excluded it.

"The way to evince the greatest hatred for vice is not indeed to allow it to prevail for a long time and then chastise it, but to crush it before its birth, that is, prevent it from showing itself anywhere. A king, for example, who put his finances in such good order that no malversation was ever committed, would thus display more hatred for the wrong done by factionaries than if, after having suffered them to batten on the blood of the people, he had them hanged."

It is always the same song, it is anthropomorphism pure and simple. A king should generally have nothing so much at heart as to keep his subjects free from oppression. One of his greatest interests is to bring good order into his finances. Nevertheless there are times when he is obliged to tolerate vice and disorders. He has a great war on his hands, he is in a state of exhaustion, he has no choice of generals, it is necessary to humor those he has, those possessed of great authority with the soldiers. He lacks money for the most pressing needs, it is necessary to turn to great financiers, who have an established credit, and he must at the same time connive at their malversations. It is true that this unfortunate necessity arises most often from previous errors. It is not the same with God: he has need of no man, he commits no error, he always does the best. One cannot even wish that things may go better, when one understands them: and it would be a vice in the Author of things if he wished to change anything whatsoever in them, if he wished to exclude the vice that was found there. Is this State with perfect government, where good is willed and performed as far as it is possible, where evil even serves the greatest good, comparable with the State of a prince whose affairs are in ruin and who escapes as best he can? Or with that of a prince who encourages oppression in order to punish it, and who delights to see the little men with begging bowls and the great on scaffolds?

"A ruler devoted to the interests of virtue, and to the good of his subjects, takes the utmost care to ensure that they never disobey his laws; and if he must needs chastise them for their disobedience, he sees to it that the penalty cures them of the inclination to evil, and restores in their soul a strong and constant tendency towards good: so far is he from any desire that the penalty for the error should incline them more and more towards evil."

To make men better, God does all that is due, and even all that can be done on his side without detriment to what is due. The most usual aim of punishment is amendment; but it is not the sole aim, nor that which God always intends. I have said a word on that above. Original sin, which disposes men towards evil, is not merely a penalty for the first sin; it is a natural consequence thereof. On that too a word has been said, in the course of an observation on the fourth theological proposition. It is like drunkenness, which is a penalty for excess in drinking and is at the same time a natural consequence that easily leads to new sins.

"To permit the evil that one could prevent is not to care whether it be committed or not, or is even to wish that it be committed."

By no means. How many times do men permit evils which they could prevent if they turned all their efforts in that direction? But other more important cares prevent them from doing so. One will rarely resolve upon adjusting irregularities in the coinage while one is involved in a great war. And the action of an English Parliament in this direction a little before the Peace of Ryswyck will be rather praised than imitated. Can one conclude from this that the State has no anxiety about this irregularity, or even that it desires it? God has a far stronger reason, and one far more worthy of him, for tolerating evils. Not only does he derive from them greater goods, but he finds them connected with the greatest goods of all those that are possible: so that it would be a fault not to permit them.

"It is a very great fault in those who govern, if they do not care whether there be disorder in their States or not. The fault is still greater if they wish and even desire disorder there. If by hidden and indirect, but infallible, ways they stirred up a sedition in their States to bring them to the brink of ruin, in order to gain for themselves the glory of showing that they have the courage and the prudence necessary for saving a great kingdom on the point of perishing, they would be most deserving of condemnation. But if they stirred up this sedition because there were no other means than that, of averting the total ruin of their subjects and of strengthening on new foundations, and for several centuries, the happiness of nations, one must needs lament the unfortunate necessity to which they were reduced, and praise them for the use that they made thereof."

This maxim, with divers others set forth here, is not applicable to the government of God. Not to mention the fact that it is only the disorders of a very small part of his kingdom which are brought up in objection, it is untrue that he has no anxiety about evils, that he desires them, that he brings them into being, to have the glory of allaying them. God wills order and good; but it happens sometimes that what is disorder in the part is order in the whole. The permission of evils comes from a kind of moral necessity: God is constrained to this by his wisdom and by his goodness; *this necessity is happy*, whereas that of the prince spoken of in the maxim is *unhappy*. His State is one of the most corrupt; and the government of God is the best State possible.

"The permission of a certain evil is only excusable when one cannot remedy it without introducing a greater evil; but it cannot be excusable in those who have in hand a remedy more efficacious against this evil, and against all the other evils that could spring from the suppression of this one."

The maxim is true, but it cannot be brought forward against the government of God. Supreme reason constrains him to permit the evil. If God chose what would not be the best absolutely and in all, that would be a greater evil than all the individual evils which he could prevent by this means. This wrong choice would destroy his wisdom and his goodness.

"The Being infinitely powerful, Creator of matter and of spirits, makes whatever he wills of this matter and these spirits. There is no situation or shape that he cannot communicate to spirits. If he then permitted a physical or a moral evil, this would not be for the reason that otherwise some other still greater physical or moral evil would be altogether inevitable. None of those reasons for the mixture of good and evil which are founded on the limitation of the forces of benefactors can apply to him."

It is true that God makes of matter and of spirits whatever he wills; but he is like a good sculptor, who will make from his block of marble only that which he judges to be the best, and who judges well. God makes of matter the most excellent of all possible machines; he makes of spirits the most excellent of all governments conceivable; and over and above all that, he establishes for their union the most perfect of all harmonies, according to the system I have proposed. Now since physical evil and moral evil occur in this perfect work, one must conclude (contrary to M. Bayle's assurance here) that *otherwise a still greater evil would have been altogether inevitable.* This great evil would be that God would have chosen ill if he had chosen otherwise than he has chosen. It is true that God is infinitely powerful; but his power is indeterminate, goodness and wisdom combined determine him to produce the best. M. Bayle makes elsewhere an objection which is peculiar to him, which he derives from the opinions of the modern Cartesians. They say that God could have given to souls what thoughts he would, without making them depend upon any relation to the body: by this means souls would be spared a great number of evils which only spring from derangement of the body. More will be said of this later; now it is sufficient to bear in mind that God cannot establish a system ill-connected and full of dissonances. It is to some extent the nature of souls to represent bodies.

"One is just as much the cause of an event when one brings it about in moral ways, as when one brings it about in physical ways. A Minister of State, who, without going out of his study, and simply by utilizing the passions of the leaders of a faction, overthrew all their plots, would thus be bringing about the ruin of this faction, no less than if he destroyed it by a surprise attack."

I have nothing to say against this maxim. Evil is always attributed to moral causes, and not always to physical causes. Here I observe simply that if I could not prevent the sin of others except by committing a sin myself, I should be justified in permitting it, and I should not be accessary thereto, or its moral cause. In God, every fault would represent a sin; it would be even more than sin, for it would destroy Divinity. And it would be a great fault in him not to choose the best. I have said so many times. He would then prevent sin by something worse than all sins.

"It is all the same whether one employ a necessary cause, or employ a free cause while choosing the moments when one knows it to be determined. If I imagine that gunpowder has the power to ignite or not to ignite when fire touches it, and if I know for certain that it will be disposed to ignite at eight o'clock in the morning, I shall be just as much the cause of its effects if I apply the fire to it at that hour, as I should be in assuming, as is the case, that it is a necessary cause. For where I am concerned it would no longer be a free cause. I should be catching it at the moment when I knew it to be necessitated by its own choice. It is impossible for a being to be free or indifferent with regard to that to which it is already determined, and at the time when it is determined thereto. All that which exists of necessity while it exists."

This maxim may pass also. I would wish only to change something in the phraseology. I would not take *free* and *indifferent* for one and the same thing, and would not place *free* and *determined* in antithesis. One is never altogether indifferent with an indifference of equipoise; one is always more inclined and consequently more determined on one side than on another: but one is never necessitated to the choice that one makes. I mean here a *necessity* absolute and metaphysical; for it must be admitted that God, that wisdom, is prompted to the best by a *moral* necessity. It must be admitted also that one is necessitated to the choice by a hypothetical necessity, when one actually makes the choice; and even before one is necessitated thereto by the very truth of the futurition, since one will do it. These hypothetical necessities do no harm. I have spoken sufficiently on this point already.

George Hayward Joyce

THE PROBLEM OF EVIL

The existence of evil in the world must at all times be the greatest of all the problems which the mind encounters when it reflects on God and His relation to the world. If He is, indeed, all-good and all-powerful, how has evil any place in the world which He has made? Why is it here? If He is all-good, why did He allow it to arise? If all-powerful, why does He not deliver us from the burden?

The actual amount of suffering which the human race endures is immense. Disease has store and to spare of torments for the body: and disease and death are the lot to which we must all look forward. Nor is the world ever free for very long from the terrible sufferings which follow in the track of war. If we concentrate our attention on human woes to the exclusion of the joys of life, we gain an appalling picture of the ills to which flesh is heir. So, too, if we fasten our attention on the sterner side of nature, on the pains which men endure from natural forces—on the storms which wreck their ships, the cold which freezes them to death, the fire which consumes them—if we contemplate this aspect of nature alone, we may be led to wonder how God came to deal so harshly with His creatures as to provide them with such a home.

Man by reason of his immaterial intellect transcends the limitations of time. He gathers up the past and the future into the present. The pain of the present moment is increased indefinitely because it is grasped as the successor of a long chain of like pangs, and because of the agonizing prospect of a like series yet to come. The multiple burden of all is apprehended as a collective whole, and is felt to be more than man is capable of enduring.

By reason of his immortal destiny each individual man is an end, irrespective of the race to which he belongs or even of the universe as a whole. Divine providence is concerned with him for his own sake. It is not enough to show that what is hurtful to the individual subserves the good of the whole. It must appear that though evil under one aspect, it is not really opposed to the highest good of the individual himself.

Of man, it is true that the balance is immensely on the side of happiness. The pessimist who declares that, in view of the suffering of life, existence is an evil, misrepresents the facts. There is plenty of joy in life, though to much of it we are so habituated that we accept it as a matter of course. Let a man be deprived, for instance, of the use of a single sense—of hearing, or sight, or of the power of speech—and he quickly becomes aware how much pleasure has hitherto streamed in through that avenue, though in all probability he seldom, if ever, adverted to the delight which he was experiencing. The problem before us is certainly not to explain why the Creator has made misery our portion. In the main our lot is such as to bear witness to His goodness and His omnipotence. We are merely concerned to learn why He has not removed suffering altogether from our life.

Much light is thrown on the question by the consideration that this life is a probation. Man's true end, as we have urged, is the possession of the supreme Good. And everything tends to show that this will not be attained by each and all without exception, but by those alone who by a right use of the gift of freedom have in some sort merited it: and that the measure of a man's recompense will correspond to his deserts. If then it can be shown that physical evil is one of the most important factors in assisting man to the attainment of his end, it at once becomes evident that

Edited from *Principles of Natural Theology,* 1922: Chapter XVII, which is now in the public domain.

there was ample reason why God should not interfere with the course of nature, but should tolerate the existence of physical suffering in view of the good which would result.

Pain is the great stimulant to action. Man, no less than the animals, is impelled to work by the sense of hunger. Experience shows that, were it not for this motive, the majority of men would be content to live in indolent ease. Man must earn his bread in the sweat of his brow. And the duty thus imposed is for most men the school of virtue. It is in fulfilling the obligation of daily toil that they learn to practice justice, diligence, patience, charity to others, obedience to those who are over them. Without the occasion thus afforded it may safely be said that virtue would have little chance. Ease is no school of moral progress. Moreover, suffering serves to call forth in man a measure of goodness which would otherwise never be realized at all. Virtue reaches its perfection when it is exercised at a severe cost to the agent. The man who gives to his neighbor, when to do so involves some painful self-denial, has attained a higher degree of charity than he whose gifts entail no inconvenience to himself. And one reason, plainly, why God permits suffering is that man may rise to a height of heroism which would otherwise have been altogether beyond his scope. Nor are these the only benefits which it confers. That sympathy for others which is one of the most precious parts of our experience and one of the most fruitful sources of well-doing has its origin in the fellow-feeling engendered by the endurance of similar trials. Furthermore, were it not for these trials, man would think little enough of a future existence, and of the need of striving after his last end. He would be perfectly content with his existence, and would reckon little of any higher good. The considerations here briefly advanced suffice at least to show how important is the office filled by pain in human life, and with what little reason it is asserted that the existence of so much suffering is irreconcilable with the wisdom of the Creator. The sufferings of men are directed primarily to the good of the sufferer himself, while they also afford to others an opportunity for the practice of virtue.

In the same way, we need feel no perplexity at the numerous instances in which human life is cut short prematurely, and the purpose of nature seems to be frustrated by death. But when life is viewed as above all else a probation, it is seen to be of little importance whether a man live out his full tale of years or not. Indeed, the shortening of the probation may be to the individual, not a loss, but an immense gain.

Much has been said of the calamities brought about by natural forces. It has often been replied that these occurrences are due to the operation of the same physical causes which have made the Earth a fit place for human habitation, and that we have no reason to demand a miraculous suspension of laws which in their general effects are so useful to us, merely because from time to time they result in a purely local disaster. This is true as far as it goes. Yet more may be said. The earthquake and the volcano serve a moral end which more than compensates for the physical evil which they cause. The awful nature of these phenomena, the overwhelming power of the forces at work, and man's utter helplessness before them, rouse him from the religious indifference to which he is so prone. They inspire a reverential awe of the Creator who made them and controls them, and a salutary fear of violating the laws which He has imposed.

It may be asked whether the Creator could not have brought man to perfection without the use of suffering. Most certainly He could have conferred upon him a similar degree of virtue without requiring any effort on his part. Yet it is easy to see that there is a special value attaching to a conquest of difficulties such as man's actual lot demands, and that in God's eyes this may well be an adequate reason for assigning this life to us in preference to another. He is not bound to ensure that our lives shall be exempt from all that we may regard as an inconvenience.

We have laid stress on the value of pain in relation to the next life, because it is in the next life, and not in this, that man must attain his last end. But it scarcely needs to be pointed out that pain is a source of many benefits in this life also. The advance of scientific discovery, the gradual improvement of the organization of the community, the growth of material civilization—all these are due in no small degree to the stimulus afforded by pain.

There will at all times be much to perplex us in the ways of providence. Much of the suffering with which the world abounds will be inexplicable to us, and we shall strive in vain to understand why this or that particular evil is permitted. But we can, at least, see that physical evil does not stand in insuperable contradiction with the divine attributes. When Mr. McTaggart writes: "There are many things in the universe which are not only intrinsically indifferent, but intrinsically bad. Such, for example, is pain," and proceeds on this ground to declare the doctrine of Divine omnipotence untenable, his reasoning is altogether unsound. It would be necessary for its validity that we should admit the principle on which optimism is based, namely, that God is under the necessity of excluding all imperfection from creation. This, as we have seen, is not the case. Pain is, it is true, an evil in relation to physical well-being. But granted that God desired to create beings endowed with sentient life, then no solid reason can be shown why He should not create them liable to pain, the natural accompaniment of such life, provided only that He turn it to good ends. It is quite arbitrary to demand that He should exclude it miraculously.

The existence of *moral evil* constitutes a far greater difficulty than does *physical evil.* It is not hard to see that God may have good reason for permitting pain and suffering, and may employ them as an instrument of good as regards the creature. But moral evil is essentially a breach of some law which He has made: and hence is of its very nature in conflict with His will. The man who sins thereby offends God. If he persists in his rebellion, the severance between the two must one day become final, and man will forfeit for ever the last end which alone can satisfy him. We are called on to explain how God came to create an order of things in which rebellion and even final rejection have a place. Since a choice from among an infinite number of possible worlds lay open to Him, how came He to choose one in which these occur? Is not such a choice in flagrant opposition to the Divine goodness?

How, then, can we account for God's permission of moral evil? It is not sufficient to say that it is due to the gift of free will which He has bestowed upon the creature. Free will need not, as is so often assumed, involve the power to choose wrong. Our ability to misuse the gift is due, as we have already argued, to the conditions under which it is exercised here. In our present state we are able to reject what is truly good and exercise our power of preference in favor of some baser attraction. Yet it is not necessary that it should be so.

The existence of moral evil, however, becomes explicable, when it is admitted that man's life is a probation. God, in other words, has created the present order such that man should have the glory of meriting his last end. We can see readily enough that in this He has conferred a great privilege upon us. To receive our final beatitude as the fruit of our labors, and as the recompense of a hard-won victory, is an incomparably higher destiny than to receive it without any effort on our part. And since God in His wisdom has seen fit to give us such a lot as this, it was inevitable that man should have the power to choose the wrong. We could not be called to merit the reward due to victory without being exposed to the possibility of defeat.

Yet the question suggests itself: Could not God have so disposed things that none should be actually defeated? It is one thing to be liable to suffer defeat: another, actually to lose the day. God in His omniscience knew which individuals, if created, would so misuse the gift bestowed on them as finally to choose the wrong and suffer definitive exclusion from beatitude. How came it that He called these beings into existence at all? Why did He not create those alone whom His foresight pointed out as victors in the struggle? How came it that the attribute of goodness did not imperatively prescribe such a course?

To this question more than one answer has been given. It is urged that if all men eventually attained their last end and secured final beatitude, probation would have little meaning. The struggle would be but a mock struggle, if it were antecedently certain that, however a man might bear himself, God would bring it about that he should be saved from ultimate disaster. It can hardly be supposed, taking human nature as it is, that with such a guarantee man would really pay the heavy price which life-long effort entails. The majority in all probability would seek, as the saying is, "to make the best of both worlds."

This argument is not without its value. Yet it will probably fail to convince the mind that no other course was open, even to Divine omnipotence: and without this, we can hardly rest satisfied. The sole reason, which is fully conclusive, would seem to be that were God to abstain from giving existence to a soul because He foresaw that that soul would choose the path to evil, the perversity of the creature would have prevailed against the goodness of the Creator, and human wickedness have compelled God to modify His purposes. Such a state of things, it would appear, is repugnant to reason. It belongs to God to determine His designs in accordance with perfect wisdom and perfect goodness, but in supreme independence of creatures. These are of necessity wholly subordinated to Him. Just as there can be nothing which does not come from God as First Efficient Cause, nor anything which does not tend to Him as the ultimate Final Cause, so it is impossible that those purposes in regard of the creature which He has made with supreme generosity and wisdom should admit of alteration because He foresees that the creature will abuse His gifts. And it would appear that the permission of moral evil, and even of final loss, is an inevitable condition of such a system.

God permits evil, but does not cause it. Yet it is impossible that He should permit anything, which He does not turn to a good end: in some way or other even the moral evil of the world must be rendered subservient to His good purposes. That He has in fact done so is abundantly plain. This employment of evil belongs not merely to exceptional cases, but is part of the ordinary disposition of providence. At all times the good are exposed to grave difficulties through the evil example which abounds around them, and through the efforts of other men to induce them to adopt a lower standard than the moral law demands. This struggle is not only the proof of their virtue, but the means of its growth. Without it man's moral development would languish. Virtue reaches a high level of perfection because it has to make headway against opposition. The attainment of perfection by those who are willing to make the effort is a good which outweighs the evil involved in the permission of moral harm. Hence we need not feel surprise that God should tolerate man's misuse of his liberty.

The existence of moral evil must ever remain the greatest of the world's mysteries: and it is idle to imagine that we can remove entirely the difficulty which we feel in its regard. Yet we know well that our human intelligence is limited in its scope, and that we must not expect to solve all problems.

David Hume

SUFFERING AND EVIL

Demea: It is my opinion that each man feels, in a manner, the truth of religion within his own breast, and, from a consciousness of his imbecility and misery, rather than from any reasoning, is led to seek protection from that Being, on whom he and all nature is dependent. So anxious or so tedious are even the best scenes of life, that futurity is still the object of all our hopes and fears. We incessantly look forward, and endeavor, by prayers, adoration, and sacrifice, to appease those unknown powers, whom we find, by experience, so able to afflict and oppress us. Wretched creatures that we are! what resource for us amidst the innumerable ills of life, did not religion suggest some methods of atonement, and appease those terrors with which we are incessantly agitated and tormented?

Philo: I am indeed persuaded that the best, and indeed the only method of bringing everyone to a due sense of religion, is by just representations of the misery and wickedness of men. And for that purpose a talent of eloquence and strong imagery is more requisite than that of reasoning and argument. For is it necessary to prove what everyone feels within himself? It is only necessary to make us feel it, if possible, more intimately and sensibly.

Demea: The people, indeed, are sufficiently convinced of this great and melancholy truth. The miseries of life; the unhappiness of man; the general corruptions of our nature; the unsatisfactory enjoyment of pleasures, riches, honors; these phrases have become almost proverbial in all languages. And who can doubt of what all men declare from their own immediate feeling and experience?

Philo: In this point the learned are perfectly agreed with the vulgar; and in all letters, sacred and profane, the topic of human misery has been insisted on with the most pathetic eloquence that sorrow and melancholy could inspire. The poets, who speak from sentiment, without a system, and whose testimony has therefore the more authority, abound in images of this nature. From Homer down to Dr. Young, the whole inspired tribe have ever been sensible, that no other representation of things would suit the feeling and observation of each individual.

Demea: As to authorities, you need not seek them. Look round this library of Cleanthes. I shall venture to affirm, that, except authors of particular sciences, such as chemistry or botany, who have no occasion to treat of human life, there is scarce one of those innumerable writers, from whom the sense of human misery has not, in some passage or other, extorted a complaint and confession of it. At least, the chance is entirely on that side; and no one author has ever, so far as I can recollect, been so extravagant as to deny it.

Philo: There you must excuse me. Leibniz has denied it; and is perhaps the first who ventured upon so bold and paradoxical an opinion; at least, the first who made it essential to his philosophical system.

Demea: And by being the first, might he not have been sensible of his error? For is this a subject in which philosophers can propose to make discoveries especially in so late an age? And can any man hope by a simple denial, for the subject scarcely admits of reasoning, to bear down the united testimony of mankind, founded on sense and consciousness? And why should man pretend to an exemption from the lot of all other animals? The whole earth, believe me, Philo, is cursed and polluted. A perpetual war is kindled amongst all living creatures. Necessity, hunger,

Edited from *Dialogues Concerning Natural Religion,* 1779, Parts 10-11, which is now in the public domain.

want, stimulate the strong and courageous; fear, anxiety, terror, agitate the weak and infirm. The first entrance into life gives anguish to the new-born infant and to its wretched parent; weakness, impotence, distress, attend each stage of that life, and it is at last finished in agony and horror.

***Philo*:** Observe too, the curious artifices of Nature in order to embitter the life of every living being. The stronger prey upon the weaker, and keep them in perpetual terror and anxiety. The weaker too, in their turn, often prey upon the stronger, and vex and molest them without relaxation. Consider that innumerable race of insects, which either are bred on the body of each animal, or, flying about, infix their stings in him. These insects have others still less than themselves, which torment them. And thus on each hand, before and behind, above and below, every animal is surrounded with enemies, which incessantly seek his misery and destruction.

***Demea*:** Man alone, seems to be, in part, an exception to this rule. For by combination in society, he can easily master lions, tigers, and bears, whose greater strength and agility naturally enable them to prey upon him.

***Philo*:** On the contrary, it is here chiefly that the uniform and equal maxims of Nature are most apparent. Man, it is true, can, by combination, surmount all his real enemies, and become master of the whole animal creation; but does he not immediately raise up to himself imaginary enemies, the demons of his fancy, who haunt him with superstitious terrors, and blast every enjoyment of life? His pleasure, as he imagines, becomes, in their eyes, a crime; his food and repose give them umbrage and offence; his very sleep and dreams furnish new materials to anxious fear; and even death, his refuge from every other ill, presents only the dread of endless and innumerable woes. Nor does the wolf molest more the timid flock, than superstition does the anxious breast of wretched mortals.

Besides, consider, Demea, this very society, by which we surmount those wild beasts, our natural enemies; what new enemies does it not raise to us? What woe and misery does it not occasion? Man is the greatest enemy of man. Oppression, injustice, contempt, contumely, violence, sedition, war, calumny, treachery, fraud; by these they mutually torment each other; and they would soon dissolve that society which they had formed, were it not for the dread of still greater ills, which must attend their separation.

***Demea*:** But though these external insults, from animals, from men, from all the elements, which assault us, form a frightful catalogue of woes, they are nothing in comparison of those which arise within ourselves, from the distempered condition of our mind and body. How many lie under the lingering torment of diseases? Hear the pathetic enumeration of the great poet:

Intestine stone and ulcer, colic-pangs,
Demoniac frenzy, moping melancholy,
And moon-struck madness, pining atrophy,
Marasmus, and wide-wasting pestilence.
Dire was the tossing, deep the groans: despair
Tended the sick, busiest from couch to couch.
And over them triumphant death his dart
Shook: but delay'd to strike, though oft invok'd
With vows, as their chief good and final hope.

The disorders of the mind, though more secret, are not perhaps less dismal and vexatious. Remorse, shame, anguish, rage, disappointment, anxiety, fear, dejection, despair; who has ever passed through life without cruel inroads from these tormentors? How many have scarcely ever felt any better sensations? Labor and poverty, so abhorred by every one, are the certain lot of the far greater number; and those few privileged persons, who enjoy ease and opulence, never reach contentment or true felicity. All the goods of life united would not make a very happy man; but all the ills united would make a wretch indeed; and any one of them almost (and who can be free from every one?) nay often the absence of one good (and who can possess all?) is sufficient to render life ineligible.

Were a stranger to drop on a sudden into this world, I would show him, as a specimen of its ills, a hospital full of diseases, a prison crowded with malefactors and debtors, a field of battle strewed with carcasses, a fleet foundering in the ocean, a nation languishing under tyranny, famine, or pestilence. To turn the gay side of life to him, and give him a notion of its pleasures; whither should I conduct him? to a ball, to an opera, to court? He might justly think, that I was only showing him a diversity of distress and sorrow.

***Philo*:** There is no evading such striking instances but by apologies, which still further aggravate the charge. Why have all men, I ask, in all ages, complained incessantly of the miseries of life? They have no just reason, says one; these complaints proceed only from their discontented, repining, anxious disposition. And can there possibly, I reply, be a more certain foundation of misery, than such a wretched temper? But if they were really as unhappy as they pretend, says my antagonist, why do they remain in life? Not satisfied with life, afraid of death. This is the secret chain, say I, that holds us. We are terrified, not bribed to the continuance of our existence. It is only a false delicacy, he may insist, which a few refined spirits indulge, and which has spread these complaints among the whole race of mankind. And what is this delicacy, I ask, which you blame? Is it any thing but a greater sensibility to all the pleasures and pains of life? And if the man of a delicate, refined temper, by being so much more alive than the rest of the world, is only so much more unhappy, what judgement must we form in general of human life? Let men remain at rest, says our adversary, and they will be easy. They are willing artificers of their own misery. No! reply I; an anxious languor follows their repose; disappointment, vexation, trouble, their activity and ambition.

***Cleanthes*:** I can observe something like what you mention in some others, but I confess I feel little or nothing of it in myself, and hope that it is not so common as you represent it.

***Demea*:** If you feel not human misery yourself, I congratulate you on so happy a singularity. Others, seemingly the most prosperous, have not been ashamed to vent their complaints in the most melancholy strains. Let us attend to the great, the fortunate emperor, Charles V, when, tired with human grandeur, he resigned all his extensive dominions into the hands of his son. In the last harangue which he made on that memorable occasion, he publicly avowed, that the greatest prosperities which he had ever enjoyed, had been mixed with so many adversities, that he might truly say he had never enjoyed any satisfaction or contentment. But did the retired life, in which he sought for shelter, afford him any greater happiness? If we may credit his son's account, his repentance commenced the very day of his resignation.

Cicero's fortune, from small beginnings, rose to the greatest luster and renown; yet what pathetic complaints of the ills of life do his familiar letters, as well as philosophical discourses, contain? And suitably to his own experience, he introduces Cato, the great, the fortunate Cato, protesting in his old age, that had he a new life in his offer, he would reject the present.

Ask yourself, ask any of your acquaintance, whether they would live over again the last ten or twenty years of their life. No! but the next twenty, they say, will be better:

> And from the dregs of life, hope to receive
> What the first sprightly running could not give.

Thus at last they find (such is the greatness of human misery, it reconciles even contradictions), that they complain at once of the shortness of life, and of its vanity and sorrow.

***Philo*:** And is it possible, Cleanthes, that after all these reflections, and infinitely more, which might be suggested, you can still persevere in your anthropomorphism, and assert the moral attributes of the Deity, his justice, benevolence, mercy, and rectitude, to be of the same nature with these virtues in human creatures? His power we allow is infinite; whatever he wills is executed; but neither man nor any other animal is happy; therefore, he does not will their happiness. His wisdom is infinite; He is never mistaken in choosing the means to any end; But the course of Nature tends not to human or animal felicity; therefore, it is not established for that purpose. Through the whole compass of human knowledge, there are no inferences more certain and infallible than these. In what respect, then, do his benevolence and mercy resemble the benevolence and mercy of men? Epicurus's old questions are yet unanswered. Is he willing to prevent evil, but not able? Then is he impotent. Is he able, but not willing? Then is he malevolent. Is he both able and willing? Whence then is evil?

You ascribe, Cleanthes (and I believe justly), a purpose and intention to Nature. But what, I beseech you, is the object of that curious artifice and machinery, which she has displayed in all animals? The preservation alone of individuals, and propagation of the species. It seems enough for her purpose, if such a rank be barely upheld in the universe, without any care or concern for the happiness of the members that compose it. No resource for this purpose, no machinery, in order merely to give pleasure or ease, no fund of pure joy and contentment, no indulgence, without some want or necessity accompanying it. At least, the few phenomena of this nature are overbalanced by opposite phenomena of still greater importance.

Our sense of music, harmony, and indeed beauty of all kinds, gives satisfaction, without being absolutely necessary to the preservation and propagation of the species. But what racking pains, on the other hand, arise from gouts, gravels, megrims, toothaches, rheumatisms, where the injury to the animal machinery is either small or incurable? Mirth, laughter, play, frolic, seem gratuitous satisfactions, which have no further tendency; spleen, melancholy, discontent, superstition, are pains of the same nature. How then does the Divine benevolence display itself, in the sense of you anthropomorphites? None but we Mystics, as you were pleased to call us, can account for this strange mixture of phenomena, by deriving it from attributes, infinitely perfect, but incomprehensible.

***Cleanthes*:** And have you at last betrayed your intentions, Philo? Your long agreement with Demea did indeed a little surprise me; but I find you were all the while erecting a concealed battery against me. And I must confess, that you have now fallen upon a subject worthy of your noble spirit of opposition and controversy. If you can make out the present point, and prove mankind to be unhappy or corrupted, there is an end at once of all religion. For to what purpose establish the natural attributes of the Deity, while the moral are still doubtful and uncertain?

***Demea*:** You take umbrage very easily, at opinions the most innocent, and the most generally received, even amongst the religious and devout themselves; and nothing can be more surprising than to find a topic like this, concerning the wickedness and misery of man, charged with no less than Atheism and profaneness. Have not all pious divines and preachers, who have indulged their rhetoric on so fertile a subject, have they not easily, I say, given a solution of any difficulties which may attend it? This world is but a point in comparison of the universe; this life but a moment in comparison of eternity. The present evil phenomena, therefore, are rectified in other regions, and in some future period of existence. And the eyes of men, being then opened to larger views of things, see the whole connection of general laws, and trace with adoration, the benevolence and rectitude of the Deity, through all the mazes and intricacies of his providence.

Cleanthes: No! No! These arbitrary suppositions can never be admitted, contrary to matter of fact, visible and uncontroverted. Whence can any cause be known but from its known effects? Whence can any hypothesis be proved but from the apparent phenomena? To establish one hypothesis upon another, is building entirely in the air, and the utmost we ever attain, by these conjectures and fictions, is to ascertain the bare possibility of our opinion; but never can we, upon such terms, establish its reality.

The only method of supporting Divine benevolence, and it is what I willingly embrace, is to deny absolutely the misery and wickedness of man. Your representations are exaggerated; your melancholy views mostly fictitious; your inferences contrary to fact and experience. Health is more common than sickness; pleasure than pain; happiness than misery. And for one vexation which we meet with, we attain, upon computation, a hundred enjoyments.

Philo: Admitting your position, which yet is extremely doubtful, you must at the same time allow, that if pain be less frequent than pleasure, it is infinitely more violent and durable. One hour of it is often able to outweigh a day, a week, a month of our common insipid enjoyments; and how many days, weeks, and months, are passed by several in the most acute torments? Pleasure, scarcely in one instance, is ever able to reach ecstasy and rapture; and in no one instance can it continue for any time at its highest pitch and altitude. The spirits evaporate, the nerves relax, the fabric is disordered, and the enjoyment quickly degenerates into fatigue and uneasiness. But pain often, good God, how often! rises to torture and agony; and the longer it continues, it becomes still more genuine agony and torture. Patience is exhausted, courage languishes, melancholy seizes us, and nothing terminates our misery but the removal of its cause, or another event, which is the sole cure of all evil, but which, from our natural folly, we regard with still greater horror and consternation.

But not to insist upon these topics, though most obvious, certain, and important, I must use the freedom to admonish you, Cleanthes, that you have put the controversy upon a most dangerous issue, and are unawares introducing a total skepticism into the most essential articles of natural and revealed theology. What! No method of fixing a just foundation for religion, unless we allow the happiness of human life, and maintain a continued existence even in this world, with all our present pains, infirmities, vexations, and follies, to be eligible and desirable! But this is contrary to every one's feeling and experience; it is contrary to an authority so established as nothing can subvert. No decisive proofs can ever be produced against this authority; nor is it possible for you to compute, estimate, and compare, all the pains and all the pleasures in the lives of all men and of all animals. And thus, by your resting the whole system of religion on a point, which, from its very nature, must for ever be uncertain, you tacitly confess, that that system is equally uncertain.

But allowing you what never will be believed, at least what you never possibly can prove, that animal, or at least human happiness, in this life, exceeds its misery, you have yet done nothing. For this is not, by any means, what we expect from infinite power, infinite wisdom, and infinite goodness. Why is there any misery at all in the world? Not by chance surely. From some cause then. Is it from the intention of the Deity? But he is perfectly benevolent. Is it contrary to his intention? But he is almighty. Nothing can shake the solidity of this reasoning, so short, so clear, so decisive; except we assert, that these subjects exceed all human capacity, and that our common measures of truth and falsehood are not applicable to them; a topic which I have all along insisted on, but which you have, from the beginning, rejected with scorn and indignation. But I will be contented to retire still from this entrenchment, for I deny that you can ever force me in it. I will allow, that pain or misery in man is compatible with infinite power and goodness in the Deity, even in your sense of these attributes. What are you advanced by all these concessions? A mere possible compatibility is not sufficient. You must prove these pure, unmixed, and uncontrollable attributes from the present mixed and confused phenomena, and from these alone. A hopeful undertaking! Were the phenomena ever so pure and unmixed, yet being finite, they would be insufficient for that purpose. How much more, where they are also so jarring and discordant!

Here, Cleanthes, I find myself at ease in my argument. Here I triumph. Formerly, when we argued concerning the natural attributes of intelligence and design, I needed all my skeptical and metaphysical subtlety to elude your grasp. In many views of the universe, and of its parts, particularly the latter, the beauty and fitness of final causes strike us with such irresistible force, that all objections appear (what I believe they really are) mere cavils and sophisms; nor can we then imagine how it was ever possible for us to repose any weight on them. But there is no view of human life, or of the condition of mankind, from which, without the greatest violence, we can infer the moral attributes, or learn that infinite benevolence, conjoined with infinite power and infinite wisdom, which we must discover by the eyes of faith alone. It is your turn now to tug the laboring oar, and to support your philosophical subtleties against the dictates of plain reason and experience.

***Cleanthes*:** I scruple not to allow that I have been apt to suspect the frequent repetition of the word *infinite*, which we meet with in all theological writers, to savor more of panegyric than of philosophy; and that any purposes of reasoning, and even of religion, would be better served, were we to rest contented with more accurate and more moderate expressions. The terms, admirable, excellent, superlatively great, wise, and holy; these sufficiently fill the imaginations of men; and any thing beyond, besides that it leads into absurdities, has no influence on the affections or sentiments. Thus, in the present subject, if we abandon all human analogy, as seems your intention, I am afraid we abandon all religion, and retain no conception of the great object of our adoration. If we preserve human analogy, we must for ever find it impossible to reconcile any mixture of evil in the universe with infinite attributes; much less can we ever prove the latter from the former. But supposing the Author of Nature to be finitely perfect, though far exceeding mankind, a satisfactory account may then be given of natural and moral evil, and every untoward phenomenon be explained and adjusted. A less evil may then be chosen, in order to avoid a greater; inconveniences be submitted to, in order to reach a desirable end; and in a word, benevolence, regulated by wisdom, and limited by necessity, may produce just such a world as the present. You, Philo, who are so prompt at starting views, and reflections, and analogies, I would gladly hear, at length, without interruption, your opinion of this new theory; and if it deserve our attention, we may afterwards, at more leisure, reduce it into form.

***Philo*:** My sentiments are not worth being made a mystery of and, therefore, without any ceremony, I shall deliver what occurs to me with regard to the present subject. It must, I think, be allowed, that if a very limited intelligence, whom we shall suppose utterly unacquainted with the universe, were assured that it were the production of a very good, wise, and powerful Being, however finite, he would, from his conjectures, form beforehand a different notion of it from what we find it to be by experience; nor would he ever imagine, merely from these attributes of the cause, of which he is informed, that the effect could be so full of vice and misery and disorder, as it appears in this life. Supposing now, that this person were brought into the world, still assured that it was the workmanship of such a sublime and benevolent Being; he might, perhaps, be surprised at the disappointment; but would never retract his former belief, if founded on any very solid argument; since such a limited intelligence must be sensible of his own blindness and ignorance, and must allow, that there may be many solutions of those phenomena, which will forever escape his comprehension. But supposing, which is the real case with regard to man, that this creature is not antecedently convinced of a supreme intelligence, benevolent, and powerful, but is left to gather such a belief from the appearances of things; this entirely alters the case, nor will he ever find any reason for such a conclusion. He may be fully convinced of the narrow limits of his understanding; but this will not help him in forming an inference concerning the goodness of superior powers, since he must form that inference from what he knows, not from what he is ignorant of. The more you exaggerate his weakness and ignorance, the more diffident you render him, and give him the greater suspicion that such subjects are beyond the reach of his faculties. You are obliged, therefore, to reason with him merely from the known phenomena, and to drop every arbitrary supposition or conjecture.

Did I show you a house or palace, where there was not one apartment convenient or agreeable; where the windows, doors, fires, passages, stairs, and the whole economy of the building, were the source of noise, confusion, fatigue, darkness, and the extremes of heat and cold; you would certainly blame the contrivance, without any further examination. The architect would in vain display his subtlety, and prove to you, that if this door or that window were altered, greater ills would ensue. What he says may be strictly true: The alteration of one particular, while the other parts of the building remain, may only augment the inconveniences. But still you would assert in general, that, if the architect had had skill and good intentions, he might have formed such a plan of the whole, and might have adjusted the parts in such a manner, as would have remedied all or most of these inconveniences. His ignorance, or even your own ignorance of such a plan, will never convince you of the impossibility of it. If you find any inconveniences and deformities in the building, you will always, without entering into any detail, condemn the architect.

In short, I repeat the question: Is the world, considered in general, and as it appears to us in this life, different from what a man, or such a limited being, would, beforehand, expect from a very powerful, wise, and benevolent Deity? It must be strange prejudice to assert the contrary. And from thence I conclude, that however consistent the world may be, allowing certain suppositions and conjectures, with the idea of such a Deity, it can never afford us an inference concerning his existence. The consistence is not absolutely denied, only the inference. Conjectures, especially where infinity is excluded from the Divine attributes, may perhaps be sufficient to prove a consistence, but can never be foundations for any inference.

There seem to be four circumstances, on which depend all, or the greatest part of the ills, that molest sensible creatures; and it is not impossible but all these circumstances may be necessary and unavoidable. We know so little beyond common life, or even of common life, that, with regard to the economy of a universe, there is no conjecture, however wild, which may not be just; nor any one, however plausible, which may not be erroneous. All that belongs to human understanding, in this deep ignorance and obscurity, is to be skeptical, or at least cautious, and not to admit of any hypothesis whatever, much less of any which is supported by no appearance of probability. Now, this I assert to be the case with regard to all the causes of evil, and the circumstances on which it depends. None of them appear to human reason in the least degree necessary or unavoidable; nor can we suppose them such, without the utmost license of imagination.

The first circumstance which introduces evil is that contrivance or economy of the animal creation, by which pains, as well as pleasures, are employed to excite all creatures to action, and make them vigilant in the great work of self-preservation. Now pleasure alone, in its various degrees, seems to human understanding sufficient for this purpose. All animals might be constantly in a state of enjoyment; but when urged by any of the necessities of nature, such as thirst, hunger, weariness, instead of pain, they might feel a diminution of pleasure, by which they might be prompted to seek that object which is necessary to their subsistence. Men pursue pleasure as eagerly as they avoid pain; at least they might have been so constituted. It seems, therefore, plainly possible to carry on the business of life without any pain. Why then is any animal ever rendered susceptible of such a sensation? If animals can be free from it an hour, they might enjoy a perpetual exemption from it; and it required as particular a contrivance of their organs to produce that feeling, as to endow them with sight, hearing, or any of the senses. Shall we conjecture, that such a contrivance was necessary, without any appearance of reason? And shall we build on that conjecture as on the most certain truth?

But a capacity of pain would not alone produce pain, were it not for the second circumstance, viz. the conducting of the world by general laws; and this seems nowise necessary to a very perfect Being. It is true, if everything were conducted by particular volitions, the course of nature would be perpetually broken, and no man could employ his reason in the conduct of life. But might not other particular volitions remedy this inconvenience? In short, might not the Deity exterminate all ill, wherever it were to be found; and produce all good, without any preparation, or long progress of causes and effects?

Besides, we must consider, that, according to the present economy of the world, the course of nature, though supposed exactly regular, yet to us appears not so, and many events are uncertain, and many disappoint our expectations. Health and sickness, calm and tempest, with an infinite number of other accidents, whose causes are unknown and variable, have a great influence both on the fortunes of particular persons and on the prosperity of public societies; and indeed all human life, in a manner, depends on such accidents. A being, therefore, who knows the secret springs of the universe, might easily, by particular volitions, turn all these accidents to the good of mankind, and render the whole world happy, without discovering himself in any operation. A fleet, whose purposes were salutary to society, might always meet with a fair wind. Good princes enjoy sound health and long life. Persons born to power and authority, be framed with good tempers and virtuous dispositions. A few such events as these, regularly and wisely conducted, would change the face of the world; and yet would no more seem to disturb the course of nature, or confound human conduct, than the present economy of things, where the causes are secret, and variable, and compounded. Some small touches given to Caligula's brain in his infancy, might have converted him into a Trajan. One wave, a little higher than the rest, by burying Caesar and his fortune in the bottom of the ocean, might have restored liberty to a considerable part of mankind. There may, for aught we know, be good reasons why Providence interposes not in this manner; but they are unknown to us; and though the mere supposition, that such reasons exist, may be sufficient to save the conclusion concerning the Divine attributes, yet surely it can never be sufficient to establish that conclusion.

If every thing in the universe be conducted by general laws, and if animals be rendered susceptible of pain, it scarcely seems possible but some ill must arise in the various shocks of matter, and the various concurrence and opposition of general laws; but this ill would be very rare, were it not for the third circumstance, which I proposed to mention, viz. the great frugality with which all powers and faculties are distributed to every particular being. So well adjusted are the organs and capacities of all animals, and so well fitted to their preservation, that, as far as history or tradition reaches, there appears not to be any single species which has yet been extinguished in the universe. Every animal has the requisite endowments; but these endowments are bestowed with so scrupulous an economy, that any considerable diminution must entirely destroy the creature. Wherever one power is increased, there is a proportional abatement in the others. Animals which excel in swiftness are commonly defective in force. Those which possess both are either imperfect in some of their senses, or are oppressed with the most craving wants. The human species, whose chief excellency is reason and sagacity, is of all others the most necessitous, and the most deficient in bodily advantages; without clothes, without arms, without food, without lodging, without any convenience of life, except what they owe to their own skill and industry. In short, nature seems to have formed an exact calculation of the necessities of her creatures; and, like a rigid master, has afforded them little more powers or endowments than what are strictly sufficient to supply those necessities. An indulgent parent would have bestowed a large stock, in order to guard against accidents, and secure the happiness and welfare of the creature in the most unfortunate concurrence of circumstances. Every course of life would not have been so surrounded with precipices, that the least departure from the true path, by mistake or necessity, must involve us in misery and ruin. Some reserve, some fund, would have been provided to ensure happiness; nor would the powers and the necessities have been adjusted with so rigid an economy. The Author of Nature is inconceivably powerful; his force is supposed great, if not altogether inexhaustible; nor is there any reason, as far as we can judge, to make him observe this strict frugality in his dealings with his creatures. It would have been better, were his power extremely limited, to have created fewer animals, and to have endowed these with more faculties for their happiness and preservation. A builder is never esteemed prudent, who undertakes a plan beyond what his stock will enable him to finish.

In order to cure most of the ills of human life, I require not that man should have the wings of the eagle, the swiftness of the stag, the force of the ox, the arms of the lion, the scales of the crocodile or rhinoceros; much less do I demand the sagacity of an angel or cherubim. I am contented to take an increase in one single power or faculty of his soul. Let him be endowed with a greater propensity to industry and labor; a more vigorous spring and activity of mind; a more constant bent to business and application. Let the whole species possess naturally an equal diligence with that which many individuals are able to attain by habit and reflection; and the most beneficial consequences, without any allay of ill, is the immediate and necessary result of this endowment. Almost all the moral, as well as natural evils of human life, arise from idleness; and were our species, by the original constitution of their frame, exempt from this vice or infirmity, the perfect cultivation of land, the improvement of arts and manufactures, the exact execution of every office and duty, immediately follow; and men at once may fully reach that state of society, which is so imperfectly attained by the best regulated government. But as industry is a power, and the most valuable of any, Nature seems determined, suitably to her usual maxims, to bestow it on men with a very sparing hand; and rather to punish him severely for his deficiency in it, than to reward him for his attainments. She has so contrived his frame, that nothing but the most violent necessity can oblige him to labor; and she employs all his other wants to overcome, at least in part, the want of diligence, and to endow him with some share of a faculty of which she has thought fit naturally to bereave him. Here our demands may be allowed very humble, and therefore the more reasonable. If we required the endowments of superior penetration and judgement, of a more delicate taste of beauty, of a nicer sensibility to benevolence and friendship; we might be told, that we impiously pretend to break the order of Nature; that we want to exalt ourselves into a higher rank of being; that the presents which we require, not being suitable to our state and condition, would only be pernicious to us. But it is hard, I dare to repeat it, it is hard, that being placed in a world so full of wants and necessities, where almost every being and element is either our foe or refuses its assistance. We should also have our own temper to struggle with, and should be deprived of that faculty which can alone fence against these multiplied evils.

The fourth circumstance, whence arises the misery and ill of the universe, is the inaccurate workmanship of all the springs and principles of the great machine of nature. It must be acknowledged, that there are few parts of the universe, which seem not to serve some purpose, and whose removal would not produce a visible defect and disorder in the whole. The parts hang all together; nor can one be touched without affecting the rest, in a greater or less degree. But at the same time, it must be observed, that none of these parts or principles, however useful, are so accurately adjusted, as to keep precisely within those bounds in which their utility consists; but they are, all of them, apt, on every occasion, to run into the one extreme or the other. One would imagine, that this grand production had not received the last hand of the maker; so little finished is every part, and so coarse are the strokes with which it is executed. Thus, the winds are requisite to convey the vapors along the surface of the globe, and to assist men in navigation; but how oft, rising up to tempests and hurricanes, do they become pernicious? Rains are necessary to nourish all the plants and animals of the earth; but how often are they defective? how often excessive? Heat is requisite to all life and vegetation; but is not always found in the due proportion. On the mixture and secretion of the humors and juices of the body depend the health and prosperity of the animal; but the parts perform not regularly their proper function. What more useful than all the passions of the mind, ambition, vanity, love, anger? But how oft do they break their bounds, and cause the greatest convulsions in society? There is nothing so advantageous in the universe, but what frequently becomes pernicious, by its excess or defect; nor has Nature guarded, with the requisite accuracy, against all disorder or confusion. The irregularity is never perhaps so great as to destroy any species; but is often sufficient to involve the individuals in ruin and misery.

On the concurrence, then, of these four circumstances, does all or the greatest part of natural evil depend. Were all living creatures incapable of pain, or were the world administered by particular volitions, evil never could have found access into the universe; and were animals endowed with a large stock of powers and faculties, beyond what strict necessity requires, or were the several springs and principles of the universe so accurately framed as to preserve always the just temperament and medium, there must have been very little ill in comparison of what we feel at present. What then shall we pronounce on this occasion? Shall we say that these circumstances are not necessary, and that they might easily have been altered in the contrivance of the universe? This decision seems too presumptuous for creatures so blind and ignorant. Let us be more modest in our conclusions. Let us allow, that, if the goodness of the Deity (I mean a goodness like the human) could be established on any tolerable reasons *a priori*, these phenomena, however untoward, would not be sufficient to subvert that principle, but might easily, in some unknown manner, be reconcilable to it. But let us still assert, that as this goodness is not antecedently established, but must be inferred from the phenomena, there can be no grounds for such an inference, while there are so many ills in the universe, and while these ills might so easily have been remedied, as far as human understanding can be allowed to judge on such a subject. I am Sceptic enough to allow, that the bad appearances, notwithstanding all my reasonings, may be compatible with such attributes as you suppose; but surely they can never prove these attributes. Such a conclusion cannot result from skepticism, but must arise from the phenomena, and from our confidence in the reasonings which we deduce from these phenomena.

Look round this universe. What an immense profusion of beings, animated and organized, sensible and active! You admire this prodigious variety and fecundity. But inspect a little more narrowly these living existences, the only beings worth regarding. How hostile and destructive to each other! How insufficient all of them for their own happiness! How contemptible or odious to the spectator! The whole presents nothing but the idea of a blind Nature, impregnated by a great vivifying principle, and pouring forth from her lap, without discernment or parental care, her maimed and abortive children!

Here the Manichaean system occurs as a proper hypothesis to solve the difficulty; and no doubt, in some respects, it is very specious, and has more probability than the common hypothesis, by giving a plausible account of the strange mixture of good and ill which appears in life. But if we consider, on the other hand, the perfect uniformity and agreement of the parts of the universe, we shall not discover in it any marks of the combat of a malevolent with a benevolent being. There is indeed an opposition of pains and pleasures in the feelings of sensible creatures; but are not all the operations of Nature carried on by an opposition of principles, of hot and cold, moist and dry, light and heavy? The true conclusion is, that the original Source of all things is entirely indifferent to all these principles; and has no more regard to good above ill, than to heat above cold, or to drought above moisture, or to light above heavy.

There may be four hypotheses framed concerning the first causes of the universe: that they are endowed with perfect goodness; that they have perfect malice; that they are opposite, and have both goodness and malice; that they have neither goodness nor malice. Mixed phenomena can never prove the two former unmixed principles; and the uniformity and steadiness of general laws seem to oppose the third. The fourth, therefore, seems by far the most probable.

What I have said concerning natural evil will apply to moral, with little or no variation; and we have no more reason to infer that the rectitude of the Supreme Being resembles human rectitude, than that his benevolence resembles the human. Nay, it will be thought, that we have still greater cause to exclude from him moral sentiments, such as we feel them, since moral evil, in the opinion of many, is much more predominant above moral good than natural evil above natural good.

But even though this should not be allowed, and though the virtue which is in mankind should be acknowledged much superior to the vice, yet so long as there is any vice at all in the universe, it will very much puzzle you anthropomorphites, how to account for it. You must assign a cause for it, without having recourse to the first cause. But as every effect must have a cause, and that cause another, you must either carry on the progression *in infinitum*, or rest on that original principle, who is the ultimate cause of all things.

***Demea*:** Hold! hold! Whither does your imagination hurry you? I joined in alliance with you, in order to prove the incomprehensible nature of the Divine Being, and refute the principles of Cleanthes, who would measure every thing by human rule and standard. But I now find you running into all the topics of the greatest libertines and infidels, and betraying that holy cause which you seemingly espoused. Are you secretly, then, a more dangerous enemy than Cleanthes himself?

***Cleanthes*:** And are you so late in perceiving it? Believe me, Demea, your friend Philo, from the beginning, has been amusing himself at both our expense; and it must be confessed, that the injudicious reasoning of our vulgar theology has given him but too just a handle of ridicule. The total infirmity of human reason, the absolute incomprehensibility of the Divine Nature, the great and universal misery, and still greater wickedness of men, these are strange topics, surely, to be so fondly cherished by orthodox divines and doctors. In ages of stupidity and ignorance, indeed, these principles may safely be espoused; and perhaps no views of things are more proper to promote superstition, than such as encourage the blind amazement, the diffidence, and melancholy of mankind. But at present...

***Philo*:** Blame not so much the ignorance of these reverend gentlemen. They know how to change their style with the times. Formerly it was a most popular theological topic to maintain that human life was vanity and misery, and to exaggerate all the ills and pains which are incident to men. But of late years, divines, we find, begin to retract this position; and maintain, though still with some hesitation, that there are more goods than evils, more pleasures than pains, even in this life. When religion stood entirely upon temper and education, it was thought proper to encourage melancholy, as indeed mankind never have recourse to superior powers so readily as in that disposition. But as men have now learned to form principles, and to draw consequences, it is necessary to change the batteries, and to make use of such arguments as will endure at least some scrutiny and examination. This variation is the same (and from the same causes) with that which I formerly remarked with regard to Skepticism.

5D. Belief

Introduction

The interplay of *belief, faith,* and *reason* raises many important questions, especially for religious discussions. As we have seen, there are many complex issues involved in attempting to prove God's existence. In this section, the role of *belief* comes to the forefront.

We begin with passages from Blaise Pascal's *Pensées* ("thoughts" or "reflections"). Pascal claims that if there is a God who is omnipotent, omniscient, perfectly benevolent, and eternal, then that supreme being would be *infinitely incomprehensible to us*. In other words, Pascal claims that our limited capacity to reason is not sufficient for us to either comprehend or prove God's existence. However, even for thinkers such as Pascal, reason does play a part. Pascal argues that it is *reasonable to believe in God* because we can rationally weigh two possible outcomes: "Let us weigh the two cases: if you gain, you gain all; if you lose, you lose nothing. Wager then unhesitatingly that He exists."

The relationship between religion, a rational fear of God, and the grounds of virtue are the subject of the reading by Damaris Cudworth Masham. According to Masham, skepticism weakens any obligation to be a virtuous person. Furthermore, skepticism is either the result of parents' negligence of their children's instruction, or from poor religious instruction. For Masham, skepticism often ends in atheism. But, argues Masham, "an irrational religion can never rationally be conceived to come from God."

The reading from Friedrich Nietzsche contains the famous statement, "God is dead." The statement is not meant to be taken literally. Nietzsche intends it to mean that Western civilization's long-standing reliance on religion as the only possible ground for morality is misguided and wrong. Nietzsche recognizes that most people think it is impossible for a moral system to be acceptable without a religious foundation. But, Nietzsche argues, we must get rid of the idea of absolute values and universal moral laws. Doing this will be liberating; it will be a "new and indescribable variety of light, happiness, relief, enlivenment, encouragement, and dawning day."

In opposition to Pascal's ideas, William Clifford argues that *belief* should be grounded on *investigation* and *doubt*; in other words, *how* we arrive at a belief is just as important as its *truth*. Clifford applies this to all types of belief, including scientific, religious, and even trivial beliefs. If we do not consistently subject our beliefs to severe scrutiny, then we become intellectually lazy. Therefore, we should not believe anything without sufficient evidence. Clifford extends this line of thought to include beliefs based on "authority." If we have no reasonable grounds for supposing that he knew the truth of what he was saying, then the so-called authority need not be believed. For example, in order to be believed, an expert's claims regarding a scientific matter must have been the result of extensive experimentation, which can easily be checked and validated by other scientists.

The article by William James argues that whenever we cannot decide an important issue, then it is understandable if we let our passions decide. However, James agrees with Clifford that we should always subject our beliefs to patient investigation. If after we exhaust all possible means of rational investigation of the evidence, and it becomes clear that it is not possible to decide a question on intellectual grounds, then we justified in letting our "passional nature" decide.

Blaise Pascal

THE WAGER

We do not need a great education of the mind to understand that there is no true and permanent satisfaction in life; that all our pleasures are but vanity, our evils infinite, and lastly, that death, which threatens us every moment, must infallibly and within a few years place us in the dread alternative of being forever either annihilated or unhappy.

Where do such feelings come from? What delight can we find in the expectation of nothing but unavailing misery? What is the cause of our boasting that we are in impenetrable darkness? How can such an argument as the following occur to a reasonable person?

> I know not who has sent me into the world, nor what the world is, nor what I myself am. I am terribly ignorant of everything. I know not what my body is, nor my senses, nor my soul, nor even that part of me which thinks, which reflects on all and on itself, yet is as ignorant of itself as everything else. I see those dreadful spaces of the universe which close me in, and I find myself fixed in one corner of this vast expanse, without knowing why I am set in this place rather than elsewhere, nor why this moment of time given me for life is assigned to this point rather than another of the whole eternity which was before me or which shall be after me. I see nothing but infinities on every side, which close me round as an atom, and as a shadow which endures but for an instant and returns no more. I know only that I must shortly die, but what I know the least is this very death which I cannot avoid.
>
> As I know not where I came from, so I know not where I go; only this I know, that on departing this world, I shall either fall forever into nothingness, or into the hands of an offended God, without knowing which of these two conditions shall eternally be my lot. Such is my state, full of weakness and uncertainty; from which I conclude that I ought to pass all the days of my life without thought of searching for what must happen to me. Perhaps I might find some ray of light in my doubts, but I will not take the trouble, nor stir a foot to seek it; and after treating with scorn those who are troubled with this care, I will go without foresight and without fear to make trial of the grand event, and allow myself to be led softly on to death, uncertain of the eternity of my future condition.

Now what do we gain in hearing some say that they do not believe there is a God who watches their actions, that they consider themselves the sole masters of their conduct and accountable for it only to themselves? Yet this eternity exists, and death is the gate of eternity for them, which threatens them every hour, and must in a short while infallibly reduce them to the dread necessity of being through eternity either nothing or miserable, without knowing which of these eternities is forever prepared for them.

When I consider the short duration of my life, swallowed up in the eternity before and after, the small space which I fill, or even can see, engulfed in the infinite immensity of spaces of which I know nothing, and which knows nothing of me, I am terrified, and wonder that I am here rather

Edited from *The Thoughts of Blaise Pascal*, Translated by Charles Kegan Paul, 1901, which is now in the public domain.

than there, for there is no reason why here rather than there, or now rather than then. Who has set me here? By whose order and design have this place and time been destined for me?

This is what I see and what troubles me. I look on all sides and see nothing but obscurity; nature offers me nothing but matter for doubt and disquiet. If I see nothing there which indicated a God, then I should decide not to believe in Him; but if I see everywhere the marks of a Creator, then I should rest peacefully in faith. But seeing too much to deny, and too little to affirm, my state is pitiful, and I have a hundred times wished that if God upheld nature, He would mark the fact unequivocally; but that if the signs which nature gives of a God are fallacious, nature would suppress them, and either say all or say nothing, that I might see what part I should take. While in my present state, ignorant of what I am, and of what I ought to do, I know neither my condition nor my duty; my heart is completely bent to know where is the true good in order to follow it, nothing would seem to me too costly for eternity.

It is incomprehensible that there should be a God, and incomprehensible that there should not be a God; that there should be a soul in the body, and that we should have no soul; that the world should have been created, and that it should not.

Do you think that it is impossible that God is infinite, without parts? "Yes." I will then make you see something which is infinite and indivisible. A point moving everywhere with infinite swiftness, for it is in all places, and is whole and entire in each situation. Perhaps this effect of nature, which seems to you impossible beforehand, may teach you to know that there may be others also which you do not yet know. Do not then draw this conclusion from your apprenticeship, that nothing remains for you to know, but rather that an infinity remains for you to know.

Infinite—nothing. The soul of man is cast into a body in which it finds number, time, and dimension. It reasons about those concepts, and calls this *nature* or *necessity*, and can believe nothing else.

Unity joined to infinity does not increase it, any more than a foot added to infinite space. The finite is annihilated in presence of the infinite and becomes simply nothing, like our intellect before God.

We know that there is an infinite, but are ignorant of its nature. We know it to be false that numbers are finite, it must therefore be true that there is an infinity in number, but what this is we do not know. It can neither be odd nor even because the addition of a unit can make no change in the nature of number; yet it is a number, and every number is either odd or even, at least this is understood of every finite number.

Therefore, we may well know that there is a God, without knowing what he is. We know then the existence and the nature of the finite, because we also are finite and have dimension. We know the existence of the infinite, and are ignorant of its nature, because it has dimension like us, but not limits like us. But we know neither the existence nor the nature of God, because he has neither dimension nor limits.

But by faith we know his existence, by glory we shall know his nature. Now I have already shown that we can know the existence of a thing without knowing its nature. Let us now speak according to the light of nature.

If there is a God, He is infinitely incomprehensible, since having neither parts nor limits he has no relation to us. We are then incapable of knowing either what He is or if He is. This being so, who will dare to undertake the solution of the question? Not we, who have no relation to him.

Who then will blame Christians for not being able to give a reason for their faith; those who profess a religion for which they cannot give a reason? They declare in putting it forth to the world that it is a foolishness, and then you complain that they do not prove it. Were they to prove it, they would not keep their word; it is in lacking proof that they are not lacking in sense. "Yes, but although this excuses those who offer it as such, and takes away from them the blame of putting it forth without reason, it does not excuse those who receive it." Let us then examine this point, and say, "God is, or He is not." But to which side shall we incline? *Reason can determine nothing about it.* There is an infinite gulf fixed between us. A game is played at the extremity of this infinite distance in which heads or tails may turn up. *What will you wager?* There is no reason for backing either one or the other, you cannot reasonably argue in favor of either.

Do not then accuse of error those who have already chosen, for you know nothing about it. "No, but I blame them for having made, not *this* choice, but *a* choice because both the man who calls 'heads' and his adversary are equally to blame, they are both in the wrong; the true course is not to wager at all."

Yes, *but you must wager.* This depends not on your will, you are embedded in the affair. Which will you choose? Let us see. Since you must choose, let us see which least interests you. You have two things to lose—truth and good—and two things to stake—your reason and your will, your knowledge and your happiness. And your nature has two things to avoid—error and misery. Since you must choose, your *reason* is *not* harmed in choosing one or the other. Here is one point cleared up. But what of your happiness? Let us weigh the gain and the loss in choosing heads that God is. Let us weigh the two cases: if you gain, you gain all; if you lose, you lose nothing. Wager then unhesitatingly that He exists.

"You are right. Yes, I must wager, but I may stake too much." Let us see. Since there is an equal chance of gain and loss, if you had only to gain two lives for one, you might still wager. But what if there were three to gain? You would have to play, and it would be imprudent not to chance your life to gain three at a game where the chances of loss or gain are even. But there is an eternity of life and happiness. And that being so, were there an infinity of chances of which one only would be for you, you would still be right to stake one to win two, and you would act foolishly, being obliged to play, if you refused to stake one life against three at a game in which out of an infinity of chances there is one for you, if there were an infinity of an infinitely happy life to win. But there is an infinity of an infinitely happy life to win, a chance of gain against a finite number of chances to lose, and what you stake is finite, that is decided. Wherever the infinite exists and there is not an infinity of chances of loss against that of gain, there is no room for hesitation, you must risk everything. Thus, when a man is forced to play, he must renounce reason to keep life, rather than risk it for infinite gain, which is as likely to happen as the loss of nothingness.

It is of no use to say that it is uncertain that we gain, and certain that we risk, and that the infinite distance between the *certainty* of that which is staked and the *uncertainty* of what we will gain, equals the finite good which is certainly staked against an uncertain infinite. This is not so. Every gambler stakes a certainty to gain an uncertainty, and yet he stakes a finite certainty against a finite uncertainty without acting unreasonably. It is false to say there is infinite distance between the certain stake and the uncertain gain. There is in truth an infinity between the certainty of gain and the certainty of loss. But the uncertainty of gain is proportional to the certainty of the stake, according to the proportion of chances of gain and loss, and if therefore there are as many chances on one side as on the other, then the game is even. And thus the certainty of the venture is equal to the uncertainty of the winnings, so far is it from the truth that there is infinite distance between them. So that our argument is of infinite force, if we stake the finite in a game where there are equal chances of gain and loss, and the infinite is the winnings. This is demonstrable, and if men are capable of any truths, this is one. You will know at last that you have wagered on a certainty, an infinity, for which you have risked nothing.

We must live differently in the world, according to these different suppositions: First, that we could always remain in it. Second, that it is certain we cannot remain here long, and uncertain if we shall remain here an hour. This last supposition is the case with us. By the law of probabilities you are bound to take pains to seek the truth; for if you die without accepting the true source of all things, then you are lost.

We know truth, not only by our reason, but also by our heart; and it is from this last that we know first principles; and reason, which has nothing to do with it, tries in vain to combat them. The skeptics who desire only truth and certainty labor in vain. We know that we do not dream, although it is impossible to prove it by reason, and this inability shows only the weakness of our reason, and not, as they declare, the general uncertainty of our knowledge. For our knowledge of first principles, such as space, time, motion, number, is as distinct as any principle derived from reason. And reason must lean necessarily on this instinctive knowledge of the heart, and must rely on it in every process. We *feel* principles, we *infer* propositions, both with certainty, though by different ways. It is as useless and absurd for reason to demand from the heart proofs of first principles before it will admit them, as it would be for the heart to ask from reason a feeling of all the propositions demonstrated before accepting them.

Damaris Cudworth Masham

A NATURAL INSCRIPTION

Religion being (as I shall take it at present for granted) the only sufficient ground or solid support of virtue; for the belief of a Superior, Omnipotent Being, inspecting our actions, and who will reward or punish us accordingly, is in all men's apprehensions the strangest, and in truth the only stable and irresistible argument for submitting our desires to a constant regulation, wherein it is that virtue does consist.

It is yet true that many who have learned, and who well remember long catechisms, with all their pretended *proofs*, are so far from having that knowledge which rational creatures ought to have of a religion they profess to believe they can only be saved by, as that they are not able to say, either what this religion does consist in, or why it is they believe it; and are so little instructed by their catechisms, as that, oftentimes, they understand not so much as the very terms they have learned in them: And more often find the proportions therein contained, so short in the information of their ignorance, or so unintelligible, to their apprehensions, or so plainly contradictory of the most obvious dictates of common sense, that religion (for the which they never think of looking beyond these systems) appears to them indeed a thing not built upon, or defensible by reason. In consequence of which *opinion*—the weakest attacks made against it—must render such persons (at the least) wavering in their belief of it; Thus, those precepts of virtue, which they have received, are, in a time wherein skepticism and vice, pass for wit and gallantry, necessarily brought under the suspicion of having no solid foundation, and the recommenders thereof, either of ignorance, or artifice.

It is indeed only a rational fear of God, and desire to approve ourselves to him, that will teach us in all things, uniformly to live as becomes our reasonable nature; to enable us to do which, must be the great business and end of a religion which comes from God.

The natural tendency of which things being to persuade men that they may please God at a cheaper rate than by the denial of their appetites, and the mortifying of their irregular affections, these misrepresentations of a pretended divine revelation have been highly prejudicial to morality. And, thereby, have also been a great occasion of skepticism; for the obligation to virtue being loosened, men easily become vicious, which when once they are, the remorse of their consciences bringing them to desire that there should be no future reckoning for their actions; and even that there should be no God to take any cognizance of them; they often come (in some degree at least) to be persuaded both of the one, and the other of these. And thus, many times, there are but a few steps between a zealous bigot, and an infidel to all religion.

Skepticism, or rather *infidelity,* is the proper disease our age, and has proceeded from diverse causes; but be the remoter or original ones what they will, it could never have prevailed as it has done, had not parents very generally contributed thereto, either by negligence of their children's instruction; or instructing them very ill in respect of religion.

It might indeed seem strange to one who had no experience of mankind, that people (however neglected in their education) could, when they came to years of judgment, be to such a degree wanting to themselves, as not to seek right information concerning truths of so great moment to them not to be ignorant of, or mistaken in, as are those of religion. Yet such is the wretched inconsideration natural to most men, that (in fact) it is no uncommon thing at all to see men live

Edited from *Occasional Thoughts*, 1705, which is now in the public domain.

day after day, in the pursuit of their inclinations, without ever exerting their reason to any other purpose than the gratification of their passions; and no wonder can it then be if they give in to the belief, or take up with a blind persuasion of such opinions as they see to be most in credit; and which will also the best suit their turn?

Absolute atheism does no doubt the best serve they who live as if there was no God in the World; but how far so great nonsense as this, has been able to obtain, is not easy to say. To me it appears (in that those who will expose themselves to argue against the existence of a God, do rarely venture to produce any hypothesis of their own to be fairly examined and compared with that which they reject. But that their opposition to a Deity, consists only in objections which may as well be retorted upon themselves, and which at best prove nothing but the shortness of human understanding) to me, I say, it appears probable that the greatest part of atheistic reasoners do rather desire, and seek to be atheists, than that in reality they are so. Men, who are accustomed to believe without any evidence of reason for what they believe, are, it is likely, more in earnest in this wild opinion: And in all appearance very many there are among us of such as a learned man calls *enthusiastic atheists,* namely, who deny the existence of an invisible, omniscient, omnipotent, first cause of all things.

But it being sufficiently obvious that want of instruction concerning religion does in a skeptical age dispose men to skepticism and infidelity, which often terminates in downright atheism, let us see whether or not all irrational instruction in regard of religion, has not the same tendency.

It is as undeniable as the difference between men's being in and out of their wits, that reason ought to be to rational creatures the guide of their belief: That is to say, that their assent to anything ought to be governed by that proof of its truth, whereof reason is the judge, be it either argument or authority, for in both cases reason must determine our assent according to the validity of the ground it finds it built on. *Reason* being here understood as that faculty in us which discovers, by the intervention of intermediate ideas, what connection those in the proposition have one with another whether *certain*, *probable*, or *none at all*, according to which we ought to regulate our assent. If we do not so, we degrade ourselves from being rational creatures; and deprive ourselves of the only guide God has given us for our conduct in our actions and opinions.

Authority yet is not hereby so subjected to reason, as that a proposition which we see not the truth of, may not nevertheless be rationally assented to by us. For although reason cannot from the evidence of the thing itself induce our assent to any proposition, where we cannot perceive the connection of the ideas there contained, yet if it appears that such a proposition was truly revealed by God, nothing can be more rational than to believe it, since we know that God can neither deceive, nor be deceived; that there are truths above our conception, and that God may (if he so pleases) communicate these to us by supernatural revelation.

The part of reason then, in regard of such a proposition as this, is, only to examine whether it be indeed a divine revelation: which should reason not attest to the truth of; it is then evidently irrational to give, or require assent to it as being so. And as plainly irrational must it be to give, or require assent to anything as a divine revelation, which is evidently contrary to reason, no less being implied than that God has made us so as to see clearly that to be a truth, which is yet a falsehood, which, were it so, would make the testimony of our reason useless to us, and thereby destroy also the credit of all revelation, for no stronger proof can be had of the truth of any revelation than the evidence of our reason that it is a revelation.

Now if the Christian religion be very often represented as teaching doctrines clearly contrary to reason, or as exacting belief of what we can neither perceive the truth of, nor do find to be revealed by Christ or his Apostles, and (what is still more) that this pretended divine religion does even consist in such a belief as this, so that a man cannot be a Christian without believing what he neither from arguments or authority has any ground for believing, what must the natural consequence of this be upon all whoever so little consult their reason, when in riper years they come to reflect upon, but to make them recall, and suspend, at least, their assent to the truth of a religion that appears to them thus irrational? *An irrational religion can never rationally be conceived to come from God.*

And if men once come to call in question such doctrines as (though but upon slender grounds for it) they had received for unquestionable truths of religion, they are ordinarily more likely to continue skeptics, or to proceed to an entire disbelief of this religion, than to take occasion to make a just search after its truth. From what has been said, I think it does appear, that irrational instruction concerning religion, as well as want of instruction, disposes to skepticism; and this being so, what wonder can it be that skepticism having once become fashionable, should continue so? The uninstructed and the ill-instructed, making by so great odds the majority. For those who have no religion themselves do not often take care that others should have any; and they who adhere to a misgrounded persuasion concerning religion, retaining a reverence for their teachers, do, in consequence, commonly presume that their children cannot be better taught than they have been before them. Instead of having their reasonable enquiries satisfied and encouraged, children are ordinarily rebuked for making any; from which, not daring in a short time to question anything that is taught them in reference to religion, they are brought to say that they *do believe* whatever their teachers tell them they must believe; but in truth they remain in an ignorant unbelief, which exposes them to be seduced by the most pitiful arguments of the atheistical, or of such as are disbelievers of revealed religion.

The foundation of all religion is the belief of a God, or of a maker and governor of the world; the evidence of which, being visible in every thing, and the general profession having usually stamped it with awe upon children's minds, they ought perhaps most commonly to be supposed to believe this, rather than have doubts raised in them by going about to prove it to them: because those who are incapable of long deductions of reason, or attending to a train of arguments, not finding the force when offered to prove what they had always taken for a clear, and obvious truth, would be rather taught thereby to suspect that a truth which they had looked on as unquestionable, might rationally be doubted of, than be any ways confirmed in the belief of it. But if any doubts concerning the existence of God do arise in their minds, they can be discovered by discoursing with them: such doubts should always be endeavored to be removed by the most solid arguments of which children are capable. Nor should they ever be rebuked for having those doubts, since not giving leave to look into the grounds of asserting any truth, whatever it be, can never be the way to establish that truth in any rational mind; but, on the contrary, must be very likely to raise a suspicion that it is not well grounded.

The belief of a Deity being entertained, what should be first taught us? It is certain that what we are in the first place concerned to know is that which is necessary to our salvation; and it is as certain that whatever God has made necessary to our salvation, we are at the same time capable of knowing. All instruction therefore which obtrudes upon anyone as necessary to their salvation, what they cannot understand or see the evidence of, is to that person, wrong instruction; and when any such unintelligible, or unevident propositions are delivered to children as if they were so visible truths that a reason or proof of them was not to be demanded by them, what effect can this produce in their minds but to teach them to silence, and to suppress their reason; from which they have afterwards no principle of virtue left, and their practices, as well as opinions, must become (as is the usual consequence) exposed to the conduct of their own, or other men's fancies. The existence of God being acknowledged a truth so early received by us, and so evident to our reason, that it looks like natural inscription. The authority of that revelation by which God has made known his will to men is to be firmly established in people's minds upon its clearest, and most rational evidence; and consequentially they are then to be referred to the scriptures themselves, to see what it is that God requires of them to *believe* and *to do*; the great obligation they are under diligently to study these divine oracles being duly represented to them. But to exhort any one to search the scriptures to the end of seeing what God requires of him, before he is satisfied that the scriptures are a revelation from God, cannot be rational, since anyone saying that the scriptures are God's Word, cannot satisfy a rational and inquisitive mind that they are so; further, that the books of the Old and New Testament were dictated by the Spirit of God, is not a self evident proposition, but a truth that demands to be made out, before it can be rationally assented to.

Friedrich Nietzsche

THE END OF AN IDEA

Have you ever heard of the madman who on a bright morning lighted a lantern and ran to the market-place calling out unceasingly: "I seek God! I seek God!"

As there were many people standing about who did not believe in God, he caused a great deal of amusement. "Why! is he lost?" said one. "Has he strayed away like a child?" said another. Or "does he keep himself hidden?" "Is he afraid of us?" "Has he taken a sea-voyage?" "Has he emigrated?" the people cried out laughingly.

The insane man jumped into their midst and transfixed them with his glances. "Where is God gone?" he called out. "I mean to tell you! We have killed him,—you and I! We are all his murderers! But how have we done it? How were we able to drink up the sea? Who gave us the sponge to wipe away the whole horizon? What did we do when we loosened this earth from its sun? Whither does it now move? Whither do we move? Away from all suns? Do we not dash on unceasingly? Backwards, sideways, forwards, in all directions? Is there still an above and below? Do we not stray, as through infinite nothingness? Does not empty space breathe upon us? Has it not become colder? Does not night come on continually, darker and darker? Shall we not have to light lanterns in the morning? Do we not hear the noise of the grave-diggers who are burying God? Do we not smell the divine putrefaction?—for even Gods putrefy! God is dead! God remains dead! And we have killed him! How shall we console ourselves, the most murderous of all murderers? The holiest and the mightiest that the world has hitherto possessed, has bled to death under our knife,—who will wipe the blood from us? With what water could we cleanse ourselves? Is not the magnitude of this deed too great for us? Shall we not ourselves have to become Gods, merely to seem worthy of it? There never was a greater event, and on account of it, all who are born after us belong to a higher history than any history hitherto!"

Here the madman was silent and looked again at his hearers; they also were silent and looked at him in surprise. At last he threw his lantern on the ground, so that it broke in pieces and was extinguished. "I come too early," he then said, "I am not yet at the right time. This prodigious event is still on its way, and is travelling, it has not yet reached men's ears. Lightning and thunder need time, the light of the stars needs time, deeds need time, even after they are done, to be seen and heard. This deed is as yet further from them than the furthest star, and yet they have done it!"

It is further stated that the madman made his way into different churches on the same day, and there intoned his Requiem *aeternam deo* [eternal god]. When led out and called to account, he always gave the reply: "What are these churches now, if they are not the tombs and monuments of God?"

The most important of more recent events—that "God is dead," that the belief in the Christian God has become unworthy of belief—already begins to cast its first shadows over Europe. To the few at least whose eye, whose suspecting glance is strong enough and subtle enough for this drama, some sun seems to have set, some old, profound confidence seems to have changed into doubt: our old world must seem to them daily more darksome, distrustful, strange and *old.*

In the main, however, one may say that the event itself is far too great, too remote, too much beyond most people's power of apprehension, for one to suppose that so much as the report of it

Edited from *The Gay Science*. Translated by Thomas Common, 1910, which is now in the public domain.

could have reached them; not to speak of many who already knew what had taken place, and what must all collapse now that this belief had been undermined—because so much was built upon it, so much rested on it, and had become one with it: for example, our entire European morality.

This lengthy, vast and uninterrupted process of crumbling, destruction, ruin and overthrow which is now imminent: who has realized it sufficiently today to have to stand up as the teacher and herald of such a tremendous logic of terror, as the prophet of a period of gloom and eclipse, the like of which has probably never taken place on earth before?

Even we, the born riddle-readers, who wait as it were on the mountains posted between today and tomorrow, and encircled by their contradiction, we, the firstlings and premature children of the coming century, into whose sight especially the shadows which must forthwith envelop Europe should already have come—how is it that even we, without genuine sympathy for this period of gloom, contemplate its advent without any personal solicitude or fear? Are we still, perhaps, too much under the immediate effects of the event—and are these effects, especially as regards ourselves, perhaps the reverse of what was to be expected—not at all sad and depressing, but rather like a new and indescribable variety of light, happiness, relief, enlivenment, encouragement, and dawning day?

In fact, we philosophers and *free spirits* feel ourselves irradiated as by a new dawn by the report that the *old God is dead*; our hearts overflow with gratitude, astonishment, presentiment and expectation. At last the horizon seems open once more, granting even that it is not bright; our ships can at last put out to sea in face of every danger; every hazard is again permitted to the discerner; the sea, our sea, again lies open before us; perhaps never before did such an *open sea* exist.

William K. Clifford

THE ETHICS OF BELIEF

A ship-owner was about to send to sea an emigrant ship. He knew that she was old, and not over-well built; that she had seen many seas and climes, and often had needed repairs. Doubts had been suggested to him that possibly she was not seaworthy. These doubts preyed upon his mind, and made him unhappy; he thought that perhaps he ought to have her thoroughly overhauled and refitted, even though this should put him at great expense. Before the ship sailed, however, he succeeded in overcoming these melancholy reflections. He said to himself that she had gone safely through so many voyages and weathered so many storms that it was idle to suppose she would not come safely home from this trip also. He would put his trust in Providence, which could hardly fail to protect all these unhappy families that were leaving their fatherland to seek for better times elsewhere. He would dismiss from his mind all ungenerous suspicions about the honesty of builders and contractors. In such ways he acquired a sincere and comfortable conviction that his vessel was thoroughly safe and seaworthy; he watched her departure with a light heart, and benevolent wishes for the success of the exiles in their strange new home that was to be; and he got his insurance-money when she went down in mid-ocean and told no tales.

What shall we say of him? Surely this, that he was verily guilty of the death of those men. It is admitted that he did sincerely believe in the soundness of his ship; but the sincerity of his conviction can in no wise help him, because he had no right to believe on such evidence as was before him. He had acquired his belief not by honestly earning it in patient investigation, but by stifling his doubts. And although in the end he may have felt so sure about it that he could not think otherwise, yet inasmuch as he had knowingly and willingly worked himself into that frame of mind, he must be held responsible for it.

Let us alter the case a little, and suppose that the ship was not unsound after all; that she made her voyage safely, and many others after it. Will that diminish the guilt of her owner? Not one jot. When an action is once done, it is right or wrong for ever; no accidental failure of its good or evil fruits can possibly alter that. The man would not have been innocent, he would only have been not found out. The question of right or wrong has to do with the *origin* of his belief, not the matter of it; not what it was, but how he got it; not whether it turned out to be true or false, but whether he had a right to believe on such evidence as was before him.

There was once an island in which some of the inhabitants professed a religion teaching neither the doctrine of original sin nor that of eternal punishment. A suspicion got abroad that the professors of this religion had made use of unfair means to get their doctrines taught to children. They were accused of wresting the laws of their country in such a way as to remove children from the care of their natural and legal guardians; and even of stealing them away and keeping them concealed from their friends and relations. A certain number of men formed themselves into a society for the purpose of agitating the public about this matter. They published grave accusations against individual citizens of the highest position and character, and did all in their power to injure these citizens in their exercise of their professions. So great was the noise they made, that a Commission was appointed to investigate the facts; but after the Commission had carefully inquired into all the evidence that could be got, it appeared that the accused were innocent. Not only had they been accused on insufficient evidence, but the evidence of their innocence was such

Edited from *Contemporary Review*, 1876, which is now in the public domain.

as the agitators might easily have obtained, if they had attempted a fair inquiry. After these disclosures the inhabitants of that country looked upon the members of the agitating society, not only as persons whose judgment was to be distrusted, but also as no longer to be counted honorable men. For although they had sincerely and conscientiously believed in the charges they had made, yet they had no right to believe on such evidence as was before them. Their sincere convictions, instead of being honestly earned by patient inquiring, were stolen by listening to the voice of prejudice and passion.

Let us vary this case also, and suppose, other things remaining as before, that a still more accurate investigation proved the accused to have been really guilty. Would this make any difference in the guilt of the accusers? Clearly not; the question is not whether their belief was true or false, but whether they entertained it on wrong grounds. They would no doubt say, "Now you see that we were right after all; next time perhaps you will believe us." And they might be believed, but they would not thereby become honorable men. They would not be innocent, they would only be not found out. Every one of them, if he chose to examine himself *in foro conscientiae* [in his conscience], would know that he had acquired and nourished a belief, when he had no right to believe on such evidence as was before him; and therein he would know that he had done a wrong thing.

It may be said, however, that in both these supposed cases it is not the belief which is judged to be wrong, but the action following upon it. The ship-owner might say, "I am perfectly certain that my ship is sound, but still I feel it my duty to have her examined, before trusting the lives of so many people to her." And it might be said to the agitator, "However convinced you were of the justice of your cause and the truth of your convictions, you ought not to have made a public attack upon any man's character until you had examined the evidence on both sides with the utmost patience and care."

In the first place, let us admit that, so far as it goes, this view of the case is right and necessary; right, because even when a man's belief is so fixed that he cannot think otherwise, he still has a choice in the action suggested by it, and so cannot escape the duty of investigating on the ground of the strength of his convictions; and necessary, because those who are not yet capable of controlling their feelings and thoughts must have a plain rule dealing with overt acts.

But this being premised as necessary, it becomes clear that it is not sufficient, and that our previous judgment is required to supplement it. For it is not possible so to sever the belief from the action it suggests as to condemn the one without condemning the other. No man holding a strong belief on one side of a question, or even wishing to hold a belief on one side, can investigate it with such fairness and completeness as if he were really in doubt and unbiased; so that the existence of a belief not founded on fair inquiry unfits a man for the performance of this necessary duty.

Nor is it that truly a belief at all which has not some influence upon the actions of him who holds it. He who truly believes that which prompts him to an action has looked upon the action to lust after it, he has committed it already in his heart. If a belief is not realized immediately in open deeds, it is stored up for the guidance of the future. It goes to make a part of that aggregate of beliefs which is the link between sensation and action at every moment of all our lives, and which is so organized and compacted together that no part of it can be isolated from the rest, but every new addition modifies the structure of the whole. No real belief, however trifling and fragmentary it may seem, is ever truly insignificant; it prepares us to receive more of its like, confirms those which resembled it before, and weakens others; and so gradually it lays a stealthy train in our inmost thoughts, which may someday explode into overt action, and leave its stamp upon our character for ever.

And no one man's belief is in any case a private matter which concerns himself alone. Our lives are guided by that general conception of the course of things which has been created by society for social purposes. Our words, our phrases, our forms and processes and modes of thought, are common property, fashioned and perfected from age to age; an heirloom which every succeeding generation inherits as a precious deposit and a sacred trust to be handled on to the next one, not unchanged but enlarged and purified, with some clear marks of its proper handiwork. Into this, for good or ill, is woven every belief of every man who has speech of his fellows. An awful privilege, and an awful responsibility, that we should help to create the world in which posterity will live.

In the two supposed cases which have been considered, it has been judged wrong to believe on insufficient evidence, or to nourish belief by suppressing doubts and avoiding investigation. The reason of this judgment is not far to seek: it is that in both these cases the belief held by one man was of great importance to other men. But forasmuch as no belief held by one man, however seemingly trivial the belief, and however obscure the believer, is ever actually insignificant or without its effect on the fate of mankind, we have no choice but to extend our judgment to all cases of belief whatever. Belief, that sacred faculty which prompts the decisions of our will, and knits into harmonious working all the compacted energies of our being, is ours not for ourselves but for humanity. It is rightly used on truths which have been established by long experience and waiting toil, and which have stood in the fierce light of free and fearless questioning. Then it helps to bind men together, and to strengthen and direct their common action. It is desecrated when given to unproved and unquestioned statements, for the solace and private pleasure of the believer; to add a tinsel splendor to the plain straight road of our life and display a bright mirage beyond it; or even to drown the common sorrows of our kind by a self-deception which allows them not only to cast down, but also to degrade us. Whoso would deserve well of his fellows in this matter will guard the purity of his beliefs with a very fanaticism of jealous care, lest at any time it should rest on an unworthy object, and catch a stain which can never be wiped away.

It is not only the leader of men, statesmen, philosopher, or poet, that owes this bounden duty to mankind. Every rustic who delivers in the village alehouse his slow, infrequent sentences, may help to kill or keep alive the fatal superstitions which clog his race. Every hard-worked wife of an artisan may transmit to her children beliefs which shall knit society together, or rend it in pieces. No simplicity of mind, no obscurity of station, can escape the universal duty of questioning all that we believe.

It is true that this duty is a hard one, and the doubt which comes out of it is often a very bitter thing. It leaves us bare and powerless where we thought that we were safe and strong. To know all about anything is to know how to deal with it under all circumstances. We feel much happier and more secure when we think we know precisely what to do, no matter what happens, than when we have lost our way and do not know where to turn. And if we have supposed ourselves to know all about anything, and to be capable of doing what is fit in regard to it, we naturally do not like to find that we are really ignorant and powerless, that we have to begin again at the beginning, and try to learn what the thing is and how it is to be dealt with—if indeed anything can be learnt about it. It is the sense of power attached to a sense of knowledge that makes men desirous of believing, and afraid of doubting.

This sense of power is the highest and best of pleasures when the belief on which it is founded is a true belief, and has been fairly earned by investigation. For then we may justly feel that it is common property, and hold good for others as well as for ourselves. Then we may be glad, not that I have learned secrets by which I am safer and stronger, but that we men have got mastery over more of the world; and we shall be strong, not for ourselves but in the name of Man and his strength. But if the belief has been accepted on insufficient evidence, the pleasure is a stolen one. Not only does it deceive ourselves by giving us a sense of power which we do not really possess, but it is sinful, because it is stolen in defiance of our duty to mankind. That duty is to guard ourselves from such beliefs as from pestilence, which may shortly master our own body and then spread to the rest of the town. What would be thought of one who, for the sake of a sweet fruit, should deliberately run the risk of delivering a plague upon his family and his neighbors?

And, as in other such cases, it is not the risk only which has to be considered; for a bad action is always bad at the time when it is done, no matter what happens afterwards. Every time we let ourselves believe for unworthy reasons, we weaken our powers of self-control, of doubting, of judicially and fairly weighing evidence. We all suffer severely enough from the maintenance and support of false beliefs and the fatally wrong actions which they lead to, and the evil born when one such belief is entertained is great and wide. But a greater and wider evil arises when the credulous character is maintained and supported, when a habit of believing for unworthy reasons is fostered and made permanent. If I steal money from any person, there may be no harm done from the mere transfer of possession; he may not feel the loss, or it may prevent him from using the money badly. But I cannot help doing this great wrong towards Man, that I make myself dishonest. What hurts society is not that it should lose its property, but that it should become a den of thieves, for then it must cease to be society. This is why we ought not to do evil, that good may come; for at any rate this great evil has come, that we have done evil and are made wicked thereby. In like manner, if I let myself believe anything on insufficient evidence, there may be no great harm done by the mere belief; it may be true after all, or I may never have occasion to exhibit it in outward acts. But I cannot help doing this great wrong towards Man, that I make myself credulous. The danger to society is not merely that it should believe wrong things, though that is great enough; but that it should become credulous, and lose the habit of testing things and inquiring into them; for then it must sink back into savagery.

The harm which is done by credulity in a man is not confined to the fostering of a credulous character in others, and consequent support of false beliefs. Habitual want of care about what I believe leads to habitual want of care in others about the truth of what is told to me. Men speak the truth of one another when each reveres the truth in his own mind and in the other's mind; but how shall my friend revere the truth in my mind when I myself am careless about it, when I believe things because I want to believe them, and because they are comforting and pleasant? Will he not learn to cry, "Peace," to me, when there is no peace? By such a course I shall surround myself with a thick atmosphere of falsehood and fraud, and in that I must live. It may matter little to me, in my cloud-castle of sweet illusions and darling lies; but it matters much to Man that I have made my neighbors ready to deceive. The credulous man is father to the liar and the cheat; he lives in the bosom of this his family, and it is no marvel if he should become even as they are. So closely are our duties knit together, that whoso shall keep the whole law, and yet offend in one point, he is guilty of all.

To sum up: *it is wrong always, everywhere, and for anyone, to believe anything upon insufficient evidence.*

If a man, holding a belief which he was taught in childhood or persuaded of afterwards, keeps down and pushes away any doubts which arise about it in his mind, purposely avoids the reading of books and the company of men that call into question or discuss it, and regards as impious those questions which cannot easily be asked without disturbing it—the life of that man is one long sin against mankind.

Inquiry into the evidence of a doctrine is not to be made once for all, and then taken as finally settled. It is never lawful to stifle a doubt; for either it can be honestly answered by means of the inquiry already made, or else it proves that the inquiry was not complete.

"But," says one, "I am a busy man; I have no time for the long course of study which would be necessary to make me in any degree a competent judge of certain questions, or even able to understand the nature of the arguments."

Then he should have no time to believe.

William James

THE WILL TO BELIEVE

I have brought with me tonight something like a sermon on justification by faith to read to you—I mean an essay in justification *of* faith, a defense of our right to adopt a believing attitude in religious matters, in spite of the fact that our merely logical intellect may not have been coerced.

Let us give the name of *hypothesis* to anything that may be proposed to our belief; and just as the electricians speak of live and dead wires, let us speak of any hypothesis as either *live* or *dead.* A live hypothesis is one which appeals as a real possibility to him to whom it is proposed. If I ask you to believe in the Mahdi, the notion makes no electric connection with your nature—it refuses to scintillate with any credibility at all. As an hypothesis it is completely dead. To an Arab, however (even if he be not one of the Madhi's followers), the hypothesis is among the mind's possibilities: it is alive. This shows that deadness and liveness in an hypothesis are *not intrinsic* properties, but *relations* to the individual thinker. They are measured by his willingness to act. The maximum of liveness in hypothesis means willingness to act irrevocably. Practically, that means belief; but there is some believing tendency wherever there is willingness to act at all.

Next, let us call the decision between two hypotheses an *option.* Options may be of several kinds. They may be (1) *living* or *dead*; (2) *forced* or *avoidable*; (3) *momentous* or *trivial*; and for our purpose we may call an option a *genuine* option when it is of the forced, living and momentous kind.

1. A *living option* is one in which both hypotheses are live ones. If I say to you: "Be a theosophist or be a Mohammedan," it is probably a dead option, because for you neither hypothesis is likely to be alive. But if I say "Be an agnostic or be a Christian," it is otherwise: trained as you are, each hypothesis makes some appeal, however small, to your belief.

2. Next, if I say to you: "Choose between going out with your umbrella or without it," I do not offer you a genuine option, for it is not forced. You can easily avoid it by not going out at all. Similarly, if I say, "Either love me or hate me," "Either call my theory true or call it false," your option is avoidable. You may remain indifferent to me, neither loving nor hating, and you may decline to offer any judgment as to my theory. But if I say, "Either accept this truth or go without it," I put on you a forced option, for there is no standing place outside of the alternative. Every dilemma based on a complete logical disjunction, with no possibility of not choosing, is an option of this forced kind.

3. Finally, if I were Dr. Nansen and proposed to you to join my North Pole expedition, your option would be momentous; for this would probably be your only similar opportunity, and your choice now would either exclude you from the North Pole sort of immortality altogether or put at least the chance of it into your hands. He who refuses to embrace a unique opportunity loses the prize as surely as if he tried and failed. *Per contra* [on the other hand], the option is trivial when the opportunity is not unique, when the stake is insignificant, or when the decision is reversible if it later prove unwise. Such trivial options abound in the scientific life. A chemist finds an hypothesis live enough to spend a year in its verification: he believes in it to that extent. But if his experiments prove inconclusive either way, he is quit for his loss of time, no vital harm being done.

The next matter to consider is the actual psychology of human opinion. When we look at certain facts, it seems as if our passional and volitional nature lay at the root of all our convictions.

Edited from *New World*, June, 1896, which is now in the public domain.

When we look at others, it seems as if they could do nothing when the intellect had once said its say. Let us take the latter facts up first.

Does it not seem preposterous on the very face of it to talk of our opinions being modifiable at will? Can our will either help or hinder our intellect in its perceptions of truth? Can we, by just willing it, believe that Abraham Lincoln's existence is a myth? Can we, by any effort of our will, or by any strength of wish that it were true, believe ourselves well and about when we are roaring with rheumatism in bed, or feel certain that the sum of the two one-dollar bills in our pocket must be a hundred dollars? We can *say* any of these things, but we are absolutely impotent to believe them; and of just such things is the whole fabric of the truths that we do believe in made up—*matters of fact*, immediate or remote, as Hume said, and *relations between ideas*, which are either there or not there for us if we see them so, and which if not there cannot be put there by any action of our own.

In Pascal's *Thoughts* there is a celebrated passage known in literature as Pascal's wager. In it he tries to force us into Christianity by reasoning as if our concern with truth resembled our concern with the stakes in a game of chance. Translated freely his words are these: "You must either believe or not believe that God is—which will you do? Your human reason cannot say. A game is going on between you and the nature of things which at the day of judgment will bring out either heads or tails. Weigh what your gains and your losses would be if you should stake all you have on heads, or God's existence: If you win in such case, you gain eternal beatitude; if you lose, you lose nothing at all."

You probably feel that when religious faith expresses itself thus, in the language of the gaming-table, it is put to its last trumps. Surely Pascal's own personal belief is but an argument for others, a last desperate snatch at a weapon against the hardness of the unbelieving heart. It is evident that unless there is some pre-existing tendency to believe in masses and holy water, the option offered to the will by Pascal is not a living option. No tendency to act on it exists in us to any degree.

The talk of believing by our volition seems, then, from one point of view, simply silly. From another point of view it is worse than silly, it is vile. When one turns to the magnificent edifice of the physical sciences, and sees how it was reared; what thousands of disinterested moral lives of men lie buried in its mere foundations; what patience and postponement, what choking down of preference, what submission to the icy laws of outer fact are wrought into its very stones and mortar; how absolutely impersonal it stands in its vast augustness—then how besotted and contemptible seems every little sentimentalist who comes blowing his voluntary smoke-wreaths, and pretending to decide things from out of his private dream! Can we wonder if those bred in the rugged and manly school of science should feel like spewing such subjectivism out of their mouths? The whole system of loyalties which grow up in the schools of science go dead against its toleration; so that it is only natural that those who have caught the scientific fever should pass over to the opposite extreme, and write sometimes as if the incorruptibly truthful intellect ought positively to prefer bitterness and unacceptableness to the heart in its cup. And that delicious *enfant terrible* William Clifford writes: "It is wrong always, everywhere, and for anyone, to believe anything upon insufficient evidence."

All this strikes one as healthy, even when expressed, as by Clifford, with somewhat too much of robust pathos in the voice. Free-will and simple wishing do seem, in the matter of our credences, to be only fifth wheels to the coach. Yet if any one should thereupon assume that intellectual insight is what remains after wish and will and sentimental preference have taken wing, or that pure reason is what then settles our opinions, he would fly quite as directly in the teeth of the facts.

It is only our already dead hypotheses that our willing nature is unable to bring to life again. But what has made them dead for us is for the most part a previous action of our willing nature of an antagonistic kind. When I say "willing nature," I do not mean only such deliberate volitions as may have set up habits of belief that we cannot now escape from—I mean all such factors of belief as fear and hope, prejudice and passion, imitation and partisanship. As a matter of fact we find ourselves believing, we hardly know how or why. Here in this room, we all of us believe in molecules and the conservation of energy, in democracy and necessary progress, all for no reasons worthy of the name. We see into these matters with no more inner clearness, and probably with much less, than any disbeliever in them might possess. His unconventionality would probably have some grounds to show for its conclusions; but for us, not insight, but the *prestige* of the opinions, is what makes the spark shoot from them and light up our sleeping magazines of faith. Our reason is quite satisfied, in nine hundred and ninety-nine cases out of every thousand of us, if it can find a few arguments that will do to recite in case our credulity is criticized by someone else. Our faith is faith in some one else's faith, and in the greatest matters this is most the case.

Our belief in truth itself, for instance, that there is a truth, and that our minds and it are made for each other—what is it but a *passionate affirmation of desire*, in which our social system backs us up? We want to have a truth; we want to believe that our experiments and studies and discussions must put us in a continually better and better position towards it; and on this line we agree to fight out our thinking lives.

Evidently, then, our non-intellectual nature does influence our convictions. There are passional tendencies and volitions which run before and others which come after belief, and it is only the latter that are too late for the fair; and they are not too late when the previous passional work has been already in their own direction. Pascal's argument, instead of being powerless, then seems a regular clincher, and is the last stroke needed to make our faith in masses and holy water complete. The state of things is evidently far from simple; and pure insight and logic, whatever they might do ideally, are not the only things that really do produce our creeds.

The thesis I defend is this: Our passional nature not only lawfully may, but must, decide an option between propositions, whenever it is a genuine option that cannot by its nature be decided on intellectual grounds; for to say, under such circumstances, "Do not decide, but leave the question open," is itself a passional decision—just like deciding yes or no—and is attended with the same risk of losing the truth.

One more point, small but important, and our preliminaries are done. There are two ways of looking at our duty in the matter of opinion—ways entirely different, and yet ways about whose difference the theory of knowledge seems hitherto to have shown very little concern. *We must know the truth;* and *we must avoid error*—these are our first and great commandments as would-be knowers.

Believe truth! Shun these, we see, are two materially different laws; and by choosing between them we may end by coloring differently our whole intellectual life. We may regard the chase for truth as paramount, and the avoidance of error as secondary; or we may, on the other hand, treat the avoidance of error as more imperative, and let truth take its chance. Clifford, in the instructive passage which I have quoted, exhorts us to the latter course. Believe nothing, he tells us, keep your mind in suspense forever, rather than by closing it on insufficient evidence incur the awful risk of believing lies. You, on the other hand, may think that the risk of being in error is a very small matter when compared with the blessings of real knowledge, and be ready to be duped many times in your investigation rather than postpone indefinitely the chance of guessing true. I myself find it impossible to go with Clifford. We must remember that these feelings of our duty about either truth or error are in any case only expressions of our passional life. Biologically considered, our minds are as ready to grind out falsehood as veracity, and he who says, "Better go without belief forever than believe a lie!" merely shows his own preponderant private horror of becoming a dupe. He may be critical of many of his desires and fears, but this fear he slavishly obeys. He cannot imagine anyone questioning its binding force. For my own part, I have also a horror of being duped; but I can believe that worse things than being duped may happen to a man in this world: so Clifford's exhortation has to my ears a thoroughly fantastic sound. It is like a general informing his soldiers that it is better to keep out of battle forever than to risk a single wound. Not so are victories either over enemies or over nature gained. Our errors are surely not such awfully solemn things. In a world where we are so certain to incur them in spite of all our caution, a certain lightness of heart seems healthier than this excessive nervousness on their behalf.

Wherever the option between losing truth and gaining it is not momentous, we can throw the chance of *gaining truth* away, and at any rate save ourselves from any chance of *believing falsehood*, by not making up our minds at all till objective evidence has come. In scientific questions, this is almost always the case; and even in human affairs in general, the need of acting is seldom so urgent that a false belief to act on is better than no belief at all. Law courts, indeed, have to decide on the best evidence attainable for the moment, because a judge's duty is to make law as well as to ascertain it, and (as a learned judge once said to me) few cases are worth spending much time over: the great thing is to have them decided on *any* acceptable principle, and got out of the way. But in our dealings with objective nature we obviously are recorders, not makers, of the truth; and decisions for the mere sake of deciding promptly and getting on to the next business would be wholly out of place. Throughout the breadth of physical nature facts are what they are quite independently of us, and seldom is there any such hurry about them that the risks of being duped by believing a premature theory need be faced. The questions here are always trivial options, the hypotheses are hardly living (at any rate not living for us spectators), the choice between believing truth or falsehood is seldom forced. The attitude of skeptical balance is therefore the absolutely wise one if we would escape mistakes. What difference, indeed, does it make to most of us whether we have or have not a theory of the Röntgen rays, whether we believe or not in mind-stuff, or have a conviction about the causality of conscious states? It makes no difference. Such options are not forced on us. On every account it is better not to make them, but still keep weighing reasons *pro et contra* [for and against] with an indifferent hand.

Human passions, however, are stronger than technical rules. "*Le cœur a ses raisons*," as Pascal says, "*que la raison ne connaît point*" [The heart has its reasons which reason does not know]; and however indifferent to all but the bare rules of the game the umpire, the abstract intellect, may be, the concrete players who furnish him the materials to judge of are usually, each one of them, in love with some pet "live hypothesis" of his own. Let us agree, however, that wherever there is no forced option, the dispassionately judicial intellect with no pet hypothesis, saving us, as it does, from dupery at any rate, ought to be our ideal.

The question next arises: Are there not somewhere forced options in our *speculative* questions, and can we always wait with impunity till the coercive evidence shall have arrived? It seems *a priori* improbable that the truth should be so nicely adjusted to our needs and powers as that.

Religions differ so much in their accidents that in discussing the religious question we must make it very generic and broad. What then do we now mean by the religious hypothesis? Science says things are; morality says some things are better than other things; and religion says essentially two things: First, she says that the best things are the more eternal things, the overlapping things, the things in the universe that throw the last stone, so to speak, and say the final word. "Perfection is eternal"—this phrase of Charles Secrétan seems a good way of putting this first affirmation of religion, an affirmation which obviously cannot yet be verified scientifically at all. The second affirmation of religion is that we are better off even now if we believe her first affirmation to be true.

Now let us consider what the logical elements of this situation are in case the religious hypothesis in both its branches be really true. (Of course, we must admit that possibility at the outset. If we are to discuss the question at all, it must involve a living option. If for any of you religion be an hypothesis that cannot, by any living possibility be true, then you need go no farther. I speak to the "saving remnant" alone.) So proceeding, we see, first, that religion offers itself as a *momentous* option. We are supposed to gain, even now, by our belief, and to lose by our non-belief, a certain vital good. Secondly, religion is a *forced* option, so far as that good goes. We cannot escape the issue by remaining skeptical and waiting for more light, because, although we do avoid error in that way *if religion be untrue*, we lose the good, *if it be true*, just as certainly as if we positively chose to disbelieve. Skepticism, then, is not avoidance of option; it is option of a certain particular kind of risk. *Better risk loss of truth than chance of error*—that is your faith-vetoer's exact position. He is actively playing his stake as much as the believer is; he is backing the field against the religious hypothesis, just as the believer is backing the religious hypothesis against the field. To preach skepticism to us as a duty until "sufficient evidence" for religion be found, is tantamount therefore to telling us, when in presence of the religious hypothesis, that to yield to our fear of its being in error is wiser and better than to yield to our hope that it may be true. It is not intellect against all passions, then; it is only intellect with one passion laying down its law. And by what, forsooth, is the supreme wisdom of this passion warranted? Dupery for dupery, what proof is there that dupery through hope is so much worse than dupery through fear? I, for one, can see no proof; and I simply refuse obedience to the scientist's command to imitate his kind of option, in a case where my own stake is important enough to give me the right to choose my own form of risk. If religion be true and the evidence for it be still insufficient, I do not wish, by putting your extinguisher upon my nature (which feels to me as if it had after all some business in this matter), to forfeit my sole chance in life of getting upon the winning side—that chance depending, of course, on my willingness to run the risk of acting as if my passional need of taking the world religiously might be prophetic and right.

Now to most of us religion comes in a still further way that makes a veto on our active faith even more illogical. The more perfect and more eternal aspect of the universe is represented in our religions as having personal form. The universe is no longer a mere *It* to us, but a *Thou*, if we are religious; and any relation that may be possible from person to person might be possible here. For instance, although in one sense we are passive portions of the universe, in another we show a curious autonomy, as if we were small active centers on our own account. We feel, too, as if the appeal of religion to us were made to our own active good-will, as if evidence might be forever withheld from us unless we met the hypothesis half-way. This feeling, forced on us we know not whence, that by obstinately believing that there are gods (although not to do so would be so easy both for our logic and our life) we are doing the universe the deepest service we can, seems part of the living essence of the religious hypothesis. If the hypothesis *were* true in all its parts, including this one, then pure intellectualism, with its veto on our making willing advances, would be an absurdity; and some participation of our sympathetic nature would be logically required. I, therefore, for one, cannot see my way to accepting the agnostic rules for truth-seeking, or willfully agree to keep my willing nature out of the game. I cannot do so for this plain reason, that a rule of thinking which would absolutely prevent me from acknowledging certain kinds of truth if those kinds of truth were really there, would be an irrational rule. That for me is the long and short of the formal logic of the situation, no matter what the kinds of truth might materially be.

The *freedom to believe* can only cover *living options* which the intellect of the individual cannot by itself resolve; and living options never seem absurdities to him who has them to consider. Indeed we *may* wait if we will—I hope you do not think that I am denying that—but if we do so, we do so at our peril as much as if we believed. In either case we *act*, taking our life in our hands. No one of us ought to issue vetoes to the other, nor should we bandy words of abuse. We ought, on the contrary, delicately and profoundly to respect one another's mental freedom—then only shall we bring about the intellectual republic; then only shall we have that spirit of inner tolerance without which all our outer tolerance is soulless, and which is empiricism's glory; then only shall we live and let live, in speculative as well as in practical things.

Part Six: Mind and Body

Introduction

If asked, most people would probably say that they have both a brain and a mind. If pressed for a more complete answer, someone might say that her brain is a physical object, but her mind is a non-physical object. Further probing might elicit other nuggets of belief: "I am *conscious* of my existence"; "I have *sensations* of physical objects"; "I *see* colors and *hear* sounds"; "The physical world sometimes *causes* me to experience pain"; "I can usually get my body to do what I want, as long as it isn't physically impossible—for example, I can't flap my arms and fly like a bird, although that would be neat."

The philosophical theory that humans have a *mind* (some philosophers use the terms "soul" or "spirit") and a *body* is called *dualism*. In opposition to dualism is the theory called *materialism*, which holds that reality is made entirely of physical objects (matter). Materialist theories are *reductive*, meaning that all physical events and properties can be explained by (reduced to) the ultimate constituents of reality; e.g., water is H_2O. In other words, the object called "water" can be reduced to two parts hydrogen and one part oxygen. Materialists claim that *consciousness* and the *mind* can be *reduced* to—and can be eventually explained by—a complete understanding of the functional nature of complex physical brain states. In contrast, dualists argue that reductionism does not, and cannot, work. We will look at several major arguments for both dualism and materialism. You can anticipate a lively discussion, especially since the topic touches on a sensitive part of most people's existence, namely, does our conscious experience of the world mean we have a mind that is independent of our brain, or are we simply "chemical bags"?

Reported cases of "near-death experiences" are often used to argue for dualism. Some people have claimed they saw bright lights; others claimed that their spirit hovered over their body, and they were able to hear conversations. Of course, these reports have been questioned; in fact, some researchers explain these "out-of-body" experiences as being caused by a release of certain chemicals in the brain of the person.

To help illustrate some of the key points of the philosophical debate, let's imagine that a dualist poses the following challenge to a materialist:

> By reducing everything to physical objects, you leave no place for mental phenomena. But my experience of the world contains *feelings* such as pain, *emotions* such as happiness, *sensations* of color and sound and taste, and many other aspects of my mental life. Also, my mind seems to have control over many (but not all) aspects of my body. My thoughts can cause my body to act. Where do all these things exist in a purely physical world?

This challenge has been taken up by many thinkers. For example, the claim that *thoughts can cause the body to act* is a key point of contention. In fact, a materialist can pose a challenge to a dualist:

> If, as you claim, the mind is non-physical, then how can it possibly *cause* the body to act? By what mechanism or force does an *immaterial* mind get a *material* object to move? In addition, how can physical nerve endings and brain states cause anything to occur in the mind? How do the mind and body *interact* with each other?

The question of how the mind and body interact has come to be known as the *mind-body problem*. The problem was raised in response to Descartes's *Meditation VI*, in which he lays the groundwork for "substance dualism," which is the theory that we exist as both a mind and a body. Descartes defines "mind" as a *thinking substance*, and "body" as an *extended substance*. But because the word "substance" is normally used to talk about physical objects, when it is attached to the term "mind" (a thinking substance), it may mislead us into thinking that the mind has dimensions, such as length, width, weight, color, texture, and so on. But this is not how Descartes conceived the mind; for Descartes, the mind has no dimensions—it is not extended, and it does not have spatial coordinates. Descartes's theory, therefore, leads directly to the mind-body interaction problem.

Perhaps we can think about mind as being like gravity. Gravity is not a thing; it is a force, or better still, a warping of space-time that affects the behavior of physical objects. In fact, we can understand and even visualize how the warping of space causes objects to behave in certain predictable ways. But does this analogy help us to understand how mind and matter interact? Physics offers the means to help us understand how gravity affects physical objects. And Descartes did offer a solution in his other writings. He proposed that the mind and matter interact by way of the pineal gland in the brain. Unfortunately, for most people, Descartes's solution is unsatisfactory; it simply pushes the problem back one step. Even if the interaction point is the pineal glad, we still are offered no idea of how the interaction works there.

It is possible to see the problem of interaction in another light. You are probably familiar with some movies about ghosts. For example, the ghost of a major character may return to visit loved ones. Of course, the ghost—being a disembodied spirit having no physical properties—is shown walking through closed doors or through walls. However, the ghost is often depicted as climbing stairs. How can that be? Walking up stairs requires having a physical body come in contact with the physical stairs. But if a ghost can walk through walls, then how can it come in contact with the stairs?

The reading from Margaret Cavendish's book *Philosophical Letters*, contains passages in which Cavendish writes letters to an imaginary friend about the philosophy of Descartes and other philosophers. Cavendish's main point of contention with Descartes is that the natural mind *cannot* be separated from the body. Cavendish agrees that we call the action of the mind "thoughts," or *rational perceptions*; however, we should also say that our bodies contain numerous *sense perceptions*. In other words, "there is a double perception, rational and sensitive." In addition, "there is a double knowledge—*rational* and *sensitive*—one belonging to the *mind*, the other to the *body*."

In the reading, "One and the Same Thing," Anne Conway claims that there is an *active* and *passive* principle in every creature. As opposed to dualists who hold that mind and body are completely different substances, Conway holds that they "differ not essentially, but gradually." Conway poses a simple question: If a spirit can exist without a body, then why does a spirit need an eye, for example, in order to see the world? Furthermore, how does a non-physical mind move a physical body? Conway's answer is that "spirit and body are originally in their first substance but one and the same thing."

William James answers the question that forms the title of his article, "Does Consciousness Exist?" in the negative. He claims that the term "consciousness" is the source of much confusion because it mistakenly separates the world into *thought* (mental) and *object* (physical). James's main argument is against the "radical dualism of thought and thing." He starts by having us consider the world as being *composed of pure experiences*. For James, "thoughts" *do not* refer to specific entities that exist in the mind; instead, the term refers to the *function of knowing*. When we talk of a certain experience as being *subjective*, we "say that the experience represents." On the other hand, when we talk of that same experience as *objective*, we say that "it is represented." However, James wants us to see that "What represents and what is represented is here numerically the same," and that "no dualism of being represented and representing resides in the experience *per se*."

The philosophical topic of *personal identity* involves questions that come about by our being *persons*. The questions are often couched in terms of an *enduring self*,, which is sometimes meant to be a non-physical *subject of consciousness*. We can ask whether the *self* is the sum total of our memories, thoughts, experiences—which of course change over time—or whether it is some unchanging essential feature that makes us an unique person.

In the reading, "Identity and Diversity," John Locke argues that in order to understand the concept of personal identity, we must get clear on what distinguishes *person*, *man*, and *substance*. For Locke, a *person* is a thinking being "which it does only by that consciousness which is inseparable from thinking." Given that consciousness is always accompanied by thinking, Locke claims "it is that which makes every one to be what he calls *self*." In other words, your personal identity depends solely on your consciousness, not on your body.

David Hume's reading, "I Am a Bundle of Perceptions," offers a unique twist on the idea of personal identity. Hume says that although most of us imagine that we are intimately conscious of our *personal identity* or *self*, we are, unfortunately, completely mistaken in this belief. What we actually experience, says Hume, is simply a *constant succession of sensations*; thus, the idea of a *self* cannot be derived from any of these impressions. Hume says that "I never can catch *myself* at any time without a perception, and never can observe any thing but the perception." For Hume, what we call our *self* is just a *bundle of different perceptions*.

René Descartes

MIND AND BODY

I rightly conclude that my essence consists only in my being a *thinking thing* [a substance whose whole essence is thinking]. And although I certainly do possess a body with which I am very closely conjoined; nevertheless, because, on the one hand, I have a clear and distinct idea of myself, in as far as I am only a thinking and *unextended thing* [mind], and as, on the other hand, I possess a distinct idea of *body*, in as far as it is only an *extended and unthinking thing*, it is certain that I [my mind] is entirely and truly distinct from my body, and may exist without it.

Moreover, I find in myself diverse faculties of thinking that have each their special mode: for example, I find I possess the faculties of imagining and perceiving, without which I can indeed clearly and distinctly conceive myself as entire, but I cannot reciprocally conceive them without conceiving myself, that is to say, without an intelligent substance in which they reside; whence I perceive that they are distinct from myself as modes are from things. I remark likewise certain other faculties, as the power of changing place, of assuming diverse figures, and the like, that cannot be conceived and cannot therefore exist, any more than the preceding, apart from a substance in which they inhere.

It is very evident, however, that these faculties, if they really exist, must belong to some corporeal or extended substance, since in their clear and distinct concept there is contained some sort of extension, but no intellection at all. Further, I cannot doubt but that there is in me a certain passive faculty of perception, that is, of receiving and taking knowledge of the ideas of sensible things; but this would be useless to me, if there did not also exist in me, or in some other thing, another active faculty capable of forming and producing those ideas. But this active faculty cannot be in me [as a thinking thing], seeing that it does not presuppose thought, and also that those ideas are frequently produced in my mind without my contributing to it in any way, and even frequently contrary to my will. This faculty must therefore exist in some substance different from me, in which all the objective reality of the ideas that are produced by this faculty is contained formally or eminently, as I before remarked; and this substance is either a body, that is to say, a corporeal nature in which is contained formally all that is objectively in those ideas; or it is God himself, or some other creature, of a rank superior to body, in which the same is contained eminently. But as God is no deceiver, it is manifest that he does not of himself and immediately communicate those ideas to me, nor even by the intervention of any creature in which their objective reality is not formally, but only eminently, contained. For as he has given me no faculty whereby I can discover this to be the case, but, on the contrary, a very strong inclination to believe that those ideas arise from corporeal objects, I do not see how he could be vindicated from the charge of deceit, if in truth they proceeded from any other source, or were produced by other causes than corporeal things: and accordingly it must be concluded, that corporeal objects exist. Nevertheless they are not perhaps exactly such as we perceive by the senses, for their comprehension by the senses is, in many instances, very obscure and confused.

But there is nothing which that nature teaches me more expressly than that I have a body which is ill affected when I feel pain, and stands in need of food and drink when I experience the sensations of hunger and thirst, etc. Nature likewise teaches me by these sensations of pain, hunger, thirst, etc., that I am not only lodged in my body as a pilot in a vessel, but that I am besides so

Edited from *Meditations on First Philosophy*: Meditation VI. Translated by John Veitch, 1901, which is now in the public domain.

intimately conjoined, and as it were intermixed with it, that my mind and body compose a certain unity. For if this were not the case, I should not feel pain when my body is hurt, seeing I am merely a thinking thing, but should perceive the wound by the understanding alone, just as a pilot perceives by sight when any part of his vessel is damaged; and when my body has need of food or drink, I should have a clear knowledge of this, and not be made aware of it by the confused sensations of hunger and thirst: for, in truth, all these sensations of hunger, thirst, pain, etc., are nothing more than certain confused modes of thinking, *arising from the union and apparent fusion of mind and body.*

To commence this examination accordingly, I here remark, in the first place, that there is a vast difference between mind and body, in respect that body, from its nature, is always divisible, and that mind is entirely indivisible. For in truth, when I consider the mind, that is, when I consider myself in so far only as I am a thinking thing, I can distinguish in myself no parts, but I very clearly discern that I am somewhat absolutely one and entire; and although the whole mind seems to be united to the whole body, yet, when a foot, an arm, or any other part is cut off, I am conscious that nothing has been taken from my mind; nor can the faculties of willing, perceiving, conceiving, etc., properly be called its parts, for it is the same mind that is exercised in willing, in perceiving, and in conceiving, etc. But quite the opposite holds in corporeal or extended things; for I cannot imagine any one of them, which I cannot easily sunder in thought, and which, therefore, I do not know to be divisible. This would be sufficient to teach me that the mind or soul of man is entirely different from the body, if I had not already been apprised of it on other grounds.

I remark, in the next place, that the mind does not immediately receive the impression from all the parts of the body, but only from the brain, or perhaps even from one small part of it, namely, that in which the common sense is said to be, which as often as it is affected in the same way, gives rise to the same perception in the mind, although meanwhile the other parts of the body may be diversely disposed, as is proved by innumerable experiments, which it is unnecessary here to enumerate.

Margaret Cavendish

A DOUBLE PERCEPTION

The mind, according to your author's opinion [Descartes], is a substance really distinct from the body, and may be actually separated from it and subsist without it. If he means that natural mind and soul of man, not the supernatural or divine, I am far from his opinion; for though the mind moves only in its own parts, and not upon or with the parts of inanimate matter, yet it cannot be separated from these parts of matter, and subsist by itself, as being part of one and the same matter the inanimate is of—for there is but only one matter, and one kind of matter, although of several degrees—only it is the self-moving part. But yet this cannot empower it to quit the same natural body whose part it is.

Neither can I apprehend that the mind's or soul's seat should be in the *glandula* [pineal gland] or kernel of the brain, and sit there like a spider in a cobweb, to whom the least motion of the cobweb gives intelligence of a fly, which he is ready to assault, and that the brain should get intelligence by the animal spirits as his servants, which run to and fro like ants to inform it; or that the mind should, according to others' opinions, be a light, and embroidered all with ideas like a herald's coat; and that the sensitive organs have no knowledge in themselves, but serve only like peeping-holes for the mind; or barn doors to receive bundles of pressures like sheaves of corn; for there being a thorough mixture of animate, rational and sensitive, and inanimate matter, we cannot assign a certain seat or place to the rational, another to the sensitive, and another to the inanimate, but they are diffused and intermixed throughout all the body; and this is the reason that sense and knowledge cannot be bound only to the head or brain. But although they are mixed together, nevertheless they do not lose their interior natures by this mixture, nor their purity or subtlety, nor their proper motions or actions, but each moves according to its own nature and substance, without confusion. The actions of the rational part in man, which is the mind or soul, are called *thoughts*, or thoughtful perceptions; and so are the sensitive perceptions, for though man, or any other animal, has but five exterior sensitive organs, yet there are numerous perceptions made in these sensitive organs and in all the body. Every single pore of the flesh is a sensitive organ, as well as the eye or the ear. But both sorts, as well the rational and sensitive, are different from each other, although both do resemble each other, as being both parts of animate matter, as I have mentioned before.

That all other animals, besides man lack reason, your author [Descartes] endeavors to prove in his *Discourse of Method*, where his chief argument is that other animals cannot express their mind, thoughts or conceptions, either by speech or any other signs, as man can do. He says that it is not for lack of the organs belonging to the framing of words, as we observe in parrots which are apt enough to express words they are taught, but understand nothing of them. My answer is, that one man expressing his mind by speech or words to another does not declare by it his excellency and supremacy above all other creatures, but for the most part more folly, for a talking man is not so wise as a contemplating man. But although other creatures cannot speak or discourse with each other as men do, should we conclude that they have neither knowledge, sense, reason, or intelligence? Certainly this is a very weak argument; for one part of a man's body, such as one hand, is not less sensible than the other, nor the heel less sensible than the heart, nor the leg less sensible than the head, but each part has its sense and reason, and consequently, its sensitive and

Edited from *Philosophical Letters,* 1664, Letters 35-37, which is now in the public domain.

rational knowledge. And although they cannot talk or give intelligence to each other by speech, nevertheless each has its own peculiar and particular knowledge, just as each particular man has his own particular knowledge, for one man's knowledge is not another man's knowledge; and if there is such a peculiar and particular knowledge in every part of one animal creature, as man, there well may be such in creatures of different kinds and sorts. But this particular knowledge belonging to each creature does not prove that there is no intelligence at all between them, no more than the want of human knowledge proves the want of reason; for reason is the rational part of matter, and makes perception, observation, and intelligence different in every creature, and every sort of creature, according to their proper natures; but perception, observation, and intelligence do not make *reason*—*reason* being the cause, and they the effects.

Although other creatures do not have speech, nor mathematical rules and demonstrations, and other arts and sciences as men, yet their perceptions and observations may be as wise as men's, and they may have as much intelligence and commerce between each other after their own manner and way, as men have after theirs. To which I leave them, and man to his conceited prerogative and excellence.

Concerning sense and perception, your author's opinion is, that it is made by a motion or impression from the object upon the sensitive organ, which impression, by means of the nerves, is brought to the brain, and so to the mind or soul, which only perceives in the brain, explaining by it the example a man being blind, or walking in dark, who by the help of his stick can perceive when he touches a stone, a tree, water, sand, and the like. By this example he brings to make a comparison with the perception of light in a shining body as nothing else but a quick and lively motion or action, which through the air and other transparent bodies tends toward the eye, in the same manner as the motion or resistance of the bodies the blind man meets them and tends through the stick toward the hand. It is no wonder that the Sun can display its rays so far in an instant, seeing that the same action, where one end of the stick is moved goes instantly to the other end, and would do the same if the stick were as long as heaven is distant from Earth. To which I answer first, that it is not only the mind that perceives in the kernel of the brain, but that there is a double perception, rational and sensitive, and that the mind perceives by the rational, but the body and the sensitive organs by the sensitive perception. And as there is a double perception, so there is a double knowledge—*rational* and *sensitive*—one belonging to the *mind*, the other to the *body*; for I believe that the eye, ear, nose, tongue, and all the body, have knowledge as well as the mind, only the rational matter, being subtle and pure is not encumbered with the grosser part of matter to work upon or with it, but leaves that to the sensitive and works or moves only in its own substance, which makes a difference between thoughts and exterior senses.

Next I say that it is not the motion or reaction of the bodies the blind man meets which makes the sensitive perception of these objects, but the sensitive corporeal motions in the hand pattern out the figure of the stick, stone, tree, sand, and the like. And as for comparing the perception of the hand when by the help of the stick it perceives the objects, with the perception of light, I confess that the sensitive perceptions do all referable each other, because all sensitive parts of matter are of one degree, as being sensible parts, only there is a difference according to the figures of the objects presented to the senses; and there is no better proof for perception being made by the sensitive motions in the body, or sensitive organ, but that all these sensitive perceptions are alike, and resemble one another; for if they were not made in the body of the sentient, but by the impression of exterior objects, then there would be so much difference between them by reason of the diversity of objects, as they would have no resemblance at all.

But for a further proof of my own opinion, if the perception proceeded merely from the motion, impression and resistance of the objects, then the hand could not perceive those objects, unless they touched the hand itself, as the stick does; for it is not probable that the motions of the stone, water, sand, etc., should leave their bodies and enter into the stick, and so into the hand; for motion must be either something or nothing; if something, then the stick and the hand would grow bigger, and the objects touched less, or else the touching and the touched must exchange their motions, which cannot be done so suddenly, especially between solid bodies. But if motion has no body, then it is nothing, and how nothing can pass or enter or move some body, I cannot conceive.

Anne Conway

ONE AND THE SAME THING

Let us examine how every creature is composed, and how the parts of its composition may be converted the one into the other; for that they have originally one and the same *essence*, or *being*. In every visible creature there is a *body* and a *spirit*, or a *more active and more passive principle*. Spirit is an eye or light beholding its own proper image, and the body is a darkness receiving that image, when the spirit looks there into, as when one sees himself in a looking-glass; for certainly he cannot so behold himself in the transparent air, nor in any diaphanous body, because the reflection of an image requires a certain opacity or darkness, which we call a body. Yet to be a body is not an essential property of any thing; as neither is it a property of any thing to be dark. Therefore as every spirit has need of a body, that it may receive and reflect its image, so also it requires a body to retain the same; for every body has this retentive nature, either more or less in itself; and by how much more perfect a body is, that is, more perfectly mixed, so much the more retentive is it.

Every reflection is made by a certain darkness, and this is a body; so the memory requires a body, to retain the spirit of the thing thought on, otherwise it would vanish as the image in a glass, which presently vanishes, the object being removed. And so likewise, when we remember any body, we see his image in us, which is a spirit that proceeded from him, while we beheld him from without; which image or spirit is retained in some body, which is the seed of our brain, and thus is made a certain spiritual generation in us.

To prove that spirit and body differ not essentially, but gradually, I shall deduce an argument from the intimate band or union, which intercedes between bodies and spirits, by means whereof the spirits have dominion over the bodies with which they are united, that they move them from one place to another, and use them as instruments in their various operations. For if spirit and body are so contrary one to another, so that a spirit is only life, or a living and sensible substance, but a body a certain mass merely dead; a spirit penetrable and indiscerpible [having no separate parts], but a body impenetrable and discerpible [having separate parts], which are all contrary attributes. What is that which joins or unite them together? Or, what are those links or chains, whereby they have so firm a connection, and that for so long a space of time? Moreover, when the spirit or soul is separated from the body, so that it has no longer dominion or power over it to move it as it had before, what is the cause of this separation? If the vital agreement the soul has to the body is the cause of the union, and that the body being corrupted that vital agreement ceases, then I answer: We must first enquire, in what this vital agreement consists; for if they cannot tell us where it does consist, they only trifle with empty words, which give a sound, but want a signification. For certainly in that sense which they take body and spirit in, there is no agreement at all between them; for a body is always a dead thing, void of life and sense, no less when the spirit is in it, than when it is gone out of it. Thus, there is no agreement at all between them, and if there is any agreement, that certainly will remain the same, both when the body is sound, and when it is corrupted. If they deny this, because a spirit requires an organized body, by means which it performs its vital acts of the external senses; moves and transports the body from place to place; which organic action ceases when the body is corrupted. Certainly by this the difficulty is never the better solved; for why does the spirit require such an organized body? Why does it require a corporeal eye so wonderfully formed and organized, that I can see by it? Why does it need a

Edited from *The Principles of the Most Ancient and Modern Philosophy,* 1692, Chapters VI-VII and IX, which is now in the public domain.

corporeal light, to see corporeal objects? Why is it requisite, that the image of the object should be sent to it, through the eye, that it may see it? If the same were entirely nothing but a spirit, and no way corporeal, then why does it need so many several corporeal organs, so far different from the nature of it?

Furthermore, how can a spirit move its body, or any of its members, if a spirit (as they affirm) is of such a nature, that no part of its body can in the least resist it, even as one body resists another, when it is moved by it, by reason of its impenetrability? For if a spirit could so easily penetrate all bodies, why does it not leave the body behind it, when it is moved from place to place, seeing it can so easily pass out without the least resistance? For certainly this is the cause of all motions which we see in the world, where one thing moves another, namely because both are impenetrable in the sense aforesaid. For were it not for this impenetrability, one creature could not move another, because this would not oppose that nor at all resist it; an example of which we have in the sails of a ship, by which the wind drives the ship. When on the contrary, if instead of sails, nets were expanded, through which the wind would have a freer passage; certainly by these the ship would be but little moved, although it blew with great violence. Thus, we see how this impenetrability causes resistance, and this makes motion. But if there were no impenetrability, as in the case of body and spirit, then there could be no resistance, and by consequence the spirit could make no motion in the body.

If it be objected, that God is altogether incorporeal and intrinsically present in all bodies, and moves bodies whenever He pleases, and is the First Mover of all things, and yet nothing is impenetrable to him, then I answer: This motion by which God moves a body, does wonderfully differ from that manner by which the soul moves the body; for the will of God which gave being to bodies, gave them motion also, so that motion itself is of God, by whose will all motion happens. For as a creature cannot give being to itself, so neither can it move itself; for in him we live, move, and have our being; so that motion and essence come from the same cause, God the creator, who remains immoveable in himself; neither is he carried from place to place, because he is equally present everywhere. But the case is far different when the soul moves the body because the soul is not the author of motion, but only determines it to this or that particular thing. And the soul itself is moved, together with the body, from place to place; and if the body is imprisoned, or held in chains, it cannot free or deliver itself out of prison or out of chains. Therefore, it would be a very unfit comparison, if one should go about to illustrate that motion the soul makes in the body, by an example of God moving his creatures; yes, so great is the difference, as if a man should go to demonstrate how a carpenter builds a ship, or a house, by an example of God creating the first matter or substance, wherein certainly there is as great a disparity or disproportion; for God gave being to creatures, but a carpenter does not give being to the wood whereby he builds a ship.

Furthermore, why is the spirit or soul so capable of feeling bodily pain? If when it is united with the body, it has nothing of a bodily nature, then why is it grieved or wounded when the body is wounded, which is quite of a different nature? For seeing the soul can so easily penetrate the body, how can any corporeal thing hurt it? If it be said, the body only feels the pain, but not the soul; this is contrary to their own principles, because they affirm, that the body has neither life nor sense: But if it is granted, that the soul is of one nature and substance with the body, although it is many degrees more excellent in regard of life and spirituality, then all the aforesaid difficulties will vanish, and it will be easily conceived, how the body and soul are united together, and how the soul moves the body, and suffers by it or with it.

From what has been said, and from diverse reasons alleged, that spirit and body are originally in their first substance but one and the same thing, it evidently appears that the philosophers which have taught otherwise, whether ancient or modern, have generally erred and laid an ill foundation in the very beginning, whence the whole house and superstructure is so feeble, and indeed so unprofitable, that the whole edifice and building must in time decay, from which absurd foundation have arose very many gross and dangerous errors, not only in philosophy, but also in divinity to the great damage of mankind.

None can object, that all this philosophy is no other than that of Descartes or Hobbes under a new mask. For, first, as touching the *Cartesian* philosophy, this holds that every body is a mere dead mass, not only void of all kind of life and sense, but utterly incapable to all eternity; this grand error also is to be imputed to all those who affirm body and spirit to be contrary things, and inconvertible one into another, so as to deny a body all life and sense; which is quite contrary to the grounds of this our philosophy. Thus, it is so far from being a *Cartesian* principle, under a new mask, that it may be truly said it is *Anti-Cartesian*, in regard of their fundamental principles; although it cannot be denied that Descartes taught many excellent and ingenious things concerning the mechanical part of natural operations, and how all natural motions proceed according to rules and laws mechanical, even as indeed nature herself. But yet in nature, and her operations, they are far more than merely mechanical; and the same is not a mere organic body, like a clock, wherein there is not a vital principle of motion; but a living body, having life and sense, which body is far more sublime than a mere mechanism, or mechanical motion.

If it is objected that this our philosophy seems, at least, very like that of Hobbes because he taught that all creatures were originally one substance, and that every creature is material and corporeal, matter and body itself, and by consequence the most noble actions are either material and corporeal. To this objection, I answer: First, I grant that all creatures are originally one substance.

Furthermore, I answer that by matter and body, here the thing is far otherwise understood, than Hobbes understood it, and which was never discovered by Descartes otherwise than in a dream: For what do they understand by matter and body? What attributes do they ascribe to them? None but extension and impenetrability, which are really one attribute; to which also may be referred figure and mobility. But, suppose those are distinct attributes, certainly this profits nothing, nor will ever help us to understand what that substance is, which they call body and matter; for they have never proceeded beyond the husk or shell, nor ever reached the kernel, they only touch the superficies, never discerning the center, they were plainly ignorant of the noblest and most excellent attributes of that substance which they call body and matter, and understood nothing of them. But if it be demanded, what are those more excellent attributes? I answer: spirit, or life, and light, under which I comprehend a capacity of all kind of feeling, sense, and knowledge, love, joy, and fruition, and all kind of power and virtue, which the noblest creatures have or can have; so that even the vilest and most contemptible creature, dust and sand, may be capable of all those perfections, through various transmutations from the one into the other; which according to the natural order of things, require long periods of time for their consummation, although the absolute power of God could have accelerated or hastened all things, and effected it in one moment: But this wisdom of God saw it to be more expedient, that all things should proceed in their natural order and course; so that after this manner, that fertility or fruitfulness, which he has endued every being with, may appear, and the creatures have time by working still to promote themselves to a greater perfection, as the instruments of divine wisdom, goodness and power, which operates in, and with them; for therein the creature has the greater joy, when it possesses what it has, as the fruit of its own labor.

Therefore, we see how every motion and action, considered in the abstract, has a wonderful subtlety or spirituality in it, beyond all created substances whatsoever, so that neither time nor place can limit the same; and yet they are nothing else but modes or manners of created substances, namely, their strength, power and virtue, whereby they are extendible into great substances, beyond what the substance itself can make. And so we may distinguish extension into material and virtual, which two-fold extension every creature has.

Material extension is that which matter, body, or substance has, as considered without all motion or action; and this extension is neither greater or lesser, because it would still remain the same. A *virtual extension* is a motion or action which a creature has, whether immediately given from God, or immediately received from its fellow creature. But every motion, proceeding from the proper life and will of the creature, is vital; and this I call a *motion of life*, which is not plainly local and mechanical as the other, but has in it a life, and vital virtue, and this is the virtual extension of a creature.

How motion or action may be transmitted from one body to another is with many a matter of great debate, because it is not a body or substance; and if it is only motion of a body, then how can motion pass properly with its own subject into another? The answer to this question is this: Motion is not propagated from one body to another by local motion, because motion itself is not moved, but only moves the body in which it is. If motion could be propagated by local motion, then this motion would be propagated of another, and this again of another, and so on *ad infinitum*, which is absurd. Therefore the manner of the said propagation is by real production or creation, and so the motion in one creature may produce motion in another. And this is all a creature can do towards moving itself or its fellow creatures, as being the instrument of God, by which motions a new substance is not created, but only new *species* of things, so that creatures may be multiplied in their kinds, while one acts upon and moves another.

William James

DOES CONSCIOUSNESS EXIST?

"Thoughts" and "things" are names for two sorts of object, which common sense will always find contrasted and will always practically oppose to each other. Philosophy, reflecting on the contrast, has varied in the past in her explanations of it, and may be expected to vary in the future. At first, "spirit and matter," "soul and body," stood for a pair of equipollent substances quite on a par in weight and interest. The spiritual principle attenuates itself to a thoroughly ghostly condition, being only a name for the fact that the "content" of experience is *known*. It loses personal form and activity—these passing over to the content—and becomes a bare "awareness," of which in its own right absolutely nothing can be said.

I believe that "consciousness," when once it has evaporated to this estate of pure diaphaneity, is on the point of disappearing altogether. It is the name of a nonentity, and has no right to a place among first principles. Those who still cling to it are clinging to a mere echo, the faint rumor left behind by the disappearing "soul" upon the air of philosophy.

To deny plumply that "consciousness" exists seems so absurd on the face of it—for undeniably "thoughts" do exist—that I fear some readers will follow me no farther. Let me then immediately explain that *I mean only to deny that the word stands for an entity*, but to insist most emphatically that *it does stand for a function*. There is, I mean, no aboriginal stuff or quality of being, contrasted with that of which material objects are made, out of which our thoughts of them are made; but there is a function in experience which thoughts perform, and for the performance of which this quality of being is invoked. That function is *knowing*. "Consciousness" is supposed necessary to explain the fact that things not only are, but get reported, are known. Whoever blots out the notion of consciousness from his list of first principles must still provide in some way for that function's being carried on.

My thesis is that if we start with the supposition that there is only one primal stuff or material in the world, a stuff of which everything is composed, and if we call that stuff "pure experience," then knowing can easily be explained as a particular sort of relation towards one another into which portions of pure experience may enter. The relation itself is a part of pure experience; one of its "terms" becomes the subject or bearer of the knowledge, the knower, the other becomes the object known. This will need much explanation before it can be understood. The best way to get it understood is to contrast it with the alternative view; and for that we may take the most recent alternative, that in which the evaporation of the definite soul-substance has proceeded as far as it can go without being yet complete.

We are supposed by almost every one to have an immediate consciousness of consciousness itself. When the world of outer fact ceases to be materially present, and we merely recall it in memory, or fancy it, the consciousness is believed to stand out and to be felt as a kind of impalpable inner flowing, which, once known in this sort of experience, may equally be detected in presentations of the outer world. "The moment we try to fix our attention upon consciousness and to *see what*, distinctly, it is," says a recent writer [G. E. Moore], "it seems to vanish: it seems as if we had before us a mere emptiness. When we try to introspect the sensation of blue, all we can see is the blue: the other element is as if it were diaphanous. Yet it *can* be distinguished if we look attentively enough, and if we know that there is something to look for." And "Consciousness,"

Edited from *Journal of Philosophy, Psychology and Scientific Methods*, 1904, which is now in the public domain.

says another philosopher [Paul Natorp], "is inexplicable and hardly describable, yet all conscious experiences have this in common, that what we call their content has a peculiar reference to a center for which 'self' is the name, in virtue of which reference alone the content is subjectively given, or appears. . . . While in this way consciousness, or reference to a self, is the only thing which distinguishes a conscious content from any sort of being that might be there with no one conscious of it, yet this only ground of the distinction defies all closer explanations. The existence of consciousness, although it is the fundamental fact of psychology, can indeed be laid down as certain, can be brought out by analysis, but can neither be defined nor deduced from anything but itself."

This supposes that the consciousness is one element, moment, factor—call it what you like—of an experience of essentially dualistic inner constitution, from which, if you abstract the content, the consciousness will remain revealed to its own eye. We operate here by physical subtraction; and the usual view is, that by mental subtraction we can separate the two factors of experience in an analogous way—not isolating them entirely, but distinguishing them enough to know that they are two.

Now my contention is exactly the reverse of this. *Experience, I believe, has no such inner duplicity; and the separation of it into consciousness and content comes, not by way of subtraction, but by way of addition*—the addition, to a given concrete piece of it, other sets of experiences, in connection with which severally its use or function may be of two different kinds. So, a given undivided portion of experience, taken in one context of associates, play the part of a knower, of a state of mind, of "consciousness," while in a different context the same undivided bit of experience plays the part of a thing known, of an objective "content." In a word, in one group it figures as a *thought*, in another group as a *thing*. And, since it can figure in both groups simultaneously we have every right to speak of it as subjective and objective both at once. The dualism connoted by such double-barreled terms as "experience," "phenomenon," "datum"—terms which, in philosophy at any rate, tend more and more to replace the single-barreled terms of "thought" and "thing"—that dualism, I say, is still preserved in this account, but reinterpreted, so that, instead of being mysterious and elusive, it becomes verifiable and concrete. It is an affair of relations, it falls outside, not inside, the single experience considered, and can always be particularized and defined.

The entering wedge for this more concrete way of understanding the dualism was fashioned by Locke when he made the word "idea" stand indifferently for *thing* and *thought*, and by Berkeley when he said that what common sense means by "realities" is exactly what the philosopher means by "ideas." Neither Locke nor Berkeley thought his truth out into perfect clearness, but it seems to me that the conception I am defending does little more than consistently carry out the "pragmatic" method which they were the first to use.

If the reader will take his own experiences, he will see what I mean. Let him begin with a perceptual experience, the "presentation," so called, of a physical object, his actual field of vision, the room he sits in, with the book he is reading as its center; and let him for the present treat this complex object in the common-sense way as being "really" what it seems to be, namely, a collection of physical things cut out from an environing world of other physical things with which these physical things have actual or potential relations. Now at the same time it is just *those self-same things* which his mind, as we say, perceives; and the whole philosophy of perception from Democritus's time downwards has just been one long wrangle over the paradox that what is evidently one reality should be in two places at once, both in outer space and in a person's mind. "Representative" theories of perception avoid the logical paradox, but on the other hand they violate the reader's sense of life, which knows no intervening mental image but seems to see the room and the book immediately just as they physically exist.

The puzzle of how the one identical room can be in two places is at bottom just the puzzle of how one identical point can be on two lines. It can, if it be situated at their intersection; and similarly, if the "pure experience" of the room were a place of intersection of two processes, which connected it with different groups of associates respectively, it could be counted twice over, as belonging to either group, and spoken of loosely as existing in two places, although it would remain all the time a numerically single thing.

Well, the experience is a member of diverse processes that can be followed away from it along entirely different lines. The one self-identical thing has so many relations to the rest of experience that you can take it in disparate systems of association, and treat it as belonging with opposite contexts. In one of these contexts it is your "field of consciousness"; in another it is "the room in which you sit," and it enters both contexts in its wholeness, giving no pretext for being said to attach itself to consciousness by one of its parts or aspects, and to out reality by another. What are the two processes, now, into which the room-experience simultaneously enters in this way?

One of them is the reader's personal biography, the other is the history of the house of which the room is part. The presentation, the experience, the *that* in short (for until we have decided *what* it is it must be a mere *that*) is the last term in a train of sensations, emotions, decisions, movements, classifications, expectations, etc., ending in the present, and the first term in a series of "inner" operations extending into the future, on the reader's part. On the other hand, the very same *that* is the final point in time of a lot of previous physical operations, carpentering, papering, furnishing, warming, etc., and the beginning point in time of a lot of future ones, in which it will be concerned when undergoing the destiny of a physical room. The physical and the mental operations form curiously incompatible groups. As a room, the experience has occupied that spot and had that environment for thirty years. As your field of consciousness it may never have existed until now. As a room, attention will go on to discover endless new details in it. As your mental state merely, few new ones will emerge under attention's eye. As a room, it will take an earthquake, or a gang of men, and in any case a certain amount of time, to destroy it. As your subjective state, the closing of your eyes, or any instantaneous play of your fancy will suffice. In the real world, fire will consume it. In your mind, you can let fire play over it without effect. As an outer object, you must pay so much a month to inhabit it. As an inner content, you may occupy it for any length of time rent-free. If, in short, you follow it in the mental direction, taking it along with events of personal biography solely, all sorts of things are true of it which are false, and false of it which are true if you treat it as a real thing experienced, follow it in the physical direction, and relate it to associates in the outer world.

So far, all seems plain sailing, but my thesis will probably grow less plausible to the reader when I pass from *percepts* to *concepts*, or from the case of things presented to that of things remote. I believe, nevertheless, that here also the same law holds good. If we take conceptual manifolds, or memories, or fancies, they also are in their first intention mere bits of pure experience, and, as such, are single *thats* which act in one context as objects, and in another context figure as mental states. By taking them in their first intention, I mean ignoring their relation to possible perceptual experiences with which they may be connected, which they may lead to and terminate in, and which then they may be supposed to "represent." Taking them in this way first, we confine the problem to a world merely "thought of" and not directly felt or seen. This world, just like the world of percepts, comes to us at first as a chaos of experiences, but lines of order soon get traced. We find that any bit of it which we may cut out as an example is connected with distinct groups of associates, just as our perceptual experiences are, that these associates link themselves with it by different relations, and that one forms the inner history of a person, while the other acts as an impersonal "objective" world, either spatial and temporal, or else merely logical or mathematical, or otherwise "ideal."

The first obstacle on the part of the reader to seeing that these non-perceptual experiences have objectivity as well as subjectivity will probably be due to the intrusion into his mind of *percepts*, that third group of associates with which the non-perceptual experiences have relations, and which, as a whole, they "represent," standing to them as thoughts to things. This important function of non-perceptual experiences complicates the question and confuses it; for, so used are we to treat percepts as the sole genuine realities that, unless we keep them out of the discussion, we tend altogether to overlook the objectivity that lies in non-perceptual experiences by themselves. We treat them, "knowing" percepts as they do, as through and through subjective, and say that they are wholly constituted of the stuff called consciousness, using this term now for a kind of entity, after the fashion which I am seeking to refute.

Abstracting, then, from percepts altogether, what I maintain is, that any single non-perceptual experience tends to get counted twice over, just as a perceptual experience does, figuring in one context as an object or field of objects, in another as a state of mind: and all this without the least internal self-division on its own part into consciousness and content. It is all consciousness in one taking; and, in the other, all content.

This certainly is the immediate, primary, or practical way of taking our thought-of world. Were there no perceptual world to serve as its "reductive," by being "stronger" and more genuinely "outer" (so that the whole merely thought-of world seems weak and inner in comparison), our world of thought would be the only world, and would enjoy complete reality in our belief. This actually happens in our dreams, and in our day-dreams so long as percepts do not interrupt them.

And yet, just as the seen room is *also* a field of consciousness, so the conceived or recollected room is *also* a state of mind; and the doubling-up of the experience has in both cases similar grounds.

The room thought-of has many thought-of couplings with many thought-of things. Some of these couplings are inconstant, others are stable. In the reader's personal history the room occupies a single date—he saw it only once perhaps, a year ago. Of the house's history, on the other hand, it forms a permanent ingredient. Grouped with the rest of its house, with the name of its town, of its owner, builder, value, decorative plan, the room maintains a definite foothold, to which, if we try to loosen it, it tends to return and to reassert itself with force. With these associates, in a word, it coheres, while to other houses, other towns, other owners, etc., it shows no tendency to cohere at all. The two collections, first of its cohesive, and, second, of its loose associates, inevitably come to be contrasted. We call the first collection the system of external realities, in the midst of which the room, as "real," exists; the other we call the stream of internal thinking, in which, as a "mental image," it for a moment floats. The room thus again gets counted twice over. It plays two different roles, being the thought-of-an-object, and the object-thought-of, both in one; and all this without paradox or mystery, just as the same material thing may be both low and high, or small and great, or bad and good, because of its relations to opposite parts of an environing world.

As "subjective" we say that the experience represents; as "objective" it is represented. What represents and what is represented is here numerically the same; but we must remember that no dualism of being represented and representing resides in the experience *per se*. In its pure state, or when isolated, there is no self-splitting of it into consciousness and what the consciousness is "of." Its subjectivity and objectivity are functional attributes solely, realized only when the experience is "taken," i.e., talked-of, twice, considered along with its two differing contexts respectively, by a new retrospective experience, of which that whole past complication now forms the fresh content.

The instant field of the present is at all times what I call the "pure" experience. It is only virtually or potentially either object or subject as yet. For the time being, it is plain, unqualified actuality, or existence, a simple *that*. In this immediacy it is of course *valid*; it is *there*, we *act* upon it; and the doubling of it in retrospection into a state of mind and a reality intended thereby, is just one of the acts. The "state of mind," first treated explicitly as such in retrospection, will stand corrected or confirmed, and the retrospective experience in its turn will get a similar treatment; but the immediate experience in its passing is "truth," practical truth, *something to act on*, at its own movement. If the world were then and there to go out like a candle, it would remain truth absolute and objective, for it would be "the last word," would have no critic, and no one would ever oppose the thought in it to the reality intended.

I think I may now claim to have made my thesis clear. "Consciousness" connotes a kind of external relation, and does not denote a special stuff or way of being. *The peculiarity of our experiences, that they not only are, but are known, which their "conscious" quality is invoked to explain, is better explained by their relations—these relations themselves being experiences—to one another.*

I will consider a few objections that are sure to be urged against the entire theory as it stands.

First of all, this will be asked: "If experience has not 'conscious' existence, if it be not partly made of 'consciousness,' of what then is it made? Matter we know, and thought we know, and conscious content we know, but neutral and simple 'pure experience' is something we know not at all. Say *what* it consists of—for it must consist of something—or be willing to give it up!"

To this challenge the reply is easy. Although for fluency's sake I myself spoke early in this article of a stuff of pure experience, I have now to say that there is no *general* stuff of which experience at large is made. There are as many stuffs as there are "natures" in the things experienced. If you ask what any one bit of pure experience is made of, the answer is always the same: It is made of *that*, of just what appears, of space, of intensity, of flatness, brownness, heaviness, or what not. "Experience" is only a collective name for all these sensible natures, and save for time and space (and, if you like, for "being") there appears no universal element of which all things are made.

The next objection is more formidable, in fact it sounds quite crushing when one first hears it. "If it is the self-same piece of pure experience, taken twice over, that serves now as thought and now as thing"—so the objection runs—"how comes it that its attributes should differ so fundamentally in the two takings. As *thing*, the experience is extended; as *thought*, it occupies no space or place. As *thing*, it is red, hard, heavy; but who ever heard of a red, hard or heavy *thought*? Yet even now you said that an experience is made of just what appears, and what appears is just such adjectives. How can the one experience in its thing-function be made of them, consist of them, carry them as its own attributes, while in its thought-function it disowns them and attributes them elsewhere? There is a self-contradiction here from which the radical dualism of thought and thing is the only truth that can save us. Only if the thought is one kind of being can the adjectives exist in it 'intentionally'; only if the thing is another kind, can they exist in it constitutively and energetically. No simple subject can take the same adjectives and at one time be qualified by it, and at another time be merely 'of' it, as of something only meant or known."

The solution insisted on by this objector, like many other common-sense solutions, grows the less satisfactory the more one turns it in one's mind. To begin with, *are* thought and thing as heterogeneous as is commonly said? No one denies that they have some categories in common. Their relations to time are identical. Both, moreover, may have parts, and both may be complex or simple. Both are of kinds, can be compared, added and subtracted and arranged in serial orders. All sorts of adjectives qualify our thoughts which appear incompatible with consciousness. For instance, they are natural and easy, or laborious. They are beautiful, happy, intense, interesting, wise, idiotic, focal, marginal, insipid, confused, vague, precise, rational, casual, general, particular, and many things besides. How, if "subject" and "object" were separated "by the whole diameter of being," and had no attributes in common, could it be so hard to tell, in a presented and recognized material object, what part comes in through the sense-organs and what part comes "out of one's own head"? Sensations and apperceptive ideas fuse here so intimately that you can no more tell where one begins and the other ends, than you can tell, in those cunning circular panoramas that have lately been exhibited, where the real foreground and the painted canvas join together.

Descartes for the first time defined thought as the absolutely unextended, and later philosophers have accepted the description as correct. But what possible meaning has it to say that, when we think of a foot-rule or a square yard, extension is not attributable to our thought? Of every extended object the *adequate* mental picture must have all the extension of the object itself. The difference between objective and subjective extension is one of relation to a context solely. In the mind the various extents maintain no necessarily stubborn order relatively to each other, while in the physical world they bound each other stably, and, added together, make the great enveloping Unit which we believe in and call real Space. As "outer," they carry themselves adversely, so to speak, to one another, exclude one another and maintain their distances; while, as "inner," their order is loose, and they form a chaos in which unity is lost. But to argue from this that inner experience is absolutely inextensive seems to me little short of absurd. The two worlds differ, not by the presence or absence of extension, but by the relations of the extensions which in both worlds exist.

Does not this case of extension now put us on the track of truth in the case of other qualities? It does; and I am surprised that the facts should not have been noticed long ago. Why, for example, do we call a fire hot, and water wet, and yet refuse to say that our mental state, when it is "of" these objects, is either wet or hot? "Intentionally," at any rate, and when the mental state is a vivid image, hotness and wetness are in it just as much as they are in the physical experience. The reason is this, that, as the general chaos of all our experiences gets sifted, we find that there are some fires that will always burn sticks and always warm our bodies, and that there are some waters that will always put out fires; while there are other fires and waters that will not act at all. The general group of experiences that *act*, that do not only possess their natures intrinsically, but wear them adjectively and energetically, turning them against one another, comes inevitably to be contrasted with the group whose members, having identically the same natures, fail to manifest them in the "energetic" way. I make for myself now an experience of blazing fire; I place it near my body; but it does not warm me in the least. I lay a stick upon it, and the stick either burns or remains green, as I please. I call up water, and pour it on the fire, and absolutely no difference ensues. I account for all such facts by calling this whole train of experiences *unreal*, a mental train. Mental fire is what won't burn real sticks; mental water is what won't necessarily (though of course it may) put out even a mental fire. Mental knives may be sharp, but they won't cut real wood. Mental triangles are pointed, but their points won't wound. With "real" objects, on the contrary, consequences always accrue; and thus the real experiences get sifted from the mental ones, the things from our thoughts of them, fanciful or true, and precipitated together as the stable part of the whole experience-chaos, under the name of the physical world. Of this our perceptual experiences are the nucleus, they being the originally *strong* experiences. We add a lot of conceptual experiences to them, making these strong also in imagination, and building out the remoter parts of the physical world by their means; and around this core of reality the world of laxly connected fancies and mere rhapsodical objects floats like a bank of clouds. In the clouds, all sorts of rules are violated which in the core are kept. Extensions there can be indefinitely located; motion there obeys no Newton's laws.

There is a peculiar class of experience to which, whether we take them as subjective or as objective, we *assign* their several natures as attributes, because in both contexts they affect their associates actively, though in neither quite as "strongly" or as sharply as things affect one another by their physical energies. I refer here to *appreciations*, which form an ambiguous sphere of being, belonging with emotion on the one hand, and having objective "value" on the other, yet seeming not quite inner nor quite outer, as if a division had begun but had not made itself complete.

Experiences of painful objects, for example, are usually also painful experiences; perceptions of loveliness, of ugliness, tend to pass muster as lovely or as ugly perceptions; intuitions of the morally lofty are lofty intuitions. Sometimes the adjective wanders as if uncertain where to fix itself. Shall we speak of seductive visions or of visions of seductive things? Of wicked desires or of desires for wickedness? Of healthy thoughts or of thoughts of healthy objects? Of good impulses, or of impulses towards the good? Of feelings of anger, or of angry feelings? Both in the mind and in the thing, these natures modify their context, exclude certain associates and determine others, have their mates and incompatibles. Yet not as stubbornly as in the case of physical qualities, for beauty and ugliness, love and hatred, pleasant and painful can, in certain complex experiences, coexist.

If one were to make an evolutionary construction of how a lot of originally chaotic pure experiences became gradually differentiated into an orderly inner and outer world, the whole theory would turn upon one's success in explaining how or why the quality of an experience, once active, could become less so, and, from being an energetic attribute in some cases, elsewhere lapse into the status of an inert or merely internal "nature." This would be the "evolution" of the psychical from the bosom of the physical, in which the aesthetic, moral and otherwise emotional experiences would represent a halfway stage.

But a last cry will probably go up from many readers. "All very pretty as a piece of ingenuity," they will say, "but our consciousness itself intuitively contradicts you. We, for our part, *know* that we are conscious. We *feel* our thought, flowing as a life within us, in absolute contrast with the objects which it so unremittingly escorts. We can not be faithless to this immediate intuition. The dualism is a fundamental *datum*: Let no man join what God has put asunder."

My reply to this is my last word, and I greatly grieve that to many it will sound materialistic. I can not help that, however, for I, too, have my intuitions and I must obey them. Let the case be what it may in others, I am as confident as I am of anything that, in myself, the stream of thinking (which I recognize emphatically as a phenomenon) is only a careless name for what, when scrutinized, reveals itself to consist chiefly of the stream of my breathing. The "I think" which Kant said must be able to accompany all my objects, is the "I breathe" which actually does accompany them. There are other internal facts besides breathing, and these increase the assets of "consciousness," so far as the latter is subject to immediate perception; but breath, which was ever the original of "spirit," breath moving outwards is, I am persuaded, the essence out of which philosophers have constructed the entity known to them as consciousness. *That entity is fictitious, while thoughts in the concrete are fully real. But thoughts in the concrete are made of the same stuff as things are.*

John Locke

IDENTITY AND DIVERSITY

If the identity of soul alone makes the same *man*; and there be nothing in the nature of matter why the same individual spirit may not be united to different bodies, it will be possible that those men, living in distant ages, and of different tempers, may have been the same man: which way of speaking must be from a very strange use of the word *man*, applied to an idea out of which body and shape are excluded.

It is not therefore unity of substance that comprehends all sorts of identity, or will determine it in every case; but to conceive and judge of it aright, we must consider what idea the word it is applied to stands for: it being one thing to be the same *substance*, another the same *man*, and a third the same *person*, if *person*, *man*, and *substance*, are three names standing for three different ideas; for such as is the idea belonging to that name, such must be the identity; which, if it had been a little more carefully attended to, would possibly have prevented a great deal of that confusion which often occurs about this matter, with no small seeming difficulties, especially concerning *personal* identity, which therefore we shall in the next place a little consider.

An animal is a living organized body; and consequently the same animal, as we have observed, is the same continued *life* communicated to different particles of matter, as they happen successively to be united to that organized living body. And whatever is talked of other definitions, ingenious observation puts it past doubt, that the idea in our minds, of which the sound *man* in our mouths is the sign, is nothing else but of an animal of such a certain form. Since I think I may be confident, that, whoever should see a creature of his own shape or make, though it had no more reason all its life than a cat or a parrot, would call him still a *man*; or whoever should hear a cat or a parrot discourse, reason, and philosophize, would call or think it nothing but a *cat* or a *parrot*; and say, the one was a dull irrational man, and the other a very intelligent rational parrot.

For I presume it is not the idea of a thinking or rational being alone that makes the *idea of a man* in most people's sense: but of a body, so and so shaped, joined to it; and if that be the idea of a man, the same successive body not shifted all at once, must, as well as the same immaterial spirit, go to the making of the same man.

This being premised, to find wherein *personal identity* consists, we must consider what *person* stands for; which, I think, is a thinking intelligent being, that has reason and reflection, and can consider itself as itself, the same thinking thing, in different times and places; which it does only by that consciousness which is inseparable from thinking, and, as it seems to me, essential to it: it being impossible for any one to perceive without *perceiving* that he does perceive. When we see, hear, smell, taste, feel, meditate, or will anything, we know that we do so. Thus it is always as to our present sensations and perceptions: and by this every one is to himself that which he calls *self*: it not being considered, in this case, whether the same self be continued in the same or diverse substances. For, since consciousness always accompanies thinking, and it is that which makes every one to be what he calls *self*, and thereby distinguishes himself from all other thinking things, in this alone consists personal identity, i.e., the sameness of a rational being: and as far as this consciousness can be extended backwards to any past action or thought, so far reaches the identity of that person; it is the same self now it was then; and it is by the same self with this present one that now reflects on it, that that action was done.

Edited from *An Essay Concerning Human Understanding,* 1690, Book II, Chapter XXVII, which is now in the public domain.

But it is further inquired, whether it be the same identical substance. This few would think they had reason to doubt of, if these perceptions, with their consciousness, always remained present in the mind, whereby the same thinking thing would be always consciously present, and, as would be thought, evidently the same to itself. But that which seems to make the difficulty is this, that this consciousness being interrupted always by forgetfulness, there being no moment of our lives wherein we have the whole train of all our past actions before our eyes in one view, but even the best memories losing the sight of one part while they are viewing another; and we sometimes, and that the greatest part of our lives, not reflecting on our past selves, being intent on our present thoughts, and in sound sleep having no thoughts at all, or at least none with that consciousness which remarks our waking thoughts—I say, in all these cases, our consciousness being interrupted, and we losing the sight of our past selves, doubts are raised whether we are the same thinking thing, i.e., the same *substance* or no. Which, however reasonable or unreasonable, concerns not *personal* identity at all. The question being what makes the same person; and not whether it be the same identical substance, which always thinks in the same person, which, in this case, matters not at all: different substances, by the same consciousness (where they do partake in it) being united into one person, as well as different bodies by the same life are united into one animal, whose identity is preserved in that change of substances by the unity of one continued life. For, it being the same consciousness that makes a man be himself to himself, personal identity depends on that only, whether it be annexed solely to one individual substance, or can be continued in a succession of several substances. For as far as any intelligent being *can* repeat the idea of any past action with the same consciousness it had of it at first, and with the same consciousness it has of any present action; so far it is the same personal self. For it is by the consciousness it has of its present thoughts and actions, that it is *self to itself* now, and so will be the same self, as far as the same consciousness can extend to actions past or to come; and would be by distance of time, or change of substance, no more two persons, than a man be two men by wearing other clothes to-day than he did yesterday, with a long or a short sleep between: the same consciousness uniting those distant actions into the same person, whatever substances contributed to their production.

That this is so, we have some kind of evidence in our very bodies, all whose particles, while vitally united to this same thinking conscious self, so that we *feel* when they are touched, and are affected by, and conscious of good or harm that happens to them, are a part of ourselves; i.e., of our thinking conscious self. Thus, the limbs of his body are to every one a part of himself; he sympathizes and is concerned for them. Cut off a hand, and thereby separate it from that consciousness he had of its heat, cold, and other affections, and it is then no longer a part of that which is himself, any more than the remotest part of matter. Thus, we see the *substance* whereof personal self consisted at one time may be varied at another, without the change of personal identity; there being no question about the same person, though the limbs which but now were a part of it, be cut off.

But the question is, Whether if the same substance which thinks be changed, it can be the same person; or, remaining the same, it can be different persons?

And to this I answer: First, this can be no question at all to those who place thought in a purely material animal constitution, void of an immaterial substance. For, whether their supposition be true or no, it is plain they conceive personal identity preserved in something else than identity of substance.

But next, as to the first part of the question, Whether, if the same thinking substance be changed, it can be the same person? I answer, that cannot be resolved but by those who know what kind of substances they are that do think; and whether the consciousness of past actions can be transferred from one thinking substance to another. I grant were the same consciousness the same individual action it could not: but it being a present representation of a past action, why it may not be possible, that that may be represented to the mind to have been which really never was, will remain to be shown. And therefore how far the consciousness of past actions is annexed to any individual agent, so that another cannot possibly have it, will be hard for us to determine, till we know what kind of action it is that cannot be done without a reflex act of perception accompanying it, and how performed by thinking substances, who cannot think without being conscious of it. But that which we call the same consciousness, not being the same individual act, why one intellectual substance may not have represented to it, as done by itself, what *it* never did, and was perhaps done by some other agent—why, I say, such a representation may not possibly be without reality of matter of fact, as well as several representations in dreams are, which yet while dreaming we take for true—will be difficult to conclude from the nature of things. But yet, to return to the question before us, it must be allowed, that, if the same consciousness can be transferred from one thinking substance to another, it will be possible that two thinking substances may make but one person. For the same consciousness being preserved, whether in the same or different substances, the personal identity is preserved.

And thus may we be able, without any difficulty, to conceive the same person at the resurrection, though in a body not exactly in make or parts the same which he had here—the same consciousness going along with the soul that inhabits it. But yet the soul alone, in the change of bodies, would scarce to any one but to him that makes the soul the man, be enough to make the same man. For should the soul of a prince, carrying with it the consciousness of the prince's past life, enter and inform the body of a cobbler, as soon as deserted by his own soul, every one sees he would be the same *person* with the prince, accountable only for the prince's actions: but who would say it was the same *man*? The body too goes to the making the man, and would, I guess, to everybody determine the man in this case, wherein the soul, with all its princely thoughts about it, would not make another man: but he would be the same cobbler to every one besides himself. I know that, in the ordinary way of speaking, the same person, and the same man, stand for one and the same thing. And indeed every one will always have a liberty to speak as he pleases, and to apply what articulate sounds to what ideas he thinks fit, and change them as often as he pleases. But yet, when we will inquire what makes the same *spirit*, *man*, or *person*, we must fix the ideas of spirit, man, or person in our minds; and having resolved with ourselves what we mean by them, it will not be hard to determine, in either of them, or the like, when it is the same, and when not.

But though the same immaterial substance or soul does not alone, wherever it be, and in whatsoever state, make the same *man*; yet it is plain, consciousness, as far as ever it can be extended—should it be to ages past—unites existences and actions very remote in time into the same *person*, as well as it does the existences and actions of the immediately preceding moment: so that whatever has the consciousness of present and past actions, is the same person to whom they both belong. Had I the same consciousness that I saw the ark and Noah's flood, as that I saw an overflowing of the Thames last winter, or as that I write now, I could no more doubt that I who write this now, that saw the Thames overflowed last winter, and that viewed the flood at the general deluge, was the same *self*—place that self in what *substance* you please—than that I who write this am the same *myself* now while I write (whether I consist of all the same substance material or immaterial, or no) that I was yesterday. For as to this point of being the same self, it matters not whether this present self be made up of the same or other substances—I being as much concerned, and as justly accountable for any action that was done a thousand years since, appropriated to me now by this self-consciousness, as I am for what I did the last moment.

Self is that conscious thinking thing—whatever substance made up of (whether spiritual or material, simple or compounded, it matters not)—which is sensible or conscious of pleasure and pain, capable of happiness or misery, and so is concerned for itself, as far as that consciousness extends. Thus every one finds that, while comprehended under that consciousness, the little finger is as much a part of himself as what is most so. Upon separation of this little finger, should this consciousness go along with the little finger, and leave the rest of the body, it is evident the little finger would be the person, the same person; and self then would have nothing to do with the rest of the body. As in this case it is the consciousness that goes along with the substance, when one part is separate from another, which makes the same person, and constitutes this inseparable self: so it is in reference to substances remote in time. That with which the consciousness of this present thinking thing *can* join itself, makes the same person, and is one self with it, and with nothing else; and so attributes to itself, and owns all the actions of that thing, as its own, as far as that consciousness reaches, and no further; as every one who reflects will perceive.

In this personal identity is founded all the right and justice of reward and punishment; happiness and misery being that for which every one is concerned for *himself*, and not mattering what becomes of any *substance*, not joined to, or affected with that consciousness. For, as it is evident in the instance I gave but now, if the consciousness went along with the little finger when it was cut off, that would be the same self which was concerned for the whole body yesterday, as making part of itself, whose actions then it cannot but admit as its own now. Though, if the same body should still live, and immediately from the separation of the little finger have its own peculiar consciousness, whereof the little finger knew nothing, it would not at all be concerned for it, as a part of itself, or could own any of its actions, or have any of them imputed to him.

This may show us wherein personal identity consists: not in the identity of substance, but, as I have said, in the identity of consciousness, wherein if Socrates and the present mayor of Queenborough agree, they are the same person: if the same Socrates waking and sleeping do not partake of the same consciousness, Socrates waking and sleeping is not the same person. And to punish Socrates waking for what sleeping Socrates thought, and waking Socrates was never conscious of, would be no more of right, than to punish one twin for what his brother-twin did, whereof he knew nothing, because their outsides were so like, that they could not be distinguished; for such twins have been seen.

But yet possibly it will still be objected—Suppose I wholly lose the memory of some parts of my life, beyond a possibility of retrieving them, so that perhaps I shall never be conscious of them again; yet am I not the same person that did those actions, had those thoughts that I once was conscious of, though I have now forgot them? To which I answer, that we must here take notice what the word *I* is applied to; which, in this case, is the *man* only. And the same man being presumed to be the same person, *I* is easily here supposed to stand also for the same person. But if it be possible for the same man to have distinct incommunicable consciousness at different times, it is past doubt the same man would at different times make different persons; which, we see, is the sense of mankind in the solemnest declaration of their opinions, human laws not punishing the mad man for the sober man's actions, nor the sober man for what the mad man did—thereby making them two persons: which is somewhat explained by our way of speaking in English when we say such an one is "not himself," or is "beside himself"; in which phrases it is insinuated, as if those who now, or at least first used them, thought that self was changed; the self-same person was no longer in that man.

But yet it is hard to conceive that Socrates, the same individual man, should be two persons. To help us a little in this, we must consider what is meant by Socrates, or the same individual *man*. First, it must be either the same individual, immaterial, thinking substance; in short, the same numerical soul, and nothing else. Secondly, or the same animal, without any regard to an immaterial soul. Thirdly, or the same immaterial spirit united to the same animal. Now, take which of these suppositions you please, it is impossible to make personal identity to consist in anything but consciousness; or reach any further than that does.

Nothing but consciousness can unite remote existences into the same person: the identity of substance will not do it; for whatever substance there is, however framed, without consciousness there is no person.

David Hume

I AM A BUNDLE OF PERCEPTIONS

There are some philosophers who imagine we are every moment intimately conscious of what we call our *Self*; that we feel its existence and its continuance in existence; and are certain, beyond the evidence of a demonstration, both of its perfect identity and simplicity. The strongest sensation, the most violent passion, say they, instead of distracting us from this view, only fix it the more intensely, and make us consider their influence on *self* either by their pain or pleasure. To attempt a farther proof of this were to weaken its evidence; since no proof can be derived from any fact, of which we are so intimately conscious; nor is there any thing, of which we can be certain, if we doubt of this.

Unluckily all these positive assertions are contrary to that very experience, which is pleaded for them, nor have we any idea of *self*, after the manner it is here explained. For from what impression could this idea be derived? This question is impossible to answer without a manifest contradiction and absurdity; and yet it is a question which must necessarily be answered if we would have the idea of self pass for clear and intelligible. It must be some one impression, that gives rise to every real idea. But self or person is not any one impression, but that to which our several impressions and ideas are supposed to have a reference. If any impression gives rise to the idea of self, that impression must continue invariably the same, through the whole course of our lives; since self is supposed to exist after that manner. But there is no impression constant and invariable. Pain and pleasure, grief and joy, passions and sensations succeed each other, and never all exist at the same time. It cannot, therefore, be from any of these impressions, or from any other, that the idea of self is derived; and consequently there is no such idea.

But farther, what must become of all our particular perceptions upon this hypothesis? All these are different, and distinguishable, and separable from each other, and may be separately considered, and may exist separately, and have no need of any thing to support their existence. After what manner, therefore, do they belong to self; and how are they connected with it? For my part, when I enter most intimately into what I call *myself*, I always stumble on some particular perception or other, of heat or cold, light or shade, love or hatred, pain or pleasure. I never can catch *myself* at any time without a perception, and never can observe any thing but the perception. When my perceptions are removed for any time, as by sound sleep; so long am I insensible of *myself*, and may truly be said not to exist. And were all my perceptions removed by death, and could I neither think, nor feel, nor see, nor love, nor hate after the dissolution of my body, I should be entirely annihilated, nor do I conceive what is farther requisite to make me a perfect non-entity. If any one, upon serious and unprejudiced reflection, thinks he has a different notion of *himself*, I must confess I can reason no longer with him. All I can allow him is, that he may be in the right as well as I, and that we are essentially different in this particular. He may, perhaps, perceive something simple and continued, which he calls *himself*; though I am certain there is no such principle in me.

I may venture to affirm of the rest of mankind, that they are nothing but a bundle or collection of different perceptions, which succeed each other with an inconceivable rapidity, and are in a perpetual flux and movement. Our eyes cannot turn in their sockets without varying our perceptions. Our thought is still more variable than our sight; and all our other senses and faculties

Edited from *A Treatise of Human Nature,* 1777, Vol. I, Book I, Part IV, Section VI, which is now in the public domain.

contribute to this change; nor is there any single power of the soul, which remains unalterably the same, perhaps for one moment. The mind is a kind of theatre, where several perceptions successively make their appearance; pass, re-pass, glide away, and mingle in an infinite variety of postures and situations. There is properly no *simplicity* in it at one time, nor *identity* in different; whatever natural propensity we may have to imagine that simplicity and identity. The comparison of the theatre must not mislead us. They are the successive perceptions only, that constitute the mind; nor have we the most distant notion of the place, where these scenes are represented, or of the materials, of which it is composed.

Part Seven: Free Will

Introduction

To most people, the strong internal feeling that we are free to make choices seems beyond doubt. When we are confronted by simple alternatives—between eating an apple or a cookie—or more series actions—between staying in a relationship or ending it—we are directly aware of our deliberations. We believe that what we ultimately choose is the result of our *free will*. Not surprisingly though, some philosophers have doubts about this.

The passages that you read will present many sides of the philosophical issues regarding free will and determinism. Let's start with determinism. One reason why science has managed to solve so many mysteries of how the world works has been its reliance on the principles of *causality*. Scientific thinking assumes that everything that happens has a physical causal network that can be discovered by using reason and experiments. Science eliminates the need for extra-physical causes—curses, superstitions, magic, angry gods, to name only a few—and instead looks to physical causes for physical events. *Determinism* is the theory that everything that happens is completely determined by the basic physical, causal laws of the universe. Thus, every event (effect) is completely determined by a physical cause.

If determinism is correct, then what place is there for free will? Since our bodies are physical objects, they are, like every other physical object in the universe, completely subject to causal laws. No one would argue that if we fell off a tall building without some device for keeping us afloat, then gravity would cause us to fall downwards. Unaided, we certainly cannot simply will ourselves not to fall. However, an advocate of free will might argue that there are other examples where the physical laws governing physical motion are not relevant. The advocate might point to our earlier example of choosing to eat either an apple or a cookie. Surely, the advocate argues, no physical laws dictate my choice; therefore, whether I eat the apple or the cookie is the result of my free choice.

The proponents of determinism can counter with evidence that your current "choices" are really the end result of your entire life. In other words, you don't really choose to like pizza and hate anchovies, for example, or choose to like swimming and dislike skiing. Nor do you choose to hate hot and humid conditions and prefer cool, dry places. You are born with a certain set of *predispositions*—a tendency to react in a certain way based on genetic and environmental factors. Predispositions are easy to understand in inorganic substances; for example, we say that sugar is predisposed to dissolve in hot water because of its chemical composition. Sugar does not choose to dissolve, and it cannot refuse to do so.

"However," the advocates of free will argue, "humans are not entirely physical. Although we have *brains*, which are physical, we also have *minds*, which are not physical, and are not subject to the physical, causal laws of nature."

The readings in this section will explore several facets of this topic. It will touch upon *mind, freedom*, *intellect*, and the *will*. Other readings will discuss the possibility that since everything in nature proceeds by necessity, humans cannot have free will. Perhaps we believe ourselves to be free because we are conscious of our volitions and desires. However, if everything that happens in our minds is determined by a cause, and every cause has a prior cause, and so on, then how are we free? These discussions impact issues such as "good and bad," "right and wrong," and "praise and blame."

So, are we free agents, or is free will an illusion? Perhaps those occasions when we seem to "deliberate," or we can't seem to "make up our minds," are simply situations where conflicting forces acting on us are not strong enough in any direction to get us to act. In other words, when the causal forces finally tip in one direction, then we act; if so, then our eventual "choice" is not based on our being free agents.

John Locke

FREE AGENTS

This, at least, I think evident—That we find in ourselves a power to begin or forbear, continue or end several actions of our minds, and motions of our bodies, barely by a thought or preference of the mind ordering, or as it were commanding, the doing or not doing such or such a particular action. This power which the mind has thus to order the consideration of any idea, or the forbearing to consider it; or to prefer the motion of any part of the body to its rest, and *vice versa*, in any particular instance, is that which we call the *Will*. The actual exercise of that power, by directing any particular action, or its forbearance, is that which we call *volition* or *willing*. The forbearance of that action, consequent to such order or command of the mind, is called *voluntary*. And whatsoever action is performed without such a thought of the mind, is called *involuntary*. The power of perception is that which we call the *understanding*.

The *understanding* and *will* are two *faculties* of the mind; a word proper enough, if it be used, as all words should be, so as not to breed any confusion in men's thoughts, by being supposed to stand for some real beings in the soul that performed those actions of understanding and volition. For when we say the *will* is the commanding and superior faculty of the soul; that it is or is not free; that it determines the inferior faculties; that it follows the dictates of the understanding, etc.,—though these and the like expressions, by those that carefully attend to their own ideas, and conduct their thoughts more by the evidence of things than the sound of words, may be understood in a clear and distinct sense—yet I suspect, I say, that this way of speaking of *faculties* has misled many into a confused notion of so many distinct agents in us, which had their several provinces and authorities, and did command, obey, and perform several actions, as so many distinct beings; which has been no small occasion of wrangling, obscurity, and uncertainty, in questions relating to them.

Everyone, I think, finds in *himself* a power to begin or forbear, continue or put an end to several actions in himself. From the consideration of the extent of this power of the mind over the actions of the man, which everyone finds in himself, arise the *ideas* of *liberty* and *necessity*.

All the actions that we have any idea of reducing themselves, as has been said, to these two, namely, *thinking* and *motion*; so far as a man has power to think or not to think, to move or not to move, according to the preference or direction of his own mind, so far is a man *free*. Wherever any performance or forbearance are not equally in a man's power; wherever doing or not doing will *not* equally *follow* upon the preference of his mind directing it, there he is *not free*, though perhaps the action may be voluntary. So that the idea of *liberty* is the idea of a power in any agent to do or forbear any particular action, according to the determination or thought of the mind, whereby either of them is preferred to the other: where either of them is not in the power of the agent to be produced by him according to his volition, there he is not at liberty; that agent is under *necessity*. So that liberty cannot be where there is no thought, no volition, no will; but there may be thought, there may be will, there may be volition, where there is no liberty. A little consideration of an obvious instance or two may make this clear.

A tennis-ball, whether in motion by the stroke of a racket, or lying still at rest, is not by any one taken to be a free agent. If we inquire into the reason, we shall find it is because we conceive not a tennis-ball to think, and consequently not to have any volition, or *preference* of motion to rest, or *vice versa*; and therefore has not liberty, is not a free agent; but all its both motion and rest come

Edited from *An Essay Concerning Human Understanding*, 1690, Book II, Chapter XXI, which is now in the public domain.

under our idea of necessary, and are so called. Likewise a man falling into the water, (a bridge breaking under him,) has not herein liberty, is not a free agent. For though he has volition, though he prefers his not falling to falling; yet the forbearance of that motion not being in his power, the stop or cessation of that motion follows not upon his volition; and therefore therein he is not free. So a man striking himself, or his friend, by a convulsive motion of his arm, which it is not in his power, by volition or the direction of his mind, to stop or forbear, nobody thinks he has in this liberty; every one pities him, as acting by necessity and constraint.

Again: suppose a man be carried, whilst fast asleep, into a room where is a person he longs to see and speak with; and be there locked fast in, beyond his power to get out: he awakes, and is glad to find himself in so desirable company, which he stays willingly in, i.e., prefers his stay to going away. I ask, is not this stay voluntary? I think nobody will doubt it: and yet, being locked fast in, it is evident he is not at liberty not to stay, he has not freedom to be gone. So that liberty is not an idea belonging to volition, or preferring; but to the person having the power of doing, or forbearing to do, according as the mind shall choose or direct. Our idea of liberty reaches as far as that power, and no farther. For wherever restraint comes to check that power, or compulsion takes away that indifferency of ability to act, or to forbear acting, there liberty, and our notion of it, presently ceases.

We have instances enough, and often more than enough, in our own bodies. A man's heart beats, and the blood circulates, which it is not in his power by any thought or volition to stop; and therefore in respect of these motions, where rest depends not on his choice, nor would follow the determination of his mind, if it should prefer it, he is not a free agent. Voluntary, then, is not opposed to necessary but to involuntary. For a man may prefer what he can do, to what he cannot do; the state he is in, to its absence or change; though necessity has made it in itself unalterable.

As it is in the motions of the body, so it is in the thoughts of our minds: where any one is such, that we have power to take it up, or lay it by, according to the preference of the mind, there we are at liberty. A waking man, being under the necessity of having some ideas constantly in his mind, is not at liberty to think or not to think; no more than he is at liberty, whether his body shall touch any other or no, but whether he will remove his contemplation from one idea to another is many times in his choice; and then he is, in respect of his ideas, as much at liberty as he is in respect of bodies he rests on; he can at pleasure remove himself from one to another. But yet some ideas to the mind, like some motions to the body, are such as in certain circumstances it cannot avoid, nor obtain their absence by the utmost effort it can use. A man on the rack is not at liberty to lay by the idea of pain, and divert himself with other contemplations: and sometimes a boisterous passion hurries our thoughts, as a hurricane does our bodies, without leaving us the liberty of thinking on other things, which we would rather choose. But as soon as the mind regains the power to stop or continue, begin or forbear, any of these motions of the body without, or thoughts within, according as it thinks fit to prefer either to the other, we then consider the man as a *free agent* again.

Wherever thought is wholly wanting, or the power to act or forbear according to the direction of thought, there necessity takes place. This, in an agent capable of volition, when the beginning or continuation of any action is contrary to that preference of his mind, is called *compulsion*; when the hindering or stopping any action is contrary to his volition, it is called *restraint*. Agents that have no thought, no volition at all, are in everything *necessary agents*.

If this be so, (as I imagine it is), I leave it to be considered, whether it may not help to put an end to that long agitated, and, I think, unreasonable, because unintelligible question: *Whether man's will be free or no?* For if I mistake not, it follows from what I have said, that the question itself is altogether improper; and it is as insignificant to ask whether man's *will* be free, as to ask whether his sleep be swift, or his virtue square: liberty being as little applicable to the will, as swiftness of motion is to sleep, or squareness to virtue. Every one would laugh at the absurdity of such a question as either of these: because it is obvious that the modifications of motion belong not to sleep, nor the difference of figure to virtue; and when any one well considers it, I think he will as plainly perceive that liberty, which is but a power, belongs only to *agents*, and cannot be an attribute or modification of the will, which is also but a power.

Such is the difficulty of explaining and giving clear notions of internal actions by sounds, that I must here warn my reader, that *ordering, directing, choosing, preferring*, etc., which I have made use of, will not distinctly enough express volition, unless he will reflect on what he himself does when he wills. For example, preferring, which seems perhaps best to express the act of volition, does it not precisely. For though a man would prefer flying to walking, yet who can say he ever wills it? Volition, it is plain, is an act of the mind knowingly exerting that dominion it takes itself to have over any part of the man, by employing it in, or withholding it from, any particular action. And what is the will, but the faculty to do this? And is that faculty anything more in effect than a power; the power of the mind to determine its thought, to the producing, continuing, or stopping any action, as far as it depends on us? For can it be denied that whatever agent has a power to think on its own actions, and to prefer their doing or omission either to other, has that faculty called will? *Will*, then, is nothing but such a power. *Liberty*, on the other side, is the power a *man* has to do or forbear doing any particular action according as its doing or forbearance has the actual preference in the mind; which is the same thing as to say, according as he himself wills it.

It is plain then that the *will* is nothing but one power or ability, and *freedom* another power or ability so that, to ask, whether the will has freedom, is to ask whether one power has another power, one ability another ability; a question at first sight too grossly absurd to make a dispute, or need an answer. For, who is it that sees not that powers belong only to agents, and are attributes only of substances, and not of powers themselves? So that this way of putting the question (whether the will be free) is in effect to ask, whether the will be a substance, an agent, or at least to suppose it, since freedom can properly be attributed to nothing else. If freedom can with any propriety of speech be applied to power, it may be attributed to the power that is in a man to produce, or forbear producing, motion in parts of his body, by choice or preference; which is that which denominates him free, and is freedom itself. But if any one should ask, whether freedom were free, he would be suspected not to understand well what he said.

However, the name *faculty*, which men have given to this power called the will, and whereby they have been led into a way of talking of the will as acting, may, by an appropriation that disguises its true sense, serve a little to palliate the absurdity; yet the will, in truth, signifies nothing but a power or ability to prefer or choose: and when the will, under the name of a faculty, is considered as it is, barely as an ability to do something, the absurdity in saying it is free, or not free, will easily discover itself. For, if it be reasonable to suppose and talk of faculties as distinct beings that can act, (as we do, when we say the will orders, and the will is free), it is fit that we should make a speaking faculty, and a walking faculty, and a dancing faculty, by which these actions are produced, which are but several modes of motion; as well as we make the will and understanding to be faculties, by which the actions of choosing and perceiving are produced, which are but several modes of thinking. And we may as properly say that it is the singing faculty sings, and the dancing faculty dances, as that the will chooses, or that the understanding conceives; or, as is usual, that the will directs the understanding, or the understanding obeys or obeys not the will: it being altogether as proper and intelligible to say that the power of speaking directs the power of singing, or the power of singing obeys or disobeys the power of speaking.

This way of talking, nevertheless, has prevailed, and, as I guess, produced great confusion. For these being all different powers in the mind, or in the man, to do several actions, he exerts them as he thinks fit: but the power to do one action is not operated on by the power of doing another action. For the power of thinking operates not on the power of choosing, nor the power of choosing on the power of thinking; no more than the power of dancing operates on the power of singing, or the power of singing on the power of dancing, as any one who reflects on it will easily perceive. And yet this is it which we say when we thus speak, that the will operates on the understanding, or the understanding on the will.

I grant, that this or that actual thought may be the occasion of volition, or exercising the power a man has to choose; or the actual choice of the mind, the cause of actual thinking on this or that thing: as the actual singing of such a tune may be the cause of dancing such a dance, and the actual dancing of such a dance the occasion of singing such a tune. But in all these it is not one *power* that operates on another: but it is the mind that operates, and exerts these powers; it is the man that does the action; it is the agent that has power, or is able to do. For powers are relations, not agents: and that which has the power or not the power to operate, is that alone which is or is not free, and not the power itself. For freedom, or not freedom, can belong to nothing but what has or has not a power to act.

To return, then, to the inquiry about liberty, I think the question is not proper, *whether the will be free*, but *whether a man be free*. Thus, I think, *First*, that so far as any one can, by the direction or choice of his mind, preferring the existence of any action to the non-existence of that action, and *vice versa*, make *it* to exist or not exist, so far *he* is free. For if I can, by a thought directing the motion of my finger, make it move when it was at rest, or *vice versa*, it is evident, that in respect of that I am free: and if I can, by a like thought of my mind, preferring one to the other, produce either words or silence, I am at liberty to speak or hold my peace: and as far as this power reaches, of acting or not acting, by the determination of his own thought preferring either, so far is a man free. For how can we think any one freer, than to have the power to do what he will? And so far as any one can, by preferring any action to its not being, or rest to any action, produce that action or rest, so far can he do what he will. For such a preferring of action to its absence, is the willing of it: and we can scarce tell how to imagine any being freer, than to be able to do what he wills. So that in respect of actions within the reach of such a power in him, a man seems as free as it is possible for freedom to make him.

But the inquisitive mind of man, willing to shift off from himself, as far as he can, all thoughts of guilt, though it be by putting himself into a worse state than that of fatal necessity, is not content with this: freedom, unless it reaches further than this, will not serve the turn: and it passes for a good plea, that a man is not free at all, if he be not as *free to will* as he is to *act what he wills*. Concerning a man's liberty, there yet, therefore, is raised this further question, *Whether a man be free to will?* which I think is what is meant, when it is disputed whether the will be free.

Secondly, that willing, or volition, being an action, and freedom consisting in a power of acting or not acting, a man in respect of willing or the act of volition, when any action in his power is once proposed to his thoughts, as presently to be done, cannot be free. The reason whereof is very manifest. For, it being unavoidable that the action depending on his will should exist or not exist, and its existence or not existence following perfectly the determination and preference of his will, he cannot avoid willing the existence or non-existence of that action; it is absolutely necessary that he will the one or the other; i.e., prefer the one to the other: since one of them must necessarily follow; and that which does follow follows by the choice and determination of his mind; that is, by his willing it: for if he did not will it, it would not be. So that, in respect of the act of willing, a man in such a case is not free: liberty consisting in a power to act or not to act; which, in regard of volition, a man, upon such a proposal has not. For it is unavoidably necessary to prefer the doing or forbearance of an action in a man's power, which is once so proposed to his thoughts; a man must necessarily will one or the other of them; upon which preference or volition, the action or its forbearance certainly follows, and is truly voluntary. But the act of volition, or preferring one of the two, being that which he cannot avoid, a man, in respect of that act of willing, is under a necessity, and so cannot be free; unless necessity and freedom can consist together, and a man can be free and bound at once. Besides to make a man free after this manner, by making the action of willing to depend on his will, there must be another antecedent will, to determine the acts of this will, and another to determine that, and so on *in infinitum*: for wherever one stops, the actions of the last will cannot be free. Nor is any being, as far as I can comprehend beings above me, capable of such a freedom of will, that it can forbear to will, i.e., to prefer the being or not being of anything in its power, which it has once considered as such.

This, then, is evident, That *a man is not at liberty to will, or not to will, anything in his power that he once considers of*: liberty consisting in a power to act or to forbear acting, and in that only. For a man that sits still is said yet to be at liberty; because he can walk if he wills it. A man that walks is at liberty also, not because he walks or moves; but because he can stand still if he wills it. But if a man sitting still has not a power to remove himself, he is not at liberty; so likewise a man falling down a precipice, though in motion, is not at liberty, because he cannot stop that motion if he would. This being so, it is plain that a man that is walking, to whom it is proposed to give off walking, is not at liberty, whether he will determine himself to walk, or give off walking or not: he must necessarily prefer one or the other of them; walking or not walking. And so it is in regard of all other actions in our power, so proposed, which are the far greater number. For, considering the vast number of voluntary actions that succeed one another every moment that we are awake in the course of our lives, there are but few of them that are thought on or proposed to the will, till the time they are to be done; and in all such actions, as I have shown, the mind, in respect of willing has not a power to act or not to act, wherein consists liberty. The mind, in that case, has not a power to forbear *willing*; it cannot avoid some determination concerning them, let the consideration be as short, the thought as quick as it will, it either leaves the man in the state he was before thinking, or changes it; continues the action, or puts an end to it. Whereby it is manifest, that *it* orders and directs one, in preference to, or with neglect of the other, and thereby either the continuation or change becomes *unavoidably* voluntary.

Since then it is plain that, in most cases, a man is not at liberty, whether he will or no, (for, when an action in his power is proposed to his thoughts, he *cannot* forbear volition; he *must* determine one way or the other); the next thing demanded is—*Whether a man be at liberty to will which of the two he pleases, motion or rest?* This question carries the absurdity of it so manifestly in itself, that one might thereby sufficiently be convinced that liberty concerns not the will. For, to ask whether a man be at liberty to will either motion or rest, speaking or silence, which he pleases, is to ask whether a man can will what he wills, or be pleased with what he is pleased with? A question which, I think, needs no answer: and they who can make a question of it must suppose one will to determine the acts of another, and another to determine that, and so on *in infinitum.*

To avoid these and the like absurdities, nothing can be of greater use than to establish in our minds determined ideas of the things under consideration. If the ideas of liberty and volition were well fixed in our understandings, and carried along with us in our minds, as they ought, through all the questions that are raised about them, I suppose a great part of the difficulties that perplex men's thoughts, and entangle their understandings, would be much easier resolved; and we should perceive where the confused signification of terms, or where the nature of the thing caused the obscurity.

First, then, it is carefully to be remembered, That *freedom* consists in the dependence of the existence, or not existence of any *action*, upon our *volition* of it; and not in the dependence of any action, or its contrary, on our *preference*. A man standing on a cliff is at liberty to leap twenty yards downwards into the sea, not because he has a power to do the contrary action, which is to leap twenty yards upwards, for that he cannot do; but he is therefore free, because he has a power to leap or not to leap. But if a greater force than his, either holds him fast, or tumbles him down, he is no longer free in that case; because the doing or forbearance of that particular action is no longer in his power. He that is a close prisoner in a room twenty feet square, being at the north side of his chamber, is at liberty to walk twenty feet southward, because he can walk or not walk it; but is not, at the same time, at liberty to do the contrary, i.e., to walk twenty feet northward. In this, then, consists *freedom*, namely in our being able to act or not to act, according as we shall choose or will.

Secondly, we must remember, that *volition* or *willing* is an act of the mind directing its thought to the production of any action, and thereby exerting its power to produce it. To avoid multiplying of words, I would crave leave here, under the word *action*, to comprehend the forbearance too of any action proposed: sitting still, or holding one's peace, when walking or speaking are proposed, though mere forbearances, requiring as much the determination of the will, and being as often weighty in their consequences, as the contrary actions, may, on that consideration, well enough pass for actions too: but this I say, that I may not be mistaken, if I speak thus.

Thirdly, the will being nothing but a power in the mind to direct the operative faculties of a man to motion or rest, as far as they depend on such direction; to the question, What is it determines the will? The true and proper answer is, The mind. For that which determines the general power of directing, to this or that particular direction, is nothing but the agent itself exercising the power it has that particular way. If this answer satisfies not, it is plain the meaning of the question, What determines the will? is this—What moves the mind, in every particular instance, to determine its general power of directing, to this or that particular motion or rest? And to this I answer—The motive for continuing in the same state or action, is only the present satisfaction in it; the motive to change is always some uneasiness: nothing setting us upon the change of state, or upon any new action, but some uneasiness. This is the great motive that works on the mind to put it upon action, which for shortness' sake we will call determining of the will.

Baruch Spinoza

EVERYTHING HAPPENS OUT OF NECESSITY

In the mind there is no absolute or free will; but the mind is determined to wish this or that by a cause, which has also been determined by another cause, and this last by another cause, and so on to infinity.

Proof: The mind is a fixed and definite mode of thought, therefore it cannot be the free cause of its actions; in other words, it cannot have an absolute faculty of positive or negative volition; but it must be determined by a cause, which has also been determined by another cause, and this last by another.

In the same way it is proved, that there is in the mind no absolute faculty of understanding, desiring, loving, etc. Whence it follows, that these and similar faculties are either entirely fictitious, or are merely abstract and general terms, such as we are accustomed to put together from particular things. Thus the intellect and the will stand in the same relation to this or that idea, or this or that volition, as "man" to Peter and Paul.

Edited from *Ethics,* Part II, Proposition XLVIII. Translated by R.H.M. Elwes, 1883, which is now in the public domain.

David Hume

OF LIBERTY AND NECESSITY

We come now to explain the direct passions, or the impressions, which arise immediately from good or evil, from pain or pleasure. Of this kind are, desire and aversion, grief and joy, hope and fear. Of all the immediate effects of pain and pleasure, there is none more remarkable than the *will*; and though properly speaking, it be not comprehended among the passions, yet as the full understanding of its nature and properties, is necessary to the explanation of them, we shall here make it the subject of our enquiry.

I desire it may be observed, that by the *will*, I mean nothing but the internal impression we feel and are conscious of, when we knowingly give rise to any new motion of our body, or new perception of our mind. This impression, like the preceding ones of pride and humility, love and hatred, it is impossible to define, and needless to describe any farther; for which reason we shall cut off all those definitions and distinctions, with which philosophers are wont to perplex rather than clear up this question; and entering at first upon the subject, shall examine that long disputed question concerning liberty and necessity; which occurs so naturally in treating of the *will*.

It is universally acknowledged, that the operations of external bodies are necessary, and that in the communication of their motion, in their attraction, and mutual cohesion, there are not the least traces of indifference or liberty. Every object is determined by an absolute fate to a certain degree and direction of its motion, and can no more depart from that precise line, in which it moves, than it can convert itself into an angel, or spirit, or any superior substance. The actions, therefore, of matter are to be regarded as instances of necessary actions; and whatever is in this respect on the same footing with matter, must be acknowledged to be necessary. That we may know whether this be the case with the actions of the *mind*, we shall begin with examining *matter*, and considering on what the idea of a necessity in its operations are founded, and why we conclude one body or action to be the infallible cause of another.

It has been observed already, that in no single instance the ultimate connection of any objects is discoverable, either by our senses or reason, and that we can never penetrate so far into the essence and construction of bodies, as to perceive the principle, on which their mutual influence depends. It is their constant union alone, with which we are acquainted; and it is from the constant union the necessity arises. If objects had not a uniform and regular conjunction with each other, we should never arrive at any idea of cause and effect; and even after all, the necessity, which enters into that idea, is nothing but a determination of the mind to pass from one object to its usual attendant, and infer the existence of one from that of the other. Here then are two particulars, which we are to consider as essential to necessity, viz, the constant union and the inference of the mind; and wherever we discover these we must acknowledge a necessity. As the actions of matter have no necessity, but what is derived from these circumstances, and it is not by any insight into the essence of bodies we discover their connection, the absence of this insight, while the union and inference remain, will never, in any case, remove the necessity. It is the observation of the union, which produces the inference; for which reason it might be thought sufficient, if we prove a constant union in the actions of the mind, in order to establish the inference, along with the necessity of these actions. But that I may bestow a greater force on my reasoning, I shall examine

Edited from *A Treatise of Human Nature,* 1777, Vol. II, Book I, Part III, Sections I-III, which is now in the public domain.

these particulars apart, and shall first prove from experience that our actions have a constant union with our motives, tempers, and circumstances, before I consider the inferences we draw from it.

To this end, a very slight and general view of the common course of human affairs will be sufficient. There is no light, in which we can take them, that does nor confirm this principle. Whether we consider mankind according to the difference of sexes, ages, governments, conditions, or methods of education; the same uniformity and regular operation of natural principles are discernible. Like causes still produce like effects; in the same manner as in the mutual action of the elements and powers of nature.

There are different trees, which regularly produce fruit, whose relish is different from each other; and this regularity will be admitted as an instance of necessity and causes in external bodies. Are the changes of our body from infancy to old age more regular and certain than those of our mind and conduct? And would a man be more ridiculous, who would expect that an infant of four years old will raise a weight of three hundred pound, than one, who from a person of the same age would look for a philosophical reasoning, or a prudent and well-concerted action?

We must certainly allow, that the cohesion of the parts of matter arises from natural and necessary principles, whatever difficulty we may find in explaining them. And for a reason we must allow, that human society is founded on like principles; and our reason in the latter case, is better than even that in the former; because we not only observe that men always seek society, but can also explain the principles on which this universal propensity is founded.

The skin, pores, muscles, and nerves of a day-laborer are different from those of a man of quality. So are his sentiments, actions and manners. The different stations of life influence the whole fabric, external and internal; and different stations arise necessarily, because uniformly, from the necessary and uniform principles of human nature. Men cannot live without society, and cannot be associated without government. Government makes a distinction of property, and establishes the different ranks of men. This produces industry, traffic, manufactures, law-suits, war, leagues, alliances, voyages, travels, cities, fleets, ports, and all those other actions and objects, which cause such a diversity, and at the same time maintain such an uniformity in human life.

Should a traveler, returning from a far country, tell us, that he had seen a climate in the fiftieth degree of northern latitude, where all the fruits ripen and come to perfection in the winter, and decay in the summer, after the same manner as in England they are produced and decay in the contrary seasons, he would find few so credulous as to believe him. I am apt to think a traveler would meet with as little credit, who should inform us of people exactly of the same character with those in Plato's republic on the one hand, or those in Hobbes's Leviathan on the other. There is a general course of nature in human actions, as well as in the operations of the sun and the climate. There are also characters peculiar to different nations and particular persons, as well as common to mankind. The knowledge of these characters is founded on the observation of an uniformity in the actions, that flow from them; and this uniformity forms the very essence of necessity.

I can imagine only one way of eluding this argument, which is by denying that uniformity of human actions, on which it is founded. As long as actions have a constant union and connection with the situation and temper of the agent, however we may in words refuse to acknowledge the necessity, we really allow the thing. Now some may, perhaps, find a pretext to deny this regular union and connection. For what is more capricious than human actions? What more inconstant than the desires of man? And what creature departs more widely, not only from right reason, but from his own character and disposition? An hour, a moment, is sufficient to make him change from one extreme to another, and overturn what cost the greatest pain and labor to establish. Necessity is regular and certain. Human conduct is irregular and uncertain. The one, therefore, proceeds not from the other.

To this I reply, that in judging of the actions of men we must proceed upon the same maxims, as when we reason concerning external objects. When any phenomena are constantly and invariably conjoined together, they acquire such a connection in the imagination, that it passes from one to the other, without any doubt or hesitation. But below this there are many inferior degrees of evidence and probability, nor does one single contrariety of experiment entirely destroy all our reasoning. The mind balances the contrary experiments, and deducting the inferior from the superior, proceeds with that degree of assurance or evidence, which remains. Even when these contrary experiments are entirely equal, we remove not the notion of causes and necessity; but supposing that the usual contrariety proceeds from the operation of contrary and concealed causes, we conclude, that the chance or indifference lies only in our judgment on account of our imperfect knowledge, not in the things themselves, which are in every case equally necessary, though to appearance not equally constant or certain. No union can be more constant and certain, than that of some actions with some motives and characters; and if in other cases the union is uncertain, it is no more than what happens in the operations of body, nor can we conclude any thing from the one irregularity, which will not follow equally from the other.

It is commonly allowed that mad-men have no liberty. But were we to judge by their actions, these have less regularity and constancy than the actions of wise-men, and consequently are farther removed from necessity. Our way of thinking in this particular is, therefore, absolutely inconsistent; but is a natural consequence of these confused ideas and undefined terms, which we so commonly make use of in our reasonings, especially on the present subject.

We must now show that as the union betwixt motives and actions has the same constancy, as that in any natural operations, so its influence on the understanding is also the same, in determining us to infer the existence of one from that of another. If this shall appear, there is no known circumstance, that enters into the connection and production of the actions of matter, that is not to be found in all the operations of the mind; and consequently we cannot, without a manifest absurdity, attribute necessity to the one, and refuse into the other.

There is no philosopher whose judgment is so riveted to this fantastical system of liberty, as not to acknowledge the force of moral evidence, and both in speculation and practice proceed upon it, as upon a reasonable foundation. Now moral evidence is nothing but a conclusion concerning the actions of men, derived from the consideration of their motives, temper and situation. Thus when we see certain characters or figures described upon paper, we infer that the person, who produced them, would affirm such facts, the death of Caesar, the success of Augustus, the cruelty of Nero; and remembering many other concurrent testimonies we conclude, that those facts were once really existent, and that so many men, without any interest, would never conspire to deceive us; especially since they must, in the attempt, expose themselves to the derision of all their contemporaries, when these facts were asserted to be recent and universally known. The same kind of reasoning runs through politics, war, commerce, economy, and indeed mixes itself so entirely in human life, that it is impossible to act or subsist a moment without having recourse to it. A prince, who imposes a tax upon his subjects, expects their compliance. A general, who conducts an army, makes account of a certain degree of courage. A merchant looks for fidelity and skill in his factory or super-cargo. A man, who gives orders for his dinner, doubts not of the obedience of his servants. In short, as nothing more nearly interests us than our own actions and those of others, the greatest part of our reasonings is employed in judgments concerning them. Now I assert, that whoever reasons after this manner, does *ipso facto* believe the actions of the *will* to arise from *necessity*, and that he knows not what he means when he denies it.

All those objects, of which we call the one cause and the other effect, considered in themselves, are as distinct and separate from each other, as any two things in nature, nor can we ever, by the most accurate survey of them, infer the existence of the one from that of the other. It is only from experience and the observation of their constant union, that we are able to form this inference; and even after all, the inference is nothing but the effects of custom on the imagination. We must not here be content with saying that the idea of cause and effect arises from objects constantly united; but must affirm, that it is the very same with the idea of those objects, and that the necessary connection is not discovered by a conclusion of the understanding, but is merely a perception of the mind. Wherever, therefore, we observe the same union, and wherever the union operates in the same manner upon the belief and opinion, we have the idea of causes and necessity, though perhaps we may avoid those expressions. Motion in one body in all past instances, that have fallen under our observation, is followed upon impulse by motion in another. It is impossible for the mind to penetrate farther. From this constant union it forms the idea of cause and effect, and by its influence feels the necessity. As there is the same constancy, and the same influence in what we call moral evidence, I ask no more. What remains can only be a dispute of words.

And indeed, when we consider how aptly natural and moral evidence cement together, and form only one chain of argument betwixt them, we shall make no scruple to allow, that they are of the same nature, and derived from the same principles. A prisoner, who has neither money nor interest, discovers the impossibility of his escape, as well from the obstinacy of the goaler, as from the walls and bars with which he is surrounded; and in all attempts for his freedom chooses rather to work upon the stone and iron of the one, than upon the inflexible nature of the other. The same prisoner, when conducted to the scaffold, foresees his death as certainly from the constancy and fidelity of his guards as from the operation of the ax or wheel. His mind runs along a certain train of ideas: The refusal of the soldiers to consent to his escape, the action of the executioner; the separation of the head and body; bleeding, convulsive motions, and death. Here is a connected chain of natural causes and voluntary actions; but the mind feels no difference betwixt them in passing from one link to another; nor is less certain of the future event than if it were connected with the present impressions of the memory and senses by a train of causes cemented together by what we are pleased to call a physical necessity. The same experienced union has the same effect on the mind, whether the united objects be motives, volitions and actions; or figure and motion. We may change the names of things; but their nature and their operation on the understanding never change.

I dare be positive no one will ever endeavor to refute these reasonings otherwise than by altering my definitions, and assigning a different meaning to the terms of *cause* and *effect*, and *necessity*, and *liberty*, and *chance*. According to my definitions, necessity makes an essential part of causation; and consequently liberty, by removing necessity, removes also causes, and is the very same thing with chance. As chance is commonly thought to imply a contradiction, and is at least directly contrary to experience, there are always the same arguments against liberty or free-will. If any one alters the definitions, I cannot pretend to argue with him, until I know the meaning he assigns to these terms.

I believe we may assign the three following reasons for the prevalence of the doctrine of liberty, however absurd it may be in one sense, and unintelligible in any other. First, after we have performed any action, though we confess we were influenced by particular views and motives, it is difficult for us to persuade ourselves we were governed by necessity, and that it was utterly impossible for us to have acted otherwise; the idea of necessity seeming to imply something of force, and violence, and constraint, of which we are not sensible. Few are capable of distinguishing betwixt the liberty of spontaneity, as it is called in the schools, and the liberty of indifference; betwixt that which is opposed to violence, and that which means a negation of necessity and causes. The first is even the most common sense of the word; and as it is only that species of liberty which it concerns us to preserve, our thoughts have been principally turned towards it, and have almost universally confounded it with the other.

Secondly, there is a false sensation or experience even of the liberty of indifference; which is regarded as an argument for its real existence. The necessity of any action, whether of *matter* or of the *mind*, is not properly a quality in the agent, but in any thinking or intelligent being, who may consider the action, and consists in the determination of his thought to infer its existence from some preceding objects. As liberty or chance, on the other hand, is nothing but the want of that determination, and a certain looseness, which we feel in passing or not passing from the idea of one to that of the other. Now we may observe that though in reflecting on human actions we seldom feel such a looseness or indifference, yet it very commonly happens, that in performing the actions themselves we are sensible of something like it. And as all related or resembling objects are readily taken for each other, this has been employed as a demonstrative or even an intuitive proof of human liberty. We feel that our actions are subject to our will on most occasions, and imagine we feel that the will itself is subject to nothing; because when by a denial of it we are provoked to try, we feel that it moves easily every way, and produces an image of itself even on that side, on which it did not settle. This image or faint motion, we persuade ourselves, could have been completed into the thing itself; because, should that be denied, we find, upon a second trial, that it can. But these efforts are all in vain; and whatever capricious and irregular actions we may perform, as the desire of showing our liberty is the sole motive of our actions, we can never free ourselves from the bonds of necessity. We may imagine we feel a liberty within ourselves; but a spectator can commonly infer our actions from our motives and character; and even where he cannot, he concludes in general, that he might, were he perfectly acquainted with every circumstance of our situation and temper, and the most secret springs of our complexion and disposition. Now this is the very essence of necessity, according to the foregoing doctrine.

A third reason why the doctrine of liberty has generally been better received in the world than its antagonist, proceeds from religion, which has been very unnecessarily interested in this question. There is no method of reasoning more common, and yet none more blamable, than in philosophical debates to endeavor to refute any hypothesis by a pretext of its dangerous consequences to religion and morality. When any opinion leads us into absurdities, it is certainly false; but it is not certain an opinion is false because it is of dangerous consequence. Such topics, therefore, ought entirely to be forborne, as serving nothing to the discovery of truth, but only to make the person of an antagonist odious. This I observe in general, without pretending to draw any advantage from it. I submit myself frankly to an examination of this kind, and dare venture to affirm, that the doctrine of necessity, according to my explication of it, is not only innocent, but even advantageous to religion and morality.

I define *necessity* two ways, conformable to the two definitions of *cause*, of which it makes an essential part. I place it either in the constant union and conjunction of like objects, or in the inference of the mind from the one to the other. Now *necessity*, in both these senses, has universally, though tacitly, in the schools, in the pulpit, and in common life, been allowed to belong to the *will* of man, and no one has ever pretended to deny, that we can draw inferences concerning human actions, and that those inferences are founded on the experienced union of like actions with like motives and circumstances. The only particular in which any one can differ from me is that perhaps he will refuse to call this necessity. But as long as the meaning is understood, I hope the word can do no harm. Or that he will maintain there is something else in the operations of matter. Now whether it be so or not is of no consequence to religion, whatever it may be to natural philosophy. I may be mistaken in asserting, that we have no idea of any other connection in the actions of body, and shall be glad to be farther instructed on that head. But sure I am, I ascribe nothing to the actions of the mind, but what must readily be allowed of. Let no one, therefore, put an invidious construction on my words, by saying simply, that I assert the necessity of human actions, and place them on the same footing with the operations of senseless matter. I *do not* ascribe to the *will* that unintelligible necessity, which is supposed to lie in matter. But I ascribe to matter that intelligible quality, call it necessity or not, which the most rigorous orthodoxy does or must allow to belong to the *will.* I change, therefore, nothing in the received systems, with regard to the will, but only with regard to material objects.

Nay I shall go farther, and assert, that this kind of necessity is so essential to religion and morality, that without it there must ensue an absolute subversion of both, and that every other supposition is entirely destructive to all laws both divine and human. It is indeed certain, that as all human laws are founded on rewards and punishments, it is supposed as a fundamental principle, that these motives have an influence on the mind, and both produce the good and prevent the evil actions. We may give to this influence what name we please; but as it is usually conjoined with the action, common sense requires it should be esteemed a cause, and be booked upon as an instance of that necessity, which I would establish.

This reasoning is equally solid, when applied to divine laws, so far as the deity is considered as a legislator, and is supposed to inflict punishment and bestow rewards with a design to produce obedience. But I also maintain, that even where he acts not in his magisterial capacity, but is regarded as the avenger of crimes merely on account of their odiousness and deformity, not only it is impossible, without the necessary connection of cause and effect in human actions, that punishments could be inflicted compatible with justice and moral equity; but also that it could ever enter into the thoughts of any reasonable being to inflict them. The constant and universal object of hatred or anger is a person or creature endowed with thought and consciousness; and when any criminal or injurious actions excite that passion, it is only by their relation to the person or connection with him. But according to the doctrine of liberty or chance, this connection is reduced to nothing, nor are men more accountable for those actions, which are designed and premeditated, than for such as are the most casual and accidental. Actions are by their very nature temporary and perishing; and where they proceed not from some cause in the characters and disposition of the person who performed them, they infix not themselves upon him, and can neither redound to his honor, if good, nor infamy, if evil. The action itself may be blamable; it may be contrary to all the rules of morality and religion; but the person is not responsible for it; and as it proceeded from nothing in him, that is durable or constant, and leaves nothing of that nature behind it, it is impossible he can, upon its account, become the object of punishment or vengeance. According to the hypothesis of liberty, therefore, a man is as pure and untainted, after having committed the most horrid crimes, as at the first moment of his birth, nor is his character any way concerned in his actions; since they are not derived from it, and the wickedness of the one can never be used as a proof of the depravity of the other. It is only upon the principles of necessity, that a person acquires any merit or demerit from his actions, however the common opinion may incline to the contrary.

But so inconsistent are men with themselves, that though they often assert that necessity utterly destroys all merit and demerit either towards mankind or superior powers, yet they continue still to reason upon these very principles of necessity in all their judgments concerning this matter. Men are not blamed for such evil actions as they perform ignorantly and casually, whatever may be their consequences. Why? Because the causes of these actions are only momentary, and terminate in them alone. Men are less blamed for such evil actions, as they perform hastily and unpremeditatedly, than for such as proceed from thought and deliberation. For what reason? Because a hasty temper, though a constant cause in the mind, operates only by intervals, and infects not the whole character. Again, repentance wipes off every crime, especially if attended with an evident reformation of life and manners. How is this to be accounted for? By asserting that actions render a person criminal, merely as they are proofs of criminal passions or principles in the mind; and when by any alteration of these principles they cease to be just proofs, they likewise cease to be criminal. But according to the doctrine of liberty or chance they never were just proofs, and consequently never were criminal.

Here then I turn to my adversary, and desire him to free his own system from these odious consequences before he charge them upon others. Or if he rather chooses, that this question should be decided by fair arguments before philosophers, than by declamations before the people, let him return to what I have advanced to prove that liberty and chance are synonymous, and concerning the nature of moral evidence and the regularity of human actions. Upon a review of these reasonings, I cannot doubt of an entire victory; and therefore having proved, that all actions of the will have particular causes, I proceed to explain what these causes are, and how they operate.

Nothing is more usual in philosophy, and even in common life, than to talk of the combat of passion and reason, to give the preference to reason, and assert that men are only so far virtuous as they conform themselves to its dictates. Every rational creature, it is said, is obliged to regulate his actions by reason; and if any other motive or principle challenge the direction of his conduct, he ought to oppose it, till it be entirely subdued, or at least brought to a conformity with that superior principle. On this method of thinking the greatest part of moral philosophy, ancient and modern, seems to be founded; nor is there an ampler field, as well for metaphysical arguments, as popular declamations, than this supposed pre-eminence of reason above passion.

The eternity, invariableness, and divine origin of the former have been displayed to the best advantage: The blindness, inconstancy, and deceitfulness of the latter have been as strongly insisted on. In order to show the fallacy of all this philosophy, I shall endeavor to prove first, *that reason alone can never be a motive to any action of the will*; and secondly, *that it can never oppose passion in the direction of the will.*

The understanding exerts itself after two different ways, as it judges from demonstration or probability; as it regards the abstract relations of our ideas, or those relations of objects, of which experience only gives us information. I believe it scarce will be asserted, that the first species of reasoning alone is ever the cause of any action. As its proper province is the world of ideas, and as the will always places us in that of realities, demonstration and volition seem, upon that account, to be totally removed, from each other. Mathematics, indeed, are useful in all mechanical operations, and arithmetic in almost every art and profession. But it is not of themselves they have any influence. Mechanics are the art of regulating the motions of bodies to some designed end or purpose; and the reason why we employ arithmetic in fixing the proportions of numbers, is only that we may discover the proportions of their influence and operation. A merchant is desirous of knowing the sum total of his accounts with any person. Why? Because that he may learn what sum will have the same effects in paying his debt, and going to market, as all the particular articles taken together. Abstract or demonstrative reasoning, therefore, never influences any of our actions, but only as it directs our judgment concerning causes and effects; which leads us to the second operation of the understanding.

It is obvious, that when we have the prospect of pain or pleasure from any object, we feel a consequent emotion of aversion or propensity, and are carried to avoid or embrace what will give us this uneasiness or satisfaction. It is also obvious, that this emotion rests not here, but making us cast our view on every side, comprehends whatever objects are connected with its original one by the relation of cause and effect. Here then reasoning takes place to discover this relation; and according as our reasoning varies, our actions receive a subsequent variation. But it is evident in this case that the impulse arises not from reason, but is only directed by it. It is from the prospect of pain or pleasure that the aversion or propensity arises towards any object. And these emotions extend themselves to the causes and effects of that object, as they are pointed out to us by reason and experience. It can never in the least concern us to know that such objects are causes, and such others effects, if both the causes and effects be indifferent to us. Where the objects themselves do not affect us, their connection can never give them any influence; and it is plain, that as reason is nothing but the discovery of this connection, it cannot be by its means that the objects are able to affect us.

Since reason alone can never produce any action, or give rise to volition, I infer, that the same faculty is as incapable of preventing volition, or of disputing the preference with any passion or emotion. This consequence is necessary. It is impossible reason could have the latter effect of preventing volition, but by giving an impulse in a contrary direction to our passion; and that impulse, had it operated alone, would have been able to produce volition. Nothing can oppose or retard the impulse of passion, but a contrary impulse; and if this contrary impulse ever arises from reason, that latter faculty must have an original influence on the *will*, and must be able to cause, as well as hinder any act of volition. But if reason has no original influence, it is impossible it can withstand any principle, which has such an efficacy, or ever keep the mind in suspense a moment. Thus it appears, that the principle, which opposes our passion, cannot be the same with reason, and is only called so in an improper sense. We speak not strictly and philosophically when we talk of the combat of passion and of reason. *Reason is, and ought only to be the slave of the passions, and can never pretend to any other office than to serve and obey them.* As this opinion may appear somewhat extraordinary, it may not be improper to confirm it by some other considerations.

A passion is an original existence, or, if you will, modification of existence, and contains not any representative quality, which renders it a copy of any other existence or modification. When I am angry, I am actually possessed with the passion, and in that emotion have no more a reference to any other object, than when I am thirsty, or sick, or more than five foot high. It is impossible, therefore, that this passion can be opposed by, or be contradictory to truth and reason; since this contradiction consists in the disagreement of ideas, considered as copies, with those objects, which they represent, what may at first occur on this head, is, that as nothing can be contrary to truth or reason, except what has a reference to it, and as the judgments of our understanding only have this reference, it must follow, that passions can be contrary to reason only so far as they are accompanied with some judgment or opinion. According to this principle, which is so obvious and natural, it is only in two senses, that any affection can be called unreasonable. First, when a passion, such as hope or fear, grief or joy, despair or security, is founded on the supposition or the existence of objects, which really do not exist. Secondly, when in exerting any passion in action, we choose means insufficient for the designed end, and deceive ourselves in our judgment of causes and effects. Where a passion is neither founded on false suppositions, nor chooses means insufficient for the end, the understanding can neither justify nor condemn it. It is not contrary to reason to prefer the destruction of the whole world to the scratching of my finger. It is not contrary to reason for me to choose my total ruin, to prevent the least uneasiness of an Indian or person wholly unknown to me. It is as little contrary to reason to prefer even my own acknowledged lesser good to my greater, and have a more ardent affection for the former than the latter. A trivial good may, from certain circumstances, produce a desire superior to what arises from the greatest and most valuable enjoyment; nor is there any thing more extraordinary in this, than in mechanics to see one pound weight raise up a hundred by the advantage of its situation. In short, a passion must be accompanied with some false judgment. in order to its being unreasonable; and even then it is not the passion, properly speaking, which is unreasonable, but the judgment.

The consequences are evident. Since a passion can never, in any sense, be called unreasonable, but when founded on a false supposition, or when it chooses means insufficient for the designed end, it is impossible, that reason and passion can ever oppose each other, or dispute for the government of the will and actions. The moment we perceive the falsehood of any supposition, or the insufficiency of any means, our passions yield to our reason without any opposition. I may desire any fruit as of an excellent relish; but whenever you convince me of my mistake, my longing ceases. I may will the performance of certain actions as means of obtaining any desired good; but as my willing of these actions is only secondary, and founded on the supposition, that they are causes of the proposed effect; as soon as I discover the falsehood of that supposition, they must become indifferent to me.

It is natural for one that does not examine objects with a strict philosophic eye, to imagine that those actions of the mind are entirely the same, which produce not a different sensation, and are not immediately distinguishable to the feeling and perception. Reason, for instance, exerts itself without producing any sensible emotion; and except in the more sublime disquisitions of philosophy, or in the frivolous subtilties of the school, scarce ever conveys any pleasure or uneasiness. Hence it proceeds, that every action of the mind, which operates with the same calmness and tranquility, is confounded with reason by all those who judge of things from the first view and appearance. Now it is certain, there are certain calm desires and tendencies, which, though they be real passions, produce little emotion in the mind, and are more known by their effects than by the immediate feeling or sensation. These desires are of two kinds: either certain instincts originally implanted in our natures, such as benevolence and resentment, the love of life, and kindness to children, or the general appetite to good, and aversion to evil, considered merely as such. When any of these passions are calm, and cause no disorder in the soul, they are very readily taken for the determinations of reason, and are supposed to proceed from the same faculty with that which judges of truth and falsehood. Their nature and principles have been supposed the same, because their sensations are not evidently different.

Beside these calm passions, which often determine the will, there are certain violent emotions of the same kind, which have likewise a great influence on that faculty. When I receive any injury from another, I often feel a violent passion of resentment, which makes me desire his punishment, independent of all considerations of pleasure and advantage to myself. When I am immediately threatened with any grievous ill, my fears, apprehensions, and aversions rise to a great height, and produce a sensible emotion.

The common error of metaphysicians has lain in ascribing the direction of the will entirely to one of these principles, and supposing the other to have no influence. Men often act knowingly against their interest: For which reason the view of the greatest possible good does not always influence them. Men often counter-act a violent passion in prosecution of their interests and designs. It is not, therefore, the present uneasiness alone which determines them. In general, we may observe that both these principles operate on the will; and where they are contrary, that either of them prevails, according to the general character or present disposition of the person. What we call strength of mind implies the prevalence of the calm passions above the violent; though we may easily observe there is no man so constantly possessed of this virtue, as never on any occasion to yield to the solicitations of passion and desire. From these variations of temper proceeds the great difficulty of deciding concerning the actions and resolutions of men, where there is any contrariety of motives and passions.

Immanuel Kant

FREEDOM OF THE WILL

The *will* is a kind of causality belonging to living beings in so far as they are *rational*, and *freedom* would be this property of such causality that it can be efficient, independently of foreign causes determining it; just as physical necessity is the property that the causality of all irrational beings has of being determined to activity by the influence of foreign causes.

The preceding definition of freedom is negative and therefore unfruitful for the discovery of its essence, but it leads to a positive conception which is so much the more full and fruitful. Since the conception of causality involves that of laws, according to which, by something that we call cause, something else, namely the effect, must be produced; hence, although freedom is not a property of the will depending on physical laws, yet it is not for that reason lawless; on the contrary it must be a causality acting according to immutable laws, but of a peculiar kind; otherwise a free will would be an absurdity. Physical necessity is a heteronomy of the efficient causes, for every effect is possible only according to this law, that something else determines the efficient cause to exert its causality. What else then can freedom of the will be but autonomy, that is, the property of the will to be a law to itself? But the proposition: "The will is in every action a law to itself," only expresses the principle: "To act on no other maxim than that which can also have as an object itself as a universal law." Now this is precisely the formula of the categorical imperative and is the principle of morality, so that a free will and a will subject to moral laws are one and the same.

On the hypothesis, then, of freedom of the will, morality together with its principle follows from it by mere analysis of the conception. However, the latter is a synthetic proposition; viz., an absolutely good will is that whose maxim can always include itself regarded as a universal law; for this property of its maxim can never be discovered by analyzing the conception of an absolutely good will. Now such synthetic propositions are only possible in this way: that the two cognitions are connected together by their union with a third in which they are both to be found. The positive concept of freedom furnishes this third cognition, which cannot, as with physical causes, be the nature of the sensible world (in the concept of which we find conjoined the concept of something in relation as cause to something else as effect). We cannot now at once show what this third is to which freedom points us and of which we have an idea *a priori*, nor can we make intelligible how the concept of freedom is shown to be legitimate from principles of pure practical reason and with it the possibility of a categorical imperative; but some further preparation is required.

It is not enough to predicate freedom of our own will, from whatever reason, if we have not sufficient grounds for predicating the same of all rational beings. For as morality serves as a law for us only because we are rational beings, it must also hold for all rational beings; and as it must be deduced simply from the property of freedom, it must be shown that freedom also is a property of all rational beings. It is not enough, then, to prove it from certain supposed experiences of human nature (which indeed is quite impossible, and it can only be shown *a priori*), but we must show that it belongs to the activity of all rational beings endowed with a will. Now I say every being that cannot act except under the idea of freedom is just for that reason in a practical point of view really free, that is to say, all laws which are inseparably connected with freedom have the same force for him as if his will had been shown to be free in itself by *a proof* theoretically conclusive. I adopt this method of assuming freedom merely as an idea which rational beings

Edited from *Fundamental Principles of the Metaphysic of Morals,* Translated by Thomas Kingsmill Abbott, 1895, which is now in the public domain.

suppose in their actions, in order to avoid the necessity of proving it in its theoretical aspect also. The former is sufficient for my purpose; for even though the speculative proof should not be made out, yet a being that cannot act except with the idea of freedom is bound by the same laws that would oblige a being who was actually free. Thus we can escape here from the onus which presses on the theory.

Now I affirm that we must attribute to every rational being which has a will that it has also the idea of freedom and acts entirely under this idea. For in such a being we conceive a reason that is practical, that is, has causality in reference to its objects. Now we cannot possibly conceive a reason consciously receiving a bias from any other quarter with respect to its judgements, for then the subject would ascribe the determination of its judgement not to its own reason, but to an impulse. It must regard itself as the author of its principles independent of foreign influences. Consequently as practical reason or as the will of a rational being it must regard itself as free, that is to say, the will of such a being cannot be a will of its own except under the idea of freedom. This idea must therefore in a practical point of view be ascribed to every rational being.

We have finally reduced the definite conception of morality to the idea of freedom. This latter, however, we could not prove to be actually a property of ourselves or of human nature; only we saw that it must be presupposed if we would conceive a being as rational and conscious of its causality in respect of its actions, i.e., as endowed with a will; and so we find that on just the same grounds we must ascribe to every being endowed with reason and will this attribute of determining itself to action under the idea of its freedom.

Now it resulted also from the presupposition of these ideas that we became aware of a law that the subjective principles of action, i.e., maxims, must always be so assumed that they can also hold as objective, that is, universal principles, and so serve as universal laws of our own dictation. But why then should I subject myself to this principle and that simply as a rational being, thus also subjecting to it all other beings endowed with reason? I will allow that no interest urges me to this, for that would not give a categorical imperative, but I must take an interest in it and discern how this comes to pass; for this properly an "I ought" is properly an "I would," valid for every rational being, provided only that reason determined his actions without any hindrance. But for beings that are in addition affected as we are by springs of a different kind, namely, sensibility, and in whose case that is not always done which reason alone would do, for these that necessity is expressed only as an "ought," and the subjective necessity is different from the objective.

It seems then as if the moral law, that is, the principle of autonomy of the will, were properly speaking only presupposed in the idea of freedom, and as if we could not prove its reality and objective necessity independently. In that case we should still have gained something considerable by at least determining the true principle more exactly than had previously been done; but as regards its validity and the practical necessity of subjecting oneself to it, we should not have advanced a step. For if we were asked why the universal validity of our maxim as a law must be the condition restricting our actions, and on what we ground the worth which we assign to this manner of acting—a worth so great that there cannot be any higher interest; and if we were asked further how it happens that it is by this alone a man believes he feels his own personal worth, in comparison with which that of an agreeable or disagreeable condition is to be regarded as nothing, to these questions we could give no satisfactory answer.

We find indeed sometimes that we can take an interest in a personal quality which does not involve any interest of external condition, provided this quality makes us capable of participating in the condition in case reason were to effect the allotment; that is to say, the mere being worthy of happiness can interest of itself even without the motive of participating in this happiness. This judgement, however, is in fact only the effect of the importance of the moral law which we before presupposed (when by the idea of freedom we detach ourselves from every empirical interest); but that we ought to detach ourselves from these interests, i.e., to consider ourselves as free in action and yet as subject to certain laws, so as to find a worth simply in our own person which can compensate us for the loss of everything that gives worth to our condition; this we are not yet able to discern in this way, nor do we see how it is possible so to act—in other words, whence the moral law derives its obligation.

It must be freely admitted that there is a sort of circle here from which it seems impossible to escape. In the order of efficient causes we assume ourselves free, in order that in the order of ends we may conceive ourselves as subject to moral laws: and we afterwards conceive ourselves as subject to these laws, because we have attributed to ourselves freedom of will: for freedom and self-legislation of will are both autonomy and, therefore, are reciprocal conceptions, and for this very reason one must not be used to explain the other or give the reason of it, but at most only logical purposes to reduce apparently different notions of the same object to one single concept (as we reduce different fractions of the same value to the lowest terms).

One resource remains to us, namely, to inquire whether we do not occupy different points of view when by means of freedom we think ourselves as causes efficient *a priori*, and when we form our conception of ourselves from our actions as effects which we see before our eyes. It is a remark which needs no subtle reflection to make, but which we may assume that even the commonest understanding can make, although it be after its fashion by an obscure discernment of judgement which it calls feeling, that all the "ideas" that come to us involuntarily (as those of the senses) do not enable us to know objects otherwise than as they affect us; so that what they may be in themselves remains unknown to us, and consequently that as regards "ideas" of this kind even with the closest attention and clearness that the understanding can apply to them, we can by them only attain to the knowledge of appearances, never to that of things in themselves. As soon as this distinction has once been made (perhaps merely in consequence of the difference observed between the ideas given us from without, and in which we are passive, and those that we produce simply from ourselves, and in which we show our own activity), then it follows of itself that we must admit and assume behind the appearance something else that is not an appearance, namely, the things in themselves; although we must admit that as they can never be known to us except as they affect us, we can come no nearer to them, nor can we ever know what they are in themselves. This must furnish a distinction, however crude, between a world of sense and the world of understanding, of which the former may be different according to the difference of the sensuous impressions in various observers, while the second which is its basis always remains the same, Even as to himself, a man cannot pretend to know what he is in himself from the knowledge he has by internal sensation. For as he does not as it were create himself, and does not come by the conception of himself *a priori* but empirically, it naturally follows that he can obtain his knowledge even of himself only by the inner sense and, consequently, only through the appearances of his nature and the way in which his consciousness is affected. At the same time beyond these characteristics of his own subject, made up of mere appearances, he must necessarily suppose something else as their basis, namely, his ego, whatever its characteristics in itself may be. Thus in respect to mere perception and receptivity of sensations he must reckon himself as belonging to the world of sense; but in respect of whatever there may be of pure activity in him (that which reaches consciousness immediately and not through affecting the senses), he must reckon himself as belonging to the intellectual world, of which, however, he has no further knowledge. To such a conclusion the reflecting man must come with respect to all the things which can be presented to him; it is probably to be met with even in persons of the commonest understanding, who, as is well known, are very much inclined to suppose behind the objects of the senses something else invisible and acting of itself. They spoil it, however, by presently sensualizing this invisible again; that is to say, wanting to make it an object of intuition, so that they do not become a whit the wiser.

Now man really finds in himself a faculty by which he distinguishes himself from everything else, even from himself as affected by objects, and that is reason. This being pure spontaneity is even elevated above the understanding. For although the latter is a spontaneity and does not, like sense, merely contain intuitions that arise when we are affected by things (and are therefore passive), yet it cannot produce from its activity any other conceptions than those which merely serve to bring the intuitions of sense under rules and, thereby, to unite them in one consciousness, and without this use of the sensibility it could not think at all; whereas, on the contrary, reason shows so pure a spontaneity in the case of what I call ideas that it thereby far transcends everything that the sensibility can give it, and exhibits its most important function in distinguishing the world of sense from that of understanding, and thereby prescribing the limits of the understanding itself.

For this reason a rational being must regard himself qua intelligence (not from the side of his lower faculties) as belonging not to the world of sense, but to that of understanding; hence he has two points of view from which he can regard himself, and recognize laws of the exercise of his faculties, and consequently of all his actions: first, so far as he belongs to the world of sense, he finds himself subject to laws of nature; secondly, as belonging to the intelligible world, under laws which being independent of nature have their foundation not in experience but in reason alone.

As a rational being, and consequently belonging to the intelligible world, man can never conceive the causality of his own will otherwise than on condition of the idea of freedom, for independence of the determinate causes of the sensible world (an independence which reason must always ascribe to itself) is freedom. Now the idea of freedom is inseparably connected with the conception of autonomy, and this again with the universal principle of morality which is ideally the foundation of all actions of rational beings, just as the law of nature is of all phenomena.

Now the suspicion is removed which we raised above, that there was a latent circle involved in our reasoning from freedom to autonomy, and from this to the moral law, viz.: that we laid down the idea of freedom because of the moral law only that we might afterwards in turn infer the latter from freedom, and that consequently we could assign no reason at all for this law, but could only show it as a *petitio principii* [a fallacy that occurs when an argument's premises assume the truth of the conclusion, instead of supporting it] which well disposed minds would gladly concede to us, but which we could never put forward as a provable proposition. For now we see that, when we conceive ourselves as free, we transfer ourselves into the world of understanding as members of it and recognize the autonomy of the will with its consequence, morality; whereas, if we conceive ourselves as under obligation, we consider ourselves as belonging to the world of sense and at the same time to the world of understanding.

All men attribute to themselves freedom of will. Hence come all judgements upon actions as being such as ought to have been done, although they have not been done. However, this freedom is not a conception of experience, nor can it be so, since it still remains, even though experience shows the contrary of what on supposition of freedom are conceived as its necessary consequences. On the other side it is equally necessary that everything that takes place should be fixedly determined according to laws of nature. This necessity of nature is likewise not an empirical conception, just for this reason, that it involves the motion of necessity and consequently of *a priori* cognition. But this conception of a system of nature is confirmed by experience; and it must even be inevitably presupposed if experience itself is to be possible, that is, a connected knowledge of the objects of sense resting on general laws. Therefore freedom is only an idea of reason, and its objective reality in itself is doubtful; while nature is a concept of the understanding which proves, and must necessarily prove, its reality in examples of experience.

There arises from this a dialectic of reason, since the freedom attributed to the will appears to contradict the necessity of nature, and placed between these two ways reason for speculative purposes finds the road of physical necessity much more beaten and more appropriate than that of freedom; yet for practical purposes the narrow footpath of freedom is the only one on which it is possible to make use of reason in our conduct; hence it is just as impossible for the subtlest philosophy as for the commonest reason of men to argue away freedom. Philosophy must then assume that no real contradiction will be found between freedom and physical necessity of the same human actions, for it cannot give up the conception of nature any more than that of freedom.

Nevertheless, even though we should never be able to comprehend how freedom is possible, we must at least remove this apparent contradiction in a convincing manner. For if the thought of freedom contradicts either itself or nature, which is equally necessary, it must in competition with physical necessity be entirely given up. It would, however, be impossible to escape this contradiction if the thinking subject, which seems to itself free, conceived itself in the same sense or in the very same relation when it calls itself free as when in respect of the same action it assumes itself to be subject to the law of nature. Hence it is an indispensable problem of speculative philosophy to show that its illusion respecting the contradiction rests on this, that we think of man in a different sense and relation when we call him free and when we regard him as subject to the laws of nature as being part and parcel of nature. It must therefore show that not only can both these very well co-exist, but that both must be thought as necessarily united in the same subject, since otherwise no reason could be given why we should burden reason with an idea which, though it may possibly without contradiction be reconciled with another that is sufficiently established, yet entangles us in a perplexity which sorely embarrasses reason in its theoretic employment. This duty, however, belongs only to speculative philosophy. The philosopher then has no option whether he will remove the apparent contradiction or leave it untouched; for in the latter case the theory respecting this would be *bonum vacans* [an unclaimed property], into the possession of which the fatalist would have a right to enter and chase all morality out of its supposed domain as occupying it without title.

We cannot however as yet say that we are touching the bounds of practical philosophy. For the settlement of that controversy does not belong to it; it only demands from speculative reason that it should put an end to the discord in which it entangles itself in theoretical questions, so that practical reason may have rest and security from external attacks which might make the ground debatable on which it desires to build.

The claims to freedom of will made even by common reason are founded on the consciousness and the admitted supposition that reason is independent of merely subjectively determined causes which together constitute what belongs to sensation only and which consequently come under the general designation of sensibility. Man considering himself in this way as an intelligence places himself thereby in a different order of things and in a relation to determining grounds of a wholly different kind when on the one hand he thinks of himself as an intelligence endowed with a will, and consequently with causality, and when on the other he perceives himself as a phenomenon in the world of sense (as he really is also), and affirms that his causality is subject to external determination according to laws of nature. Now he soon becomes aware that both can hold good, nay, must hold good at the same time. For there is not the smallest contradiction in saying that a thing in appearance (belonging to the world of sense) is subject to certain laws, of which the very same as a thing or being in itself is independent, and that he must conceive and think of himself in this twofold way, rests as to the first on the consciousness of himself as an object affected through the senses, and as to the second on the consciousness of himself as an intelligence, i.e., as independent on sensible impressions in the employment of his reason (in other words as belonging to the world of understanding). Hence it comes to pass that man claims the possession of a will which takes no account of anything that comes under the head of desires and inclinations and, on the contrary, conceives actions as possible to him, nay, even as necessary which can only be done by disregarding all desires and sensible inclinations. The causality of such actions lies in him as an intelligence and in the laws of effects and actions dependent on the principles of an intelligible world, of which indeed he knows nothing more than that in it pure reason alone independent of sensibility gives the law; moreover since it is only in that world, as an intelligence, that he is his proper self (being as man only the appearance of himself), those laws apply to him directly and categorically, so that the incitements of inclinations and appetites (in other words the whole nature of the world of sense) cannot impair the laws of his volition as an intelligence. Nay, he does not even hold himself responsible for the former or ascribe them to his proper self, i.e., his will: he only ascribes to his will any indulgence which he might yield them if he allowed them to influence his maxims to the prejudice of the rational laws of the will.

When practical reason thinks itself into a world of understanding, it does not thereby transcend its own limits, as it would if it tried to enter it by intuition or sensation. The former is only a negative thought in respect of the world of sense, which does not give any laws to reason in determining the will and is positive only in this single point that this freedom as a negative characteristic is at the same time conjoined with a (positive) faculty and even with a causality of reason, which we designate a *will*, namely a faculty of so acting that the principle of the actions shall conform to the essential character of a rational motive, i.e., the condition that the maxim have universal validity as a law. But were it to borrow an object of will, that is, a motive, from the world of understanding, then it would overstep its bounds and pretend to be acquainted with something of which it knows nothing. The conception of a world of the understanding is then only a point of view which reason finds itself compelled to take outside the appearances in order to conceive itself as practical, which would not be possible if the influences of the sensibility had a determining power on man, but which is necessary unless he is to be denied the consciousness of himself as an intelligence and, consequently, as a rational cause, energizing by reason, that is, operating freely. This thought certainly involves the idea of an order and a system of laws different from that of the mechanism of nature which belongs to the sensible world; and it makes the conception of an intelligible world necessary (that is to say, the whole system of rational beings as things in themselves). But it does not in the least authorize us to think of it further than as to its formal condition only, that is, the universality of the maxims of the will as laws, and consequently the autonomy of the latter, which alone is consistent with its freedom; whereas, on the contrary, all laws that refer to a definite object give heteronomy, which only belongs to laws of nature and can only apply to the sensible world.

But reason would overstep all its bounds if it undertook to explain how pure reason can be practical, which would be exactly the same problem as to explain how freedom is possible. For we can explain nothing but that which we can reduce to laws, the object of which can be given in some possible experience. But freedom is a mere idea, the objective reality of which can in no wise be shown according to laws of nature, and consequently not in any possible experience; and for this reason it can never be comprehended or understood, because we cannot support it by any sort of example or analogy. It holds good only as a necessary hypothesis of reason in a being that believes itself conscious of a will, that is, of a faculty distinct from mere desire (namely, a faculty of determining itself to action as an intelligence, in other words, by laws of reason independently on natural instincts). Now where determination according to laws of nature ceases, there all explanation ceases also, and nothing remains but defense, i.e., the removal of the objections of those who pretend to have seen deeper into the nature of things, and thereupon boldly declare freedom impossible. We can only point out to them that the supposed contradiction that they have discovered in it arises only from this, that in order to be able to apply the law of nature to human actions, they must necessarily consider man as an appearance: then when we demand of them that they should also think of him qua intelligence as a thing in itself, they still persist in considering him in this respect also as an appearance. In this view it would no doubt be a contradiction to suppose the causality of the same subject (that is, his will) to be withdrawn from all the natural laws of the sensible world. But this contradiction disappears, if they would only bethink themselves and admit, as is reasonable, that behind the appearances there must also lie at their root (although hidden) the things in themselves, and that we cannot expect the laws of these to be the same as those that govern their appearances. The subjective impossibility of explaining the freedom of the will is identical with the impossibility of discovering and explaining an interest which man can take in the moral law. Nevertheless he does actually take an interest in it, the basis of which in us we call the moral feeling, which some have falsely assigned as the standard of our moral judgement, whereas it must rather be viewed as the subjective effect that the law exercises on the will, the objective principle of which is furnished by reason alone.

In order indeed that a rational being who is also affected through the senses should will what reason alone directs such beings that they ought to will, it is no doubt requisite that reason should have a power to infuse a feeling of pleasure or satisfaction in the fulfilment of duty, that is to say, that it should have a causality by which it determines the sensibility according to its own principles. But it is quite impossible to discern, i.e., to make it intelligible *a priori*, how a mere thought, which itself contains nothing sensible, can itself produce a sensation of pleasure or pain; for this is a particular kind of causality of which as of every other causality we can determine nothing whatever *a priori*; we must only consult experience about it. But as this cannot supply us with any relation of cause and effect except between two objects of experience, whereas in this case, although indeed the effect produced lies within experience, yet the cause is supposed to be pure reason acting through mere ideas which offer no object to experience, it follows that for us men it is quite impossible to explain how and why the universality of the maxim as a law, that is, morality, interests. This only is certain, that it is not because it interests us that it has validity for us (for that would be heteronomy and dependence of practical reason on sensibility, namely, on a feeling as its principle, in which case it could never give moral laws), but that it interests us because it is valid for us as men, inasmuch as it had its source in our will as intelligences, in other words, in our proper self, and what belongs to mere appearance is necessarily subordinated by reason to the nature of the thing in itself.

The question then, "How a categorical imperative is possible," can be answered to this extent, that we can assign the only hypothesis on which it is possible, namely, the idea of freedom; and we can also discern the necessity of this hypothesis, and this is sufficient for the practical exercise of reason, that is, for the conviction of the validity of this imperative, and hence of the moral law; but how this hypothesis itself is possible can never be discerned by any human reason. On the hypothesis, however, that the will of an intelligence is free, its autonomy, as the essential formal condition of its determination, is a necessary consequence. Moreover, this freedom of will is not merely quite possible as a hypothesis (not involving any contradiction to the principle of physical necessity in the connection of the phenomena of the sensible world) as speculative philosophy can show: but further, a rational being who is conscious of causality through reason, that is to say, of a will (distinct from desires), must of necessity make it practically, that is, in idea, the condition of all his voluntary actions. But to explain how pure reason can be of itself practical without the aid of any spring of action that could be derived from any other source, i.e., how the mere principle of the universal validity of all its maxims as laws (which would certainly be the form of a pure practical reason) can of itself supply a spring, without any matter (object) of the will in which one could antecedently take any interest; and how it can produce an interest which would be called purely moral; or in other words, how pure reason can be practical—to explain this is beyond the power of human reason, and all the labor and pains of seeking an explanation of it are lost.

It is just the same as if I sought to find out how freedom itself is possible as the causality of a will. For then I quit the ground of philosophical explanation, and I have no other to go upon. I might indeed revel in the world of intelligences which still remains to me, but although I have an idea of it which is well founded, yet I have not the least knowledge of it, nor an I ever attain to such knowledge with all the efforts of my natural faculty of reason. It signifies only a something that remains over when I have eliminated everything belonging to the world of sense from the actuating principles of my will, serving merely to keep in bounds the principle of motives taken from the field of sensibility; fixing its limits and showing that it does not contain all in all within itself, but that there is more beyond it; but this something more I know no further. Of pure reason which frames this ideal, there remains after the abstraction of all matter, i.e., knowledge of objects, nothing but the form, namely, the practical law of the universality of the maxims, and in conformity with this conception of reason in reference to a pure world of understanding as a possible efficient cause, that is a cause determining the will. There must here be a total absence of springs; unless this idea of an intelligible world is itself the spring, or that in which reason primarily takes an interest; but to make this intelligible is precisely the problem that we cannot solve.

Here now is the extreme limit of all moral inquiry, and it is of great importance to determine it even on this account, in order that reason may not on the one hand, to the prejudice of morals, seek about in the world of sense for the supreme motive and an interest comprehensible but empirical; and on the other hand, that it may not impotently flap its wings without being able to move in the (for it) empty space of transcendent concepts which we call the intelligible world, and so lose itself amidst chimeras. For the rest, the idea of a pure world of understanding as a system of all intelligences, and to which we ourselves as rational beings belong (although we are likewise on the other side members of the sensible world), this remains always a useful and legitimate idea for the purposes of rational belief, although all knowledge stops at its threshold, useful, namely, to produce in us a lively interest in the moral law by means of the noble ideal of a universal kingdom of ends in themselves (rational beings), to which we can belong as members then only when we carefully conduct ourselves according to the maxims of freedom as if they were laws of nature.

Paul-Henri d'Holbach

A SERIES OF NECESSARY MOMENTS

Those who have pretended that the soul is distinguished from the body, is immaterial, draws its ideas from its own peculiar source, acts by its own energies, without the aid of any exterior object, have, by a consequence of their own system, enfranchised it from those physical laws according to which all beings of which we have a knowledge are obliged to act. They have believed that the soul is mistress of its own conduct, is able to regulate its own peculiar operations, has the faculty to determine its will by its own natural energy; in a word, they have pretended that man is a *free agent.*

It has been already sufficiently proved that the soul is nothing more than the body considered relatively to some of its functions more concealed than others: it has been shown that this soul, even when it shall be supposed immaterial, is continually modified conjointly with the body, is submitted to all its motion, and that without this it would remain inert and dead: that, consequently, it is subjected to the influence of those material and physical causes which give impulse to the body; of which the mode of existence, whether habitual or transitory, depends upon the material elements by which it is surrounded, that form its texture, constitute its temperament, enter into it by means of the aliments, and penetrate it by their subtility. The faculties which are called intellectual, and those qualities which are styled moral, have been explained in a manner purely physical and natural. In the last place it has been demonstrated that all the ideas, all the systems, all the affections, all the opinions, whether true or false, which man forms to himself, are to be attributed to his physical and material senses. Thus man is a being purely physical; in whatever manner he is considered, he is connected to universal nature, and submitted to the necessary and immutable laws that she imposes on all the beings she contains, according to their peculiar essences or to the respective properties with which, without consulting them, she endows each particular species. Man's life is a line that nature commands him to describe upon the surface of the earth, without his ever being able to swerve from it, even for an instant. He is born without his own consent; his organization does in nowise depend upon himself; his ideas come to him involuntarily; his habits are in the power of those who cause him to contract them; he is unceasingly modified by causes, whether visible or concealed, over which he has no control, which necessarily regulate his mode of existence, give the hue to his way of thinking, and determine his manner of acting. He is good or bad, happy or miserable, wise or foolish, reasonable or irrational, without his will being for any thing in these various states. Nevertheless, in despite of the shackles by which he is bound, it is pretended he is a free agent, or that independent of the causes by which he is moved, he determines his own will, and regulates his own condition.

However slender the foundation of this opinion, of which everything ought to point out to him the error, it is current at this day and passes for an incontestable truth with a great number of people, otherwise extremely enlightened; it is the basis of religion, which, supposing relations between man and the unknown being she has placed above nature, has been incapable of imagining how man could either merit reward or deserve punishment from this being, if he was not a free agent. Society has been believed interested in this system; because an idea has gone abroad, that if all the actions of man were to be contemplated as necessary, the right of punishing those who injure their associates would no longer exist. At length human vanity accommodated itself to a

Edited from *The System of Nature,* Chapter XI. Translated by H. D. Robinson, 1868, which is now in the public domain.

hypothesis which, unquestionably, appears to distinguish man from all other physical beings, by assigning to him the special privilege of a total independence of all other causes, but of which a very little reflection would have shown him the impossibility.

The will, as we have elsewhere said, is a modification of the brain, by which it is disposed to action, or prepared to give play to the organs. This will is necessarily determined by the qualities, good or bad, agreeable or painful, of the object or the motive that acts upon his senses, or of which the idea remains with him, and is resuscitated by his memory. In consequence, he acts necessarily, his action is the result of the impulse he receives either from the motive, from the object, or from the idea which has modified his brain, or disposed his will. When he does not act according to this impulse, it is because there comes some new cause, some new motive, some new idea, which modifies his brain in a different manner, gives him a new impulse, determines his will in another way, by which the action of the former impulse is suspended: thus, the sight of an agreeable object, or its idea, determines his will to set him in action to procure it; but if a new object or a new idea more powerfully attracts him, it gives a new direction to his will, annihilates the effect of the former, and prevents the action by which it was to be procured. This is the mode in which reflection, experience, reason, necessarily arrests or suspends the action of man's will: without this he would of necessity have followed the anterior impulse which carried him towards a then desirable object. In all this he always acts according to necessary laws, from which he has no means of emancipating himself.

If when tormented with violent thirst, he figures to himself in idea, or really perceives a fountain, whose limpid streams might cool his feverish want, is he sufficient master of himself to desire or not to desire the object competent to satisfy so lively a want? It will no doubt be conceded, that it is impossible he should not be desirous to satisfy it; but it will be said—if at this moment it is announced to him that the water he so ardently desires is poisoned, he will, notwithstanding his vehement thirst, abstain from drinking it: and it has, therefore, been falsely concluded that he is a free agent. The fact, however, is, that the motive in either case is exactly the same: his own conservation. The same necessity that determined him to drink before he knew the water was deleterious, upon this new discovery equally determines him not to drink; the desire of conserving himself either annihilates or suspends the former impulse; the second motive becomes stronger than the preceding, that is, the fear of death, or the desire of preserving himself, necessarily prevails over the painful sensation caused by his eagerness to drink: but, it will be said, if the thirst is very parching, an inconsiderate man without regarding the danger will risk swallowing the water. Nothing is gained by this remark: in this case, the anterior impulse only regains the ascendency; he is persuaded that life may possibly be longer preserved, or that he shall derive a greater good by drinking the poisoned water than by enduring the torment, which, to his mind, threatens instant dissolution: thus the first becomes the strongest and necessarily urges him on to action. Nevertheless, in either case, whether he partakes of the water, or whether he does not, the two actions will be equally necessary; they will be the effect of that motive which finds itself most puissant; which consequently acts in the most coercive manner upon his will.

This example will serve to explain the whole phenomena of the human will. This *will*, or rather the *brain*, finds itself in the same situation as a bowl, which, although it has received an impulse that drives it forward in a straight line, is deranged in its course whenever a force superior to the first obliges it to change its direction. The man who drinks the poisoned water appears a madman; but the actions of fools are as necessary as those of the most prudent individuals. The motives that determine the voluptuary and the debauchee to risk their health, are as powerful, and their actions are as necessary, as those which decide the wise man to manage his. But, it will be insisted, the debauchee may be prevailed on to change his conduct: this does not imply that he is a free agent;

but that motives may be found sufficiently powerful to annihilate the effect of those that previously acted upon him; then these new motives determine his will to the new mode of conduct he may adopt as necessarily as the former did to the old mode.

Man is said to *deliberate*, when the action of the will is suspended; this happens when two opposite motives act alternately upon him. To deliberate, is to hate and to love in succession; it is to be alternately attracted and repelled; it is to be moved, sometimes by one motive, sometimes by another. Man only deliberates when he does not distinctly understand the quality of the objects from which he receives impulse, or when experience has not sufficiently apprised him of the effects, more or less remote, which his actions will produce. He would take the air, but the weather is uncertain; he deliberates in consequence; he weighs the various motives that urge his will to go out or to stay at home; he is at length determined by that motive which is most probable; this removes his indecision, which necessarily settles his will, either to remain within or to go abroad: this motive is always either the immediate or ultimate advantage he finds, or thinks he finds, in the action to which he is persuaded.

Man's will frequently fluctuates between two objects, of which either the presence or the ideas move him alternately: he waits until he has contemplated the objects, or the ideas they have left in his brain which solicit him to different actions; he then compares these objects or ideas; but even in the time of deliberation, during the comparison, pending these alternatives of love and hatred which succeed each other, sometimes with the utmost rapidity, he is not a free agent for a single instant; the good or the evil which he believes he finds successively in the objects, are the necessary motives of these momentary wills; of the rapid motion of desire or fear, that he experiences as long as his uncertainty continues. From this it will be obvious that deliberation is necessary; that uncertainty is necessary; that whatever part he takes, in consequence of this deliberation, it will always necessarily be that which he has judged, whether well or ill, is most probable to turn to his advantage.

When the soul is assailed by two motives that act alternately upon it, or modify it successively, it deliberates; the brain is in a sort of equilibrium, accompanied with perpetual oscillations, sometimes towards one object, sometimes towards the other, until the most forcible carries the point, and thereby extricates it from this state of suspense, in which consists the indecision of his will. But when the brain is simultaneously assailed by causes equally strong that move it in opposite directions, agreeable to the general law of all bodies when they are struck equally by contrary powers, it stops; it is neither capable to will nor to act; it waits until one of the two causes has obtained sufficient force to overpower the other; to determine its will; to attract it in such a manner that it may prevail over the efforts of the other cause.

This mechanism, so simple, so natural, suffices to demonstrate why uncertainty is painful, and why suspense is always a violent state for man. The brain, an organ so delicate and so mobile, experiences such rapid modifications that it is fatigued; or when it is urged in contrary directions, by causes equally powerful, it suffers a kind of compression, that prevents the activity which is suitable to the preservation of the whole, and which is necessary to procure what is advantageous to its existence. This mechanism will also explain the irregularity, the indecision, the inconstancy of man, and account for that conduct which frequently appears an inexplicable mystery, and which is, indeed, the effect of the received systems. In consulting experience, it will be found that the soul is submitted to precisely the same physical laws as the material body. If the will of each individual, during a given time, was only moved by a single cause or passion, nothing would be more easy than to foresee his actions; but his heart is frequently assailed by contrary powers, by adverse motives, which either act on him simultaneously or in succession; then his brain, attracted in opposite directions, is either fatigued, or else tormented by a state of compression, which deprives it of activity. Sometimes it is in a state of incommodious inaction; sometimes it is the sport of the alternate shocks it undergoes. Such, no doubt, is the state in which man finds himself when a lively passion solicits him to the commission of crime, whilst fear points out to him the danger by which it is attended: such, also, is the condition of him whom remorse, by the continued labor of his distracted soul, prevents from enjoying the objects he has criminally obtained.

If the powers or causes, whether exterior or interior, acting on the mind of man, tend towards opposite points, his soul, as well as all other bodies, will take a mean direction between the two; and in consequence of the violence with which his soul is urged, his condition becomes sometimes so painful that his existence is troublesome: he has no longer a tendency to his own peculiar conservation; he seeks after death as a sanctuary against himself, and as the only remedy to his despair: it is thus we behold men, miserable and discontented, voluntarily destroy themselves whenever life becomes insupportable.

Choice by no means proves the free agency of man: he only deliberates when he does not yet know which to choose of the many objects that move him, he is then in an embarrassment, which does not terminate until his will is decided by the greater advantage he believes he shall find in the object he chooses, or the action he undertakes. From whence it may be seen, that choice is necessary, because he would not determine for an object, or for an action, if he did not believe that he should find in it some direct advantage. That man should have free agency it were needful that he should be able to will or choose without motive, or that he could prevent motives coercing his will. Action always being the effect of his will once determined, and as his will cannot be determined but by a motive which is not in his own power, it follows that he is never the master of the determination of his own peculiar will; that consequently he never acts as a free agent. It has been believed that man was a free agent because he had a will with the power of choosing; but attention has not been paid to the fact that even his will is moved by causes independent of himself; is owing to that which is inherent in his own organization, or which belongs to the nature of the beings acting on him. Is he the master of willing not to withdraw his hand from the fire when he fears it will be burnt? Or has he the power to take away from fire the property which makes him fear it? Is he the master of not choosing a dish of meat, which he knows to be agreeable, or analogous to his palate; of not preferring it to that which he knows to be disagreeable or dangerous? It is always according to his sensations, to his own peculiar experience, or to his suppositions, that he judges of things, either well or ill; but whatever may be his judgment, it depends necessarily on his mode of feeling, whether habitual or accidental, and the qualities he finds in the causes that move him, which exist in despite of himself.

All the causes by which his will is actuated, must act upon him in a manner sufficiently marked to give him some sensation, some perception, some idea; whether complete or incomplete, true or false: as soon as his will is determined, he must have felt either strongly or feebly; if this was not the case he would have determined without motive: thus, to speak correctly, there are no causes which are truly indifferent to the will: however faint the impulse he receives, whether on the part of the objects themselves, or on the part of their images or ideas, as soon as his will acts, the impulse has been competent to determine him.

When it is said, that man is not a free agent, it is not pretended to compare him to a body moved by a simple impulsive cause: he contains within himself causes inherent to his existence; he is moved by an interior organ, which has its own peculiar laws, and is itself necessarily determined in consequence of ideas formed from perceptions resulting from sensations which it receives from exterior objects. As the mechanism of these sensations, of these perceptions, and the manner they engrave ideas on the brain of man, are not known to him; because he is unable to unravel all these motions; because he cannot perceive the chain of operations in his soul, or the motive principle that acts within him, he supposes himself a free agent; which, literally translated, signifies, that he moves himself by himself; that he determines himself without cause: when he rather ought to say, that he is ignorant how or for why he acts in the manner he does. It is true the soul enjoys an activity peculiar to itself: but it is equally certain that this activity would never be displayed, if some motive or some cause did not put it in a condition to exercise itself: at least it will not be pretended that the soul is able either to love or to hate without being moved, without knowing the objects, without having some idea of their qualities. Gunpowder has unquestionably a particular activity, but this activity will never display itself, unless fire be applied to it; this, however, immediately sets it in motion.

It is the great complication of motion in man, it is the variety of his action, it is the multiplicity of causes that move him, whether simultaneously or in continual succession, that persuades him he is a free agent: if all his motions were simple, if the causes that move him did not confound themselves with each other, if they were distinct, if his machine were less complicated, he would perceive that all his actions were necessary, because he would be enabled to recur instantly to the cause that made him act. A man who should be always obliged to go towards the west, would always go on that side; but he would feel that, in so going, he was not a free agent: if he had another sense, as his actions or his motion, augmented by a sixth, would be still more varied and much more complicated, he would believe himself still more a free agent than he does with his five senses.

It is, then, for want of recurring to the causes that move him; for want of being able to analyze, from not being competent to decompose the complicated motion of his machine, that man believes himself a free agent: it is only upon his own ignorance that he founds the profound yet deceitful notion he has of his free agency; that he builds those opinions which he brings forward as a striking proof of his pretended freedom of action. If, for a short time, each man was willing to examine his own peculiar actions, search out their true motives to discover their concatenation, he would remain convinced that the sentiment he has of his natural free agency, is a chimera that must speedily be destroyed by experience.

Nevertheless it must be acknowledged that the multiplicity and diversity of the causes which continually act upon man, frequently without even his knowledge, render it impossible, or at least extremely difficult for him to recur to the true principles of his own peculiar actions, much less the actions of others: they frequently depend upon causes so fugitive, so remote from their effects, and which, superficially examined, appear to have so little analogy, so slender a relation with them, that it requires singular sagacity to bring them into light. This is what renders the study of the moral man a task of such difficulty; this is the reason why his heart is an abyss, of which it is frequently impossible for him to fathom the depth. He is then obliged to content himself with a knowledge of the general and necessary laws by which the human heart is regulated: for the individuals of his own species these laws are pretty nearly the same; they vary only in consequence of the organization that is peculiar to each, and of the modification it undergoes: this, however, cannot be rigorously the same in any two. It suffices to know, that by his essence, man tends to conserve himself, and to render his existence happy: this granted, whatever may be his actions, if he recur back to this first principle, to this general, this necessary tendency of his will, he never can be deceived with regard to his motives.

From all that has been advanced, it results, that in no one moment of his existence is man a free agent. He is not the architect of his own conformation, which he holds from nature; he has no control over his own ideas, or over the modification of his brain; these are due to causes, that, in despite of him, and without his own knowledge, unceasingly act upon him; he is not the master of not loving or coveting that which he finds amiable or desirable; he is not capable of refusing to deliberate, when he is uncertain of the effects certain objects will produce upon him; he cannot avoid choosing that which he believes will be most advantageous to him; in the moment when his will is determined by his choice he is not competent to act otherwise than he does.

This is a principle the truth of which no thinking being will be able to refuse accrediting: his life is a series of necessary moments; his conduct, whether good or bad, virtuous or vicious, useful or prejudicial, either to himself or to others, is a concatenation of action, as necessary as all the moments of his existence. To live, is to exist in a necessary mode during the points of that duration which succeed each other necessarily: to will, is to acquiesce or not in remaining such as he is: to be free, is to yield to the necessary motives he carries within himself. If he understood the play of his organs, if he was able to recall to himself all the impulsions they have received, all the modifications they have undergone, all the effects they have produced, he would perceive that all his actions are submitted to that fatality, which regulates his own particular system, as it does the entire system of the universe: no one effect in him, any more than in nature, produces itself by chance; this, as has been before proved, is a word void of sense. All that passes in him; all that is done by him; as well as all that happens in nature, or that is attributed to her, is derived from necessary causes, which act according to necessary laws, and which produce necessary effects from whence necessarily flow others. Fatality, is the eternal, the immutable, the necessary order, established in nature; or the indispensable connection of causes that act, with the effects they operate. In the moral as well as in the physical world, every thing that happens is a necessary consequence of causes, either visible or concealed, which are of necessity obliged to act after their peculiar essences. In man, free agency is nothing more than necessity contained within himself.

Part Eight: Morality

Introduction

Ethical theories are concerned with human actions; not only with what we do but what we *ought* to do. Questions about morality include moral concepts and principles—right and wrong, good and bad, ought and ought not—and moral prescriptions—"You *should not* kill an innocent human," and "You *should* always tell the truth." A moral theory does not have to rely on the authority of any particular religious belief; it can provide reasons and arguments to justify its position and principles.

Whether or not we have free will has a direct impact on many ethical questions, such as the role of responsibility for moral actions and the punishment of unwanted acts. Most people believe that we do not hold very young children morally responsible for their actions because children are not yet fully capable of rationally understanding right from wrong. This belief recognizes that the ability or capacity to understand the difference between right and wrong requires a mature, rational mind. This is also why most people do not hold animals morally responsible for their actions, because we do not think that animals have any conception of right and wrong, and because most people doubt that animals have free will. Therefore, if a dog seriously hurts or kills a human, then we say the dog is *physically responsible*, but *not morally responsible* for the harm done. If we determine that the dog might harm others, then we might decide that the dog should be put to death. In contrast, we generally hold an adult to be not only physically responsible for a murder, but also morally responsible, especially if we believe that the person acted on her free will. One of the basic justifications for moral principles, laws, and punishments is the assumption that humans have free will; therefore, we are responsible for our actions.

Additional factors in the questions concerning ethics and responsibility are the respective roles of consciousness and the self. It seems apparent that free will can only act if we are conscious of our deliberations, otherwise our action will be similar to a knee-jerk reaction instead of a conscious act of deliberation. Given this general outline, it should be clear that there are many important interrelated questions.

In the first reading by Plato, Socrates is challenged to defend the idea that we should be good because it is the right thing to do. The challenge comes by way of a story about a ring that has the power to make its wearer invisible. It is argued that the power of invisibility will eventually corrupt the wearer by making it possible to do whatever he wants without ever getting caught. In reply to this, Socrates offers an argument supporting the idea that being a moral or just person has *intrinsic* value, that is, it has value *in itself*, regardless of the outcome of our actions.

In a passage from his *Nicomachean Ethics,* Aristotle explains that *intellectual virtue* results from experience and teaching, whereas *moral virtue* results from habit. Also, moral excellence is intimately connected with pleasure and pain which often are the result of human actions. For Aristotle, since virtues involve choice of action, what we choose leads to the state of our character. The result is that moral virtues are defined as the mean between two vices; this mean is also referred to as *temperance* or *moderation*.

The philosopher David Hume's *An Enquiry Concerning the Principles of Morals* offers an empirical look at how humans make moral judgments. For Hume, moral decisions and judgments cannot be based on reason alone. He argues that since reason deals with facts, it cannot decide whether to choose one moral option over another. Therefore, "morality is determined by sentiment. It defines virtue to be whatever mental action or quality gives to a spectator the pleasing sentiment of approbation; and vice the contrary."

In the next reading, Immanuel Kant defines ethics as a system of the *ends* of practical reason. For Kant, the study of morality involves the investigation of the distinction between *ends of action* and the *duties of constraint*. Kant claims that humans are free moral beings; thus duty involves self-constraint. In this manner, we can connect self-constraint with the freedom of the will.

John Stuart Mill presents the moral theory of *utilitarianism*, which is captured by this principle: We should always choose the act that is most likely to bring about the greatest amount of happiness and the least amount of pain. Under utilitarianism, you can determine whether your action is right or wrong by comparing the consequences of all the actions that are available to you in any given situation. Therefore, according to the principle of utility, it is is not your individual happiness that you should consider; instead, it is the greatest amount of happiness for the greatest number of people.

The reading by Friedrich Nietzsche offers an opportunity to contrast what he calls a *pre-moral society* (where the value of an action is determined by its consequences), with a *moral society* (where the value of an action is found in its motives). In fact, Nietzsche argues that we need to overcome morality by recognizing that our conscious intentions are just the surface appearance of the drives that actually determine our actions. Therefore, you should strive for independence; you should free yourself from the chains of *accepted truths,* so you can become a *free spirit.*

The reading by Thomas Huxley looks at morality through a different lens. Huxley argues that although evolution may show us how good and evil tendencies have come about, it cannot "furnish any better reason why what we call *good* is preferable to what we call *evil.*" In other words, the biological and environmental methods at work in the struggle for existence are not reconcilable with ethical principles. In fact, Huxley holds that social progress requires that the struggle for existence needs to be substituted by the "*ethical process*; the end of which is not the survival of those who may happen to be the fittest, in respect of the whole of the conditions which obtain, but of those who are ethically the best."

Plato

WHY SHOULD WE BE GOOD?

Socrates, do you wish really to persuade us, or only to seem to have persuaded us, that to be just is always better than to be unjust?

I should wish really to persuade you, Glaucon, if I could.

But to my mind, Socrates. the nature of justice and injustice have not yet been made clear. Setting aside their rewards and results, I want to know what they are in themselves, and how they inwardly work in the soul. If you, please, then, I will revive the argument of Thrasymachus. And first I will speak of the nature and origin of justice according to the common view of them. Secondly, I will show that all men who practice justice do so against their will, of necessity, but not as a good. And thirdly, I will argue that there is reason in this view, for the life of the unjust is after all far better than the life of the just—if what they say is true, Socrates, since I myself am not of their opinion. But still, I acknowledge that I am perplexed when I hear the voices of Thrasymachus and myriads of others in my ears; and, on the other hand, I have never yet heard the superiority of justice to injustice maintained by any one in a satisfactory way. I want to hear justice praised in respect of itself; then I shall be satisfied, and you are the person from whom I think that I am most likely to hear this; and therefore I will praise the unjust life to the utmost of my power, and my manner of speaking will indicate the manner in which I desire to hear you too praising justice and censuring injustice. Will you say whether you approve of my proposal?

Indeed I do, Glaucon; nor can I imagine any theme about which a man of sense would oftener wish to converse.

I am delighted to hear you say so, and shall begin by speaking, as I proposed, of the nature and origin of justice. They say that to do injustice is, by nature, good; to suffer injustice, evil; but that the evil is greater than the good. And so when men have both done and suffered injustice and have had experience of both, not being able to avoid the one and obtain the other, they think that they had better agree among themselves to have neither; hence there arise laws and mutual covenants; and that which is ordained by law is termed by them lawful and just. This they affirm to be the origin and nature of justice; it is a mean or compromise, between the best of all, which is to do injustice and not be punished, and the worst of all, which is to suffer injustice without the power of retaliation; and justice, being at a middle point between the two, is tolerated not as a good, but as the lesser evil, and honored by reason of the inability of men to do injustice. For no man who is worthy to be called a man would ever submit to such an agreement if he were able to resist; he would be mad if he did. Such is the received account, Socrates, of the nature and origin of justice.

Now that those who practice justice do so involuntarily and because they have not the power to be unjust will best appear if we imagine something of this kind: having given both to the just and the unjust power to do what they will, let us watch and see whither desire will lead them; then we shall discover in the very act the just and unjust man to be proceeding along the same road, following their interest, which all natures deem to be their good, and are only diverted into the path of justice by the force of law. The liberty which we are supposing may be most completely given *to them in the form of such a power as is said to have been possessed by Gyges. According to the tradition, Gyges was a shepherd in the service of the king of Lydia; there was a great storm, and an earthquake made an opening in the earth at the place where he was feeding his flock. Amazed at the sight, he descended into the opening, where,*

Edited from *Republic,* Books II and IX. Translated by Benjamin Jowett, 1892, which is now in the public domain.

among other marvels, he beheld a hollow brass horse, having doors, at which he stooping and looking in saw a dead body of stature, as appeared to him, more than human, and having nothing on but a gold ring; this he took from the finger of the dead and reascended.

Now the shepherds met together, according to custom, that they might send their monthly report about the flocks to the king; into their assembly he came having the ring on his finger, and as he was sitting among them he chanced to turn the collet of the ring inside his hand, when instantly he became invisible to the rest of the company and they began to speak of him as if he were no longer present. He was astonished at this, and again touching the ring he turned the collet outwards and reappeared; he made several trials of the ring, and always with the same result—when he turned the collet inwards he became invisible, when outwards he reappeared. Whereupon he contrived to be chosen one of the messengers who were sent to the court; where as soon as he arrived he seduced the queen, and with her help conspired against the king and slew him, and took the kingdom.

Suppose now that there were two such magic rings, and the just put on one of them and the unjust the other; no man can be imagined to be of such an iron nature that he would stand fast in justice. No man would keep his hands off what was not his own when he could safely take what he liked out of the market, or go into houses and lie with any one at his pleasure, or kill or release from prison whom he would, and in all respects be like a God among men. Then the actions of the just would be as the actions of the unjust; they would both come at last to the same point. And this we may truly affirm to be a great proof that a man is just, not willingly or because he thinks that justice is any good to him individually, but of necessity, for wherever any one thinks that he can safely be unjust, there he is unjust. For all men believe in their hearts that injustice is far more profitable to the individual than justice, and he who argues as I have been supposing, will say that they are right. If you could imagine any one obtaining this power of becoming invisible, and never doing any wrong or touching what was another's, he would be thought by the onlookers to be a most wretched idiot, although they would praise him to one another's faces, and keep up appearances with one another from a fear that they too might suffer injustice.

Now, if we are to form a real judgment of the life of the just and unjust, we must isolate them; there is no other way; and how is the isolation to be effected? I answer: Let the unjust man be entirely unjust, and the just man entirely just; nothing is to be taken away from either of them, and both are to be perfectly furnished for the work of their respective lives. First, let the unjust be like other distinguished masters of craft; like the skillful pilot or physician, who knows intuitively his own powers and keeps within their limits, and who, if he fails at any point, is able to recover himself. So let the unjust make his unjust attempts in the right way, and lie hidden if he means to be great in his injustice (he who is found out is nobody): for the highest reach of injustice is to be deemed just when you are not. Therefore I say that in the perfectly unjust man we must assume the most perfect injustice; there is to be no deduction, but we must allow him, while doing the most unjust acts, to have acquired the greatest reputation for justice. If he has taken a false step he must be able to recover himself; he must be one who can speak with effect, if any of his deeds come to light, and who can force his way where force is required his courage and strength, and command of money and friends. And at his side let us place the just man in his nobleness and simplicity, wishing, as Aeschylus says, to be and not to seem good. There must be no seeming, for if he seems to be just he will be honored and rewarded, and then we shall not know whether he is just for the sake of justice or for the sake of honors and rewards; therefore, let him be clothed in justice only, and have no other covering; and he must be imagined in a state of life the opposite of the former. Let him be the best of men, and let him be thought the worst; then he will have been put to the proof; and we shall see whether he will be affected by the fear of infamy and its consequences. And let him continue thus to the hour of death; being just and seeming to be unjust. When both have reached the uttermost extreme, the one of justice and the other of injustice, let judgment be given which of them is the happier of the two.

Heavens, Glaucon! How energetically you polish them up for the decision, first one and then the other, as if they were two statues.

I do my best, Socrates. And now that we know what they are like, there is no difficulty in tracing out the sort of life which awaits either of them. This I will proceed to describe; but as you may think the description a little too coarse, I ask you to suppose, Socrates, that the words which follow are not mine. Let me put them into the mouths of the eulogists of injustice: They will tell you that the just man who is thought unjust will be scourged, racked, bound—will have his eyes burnt out; and, at last, after suffering every kind of evil, he will be impaled: Then he will understand that he ought to seem only, and not to be, just; the words of Aeschylus may be more truly spoken of the unjust than of the just. For the unjust is pursuing a reality; he does not live with a view to appearances—he wants to be really unjust and not to seem only.

In the first place, he is thought just, and therefore bears rule in the city; he can marry whom he will, and give in marriage to whom he will; also he can trade and deal where he likes, and always to his own advantage, because he has no misgivings about injustice and at every contest, whether in public or private, he gets the better of his antagonists, and gains at their expense, and is rich, and out of his gains he can benefit his friends, and harm his enemies; moreover, he can offer sacrifices, and dedicate gifts to the gods abundantly and magnificently, and can honor the gods or any man whom he wants to honor in a far better style than the just, and therefore he is likely to be dearer than they are to the gods. And thus, Socrates, gods and men are said to unite in making the life of the unjust better than the life of the just.

On what principle, then, shall we any longer choose justice rather than the worst injustice, when, if we only unite the latter with a deceitful regard to appearances, we shall fare to our mind both with gods and men, in life and after death, as the most numerous and the highest authorities tell us. Knowing all this, Socrates, how can a man who has any superiority of mind or person or rank or wealth, be willing to honor justice; or indeed to refrain from laughing when he hears justice praised? And even if there should be some one who is able to disprove the truth of my words, and who is satisfied that justice is best, still he is not angry with the unjust, but is very ready to forgive them, because he also knows that men are not just of their own free will; unless, there be some one whom the divinity within him may have inspired with a hatred of injustice, or who has attained knowledge of the truth—but no other man. He only blames injustice who, owing to cowardice or age or some weakness, has not the power of being unjust. And this is proved by the fact that when he obtains the power, he immediately becomes unjust as far as he can be.

Now as you have admitted that justice is one of that highest class of goods which are desired indeed for their results, but in a far greater degree for their own sakes—like sight or hearing or knowledge or health, or any other real and natural and not merely conventional good—I would ask you in your praise of justice to regard one point only: I mean the essential good and evil which justice and injustice work in the possessors of them. Let others praise justice and censure injustice, magnifying the rewards and honors of the one and abusing the other; that is a manner of arguing which, coming from them, I am ready to tolerate, but from you who have spent your whole life in the consideration of this question, unless I hear the contrary from your own lips, I expect something better. And therefore, I say, not only prove to us that justice is better than injustice, but show what they either of them do to the possessor of them, which makes the one to be a good and the other an evil, whether seen or unseen by gods and men.

Having now arrived at this stage of the argument, Glaucon, we may revert to the words which brought us hither. You say that some people believe that injustice was a gain to the perfectly unjust who was reputed to be just?

Yes, that was said.

Now then, having determined the power and quality of justice and injustice, let us have a little conversation. Let us make an image of the soul, that he may have his own words presented before his eyes.

Of what sort?

An ideal image of the soul, like the composite creations of ancient mythology, such as the Chimera or Scylla or Cerberus, and there are many others in which two or more different natures are said to grow into one.

There are said of have been such unions.

Then now model the form of a multitudinous, many-headed monster, having a ring of heads of all manner of beasts, tame and wild, which he is able to generate and metamorphose at will.

You suppose marvelous powers in the artist, Socrates, but as language is more pliable than wax or any similar substance, let there be such a model as you propose.

Suppose now that you make a second form as of a lion, and a third of a man, the second smaller than the first, and the third smaller than the second.

That is an easier task; and I have made them as you say.

And now join them, and let the three grow into one.

That has been accomplished.

Next, fashion the outside of them into a single image, as of a man, so that he who is not able to look within, and sees only the outer hull, may believe the beast to be a single human creature.

I have done so.

And now, to him who maintains that it is profitable for the human creature to be unjust, and unprofitable to be just, let us reply that, if he be right, it is profitable for this creature to feast the multitudinous monster and strengthen the lion and the lion-like qualities, but to starve and weaken the man, who is consequently liable to be dragged about at the mercy of either of the other two; and he is not to attempt to familiarize or harmonize them with one another—he ought rather to suffer them to fight and bite and devour one another.

Certainly, that is what the approver of injustice says.

To him, the supporter of justice makes answer that he should ever so speak and act as to give the man within him in some way or other the most complete mastery over the entire human creature. He should watch over the many-headed monster like a good husbandman, fostering and cultivating the gentle qualities, and preventing the wild ones from growing; he should be making the lion-heart his ally, and in common care of them all should be uniting the several parts with one another and with himself.

Yes, that is quite what the maintainers of justice say.

And so from every point of view, whether of pleasure, honor, or advantage, the approver of justice is right and speaks the truth, and the disapprover is wrong and false and ignorant.

Yes, from every point of view.

Come, now, and let us gently reason with the unjust, who is not intentionally in error. "Sweet Sir," we will say to him, "what think you of things esteemed noble and ignoble? Is not the noble that which subjects the beast to the man, or rather to the god in man; and the ignoble that which subjects the man to the beast?" He can hardly avoid saying yes—can he now?

Not if he has any regard for my opinion.

But, if he agrees so far, we may ask him to answer another question: "Then how would a man profit if he received gold and silver on the condition that he was to enslave the noblest part of him to the worst? Who can imagine that a man who sold his son or daughter into slavery for money, especially if he sold them into the hands of fierce and evil men, would be the gainer, however large might be the sum which he received? And will any one say that he is not a miserable and despicable person who remorselessly sells his own divine being to that which is most godless and detestable? Eriphyle took the necklace as the price of her husband's life, but he is taking a bribe in order to compass a worse ruin."

Yes, far worse—I will answer for him.

Has not the intemperate been censured of old, because in him the huge multiform monster is allowed to be too much at large?

Clearly.

And men are blamed for pride and bad temper when the lion and serpent element in them disproportionately grows and gains strength?

Yes.

And luxury and softness are blamed, because they relax and weaken this same creature, and make a coward of him?

Very true.

And is not a man reproached for flattery and meanness who subordinates the spirited animal to the unruly monster, and, for the sake of money, of which he can never have enough, habituates him in the days of his youth to be trampled in the mire, and from being a lion to become a monkey?

True.

And why are mean employments and manual arts a reproach? Only because they imply a natural weakness of the higher principle; the individual is unable to control the creatures within him, but has to court them, and his great study is how to flatter them.

Such appears to be the reason.

And therefore, being desirous of placing him under a rule like that of the best, we say that he ought to be the servant of the best, in whom the Divine rules; not to the injury of the servant, but because every one had better be ruled by divine wisdom dwelling within him; or, if this be impossible, then by an external authority, in order that we may be all, as far as possible, under the same government, friends and equals.

True.

And this is clearly seen to be the intention of the law, which is the ally of the whole city; and is seen also in the authority which we exercise over children, and the refusal to let them be free until we have established in them a principle analogous to the constitution of a state, and by cultivation of this higher element have set up in their hearts a guardian and ruler like our own, and when this is done they may go their ways.

Yes, the purpose of the law is manifest.

From what point of view, then, and on what ground can we say that a man is profited by injustice or intemperance or other baseness, which will make him a worse man, even though he acquire money or power by his wickedness?

From no point of view at all.

What shall he profit, if his injustice be undetected and unpunished? He who is undetected only gets worse, whereas he who is detected and punished has the brutal part of his nature silenced and humanized; the gentler element in him is liberated, and his whole soul is perfected and ennobled by the acquirement of justice and temperance and wisdom, more than the body ever is by receiving gifts of beauty, strength and health, in proportion as the soul is more honorable than the body.

Certainly.

To this nobler purpose the man of understanding will devote the energies of his life. And in the first place, he will honor studies which impress these qualities on his soul and disregard others. In the next place, he will regulate his bodily habit and training, and so far will he be from yielding to brutal and irrational pleasures, that he will regard even health as quite a secondary matter; his first object will be not that he may be fair or strong or well, unless he is likely thereby to gain temperance, but he will always desire so to temper the body as to preserve the harmony of the soul. And in the acquisition of wealth there is a principle of order and harmony which he will also observe; he will not allow himself to be dazzled by the foolish applause of the world, and heap up riches to his own infinite harm.

Certainly not.

He will look at the city which is within him, and take heed that no disorder occur in it, such as might arise either from superfluity or from want; and upon this principle he will regulate his property and gain or spend according to his means.

Very true.

Aristotle

VIRTUES

Since happiness is an activity of soul in accordance with perfect virtue, we must consider the nature of virtue; for perhaps we shall thus see better the nature of happiness. But clearly the virtue we must study is human virtue; for the good we were seeking was human good and the happiness human happiness. By human virtue we mean not that of the body but that of the soul; and happiness also we call an activity of soul.

Virtue is distinguished into kinds; we say that some of the virtues are intellectual and others moral—philosophic wisdom and understanding and practical wisdom being intellectual, liberality and temperance moral. For in speaking about a man's character we do not say that he is wise or has understanding but that he is good-tempered or temperate; yet we praise the wise man also with respect to his state of mind; and of states of mind we call those which merit praise virtues.

Virtue, then, being of two kinds, intellectual and moral, intellectual virtue in the main owes both its birth and its growth to teaching (for which reason it requires experience and time), while moral virtue comes about as a result of habit. From this it is also plain that none of the moral virtues arises in us by nature; for nothing that exists by nature can form a habit contrary to its nature. For instance, the stone which by nature moves downwards cannot be habituated to move upwards, not even if one tries to train it by throwing it up ten thousand times. Neither by nature, then, nor contrary to nature do the virtues arise in us; rather we are adapted by nature to receive them, and are made perfect by habit.

Again, of all the things that come to us by nature we first acquire the potentiality and later exhibit the activity (this is plain in the case of the senses; for it was not by often seeing or often hearing that we got these senses, but on the contrary we had them before we used them, and did not come to have them by using them); but the virtues we get by first exercising them, as also happens in the case of the arts as well. For the things we have to learn before we can do them, we learn by doing them; for example, men become builders by building; so too we become just by doing just acts, temperate by doing temperate acts, brave by doing brave acts.

For if this were not so, there would have been no need of a teacher, but all men would have been born good or bad at their craft. This, then, is the case with the virtues also; by doing the acts that we do in our transactions with other men we become just or unjust, and by doing the acts that we do in the presence of danger, and being habituated to feel fear or confidence, we become brave or cowardly. Thus, in one word, states of character arise out of like activities.

Since, then, the present inquiry does not aim at theoretical knowledge like the others (for we are inquiring not in order to know what virtue is, but in order to become good, since otherwise our inquiry would have been of no use), we must examine the nature of actions, namely how we ought to do them; for these determine also the nature of the states of character that are produced, as we have said. Now, that we must act according to the right rule is a common principle and must be assumed.

By abstaining from pleasures we become temperate, and it is when we have become so that we are most able to abstain from them; and similarly too in the case of courage; for by being habituated to despise things that are terrible and to stand our ground against them we become

Edited from *Nicomachean Ethics,* Books I and II. Translated by W. D. Ross, 1908, which is now in the public domain.

brave, and it is when we have become so that we shall be most able to stand our ground against them.

We must take as a sign of states of character the pleasure or pain that ensues on acts. For moral excellence is concerned with pleasures and pains; it is on account of the pleasure that we do bad things, and on account of the pain that we abstain from noble ones. Hence we ought to have been brought up in a particular way from our very youth, as Plato says, so as both to delight in and to be pained by the things that we ought; for this is the right education.

Again, if the virtues are concerned with actions and passions, and every passion and every action is accompanied by pleasure and pain, for this reason also virtue will be concerned with pleasures and pains.

The question might be asked, "What do we mean by saying that we must become just by doing just acts, and temperate by doing temperate acts?" For if men do just and temperate acts, they are already just and temperate.

But if the acts that are in accordance with the virtues have themselves a certain character, it does not follow that they are done justly or temperately. The agent also must be in a certain condition when he does them; in the first place he must have knowledge, secondly he must choose the acts, and choose them for their own sakes, and thirdly his action must proceed from a firm and unchangeable character.

Actions, then, are called just and temperate when they are such as the just or the temperate man would do; but it is not the man who does these that is just and temperate, but the man who also does them as just and temperate men do them. It is well said, then, that it is by doing just acts that the just man is produced, and by doing temperate acts the temperate man; without doing these no one would have even a prospect of becoming good.

But most people do not do these, but take refuge in theory and think they are being philosophers and will become good in this way, behaving somewhat like patients who listen attentively to their doctors, but do none of the things they are ordered to do. As the latter will not be made well in body by such a course of treatment, the former will not be made well in soul by such a course of philosophy.

Next we must consider what virtue is. Since things that are found in the soul are of three kinds—passions, faculties, and states of character—virtue must be one of these. By *passions* I mean appetite, anger, fear, confidence, envy, joy, friendly feeling, hatred, longing, emulation, pity, and in general the feelings that are accompanied by pleasure or pain. By *faculties*, the things in virtue of which we are said to be capable of feeling these, e.g., of becoming angry or being pained or feeling pity. By *states of character*, the things in virtue of which we stand well or badly with reference to the passions, e.g., with reference to anger we stand badly if we feel it violently or too weakly, and well if we feel it moderately; and similarly with reference to the other passions.

Now neither the virtues nor the vices are passions, because we are not called good or bad on the ground of our passions, but are so called on the *ground* of our virtues and our vices, and because we are neither praised nor blamed for our passions (for the man who feels fear or anger is not praised, nor is the man who simply feels anger blamed, but the man who feels it in a certain way), but for our virtues and our vices we are praised or blamed. Again, we feel anger and fear without choice, but the virtues are modes of choice or involve choice. Further, in respect of the passions we are said to be moved, but in respect of the virtues and the vices we are said not to be moved but to be disposed in a particular way.

For these reasons also they are not faculties; for we are neither called good nor bad, nor praised nor blamed, for the simple capacity of feeling the passions; again, we have the faculties by nature, but we are not made good or bad by nature. If, then, the virtues are neither passions nor faculties, all that remains is that they should be states of character.

We must, however, not only describe virtue as a state of character, but also say what sort of state it is. We may remark, then, that every virtue or excellence both brings into good condition the thing of which it is the excellence and makes the work of that thing be done well; e.g., the excellence of the eye makes both the eye and its work good; for it is by the excellence of the eye that we see well. Similarly the excellence of the horse makes a horse both good in itself and good at running and at carrying its rider and at awaiting the attack of the enemy. Therefore, if this is true in every case, the virtue of man also will be the state of character which makes a man good and which makes him do his own work well.

If it is thus, then, that every art does its work well, and if, further, virtue is more exact and better than any art, as nature also is, then virtue must have the quality of aiming at the intermediate. I mean *moral virtue*; for it is this that is concerned with passions and actions, and in these there is excess, defect, and the intermediate. For instance, both fear and confidence, and appetite and anger and pity, and in general pleasure and pain may be felt both too much and too little, and in both cases not well; but to feel them at the right times, with reference to the right objects, towards the right people, with the right motive, and in the right way, is what is both intermediate and best, and this is characteristic of virtue. Similarly with regard to actions also there is excess, defect, and the intermediate. Now virtue is concerned with passions and actions, in which excess is a form of failure, and so is defect, while the intermediate is praised and is a form of success; and being praised and being successful are both characteristics of virtue. Therefore virtue is a kind of mean, since, as we have seen, it aims at what is intermediate.

Again, it is possible to fail in many ways (for evil belongs to the class of the unlimited, as the Pythagoreans conjectured, and good to that of the limited), while to succeed is possible only in one way (for which reason also one is easy and the other difficult—to miss the mark easy, to hit it difficult); for these reasons also, then, excess and defect are characteristic of vice, and the mean of virtue; For men are good in but one way, but bad in many.

Virtue, then, is a state of character concerned with choice, lying in a mean, i.e., the mean relative to us, this being determined by a rational principle, and by that principle by which the man of practical wisdom would determine it. Now it is a mean between two vices, that which depends on excess and that which depends on defect; and again it is a mean because the vices respectively fall short of or exceed what is right in both passions and actions, while virtue both finds and chooses that which is intermediate. Hence in respect of its substance and the definition which states its essence virtue is a mean, with regard to what is best and right an extreme.

But not every action nor every passion admits of a mean; for some have names that already imply badness, e.g., spite, shamelessness, envy, and in the case of actions adultery, theft, murder; for all of these and suchlike things imply by their names that they are themselves bad, and not the excesses or deficiencies of them. It is not possible, then, ever to be right with regard to them; one must always be wrong. Nor does goodness or badness with regard to such things depend on committing adultery with the right woman, at the right time, and in the right way, but simply to do any of them is to go wrong. It would be equally absurd, then, to expect that in unjust, cowardly, and voluptuous action there should be a mean, an excess, and a deficiency; for at that rate there would be a mean of excess and of deficiency, an excess of excess, and a deficiency of deficiency. But as there is no excess and deficiency of temperance and courage because what is intermediate is in a sense an extreme, so too of the actions we have mentioned there is no mean nor any excess and deficiency, but however they are done they are wrong; for in general there is neither a mean of excess and deficiency, nor excess and deficiency of a mean.

We must, however, not only make this general statement, but also apply it to the individual facts. For among statements about conduct those which are general apply more widely, but those which are particular are more genuine, since conduct has to do with individual cases, and our statements must harmonize with the facts in these cases. We may take these cases from our table. With regard to feelings of fear and confidence courage is the mean; of the people who exceed, he who exceeds in fearlessness has no name (many of the states have no name), while the man who exceeds in confidence is rash, and he who exceeds in fear and falls short in confidence is a coward. With regard to pleasures and pains—not all of them, and not so much with regard to the pains—the mean is temperance, the excess self-indulgence. Persons deficient with regard to the pleasures are not often found; hence such persons also have received no name. But let us call them "insensible."

With regard to giving and taking of money the mean is liberality, the excess and the defect prodigality and meanness. In these actions people exceed and fall short in contrary ways; the prodigal exceeds in spending and falls short in taking, while the mean man exceeds in taking and falls short in spending.

With regard to honor and dishonor the mean is proper pride, the excess is known as a sort of "empty vanity," and the deficiency is undue humility, so there is a state similarly related to proper pride, being concerned with small honors while that is concerned with great. For it is possible to desire honor as one ought, and more than one ought, and less, and the man who exceeds in his desires is called ambitious, the man who falls short unambitious, while the intermediate person has no name. The dispositions also are nameless, except that that of the ambitious man is called "ambition." Hence the people who are at the extremes lay claim to the middle place; and we ourselves sometimes call the intermediate person *ambitious* and sometimes *unambitious*, and sometimes praise the ambitious man and sometimes the unambitious. The reason of our doing this will be stated in what follows; but now let us speak of the remaining states according to the method which has been indicated.

With regard to anger also there is an excess, a deficiency, and a mean. Although they can scarcely be said to have names, yet since we call the intermediate person good-tempered let us call the mean good temper; of the persons at the extremes let the one who exceeds be called irascible, and his vice irascibility, and the man who falls short an inirascible sort of person, and the deficiency inirascibility.

There are also three other means, which have a certain likeness to one another, but differ from one another: for they are all concerned with intercourse in words and actions, but differ in that one is concerned with truth in this sphere, the other two with pleasantness; and of this one kind is exhibited in giving amusement, the other in all the circumstances of life. We must therefore speak of these too, that we may the better see that in all things the mean is praiseworthy, and the extremes neither praiseworthy nor right, but worthy of blame.

Now most of these states also have no names, but we must try, as in the other cases, to invent names ourselves so that we may be clear and easy to follow. With regard to truth, then, the intermediate is a truthful sort of person and the mean may be called truthfulness, while the pretense which exaggerates is boastfulness and the person characterized by it a boaster, and that which understates is mock modesty and the person characterized by it mock-modest. With regard to pleasantness in the giving of amusement the intermediate person is ready-witted and the disposition ready wit, the excess is buffoonery and the person characterized by it a buffoon, while the man who falls short is a sort of boor and his state is boorishness. With regard to the remaining kind of pleasantness, that which is exhibited in life in general, the man who is pleasant in the right way is friendly and the mean is friendliness, while the man who exceeds is an obsequious person if he has no end in view, a flatterer if he is aiming at his own advantage, and the man who falls short and is unpleasant in all circumstances is a quarrelsome and surly sort of person.

There are also means in the passions and concerned with the passions; since shame is not a virtue, and yet praise is extended to the modest man. For even in these matters one man is said to be intermediate, and another to exceed, as for instance the bashful man who is ashamed of everything; while he who falls short or is not ashamed of anything at all is shameless, and the intermediate person is modest. Righteous indignation is a mean between envy and spite, and these states are concerned with the pain and pleasure that are felt at the fortunes of our neighbors; the man who is characterized by righteous indignation is pained at undeserved good fortune, the envious man, going beyond him, is pained at all good fortune, and the spiteful man falls so far short of being pained that he even rejoices.

That moral virtue is a mean, then, and in what sense it is so, and that it is a mean between two vices, the one involving excess, the other deficiency, and that it is such because its character is to aim at what is intermediate in passions and in actions, has been sufficiently stated. Hence also it is no easy task to be good. For in everything it is no easy task to find the middle, e.g., to find the middle of a circle is not for every one but for him who knows; so, too, any one can get angry—that is easy—or give or spend money; but to do this to the right person, to the right extent, at the right time, with the right motive, and in the right way, that is not for every one, nor is it easy; wherefore goodness is both rare and laudable and noble.

Hence he who aims at the intermediate must first depart from what is the more contrary to it. For of the extremes, one is more erroneous, one less so; therefore, since to hit the mean is hard in the extreme, we must as a second best, as people say, take the least of the evils; and this will be done best in the way we describe. But we must consider the things towards which we ourselves also are easily carried away; for some of us tend to one thing, some to another; and this will be recognizable from the pleasure and the pain we feel. We must drag ourselves away to the contrary extreme; for we shall get into the intermediate state by drawing well away from error, as people do in straightening sticks that are bent.

Now in everything the pleasant or pleasure is most to be guarded against; for we do not judge it impartially; for if we dismiss pleasure thus we are less likely to go astray. It is by doing this, then, (to sum the matter up) that we shall best be able to hit the mean. But this is no doubt difficult, and especially in individual cases; for or is not easy to determine both how and with whom and on what provocation and how long one should be angry; for we too sometimes praise those who fall short and call them good-tempered, but sometimes we praise those who get angry and call them manly. The man, however, who deviates little from goodness is not blamed, whether he does so in the direction of the more or of the less, but only the man who deviates more widely; for he does not fail to be noticed. But up to what point and to what extent a man must deviate before he becomes blameworthy it is not easy to determine by reasoning, any more than anything else that is perceived by the senses; such things depend on particular facts, and the decision rests with perception. So much, then, is plain, that the intermediate state is in all things to be praised, but that we must incline sometimes towards the excess, sometimes towards the deficiency; for so shall we most easily hit the mean and what is right.

David Hume

MORALITY IS DETERMINED BY SENTIMENT

There has been a controversy started of late concerning the general foundation of Morals; whether they be derived from Reason, or from Sentiment; whether we attain the knowledge of them by a chain of argument and induction, or by an immediate feeling and finer internal sense; whether, like all sound judgment of truth and falsehood, they should be the same to every rational intelligent being; or whether, like the perception of beauty and deformity, they be founded entirely on the particular fabric and constitution of the human species.

It must be acknowledged, that both sides of the question are susceptible of specious arguments. Moral distinctions, it may be said, are discernible by pure reason: the long chain of proofs often produced on both sides; the examples cited, the authorities appealed to, the analogies employed, the fallacies detected, the inferences drawn, and the several conclusions adjusted to their proper principles. Truth is disputable; not taste: what exists in the nature of things is the standard of our judgment; what each man feels within himself is the standard of sentiment. Propositions in geometry may be proved, systems in physics may be controverted; but the harmony of verse, the tenderness of passion, the brilliancy of wit, must give immediate pleasure. No man reasons concerning another's beauty; but frequently concerning the justice or injustice of his actions. In every criminal trial the first object of the prisoner is to disprove the facts alleged, and deny the actions imputed to him: the second to prove, that, even if these actions were real, they might be justified, as innocent and lawful. It is confessedly by deductions of the understanding, that the first point is ascertained: how can we suppose that a different faculty of the mind is employed in fixing the other? On the other hand, those who would resolve all moral determinations into sentiment, may endeavor to show, that it is impossible for reason ever to draw conclusions of this nature. To virtue, say they, it belongs to be amiable, and vice odious. This forms their very nature or essence. But can reason or argumentation distribute these different epithets to any subjects, and pronounce beforehand, that this must produce love, and that hatred? Or what other reason can we ever assign for these affections, but the original fabric and formation of the human mind, which is naturally adapted to receive them?

The end of all moral speculations is to teach us our duty; and, by proper representations of the deformity of vice and beauty of virtue, beget correspondent habits, and engage us to avoid the one, and embrace the other. But is this ever to be expected from inferences and conclusions of the understanding, which of themselves have no hold of the affections or set in motion the active powers of men? They discover truths: but where the truths which they discover are indifferent, and beget no desire or aversion, they can have no influence on conduct and behavior. What is honorable, what is fair, what is becoming, what is noble, what is generous, takes possession of the heart, and animates us to embrace and maintain it. What is intelligible, what is evident, what is probable, what is true, procures only the cool assent of the understanding; and gratifying a speculative curiosity, puts an end to our researches.

Extinguish all the warm feelings and prepossessions in favor of virtue, and all disgust or aversion to vice: render men totally indifferent towards these distinctions; and morality is no longer a practical study, nor has any tendency to regulate our lives and actions.

These arguments on each side (and many more might be produced) are so plausible, that I am apt to suspect, they may, the one as well as the other, be solid and satisfactory, and that reason and sentiment concur in almost all moral determinations and conclusions. The final sentence, it is probable, which pronounces characters and actions amiable or odious, praise-worthy or blameable; that which stamps on them the mark of honor or infamy, approbation or censure; that which renders morality an active principle and constitutes virtue our happiness, and vice our misery; it is probable, I say, that this final sentence depends on some internal sense or feeling, which nature has made universal in the whole species. For what else can have an influence of this nature? But in order to pave the way for such a sentiment, and give a proper discernment of its object, it is often necessary, we find, that much reasoning should precede, that nice distinctions be made, just conclusions drawn, distant comparisons formed, complicated relations examined, and general facts fixed and ascertained.

But though this question, concerning the general principles of morals, be curious and important, it is needless for us, at present, to employ farther care in our researches concerning it. For if we can be so happy, in the course of this enquiry, as to discover the true origin of morals, it will then easily appear how far either sentiment or reason enters into all determinations of this nature. In order to attain this purpose, we shall endeavor to follow a very simple method: we shall analyze that complication of mental qualities, which form what, in common life, we call Personal Merit: we shall consider every attribute of the mind, which renders a man an object either of esteem and affection, or of hatred and contempt; every habit or sentiment or faculty, which, if ascribed to any person, implies either praise or blame.

The only object of reasoning is to discover the circumstances on both sides, which are common to these qualities; to observe that particular in which the estimable qualities agree on the one hand, and the blameable on the other; and thence to reach the foundation of ethics, and find those universal principles, from which all censure or approbation is ultimately derived. As this is a *question of fact*, not of abstract science, we can only expect success, by following the experimental method, and deducing general maxims from a comparison of particular instances. The other scientific method, where a general abstract principle is first established, and is afterwards branched out into a variety of inferences and conclusions, may be more perfect in itself, but suits less the imperfection of human nature, and is a common source of illusion and mistake in this as well as in other subjects. Men are now cured of their passion for hypotheses and systems in natural philosophy, and will hearken to no arguments but those which are derived from experience. It is full time they should attempt a like reformation in all moral disquisitions; and reject every system of ethics, however subtle or ingenious, which is not founded on fact and observation.

If the foregoing hypothesis be received, it will now be easy for us to determine the question first started, concerning the general principles of morals, and examine how far either reason or sentiment enters into all decisions of praise or censure.

One principal foundation of moral praise being supposed to lie in the usefulness of any quality or action, it is evident that *reason* must enter for a considerable share in all decisions of this kind; since nothing but that faculty can instruct us in the tendency of qualities and actions, and point out their beneficial consequences to society and to their possessor. In many cases this is an affair liable to great controversy: doubts may arise; opposite interests may occur; and a preference must be given to one side, from very nice views, and a small overbalance of utility. This is particularly remarkable in questions with regard to justice; as is, indeed, natural to suppose, from that species of utility which attends this virtue. Were every single instance of justice, like that of benevolence, useful to society; this would be a more simple state of the case, and seldom liable to great controversy. But as single instances of justice are often pernicious in their first and immediate tendency, and as the advantage to society results only from the observance of the general rule, and from the concurrence and combination of several persons in the same equitable conduct; the case here becomes more intricate and involved. The various circumstances of society; the various consequences of any practice; the various interests which may be proposed; these, on many occasions, are doubtful, and subject to great discussion and inquiry. The object of municipal laws is to fix all the questions with regard to justice: the debates of civilians; the reflections of politicians; the precedents of history and public records, are all directed to the same purpose. And a very accurate reason or judgment is often requisite, to give the true determination, amidst such intricate doubts arising from obscure or opposite utilities.

But though reason, when fully assisted and improved, be sufficient to instruct us in the pernicious or useful tendency of qualities and actions; it is not alone sufficient to produce any moral blame or approbation. Utility is only a tendency to a certain end; and were the end totally indifferent to us, we should feel the same indifference towards the means. It is requisite a sentiment should here display itself, in order to give a preference to the useful above the pernicious tendencies. This sentiment can be no other than a feeling for the happiness of mankind, and a resentment of their misery; since these are the different ends which virtue and vice have a tendency to promote. Here therefore reason instructs us in the several tendencies of actions, and humanity makes a distinction in favor of those which are useful and beneficial.

This partition between the faculties of understanding and sentiment, in all moral decisions, seems clear from the preceding hypothesis. But I shall suppose that hypothesis false: it will then be requisite to look out for some other theory that may be satisfactory; and I dare venture to affirm that none such will ever be found, so long as we suppose reason to be the sole source of morals. To prove this, it will be proper to weigh the five following considerations.

1. Examine the crime of ingratitude, for instance; which has place, wherever we observe good-will, expressed and known, together with good-offices performed, on the one side, and a return of ill-will or indifference, with ill-offices or neglect on the other: anatomize all these circumstances, and examine, by your reason alone, in what consists the demerit or blame. You never will come to any issue or conclusion.

Reason judges either of *matters of fact* or of *relations*. Enquire then, first, where is that matter of fact which we here call crime; point it out; determine the time of its existence; describe its essence or nature; explain the sense or faculty to which it discovers itself. It resides in the mind of the person who is ungrateful. He must, therefore, feel it, and be conscious of it. But nothing is there, except the passion of ill-will or absolute indifference. You cannot say that these, of themselves, always, and in all circumstances, are crimes. No, they are only crimes when directed towards persons who have before expressed and displayed good-will towards us. Consequently, we may infer, that the crime of ingratitude is not any particular individual fact; but arises from a complication of circumstances, which, being presented to the spectator, excites the sentiment of blame, by the particular structure and fabric of his mind.

This representation, you say, is false. Crime, indeed, consists not in a particular fact, of whose reality we are assured by reason; but it consists in certain moral relations, discovered by reason, in the same manner as we discover by reason the truths of geometry or algebra. But what are the relations, I ask, of which you here talk? In the case stated above, I see first good-will and good-offices in one person; then ill-will and ill-offices in the other. Between these, there is a relation of contrariety. Does the crime consist in that relation? But suppose a person bore me ill-will or did me ill-offices; and I, in return, were indifferent towards him, or did him good offices. Here is the same relation of contrariety; and yet my conduct is often highly laudable. Twist and turn this matter as much as you will, you can never rest the morality on relation; but must have recourse to the decisions of sentiment.

When it is affirmed that two and three are equal to the half of ten, this relation of equality I understand perfectly. I conceive, that if ten be divided into two parts, of which one has as many units as the other; and if any of these parts be compared to two added to three, it will contain as many units as that compound number. But when you draw thence a comparison to moral relations, I own that I am altogether at a loss to understand you. A moral action, a crime, such as ingratitude, is a complicated object. Does the morality consist in the relation of its parts to each other? How? After what manner? Specify the relation: be more particular and explicit in your propositions, and you will easily see their falsehood.

No, say you, the morality consists in the relation of actions to the rule of right; and they are denominated good or ill, according as they agree or disagree with it. What then is this rule of right? In what does it consist? How is it determined? By reason, you say, which examines the moral relations of actions. So that moral relations are determined by the comparison of action to a rule. And that rule is determined by considering the moral relations of objects. Is not this fine reasoning?

All this is metaphysics, you cry. That is enough; there needs nothing more to give a strong presumption of falsehood. Yes, reply I, here are metaphysics surely; but they are all on your side, who advance an abstruse hypothesis, which can never be made intelligible with any particular instance or illustration. The hypothesis which we embrace is plain. It maintains that morality is determined by sentiment. It defines virtue to be whatever mental action or quality gives to a spectator the pleasing sentiment of approbation; and vice the contrary. We then proceed to examine a plain matter of fact, to wit, what actions have this influence. We consider all the circumstances in which these actions agree, and thence endeavor to extract some general observations with regard to these sentiments. If you call this metaphysics, and find anything abstruse here, you need only conclude that your turn of mind is not suited to the moral sciences.

2. When a man, at any time, deliberates concerning his own conduct (as, whether he had better, in a particular emergency, assist a brother or a benefactor), he must consider these separate relations, with all the circumstances and situations of the persons, in order to determine the superior duty and obligation; and in order to determine the proportion of lines in any triangle, it is necessary to examine the nature of that figure, and the relation which its several parts bear to each other. But notwithstanding this appearing similarity in the two cases, there is, at bottom, an extreme difference between them. A speculative reasoner concerning triangles or circles considers the several known and given relations of the parts of these figures; and thence infers some unknown relation, which is dependent on the former. But in moral deliberations we must be acquainted beforehand with all the objects, and all their relations to each other; and from a comparison of the whole, fix our choice or approbation. No new fact to be ascertained; no new relation to be discovered. All the circumstances of the case are supposed to be laid before us, so we can fix any sentence of blame or approbation. If any material circumstance be yet unknown or doubtful, we must first employ our inquiry or intellectual faculties to assure us of it; and must suspend for a time all moral decision or sentiment. While we are ignorant whether a man were aggressor or not, how can we determine whether the person who killed him be criminal or innocent? But after every circumstance, every relation is known, the understanding has no further room to operate, nor any object on which it could employ itself. The approbation or blame which then ensues, cannot be the work of the judgment, but of the heart; and is not a speculative proposition or affirmation, but an active feeling or sentiment. In the disquisitions of the understanding, from known circumstances and relations, we infer some new and unknown. In moral decisions, all the circumstances and relations must be previously known; and the mind, from

the contemplation of the whole, feels some new impression of affection or disgust, esteem or contempt, approbation or blame. Hence the great difference between a mistake of fact and one of right; and hence the reason why the one is commonly criminal and not the other.

In these sentiments then, not in a discovery of relations of any kind, do all moral determinations consist. Before we can pretend to form any decision of this kind, everything must be known and ascertained on the side of the object or action. Nothing remains but to feel, on our part, some sentiment of blame or approbation; whence we pronounce the action criminal or virtuous.

3. This doctrine will become still more evident, if we compare moral beauty with natural, to which in many particulars it bears so near a resemblance. It is on the proportion, relation, and position of parts, that all natural beauty depends; but it would be absurd thence to infer, that the perception of beauty, like that of truth in geometrical problems, consists wholly in the perception of relations, and was performed entirely by the understanding or intellectual faculties. In all the sciences, our mind from the known relations investigates the unknown. But in all decisions of taste or external beauty, all the relations are beforehand obvious to the eye; and we thence proceed to feel a sentiment of complacency or disgust, according to the nature of the object, and disposition of our organs.

Euclid has fully explained all the qualities of the circle; but has not in any proposition said a word of its beauty. The reason is evident. The beauty is not a quality of the circle. It lies not in any part of the line, whose parts are equally distant from a common center. It is only the effect which that figure produces upon the mind, whose peculiar fabric of structure renders it susceptible of such sentiments. In vain would you look for it in the circle, or seek it, either by your senses or by mathematical reasoning, in all the properties of that figure.

No satisfactory answer can be given to any of these questions, upon the abstract hypothesis of morals; and we must at last acknowledge, that the crime or immorality is no particular fact or relation, which can be the object of the understanding, but arises entirely from the sentiment of disapprobation, which, by the structure of human nature, we unavoidably feel on the apprehension of barbarity or treachery.

4. Inanimate objects may bear to each other all the same relations which we observe in moral agents; though the former can never be the object of love or hatred, nor are consequently susceptible of merit or iniquity. A young tree, which over-tops and destroys its parent, stands in all the same relations with Nero, when he murdered Agrippina; and if morality consisted merely in relations, would no doubt be equally criminal.

5. It appears evident that the ultimate ends of human actions can never, in any case, be accounted for by reason, but recommend themselves entirely to the sentiments and affections of mankind, without any dependence on the intellectual faculties. Ask a man why he exercises; he will answer, because he desires to keep his health. If you then enquire, why he desires health, he will readily reply, because sickness is painful. If you push your enquiries farther, and desire a reason why he hates pain, it is impossible he can ever give any. This is an ultimate end, and is never referred to any other object.

Perhaps to your second question, why he desires health, he may also reply, that it is necessary for the exercise of his calling. If you ask, why he is anxious on that head, he will answer, because he desires to get money. If you demand Why? It is the instrument of pleasure, says he. And beyond this it is an absurdity to ask for a reason. It is impossible there can be a progress *in infinitum*; and that one thing can always be a reason why another is desired. Something must be desirable on its own account, and because of its immediate accord or agreement with human sentiment and affection.

Now as virtue is an end, and is desirable on its own account, without fee and reward, merely for the immediate satisfaction which it conveys; it is requisite that there should be some sentiment which it touches, some internal taste or feeling, or whatever you may please to call it, which distinguishes moral good and evil, and which embraces the one and rejects the other.

Thus the distinct boundaries and offices of reason and of taste are easily ascertained. The former conveys the knowledge of truth and falsehood: the latter gives the sentiment of beauty and deformity, vice and virtue. The one discovers objects as they really stand in nature, without addition and diminution: the other has a productive faculty, and gilding or staining all natural objects with the colors, borrowed from internal sentiment, raises in a manner a new creation. Reason being cool and disengaged, is no motive to action, and directs only the impulse received from appetite or inclination, by showing us the means of attaining happiness or avoiding misery: Taste, as it gives pleasure or pain, and thereby constitutes happiness or misery, becomes a motive to action, and is the first spring or impulse to desire and volition. From circumstances and relations, known or supposed, the former leads us to the discovery of the concealed and unknown: after all circumstances and relations are laid before us, the latter makes us feel from the whole a new sentiment of blame or approbation.

Immanuel Kant

DUTY

The notion of duty is in itself already the notion of a constraint of the free elective will by the law; whether this constraint be an external one or be self-constraint. The moral imperative, by its categorical (the unconditional *ought*) announces this constraint, which therefore does not apply to all rational beings (for there may also be holy beings), but applies to men as rational physical beings who are unholy enough to be seduced by pleasure to the transgression of the moral law, although they themselves recognize its authority; and when they do obey it, to obey it unwillingly (with resistance of their inclination); and it is in this that the constraint properly consists. Now, as man is a free (moral) being, the notion of duty can contain only self-constraint (by the idea of the law itself), when we look to the internal determination of the will (the spring), for thus only is it possible to combine that constraint (even if it were external) with the freedom of the elective will. The notion of duty then must be an ethical one.

The impulses of nature, then, contain hindrances to the fulfilment of duty in the mind of man, and resisting forces, some of them powerful; and he must judge himself able to combat these and to conquer them by means of reason, not in the future, but in the present, simultaneously with the thought; he must judge that he can do what the law unconditionally commands that be ought.

Now the power and resolved purpose to resist a strong but unjust opponent is called *fortitude*, and when concerned with the opponent of the moral character within us, it is *virtue*. Accordingly, general deontology [duty or rule-based ethics], in that part which brings not external, but internal, freedom under laws is the doctrine of virtue.

Jurisprudence had to do only with the formal condition of external freedom (the condition of consistency with itself, if its maxim became a universal law), that is, with law. Ethics, on the contrary, supplies us with a matter (an object of the free elective will), an end of pure reason which is at the same time conceived as an objectively necessary end, i.e., as duty for all men. For, as the sensible inclinations mislead us to ends (which are the matter of the elective will) that may contradict duty, the legislating reason cannot otherwise guard against their influence than by an opposite moral end, which therefore must be given *a priori* independently on inclination.

An end is an object of the elective will (of a rational being) by the idea of which this will is determined to an action for the production of this object. Now I may be forced by others to actions which are directed to an end as means, but I cannot be forced to have an end; I can only make something an end to myself. If, however, I am also bound to make something which lies in the notions of practical reason an end to myself, and therefore besides the formal determining principle of the elective will (as contained in law) to have also a material principle, an end which can be opposed to the end derived from sensible impulses; then this gives the notion of an end which is in itself a duty. The doctrine of this cannot belong to jurisprudence, but to ethics, since this alone includes in its conception self-constraint according to moral laws.

For this reason, "ethics" may also be defined as the system of the ends of the pure practical reason. The two parts of moral philosophy are distinguished as treating respectively of ends and of duties of constraint. That ethics contains duties to the observance of which one cannot be (physically) forced by others, is merely the consequence of this, that it is a doctrine of ends, since to be forced to have ends or to set them before one's self is a contradiction.

Edited from *The Metaphysical Elements of Ethics,* Introduction. Translated by Thomas Kingsmill Abbott, 1909, which is now in the public domain.

Now that ethics is a doctrine of virtue follows from the definition of virtue given above compared with the obligation, the peculiarity of which has just been shown. There is in fact no other determination of the elective will, except that to an end, which in the very notion of it implies that I cannot even physically be forced to it by the elective will of others. Another may indeed force me to do something which is not my end (but only means to the end of another), but he cannot force me to make it my own end, and yet I can have no end except of my own making. The latter supposition would be a contradiction—an act of freedom which yet at the same time would not be free. But there is no contradiction in setting before one's self an end which is also a duty: for in this case I constrain myself, and this is quite consistent with freedom. But how is such an end possible? That is now the question. For the possibility of the notion of the thing (namely, that it is not self-contradictory) is not enough to prove the possibility of the thing itself (the objective reality of the notion).

We can conceive the relation of end to duty in two ways; either starting from the end to find the maxim of the dutiful actions; or conversely, setting out from this to find the end which is also duty. Jurisprudence proceeds in the former way. It is left to everyone's free elective will what end he will choose for his action. But its maxim is determined *a priori*; namely, that the freedom of the agent must be consistent with the freedom of every other according to a universal law.

Ethics, however, proceeds in the opposite way. It cannot start from the ends which the man may propose to himself, and hence give directions as to the maxims he should adopt, that is, as to his duty; for that would be to take empirical principles of maxims, and these could not give any notion of duty; since this, the categorical ought, has its root in pure reason alone. Indeed, if the maxims were to be adopted in accordance with those ends (which are all selfish), we could not properly speak of the notion of duty at all. Hence in ethics the notion of duty must lead to ends, and must on moral principles give the foundation of maxims with respect to the ends which we ought to propose to ourselves.

Setting aside the question what sort of end that is which is in itself a duty, and how such an end is possible, it is here only necessary to show that a duty of this kind is called a duty of virtue, and why it is so called.

To every duty corresponds a right of action, but all duties do not imply a corresponding right of another to compel any one, but only the duties called legal duties. Similarly to all ethical obligation corresponds the notion of virtue, but it does not follow that all ethical duties are duties of virtue. Those, in fact, are not so which do not concern so much a certain end (matter, object of the elective will), but merely that which is formal in the moral determination of the will (e.g., that the dutiful action must also be done from duty). It is only an end which is also duty that can be called a duty of virtue. Hence there are several of the latter kind (and thus there are distinct virtues); on the contrary, there is only one duty of the former kind, but it is one which is valid for all actions (only one virtuous disposition).

The duty of virtue is essentially distinguished from the duty of justice in this respect; that it is morally possible to be externally compelled to the latter, whereas the former rests on free self-constraint only. For finite holy beings (which cannot even be tempted to the violation of duty) there is no doctrine of virtue, but only moral philosophy, the latter being an autonomy of practical reason, whereas the former is also an autocracy of it. That is, it includes a consciousness—not indeed immediately perceived, but rightly concluded, from the moral categorical imperative—of the power to become master of one's inclinations which resist the law; so that human morality in its highest stage can yet be nothing more than virtue; even if it were quite pure (perfectly free from the influence of a spring foreign to duty), a state which is poetically personified under the name of the wise man (as an ideal to which one should continually approximate).

Virtue, however, is *not* to be defined and esteemed merely as habit, and as a long custom acquired by practice of morally good actions. For, if this is not an effect of well-resolved and firm principles ever more and more purified, then, like any other mechanical arrangement brought about by technical practical reason, it is neither armed for all circumstances nor adequately secured against the change that may be wrought by new allurements.

John Stuart Mill

THE PRINCIPLE OF UTILITY

The creed which accepts as the foundation of morals, Utility, or the Greatest Happiness Principle, holds that actions are right in proportion as they tend to promote happiness, wrong as they tend to produce the reverse of happiness. By happiness is intended pleasure, and the absence of pain; by unhappiness, pain, and the privation of pleasure. To give a clear view of the moral standard set up by the theory, much more requires to be said; in particular, what things it includes in the ideas of pain and pleasure; and to what extent this is left an open question. But these supplementary explanations do not affect the theory of life on which this theory of morality is grounded—namely, that pleasure, and freedom from pain, are the only things desirable as ends; and that all desirable things (which are as numerous in the utilitarian as in any other scheme) are desirable either for the pleasure inherent in themselves, or as means to the promotion of pleasure and the prevention of pain.

Now, such a theory of life excites in many minds, and among them in some of the most estimable in feeling and purpose, inveterate dislike. To suppose that life has (as they express it) no higher end than pleasure—no better and nobler object of desire and pursuit—they designate as utterly mean and groveling; as a doctrine worthy only of swine, to whom the followers of Epicurus were, at a very early period, contemptuously likened; and modern holders of the doctrine are occasionally made the subject of equally polite comparisons by its German, French, and English assailants.

When thus attacked, the Epicureans have always answered, that it is not they, but their accusers, who represent human nature in a degrading light; since the accusation supposes human beings to be capable of no pleasures except those of which swine are capable. If this supposition were true, the charge could not be gainsaid, but would then be no longer an imputation; for if the sources of pleasure were precisely the same to human beings and to swine, the rule of life which is good enough for the one would be good enough for the other. The comparison of the Epicurean life to that of beasts is felt as degrading, precisely because a beast's pleasures do not satisfy a human being's conceptions of happiness. Human beings have faculties more elevated than the animal appetites, and when once made conscious of them, do not regard anything as happiness which does not include their gratification. I do not, indeed, consider the Epicureans to have been by any means faultless in drawing out their scheme of consequences from the utilitarian principle. To do this in any sufficient manner, many Stoic, as well as Christian elements require to be included. But there is no known Epicurean theory of life which does not assign to the pleasures of the intellect; of the feelings and imagination, and of the moral sentiments, a much higher value as pleasures than to those of mere sensation. It must be admitted, however, that utilitarian writers in general have placed the superiority of mental over bodily pleasures chiefly in the greater permanency, safety, uncostliness, etc., of the former—that is, in their circumstantial advantages rather than in their intrinsic nature. And on all these points utilitarians have fully proved their case; but they might have taken the other, and, as it may be called, higher ground, with entire consistency. It is quite compatible with the principle of utility to recognize the fact, that some *kinds* of pleasure are more desirable and more valuable than others. It would be absurd that while, in estimating all other

Edited from *Utilitarianism,* 1861, Chapters II and IV, which is now in the public domain.

things, quality is considered as well as quantity, the estimation of pleasures should be supposed to depend on quantity alone.

If I am asked, what I mean by difference of quality in pleasures, or what makes one pleasure more valuable than another, merely as a pleasure, except its being greater in amount, there is but one possible answer. Of two pleasures, if there be one to which all or almost all who have experience of both give a decided preference, irrespective of any feeling of moral obligation to prefer it, that is the more desirable pleasure. If one of the two is, by those who are competently acquainted with both, placed so far above the other that they prefer it, even though knowing it to be attended with a greater amount of discontent, and would not resign it for any quantity of the other pleasure which their nature is capable of, we are justified in ascribing to the preferred enjoyment a superiority in quality, so far outweighing quantity as to render it, in comparison, of small account.

Now it is an unquestionable fact that those who are equally acquainted with, and equally capable of appreciating and enjoying both, do give a most marked preference to the manner of existence which employs their higher faculties. Few human creatures would consent to be changed into any of the lower animals, for a promise of the fullest allowance of a beast's pleasures; no intelligent human being would consent to be a fool, no instructed person would be an ignoramus, no person of feeling and conscience would be selfish and base, even though they should be persuaded that the fool, the dunce, or the rascal is better satisfied with his lot than they are with theirs. They would not resign what they possess more than he, for the most complete satisfaction of all the desires which they have in common with him. If they ever fancy they would, it is only in cases of unhappiness so extreme, that to escape from it they would exchange their lot for almost any other, however undesirable in their own eyes. A being of higher faculties requires more to make him happy, is capable probably of more acute suffering, and is certainly accessible to it at more points, than one of an inferior type; but in spite of these liabilities, he can never really wish to sink into what he feels to be a lower grade of existence. We may give what explanation we please of this unwillingness; we may attribute it to pride, a name which is given indiscriminately to some of the most and to some of the least estimable feelings of which mankind are capable; we may refer it to the love of liberty and personal independence, an appeal to which was with the Stoics one of the most effective means for the inculcation of it; to the love of power, or to the love of excitement, both of which do really enter into and contribute to it: but its most appropriate appellation is a sense of dignity, which all human beings possess in one form or other, and in some, though by no means in exact, proportion to their higher faculties, and which is so essential a part of the happiness of those in whom it is strong, that nothing which conflicts with it could be, otherwise than momentarily, an object of desire to them. Whoever supposes that this preference takes place at a sacrifice of happiness—that the superior being, in anything like equal circumstances, is not happier than the inferior—confounds the two very different ideas, of happiness, and content. It is indisputable that the being whose capacities of enjoyment are low, has the greatest chance of having them fully satisfied; and a highly-endowed being will always feel that any happiness which he can look for, as the world is constituted, is imperfect. But he can learn to bear its imperfections, if they are at all bearable; and they will not make him envy the being who is indeed unconscious of the imperfections, but only because he feels not at all the good which those imperfections qualify. It is better to be a human being dissatisfied than a pig satisfied; better to be Socrates dissatisfied than a fool satisfied. And if the fool, or the pig, is of a different opinion, it is because they only know their own side of the question. The other party to the comparison knows both sides.

It may be objected, that many who are capable of the higher pleasures, occasionally, under the influence of temptation, postpone them to the lower. But this is quite compatible with a full appreciation of the intrinsic superiority of the higher. Men often, from infirmity of character, make their election for the nearer good, though they know it to be the less valuable; and this no less when the choice is between two bodily pleasures, than when it is between bodily and mental. They pursue sensual indulgences to the injury of health, though perfectly aware that health is the greater good. It may be further objected, that many who begin with youthful enthusiasm for everything noble, as they advance in years sink into indolence and selfishness. But I do not believe that those who undergo this very common change, voluntarily choose the lower description of pleasures in preference to the higher. I believe that before they devote themselves exclusively to the one, they have already become incapable of the other. Capacity for the nobler feelings is in most natures a very tender plant, easily killed, not only by hostile influences, but by mere want of sustenance; and in the majority of young persons it speedily dies away if the occupations to which their position in life has devoted them, and the society into which it has thrown them, are not favorable to keeping that higher capacity in exercise. Men lose their high aspirations as they lose their intellectual tastes, because they have not time or opportunity for indulging them; and they addict themselves to inferior pleasures, not because they deliberately prefer them, but because they are either the only ones to which they have access, or the only ones which they are any longer capable of enjoying. It may be questioned whether any one who has remained equally susceptible to both classes of pleasures, ever knowingly and calmly preferred the lower; though many, in all ages, have broken down in an ineffectual attempt to combine both.

From this verdict of the only competent judges, I apprehend there can be no appeal. On a question which is the best worth having of two pleasures, or which of two modes of existence is the most grateful to the feelings, apart from its moral attributes and from its consequences, the judgment of those who are qualified by knowledge of both, or, if they differ, that of the majority among them, must be admitted as final. And there needs be the less hesitation to accept this judgment respecting the quality of pleasures, since there is no other tribunal to be referred to even on the question of quantity. What means are there of determining which is the acutest of two pains, or the more intense of two pleasurable sensations, except the general suffrage of those who are familiar with both? Neither pains nor pleasures are homogeneous, and pain is always heterogeneous with pleasure. What is there to decide whether a particular pleasure is worth purchasing at the cost of a particular pain, except the feelings and judgment of the experienced? When, therefore, those feelings and judgment declare the pleasures derived from the higher faculties to be preferable *in kind*, apart from the question of intensity, to those of which the animal nature, disjoined from the higher faculties, is susceptible, they are entitled on this subject to the same regard.

I have dwelt on this point, as being a necessary part of a perfectly just conception of Utility or Happiness, considered as the directive rule of human conduct. But it is by no means an indispensable condition to the acceptance of the utilitarian standard; for that standard is not the agent's own greatest happiness, but the greatest amount of happiness altogether; and if it may possibly be doubted whether a noble character is always the happier for its nobleness, there can be no doubt that it makes other people happier, and that the world in general is immensely a gainer by it. Utilitarianism, therefore, could only attain its end by the general cultivation of nobleness of character, even if each individual were only benefited by the nobleness of others, and his own, so far as happiness is concerned, were a sheer deduction from the benefit. But the bare enunciation of such an absurdity as this last, renders refutation superfluous.

According to the Greatest Happiness Principle, as above explained, the ultimate end, with reference to and for the sake of which all other things are desirable (whether we are considering our own good or that of other people), is an existence exempt as far as possible from pain, and as rich as possible in enjoyments, both in point of quantity and quality; the test of quality, and the rule for measuring it against quantity, being the preference felt by those who, in their opportunities of experience, to which must be added their habits of self-consciousness and self-observation, are best furnished with the means of comparison. This, being, according to the utilitarian opinion, the end of human action, is necessarily also the standard of morality; which may accordingly be defined, the rules and precepts for human conduct, by the observance of which an existence such as has been described might be, to the greatest extent possible, secured to all mankind; and not to them only, but, so far as the nature of things admits, to the whole sentient creation.

Against this doctrine, however, arises another class of objectors, who say that happiness, in any form, cannot be the rational purpose of human life and action; because, in the first place, it is unattainable: and they contemptuously ask, "What right hast thou to be happy?" a question which Mr. Carlyle clenches by the addition, "What right, a short time ago, hadst thou even *to be*?" Next, they say, that men can do *without* happiness; that all noble human beings have felt this, and could not have become noble but by learning the lesson of Entsagen, or renunciation; which lesson, thoroughly learnt and submitted to, they affirm to be the beginning and necessary condition of all virtue.

The first of these objections would go to the root of the matter were it well founded; for if no happiness is to be had at all by human beings, the attainment of it cannot be the end of morality, or of any rational conduct. Though, even in that case, something might still be said for the utilitarian theory; since utility includes not solely the pursuit of happiness, but the prevention or mitigation of unhappiness; and if the former aim be chimerical, there will be all the greater scope and more imperative need for the latter, so long at least as mankind think fit to live, and do not take refuge in the simultaneous act of suicide recommended under certain conditions by Novalis. When, however, it is thus positively asserted to be impossible that human life should be happy, the assertion, if not something like a verbal quibble, is at least an exaggeration. If by happiness be meant a continuity of highly pleasurable excitement, it is evident enough that this is impossible. A state of exalted pleasure lasts only moments, or in some cases, and with some intermissions, hours or days, and is the occasional brilliant flash of enjoyment, not its permanent and steady flame. Of this the philosophers who have taught that happiness is the end of life were as fully aware as those who taunt them. The happiness which they meant was not a life of rapture, but moments of such, in an existence made up of few and transitory pains, many and various pleasures, with a decided predominance of the active over the passive, and having as the foundation of the whole, not to expect more from life than it is capable of bestowing. A life thus composed, to those who have been fortunate enough to obtain it, has always appeared worthy of the name of happiness. And such an existence is even now the lot of many, during some considerable portion of their lives. The present wretched education, and wretched social arrangements, are the only real hindrance to its being attainable by almost all.

The objectors perhaps may doubt whether human beings, if taught to consider happiness as the end of life, would be satisfied with such a moderate share of it. But great numbers of mankind have been satisfied with much less. The main constituents of a satisfied life appear to be two, either of which by itself is often found sufficient for the purpose: tranquility, and excitement. With much tranquility, many find that they can be content with very little pleasure: with much excitement, many can reconcile themselves to a considerable quantity of pain. There is assuredly no inherent impossibility in enabling even the mass of mankind to unite both; since the two are so far from being incompatible that they are in natural alliance, the prolongation of either being a preparation for, and exciting a wish for, the other. It is only those in whom indolence amounts to a vice, that do not desire excitement after an interval of repose; it is only those in whom the need of excitement is a disease, that feel the tranquility which follows excitement dull and insipid, instead of pleasurable in direct proportion to the excitement which preceded it. When people who are tolerably fortunate in their outward lot do not find in life sufficient enjoyment to make it valuable to them, the cause generally is, caring for nobody but themselves. To those who have neither public nor private affections, the excitements of life are much curtailed, and in any case dwindle in value as the time approaches when all selfish interests must be terminated by death: while those who leave after them objects of personal affection, and especially those who have also cultivated a fellow-feeling with the collective interests of mankind, retain as lively an interest in life on the eve of death as in the vigor of youth and health. Next to selfishness, the principal cause which makes life unsatisfactory, is want of mental cultivation. A cultivated mind—I do not mean that of a philosopher, but any mind to which the fountains of knowledge have been opened, and which has been taught, in any tolerable degree, to exercise its faculties—finds sources of inexhaustible interest in all that surrounds it; in the objects of nature, the achievements of art, the imaginations of poetry, the incidents of history, the ways of mankind past and present, and their prospects in the future. It is possible, indeed, to become indifferent to all this, and that too without having exhausted a thousandth part of it; but only when one has had from the beginning no moral or human interest in these things, and has sought in them only the gratification of curiosity.

Now there is absolutely no reason in the nature of things why an amount of mental culture sufficient to give an intelligent interest in these objects of contemplation, should not be the inheritance of every one born in a civilized country. As little is there an inherent necessity that any human being should be a selfish egotist, devoid of every feeling or care but those which center in his own miserable individuality. Something far superior to this is sufficiently common even now, to give ample earnest of what the human species may be made. Genuine private affections, and a sincere interest in the public good, are possible, though in unequal degrees, to every rightly brought-up human being. In a world in which there is so much to interest, so much to enjoy, and so much also to correct and improve, every one who has this moderate amount of moral and intellectual requisites is capable of an existence which may be called enviable; and unless such a person, through bad laws, or subjection to the will of others, is denied the liberty to use the sources of happiness within his reach, he will not fail to find this enviable existence, if he escape the positive evils of life, the great sources of physical and mental suffering—such as indigence, disease, and the unkindness, worthlessness, or premature loss of objects of affection. The main stress of the problem lies, therefore, in the contest with these calamities, from which it is a rare good fortune entirely to escape; which, as things now are, cannot be obviated, and often cannot be in any material degree mitigated. Yet no one whose opinion deserves a moment's consideration can doubt that most of the great positive evils of the world are in themselves removable, and will, if human affairs continue to improve, be in the end reduced within narrow limits. Poverty, in any sense implying suffering, may be completely extinguished by the wisdom of society, combined with the good sense and providence of individuals. Even that most intractable of enemies, disease, may be indefinitely reduced in dimensions by good physical and moral education, and proper control of noxious influences; while the progress of science holds out a promise for the future of still more direct conquests over this detestable foe. And every advance in that direction relieves us from some, not only of the chances which cut short our own lives, but, what concerns us still more, which deprive us of those in whom our happiness is wrapped up. As for vicissitudes of fortune, and other disappointments connected with worldly circumstances, these are principally the effect either of gross imprudence, of ill-regulated desires, or of bad or imperfect social institutions. All the grand sources, in short, of human suffering are in a great degree, many of them almost entirely, conquerable by human care and effort; and though their removal is grievously slow—though a long succession of generations will perish in the breach before the conquest is completed, and this world becomes all that, if will and knowledge were not wanting, it might easily be made—yet every mind sufficiently intelligent and generous to bear a part, however small and inconspicuous, in the endeavor, will draw a noble enjoyment from the contest itself, which he would not for any bribe in the form of selfish indulgence consent to be without.

I must again repeat, what the assailants of utilitarianism seldom have the justice to acknowledge, that the happiness which forms the utilitarian standard of what is right in conduct, is not the agent's own happiness, but that of all concerned. As between his own happiness and that of others, utilitarianism requires him to be as strictly impartial as a disinterested and benevolent spectator. In the golden rule of Jesus of Nazareth, we read the complete spirit of the ethics of utility. To do as one would be done by, and to love one's neighbor as oneself, constitute the ideal perfection of utilitarian morality. As the means of making the nearest approach to this ideal, utility would enjoin, first, that laws and social arrangements should place the happiness, or (as speaking practically it may be called) the interest, of every individual, as nearly as possible in harmony with the interest of the whole; and secondly, that education and opinion, which have so vast a power over human character, should so use that power as to establish in the mind of every individual an indissoluble association between his own happiness and the good of the whole; especially between his own happiness and the practice of such modes of conduct, negative and positive, as regard for the universal happiness prescribes: so that not only he may be unable to conceive the possibility of happiness to himself, consistently with conduct opposed to the general good, but also that a direct impulse to promote the general good may be in every individual one of the habitual motives of action, and the sentiments connected therewith may fill a large and prominent place in every human being's sentient existence. If the impugners of the utilitarian morality represented it to their own minds in this its true character, I know not what recommendation possessed by any other morality they could possibly affirm to be wanting to it: what more beautiful or more exalted developments of human nature any other ethical system can be supposed to foster, or what springs of action, not accessible to the utilitarian, such systems rely on for giving effect to their mandates.

The utilitarian doctrine is that happiness is desirable, and the only thing desirable, as an end; all other things being only desirable as means to that end. What ought to be required of this doctrine—what conditions is it requisite that the doctrine should fulfil—to make good its claim to be believed?

The only proof capable of being given that an object is visible, is that people actually see it. The only proof that a sound is audible, is that people hear it: and so of the other sources of our experience. In like manner, I apprehend, the sole evidence it is possible to produce that anything is desirable, is that people do actually desire it. If the end which the utilitarian doctrine proposes to itself were not, in theory and in practice, acknowledged to be an end, nothing could ever convince any person that it was so. No reason can be given why the general happiness is desirable, except that each person, so far as he believes it to be attainable, desires his own happiness. This, however, being a fact, we have not only all the proof which the case admits of, but all which it is possible to require, that happiness is a good: that each person's happiness is a good to that person, and the general happiness, therefore, a good to the aggregate of all persons. Happiness has made out its title as *one* of the ends of conduct, and consequently one of the criteria of morality.

But it has not, by this alone, proved itself to be the sole criterion. To do that, it would seem, by the same rule, necessary to show, not only that people desire happiness, but that they never desire anything else. Now it is palpable that they do desire things which, in common language, are decidedly distinguished from happiness. They desire, for example, virtue, and the absence of vice, no less really than pleasure and the absence of pain. The desire of virtue is not as universal, but it is as authentic a fact, as the desire of happiness. And hence the opponents of the utilitarian standard deem that they have a right to infer that there are other ends of human action besides happiness, and that happiness is not the standard of approbation and disapprobation.

But does the utilitarian doctrine deny that people desire virtue, or maintain that virtue is not a thing to be desired? The very reverse. It maintains not only that virtue is to be desired, but that it is to be desired disinterestedly, for itself. Whatever may be the opinion of utilitarian moralists as to the original conditions by which virtue is made virtue; however they may believe (as they do) that actions and dispositions are only virtuous because they promote another end than virtue; yet this being granted, and it having been decided, from considerations of this description, what *is* virtuous, they not only place virtue at the very head of the things which are good as means to the ultimate end, but they also recognize as a psychological fact the possibility of its being, to the individual, a good in itself, without looking to any end beyond it; and hold, that the mind is not in a right state, not in a state conformable to Utility, not in the state most conducive to the general happiness, unless it does love virtue in this manner—as a thing desirable in itself, even although, in the individual instance, it should not produce those other desirable consequences which it tends to produce, and on account of which it is held to be virtue. This opinion is not, in the smallest degree, a departure from the Happiness principle. The ingredients of happiness are very various, and each of them is desirable in itself, and not merely when considered as swelling an aggregate. The principle of utility does not mean that any given pleasure, as music, for instance, or any given exemption from pain, as for example health, are to be looked upon as means to a collective something termed happiness, and to be desired on that account. They are desired and desirable in and for themselves; besides being means, they are a part of the end. Virtue, according to the utilitarian doctrine, is not naturally and originally part of the end, but it is capable of becoming so; and in those who love it disinterestedly it has become so, and is desired and cherished, not as a means to happiness, but as a part of their happiness.

To illustrate this farther, we may remember that virtue is not the only thing, originally a means, and which if it were not a means to anything else, would be and remain indifferent, but which by association with what it is a means to, comes to be desired for itself, and that too with the utmost intensity. What, for example, shall we say of the love of money? There is nothing originally more desirable about money than about any heap of glittering pebbles. Its worth is solely that of the things which it will buy; the desires for other things than itself, which it is a means of gratifying. Yet the love of money is not only one of the strongest moving forces of human life, but money is, in many cases, desired in and for itself; the desire to possess it is often stronger than the desire to use it, and goes on increasing when all the desires which point to ends beyond it, to be compassed by it, are falling off. It may be then said truly, that money is desired not for the sake of an end, but as part of the end. From being a means to happiness, it has come to be itself a principal ingredient of the individual's conception of happiness. The same may be said of the majority of the great objects of human life—power, for example, or fame; except that to each of these there is a certain amount of immediate pleasure annexed, which has at least the semblance of being naturally inherent in them; a thing which cannot be said of money. Still, however, the strongest natural attraction, both of power and of fame, is the immense aid they give to the attainment of our other wishes; and it is the strong association thus generated between them and all our objects of desire, which gives to the direct desire of them the intensity it often assumes, so as in some characters to surpass in strength all other desires. In these cases the means have become a part of the end, and a more important part of it than any of the things which they are means to. What was once desired as an instrument for the attainment of happiness, has come to be desired for its own sake. In being desired for its own sake it is, however, desired as part of happiness. The person is made, or thinks he would be made, happy by its mere possession; and is made unhappy by failure to obtain it. The desire of it is not a different thing from the desire of happiness, any more than the love of music, or the desire of health. They are included in happiness. They are some of the elements of which the desire of happiness is made up. Happiness is not an abstract idea, but a concrete whole; and these are some of its parts. And the utilitarian standard sanctions and approves their being so. Life would be a poor thing, very ill provided with sources of happiness, if there were not this provision of nature, by which things originally indifferent, but conducive to, or otherwise associated with, the satisfaction of our primitive desires, become in themselves sources of pleasure more valuable than the primitive pleasures, both in permanency, in the space of human existence that they are capable of covering, and even in intensity. Virtue, according to the utilitarian conception, is a good of this description. There was no original desire of it, or motive to it, save its conduciveness to pleasure, and especially to protection from pain. But through the association thus formed, it may be felt a good in itself, and desired as such with as great intensity as any other good; and with this difference between it and the love of money, of power, or of fame, that all of these may, and often do, render the individual noxious to the other members of the society to which he belongs, whereas there is nothing which makes him so much a blessing to them as the cultivation of the disinterested, love of virtue. And consequently, the utilitarian standard, while it tolerates and approves those other acquired desires, up to the point beyond which they would be more injurious to the general happiness than promotive of it, enjoins and requires the cultivation of the love of virtue up to the greatest strength possible, as being above all things important to the general happiness.

It results from the preceding considerations, that there is in reality nothing desired except happiness. Whatever is desired otherwise than as a means to some end beyond itself, and ultimately to happiness, is desired as itself a part of happiness, and is not desired for itself until it has become so. Those who desire virtue for its own sake, desire it either because the consciousness of it is a pleasure, or because the consciousness of being without it is a pain, or for both reasons united; as in truth the pleasure and pain seldom exist separately, but almost always together, the same person feeling pleasure in the degree of virtue attained, and pain in not having attained more. If one of these gave him no pleasure, and the other no pain, he would not love or desire virtue, or would desire it only for the other benefits which it might produce to himself or to persons whom he cared for.

We have now, then, an answer to the question, of what sort of proof the principle of utility is susceptible. If the opinion which I have now stated is psychologically true—if human nature is so constituted as to desire nothing which is not either a part of happiness or a means of happiness, we can have no other proof, and we require no other, that these are the only things desirable. If so, happiness is the sole end of human action, and the promotion of it the test by which to judge of all human conduct; from whence it necessarily follows that it must be the criterion of morality, since a part is included in the whole.

And now to decide whether this is really so; whether mankind do desire nothing for itself but that which is a pleasure to them, or of which the absence is a pain; we have evidently arrived at a question of fact and experience, dependent, like all similar questions, upon evidence. It can only be determined by practiced self-consciousness and self-observation, assisted by observation of others. I believe that these sources of evidence, impartially consulted, will declare that desiring a thing and finding it pleasant, aversion to it and thinking of it as painful, are phenomena entirely inseparable, or rather two parts of the same phenomenon; in strictness of language, two different modes of naming the same psychological fact: that to think of an object as desirable (unless for the sake of its consequences), and to think of it as pleasant, are one and the same thing; and that to desire anything, except in proportion as the idea of it is pleasant, is a physical and metaphysical impossibility.

So obvious does this appear to me, that I expect it will hardly be disputed: and the objection made will be, not that desire can possibly be directed to anything ultimately except pleasure and exemption from pain, but that the will is a different thing from desire; that a person of confirmed virtue, or any other person whose purposes are fixed, carries out his purposes without any thought of the pleasure he has in contemplating them, or expects to derive from their fulfilment; and persists in acting on them, even though these pleasures are much diminished, by changes in his character or decay of his passive sensibilities, or are outweighed by the pains which the pursuit of the purposes may bring upon him. All this I fully admit, and have stated it elsewhere, as positively and emphatically as any one. Will, the active phenomenon, is a different thing from desire, the state of passive sensibility, and though originally an offshoot from it, may in time take root and detach itself from the parent stock; so much so, that in the case of an habitual purpose, instead of willing the thing because we desire it, we often desire it only because we will it. This, however, is but an instance of that familiar fact, the power of habit, and is nowise confined to the case of virtuous actions. Many indifferent things, which men originally did from a motive of some sort, they continue to do from habit. Sometimes this is done unconsciously, the consciousness coming only after the action: at other times with conscious volition, but volition which has become habitual, and is put into operation by the force of habit, in opposition perhaps to the deliberate preference, as often happens with those who have contracted habits of vicious or hurtful indulgence. Third and last comes the case in which the habitual act of will in the individual instance is not in contradiction to the general intention prevailing at other times, but in fulfilment of it; as in the case of the person of confirmed virtue, and of all who pursue deliberately and consistently any determinate end. The distinction between will and desire thus understood, is an authentic and highly important psychological fact; but the fact consists solely in this—that will, like all other parts of our constitution, is amenable to habit, and that we may will from habit what we no longer desire for itself, or desire only because we will it. It is not the less true that will, in the beginning, is entirely produced by desire; including in that term the repelling influence of pain as well as the attractive one of pleasure. Let us take into consideration, no longer the person who has a confirmed will to do right, but him in whom that virtuous will is still feeble, conquerable by temptation, and not to be fully relied on; by what means can it be strengthened? How can the will to be virtuous, where it does not exist in sufficient force, be implanted or awakened? Only by making the person *desire* virtue—by making him think of it in a pleasurable light, or of its absence in a painful one. It is by associating the doing right with pleasure, or the doing wrong with pain, or by eliciting and impressing and bringing home to the person's experience the pleasure naturally involved in the one or the pain in the other, that it is possible to call forth that will to be virtuous, which, when confirmed, acts without any thought of either pleasure or pain. Will is the child of desire, and passes out of the dominion of its parent only to come under that of habit. That which is the result of habit affords no presumption of being intrinsically good; and there would be no reason for wishing that the purpose of virtue should become independent of pleasure and pain, were it not that the influence of the pleasurable and painful associations which prompt to virtue is not sufficiently to be depended on for unerring constancy of action until it has acquired the support of habit. Both in feeling and in conduct, habit is the only thing which imparts certainty; and it is because of the importance to others of being able to rely absolutely on one's feelings and conduct, and to oneself of being able to rely on one's own, that the will to do right ought to be cultivated into this habitual independence. In other words, this state of the will is a means to good, not intrinsically a good; and does not contradict the doctrine that nothing is a good to human beings but in so far as it is either itself pleasurable, or a means of attaining pleasure or averting pain.

But if this doctrine be true, the principle of utility is proved. Whether it is so or not, must now be left to the consideration of the thoughtful reader.

Friedrich Nietzsche

A FREE SPIRIT

It is the business of the very few to be independent; it is a privilege of the strong. And whoever attempts it, even with the best right, but without being *obliged* to do so, proves that he is probably not only strong, but also daring beyond measure. He enters into a labyrinth, he multiplies a thousand-fold the dangers which life in itself already brings with it; not the least of which is that no one can see how and where he loses his way, becomes isolated, and is torn piecemeal by some minotaur of conscience. Supposing such a one comes to grief, it is so far from the comprehension of men that they neither feel it, nor sympathize with it. And he cannot any longer go back! He cannot even go back again to the sympathy of men!

In our youthful years, we still venerate and despise without the art of *nuance*, which is the best gain of life, and we have rightly to do hard penance for having fallen upon men and things with Yea and Nay. Everything is so arranged that the worst of all tastes, *the taste for the unconditional*, is cruelly befooled and abused, until a man learns to introduce a little art into his sentiments, and prefers to try conclusions with the artificial, as do the real artists of life. The angry and reverent spirit peculiar to youth appears to allow itself no peace, until it has suitably falsified men and things, to be able to vent its passion upon them: youth in itself even, is something falsifying and deceptive. Later on, when the young soul, tortured by continual disillusions, finally turns suspiciously against itself—still ardent and savage even in its suspicion and remorse of conscience: how it upbraids itself, how impatiently it tears itself, how it revenges itself for its long self-blinding, as though it had been a voluntary blindness! In this transition one punishes oneself by distrust of one's sentiments; one tortures one's enthusiasm with doubt, one feels even the good conscience to be a danger, as if it were the self-concealment and lassitude of a more refined uprightness; and above all, one espouses upon principle the cause *against* "youth." A decade later, and one comprehends that all this was also still—youth!

Throughout the longest period of human history—one calls it the prehistoric period—the value or non-value of an action was inferred from its *consequences*; the action in itself was not taken into consideration, any more than its origin; but pretty much as in China at present, where the distinction or disgrace of a child redounds to its parents, the retro-operating power of success or failure was what induced men to think well or ill of an action. Let us call this period the *pre-moral* period of mankind; the imperative, "Know thyself!" was then still unknown. In the last ten thousand years, on the other hand, on certain large portions of the earth, one has gradually got so far, that one no longer lets the consequences of an action, but its origin, decide with regard to its worth: a great achievement as a whole, an important refinement of vision and of criterion, the unconscious effect of the supremacy of aristocratic values and of the belief in "origin," the mark of a period which may be designated in the narrower sense as the *moral* one: the first attempt at self-knowledge is thereby made. Instead of the consequences, the origin—what an inversion of perspective! And assuredly an inversion effected only after long struggle and wavering! To be sure, an ominous new superstition, a peculiar narrowness of interpretation, attained supremacy precisely thereby: the origin of an action was interpreted in the most definite sense possible, as origin out of an *intention*; people were agreed in the belief that the value of an action lay in the value of its intention. The intention as the sole origin and antecedent history of an action: under the influence

Edited from *Beyond Good and Evil,* Chapter II. Translated by Helen Zimmern, 1913, which is now in the public domain.

of this prejudice, moral praise and blame have been bestowed, and men have judged and even philosophized almost up to the present day.

Is it not possible, however, that the necessity may now have arisen of again making up our minds with regard to the reversing and fundamental shifting of values, owing to a new self-consciousness and acuteness in man—is it not possible that we may be standing on the threshold of a period which, to begin with, would be distinguished negatively as *ultra-moral*: nowadays when, at least among us immoralists, the suspicion arises that the decisive value of an action lies precisely in that which is *not intentional*, and that all its intentionalness, all that is seen, sensible, or "sensed" in it, belongs to its surface or skin—which, like every skin, betrays something, but *conceals* still more? In short, we believe that the intention is only a sign or symptom, which first requires an explanation—a sign, moreover, which has too many interpretations, and consequently hardly any meaning in itself alone: that morality, in the sense in which it has been understood hitherto, as intention-morality, has been a prejudice, perhaps a prematureness or preliminariness, probably something of the same rank as astrology and alchemy, but in any case something which must be surmounted. The surmounting of morality, in a certain sense even the self-mounting of morality—let that be the name for the long-secret labor which has been reserved for the most refined, the most upright, and also the most wicked consciences of today, as the living touchstones of the soul.

It cannot be helped: the sentiment of surrender, of sacrifice for one's neighbor, and all self-renunciation-morality, must be mercilessly called to account, and brought to judgment; just as the aesthetics of "disinterested contemplation," under which the emasculation of art nowadays seeks insidiously enough to create itself a good conscience. There is far too much witchery and sugar in the sentiments "for others" and "*not* for myself," for one not needing to be doubly distrustful here, and for one asking promptly: "Are they not perhaps—*deceptions*?" That they *please*—he who has them, and he who enjoys their fruit, and also the mere spectator—that is still no argument in their *favor*, but just calls for caution. Let us therefore be cautious!

At whatever standpoint of philosophy one may place oneself nowadays, seen from every position, the *erroneousness* of the world in which we think we live is the surest and most certain thing our eyes can light upon: we find proof after proof thereof, which would fain allure us into surmises concerning a deceptive principle in the "nature of things." He, however, who makes thinking itself, and consequently "the spirit," responsible for the falseness of the world—an honorable exit, which every conscious or unconscious advocate of God avails himself of—he who regards this world, including space, time, form, and movement, as falsely *deduced*, would have at least good reason in the end to become distrustful also of all thinking; has it not hitherto been playing upon us the worst of scurvy tricks? And what guarantee would it give that it would not continue to do what it has always been doing? In all seriousness, the innocence of thinkers has something touching and respect-inspiring in it, which even nowadays permits them to wait upon consciousness with the request that it will give them *honest* answers: for example, whether it be "real" or not, and why it keeps the outer world so resolutely at a distance, and other questions of the same description. The belief in "immediate certainties" is a *moral naïveté* which does honor to us philosophers; but—we have now to cease being "*merely* moral" men! Apart from morality, such belief is a folly which does little honor to us! If in middle-class life an ever-ready distrust is regarded as the sign of a "bad character," and consequently as an imprudence, here among us, beyond the middle-class world and its Yeas and Nays, what should prevent our being imprudent and saying: the philosopher has at length a *right* to "bad character," as the being who has hitherto been most befooled on earth—he is now under *obligation* to distrustfulness, to the wickedest squinting out of every abyss of suspicion.

Forgive me the joke of this gloomy grimace and turn of expression; for I myself have long ago learned to think and estimate differently with regard to deceiving and being deceived, and I keep at least a couple of pokes in the ribs ready for the blind rage with which philosophers struggle against being deceived. Why *not*? It is nothing more than a moral prejudice that truth is worth more than semblance; it is, in fact, the worst proved supposition in the world. So much must be conceded: there could have been no life at all except upon the basis of perspective estimates and semblances; and if, with the virtuous enthusiasm and stupidity of many philosophers, one wished to do away altogether with the "seeming world"—well, granted that *you* could do that—at least nothing of your "truth" would thereby remain! Indeed, what is it that forces us in general to the supposition that there is an essential opposition of "true" and "false"? Is it not enough to suppose degrees of seemingness, and as it were lighter and darker shades and tones of semblance—different values, as the painters say? Why might not the world *which concerns us*—be a fiction? And to any one who suggested: "But to a fiction belongs an originator?"—might it not be bluntly replied: *Why*? May not this "belong" also belong to the fiction? Is it not at length permitted to be a little ironical towards the subject, just as towards the predicate and object? Might not the philosopher elevate himself above faith in grammar? All respect to governesses, but is it not time that philosophy should renounce governess-faith?

Oh, Voltaire! Oh, humanity! Oh, idiocy! There is something ticklish in "the truth," and in the *search* for the truth; and if man goes about it too humanely—*he seeks the true only to do the good*—I wager he finds nothing!

Supposing that nothing else is "given" as real but our world of desires and passions, that we cannot sink or rise to any other "reality" but just that of our impulses—for thinking is only a relation of these impulses to one another—are we not permitted to make the attempt and to ask the question whether this which is "given" does not *suffice*, by means of our counterparts, for the understanding even of the so-called mechanical (or "material") world? I do not mean as an illusion, a "semblance," a "representation" (in the Berkeleyan and Schopenhauerian sense), but as possessing the same degree of reality as our emotions themselves—as a more primitive form of the world of emotions, in which everything still lies locked in a mighty unity, which afterwards branches off and develops itself in organic processes (naturally also, refines and debilitates), as a kind of instinctive life in which all organic functions, including self-regulation, assimilation, nutrition, secretion, and change of matter, are still synthetically united with one another—as a *primary form* of life? In the end, it is not only permitted to make this attempt, it is commanded by the conscience of *logical method*. Not to assume several kinds of causality, so long as the attempt to get along with a single one has not been pushed to its furthest extent (to absurdity, if I may be allowed to say so); that is a morality of method which one may not repudiate nowadays—it follows "from its definition," as mathematicians say. The question is ultimately whether we really recognize the *will* as *operating*, whether we believe in the causality of the *will*; if we do so—and fundamentally our belief *in this* is just our belief in causality itself—we *must* make the attempt to posit hypothetically the causality of the *will* as the only causality. *Will* can naturally only operate on *will*—and not on matter (not on nerves, for instance). In short, the hypothesis must be hazarded, whether *will* does not operate on *will* wherever *effects* are recognized—and whether all mechanical action, inasmuch as a power operates therein, is not just the power of *will*, the effect of *will*. Granted, finally, that we succeeded in explaining our entire instinctive life as the development and ramification of one fundamental form of *will*—namely, the *Will to Power*, as my thesis puts it; granted that all organic functions could be traced back to this *Will to Power*, and that the solution of the problem of generation and nutrition—it is one problem—could also be found therein: one would thus have acquired the right to define *all* active force unequivocally as *Will to Power*. The world seen from within, the world defined and designated according to its "intelligible character"—it would simply be *Will to Power*, and nothing else.

"What? Does not that mean in popular language: God is disproved, but not the devil?" On the contrary! On the contrary, my friends! And who the devil also compels you to speak popularly!

As happened finally in all the enlightenment of modern times with the French Revolution (that terrible farce, quite superfluous when judged close at hand, into which, however, the noble and visionary spectators of all Europe have interpreted from a distance their own indignation and enthusiasm so long and passionately, *until the text has disappeared under the interpretation*), so a noble posterity might once more misunderstand the whole of the past, and perhaps only thereby make *its* aspect endurable. Or rather, has not this already happened? Have not we ourselves been that "noble posterity"? And, in so far as we now comprehend this, is it not thereby already past?

Nobody will very readily regard a doctrine as true merely because it makes people happy or virtuous—excepting, perhaps, the amiable "Idealists," who are enthusiastic about the good, true, and beautiful, and let all kinds of motley, coarse, and good-natured desirabilities swim about promiscuously in their pond. Happiness and virtue are no arguments. It is willingly forgotten, however, even on the part of thoughtful minds, that to make unhappy and to make bad are just as little counter-arguments. A thing could be *true*, although it were in the highest degree injurious and dangerous; indeed, the fundamental constitution of existence might be such that one succumbed by a full knowledge of it—so that the strength of a mind might be measured by the amount of *truth* it could endure—or to speak more plainly, by the extent to which it *required* truth attenuated, veiled, sweetened, damped, and falsified. But there is no doubt that for the discovery of certain *portions* of truth, the wicked and unfortunate are more favorably situated and have a greater likelihood of success; not to speak of the wicked who are happy—a species about whom moralists are silent. Perhaps severity and craft are more favorable conditions for the development of strong, independent spirits and philosophers than the gentle, refined, yielding good-nature, and habit of taking things easily, which are prized, and rightly prized in a learned man. Presupposing always, to begin with, that the term "philosopher" be not confined to the philosopher who writes books, or even introduces *his* philosophy into books! Stendhal furnishes a last feature of the portrait of the free-spirited philosopher, which for the sake of German taste, I will not omit to underline—for it is *opposed* to German taste. "To be a good philosopher, one must be clear and without illusion. A banker who has made a fortune has a characteristic that is needed for making philosophical discoveries, namely, for seeing clearly into what is," said this last great psychologist.

Everything that is profound loves the mask: the profoundest things have a hatred even of figure and likeness. Should not the *contrary* only be the right disguise for the shame of a God to go about in? A question worth asking! It would be strange if some mystic has not already ventured on the same kind of thing. There are proceedings of such a delicate nature that it is well to overwhelm them with coarseness and make them unrecognizable; there are actions of love and of an extravagant magnanimity after which nothing can be wiser than to take a stick and thrash the witness soundly: one thereby obscures his recollection. Many a one is able to obscure and abuse his own memory, in order at least to have vengeance on this sole party in the secret: shame is inventive. They are not the worst things of which one is most ashamed: there is not only deceit behind a mask; there is so much goodness in craft. I could imagine that a man with something costly and fragile to conceal, would roll through life clumsily and rotundly like an old, green, heavily-hooped wine-cask—the refinement of his shame requiring it to be so. A man who has depths in his shame meets his destiny and his delicate decisions upon paths which few ever reach, and with regard to the existence of which his nearest and most intimate friends may be ignorant; his mortal danger conceals itself from their eyes, and equally so his regained security. Such a hidden nature, which instinctively employs speech for silence and concealment, and is inexhaustible in evasion of communication, *desires* and insists that a mask of himself shall occupy his place in the hearts and heads of his friends; and supposing he does not desire it, his eyes will some day be opened to the fact that there is nevertheless a mask of him there—and that it is well to be so. Every profound spirit needs a mask; nay, more, around every profound spirit there continually grows a mask, owing to the constantly false, that is to say, *superficial* interpretation of every word he utters, every step he takes, every sign of life he manifests.

One must subject oneself to one's own tests that one is destined for independence and command, and do so at the right time. One must not avoid one's tests, although they constitute perhaps the most dangerous game one can play, and are in the end tests made only before ourselves and before no other judge. Not to cleave to any person, be it even the dearest—every person is a prison and also a recess. Not to cleave to a fatherland, be it even the most suffering and necessitous—it is even less difficult to detach one's heart from a victorious fatherland. Not to cleave to a sympathy, be it even for higher men, into whose peculiar torture and helplessness chance has given us an insight. Not to cleave to a science, though it tempt one with the most valuable discoveries, apparently specially reserved for us. Not to cleave to one's own liberation, to the voluptuous distance and remoteness of the bird, which always flies further aloft in order always to see more under it—the danger of the flier. Not to cleave to our own virtues, nor become as a whole a victim to any of our specialties, to our "hospitality" for instance, which is the danger of dangers for highly developed and wealthy souls, who deal prodigally, almost indifferently with themselves, and push the virtue of liberality so far that it becomes a vice. One must know how to *conserve oneself*—the best test of independence.

A new order of philosophers is appearing; I shall venture to baptize them by a name not without danger. As far as I understand them, as far as they allow themselves to be understood—for it is their nature to *wish* to remain something of a puzzle—these philosophers of the future might rightly, perhaps also wrongly, claim to be designated as "tempters." This name itself is after all only an attempt, or, if it be preferred, a temptation.

Will they be new friends of "truth," these coming philosophers? Very probably, for all philosophers hitherto have loved their truths. But assuredly they will not be dogmatists. It must be contrary to their pride, and also contrary to their taste, that their truth should still be truth for everyone—that which has hitherto been the secret wish and ultimate purpose of all dogmatic efforts. "My opinion is *my* opinion: another person has not easily a right to it"—such a philosopher of the future will say, perhaps. One must renounce the bad taste of wishing to agree with many people. "Good" is no longer good when one's neighbor takes it into his mouth. And how could there be a "common good"! The expression contradicts itself; that which can be common is always of small value. In the end, things must be as they are and have always been—the great things remain for the great, the abysses for the profound, the delicacies and thrills for the refined, and, to sum up shortly, everything rare for the rare.

Need I say expressly after all this that they will be free, *very free spirits*, these philosophers of the future—as certainly also they will not be merely free spirits, but something more, higher, greater, and fundamentally different, which does not wish to be misunderstood and mistaken? But while I say this, I feel under obligation almost as much to them as to ourselves (we free spirits who are their heralds and forerunners), to sweep away from ourselves altogether a stupid old prejudice and misunderstanding, which, like a fog, has too long made the conception of "free spirit" obscure. In every country of Europe, and the same in America, there is at present something which makes an abuse of this name a very narrow, prepossessed, enchained class of spirits, who desire almost the opposite of what our intentions and instincts prompt—not to mention that in respect to the *new* philosophers who are appearing, they must still more be closed windows and bolted doors. Briefly and regrettably, they belong to the levelers, these wrongly named "free spirits"—as glib-tongued and scribe-fingered slaves of the democratic taste and its "modern ideas" all of them men without solitude, without personal solitude, blunt honest fellows to whom neither courage nor honorable conduct ought to be denied, only, they are not free, and are ludicrously superficial, especially in their innate partiality for seeing the cause of almost *all* human misery and failure in the old forms in which society has hitherto existed—a notion which happily inverts the truth entirely! What they would fain attain with all their strength is the universal, green-meadow happiness of the herd, together with security, safety, comfort, and alleviation of life for everyone, their two most frequently chanted songs and doctrines are called "Equality of Rights" and "Sympathy with All Sufferers"—and suffering itself is looked upon by them as something which must be *done away with*. We opposite ones, however, who have opened our eye and conscience to the question how and where the plant "man" has hitherto grown most vigorously, believe that this has always taken place under the opposite conditions, that for this end the dangerousness of his situation had to be increased enormously, his inventive faculty and dissembling power (his "spirit") had to develop into subtlety and daring under long oppression and compulsion, and his Will to Life had to be increased to the unconditioned Will to Power—we believe that severity, violence, slavery, danger in the street and in the heart, secrecy, stoicism, tempter's art and devilry of every kind—that everything wicked, terrible, tyrannical, predatory, and serpentine in man, serves as well for the elevation of the human species as its opposite—we do not even say enough when we only say this much, and in any case we find ourselves here, both with our speech and our silence, at the other extreme of all modern ideology and gregarious desirability, as their antipodes perhaps? What wonder that we "free spirits" are not exactly the most communicative spirits? That we do not wish to betray in every respect *what* a spirit can free itself from, and *where* perhaps it will then be driven? And as to the import of the dangerous formula, "Beyond Good and Evil," with which we at least avoid confusion, we *are* something else than "free-thinkers," and whatever these honest advocates of "modern ideas" like to call themselves. Having been at home, or at least guests, in many realms of the spirit, having escaped again and again from the gloomy, agreeable nooks in which preferences and prejudices, youth, origin, the accident of men and books, or even the weariness of travel seemed to confine us, full of malice against the seductions of dependency which he concealed in honors, money, positions, or exaltation of the senses, grateful even for distress and the vicissitudes of illness, because they always free us from some rule, and its "prejudice," grateful to the God, devil, sheep, and worm in us, inquisitive to a fault, investigators to the point of cruelty, with unhesitating fingers for the intangible, with teeth and stomachs for the most indigestible, ready for any business that requires sagacity and acute senses, ready for every adventure, owing to an excess of "free will," with anterior and posterior souls, into the ultimate intentions of which it is difficult to pry, with foregrounds and backgrounds to the end of which no foot may run, hidden ones under the mantles of light, appropriators, although we resemble heirs and spendthrifts, arrangers and collectors from morning till night, misers of our wealth and our full-crammed drawers, economical in learning and forgetting, inventive in scheming, sometimes proud of tables of categories, sometimes pedants, sometimes night-owls of work even in full day, yes, if necessary, even scarecrows—and it is necessary nowadays, that is to say, inasmuch as we are the born, sworn, jealous friends of *solitude*, of our own profoundest midnight and midday solitude—such kind of men are we, we free spirits! And perhaps you are also something of the same kind, you coming ones. You *new* philosophers.

Thomas H. Huxley

EVOLUTION AND ETHICS

Man, the animal, has worked his way to the headship of the sentient world, and has become the superb animal which he is, in virtue of his success in the struggle for existence. The conditions having been of a certain order, man's organization has adjusted itself to them better than that of his competitors in the cosmic strife. In the case of mankind, the self-assertion, the unscrupulous seizing upon all that can be grasped, the tenacious holding of all that can be kept, which constitute the essence of the struggle for existence, have answered. For his successful progress, throughout the savage state, man has been largely indebted to those qualities which he shares with the ape and the tiger; his exceptional physical organization; his cunning, his sociability, his curiosity, and his imitativeness; his ruthless and ferocious destructiveness when his anger is roused by opposition.

But, in proportion as men have passed from anarchy to social organization, and in proportion as civilization has grown in worth, these deeply ingrained serviceable qualities have become defects. After the manner of successful persons, civilized man would gladly kick down the ladder by which he has climbed. He would be only too pleased to see "the ape and tiger die." But they decline to suit his convenience; and the unwelcome intrusion of these boon companions of his hot youth into the ranged existence of civil life adds pains and griefs, innumerable and immeasurably great, to those which the cosmic process necessarily brings on the mere animal. In fact, civilized man brands all these ape and tiger promptings with the name of sins; he punishes many of the acts which flow from them as crimes; and, in extreme cases, he does his best to put an end to the survival of the fittest of former days by axe and rope.

I have said that civilized man has reached this point; the assertion is perhaps too broad and general; I had better put it that ethical man has attained thereto. The science of ethics professes to furnish us with a reasoned rule of life; to tell us what is right action and why it is so. Whatever differences of opinion may exist among experts there is a general consensus that the ape and tiger methods of the struggle for existence are not reconcilable with sound ethical principles.

Thousands upon thousands of our fellows, thousands of years ago, have preceded us in finding themselves face to face with the same dread problem of evil. They also have seen that *the cosmic process is evolution*; that it is full of wonder, full of beauty, and, at the same time, full of pain. They have sought to discover the bearing of these great facts on ethics; to find out whether there is, or is not, a sanction for morality in the ways of the cosmos.

To the struggle for bare existence, which never ends, though it may be alleviated and partially disguised for a fortunate few, succeeded the struggle to make existence intelligible and to bring the order of things into harmony with the moral sense of man, which also never ends, but, for the thinking few, becomes keener with every increase of knowledge and with every step towards the realization of a worthy ideal of life.

Two thousand five hundred years ago, the value of civilization was as apparent as it is now; then, as now, it was obvious that only in the garden of an orderly polity can the finest fruits humanity is capable of bearing be produced. But it had also become evident that the blessings of culture were not unmixed. The garden was apt to turn into a hothouse. The stimulation of the senses, the pampering of the emotions, endlessly multiplied the sources of pleasure. The constant widening of the intellectual field indefinitely extended the range of that especially human faculty of looking before and after, which adds to the fleeting present those old and new worlds of the past and the future, wherein men dwell the more the higher their culture. But that very sharpening of the sense and that subtle refinement of emotion, which brought such a wealth of pleasures, were fatally attended by a proportional enlargement of the capacity for suffering; and the divine faculty of imagination, while it created new heavens and new earths, provided them with the corresponding hells of futile regret for the past and morbid anxiety for the future. Finally, the inevitable penalty of over-stimulation, exhaustion, opened the gates of civilization to its great enemy, *ennui*; the stale and flat weariness when man delights not, nor woman neither; when all things are vanity and vexation; and life seems not worth living except to escape the bore of dying.

Even purely intellectual progress brings about its revenges. Problems settled in a rough and ready way by rude men, absorbed in action, demand renewed attention and show themselves to be still unread riddles when men have time to think. Sacred customs, venerable dooms of ancestral wisdom, hallowed by tradition and professing to hold good for all time, are put to the question. Cultured reflection asks for their credentials; judges them by its own standards; finally, gathers those of which it approves into ethical systems, in which the reasoning is rarely much more than a decent pretext for the adoption of foregone conclusions.

One of the oldest and most important elements in such systems is the conception of justice. Society is impossible unless those who are associated agree to observe certain rules of conduct towards one another; its stability depends on the steadiness with which they abide by that agreement; and, so far as they waver, that mutual trust which is the bond of society is weakened or destroyed. Wolves could not hunt in packs except for the real, though unexpressed, understanding that they should not attack one another during the chase. The most rudimentary polity is a pack of men living under the like tacit, or expressed, understanding; and having made the very important advance upon wolf society, that they agree to use the force of the whole body against individuals who violate it and in favor of those who observe it. This observance of a common understanding, with the consequent distribution of punishments and rewards according to accepted rules, received the name of justice, while the contrary was called injustice. Early ethics did not take much note of the animus of the violator of the rules. But civilization could not advance far, without the establishment of a capital distinction between the case of involuntary and that of willful misdeed; between a merely wrong action and a guilty one. And, with increasing refinement of moral appreciation, the problem of desert, which arises out of this distinction, acquired more and more theoretical and practical importance. If life must be given for life, yet it was recognized that the unintentional slayer did not altogether deserve death; and, by a sort of compromise between the public and the private conception of justice, a sanctuary was provided in which he might take refuge from the avenger of blood.

The idea of justice thus underwent a gradual sublimation from punishment and reward according to acts, to punishment and reward according to desert; or, in other words, according to motive. Righteousness, that is, action from right motive, not only became synonymous with justice, but the positive constituent of innocence and the very heart of goodness.

Now when the ancient sage, who had attained to this conception of goodness, looked the world, and especially human life, in the face, he found it as hard as we do to bring the course of evolution into harmony with even the elementary requirement of the ethical ideal of the just and the good.

If there is one thing plainer than another, it is that neither the pleasures nor the pains of life, in the merely animal world, are distributed according to desert; for it is admittedly impossible for the lower orders of sentient beings, to deserve either the one or the other. If there is a generalization from the facts of human life which has the assent of thoughtful men in every age and country, it is that the violator of ethical rules constantly escapes the punishment which he deserves; that the wicked flourishes like a green bay tree, while, the righteous begs his bread; that the sins of the fathers are visited upon the children; that, in the realm of nature, ignorance is punished just as severely as willful wrong; and that thousands upon thousands of innocent beings suffer for the crime, or the unintentional trespass of one.

Thus, brought before the tribunal of ethics, the cosmos might well seem to stand condemned. The conscience of man revolted against the moral indifference of nature, and the microcosmic atom should have found the illimitable macrocosm guilty. But few, or none, ventured to record that verdict.

The majority of us profess neither pessimism nor optimism. We hold that the world is neither so good, nor so bad, as it conceivably might be; and, as most of us have reason, now and again, to discover that it can be. Those who have failed to experience the joys that make life worth living are, probably, in as small a minority as those who have never known the griefs that rob existence of its savor and turn its richest fruits into mere dust and ashes.

Further, I think I do not err in assuming that, however diverse their views on philosophical and religious matters, most men are agreed that the proportion of good and evil in life may be very sensibly affected by human action. I never heard anybody doubt that the evil may be thus increased, or diminished; and it would seem to follow that good must be similarly susceptible of addition or subtraction. Finally, to my knowledge, nobody professes to doubt that, so far forth as we possess a power of bettering things, it is our paramount duty to use it and to train all our intellect and energy to this supreme service of our kind.

Hence the pressing interest of the question, to what extent modern progress in natural knowledge, and, more especially, the general outcome of that progress in the doctrine of evolution, is competent to help us in the great work of helping one another?

The propounders of what are called the "ethics of evolution," when the "evolution of ethics" would usually better express the object of their speculations, adduce a number of more or less interesting facts and more or less sound arguments in favor of the origin of the moral sentiments, in the same way as other natural phenomena, by a process of evolution. I have little doubt, for my own part, that they are on the right track; but as the immoral sentiments have no less been evolved, there is, so far, as much natural sanction for the one as the other. The thief and the murderer follow nature just as much as the philanthropist. Cosmic evolution may teach us how the good and the evil tendencies of man may have come about; but, in itself, it is incompetent to furnish any better reason why what we call *good* is preferable to what we call *evil* than we had before. Some day, I doubt not, we shall arrive at an understanding of the evolution of the Aesthetic faculty; but all the understanding in the world will neither increase nor diminish the force of the intuition that this is beautiful and that is ugly.

There is another fallacy which appears to me to pervade the so-called "ethics of evolution." It is the notion that because, on the whole, animals and plants have advanced in perfection of organization by means of the struggle for existence and the consequent "survival of the fittest"; therefore men in society, men as *ethical beings*, must look to the same process to help them towards perfection. I suspect that this fallacy has arisen out of the unfortunate ambiguity of the phrase "survival of the fittest." "Fittest" has a connotation of "best"; and about "best" there hangs a moral flavor. In cosmic nature, however, what is "fittest" depends upon the conditions.

Men in society are undoubtedly subject to the cosmic process. As among other animals, multiplication goes on without cessation, and involves severe competition for the means of support. The struggle for existence tends to eliminate those less fitted to adapt themselves to the circumstances of their existence. The strongest, the most self-assertive, tend to tread down the weaker. But the influence of the cosmic process on the evolution of society is the greater the more rudimentary its civilization. Social progress means a checking of the cosmic, process at every step and the substitution for it of another, which may be called the *ethical process*; the end of which is not the survival of those who may happen to be the fittest, in respect of the whole of the conditions which obtain, but of those who are ethically the best.

As I have already urged, the practice of that which is ethically best—what we call goodness or virtue—involves a course of conduct which, in all respects, is opposed to that which leads to success in the cosmic struggle for existence. In place of ruthless self-assertion it demands self-restraint; in place of thrusting aside, or treading down, all competitors, it requires that the individual shall not merely respect, but shall help his fellows; its influence is directed, not so much to the survival of the fittest, as to the fitting of as many as possible to survive. It repudiates the gladiatorial theory of existence. It demands that each man who enters into the enjoyment of the advantages of a polity shall be mindful of his debt to those who have laboriously constructed it; and shall take heed that no act of his weakens the fabric in which he has been permitted to live. Laws and moral precepts are directed to the end of curbing the cosmic process and reminding the individual of his duty to the community, to the protection and influence of which he owes, if not existence itself, at least the life of something better than a brutal savage.

It is from neglect of these plain considerations that the fanatical individualism of our time attempts to apply the analogy of cosmic nature to society. Once more we have a misapplication of the stoical injunction to follow nature; the duties of the individual to the state are forgotten, and his tendencies to self-assertion are dignified by the name of rights. It is seriously debated whether the members of a community are justified in using their combined strength to constrain one of their number to contribute his share to the maintenance of it; or even to prevent him from doing his best to destroy it. The struggle for existence which has done such admirable work in cosmic nature, must, it appears, be equally beneficent in the ethical sphere. Yet if that which I have insisted upon is true; if the cosmic process has no sort of relation to moral ends; if the imitation of it by man is inconsistent with the first principles of ethics; what becomes of this surprising theory?

Let us understand, once for all, that the ethical progress of society depends, not on imitating the cosmic process, still less in running away from it, but in combating it. It may seem an audacious proposal thus to pit the microcosm against the macrocosm and to set man to subdue nature to his higher ends; but I venture to think that the great intellectual difference between the ancient times and our day, lies in the solid foundation we have acquired for the hope that such an enterprise may meet with a certain measure of success.

The history of civilization details the steps by which men have succeeded in building up an artificial world within the cosmos. Fragile reed as he may be, man, as Pascal says, is a thinking reed: there lies within him a fund of energy operating intelligently and so far akin to that which pervades the universe, that it is competent to influence and modify the cosmic process. In every family, in every polity that has been established, the cosmic process in man has been restrained and otherwise modified by law and custom; in surrounding nature, it has been similarly influenced by the art of the shepherd, the agriculturist, the artisan. As civilization has advanced, so has the extent of this interference increased; until the organized and highly developed sciences and arts of the present day have endowed man with a command over the course of non-human nature greater than that once attributed to the magicians. The most impressive, I might say startling, of these changes have been brought about in the course of the last two centuries; while a right comprehension of the process of life and of the means of influencing its manifestations is only just dawning upon us. We do not yet see our way beyond generalities; and we are befogged by the obtrusion of false analogies and crude anticipations. But Astronomy, Physics, Chemistry, have all had to pass through similar phases, before they reached the stage at which their influence became an important factor in human affairs. Physiology, Psychology, Ethics, Political Science, must submit to the same ordeal. Yet it seems to me irrational to doubt that, at no distant period, they will work as great a revolution in the sphere of practice.

The theory of evolution encourages no millennial anticipations. If, for millions of years, our globe has taken the upward road, yet, some time, the summit will be reached and the downward route will be commenced. The most daring imagination will hardly venture upon the suggestion that the power and the intelligence of man can ever arrest the procession of the great year.

Moreover, the cosmic nature born with us and, to a large extent, necessary for our maintenance, is the outcome of millions of years of severe training, and it would be folly to imagine that a few centuries will suffice to subdue its masterfulness to purely ethical ends. Ethical nature may count upon having to reckon with a tenacious and powerful enemy as long as the world lasts. But, on the other hand, I see no limit to the extent to which intelligence and will, guided by sound principles of investigation, and organized in common effort, may modify the conditions of existence, for a period longer than that now covered by history. And much may be done to change the nature of man himself. The intelligence which has converted the brother of the wolf into the faithful guardian of the flock ought to be able to do something towards curbing the instincts of savagery in civilized men.

Part Nine: Political and Social Philosophy

Introduction

Humans seem to have a difficult time balancing the desire to be independent individuals with the desire to be members of a group. These desires often clash, especially when it comes to politics, government, and social issues. A fundamental question that people have argued about for centuries is, "How much freedom should individuals have?" Positions range from those who advocate absolute freedom, to those who advocate that we cannot be trusted with any freedom to decide our actions or how we should live our lives.

The first reading by Plato raises several important philosophical issues. The setting is Socrates's trial where he has been accused of "corrupting the youth." This provides the opportunity for Plato to discuss the social and political aspects of an individual's behavior, the role of duty, justice and injustice, honor, and the relationship between religion and government. Socrates defends his actions by showing that his entire life has been dedicated to the search for wisdom, which, Socrates asserts, should be the goal of everyone.

If humans decide to enter into a "social contract" whereby they agree to honor a set of fundamental rights, obligations, and laws, then they voluntarily give up certain freedoms that might exist without such contractual agreements. This is the basis for the second reading by Plato, in which Socrates is urged to escape prison to avoid his death sentence. Socrates outlines both the reasons that support his escape and the reasons why he should not escape. Socrates asserts the responsibility of every citizen to obey the laws of the state because each citizen has entered into an implied contract that he will obey the laws. Therefore, if Socrates escapes, then he is doing an injustice to the state; but if he stays and accepts his punishment, then he departs "in innocence, a sufferer and not a doer of evil; a victim, not of the laws, but of men."

According to Aristotle, "man is by nature a political animal." Since humans act in order to bring about a good life, it is natural for humans to create governments and laws. If this is correct, then it leads us to inquire about the best form of government. As you can imagine, great debates have occurred over the definition of the term "best" when it comes to forms of government. A few of the most well-known and championed forms are monarchy, democracy, communism, and socialism.

The reading by Thomas Hobbes offers another explanation of how politics arises out of a social contract. According to Hobbes, humans always act in their own self-interest. However, if we live in a *state of nature* in which everyone is in constant fear and at war with everyone else, then we cannot always obtain what we desire. Hobbes holds that a society run by a strong *sovereign* who has complete power to impose penalties for the protection and safety of everyone is the best form of government.

The concept of *human freedom* has several aspects, including the ability to make choices. "Choosing" seems to imply having purposes or goals that one wishes to attain. But must individual choices conform to some definition of "rationality"? In other words, are irrational choices really free? Likewise, if the laws of my country constrain my free action, then is my constrained action coerced? John Locke asks the question, "Why would anyone give up his freedom and be under the control of others?" The answer, for Locke, is that since the state of nature is unsafe and insecure, therefore, we put ourselves under a government to preserve and protect our property. We consent to laws that bind everyone, demand an impartial authority to decide disputes between citizens and the power to enforce laws and judicial decisions.

But what if the social contract gets corrupted by those in power? According to Catherine Macaulay, abuse of power is common and it is the foundation of every tyranny. If this happens, then the people can reassert "their native right of forming a government for themselves."

Another important political question is whether there should be constraints on free speech. John Stuart Mill argues that freedom of thought and open discussions of ideas and opinions is a necessary condition for a democratic society. However, we must also guard against the *tyranny of the majority*—the tendency of society to impose the majority views on those who dissent from them.

We can ask, "Should *property* be owned by individuals who can do whatever they wish with it, or should it be controlled by a government?" We can also ask, "Should *wealth* be allowed to be controlled by a few individuals, or should government 'redistribute' wealth amongst the citizens?" According to Karl Marx and Friedrich Engels, political power is simply the organized power of one class to oppress another. In the passage from the *Communist Manifesto,* Marx and Engels present an historical analysis of social class struggle that they claim will lead inevitably to the overthrow of the "oppressive bourgeoisie," who own the means of production, by the "proletariat," the workers.

But what if a large part of society is shut out of politics and are barred from participating? The fight for women's rights has a long history. Mary Wollstonecraft, writing in 1792, long before women had any recognized social rights, argued that one of the first things a society must do, in order to make women truly full members of society, is to provide equal access to education. Thus, women should have rights in common with men, and should be "free in a physical, moral, and civil sense."

Plato

APOLOGY

How you have felt, O men of Athens, at hearing the speeches of my accusers, I cannot tell; but I know that their persuasive words almost made me forget who I was—such was the effect of them; and yet they have hardly spoken a word of truth. But many as their falsehoods were, there was one of them which quite amazed me; I mean when they told you to be upon your guard, and not to let yourselves be deceived by the force of my eloquence. They ought to have been ashamed of saying this, because they were sure to be detected as soon as I opened my lips and displayed my deficiency; they certainly did appear to be most shameless in saying this, unless by the force of eloquence they mean the force of truth; for then I do indeed admit that I am eloquent. But in how different a way from theirs! Well, as I was saying, they have hardly uttered a word, or not more than a word, of truth; but you shall hear from me the whole truth: not, however, delivered after their manner, in a set oration duly ornamented with words and phrases. No indeed! but I shall use the words and arguments which occur to me at the moment; for I am certain that this is right, and that at my time of life I ought not to be appearing before you, O men of Athens, in the character of a juvenile orator—let no one expect this of me. And I must beg of you to grant me one favor, which is this—If you hear me using the same words in my defense which I have been in the habit of using, and which most of you may have heard in the agora, and at the tables of the moneychangers, or anywhere else, I would ask you not to be surprised at this, and not to interrupt me. For I am more than seventy years of age, and this is the first time that I have ever appeared in a court of law, and I am quite a stranger to the ways of the place; and therefore I would have you regard me as if I were really a stranger, whom you would excuse if he spoke in his native tongue, and after the fashion of his country; that I think is not an unfair request. Never mind the manner, which may or may not be good; but think only of the justice of my cause, and give heed to that: let the judge decide justly and the speaker speak truly.

And first, I have to reply to the older charges and to my first accusers, and then I will go to the later ones. For I have had many accusers, who accused me of old, and their false charges have continued during many years; and I am more afraid of them than of Anytus and his associates, who are dangerous, too, in their own way. But far more dangerous are these, who began when you were children, and took possession of your minds with their falsehoods, telling of one Socrates, a wise man, who speculated about the heaven above, and searched into the earth beneath, and made the worse appear the better cause. These are the accusers whom I dread; for they are the circulators of this rumor, and their hearers are too apt to fancy that speculators of this sort do not believe in the gods. And they are many, and their charges against me are of ancient date, and they made them in days when you were impressible—in childhood, or perhaps in youth—and the cause when heard went by default, for there was none to answer. And, hardest of all, their names I do not know and cannot tell; unless in the chance of a comic poet. But the main body of these slanderers who from envy and malice have wrought upon you—and there are some of them who are convinced themselves, and impart their convictions to others—all these, I say, are most difficult to deal with; for I cannot have them up here, and examine them, and therefore I must simply fight with shadows in my own defense, and examine when there is no one who answers. I will ask you then to assume with me, as I was saying, that my opponents are of two kinds—one recent, the other ancient; and

Edited from *Apology*. Translated by Benjamin Jowett, 1891, which is now in the public domain.

I hope that you will see the propriety of my answering the latter first, for these accusations you heard long before the others, and much oftener.

Well, then, I will make my defense, and I will endeavor in the short time which is allowed to do away with this evil opinion of me which you have held for such a long time; and I hope I may succeed, if this be well for you and me, and that my words may find favor with you. But I know that to accomplish this is not easy—I quite see the nature of the task. Let the event be as God wills: in obedience to the law I make my defense.

I will begin at the beginning, and ask what the accusation is which has given rise to this slander of me, and which has encouraged Meletus to proceed against me. What do the slanderers say? They shall be my prosecutors, and I will sum up their words in an affidavit. "Socrates is an evil-doer, and a curious person, who searches into things under the earth and in heaven, and he makes the worse appear the better cause; and he teaches the aforesaid doctrines to others." That is the nature of the accusation, and that is what you have seen yourselves in the comedy of Aristophanes; who has introduced a man whom he calls Socrates, going about and saying that he can walk in the air, and talking a deal of nonsense concerning matters of which I do not pretend to know either much or little—not that I mean to say anything disparaging of anyone who is a student of natural philosophy. I should be very sorry if Meletus could lay that to my charge. But the simple truth is, O Athenians, that I have nothing to do with these studies. Very many of those here present are witnesses to the truth of this, and to them I appeal. Speak then, you who have heard me, and tell your neighbors whether any of you have ever known me hold forth in few words or in many upon matters of this sort. You hear their answer. And from what they say of this you will be able to judge of the truth of the rest.

As little foundation is there for the report that I am a teacher, and take money; that is no more true than the other. Although, if a man is able to teach, I honor him for being paid. For example, there are those who go the round of the cities, and are able to persuade the young men to leave their own citizens, by whom they might be taught for nothing, and come to them, whom they not only pay, but are thankful if they may be allowed to pay them. I met a man who has spent a world of money on the Sophists, and I asked him: "Callias," I said, "if your two sons were foals or calves, there would be no difficulty in finding someone to put over them; we should hire a trainer of horses or a farmer probably who would improve and perfect them in their own proper virtue and excellence; but as they are human beings, whom are you thinking of placing over them? Is there anyone who understands human and political virtue? You must have thought about this as you have sons; is there anyone?" "There is," he said. "Who is he?" said I, "and of what country? and what does he charge?" "Evenus the Parian," he replied; "he is the man, and his charge is five minae." Happy is Evenus, I said to myself, if he really has this wisdom, and teaches at such a modest charge. Had I the same, I should have been very proud and conceited; but the truth is that I have no knowledge of the kind.

I dare say, Athenians, that someone among you will reply, "Why is this, Socrates, and what is the origin of these accusations of you: for there must have been something strange which you have been doing? All this great fame and talk about you would never have arisen if you had been like other men: tell us, then, why this is, as we should be sorry to judge hastily of you." Now I regard this as a fair challenge, and I will endeavor to explain to you the origin of this name of "wise," and of this evil fame. Please to attend then. And although some of you may think I am joking, I declare that I will tell you the entire truth. Men of Athens, this reputation of mine has come of a certain sort of wisdom which I possess. If you ask me what kind of wisdom, I reply, such wisdom as is attainable by man, for to that extent I am inclined to believe that I am wise; whereas the persons of whom I was speaking have a superhuman wisdom, which I may fail to describe, because I have it not myself; and he who says that I have, speaks falsely, and is taking away my character. And here, O men of Athens, I must beg you not to interrupt me, even if I seem to say something extravagant. For the word which I will speak is not mine. I will refer you to a witness who is worthy of credit, and will tell you about my wisdom—whether I have any, and of what sort—and that witness shall be the god of Delphi. You must have known Chaerephon; he was early a friend of mine, and also a friend of yours, for he shared in the exile of the people, and returned with you. Well, Chaerephon, as you know, was very impetuous in all his doings, and he went to Delphi and boldly asked the oracle to tell him whether—as I was saying, I must beg you not to interrupt—he asked the oracle to tell him whether there was anyone wiser than I was, and the Pythian prophetess answered that there was no man wiser. Chaerephon is dead himself, but his brother, who is in court, will confirm the truth of this story.

Why do I mention this? Because I am going to explain to you why I have such an evil name. When I heard the answer, I said to myself, What can the god mean? and what is the interpretation of this riddle? for I know that I have no wisdom, small or great. What can he mean when he says that I am the wisest of men? And yet he is a god and cannot lie; that would be against his nature. After a long consideration, I at last thought of a method of trying the question. I reflected that if I could only find a man wiser than myself, then I might go to the god with a refutation in my hand. I should say to him, "Here is a man who is wiser than I am; but you said that I was the wisest." Accordingly I went to one who had the reputation of wisdom, and the result was as follows: When I began to talk with him, I could not help thinking that he was not really wise, although he was thought wise by many, and wiser still by himself; and I went and tried to explain to him that he thought himself wise, but was not really wise; and the consequence was that he hated me, and his enmity was shared by several who were present and heard me. So I left him, saying to myself, as I went away: Well, although I do not suppose that either of us knows anything really beautiful and good, I am better off than he is—for he knows nothing, and thinks that he knows. I neither know nor think that I know. In this latter particular, then, I seem to have slightly the advantage of him. Then I went to another, who had still higher philosophical pretensions, and my conclusion was exactly the same. I made another enemy of him, and of many others besides him.

After this I went to one man after another, being not unconscious of the enmity which I provoked, and I lamented and feared this: but necessity was laid upon me—the word of God, I thought, ought to be considered first. And I said to myself, Go I must to all who appear to know, and find out the meaning of the oracle. And I swear to you, Athenians, by the dog I swear!—for I must tell you the truth—the result of my mission was just this: I found that the men most in repute were all but the most foolish; and that some inferior men were really wiser and better. I will tell you the tale of my wanderings and of the "Herculean" labors, as I may call them, which I endured only to find at last the oracle irrefutable. When I left the politicians, I went to the poets. And there, I said to myself, you will be detected; now you will find out that you are more ignorant than they are. Accordingly, I took them some of the most elaborate passages in their own writings, and asked what was the meaning of them—thinking that they would teach me something. Will you believe me? I am almost ashamed to speak of this, but still I must say that there is hardly a person present who would not have talked better about their poetry than they did themselves. That showed me in an instant that not by wisdom do poets write poetry, but by a sort of genius and inspiration; they are like diviners or soothsayers who also say many fine things, but do not understand the meaning of them. And the poets appeared to me to be much in the same case; and I further observed that upon the strength of their poetry they believed themselves to be the wisest of men in other things in which they were not wise. So I departed, conceiving myself to be superior to them for the same reason that I was superior to the politicians.

At last I went to the artisans, for I was conscious that I knew nothing at all, as I may say, and I was sure that they knew many fine things; and in this I was not mistaken, for they did know many things of which I was ignorant, and in this they certainly were wiser than I was. But I observed that even the good artisans fell into the same error as the poets; because they were good workmen they thought that they also knew all sorts of high matters, and this defect in them overshadowed their wisdom—therefore I asked myself on behalf of the oracle, whether I would like to be as I was, neither having their knowledge nor their ignorance, or like them in both; and I made answer to myself and the oracle that I was better off as I was.

This investigation has led to my having many enemies of the worst and most dangerous kind, and has given occasion also to many calumnies, and I am called wise, for my hearers always imagine that I myself possess the wisdom which I find wanting in others: but the truth is, O men of Athens, that God only is wise; and in this oracle he means to say that the wisdom of men is little or nothing; he is not speaking of Socrates, he is only using my name as an illustration, as if he said, He, O men, is the wisest, who, like Socrates, knows that his wisdom is in truth worth nothing. And so I go my way, obedient to the god, and make inquisition into the wisdom of anyone, whether citizen or stranger, who appears to be wise; and if he is not wise, then in vindication of the oracle I show him that he is not wise; and this occupation quite absorbs me, and I have no time to give either to any public matter of interest or to any concern of my own, but I am in utter poverty by reason of my devotion to the god.

There is another thing: young men of the richer classes, who have not much to do, come about me of their own accord; they like to hear the pretenders examined, and they often imitate me, and examine others themselves; there are plenty of persons, as they soon enough discover, who think that they know something, but really know little or nothing: and then those who are examined by them instead of being angry with themselves are angry with me: This confounded Socrates, they say; this villainous misleader of youth! And then if somebody asks them, Why, what evil does he practice or teach? they do not know, and cannot tell; but in order that they may not appear to be at a loss, they repeat the ready-made charges which are used against all philosophers about teaching things up in the clouds and under the earth, and having no gods, and making the worse appear the better cause; for they do not like to confess that their pretense of knowledge has been detected—which is the truth: and as they are numerous and ambitious and energetic, and are all in battle array and have persuasive tongues, they have filled your ears with their loud and inveterate calumnies. And this is the reason why my three accusers, Meletus and Anytus and Lycon, have set upon me; Meletus, who has a quarrel with me on behalf of the poets; Anytus, on behalf of the craftsmen; Lycon, on behalf of the rhetoricians: and as I said at the beginning, I cannot expect to get rid of this mass of calumny all in a moment. And this, O men of Athens, is the truth and the whole truth; I have concealed nothing, I have dissembled nothing. And yet I know that this plainness of speech makes them hate me, and what is their hatred but a proof that I am speaking the truth? This is the occasion and reason of their slander of me, as you will find out either in this or in any future inquiry.

I have said enough in my defense against the first class of my accusers; I turn to the second class, who are headed by Meletus, that good and patriotic man, as he calls himself. And now I will try to defend myself against them: these new accusers must also have their affidavit read. What do they say? Something of this sort: That Socrates is a doer of evil, and corrupter of the youth, and he does not believe in the gods of the state, and has other new divinities of his own. That is the sort of charge; and now let us examine the particular counts. He says that I am a doer of evil, who corrupt the youth; but I say, O men of Athens, that Meletus is a doer of evil, and the evil is that he makes a joke of a serious matter, and is too ready at bringing other men to trial from a pretended zeal and interest about matters in which he really never had the smallest interest. And the truth of this I will endeavor to prove.

Come hither, Meletus, and let me ask a question of you. You think a great deal about the improvement of youth?

Yes, I do.

Tell the judges, then, who is their improver; for you must know, as you have taken the pains to discover their corrupter, and are citing and accusing me before them. Speak, then, and tell the judges who their improver is. Observe, Meletus, that you are silent, and have nothing to say. But is not this rather disgraceful, and a very considerable proof of what I was saying, that you have no interest in the matter? Speak up, friend, and tell us who their improver is.

The laws.

But that, my good sir, is not my meaning. I want to know who the person is, who, in the first place, knows the laws.

The judges, Socrates, who are present in court.

What do you mean to say, Meletus, that they are able to instruct and improve youth?

Certainly they are.

What, all of them, or some only and not others?

All of them.

By the goddess Hera, that is good news! There are plenty of improvers, then. And what do you say of the audience, do they improve them?

Yes, they do.

And the senators?

Yes, the senators improve them.

But perhaps the members of the citizen assembly corrupt them? Or do they too improve them?

They improve them.

Then every Athenian improves and elevates them; all with the exception of myself; and I alone am their corrupter? Is that what you affirm?

That is what I stoutly affirm.

I am very unfortunate if that is true. But suppose I ask you a question: Would you say that this also holds true in the case of horses? Does one man do them harm and all the world good? Is not the exact opposite of this true? One man is able to do them good, or at least not many; the trainer of horses, that is to say, does them good, and others who have to do with them rather injure them? Is not that true, Meletus, of horses, or any other animals? Yes, certainly. Whether you and Anytus say yes or no, that is no matter. Happy indeed would be the condition of youth if they had one corrupter only, and all the rest of the world were their improvers. And you, Meletus, have sufficiently shown that you never had a thought about the young: your carelessness is seen in your not caring about matters spoken of in this very indictment.

And now, Meletus, I must ask you another question: Which is better, to live among bad citizens, or among good ones? Answer, friend, I say; for that is a question which may be easily answered. Do not the good do their neighbors good, and the bad do them evil?

Certainly.

And is there anyone who would rather be injured than benefited by those who live with him? Answer, my good friend; the law requires you to answer, does anyone like to be injured?

Certainly not.

And when you accuse me of corrupting and deteriorating the youth, do you allege that I corrupt them intentionally or unintentionally?

Intentionally, I say.

But you have just admitted that the good do their neighbors good, and the evil do them evil. Now is that a truth which your superior wisdom has recognized thus early in life, and am I, at my age, in such darkness and ignorance as not to know that if a man with whom I have to live is corrupted by me, I am very likely to be harmed by him, and yet I corrupt him, and intentionally, too; that is what you are saying, and of that you will never persuade me or any other human being. But either I do not corrupt them, or I corrupt them unintentionally, so that on either view of the case you lie. If my offence is unintentional, the law has no cognizance of unintentional offences: you ought to have taken me privately, and warned and admonished me; for if I had been better advised, I should have left off doing what I only did unintentionally, no doubt I should; whereas you hated to converse with me or teach me, but you indicted me in this court, which is a place not of instruction, but of punishment.

I have shown, Athenians, as I was saying, that Meletus has no care at all, great or small, about the matter. But still I should like to know, Meletus, in what I am affirmed to corrupt the young. I suppose you mean, as I infer from your indictment, that I teach them not to acknowledge the gods which the state acknowledges, but some other new divinities or spiritual agencies in their stead. These are the lessons which corrupt the youth, as you say.

Yes, that I say emphatically.

Then, by the gods, Meletus, of whom we are speaking, tell me and the court, in somewhat plainer terms, what you mean! for I do not as yet understand whether you affirm that I teach others to acknowledge some gods, and therefore do believe in gods and am not an entire atheist—this you do not lay to my charge; but only that they are not the same gods which the city recognizes—the charge is that they are different gods. Or, do you mean to say that I am an atheist simply, and a teacher of atheism?

I mean the latter, that you are a complete atheist.

That is an extraordinary statement, Meletus. Why do you say that? Do you mean that I do not believe in the godhead of the sun or moon, which is the common creed of all men?

I assure you, judges, that he does not believe in them; for he says that the sun is stone, and the moon earth.

Friend Meletus, you think that you are accusing Anaxagoras; and you have but a bad opinion of the judges, if you fancy them ignorant to such a degree as not to know that those doctrines are found in the books of Anaxagoras. And these are the doctrines which the youth are said to learn of Socrates, when there are not unfrequently exhibitions of them at the theatre, and they might cheaply purchase them, and laugh at Socrates if he pretends to father such eccentricities. And so, Meletus, you really think that I do not believe in any god?

I swear by Zeus that you believe absolutely in none at all.

You are a liar, Meletus, not believed even by yourself. For I cannot help thinking, O men of Athens, that Meletus is reckless and impudent, and that he has written this indictment in a spirit of mere wantonness and youthful bravado. Has he not compounded a riddle, thinking to try me? He said to himself: I shall see whether this wise Socrates will discover my ingenious contradiction, or whether I shall be able to deceive him and the rest of them. For he certainly does appear to me to contradict himself in the indictment as much as if he said that Socrates is guilty of not believing in the gods, and yet of believing in them—but this surely is a piece of fun.

I should like you, O men of Athens, to join me in examining what I conceive to be his inconsistency; and do you, Meletus, answer. And I must remind you that you are not to interrupt me if I speak in my accustomed manner.

Did ever man, Meletus, believe in the existence of human beings, and not of human beings? I wish, men of Athens, that he would answer, and not be always trying to get up an interruption. Did ever any man believe in horsemanship, and not in horses? Or in flute-playing, and not in flute-players? No, my friend; I will answer to you and to the court, as you refuse to answer for yourself. There is no man who ever did. But now please to answer the next question: Can a man believe in spiritual and divine agencies, and not in spirits or demigods?

He cannot.

I am glad that I have extracted that answer, by the assistance of the court; nevertheless you swear in the indictment that I teach and believe in divine or spiritual agencies (new or old, no matter for that); at any rate, I believe in spiritual agencies, as you say and swear in the affidavit; but if I believe in divine beings, I must believe in spirits or demigods; is not that true? Yes, that is true, for I may assume that your silence gives assent to that. Now what are spirits or demigods? Are they not either gods or the sons of gods? Is that true?

Yes, that is true.

But this is just the ingenious riddle of which I was speaking: the demigods or spirits are gods, and you say first that I don't believe in gods, and then again that I do believe in gods; that is, if I believe in demigods. For if the demigods are the illegitimate sons of gods, whether by the Nymphs or by any other mothers, as is thought, that, as all men will allow, necessarily implies the existence of their parents. You might as well affirm the existence of mules, and deny that of horses and asses. Such nonsense, Meletus, could only have been intended by you as a trial of me. You have put this into the indictment because you had nothing real of which to accuse me. But no one who has a particle of understanding will ever be convinced by you that the same man can believe in divine and superhuman things, and yet not believe that there are gods and demigods and heroes.

I have said enough in answer to the charge of Meletus: any elaborate defense is unnecessary; but as I was saying before, I certainly have many enemies, and this is what will be my destruction, if I am destroyed; of that I am certain; not Meletus, nor yet Anytus, but the envy and detraction of the world, which has been the death of many good men, and will probably be the death of many more; there is no danger of my being the last of them.

Someone will say: And are you not ashamed, Socrates, of a course of life which is likely to bring you to an untimely end? To him I may fairly answer: There you are mistaken: a man who is good for anything ought not to calculate the chance of living or dying; he ought only to consider whether in doing anything he is doing right or wrong—acting the part of a good man or of a bad. Whereas, according to your view, the heroes who fell at Troy were not good for much, and the son of Thet is above all, who altogether despised danger in comparison with disgrace; and when his goddess mother said to him, in his eagerness to slay Hector, that if he avenged his companion Patroclus, and slew Hector, he would die himself. "Fate," as she said, "waits upon you next after Hector"; he, hearing this, utterly despised danger and death, and instead of fearing them, feared rather to live in dishonor, and not to avenge his friend. "Let me die next," he replies, "and be avenged of my enemy, rather than abide here by the beaked ships, a scorn and a burden of the earth." Had Achilles any thought of death and danger? For wherever a man's place is, whether the place which he has chosen or that in which he has been placed by a commander, there he ought to remain in the hour of danger; he should not think of death or of anything, but of disgrace. And this, O men of Athens, is a true saying.

Strange, indeed, would be my conduct, O men of Athens, if I who, when I was ordered by the generals whom you chose to command me at Potidaea and Amphipolis and Delium, remained where they placed me, like any other man, facing death; if, I say, now, when, as I conceive and imagine, God orders me to fulfil the philosopher's mission of searching into myself and other men, I were to desert my post through fear of death, or any other fear; that would indeed be strange, and I might justly be arraigned in court for denying the existence of the gods, if I disobeyed the oracle because I was afraid of death: then I should be fancying that I was wise when I was not wise. For this fear of death is indeed the pretense of wisdom, and not real wisdom, being the appearance of knowing the unknown; since no one knows whether death, which they in their fear apprehend to be the greatest evil, may not be the greatest good. Is there not here conceit of knowledge, which is a disgraceful sort of ignorance? And this is the point in which, as I think, I am superior to men in general, and in which I might perhaps fancy myself wiser than other men, that whereas I know but little of the world below, I do not suppose that I know: but I do know that injustice and disobedience to a better, whether God or man, is evil and dishonorable, and I will never fear or avoid a possible good rather than a certain evil. And therefore if you let me go now, and reject the counsels of Anytus, who said that if I were not put to death I ought not to have been prosecuted, and that if I escape now, your sons will all be utterly ruined by listening to my words; if you say to me, Socrates, this time we will not mind Anytus, and will let you off, but upon one condition, that you are not to inquire and speculate in this way any more, and that if you are caught doing this again you shall die; if this was the condition on which you let me go, I should reply: Men of Athens, I honor and love you; but I shall obey God rather than you, and while I have life and strength I shall never cease from the practice and teaching of philosophy, exhorting anyone whom I meet after my manner, and convincing him, saying: O my friend, why do you who are a citizen of the great and mighty and wise city of Athens, care so much about laying up the greatest amount of money and honor and reputation, and so little about wisdom and truth and the greatest improvement of the soul, which you never regard or heed at all? Are you not ashamed of this? And if the person with whom I am arguing says: Yes, but I do care; I do not depart or let him go at once; I interrogate and examine and cross-examine him, and if I think that he has no virtue, but only says that he has, I reproach him with undervaluing the greater, and overvaluing the less. And this I should say to everyone whom I meet, young and old, citizen and alien, but especially to the citizens, inasmuch as they are my brethren. For this is the command of God, as I would have you know; and I believe that to this day no greater good has ever happened in the state than my service to the God. For I do nothing but go about persuading you all, old and young alike, not to take thought for your persons and your properties, but first and chiefly to care about the greatest improvement of the soul. I tell you that virtue is not given by money, but that from virtue come money and every other good of man, public as well as private. This is my teaching, and if this is the doctrine which corrupts the youth, my influence is ruinous indeed. But if anyone says that this is not my teaching, he is speaking an untruth. Wherefore, O men of Athens, I say to you, do as Anytus bids or not as Anytus bids, and either acquit me or not; but whatever you do, know that I shall never alter my ways, no t even if I have to die many times.

Men of Athens, do not interrupt, but hear me; there was an agreement between us that you should hear me out. And I think that what I am going to say will do you good: for I have something more to say, at which you may be inclined to cry out; but I beg that you will not do this. I would have you know that, if you kill such a one as I am, you will injure yourselves more than you will injure me. Meletus and Anytus will not injure me: they cannot; for it is not in the nature of things that a bad man should injure a better than himself. I do not deny that he may, perhaps, kill him, or drive him into exile, or deprive him of civil rights; and he may imagine, and others may imagine, that he is doing him a great injury: but in that I do not agree with him; for the evil of doing as Anytus is doing—of unjustly taking away another man's life—is greater far. And now, Athenians, I am not going to argue for my own sake, as you may think, but for yours, that you may not sin against the God, or lightly reject his boon by condemning me. For if you kill me you will not easily find another like me, who, if I may use such a ludicrous figure of speech, am a sort of gadfly, given to the state by the God; and the state is like a great and noble steed who is tardy in his motions owing to his very size, and requires to be stirred into life. I am that gadfly which God has given the state and all day long and in all places am always fastening upon you, arousing and persuading and reproaching you. And as you will not easily find another like me, I would advise you to spare me. I dare say that you may feel irritated at being suddenly awakened when you are caught napping; and you may think that if you were to strike me dead, as Anytus advises, which you easily might, then you would sleep on for the remainder of your lives, unless God in his care of you gives you another gadfly. And that I am given to you by God is proved by this: that if I had been like other men, I should not have neglected all my own concerns, or patiently seen the neglect of them during all these years, and have been doing yours, coming to you individually, like a father or elder brother, exhorting you to regard virtue; this I say, would not be like human nature. And had I gained anything, or if my exhortations had been paid, there would have been some sense in that: but now, as you will perceive, not even the impudence of my accusers dares to say that I have ever exacted or sought pay of anyone; they have no witness of that. And I have a witness of the truth of what I say; my poverty is a sufficient witness.

Someone may wonder why I go about in private, giving advice and busying myself with the concerns of others, but do not venture to come forward in public and advise the state. I will tell you the reason of this. You have often heard me speak of an oracle or sign which comes to me, and is the divinity which Meletus ridicules in the indictment. This sign I have had ever since I was a child. The sign is a voice which comes to me and always forbids me to do something which I am going to do, but never commands me to do anything, and this is what stands in the way of my being a politician. And rightly, as I think. For I am certain, O men of Athens, that if I had engaged in politics, I should have perished long ago and done no good either to you or to myself. And don't be offended at my telling you the truth: for the truth is that no man who goes to war with you or any other multitude, honestly struggling against the commission of unrighteousness and wrong in the state, will save his life; he who will really fight for the right, if he would live even for a little while, must have a private station and not a public one.

I can give you as proofs of this, not words only, but deeds, which you value more than words. Let me tell you a passage of my own life, which will prove to you that I should never have yielded to injustice from any fear of death, and that if I had not yielded I should have died at once. I will tell you a story—tasteless, perhaps, and commonplace, but nevertheless true. The only office of state which I ever held, O men of Athens, was that of senator; the tribe Antiochis, which is my tribe, had the presidency at the trial of the generals who had not taken up the bodies of the slain after the battle of Arginusae; and you proposed to try them all together, which was illegal, as you all thought afterwards; but at the time I was the only one of the Prytanes who was opposed to the illegality, and I gave my vote against you; and when the orators threatened to impeach and arrest me, and have me taken away, and you called and shouted, I made up my mind that I would run the risk, having law and justice with me, rather than take part in your injustice because I feared imprisonment and death. This happened in the days of the democracy. But when the oligarchy of the Thirty was in power, they sent for me and four others into the rotunda, and bade us bring Leon the Salaminian from Salamis, as they wanted to execute him. This was a specimen of the sort of commands which they were always giving with the view of implicating as many as possible in their crimes; and then I showed, not in words only, but in deed, that, if I may be allowed to use such an expression, I cared not a straw for death, and that my only fear was the fear of doing an unrighteous or unholy thing. For the strong arm of that oppressive power did not frighten me into doing wrong; and when we came out of the rotunda the other four went to Salamis and fetched Leon, but I went quietly home. For which I might have lost my life, had not the power of the Thirty shortly afterwards come to an end. And to this many will witness.

Now do you really imagine that I could have survived all these years, if I had led a public life, supposing that like a good man I had always supported the right and had made justice, as I ought, the first thing? No, indeed, men of Athens, neither I nor any other. But I have been always the same in all my actions, public as well as private, and never have I yielded any base compliance to those who are slanderously termed my disciples or to any other. For the truth is that I have no regular disciples: but if anyone likes to come and hear me while I am pursuing my mission, whether he be young or old, he may freely come. Nor do I converse with those who pay only, and not with those who do not pay; but anyone, whether he be rich or poor, may ask and answer me and listen to my words; and whether he turns out to be a bad man or a good one, that cannot be justly laid to my charge, as I never taught him anything. And if anyone says that he has ever learned or heard anything from me in private which all the world has not heard, I should like you to know that he is speaking an untruth.

But I shall be asked, Why do people delight in continually conversing with you? I have told you already, Athenians, the whole truth about this: they like to hear the cross-examination of the pretenders to wisdom; there is amusement in this. And this is a duty which the God has imposed upon me, as I am assured by oracles, visions, and in every sort of way in which the will of divine power was ever signified to anyone. This is true, O Athenians; or, if not true, would be soon refuted. For if I am really corrupting the youth, and have corrupted some of them already, those of them who have grown up and have become sensible that I gave them bad advice in the days of their youth should come forward as accusers and take their revenge; and if they do not like to come themselves, some of their relatives, fathers, brothers, or other kinsmen, should say what evil their families suffered at my hands. Now is their time. Many of them I see in the court. There is Crito, who is of the same age and of the same deme with myself. I might mention a great many others, any of whom Meletus should have produced as witnesses in the course of his speech; and let him still produce them, if he has forgotten—I will make way for him. And let him say, if he has any testimony of the sort which he can produce. Nay, Athenians, the very opposite is the truth. For all these are ready to witness on behalf of the corrupter, of the destroyer of their kindred, as Meletus and Anytus call me; not the corrupted youth only—there might have been a motive for that—but their uncorrupted elder relatives. Why should they too support me with their testimony? Why, indeed, except for the sake of truth and justice, and because they know that I am speaking the truth, and that Meletus is lying.

Well, Athenians, this and the like of this is nearly all the defense which I have to offer. Yet a word more. Perhaps there may be someone who is offended at me, when he calls to mind how he himself, on a similar or even a less serious occasion, had recourse to prayers and supplications with many tears, and how he produced his children in court, which was a moving spectacle, together with a posse of his relations and friends; whereas I, who am probably in danger of my life, will do none of these things. Perhaps this may come into his mind, and he may be set against me, and vote in anger because he is displeased at this. Now if there be such a person among you, which I am far from affirming, I may fairly reply to him: My friend, I am a man, and like other men, a creature of flesh and blood, and not of wood or stone, as Homer says; and I have a family, yes, and sons. O Athenians, three in number, one of whom is growing up, and the two others are still young; and yet I will not bring any of them hither in order to petition you for an acquittal. And why not? Not from any self-will or disregard of you. Whether I am or am not afraid of death is another question, of which I will not now speak. But my reason simply is that I feel such conduct to be discreditable to myself, and you, and the whole state. One who has reached my years, and who has a name for wisdom, whether deserved or not, ought not to debase himself. At any rate, the world has decided that Socrates is in some way superior to other men. And if those among you who are said to be superior in wisdom and courage, and any other virtue, demean themselves in this way, how shameful is their conduct! I have seen men of reputation, when they have been condemned, behaving in the strangest manner: they seemed to fancy that they were going to suffer something dreadful if they died, and that they could be immortal if you only allowed them to live; and I think that they were a dishonor to the state, and that any stranger coming in would say of them that the most eminent men of Athens, to whom the Athenians themselves give honor and command, are no better than women. And I say that these things ought not to be done by those of us who are of reputation; and if they are done, you ought not to permit them; you ought rather to show that you are more inclined to condemn, not the man who is quiet, but the man who gets up a doleful scene, and makes the city ridiculous.

But, setting aside the question of dishonor, there seems to be something wrong in petitioning a judge, and thus procuring an acquittal instead of informing and convincing him. For his duty is, not to make a present of justice, but to give judgment; and he has sworn that he will judge according to the laws, and not according to his own good pleasure; and neither he nor we should get into the habit of perjuring ourselves—there can be no piety in that. Do not then require me to do what I consider dishonorable and impious and wrong, especially now, when I am being tried for impiety on the indictment of Meletus. For if, O men of Athens, by force of persuasion and entreaty, I could overpower your oaths, then I should be teaching you to believe that there are no gods, and convict myself, in my own defense, of not believing in them. But that is not the case; for I do believe that there are gods, and in a far higher sense than that in which any of my accusers believe in them. And to you and to God I commit my cause, to be determined by you as is best for you and me.

[At this point, the jury finds Socrates guilty. Socrates now offers a proposal for his sentence.]

There are many reasons why I am not grieved, O men of Athens, at the vote of condemnation. I expected it, and am only surprised that the votes are so nearly equal; for I had thought that the majority against me would have been far larger; but now, had thirty votes gone over to the other side, I should have been acquitted. And I may say that I have escaped Meletus. And I may say more; for without the assistance of Anytus and Lycon, he would not have had a fifth part of the votes, as the law requires, in which case he would have incurred a fine of a thousand drachmae, as is evident.

And so he proposes death as the penalty. And what shall I propose on my part, O men of Athens? Clearly that which is my due. And what is that which I ought to pay or to receive? What shall be done to the man who has never had the wit to be idle during his whole life; but has been careless of what the many care about—wealth, and family interests, and military offices, and speaking in the assembly, and magistracies, and plots, and parties. Reflecting that I was really too honest a man to follow in this way and live, I did not go where I could do no good to you or to myself; but where I could do the greatest good privately to everyone of you, thither I went, and sought to persuade every man among you that he must look to himself, and seek virtue and wisdom before he looks to his private interests, and look to the state before he looks to the interests of the state; and that this should be the order which he observes in all his actions. What shall be done to such a one? Doubtless some good thing, O men of Athens, if he has his reward; and the good should be of a kind suitable to him. What would be a reward suitable to a poor man who is your benefactor, who desires leisure that he may instruct you? There can be no more fitting reward than maintenance in the Prytaneum, O men of Athens, a reward which he deserves far more than the citizen who has won the prize at Olympia in the horse or chariot race, whether the chariots were drawn by two horses or by many. For I am in want, and he has enough; and he only gives you the appearance of happiness, and I give you the reality. And if I am to estimate the penalty justly, I say that maintenance in the Prytaneum is the just return.

Perhaps you may think that I am braving you in saying this, as in what I said before about the tears and prayers. But that is not the case. I speak rather because I am convinced that I never intentionally wronged anyone, although I cannot convince you of that—for we have had a short conversation only; but if there were a law at Athens, such as there is in other cities, that a capital cause should not be decided in one day, then I believe that I should have convinced you; but now the time is too short. I cannot in a moment refute great slanders; and, as I am convinced that I never wronged another, I will assuredly not wrong myself. I will not say of myself that I deserve any evil, or propose any penalty. Why should I? Because I am afraid of the penalty of death which Meletus proposes? When I do not know whether death is a good or an evil, why should I propose a penalty which would certainly be an evil? Shall I say imprisonment? And why should I live in prison, and be the slave of the magistrates of the year—of the Eleven? Or shall the penalty be a fine, and imprisonment until the fine is paid? There is the same objection. I should have to lie in prison, for money I have none, and I cannot pay. And if I say exile. and this may possibly be the penalty which you will affix, I must indeed be blinded by the love of life if I were to consider that when you, who are my own citizens, cannot endure my discourses and words, and have found them so grievous and odious that you would have done with them, others are likely to endure me. No, indeed, men of Athens, that is not very likely. And what a life should I lead, at my age, wandering from city to city, living in ever-changing exile, and always being driven out! For I am quite sure that into whatever place I go, as here so also there, the young men will come to me; and if I drive them away, their elders will drive me out at their desire: and if I let them come, their fathers and friends will drive me out for their sakes.

Someone will say: Yes, Socrates, but cannot you hold your tongue, and then you may go into a foreign city, and no one will interfere with you? Now I have great difficulty in making you understand my answer to this. For if I tell you that this would be a disobedience to a divine command, and therefore that I cannot hold my tongue, you will not believe that I am serious; and if I say again that the greatest good of man is daily to converse about virtue, and all that concerning which you hear me examining myself and others, and that the life which is unexamined is not worth living—that you are still less likely to believe. And yet what I say is true, although a thing of which it is hard for me to persuade you. Moreover, I am not accustomed to think that I deserve any punishment. Had I money I might have proposed to give you what I had, and have been none the worse. But you see that I have none, and can only ask you to proportion the fine to my means. However, I think that I could afford a minae, and therefore I propose that penalty; Plato, Crito, Critobulus, and Apollodorus, my friends here, bid me say thirty minae, and they will be the sureties. Well then, say thirty minae, let that be the penalty; for that they will be ample security to you.

[At this point, the jury condemns Socrates to death. Socrates then comments on his sentence.]

Not much time will be gained, O Athenians, in return for the evil name which you will get from the detractors of the city, who will say that you killed Socrates, a wise man; for they will call me wise even although I am not wise when they want to reproach you. If you had waited a little while, your desire would have been fulfilled in the course of nature. For I am far advanced in years, as you may perceive, and not far from death. I am speaking now only to those of you who have condemned me to death. And I have another thing to say to them: You think that I was convicted through deficiency of words; I mean, that if I had thought fit to leave nothing undone, nothing unsaid, I might have gained an acquittal. Not so; the deficiency which led to my conviction was not of words; certainly not. But I had not the boldness or impudence or inclination to address you as you would have liked me to address you, weeping and wailing and lamenting, and saying and doing many things which you have been accustomed to hear from others, and which, as I say, are unworthy of me. But I thought that I ought not to do anything common or mean in the hour of danger: nor do I now repent of the manner of my defense, and I would rather die having spoken after my manner, than speak in your manner and live. For neither in war nor yet at law ought any man to use every way of escaping death. For often in battle there is no doubt that if a man will throw away his arms, and fall on his knees before his pursuers, he may escape death; and in other dangers there are other ways of escaping death, if a man is willing to say and do anything. The difficulty, my friends, is not in avoiding death, but in avoiding unrighteousness; for that runs faster than death. I am old and move slowly, and the slower runner has overtaken me, and my accusers are keen and quick, and the faster runner, who is unrighteousness, has overtaken them. And now I depart hence condemned by you to suffer the penalty of death, and they, too, go their ways condemned by the truth to suffer the penalty of villainy and wrong; and I must abide by my award; let them abide by theirs. I suppose that these things may be regarded as fated, and I think that they are well.

And now, O men who have condemned me, I would offer a prophesy to you; for I am about to die, and that is the hour in which men are gifted with prophetic power. And I prophesy to you who are my murderers, that immediately after my death punishment far heavier than you have inflicted on me will surely await you. Me you have killed because you wanted to escape the accuser, and not to give an account of your lives. But that will not be as you suppose: far otherwise. For I say that there will be more accusers of you than there are now; accusers whom hitherto I have restrained: and as they are younger they will be more severe with you, and you will be more offended at them. For if you think that by killing me you can avoid the accuser censuring your lives, you are mistaken; that is not a way of escape which is either possible or honorable; the easiest and noblest way is not to be crushing others, but to be improving yourselves. This is the prophecy which I utter before my departure, to the judges who have condemned me.

Friends, who would have acquitted me, I would like also to talk with you about this thing which has happened, while the magistrates are busy, and before I go to the place at which I must die. Stay then awhile, for we may as well talk with one another while there is time. You are my friends, and I should like to show you the meaning of this event which has happened to me. O my judges—for you I may truly call judges—I should like to tell you of a wonderful circumstance. Hitherto the familiar oracle within me has constantly been in the habit of opposing me even about trifles, if I was going to make a slip or error about anything; and now as you see there has come upon me that which may be thought, and is generally believed to be, the last and worst evil. But the oracle made no sign of opposition, either as I was leaving my house and going out in the morning, or when I was going up into this court, or while I was speaking, at anything which I was going to say; and yet I have often been stopped in the middle of a speech; but now in nothing I either said or did touching this matter has the oracle opposed me. What do I take to be the explanation of this? I will tell you. I regard this as a proof that what has happened to me is a good, and that those of us who think that death is an evil are in error. This is a great proof to me of what I am saying, for the customary sign would surely have opposed me had I been going to evil and not to good.

Let us reflect in another way, and we shall see that there is great reason to hope that death is a good, for one of two things: either death is a state of nothingness and utter unconsciousness, or, as men say, there is a change an d migration of the soul from this world to another. Now if you suppose that there is no consciousness, but a sleep like the sleep of him who is undisturbed even by the sight of dreams, death will be an unspeakable gain. For if a person were to select the night in which his sleep was undisturbed even by dreams, and were to compare with this the other days and nights of his life, and then were to tell us how many days and nights he had passed in the course of his life better and more pleasantly than this one, I think that any man, I will not say a private man, but even the great king, will not find many such days or nights, when compared with the others. Now if death is like this, I say that to die is gain; for eternity is then only a single night. But if death is the journey to another place, and there, as men say, all the dead are, what good, O my friends and judges, can be greater than this? If indeed when the pilgrim arrives in the world below, he is delivered from the professors of justice in this world, and finds the true judges who are said to give judgment there, that pilgrimage will be worth making. What would not a man give if he might converse with Orpheus and Musaeus and Hesiod and Homer? If this is true, let me die again and again. I, too, shall have a wonderful interest in a place where I can converse with Palamedes, and Ajax the son of Telamon, and other heroes of old, who have suffered death through an unjust judgment; and there will be no small pleasure, as I think, in comparing my own sufferings with theirs. Above all, I shall be able to continue my search into true and false knowledge; as in this world, so also in that; I shall find out who is wise, and who pretends to be wise, and is not. What would not a man give, O judges, to be able to examine the leader of the great Trojan expedition; or Odysseus or Sisyphus, or numberless others, men and women too! What infinite delight would there be in conversing with them and asking them questions! For in that world they do not put a man to death for this; certainly not. For besides being happier in that world than in this, they will be immortal, if what is said is true.

So, be of good cheer about death, and know this of a truth—that no evil can happen to a good man, either in life or after death. He and his are not neglected by the gods; nor has my own approaching end happened by mere chance. But I see clearly that to die and be released was better for me; and therefore the oracle gave no sign. For which reason also, I am not angry with my accusers, or my condemners; they have done me no harm, although neither of them meant to do me any good; and for this I may gently blame them.

Still I have a favor to ask of them. When my sons are grown up, I would ask you, O my friends, to punish them; and I would have you trouble them, as I have troubled you, if they seem to care about riches, or anything, more than about virtue; or if they pretend to be something when they are really nothing, then reprove them, as I have reproved you, for not caring about that for which they ought to care, and thinking that they are something when they are really nothing. And if you do this, I and my sons will have received justice at your hands.

The hour of departure has arrived, and we go our ways—I to die, and you to live. Which is better, God only knows.

Plato

SHOULD I OBEY THE LAWS?

[The scene is the prison where Socrates is being held.]

Why have you come at this hour, Crito? It must be quite early.

The dawn is breaking, Socrates.

I wonder that the keeper of the prison would let you in.

He knows me, because I often come, Socrates; moreover, I have done him a kindness.

And are you only just arrived?

No, I came some time ago.

Then why did you sit and say nothing, instead of at once awakening me?

I have been watching with amazement your peaceful slumbers; and for that reason I did not awake you, because I wished to minimize the pain. I have always thought you to be of a happy disposition; but never did I see anything like the easy, tranquil manner in which you bear this calamity.

Why, Crito, when a man has reached my age he ought not to be fretting and worrying about the approach of death.

And yet other old men find themselves in similar misfortunes, and age does not prevent them from worrying.

That is true. But you have not told me why you come at this early hour.

I come to bring you a message which is sad and painful; not, as I believe, to yourself, but to all of us who are your friends, and saddest of all to me.

What? Has the ship come from Delos, on the arrival of which I am to die?

No, the ship has not actually arrived, but she will probably be here today; therefore, tomorrow, Socrates, will be the last day of your life.

Very well, Crito; if such is the will of God, I am willing; but my belief is that there will be a delay of a day.

Why do you think so?

Edited from *Crito*. Translated by Benjamin Jowett, 1892, which is now in the public domain.

I will tell you. I am to die on the day after the arrival of the ship.

Yes; that is what the authorities say.

But I do not think that the ship will be here until tomorrow; this I infer from a vision which I had last night, or rather only just now, when you fortunately allowed me to sleep.

And what was the nature of the vision?

There appeared to me the likeness of a woman, fair and comely, clothed in bright clothing, who called to me and said, "Socrates, the third day hence to fertile Phthia shalt thou go."

What a singular dream, Socrates!

There can be no doubt about the meaning, Crito.

Yes; the meaning is only too clear. But, oh my beloved Socrates, let me urge you once more to take my advice and escape. For if you die, I shall not only lose a friend who can never be replaced, but there is another evil; people who do not know you and me will believe that I might have saved you if I had been willing to give money, but that I did not care. Now, can there be a worse disgrace than this—that I should be thought to value money more than the life of a friend? For many people will not be persuaded that I wanted you to escape, and that you refused.

But why, my dear Crito, should we care about the opinion of the many? Good men, and they are the only persons who are worth considering, will think of these things truly as they occurred.

But the opinion of the many must be regarded, for what is now happening shows that they can do the greatest evil to anyone who has lost their good opinion.

I only wish it were so, Crito; and that the many could do the greatest evil; for then they would also be able to do the greatest good—and what a fine thing this would be! But in reality they can do neither; for they cannot make a man either wise or foolish; and whatever they do is the result of chance.

Well, I will not dispute with you; but please to tell me, Socrates, whether you are not acting out of regard to me and your other friends: are you not afraid that if you escape from prison we may get into trouble for having stolen you away, and lose either the whole or a great part of our property; or that even a worse evil may happen to us? Now, if you fear on our account, be at ease; for in order to save you, we ought surely to run this, or even a greater risk; be persuaded, then, and do as I say.

Yes, Crito, that is one fear which you mention, but by no means the only one.

Fear not—there are persons who are willing to get you out of prison at no great cost; and as for the informers, they are far from being exorbitant in their demands—a little money will satisfy them. My means, which are certainly ample, are at your service, and if you have a scruple about spending all mine, there are other who will give you the use of theirs. I say, therefore, do not hesitate on our account, and do not say, as you did in the court that you will have a difficulty in knowing what to do with yourself anywhere else. For men will love you in other places to which you may go, and not in Athens only; there are friends of mine in Thessaly, if you like to go to them, who will value and protect you, and no Thessalian will give you any trouble. Nor can I think that you are at all justified, Socrates, in betraying your own life when you might be saved; in acting thus you are playing into the hands of your enemies, who are hurrying on your destruction. And further I should say that you are deserting your own children; for you might bring them up and educate them; instead of which you go away and leave them, and they will have to take their chance; and if they do not meet with the usual fate of orphans, there will be small thanks to you. No man should bring children into the world who is unwilling to persevere to the end in their nurture and education. But you appear to be choosing the easier part, not the better and manlier, which would have been more becoming in one who professes to care for virtue in all his actions, like yourself. And indeed, I am ashamed not only of you, but of us who are your friends, when I reflect that the whole business will be attributed entirely to our want of courage. The trial need never have come on, or might have been managed differently; and this last act, or crowning folly, will seem to have occurred through our negligence and cowardice, who might have saved you, if we had been good for anything; and you might have saved yourself, for there was no difficulty at all. See now, Socrates, how sad and discreditable are the consequences, both to us and you. Make up your mind then, or rather have your mind already made up, for the time of deliberation is over, and there is only one thing to be done, which must be done this very night, and if we delay at all will be no longer practicable or possible; I beseech you therefore, Socrates, be persuaded by me, and do as I say.

Dear Crito, your zeal is invaluable, if a right one; but if wrong, the greater the zeal the greater the danger; and therefore we ought to consider whether I shall or shall not do as you say. For I am and always have been one of those natures who must be guided by reason, whatever the reason may be which upon reflection appears to me to be the best; and now that this chance has befallen me, I cannot repudiate my own words: the principles which I have always honored and revered I still honor, and unless we can at once find other and better principles, I am certain not to agree with you; no, not even if the power of the multitude could inflict many more imprisonments, confiscations, deaths, frightening us like children with hobgoblin terrors. What will be the fairest way of considering the question? Shall I return to your old argument about the opinions of men? We were saying that some of them are to be regarded, and others not. Now were we right in maintaining this before I was condemned? And has the argument which was once good now proved to be talk for the sake of talking—mere childish nonsense? That is what I want to consider with your help, Crito, whether, under my present circumstances, the argument appears to be in any way different or not, and is to be allowed by me or disallowed. That argument, which, as I believe, is maintained by many persons of authority, was to the effect that the opinions of some men are to be regarded and of other men not to be regarded. Now you, Crito, are not going to die tomorrow—at least, there is no human probability of this—and therefore you are disinterested and not liable to be deceived by the circumstances in which you are placed. Tell me then, whether I am right in saying that some opinions, and the opinions of some men only, are to be valued, and that other opinions, and the opinions of other men, are not to be valued. I ask you whether I was right in maintaining this?

Certainly.

The good are to be regarded, and not the bad?

Yes.

And the opinions of the wise are good, and the opinions of the unwise are evil?

Certainly.

And what was said about another matter? Is the pupil who devotes himself to the practice of gymnastics supposed to attend to the praise and blame and opinion of every man, or of one man only—his physician or trainer, whoever he may be?

Of one man only.

And he ought to fear the censure and welcome the praise of that one only, and not of the many?

Clearly so.

And he ought to act and train, and eat and drink in the way which seems good to his single master who has understanding, rather than according to the opinion of all other men put together?

True.

And if he disobeys and disregards the opinion and approval of the one, and regards the opinion of the many who have no understanding, will he not suffer evil?

Certainly he will.

And what will the evil be in the disobedient person?

Clearly, affecting the body; that is what is destroyed by the evil.

Very good. And is not this true, Crito, of other things which we need not separately enumerate? In questions of just and unjust, fair and foul, good and evil, which are the subjects of our present discussion, ought we to follow the opinion of the many and to fear them; or the opinion of the one man who has understanding? Ought we not to fear and reverence him more than all the rest of the world: and if we desert him shall we not destroy and injure that principle in us which may be assumed to be improved by justice and deteriorated by injustice—there is such a principle?

Certainly there is, Socrates.

Take a parallel instance:—if, acting under the advice of those who have no understanding, we destroy that which is improved by health and is deteriorated by disease, would life be worth having? And that which has been destroyed is the body?

Yes.

Could we live, having an evil and corrupted body?

Certainly not.

And will life be worth having, if that higher part of man is destroyed, which is improved by justice and depraved by injustice? Do we suppose that principle, whatever it may be in man, which has to do with justice and injustice, to be inferior to the body?

Certainly not.

More honorable than the body?

Far more.

Then, my friend, we must not regard what the many say of us; but what he, the one man who has understanding of just and unjust, will say, and what the truth will say. And therefore you begin in error when you advise that we should regard the opinion of the many about just and unjust, good and evil, honorable and dishonorable. "Well," someone will say, "but the many can kill us."

Yes, Socrates, that will clearly be the answer.

And it is true. But still I find with surprise that the old argument is unshaken as ever. And I should like to know whether I may say the same of another proposition—that not life, but a good life, is to be chiefly valued?

Yes, that also remains unshaken.

And a good life is equivalent to a just and honorable one—that holds also?

Yes, it does.

From these premises, I proceed to argue the question whether I ought or ought not to try and escape without the consent of the Athenians; and if I am clearly right in escaping, then I will make the attempt, but if not, then I will abstain. The other considerations which you mention, of money and loss of character and the duty of educating one's children, are, I fear, only the doctrines of the multitude, who would be as ready to restore people to life, if they were able, as they are to put them to death—and with as little reason. But now, since the argument has thus far prevailed, the only question which remains to be considered is whether we shall do rightly either in escaping or in having others aid in our escape and paying them in money and thanks, or whether in reality we shall not do rightly; and if the latter, then death or any other calamity which may ensue on my remaining here must not be allowed to enter into the calculation.

I think that you are right, Socrates. How, then, shall we proceed?

Let us consider the matter together, and either refute me if you can, and I will be convinced; or else cease, my dear friend, from repeating to me that I ought to escape against the wishes of the Athenians; for I highly value your attempts to persuade me to do so, but I may not be persuaded against my own better judgment. And now please consider my first position, and try your best to answer me.

I will.

Are we to say that we are never intentionally to do wrong, or that in one way we ought and in another way we ought not to do wrong, or is doing wrong always evil and dishonorable, as has been already acknowledged by us? Are all our former admissions to be thrown away? And have we, at our age, been earnestly discoursing with one another all our life long, only to discover that we are no better than children? Or, in spite of the opinion of the many, and in spite of consequences whether better or worse, shall we insist on the truth of what was then said, that injustice is always an evil and dishonor to him who acts unjustly? Shall we say so or not?

Yes.

Then we must do no wrong?

Certainly not.

Nor, when we are injured, injure others in return, as the many imagine; for we must injure no one at all?

Clearly not.

Again, Crito, may we do evil?

Surely not, Socrates.

And what of doing evil in return for evil, which is the morality of the many—is that just or not?

Not just.

For doing evil to another is the same as injuring him?

Very true.

Then we ought not to retaliate or render evil for evil to anyone, whatever evil we may have suffered from him. But I would have you consider, Crito, whether you really mean what you are saying. For this opinion has never been held, and never will be held, by any considerable number of persons; and those who are agreed and those who are not agreed upon this point have no common ground, and can only despise one another when they see how widely they differ. Tell me, then, whether you agree with and assent to my first principle, that neither injury, nor retaliation, nor warding off evil by evil is ever right. And shall that be the premise of our argument? Or do you decline and dissent from this? For so I have ever thought, and continue to think; but, if you are of another opinion, let me hear what you have to say. If, however, you remain of the same mind as formerly, I will proceed to the next step.

You may proceed, for I have not changed my mind.

Then I will go on to the next point, which may be put in the form of a question: Ought a man to do what he admits to be right, or ought he to betray the right?

He ought to do what he thinks right.

But if this is true, what is the application? In leaving the prison against the will of the Athenians, do I wrong any? Or rather, do I not wrong those whom I ought least to wrong? Do I not desert the principles which were acknowledged by us to be just—what do you say?

I cannot tell, Socrates; for I do not know.

Then consider the matter in this way: Imagine that I am about to play truant (you may call the proceeding by any name which you like), and the Laws and the government come and interrogate me: "Tell us, Socrates," they say; "what are you doing? Are you not doing by an act of yours to overturn us—the laws, and the whole state, as far as in you lies? Do you imagine that a state can subsist and not be overthrown, in which the decisions of law have no power, but are set aside and trampled upon by individuals?" What will be our answer, Crito, to these and the like words? Any one, and especially a rhetorician, will have a good deal to say on behalf of the law which requires a sentence to be carried out. He will argue that this law should not be set aside; and shall we reply, "Yes; but the state has injured us and given an unjust sentence." Suppose I say that?

Very good, Socrates.

"And was that our agreement with you?" the Law would answer; "or were you to abide by the sentence of the state?" And if I were to express my astonishment at their words, the Law would probably add, "Answer, Socrates, you who are in the habit of asking and answering questions. Tell us what complaint have you to make against us which justifies you in attempting to destroy us and the state? In the first place did we not bring you into existence? Your father married your mother by our aid and gave birth to you. Say whether you have any objection to urge against those of us who regulate marriage?" None, I should reply. "Or against those of us who after birth regulate the nurture and education of children, in which you also were trained? Were not the laws, which have the charge of education, right in commanding your father to train you in music and gymnastic?" Right, I should reply. "Well then, since you were brought into the world and nurtured and educated by us, can you deny in the first place that you are our child and slave, as your fathers were before you? And if this is true you are not on equal terms with us; nor can you think that you have a right to do to us what we are doing to you. Would you have any right to strike or revile or do any other evil to your father or your master, if you had one, because you have been struck or reviled by him, or received some other evil at his hands? No, you would not say this. And because we think right to destroy you, do you think that you have any right to destroy us in return, and your country as far as in you lies? Will you, professor of true virtue, pretend that you are justified in this? Has a philosopher like you failed to discover that our country is more to be valued and higher and holier far than mother or father or any ancestor, and more to be regarded in the eyes of the gods and of men of understanding? Also to be soothed, and gently and reverently entreated when angry, even more than a father, and either to be persuaded, or if not persuaded, to be obeyed? And when we are punished by her, whether with imprisonment or whips, the punishment is to be endured in silence; and if she lead us to wounds or death in battle, there we follow as is right; neither may anyone yield or retreat or leave his rank, but whether in battle or in a court of law, or in any other place, he must do what his city and his country order him; or he must change their view of what is just: and if he may do no violence to his father or mother, much less may he do violence to his country." What answer shall we make to this, Crito? Does the Law speak truly, or does it not?

I think that it does.

Then the Law will say: "Consider, Socrates, if we are speaking truly that in your present attempt you are going to do us an injury. For, having brought you into the world, and nurtured and educated you, and given you and every other citizen a share in every good which we had to give, we further proclaim to any Athenian by the liberty which we allow him, that if he does not like us when he has become of age and has seen the ways of the city, and made our acquaintance, he may go where he pleases and take his goods with him. None of us laws will forbid him or interfere with him. Anyone who does not like us and the city, and who wants to emigrate to a colony or to any other city, may go where he likes, retaining his property. But he who has experience of the manner in which we order justice and administer the state, and still remains, has entered into an implied contract that he will do as we command him. And he who disobeys us is, as we maintain, thrice wrong; first, because in disobeying us he is disobeying his parents; secondly, because we are the authors of his education; thirdly, because he has made an agreement with us that he will duly obey our commands; and he neither obeys them nor convinces us that our commands are unjust; and we do not rudely impose them, but give him the alternative of obeying or convincing us; that is what we offer, and he does neither. These are the sort of accusations to which, as we were saying, you, Socrates, will be exposed if you accomplish your intentions; you, above all other Athenians."

Suppose now I ask, why I rather than anybody else? The Law will justly reply that I above all other men have acknowledged the agreement. "There is clear proof, Socrates, that we and the city were not displeasing to you. Of all Athenians, you have been the most constant resident in the city, which, as you never leave, you may be supposed to love. For you never went out of the city either to see the games, except once when you went to the Isthmus, or to any other place unless when you were on military service; nor did you travel as other men do. Nor had you any curiosity to know other states or their laws: your affections did not go beyond us and our state; we were your special favorites, and you acquiesced in our government of you; and here in this city you had your children, which is a proof of your satisfaction. Moreover, you might in the course of the trial, if you had liked, have fixed the penalty at banishment; the state, which refuses to let you go now, would have let you go then. But you pretended that you preferred death to exile, and that you were willing to die. And now you have forgotten these fine sentiments, and pay no respect to us the laws, of whom you are the destroyer; and are doing what only a miserable slave would do, running away and turning your back upon the compacts and agreements which you made as a citizen. And first of all answer this very question: Are we right in saying that you agreed to be governed according to us in deed, and not in word only? Is that true or not?" How shall we answer, Crito? Must we not assent?

We cannot help it, Socrates.

Then will the Law not say, "You, Socrates, are breaking the covenants and agreements which you made with us at your leisure, not in any haste or under any compulsion or deception, but after you have had seventy years to think of them, during which time you were at liberty to leave the city, if we were not to your mind, or if our covenants appeared to you to be unfair. You had your choice. But you, above all other Athenians, seemed to be so fond of the state, or, in other words, of us her laws (and who would care about a state which has no laws?), that you never stirred out of her; the halt, the blind, the maimed were not more stationary in her than you were. And now you run away and forsake your agreements. Socrates, if you will take our advice; do not make yourself ridiculous by escaping out of the city. For just consider, if you transgress and err in this sort of way, what good will you do either to yourself or to your friends? That your friends will be driven into exile and deprived of citizenship, or will lose their property, is fairly certain; and you yourself, if you fly to one of the neighboring cities, will come to them as an enemy, Socrates, and their government will be against you, and all patriotic citizens will cast an evil eye upon you as a subverter of the laws, and you will confirm in the minds of the judges the justice of their own condemnation of you. For he who is a corrupter of the laws is more than likely to be a corrupter of the young and foolish portion of mankind. Will you then flee from well-ordered cities and virtuous men? Is existence worth having on these terms? Or will you go to them without shame, and talk to them, Socrates? And what will you say to them? What you say here about virtue and justice and institutions and laws being the best things among men? Would that be decent of you? Surely not. But if you go away from well-governed states to Crito's friends in Thessaly, where there is great disorder, they will be charmed to hear the tale of your escape from prison, set off with ludicrous particulars of the manner in which you were wrapped in a goatskin or some other disguise, and metamorphosed as the manner is of runaways; but will there be no one to remind you that in your old age you were not ashamed to violate the most sacred laws from a miserable desire of a little more life? Perhaps not, if you keep them in a good temper; but if they are out of temper you will hear many degrading things; you will live, but how? As the flatterer of all men, and the servant of all men; and doing what? Eating and drinking in Thessaly, having gone abroad in order that you may get a dinner. And where will be your fine sentiments about justice and virtue? Say that you wish to live for the sake of your children—you want to bring them up and educate them—will you take them into Thessaly and deprive them of Athenian citizenship? Is this the benefit which you will confer upon them? Or are you under the impression that they will be better cared for and educated here if you are still alive, although absent from them; for your friends will take care of them? Do you fancy that if you are an inhabitant of Thessaly they will take care of them, and if you are an inhabitant of the other world that they will not take care of them? No; but if they who call themselves friends are good for anything, they will—to be sure they will. Listen, then, Socrates, to us who have brought you up. Think not of life and children first, and of justice afterwards, but of justice first, that you may be justified before the princes of the world below. For neither will you nor any that belong to you be happier or holier or more just in this life, or happier in another, if you do as Crito bids. Now you depart in innocence, a sufferer and not a doer of evil; a victim, not of the laws, but of men. But if you go forth, returning evil for evil, and injury for injury, breaking the covenants and agreements which you have made with us, and wronging those whom you ought least of all to wrong, that is to say, yourself, your friends, your country, and us, we shall be angry with you while you live, and our brethren, the laws in the world below, will receive you as an enemy; for they will know that you have done your best to destroy us. Listen, then, to us and not to Crito."

This, dear Crito, is the voice which I seem to hear murmuring in my ears, like the sound of the flute in the ears of the mystic; that voice, I say, is humming in my ears, and prevents me from hearing any other. And I know that anything more which you may say will be vain. Yet speak, if you have anything to say.

I have nothing to say, Socrates.

Leave me then, Crito, to fulfil the will of God, and to follow where he leads.

Aristotle

A POLITICAL ANIMAL

Every state is a community of some kind, and every community is established with a view to some good; for mankind always act in order to obtain that which they think good. But, if all communities aim at some good, the state or political community, which is the highest of all, and which embraces all the rest, aims at good in a greater degree than any other, and at the highest good.

When several families are united, and the association aims at something more than the supply of daily needs, the first society to be formed is the village. When several villages are united in a single complete community, large enough to be nearly or quite self-sufficient, the state comes into existence, originating in the bare needs of life, and continuing in existence for the sake of a good life. And therefore, if the earlier forms of society are natural, so is the state, for it is the end of them, and the nature of a thing is its end.

Hence it is evident that the state is a creation of nature, and that *man is by nature a political animal.* Nature, as we often say, makes nothing in vain, and man is the only animal whom she has endowed with the gift of speech. And whereas mere voice is but an indication of pleasure or pain, and is therefore found in other animals (for their nature attains to the perception of pleasure and pain and the intimation of them to one another, and no further), the power of speech is intended to set forth the expedient and inexpedient, and therefore likewise the just and the unjust. And it is a characteristic of man that he alone has any sense of good and evil, of just and unjust, and the like, and the association of living beings who have this sense makes a family and a state.

Further, the state is by nature clearly prior to the family and to the individual, since the whole is of necessity prior to the part. The proof that the state is a creation of nature and prior to the individual is that the individual, when isolated, is not self-sufficient; and therefore he is like a part in relation to the whole. A social instinct is implanted in all men by nature, and yet he who first founded the state was the greatest of benefactors. For man, when perfected, is the best of animals, but, when separated from law and justice, he is the worst of all; since armed injustice is the more dangerous. Therefore, if he does not have virtue, he is the most unholy and the most savage of animals, and the most full of lust and gluttony. But justice is the bond of men in states, for the administration of justice, which is the determination of what is just, is the principle of order in political society.

In all governments, two points have to be considered: first, whether any particular law is good or bad, when compared with the perfect state; secondly, whether it is or is not consistent with the idea and character which the lawgiver has set before his citizens. That in a well-ordered state the citizens should have leisure and not have to provide for their daily wants is generally acknowledged, but there is a difficulty in seeing how this leisure is to be attained.

Edited from *Politics,* Book I, Parts I, II and IX. Translated by Benjamin Jowett, 1885, which is now in the public domain.

Thomas Hobbes

SOLITARY, POOR, NASTY, BRUTISH, AND SHORT

In the nature of man, we find three principal causes of quarrel. First, *competition*; secondly, *diffidence*; thirdly, *glory*. The first makes men invade for gain; the second, for safety; and the third, for reputation. The first use violence to make themselves masters of other men's persons, wives, children, and cattle; the second, to defend them; the third, for trifles, as a word, a smile, a different opinion, and any other sign of undervalue, either direct in their persons, or by reflection in their kindred, their friends, their nation, their profession, or their name.

Hereby it is manifest that during the time men live without a common power to keep them all in awe, they are in that condition which is called *war*; and such a war is of *every man against every man*. For war consists not in battle only, or the act of fighting; but in a tract of time, where the will to contend by battle is sufficiently known: and therefore, the notion of time is to be considered in the nature of war; as it is in the nature of weather. For as the nature of foul weather lies not in a shower or two of rain; but in an inclination of many days together: so the nature of war consists not in actual fighting; but in the known disposition of it, and during all the time there is no assurance to the contrary. All other time is peace.

Whatever therefore is consequent to a time of war, where every man is enemy to every man; the same is consequent to the time, where men live without security except their own strength and their own invention shall furnish them with. In such condition, there is no place for industry; because the fruit of it is uncertain; and consequently no culture of the earth, no navigation, nor use of the commodities that may be imported by sea, no commodious building, no instruments of moving and removing such things as require much force, no knowledge of the face of the earth, no account of time, no arts, no letters, no society, and which is worst of all, continual fear and danger of violent death; *and the life of man—solitary, poor, nasty, brutish, and short.*

It may seem strange to some man, who has not well weighed these things, that nature should thus dissociate, and render men apt to invade and destroy one another: and he may therefore, not trusting to this inference made from the passions, desire perhaps to have the same confirmed by experience. Let him therefore consider: when taking a journey, he arms himself and seeks to go well accompanied; when going to sleep, he locks his doors; when even in his house he locks his chests; and this when he knows there are laws, and public officers, armed, to revenge all injuries that are done to him; what opinion he has of his fellow subjects when he rides armed; of his fellow citizens, when he locks his doors; and of his children and servants, when he locks his chests. Does he not there as much accuse mankind by his actions, as I do by my words? But neither of us accuse man's nature in it. The desires and other passions of man are in themselves no sin. No more are the actions that proceed from those passions, until they know a law that forbids them; which until laws are made they cannot know: nor can any law be made until they have agreed upon the person that shall make it.

To this *war of every man against every man*, this also is consequent; that nothing can be unjust. The notions of right and wrong, justice and injustice, have no place there. Where there is no common power, there is no law: where no law, no injustice. Force and fraud are in war the two cardinal virtues. Justice and injustice are none of the faculties either of the body, nor mind. If they were, they might be in a man that were alone in the world, as well as his senses and passions. They

Edited from *Leviathan,* 1651, Chapters XIII-XV, and XVII, which is now in the public domain.

are qualities that relate to men in society, not in solitude. It is consequent also to the same condition, that there is no propriety, no dominion, no mine and thine distinct; but only that to be every man's that he can get; and for so long as he can keep it. And thus much for the ill condition, which man by mere nature is actually placed in; though with a possibility to come out of it, consisting partly in the passions, partly in his reason.

The passions that incline men to peace are fear of death, desire of such things as are necessary to commodious living, and a hope by their industry to obtain them. And reason suggests convenient Articles of Peace, upon which men may be drawn to agreement. These articles are those which otherwise are called the Laws of Nature.

The Right of Nature is the liberty each man has to use his own power for the preservation of his own nature; that is to say, of his own life; and consequently, of doing anything which in his own judgement and reason he shall conceive to be the most apt means necessary.

By *liberty* is understood the absence of external impediments; impediments which may often take away part of a man's power to do what he would, but cannot hinder him from using the power left him, according as his judgement and reason shall dictate to him.

A law of nature is a precept or general rule found out by reason, by which a man is forbidden to do that which is destructive of his life, or takes away the means of preserving the same; and to omit that by which he thinks it may be best preserved. For though they that speak of this subject, use to confound right and law, yet they ought to be distinguished because *right* consists in liberty to do, or to forbear, whereas *law* determines and binds to one of them, so that law and right differ as much as obligation and liberty; which in one and the same matter are inconsistent.

And because the condition of man is a condition of war of everyone against every one, in which case everyone is governed by his own reason, and there is nothing he can make use of that may not be a help to him in preserving his life against his enemies, it follows that in such a condition, every man has a right to every thing, even to one another's body. And therefore, as long as this natural right of every man to every thing endures, there can be no security to any man (how strong or wise he might be) of living out the time which nature ordinarily allows men to live.

Consequently, it is a precept or general rule of reason, "That every man ought to endeavor peace, as far as he has hope of obtaining it; and when he cannot obtain it, that he may seek, and use, all help and advantages of war." The first branch of this rule contains the first and fundamental law of nature, which is "To seek peace and follow it." The second, the sum of the right of nature, which is "By all means we can, to defend ourselves."

From this fundamental law of nature, by which men are commanded to endeavor peace, is derived this second law: "That a man is willing, when others are so too, for peace and defense of himself he shall think it necessary, to lay down this right to all things, and be content with so much liberty against other men as he would allow other men against himself." For as long as every man holds this right, of doing anything he likes, so long are all men in the condition of war. But if other men will not lay down their right, as well as he, then there is no reason for anyone, to divest himself of his, for that would expose him to prey (which no man is bound to) rather than to dispose himself to peace.

To lay down a man's right to any thing is to divest himself of the liberty of hindering another of the benefit of his own right to the same. For he that renounces or passes away his right gives not to any other man a right which he had not before, because there is nothing to which every man had not right by nature, but only stands out of his way, that he may enjoy his own original right without hindrance from him, not without hindrance from another. So that the effect which redounds to one man by another man's defect of right is but so much diminution of impediments to the use of his own original right.

Right is laid aside, either by simply renouncing it or by transferring it to another. By simply *renouncing*—when he cares not to whom the benefit goes; by *transferring*—when he intends the benefit to some certain person or persons. And when a man has in either manner abandoned, or granted away his right, then is he said to be *obliged* or *bound* not to hinder those to whom such right is granted or abandoned from the benefit of it: and that he *ought*, and it is his *duty*, not to make void that voluntary act of his own: such hindrance is *injustice* and *injury*. So that injury or injustice in the controversies of the world is somewhat like that which in the disputations of scholars is called absurdity. For as an *absurdity* is to contradict what one maintained in the beginning, so in the world it is called *injustice* and *injury*, voluntarily to undo that which from the beginning he had voluntarily done. The way by which a man either simply renounces or transfers his right, is a declaration or signification by some voluntary and sufficient sign or signs that he does so renounce or transfer, or has so renounced or transferred the same, to him that accepts it. And these signs are either words only, or actions only; or (as it happens most often) both words and actions. And these are the *bonds* by which men are bound and obliged. Bonds that have their strength, not from their own nature (for nothing is more easily broken then a man's word) but from fear of some evil consequence upon the rupture.

Whenever a man transfers his right, or renounces it, it is either in consideration of some right reciprocally transferred to himself; or for some other good he hopes to attain. For it is a voluntary act, and of the voluntary acts of every man, the object is some good to himself. Therefore, there are some rights which no man can be understood by any words or other signs to have abandoned or transferred. A man cannot lay down the right of resisting those who assault him by force in order to take away his life, because he cannot be understood to aim to any good to himself. The same may be said of wounds and chains and imprisonment, because there is no benefit consequent to such patience, as there is to the patience of suffering another to be wounded or imprisoned, but also because a man cannot tell, when he sees men proceed against him by violence, whether they intend his death or not. And lastly, the motive and end for which this renouncing and transferring of right is introduced is nothing else but the security of a man's person in his life and in the means of so preserving life, as not to be weary of it. Therefore, if a man by words or other signs seems to despoil himself of the end for which those signs were intended, then he is not to be understood as if he meant it, or that it was his will; but that he was ignorant of how such words and actions were to be interpreted.

The mutual transferring of right is that which men call *contract*. There is a difference between transferring of the right to the thing, and transferring of the thing itself. The thing may be delivered together with the translation of the right, as in buying and selling with money, or exchange of goods or lands, and it may be delivered some time after.

Again, one of the contractors may deliver the thing contracted for on his part, and leave the other to perform his part at some determinate time after, and in the meantime be trusted; and then the contract on his part is called *pact*, or *covenant*: Or both parts may contract now to perform hereafter, in which cases he that is to perform in time to come, being trusted, his performance is called *keeping of promise*, or *faith*; and the failing of performance (if it be voluntary) *violation of faith*.

When the transferring of right is not mutual, but one of the parties transfers in hope to gain friendship or service from another, or from his friends, or in hope to gain the reputation of charity or magnanimity, or to deliver his mind from the pain of compassion, or in hope of reward in heaven, then this is not contract, but a *gift*, *free-gift*, or *grace*, words that signify one and the same thing.

Signs of contract are either expressed or by inference; *expressed* are words spoken with understanding of what they signify, and such words are either of the time present or past, such as

I Give, I Grant, I Have Given, I Have Granted, I Will That This Be Yours, or of the future, such as, *I Will Give, I Will Grant*; which are words of the future and are called *promise.*

Signs by inference are sometimes the consequence of words, sometimes the consequence of silence; sometimes the consequence of actions, sometimes the consequence of forbearing an action, and generally, a sign by inference of any contract is whatsoever sufficiently argues the will of the contractor.

If a covenant is made where neither of the parties perform presently, but trust one another in the condition of mere nature (which is a condition of war of every man against every man) upon any reasonable suspicion it is void. But if there is a common power set over them both, with right and force sufficient to compel performance, then it is not void. For he that performs first has no assurance the other will perform after, because the bonds of words are too weak to bridle men's ambition, avarice, anger, and other passions, without the fear of some coercive power, which in the condition of mere nature where all men are equal, and judges of the justness of their own fears, cannot possibly be supposed. Therefore, he that performs first betrays himself to his enemy, contrary to the right (he can never abandon) of defending his life and means of living.

But in a civil state, where there is a power set up to constrain those that would otherwise violate their faith, that fear is no more reasonable; and for that cause, he who by the covenant is to perform first is obliged so to do.

The cause of fear which makes such a covenant invalid must always be something arising after the covenant made; as some new fact or other sign of the will not to perform, or else it cannot make the covenant void. For that which could not hinder a man from promising, ought not to be admitted as a hindrance of performing.

Whoever transfers any right transfers the means of enjoying it as far as it lies in his power. As he that sells land is understood to transfer whatever grow upon it. Nor can he that sells a mill turn away the stream that drives it. And they that give to a man the right of government in *sovereignty* are understood to give him the right of levying money to maintain soldiers, and of appointing magistrates for the administration of justice.

From that law of nature, by which we are obliged to transfer to another such rights as being retained, hinder the peace of mankind, there follows a third, which is this: "That men perform their covenants made," without which covenants are in vain and but empty words, and the right of all men to all things remaining means that we are still in the condition of war.

And in this law of nature consists the fountain and origin of *justice.* For where no covenant has preceded, no right been transferred, and every man has right to every thing. Consequently, no action can be unjust. But when a covenant is made, then to break it is unjust. The definition of *injustice* is no other than the lack of performance of covenant. And whatsoever is not unjust is just.

The only way to erect such a common power as may be able to defend them from the invasion of foreigners, and the injuries of one another, and thereby to secure them in such sort, as that by their own industry, and by the fruits of the Earth they may nourish themselves and live contentedly is to confer all their power and strength upon one man, or upon one assembly of men, that may reduce all their wills, by plurality of voices unto one will, which is as much as to say, to appoint one man, or assembly of men, to bear their person, and every one to acknowledge himself to be author of whatsoever he that so bears their person, shall act, or cause to be acted, in those things which concerns the *common peace and safety*; and therein to submit their wills, every one to his will, and their judgments to his judgment. This is more than consent, or concord; it is a real unity of them all in one and the same person, made by covenant of every man with every man, in such manner, as if every man should say to every man, "I authorize and give up my right of governing myself to this man, or to this assembly of men, on this condition: that you give up your right to him, and authorize all his actions in like manner." This done, the multitude so united in one person, is called a *commonwealth*. This is the generation of that great *leviathan*, or rather (to speak more reverently) of that *mortal god*, to which we owe under the immortal God our peace and defense. For by this authority, given him by every particular man in the commonwealth, he has the use of so much power and strength conferred on him, that by terror thereof, he is enabled to form the wills of them all to peace at home and mutual aid against their enemies abroad.

In him consists the essence of the commonwealth, which is "One person, of whose acts a great multitude, by mutual covenants one with another, have made themselves every one the author, to the end he may use the strength and means of them all, as he shall think expedient, for their peace and common defense." And he that carries this person is called *sovereign*, and is said to have *sovereign power*; and every one besides, his *subject*.

John Locke

FOR THE GOOD OF THE PEOPLE

Wherever any number of men are so united into one society, as to quit every one his executive power of the law of nature, and to resign it to the public, there and there only is a political, or civil society. For hereby he authorizes the society to make laws for him, as the public good of the society shall require. And this puts men out of a state of nature into that of a commonwealth, by setting up a judge on earth, with authority to determine all the controversies, and redress the injuries that may happen to any member of the commonwealth.

Hence it is evident, that absolute monarchy, which by some men is counted the only government in the world, is indeed inconsistent with civil society, and so can be no form of civil-government at all: for the end of civil society, being to avoid, and remedy those inconveniencies of the state of nature, which necessarily follow from every man's being judge in his own case, by setting up a known authority, to which every one of that society may appeal upon any injury received, or controversy that may arise, and which every one of the society ought to obey; wherever any persons are, who have not such an authority to appeal to, for the decision of any difference between them, there those persons are still in the state of nature; and so is every absolute prince, in respect of those who are under his dominion.

For he being supposed to have all, both legislative and executive power in himself alone, there is no judge to be found, no appeal lies open to any one, who may fairly, and indifferently, and with authority decide, and from whose decision relief and redress may be expected of any injury or inconvenience, that may be suffered from the prince, or by his order: so that such a man, however entitled, Czar, or how you please, is as much in the state of nature, with all under his dominion, as he is with the rest of mankind: for wherever any two men are, who have no standing rule, and common judge to appeal to on earth, for the determination of controversies of right between them, there they are still in the state of nature, and under all the inconveniencies of it, with only this woeful difference to the subject, or rather slave of an absolute prince: that whereas, in the ordinary state of nature, he has a liberty to judge of his right, and according to the best of his power, to maintain it; now, whenever his property is invaded by the will and order of his monarch, he has not only no appeal, as those in society ought to have, but as if he were degraded from the common state of rational creatures, is denied a liberty to judge of, or to defend his right; and so is exposed to all the misery and inconveniencies, that a man can fear from one, who being in the unrestrained state of nature, is yet corrupted with flattery, and armed with power.

If man in the state of Nature be so free, if he be absolute lord of his own person and possessions, equal to the greatest and subject to nobody, why will he part with his freedom, this empire, and subject himself to the dominion and control of any other power? To which it is obvious to answer, that though in the state of Nature he has such a right, yet the enjoyment of it is very uncertain and constantly exposed to the invasion of others; for all being kings as much as he, every man his equal, and the greater part no strict observers of equity and justice, the enjoyment of the property he has in this state is very unsafe, very insecure. This makes him willing to quit this condition which, however free, is full of fears and continual dangers; and it is not without reason that he seeks out and is willing to join in society with others who are already united, or have a mind to unite for the mutual preservation of their lives, liberties and estates, which I call by the general

Edited from *Second Treatise of Civil Government,* 1689, Chapters VII, IX, and XIX, which is now in the public domain.

name—*property*. The great and chief end, therefore, of men uniting into commonwealths, and putting themselves under government, is the preservation of their property; to which in the state of Nature there are many things wanting.

Firstly, there wants an established, settled, known law, received and allowed by common consent to be the standard of right and wrong, and the common measure to decide all controversies between them. For though the law of Nature be plain and intelligible to all rational creatures, yet men, being biased by their interest, as well as ignorant for want of study of it, are not apt to allow of it as a law binding to them in the application of it to their particular cases.

Secondly, in the state of Nature there wants a known and indifferent judge, with authority to determine all differences according to the established law. For every one in that state being both judge and executioner of the law of Nature, men being partial to themselves, passion and revenge is very apt to carry them too far, and with too much heat in their own cases, as well as negligence and unconcernedness, make them too remiss in other men's.

Thirdly, in the state of Nature there often wants power to back and support the sentence when right, and to give it due execution. They who by any injustice offended will seldom fail where they are able by force to make good their injustice. Such resistance many times makes the punishment dangerous, and frequently destructive to those who attempt it.

Thus mankind, notwithstanding all the privileges of the state of Nature, being but in an ill condition while they remain in it are quickly driven into society. Hence it comes to pass, that we seldom find any number of men live any time together in this state. The inconveniencies that they are therein exposed to by the irregular and uncertain exercise of the power every man has of punishing the transgressions of others, make them take sanctuary under the established laws of government, and therein seek the preservation of their property. It is this that makes them so willingly give up every one his single power of punishing to be exercised by such alone as shall be appointed to it amongst them, and by such rules as the community, or those authorized by them to that purpose, shall agree on. And in this we have the original right and rise of both the legislative and executive power as well as of the governments and societies themselves.

For in the state of Nature to omit the liberty he has of innocent delights, a man has two powers. The first is to do whatsoever he thinks fit for the preservation of himself and others within the permission of the law of Nature; by which law, common to them all, he and all the rest of mankind are one community, make up one society distinct from all other creatures, and were it not for the corruption and viciousness of degenerate men, there would be no need of any other, no necessity that men should separate from this great and natural community, and associate into lesser combinations. The other power a man has in the state of Nature is the power to punish the crimes committed against that law. Both these he gives up when he joins in a private, if I may so call it, or particular political society, and incorporates into any commonwealth separate from the rest of mankind.

The first power, namely, of doing whatsoever he thought fit for the preservation of himself and the rest of mankind, he gives up to be regulated by laws made by the society, so far forth as the preservation of himself and the rest of that society shall require; which laws of the society in many things confine the liberty he had by the law of Nature.

Secondly, the power of punishing he wholly gives up, and engages his natural force, which he might before employ in the execution of the law of Nature, by his own single authority, as he thought fit, to assist the executive power of the society as the law thereof shall require. For being now in a new state, wherein he is to enjoy many conveniences from the labor, assistance, and society of others in the same community, as well as protection from its whole strength, he is to part also with as much of his natural liberty, in providing for himself, as the good, prosperity, and safety of the society shall require, which is not only necessary but just, since the other members of the society do the like.

But though men when they enter into society give up the equality, liberty, and executive power they had in the state of Nature into the hands of the society, to be so far disposed of by the legislative as the good of the society shall require, yet it being only with an intention in every one the better to preserve himself, his liberty and property (for no rational creature can be supposed to change his condition with an intention to be worse), the power of the society or legislative constituted by them can never be supposed to extend farther than the common good, but is obliged to secure everyone's property by providing against those three defects above mentioned that made the state of Nature so unsafe and uneasy. And so, whoever has the legislative or supreme power of any commonwealth, is bound to govern by established standing laws, promulgated and known to the people, and not by extemporary decrees, by indifferent and upright judges, who are to decide controversies by those laws; and to employ the force of the community at home only in the execution of such laws, or abroad to prevent or redress foreign injuries and secure the community from inroads and invasion. And all this to be directed to no other end but the peace, safety, and public good of the people.

The reason why men enter into society is the preservation of their property; and the end why they choose and authorize a legislative is that there may be laws made, and rules set, as guards and fences to the properties of all the members of the society, to limit the power, and moderate the dominion, of every part and member of the society: for since it can never be supposed to be the will of the society, that the legislative should have a power to destroy that which every one designs to secure, by entering into society, and for which the people submitted themselves to legislators of their own making; whenever the legislators endeavor to take away, and destroy the property of the people, or to reduce them to slavery under arbitrary power, they put themselves into a state of war with the people, who are thereupon absolved from any farther obedience, and are left to the common refuge, which God hath provided for all men, against force and violence. Whenever therefore the legislative shall transgress this fundamental rule of society; and either by ambition, fear, folly or corruption, endeavor to grasp themselves, or put into the hands of any other, an absolute power over the lives, liberties, and estates of the people; by this breach of trust they forfeit the power the people had put into their hands for quite contrary ends, and it devolves to the people, who have a right to resume their original liberty, and, by the establishment of a new legislative, provide for their own safety and security, which is the end for which they are in society. What I have said here, concerning the legislative in general, holds true also concerning the supreme executor, who having a double trust put in him, both to have a part in the legislative, and the supreme execution of the law, acts against both, when he goes about to set up his own arbitrary will as the law of the society. He acts also contrary to his trust, when he either employs the force, treasure, and offices of the society, to corrupt the representatives, and gain them to his purposes; or openly engages the electors, and prescribes to their choice, such, whom he has, by solicitations, threats, promises, or otherwise, won to his designs; and employs them to bring in such, who have promised beforehand what to vote, and what to enact.

To conclude, the power that every individual gave the society, when he entered into it, can never revert to the individuals again, as long as the society lasts, but will always remain in the community; because without this there can be no community, no commonwealth, which is contrary to the original agreement: so also when the society has placed the legislative in any assembly of men, to continue in them and their successors, with direction and authority for providing such successors, the legislative can never revert to the people while that government lasts; because having provided a legislative with power to continue forever, they have given up their political power to the legislative, and cannot resume it. But if they have set limits to the duration of their legislative, and made this supreme power in any person, or assembly, only temporary, or else, when by the miscarriages of those in authority, it is forfeited; upon the forfeiture, or at the determination of the time set, it reverts to the society, and the people have a right to act as supreme, and continue the legislative in themselves, or erect a new form, or under the old form place it in new hands, as they think good.

Catharine Macaulay

OBSERVATIONS ON REVOLUTION

However strongly the warm friends of freedom might wish that this abstract right of the people, of choosing their own magistrates, and deposing them for ill conduct, had been laid open to the public by a formal declaration of such a right in the acts of succession, this certainly was not a period of time for carrying these wishes into execution.

It is not my intention to make any formal comparison between the new constitution of France, and the present existing constitution of England; or to presume to censure a government, from which an industrious people receive protection, and with which the large majority of the nation are entirely satisfied. Yet it may not be inexpedient to observe, that we cannot with any grounds of reason or propriety, set up our own constitution as the model which all other nations ought implicitly to follow, unless we are certain that it bestows the greatest possible happiness on the people which in the nature of things any government can bestow. We ought to be certain, that this model will bear the most critical examination. It ought to be void of any of those obvious, or more concealed causes, which produce present evils, and carry the mind to apprehensions of future mischiefs. We ought not at least to have had a national debt, swelled to a magnitude which terrifies even the most sanguine for its consequences. Our parliaments ought to have been eminently distinguished for their integrity, and a total independence of any corrupt influence; and no necessity ought to have existed in our affairs, which have obliged us to endure imposts which our ancestors would have rejected with horror, and resisted. If an Englishman sees any thing which is amiss in his own government, he ought not undoubtedly to look forward to any other remedy than those which the lenient hand of reformation will supply. But when the old vessel of a commonwealth is torn to pieces by the shocks it has sustained from contending parties; when the people, disdaining and rejecting all those fond opinions by which they have been enslaved to misery, assert their native right of forming a government for themselves; surely in such a case the builders are bound by no law of duty or reason to make use of these old materials in the structure of their new constitution, which they suppose to have been of an injurious tendency.

The legitimate power by which governments are made or altered, must either stand on the native rights of the species, or it must stand on an authority vested in an individual, or in a limited number of individuals, exalted to this authority, either by the positive law of a revealed will, or by some native superiority evidently attached to their persons. That this sacred trust has never been so formally vested in any individual, or in any given number of individuals, is in a manner acknowledged by the most strenuous advocates for passive obedience; for all their arguments are built on presumptive grounds.

The contrary proposition to this, namely, that native right in the social body to choose its own government, which Mr. Burke condemns under the description of a metaphysical foolery, is allowed with all its weight of authority by the greatest part of the English Revolutionists; nor can any other reasonable ground of persuasion be made use of, to bring the people to concur in any plan of salutary or necessary reformation. With what pretense then, can Mr. Burke charge Dr. Price, or any of his adherents or admirers, with advancing a novel or a mischievous doctrine, when they assert that all legitimate power is founded on the rights of nature?

Edited from *Observations on the Reflections of the Right Hon. Edmund Burke, on the Revolution in France*, 1791, which is now in the public domain.

> But government (says Mr. Burke) is not made in virtue of natural rights, which may and do exist in total independence of it; and exist in much greater clearness, and in a much greater degree of abstract perfection; but their abstract perfection is their practical defect. By having a right to every thing, they want every thing. Government is a contrivance of human wisdom, to provide for human wants. Men have a right that these wants should be provided for by this wisdom. Among these wants is to be reckoned the want out of a civil society, of a sufficient restraint upon their passions. Society requires not only that the passions of individuals should be subjected, but even in the mass and body, as well as in the individuals, the inclinations of men should frequently be thwarted, their will controlled, and their passions brought into subjection. This can only be done by a power out of themselves, and not in the exercise of its functions, subject to that will, and to those passions, which it is in its office to bridle and subdue. In this sense, the restraints of men, as well as their liberties, are to be reckoned among their rights.

To this very ingenious reasoning, and these refined distinctions between natural and social rights, the people may possibly object, that in delivering themselves passively over to the unrestrained rule of others on the plea of controlling their inordinate inclinations and passions, they deliver themselves over to men, who, as men, and partaking of the same nature as themselves, are as liable to be governed by the same principles and errors; and to men who, by the great superiority of their station, having no common interest with themselves which might lead them to preserve a salutary check over their vices, must be inclined to abuse in the grossest manner their trust. To proceed with Mr. Burke's argument—should the rich and opulent in the nation plead their right to the predominant sway in society, from its being a necessary circumstance to guard their wealth from the gripe of poverty, the men in an inferior state of fortune might argue, that should they give way to this plea in all its extent, their moderate possessions would be exposed to the burden of unequal taxes; for the rich, when possessed of the whole authority of the state, would be sure to take the first care of themselves, if they should not be tempted to secure an exoneration of all burthens, by dividing the spoils of the public; and that the abuse of such high trusts must necessarily arise, because to act by selfish considerations, is in the very constitution of our nature.

To such pleas, so plausibly urged on all sides, I know of no rational objection; nor can I think of any expedient to remove the well grounded apprehensions of the different interests which compose a commonwealth, than a fair and equal representation of the whole people—a circumstance which appears very peculiarly necessary in a mixed form of government, where the democratic part of the constitution will ever be in danger of being overborne by the energy attending on its higher constituent parts.

On such grounds of reasoning, there will be found no insuperable objections to those propositions of Dr. Price, which are so highly censured by Mr. Burke, as containing principles of the most seditious and dangerous nature; even though we should allow that every government which accords with the opinions and the inclinations of the large majority of the people, is, in an high sense of the term, a legitimate government.

But this is not the point of view in which the friends of equal representation see the necessity of a reform. The subject of their complaint is, that the important interests of the great body of the Commons is, by our present inadequate state of representation, sacrificed to the ambition of private individuals, who by their command over boroughs, may make their market with government at the expense of the public. The strong and firm opposition which the ruling powers have given to every step towards this reasonable reformation, is not one of the happiest effects which arise from that continual war of interests so much admired by Mr. Burke and others. The jealousy it manifests of the people, is without all bounds of moderation; for the organ by which the democratic influence is exerted, has no very formidable energy. Its power is circumscribed and shut in by the immoveable barrier of laws, usages, positive rules of doctrine and practice, counterpoised by the House of Lords, and in a manner subjected to the Crown by the prerogative of calling and dissolving parliaments.

Thus, in every light in which we can place the argument, in every possible mode of reasoning, we shall be driven back to elect either the first or the second of these propositions; either that an individual, or some privileged persons, have an inherent and indefeasible right to make laws for the community, or that this authority rests in the unalienable and indefeasible rights of man.

That the people have often abused their power, it must be granted; for they have often sacrificed themselves and their posterity to the wanton will of an individual, and this is the foundation of all the regal tyrannies which have subsisted in society; but no abuse of their power can take away their right, because their right exists in the very constitution of things. If the French people therefore should be so capricious as to fling off their new constitution, and subject themselves to more unequal forms of government, or even to tyranny, it will be agreeable to the course of past experience. But such an exertion of power cannot injure their right; and whatever form or complexion any future government in France may bear, it can have no legitimate source, but in the will of the people.

John Stuart Mill

LIBERTY

The subject of this Essay is not the so-called Liberty of the Will, so unfortunately opposed to the misnamed doctrine of Philosophical Necessity; but Civil, or Social Liberty: the nature and limits of the power which can be legitimately exercised by society over the individual. A question seldom stated, and hardly ever discussed, in general terms, but which profoundly influences the practical controversies of the age by its latent presence, and is likely soon to make itself recognized as the vital question of the future. It is so far from being new, that in a certain sense, it has divided mankind, almost from the remotest ages; but in the stage of progress into which the more civilized portions of the species have now entered, it presents itself under new conditions, and requires a different and more fundamental treatment.

The struggle between Liberty and Authority is the most conspicuous feature in the portions of history with which we are earliest familiar, particularly in that of Greece, Rome, and England. But in old times this contest was between subjects, or some classes of subjects, and the government. By liberty, was meant protection against the tyranny of the political rulers. The rulers were conceived (except in some of the popular governments of Greece) as in a necessarily antagonistic position to the people whom they ruled. They consisted of a governing One, or a governing tribe or caste, who derived their authority from inheritance or conquest, who, at all events, did not hold it at the pleasure of the governed, and whose supremacy men did not venture, perhaps did not desire, to contest, whatever precautions might be taken against its oppressive exercise. Their power was regarded as necessary, but also as highly dangerous; as a weapon which they would attempt to use against their subjects, no less than against external enemies. To prevent the weaker members of the community from being preyed upon by innumerable vultures, it was needful that there should be an animal of prey stronger than the rest, commissioned to keep them down. But as the king of the vultures would be no less bent upon preying on the flock than any of the minor harpies, it was indispensable to be in a perpetual attitude of defense against his beak and claws. The aim, therefore, of patriots, was to set limits to the power which the ruler should be suffered to exercise over the community; and this limitation was what they meant by liberty. It was attempted in two ways. First, by obtaining a recognition of certain immunities, called political liberties or rights, which it was to be regarded as a breach of duty in the ruler to infringe, and which if he did infringe, specific resistance, or general rebellion, was held to be justifiable. A second, and generally a later expedient, was the establishment of constitutional checks; by which the consent of the community, or of a body of some sort, supposed to represent its interests, was made a necessary condition to some of the more important acts of the governing power. To the first of these modes of limitation, the ruling power, in most European countries, was compelled, more or less, to submit. It was not so with the second; and to attain this, or when already in some degree possessed, to attain it more completely, became everywhere the principal object of the lovers of liberty. And so long as mankind were content to combat one enemy by another, and to be ruled by a master, on condition of being guaranteed more or less efficaciously against his tyranny, they did not carry their aspirations beyond this point.

A time, however, came, in the progress of human affairs, when men ceased to think it a necessity of nature that their governors should be an independent power, opposed in interest to

Edited from *On Liberty,* 1859, Chapter I, which is now in the public domain.

themselves. It appeared to them much better that the various magistrates of the State should be their tenants or delegates, revocable at their pleasure. In that way alone, it seemed, could they have complete security that the powers of government would never be abused to their disadvantage. By degrees, this new demand for elective and temporary rulers became the prominent object of the exertions of the popular party, wherever any such party existed; and superseded, to a considerable extent, the previous efforts to limit the power of rulers. As the struggle proceeded for making the ruling power emanate from the periodical choice of the ruled, some persons began to think that too much importance had been attached to the limitation of the power itself. That (it might seem) was a resource against rulers whose interests were habitually opposed to those of the people. What was now wanted was, that the rulers should be identified with the people; that their interest and will should be the interest and will of the nation. The nation did not need to be protected against its own will. There was no fear of its tyrannizing over itself. Let the rulers be effectually responsible to it, promptly removable by it, and it could afford to trust them with power of which it could itself dictate the use to be made. Their power was but the nation's own power, concentrated, and in a form convenient for exercise.

But, in political and philosophical theories, as well as in persons, success discloses faults and infirmities which failure might have concealed from observation. The notion, that the people have no need to limit their power over themselves, might seem axiomatic, when popular government was a thing only dreamed about, or read of as having existed at some distant period of the past. Neither was that notion necessarily disturbed by such temporary aberrations as those of the French Revolution, the worst of which were the work of a usurping few, and which, in any case, belonged, not to the permanent working of popular institutions, but to a sudden and convulsive outbreak against monarchical and aristocratic despotism. In time, however, a democratic republic came to occupy a large portion of the earth's surface, and made itself felt as one of the most powerful members of the community of nations; and elective and responsible government became subject to the observations and criticisms which wait upon a great existing fact. It was now perceived that such phrases as "self-government," and "the power of the people over themselves," do not express the true state of the case. The "people" who exercise the power are not always the same people with those over whom it is exercised; and the "self-government" spoken of is not the government of each by himself, but of each by all the rest. The will of the people, moreover, practically means, the will of the most numerous or the most active *part* of the people; the majority, or those who succeed in making themselves accepted as the majority: the people, consequently, *may* desire to oppress a part of their number; and precautions are as much needed against this, as against any other abuse of power. The limitation, therefore, of the power of government over individuals, loses none of its importance when the holders of power are regularly accountable to the community, that is, to the strongest party therein. This view of things, recommending itself equally to the intelligence of thinkers and to the inclination of those important classes in European society to whose real or supposed interests democracy is adverse, has had no difficulty in establishing itself; and in political speculations "the tyranny of the majority" is now generally included among the evils against which society requires to be on its guard.

Like other tyrannies, the tyranny of the majority was at first, and is still vulgarly, held in dread, chiefly as operating through the acts of the public authorities. But reflecting persons perceived that when society is itself the tyrant—society collectively, over the separate individuals who compose it—its means of tyrannizing are not restricted to the acts which it may do by the hands of its political functionaries. Society can and does execute its own mandates: and if it issues wrong mandates instead of right, or any mandates at all in things with which it ought not to meddle, it practices a social tyranny more formidable than many kinds of political oppression, since, though not usually upheld by such extreme penalties, it leaves fewer means of escape, penetrating much more deeply into the details of life, and enslaving the soul itself. Protection, therefore, against the tyranny of the magistrate is not enough: there needs protection also against the tyranny of the prevailing opinion and feeling; against the tendency of society to impose, by other means than civil penalties, its own ideas and practices as rules of conduct on those who dissent from them; to fetter the development, and, if possible, prevent the formation, of any individuality not in harmony with its ways, and compel all characters to fashion themselves upon the model of its own.

There is a limit to the legitimate interference of collective opinion with individual independence: and to find that limit, and maintain it against encroachment, is as indispensable to a good condition of human affairs, as protection against political despotism. But though this proposition is not likely to be contested in general terms, the practical question, where to place the limit—how to make the fitting adjustment between individual independence and social control—is a subject on which nearly everything remains to be done. All that makes existence valuable to any one, depends on the enforcement of restraints upon the actions of other people. Some rules of conduct, therefore, must be imposed, by law in the first place, and by opinion on many things which are not fit subjects for the operation of law. What these rules should be, is the principal question in human affairs; but if we except a few of the most obvious cases, it is one of those which least progress has been made in resolving. No two ages, and scarcely any two countries, have decided it alike; and the decision of one age or country is a wonder to another. Yet the people of any given age and country no more suspect any difficulty in it, than if it were a subject on which mankind had always been agreed. The rules which obtain among themselves appear to them self-evident and self-justifying. This all but universal illusion is one of the examples of the magical influence of custom, which is not only, as the proverb says, a second nature, but is continually mistaken for the first. The effect of custom, in preventing any misgiving respecting the rules of conduct which mankind impose on one another, is all the more complete because the subject is one on which it is not generally considered necessary that reasons should be given, either by one person to others, or by each to himself. People are accustomed to believe, and have been encouraged in the belief by some who aspire to the character of philosophers, that their feelings, on subjects of this nature, are better than reasons, and render reasons unnecessary. The practical principle which guides them to their opinions on the regulation of human conduct, is the feeling in each person's mind that everybody should be required to act as he, and those with whom he sympathizes, would like them to act. No one, indeed, acknowledges to himself that his standard of judgment is his own liking; but an opinion on a point of conduct, not supported by reasons, can only count as one person's preference; and if the reasons, when given, are a mere appeal to a similar preference felt by other people, it is still only many people's liking instead of one. To an ordinary man, however, his own preference, thus supported, is not only a perfectly satisfactory reason, but the only one he generally has for any of his notions of morality, taste, or propriety, which are not expressly written in his religious creed; and his chief guide in the interpretation even of that. Men's opinions, accordingly, on what is laudable or blamable, are affected by all the multifarious causes which influence their wishes in regard to the conduct of others, and which are as numerous as those which determine their wishes on any other subject. Sometimes their reason, at other times their prejudices or superstitions, often their social affections, not seldom their anti-social ones, their envy or jealousy, their arrogance or contemptuousness: but most commonly, their desires or fears for themselves, their legitimate or illegitimate self-interest.

Wherever there is an ascendant class, a large portion of the morality of the country emanates from its class interests, and its feelings of class superiority. The morality between Spartans and Helots, between planters and negroes, between princes and subjects, between nobles and roturiers [those who are not of noble birth], between men and women, has been for the most part the creation of these class interests and feelings: and the sentiments thus generated, react in turn upon the moral feelings of the members of the ascendant class, in their relations among themselves. Where, on the other hand, a class, formerly ascendant, has lost its ascendancy, or where its ascendancy is unpopular, the prevailing moral sentiments frequently bear the impress of an impatient dislike of superiority.

Another grand determining principle of the rules of conduct, both in act and forbearance, which have been enforced by law or opinion, has been the servility of mankind towards the supposed preferences or aversions of their temporal masters, or of their gods. This servility, though essentially selfish, is not hypocrisy; it gives rise to perfectly genuine sentiments of abhorrence; it made men burn magicians and heretics. Among so many baser influences, the general and obvious interests of society have of course had a share, and a large one, in the direction of the moral sentiments: less, however, as a matter of reason, and on their own account, than as a consequence of the sympathies and antipathies which grew out of them: and sympathies and antipathies which had little or nothing to do with the interests of society, have made themselves felt in the establishment of moralities with quite as great force.

The likings and dislikings of society, or of some powerful portion of it, are thus the main thing which has practically determined the rules laid down for general observance, under the penalties of law or opinion. And in general, those who have been in advance of society in thought and feeling have left this condition of things unassailed in principle, however they may have come into conflict with it in some of its details. They have occupied themselves rather in inquiring what things society ought to like or dislike, than in questioning whether its likings or dislikings should be a law to individuals. They preferred endeavoring to alter the feelings of mankind on the particular points on which they were themselves heretical, rather than make common cause in defense of freedom, with heretics generally. The only case in which the higher ground has been taken on principle and maintained with consistency, by any but an individual here and there, is that of religious belief: a case instructive in many ways, and not least so as forming a most striking instance of the fallibility of what is called the moral sense: for the *odium theologicum* [hatred between those holding different religious beliefs], in a sincere bigot, is one of the most unequivocal cases of moral feeling. Those who first broke the yoke of what called itself the Universal Church, were in general as little willing to permit difference of religious opinion as that church itself. But when the heat of the conflict was over, without giving a complete victory to any party, and each church or sect was reduced to limit its hopes to retaining possession of the ground it already occupied; minorities, seeing that they had no chance of becoming majorities, were under the necessity of pleading to those whom they could not convert, for permission to differ. It is accordingly on this battle-field, almost solely, that the rights of the individual against society have been asserted on broad grounds of principle, and the claim of society to exercise authority over dissentients, openly controverted. The great writers to whom the world owes what religious liberty it possesses, have mostly asserted freedom of conscience as an indefeasible right, and denied absolutely that a human being is accountable to others for his religious belief. Yet so natural to mankind is intolerance in whatever they really care about, that religious freedom has hardly anywhere been practically realized, except where religious indifference, which dislikes to have its peace disturbed by theological quarrels, has added its weight to the scale. In the minds of almost all religious persons, even in the most tolerant countries, the duty of toleration is admitted with tacit reserves. One person will bear with dissent in matters of church government, but not of dogma; another can tolerate everybody, short of a Papist or a Unitarian; another, every one who believes in revealed religion; a few extend their charity a little further, but stop at the belief in a God and in a future state. Wherever the sentiment of the majority is still genuine and intense, it is found to have abated little of its claim to be obeyed.

In England, from the peculiar circumstances of our political history, though the yoke of opinion is perhaps heavier, that of law is lighter, than in most other countries of Europe; and there is considerable jealousy of direct interference, by the legislative or the executive power, with private conduct; not so much from any just regard for the independence of the individual, as from the still subsisting habit of looking on the government as representing an opposite interest to the public. The majority have not yet learnt to feel the power of the government their power, or its opinions their opinions. When they do so, individual liberty will probably be as much exposed to invasion from the government, as it already is from public opinion. But, as yet, there is a considerable amount of feeling ready to be called forth against any attempt of the law to control individuals in things in which they have not hitherto been accustomed to be controlled by it; and this with very little discrimination as to whether the matter is, or is not, within the legitimate sphere of legal control; insomuch that the feeling, highly salutary on the whole, is perhaps quite as often misplaced as well grounded in the particular instances of its application. There is, in fact, no recognized principle by which the propriety or impropriety of government interference is customarily tested. People decide according to their personal preferences. Some, whenever they see any good to be done, or evil to be remedied, would willingly instigate the government to undertake the business; while others prefer to bear almost any amount of social evil, rather than add one to the departments of human interests amenable to governmental control. And men range themselves on one or the other side in any particular case, according to this general direction of their sentiments; or according to the degree of interest which they feel in the particular thing which it is proposed that the government should do, or according to the belief they entertain that the government would, or would not, do it in the manner they prefer; but very rarely on account of any opinion to which they consistently adhere, as to what things are fit to be done by a government. And it seems to me that in consequence of this absence of rule or principle, one side is at present as often wrong as the other; the interference of government is, with about equal frequency, improperly invoked and improperly condemned.

The object of this essay is to assert one very simple principle, as entitled to govern absolutely the dealings of society with the individual in the way of compulsion and control, whether the means used be physical force in the form of legal penalties, or the moral coercion of public opinion. *That principle is, that the sole end for which mankind are warranted, individually or collectively, in interfering with the liberty of action of any of their number, is self-protection. That the only purpose for which power can be rightfully exercised over any member of a civilized community, against his will, is to prevent harm to others.* His own good, either physical or moral, is not a sufficient warrant. He cannot rightfully be compelled to do or forbear because it will be better for him to do so, because it will make him happier, because, in the opinions of others, to do so would be wise, or even right. These are good reasons for remonstrating with him, or reasoning with him, or persuading him, or entreating him, but not for compelling him, or visiting him with any evil in case he do otherwise. To justify that, the conduct from which it is desired to deter him must be calculated to produce evil to some one else. The only part of the conduct of any one, for which he is amenable to society, is that which concerns others. In the part which merely concerns himself, his independence is, of right, absolute. Over himself, over his own body and mind, the individual is sovereign.

It is, perhaps, hardly necessary to say that this doctrine is meant to apply only to human beings in the maturity of their faculties. We are not speaking of children, or of young persons below the age which the law may fix as that of manhood or womanhood. Those who are still in a state to require being taken care of by others, must be protected against their own actions as well as against external injury. For the same reason, we may leave out of consideration those backward states of society in which the race itself may be considered as in its nonage. The early difficulties in the way of spontaneous progress are so great, that there is seldom any choice of means for overcoming them; and a ruler full of the spirit of improvement is warranted in the use of any expedients that will attain an end, perhaps otherwise unattainable. Despotism is a legitimate mode of government in dealing with barbarians, provided the end be their improvement, and the means justified by actually effecting that end. Liberty, as a principle, has no application to any state of things anterior to the time when mankind have become capable of being improved by free and equal discussion. Until then, there is nothing for them but implicit obedience to an Akbar or a Charlemagne, if they are so fortunate as to find one. But as soon as mankind have attained the capacity of being guided to their own improvement by conviction or persuasion (a period long since reached in all nations with whom we need here concern ourselves), compulsion, either in the direct form or in that of pains and penalties for non-compliance, is no longer admissible as a means to their own good, and justifiable only for the security of others.

It is proper to state that I forego any advantage which could be derived to my argument from the idea of abstract right, as a thing independent of utility. I regard utility as the ultimate appeal on all ethical questions; but it must be utility in the largest sense, grounded on the permanent interests of man as a progressive being. Those interests, I contend, authorize the subjection of individual spontaneity to external control, only in respect to those actions of each, which concern the interest of other people. If any one does an act hurtful to others, there is a *prima facie* case for punishing him, by law, or, where legal penalties are not safely applicable, by general disapprobation. There are also many positive acts for the benefit of others, which he may rightfully be compelled to perform; such as, to give evidence in a court of justice; to bear his fair share in the common defense, or in any other joint work necessary to the interest of the society of which he enjoys the protection; and to perform certain acts of individual beneficence, such as saving a fellow-creature's life, or interposing to protect the defenseless against ill-usage, things which whenever it is obviously a man's duty to do, he may rightfully be made responsible to society for not doing. A person may cause evil to others not only by his actions but by his inaction, and in either case he is justly accountable to them for the injury. The latter case, it is true, requires a much more cautious exercise of compulsion than the former. To make any one answerable for doing evil to others, is the rule; to make him answerable for not preventing evil, is, comparatively speaking, the exception. Yet there are many cases clear enough and grave enough to justify that exception. In all things which regard the external relations of the individual, he is *de jure* [by right, according to law] amenable to those whose interests are concerned, and if need be, to society as their protector. There are often good reasons for not holding him to the responsibility; but these reasons must arise from the special expediencies of the case: either because it is a kind of case in which he is on the whole likely to act better, when left to his own discretion, than when controlled in any way in which society have it in their power to control him; or because the attempt to exercise control would produce other evils, greater than those which it would prevent. When such reasons as these preclude the enforcement of responsibility, the conscience of the agent himself should step into the vacant judgment seat, and protect those interests of others which have no external protection; judging himself all the more rigidly, because the case does not admit of his being made accountable to the judgment of his fellow-creatures.

But there is a sphere of action in which society, as distinguished from the individual, has, if any, only an indirect interest; comprehending all that portion of a person's life and conduct which affects only himself, or if it also affects others, only with their free, voluntary, and undeceived consent and participation. When I say only himself, I mean directly, and in the first instance: for whatever affects himself, may affect others *through* himself; and the objection which may be grounded on this contingency, will receive consideration in the sequel. This, then, is the appropriate region of human liberty. It comprises, first, the inward domain of consciousness; demanding liberty of conscience, in the most comprehensive sense; liberty of thought and feeling; absolute freedom of opinion and sentiment on all subjects, practical or speculative, scientific, moral, or theological. The liberty of expressing and publishing opinions may seem to fall under a different principle, since it belongs to that part of the conduct of an individual which concerns other people; but, being almost of as much importance as the liberty of thought itself, and resting in great part on the same reasons, is practically inseparable from it. Secondly, the principle requires liberty of tastes and pursuits; of framing the plan of our life to suit our own character; of doing as we like, subject to such consequences as may follow: without impediment from our fellow-creatures, so long as what we do does not harm them, even though they should think our conduct foolish, perverse, or wrong. Thirdly, from this liberty of each individual, follows the liberty, within the same limits, of combination among individuals; freedom to unite, for any purpose not involving harm to others: the persons combining being supposed to be of full age, and not forced or deceived.

No society in which these liberties are not, on the whole, respected, is free, whatever may be its form of government; and none is completely free in which they do not exist absolute and unqualified. The only freedom which deserves the name, is that of pursuing our own good in our own way, so long as we do not attempt to deprive others of theirs, or impede their efforts to obtain it. Each is the proper guardian of his own health, whether bodily, or mental and spiritual. Mankind are greater gainers by suffering each other to live as seems good to themselves, than by compelling each to live as seems good to the rest.

Though this doctrine is anything but new, and, to some persons, may have the air of a truism, there is no doctrine which stands more directly opposed to the general tendency of existing opinion and practice. Society has expended fully as much effort in the attempt (according to its lights) to compel people to conform to its notions of personal, as of social excellence. The ancient commonwealths thought themselves entitled to practice, and the ancient philosophers countenanced, the regulation of every part of private conduct by public authority, on the ground that the State had a deep interest in the whole bodily and mental discipline of every one of its citizens; a mode of thinking which may have been admissible in small republics surrounded by powerful enemies, in constant peril of being subverted by foreign attack or internal commotion, and to which even a short interval of relaxed energy and self-command might so easily be fatal, that they could not afford to wait for the salutary permanent effects of freedom. In the modern world, the greater size of political communities, and above all, the separation between spiritual and temporal authority (which placed the direction of men's consciences in other hands than those which controlled their worldly affairs), prevented so great an interference by law in the details of private life; but the engines of moral repression have been wielded more strenuously against divergence from the reigning opinion in self-regarding, than even in social matters; religion, the most powerful of the elements which have entered into the formation of moral feeling, having almost always been governed either by the ambition of a hierarchy, seeking control over every department of human conduct, or by the spirit of Puritanism. And some of those modern reformers who have placed themselves in strongest opposition to the religions of the past, have been no way behind either churches or sects in their assertion of the right of spiritual domination: M. Comte, in particular, whose social system, as unfolded in his *The System of Positive Polity*, aims at establishing (though by moral more than by legal appliances) a despotism of society over the individual, surpassing anything contemplated in the political ideal of the most rigid disciplinarian among the ancient philosophers.

Apart from the peculiar tenets of individual thinkers, there is also in the world at large an increasing inclination to stretch unduly the powers of society over the individual, both by the force of opinion and even by that of legislation: and as the tendency of all the changes taking place in the world is to strengthen society, and diminish the power of the individual, this encroachment is not one of the evils which tend spontaneously to disappear, but, on the contrary, to grow more and more formidable. The disposition of mankind, whether as rulers or as fellow-citizens to impose their own opinions and inclinations as a rule of conduct on others, is so energetically supported by some of the best and by some of the worst feelings incident to human nature, that it is hardly ever kept under restraint by anything but want of power; and as the power is not declining, but growing, unless a strong barrier of moral conviction can be raised against the mischief, we must expect, in the present circumstances of the world, to see it increase.

Karl Marx and Friedrich Engels

WORKERS OF THE WORLD, UNITE!

A spectre is haunting Europe—the spectre of communism. All the powers of old Europe have entered into a holy alliance to exorcise this spectre. Where is the party in opposition that has not been decried as communistic by its opponents in power? Where is the opposition that has not hurled back the branding reproach of communism, against the more advanced opposition parties, as well as against its reactionary adversaries?

Two things result from this fact: 1. Communism is already acknowledged by all European powers to be itself a power; 2. It is high time that Communists should openly, in the face of the whole world, publish their views, their aims, their tendencies, and meet this nursery tale of the Spectre of Communism with a manifesto of the party itself.

The history of all hitherto existing society is the history of class struggles. Freeman and slave, patrician and plebeian, lord and serf, guild-master and journeyman, in a word, oppressor and oppressed, stood in constant opposition to one another, carried on an uninterrupted, now hidden, now open fight, a fight that each time ended, either in a revolutionary reconstitution of society at large, or in the common ruin of the contending classes.

In the earlier epochs of history, we find almost everywhere a complicated arrangement of society into various orders, a manifold gradation of social rank. In ancient Rome, we have patricians, knights, plebeians, slaves; in the Middle Ages, feudal lords, vassals, guild-masters, journeymen, apprentices, serfs; in almost all of these classes, again, subordinate gradations.

The modern bourgeois society that has sprouted from the ruins of feudal society has not done away with class antagonisms. It has but established new classes, new conditions of oppression, new forms of struggle in place of the old ones.

Our epoch, the epoch of the bourgeoisie, possesses, however, this distinct feature: it has simplified class antagonisms. Society as a whole is more and more splitting up into two great hostile camps, into two great classes directly facing each other: Bourgeoisie and Proletariat.

From the serfs of the Middle Ages sprang the chartered burghers of the earliest towns. From these burgesses the first elements of the bourgeoisie were developed. The discovery of America, the rounding of the Cape, opened up fresh ground for the rising bourgeoisie. The East-Indian and Chinese markets, the colonisation of America, trade with the colonies, the increase in the means of exchange and in commodities generally, gave to commerce, to navigation, to industry, an impulse never before known, and thereby, to the revolutionary element in the tottering feudal society, a rapid development.

The feudal system of industry, in which industrial production was monopolised by closed guilds, now no longer sufficed for the growing wants of the new markets. The manufacturing system took its place. The guild-masters were pushed on one side by the manufacturing middle class; division of labor between the different corporate guilds vanished in the face of division of labor in each single workshop.

Meantime, the markets kept ever growing, the demand ever rising. Even manufacturers no longer sufficed. Thereupon, steam and machinery revolutionised industrial production. The place of manufacture was taken by the giant, Modern Industry; the place of the industrial middle class by industrial millionaires, the leaders of the whole industrial armies, the modern bourgeois.

Edited from *Manifesto of the Communist Party*, 1888, Chapters I, II, and IV, which is now in the public domain.

Modern industry has established the world market, for which the discovery of America paved the way. This market has given an immense development to commerce, to navigation, to communication by land. This development has, in its turn, reacted on the extension of industry; and in proportion as industry, commerce, navigation, railways extended, in the same proportion the bourgeoisie developed, increased its capital, and pushed into the background every class handed down from the Middle Ages. We see, therefore, how the modern bourgeoisie is itself the product of a long course of development, of a series of revolutions in the modes of production and of exchange.

The bourgeoisie, wherever it has got the upper hand, has put an end to all feudal, patriarchal, idyllic relations. It has pitilessly torn asunder the motley feudal ties that bound man to his "natural superiors," and has left remaining no other nexus between man and man than naked self-interest, than callous "cash payment." It has drowned the most heavenly ecstasies of religious fervor, of chivalrous enthusiasm, of philistine sentimentalism, in the icy water of egotistical calculation. It has resolved personal worth into exchange value, and in place of the numberless indefeasible chartered freedoms, has set up that single, unconscionable freedom—Free Trade. In one word, for exploitation, veiled by religious and political illusions, it has substituted naked, shameless, direct, brutal exploitation.

The bourgeoisie has stripped of its halo every occupation hitherto honored and looked up to with reverent awe. It has converted the physician, the lawyer, the priest, the poet, the man of science, into its paid wage laborers. The bourgeoisie has torn away from the family its sentimental veil, and has reduced the family relation to a mere money relation. The bourgeoisie has disclosed how it came to pass that the brutal display of vigor in the Middle Ages, which reactionaries so much admire, found its fitting complement in the most slothful indolence. It has been the first to show what man's activity can bring about. It has accomplished wonders far surpassing Egyptian pyramids, Roman aqueducts, and Gothic cathedrals; it has conducted expeditions that put in the shade all former Exoduses of nations and crusades.

The bourgeoisie cannot exist without constantly revolutionising the instruments of production, and thereby the relations of production, and with them the whole relations of society. Conservation of the old modes of production in unaltered form, was, on the contrary, the first condition of existence for all earlier industrial classes. Constant revolutionising of production, uninterrupted disturbance of all social conditions, everlasting uncertainty and agitation distinguish the bourgeois epoch from all earlier ones. All fixed, fast-frozen relations, with their train of ancient and venerable prejudices and opinions, are swept away, all new-formed ones become antiquated before they can ossify. All that is solid melts into air, all that is holy is profaned, and man is at last compelled to face with sober senses his real conditions of life, and his relations with his kind.

The need of a constantly expanding market for its products chases the bourgeoisie over the entire surface of the globe. It must nestle everywhere, settle everywhere, establish connections everywhere. The bourgeoisie has through its exploitation of the world market given a cosmopolitan character to production and consumption in every country. To the great chagrin of Reactionists, it has drawn from under the feet of industry the national ground on which it stood. All old-established national industries have been destroyed or are daily being destroyed. They are dislodged by new industries, whose introduction becomes a life and death question for all civilized nations, by industries that no longer work up indigenous raw material, but raw material drawn from the remotest zones; industries whose products are consumed, not only at home, but in every quarter of the globe. In place of the old wants, satisfied by the production of the country, we find new wants, requiring for their satisfaction the products of distant lands and climes. In place of the old local and national seclusion and self-sufficiency, we have intercourse in every direction, universal inter-dependence of nations. And as in material, so also in intellectual production. The intellectual creations of individual nations become common property. National one-sidedness and narrow-mindedness become more and more impossible, and from the numerous national and local literatures, there arises a world literature.

The bourgeoisie, by the rapid improvement of all instruments of production, by the immensely facilitated means of communication, draws all, even the most barbarian, nations into civilization. The cheap prices of commodities are the heavy artillery with which it batters down all Chinese walls, with which it forces the barbarians' intensely obstinate hatred of foreigners to capitulate. It compels all nations, on pain of extinction, to adopt the bourgeois mode of production; it compels them to introduce what it calls civilization into their midst, i.e., to become bourgeois themselves. In one word, it creates a world after its own image.

The bourgeoisie has subjected the country to the rule of the towns. It has created enormous cities, has greatly increased the urban population as compared with the rural, and has thus rescued a considerable part of the population from the idiocy of rural life. Just as it has made the country dependent on the towns, so it has made barbarian and semi-barbarian countries dependent on the civilized ones, nations of peasants on nations of bourgeois, the East on the West.

The bourgeoisie keeps more and more doing away with the scattered state of the population, of the means of production, and of property. It has agglomerated population, centralized the means of production, and has concentrated property in a few hands. The necessary consequence of this was political centralisation. Independent, or but loosely connected provinces, with separate interests, laws, governments, and systems of taxation, became lumped together into one nation, with one government, one code of laws, one national class-interest, one frontier, and one customs-tariff.

The bourgeoisie, during its rule of scarce one hundred years, has created more massive and more colossal productive forces than have all preceding generations together. Subjection of Nature's forces to man, machinery, application of chemistry to industry and agriculture, steam-navigation, railways, electric telegraphs, clearing of whole continents for cultivation, canalization of rivers, whole populations conjured out of the ground—what earlier century had even a presentiment that such productive forces slumbered in the lap of social labor?

We see then: the means of production and of exchange, on whose foundation the bourgeoisie built itself up, were generated in feudal society. At a certain stage in the development of these means of production and of exchange, the conditions under which feudal society produced and exchanged, the feudal organization of agriculture and manufacturing industry, in one word, the feudal relations of property became no longer compatible with the already developed productive forces; they became so many fetters. They had to be burst asunder; they were burst asunder. Into their place stepped free competition, accompanied by a social and political constitution adapted in it, and the economic and political sway of the bourgeois class.

A similar movement is going on before our own eyes. Modern bourgeois society, with its relations of production, of exchange and of property, a society that has conjured up such gigantic means of production and of exchange, is like the sorcerer who is no longer able to control the powers of the nether world whom he has called up by his spells. For many a decade past the history of industry and commerce is but the history of the revolt of modern productive forces against modern conditions of production, against the property relations that are the conditions for the existence of the bourgeois and of its rule. It is enough to mention the commercial crises that by their periodical return put the existence of the entire bourgeois society on its trial, each time more threateningly. In these crises, a great part not only of the existing products, but also of the previously created productive forces, are periodically destroyed. In these crises, there breaks out an epidemic that, in all earlier epochs, would have seemed an absurdity—the epidemic of over-production. Society suddenly finds itself put back into a state of momentary barbarism; it appears as if a famine, a universal war of devastation, had cut off the supply of every means of subsistence; industry and commerce seem to be destroyed; and why? Because there is too much civilization, too much means of subsistence, too much industry, too much commerce. The productive forces at the disposal of society no longer tend to further the development of the conditions of bourgeois property; on the contrary, they have become too powerful for these conditions, by which they are fettered, and so soon as they overcome these fetters, they bring disorder into the whole of bourgeois society, endanger the existence of bourgeois property. The conditions of bourgeois society are too narrow to comprise the wealth created by them. And how does the bourgeoisie get over these crises? On the one hand by enforced destruction of a mass of productive forces; on the other, by the conquest of new markets, and by the more thorough exploitation of the old ones. That is to say, by paving the way for more extensive and more destructive crises, and by diminishing the means whereby crises are prevented.

The weapons with which the bourgeoisie felled feudalism to the ground are now turned against the bourgeoisie itself. But not only has the bourgeoisie forged the weapons that bring death to itself; it has also called into existence the men who are to wield those weapons—the modern working class—the proletarians.

In proportion as the bourgeoisie, i.e., capital, is developed, in the same proportion is the proletariat, the modern working class, developed—a class of laborers, who live only so long as they find work, and who find work only so long as their labor increases capital. These laborers, who must sell themselves piecemeal, are a commodity, like every other article of commerce, and are consequently exposed to all the vicissitudes of competition, to all the fluctuations of the market.

Owing to the extensive use of machinery, and to the division of labor, the work of the proletarians has lost all individual character, and, consequently, all charm for the workman. He becomes an appendage of the machine, and it is only the most simple, most monotonous, and most easily acquired knack, that is required of him. Hence, the cost of production of a workman is restricted, almost entirely, to the means of subsistence that he requires for maintenance, and for the propagation of his race. But the price of a commodity, and therefore also of labor, is equal to its cost of production. In proportion, therefore, as the repulsiveness of the work increases, the wage decreases. Nay more, in proportion as the use of machinery and division of labor increases, in the same proportion the burden of toil also increases, whether by prolongation of the working hours, by the increase of the work exacted in a given time or by increased speed of machinery, etc.

Modern industry has converted the little workshop of the patriarchal master into the great factory of the industrial capitalist. Masses of laborers, crowded into the factory, are organized like soldiers. As privates of the industrial army they are placed under the command of a perfect hierarchy of officers and sergeants. Not only are they slaves of the bourgeois class, and of the bourgeois State; they are daily and hourly enslaved by the machine, by the overlooker, and, above all, by the individual bourgeois manufacturer himself. The more openly this despotism proclaims gain to be its end and aim, the more petty, the more hateful and the more embittering it is.

The less the skill and exertion of strength implied in manual labor, in other words, the more modern industry becomes developed, the more is the labor of men superseded by that of women. Differences of age and sex have no longer any distinctive social validity for the working class. All are instruments of labor, more or less expensive to use, according to their age and sex. No sooner is the exploitation of the laborer by the manufacturer, so far, at an end, that he receives his wages in cash, than he is set upon by the other portions of the bourgeoisie, the landlord, the shopkeeper, the pawnbroker, etc.

The lower strata of the middle class—the small tradespeople, shopkeepers, and retired tradesmen generally, the handicraftsmen and peasants—all these sink gradually into the proletariat, partly because their diminutive capital does not suffice for the scale on which Modern Industry is carried on, and is swamped in the competition with the large capitalists, partly because their specialised skill is rendered worthless by new methods of production. Thus the proletariat is recruited from all classes of the population.

The proletariat goes through various stages of development. With its birth begins its struggle with the bourgeoisie. At first the contest is carried on by individual laborers, then by the workpeople of a factory, then by the operative of one trade, in one locality, against the individual bourgeois who directly exploits them. They direct their attacks not against the bourgeois conditions of production, but against the instruments of production themselves; they destroy imported wares that compete with their labor, they smash to pieces machinery, they set factories ablaze, they seek to restore by force the vanished status of the workman of the Middle Ages.

At this stage, the laborers still form an incoherent mass scattered over the whole country, and broken up by their mutual competition. If anywhere they unite to form more compact bodies, this is not yet the consequence of their own active union, but of the union of the bourgeoisie, which class, in order to attain its own political ends, is compelled to set the whole proletariat in motion, and is moreover yet, for a time, able to do so. At this stage, therefore, the proletarians do not fight their enemies, but the enemies of their enemies, the remnants of absolute monarchy, the landowners, the non-industrial bourgeois, the petty bourgeois. Thus, the whole historical movement is concentrated in the hands of the bourgeoisie; every victory so obtained is a victory for the bourgeoisie.

But with the development of industry, the proletariat not only increases in number; it becomes concentrated in greater masses, its strength grows, and it feels that strength more. The various interests and conditions of life within the ranks of the proletariat are more and more equalized, in proportion as machinery obliterates all distinctions of labor, and nearly everywhere reduces wages to the same low level. The growing competition among the bourgeois, and the resulting commercial crises, make the wages of the workers ever more fluctuating. The increasing improvement of machinery, ever more rapidly developing, makes their livelihood more and more precarious; the collisions between individual workmen and individual bourgeois take more and more the character of collisions between two classes. Thereupon, the workers begin to form combinations (Trade Unions) against the bourgeois; they club together in order to keep up the rate of wages; they found permanent associations in order to make provision beforehand for these occasional revolts. Here and there, the contest breaks out into riots.

Now and then the workers are victorious, but only for a time. The real fruit of their battles lies, not in the immediate result, but in the ever expanding union of the workers. This union is helped on by the improved means of communication that are created by modern industry, and that places the workers of different localities in contact with one another. It was just this contact that was needed to centralize the numerous local struggles, all of the same character, into one national struggle between classes. But every class struggle is a political struggle. And that union, to attain which the burghers of the Middle Ages, with their miserable highways, required centuries, the modern proletarian, thanks to railways, achieve in a few years.

This organisation of the proletarians into a class, and, consequently into a political party, is continually being upset again by the competition between the workers themselves. But it ever rises up again, stronger, firmer, mightier. It compels legislative recognition of particular interests of the workers, by taking advantage of the divisions among the bourgeoisie itself. Thus, the ten-hours' bill in England was carried.

Collisions between the classes of the old society further, in many ways, the course of development of the proletariat. The bourgeoisie finds itself involved in a constant battle. At first with the aristocracy; later on, with those portions of the bourgeoisie itself, whose interests have become antagonistic to the progress of industry; at all time with the bourgeoisie of foreign countries. In all these battles, it sees itself compelled to appeal to the proletariat, to ask for help, and thus, to drag it into the political arena. The bourgeoisie itself, therefore, supplies the proletariat with its own elements of political and general education, in other words, it furnishes the proletariat with weapons for fighting the bourgeoisie.

Further, as we have already seen, entire sections of the ruling class are, by the advance of industry, precipitated into the proletariat, or are at least threatened in their conditions of existence. These also supply the proletariat with fresh elements of enlightenment and progress.

Finally, in times when the class struggle nears the decisive hour, the progress of dissolution going on within the ruling class, in fact within the whole range of old society, assumes such a violent, glaring character, that a small section of the ruling class cuts itself adrift, and joins the revolutionary class, the class that holds the future in its hands. Just as, therefore, at an earlier period, a section of the nobility went over to the bourgeoisie, so now a portion of the bourgeoisie goes over to the proletariat, and in particular, a portion of the bourgeois ideologists, who have raised themselves to the level of comprehending theoretically the historical movement as a whole.

Of all the classes that stand face to face with the bourgeoisie today, the proletariat alone is a really revolutionary class. The other classes decay and finally disappear in the face of Modern Industry; the proletariat is its special and essential product.

The lower middle class, the small manufacturer, the shopkeeper, the artisan, the peasant, all these fight against the bourgeoisie, to save from extinction their existence as fractions of the middle class. They are therefore not revolutionary, but conservative. Nay more, they are reactionary, for they try to roll back the wheel of history. If by chance, they are revolutionary, they are only so in view of their impending transfer into the proletariat; they thus defend not their present, but their future interests, they desert their own standpoint to place themselves at that of the proletariat.

The "dangerous class," the social scum, that passively rotting mass thrown off by the lowest layers of the old society, may, here and there, be swept into the movement by a proletarian revolution; its conditions of life, however, prepare it far more for the part of a bribed tool of reactionary intrigue.

In the condition of the proletariat, those of old society at large are already virtually swamped. The proletarian is without property; his relation to his wife and children has no longer anything in common with the bourgeois family relations; modern industry labor, modern subjection to capital, the same in England as in France, in America as in Germany, has stripped him of every trace of national character. Law, morality, religion, are to him so many bourgeois prejudices, behind which lurk in ambush just as many bourgeois interests.

All the preceding classes that got the upper hand sought to fortify their already acquired status by subjecting society at large to their conditions of appropriation. The proletarians cannot become masters of the productive forces of society, except by abolishing their own previous mode of appropriation, and thereby also every other previous mode of appropriation. They have nothing of their own to secure and to fortify; their mission is to destroy all previous securities for, and insurances of, individual property.

All previous historical movements were movements of minorities, or in the interest of minorities. The proletarian movement is the self-conscious, independent movement of the immense majority, in the interest of the immense majority. The proletariat, the lowest stratum of our present society, cannot stir, cannot raise itself up, without the whole superincumbent strata of official society being sprung into the air. Though not in substance, yet in form, the struggle of the proletariat with the bourgeoisie is at first a national struggle. The proletariat of each country must, of course, first of all settle matters with its own bourgeoisie.

In depicting the most general phases of the development of the proletariat, we traced the more or less veiled civil war, raging within existing society, up to the point where that war breaks out into open revolution, and where the violent overthrow of the bourgeoisie lays the foundation for the sway of the proletariat.

Hitherto, every form of society has been based, as we have already seen, on the antagonism of oppressing and oppressed classes. But in order to oppress a class, certain conditions must be assured to it under which it can, at least, continue its slavish existence. The serf, in the period of serfdom, raised himself to membership in the commune, just as the petty bourgeois, under the yoke of the feudal absolutism, managed to develop into a bourgeois. The modern laborer, on the contrary, instead of rising with the process of industry, sinks deeper and deeper below the conditions of existence of his own class. He becomes a pauper, and pauperism develops more rapidly than population and wealth. And here it becomes evident, that the bourgeoisie is unfit any longer to be the ruling class in society, and to impose its conditions of existence upon society as an over-riding law. It is unfit to rule because it is incompetent to assure an existence to its slave within his slavery, because it cannot help letting him sink into such a state, that it has to feed him, instead of being fed by him. Society can no longer live under this bourgeoisie, in other words, its existence is no longer compatible with society.

The essential conditions for the existence and for the sway of the bourgeois class is the formation and augmentation of capital; the condition for capital is wage-labor. Wage-labor rests exclusively on competition between the laborers. The advance of industry, whose involuntary promoter is the bourgeoisie, replaces the isolation of the laborers, due to competition, by the revolutionary combination, due to association. The development of Modern Industry, therefore, cuts from under its feet the very foundation on which the bourgeoisie produces and appropriates products. What the bourgeoisie therefore produces, above all, are its own grave-diggers. Its fall and the victory of the proletariat are equally inevitable.

In what relation do the Communists stand to the proletarians as a whole? The Communists do not form a separate party opposed to the other working-class parties. They have no interests separate and apart from those of the proletariat as a whole. They do not set up any sectarian principles of their own, by which to shape and mold the proletarian movement.

The Communists are distinguished from the other working-class parties by this only: 1. In the national struggles of the proletarians of the different countries, they point out and bring to the front the common interests of the entire proletariat, independently of all nationality; 2. In the various stages of development which the struggle of the working class against the bourgeoisie has to pass through, they always and everywhere represent the interests of the movement as a whole.

The Communists, therefore, are on the one hand, practically, the most advanced and resolute section of the working-class parties of every country, that section which pushes forward all others; on the other hand, theoretically, they have over the great mass of the proletariat the advantage of clearly understanding the line of march, the conditions, and the ultimate general results of the proletarian movement.

The immediate aim of the Communists is the same as that of all other proletarian parties: formation of the proletariat into a class, overthrow of the bourgeois supremacy, conquest of political power by the proletariat. The proletariat will use its political supremacy to wrest, by degree, all capital from the bourgeoisie, to centralize all instruments of production in the hands of the

State, i.e., of the proletariat organized as the ruling class; and to increase the total productive forces as rapidly as possible.

Of course, in the beginning, this cannot be effected except by means of despotic inroads on the rights of property, and on the conditions of bourgeois production; by means of measures, therefore, which appear economically insufficient and untenable, but which, in the course of the movement, outstrip themselves, necessitate further inroads upon the old social order, and are unavoidable as a means of entirely revolutionizing the mode of production.

These measures will, of course, be different in different countries. Nevertheless, in most advanced countries, the following will be generally applicable.

1. Abolition of property in land and application of all rents of land to public purposes.
2. A heavy progressive or graduated income tax.
3. Abolition of all rights of inheritance.
4. Confiscation of the property of all emigrants and rebels.
5. Centralization of credit in the hands of the state, by means of a national bank with State capital and an exclusive monopoly.
6. Centralization of the means of communication and transport in the hands of the State.
7. Extension of factories and instruments of production owned by the State; the bringing into cultivation of waste-lands, and the improvement of the soil generally in accordance with a common plan.
8. Equal liability of all to work. Establishment of industrial armies, especially for agriculture.
9. Combination of agriculture with manufacturing industries; gradual abolition of all the distinction between town and country by a more equable distribution of the populace over the country.
10. Free education for all children in public schools. Abolition of children's factory labor in its present form. Combination of education with industrial production, etc.

When, in the course of development, class distinctions have disappeared, and all production has been concentrated in the hands of a vast association of the whole nation, the public power will lose its political character. Political power, properly so called, is merely the organized power of one class for oppressing another. If the proletariat during its contest with the bourgeoisie is compelled, by the force of circumstances, to organize itself as a class, if, by means of a revolution, it makes itself the ruling class, and, as such, sweeps away by force the old conditions of production, then it will, along with these conditions, have swept away the conditions for the existence of class antagonisms and of classes generally, and will thereby have abolished its own supremacy as a class. In place of the old bourgeois society, with its classes and class antagonisms, we shall have an association, in which the free development of each is the condition for the free development of all.

The Communists disdain to conceal their views and aims. They openly declare that their ends can be attained only by the forcible overthrow of all existing social conditions. Let the ruling classes tremble at a Communistic revolution. The proletarians have nothing to lose but their chains. They have a world to win.

Working Men of All Countries, Unite!

Mary Wollstonecraft

A VINDICATION OF THE RIGHTS OF WOMAN

The discussion of this subject merely consists in opening a few simple principles, and clearing away the rubbish which obscured them. But, as all readers are not sagacious, I must be allowed to add some explanatory remarks to bring the subject home to reason—to that sluggish reason, which supinely takes opinions on trust, and obstinately supports them to spare itself the labor of thinking.

Moralists have unanimously agreed, that unless virtue be nursed by liberty, it will never attain due strength—and what they say of man I extend to mankind, insisting, that in all cases morals must be fixed on immutable principles; and that the being cannot be termed rational or virtuous, who obeys any authority but that of reason.

To render women truly useful members of society, I argue, that they should be led, by having their understandings cultivated on a large scale, to acquire a rational affection for their country, founded on knowledge, because it is obvious, that we are little interested about what we do not understand. And to render this general knowledge of due importance, I have endeavored to show that private duties are never properly fulfilled, unless the understanding enlarges the heart; and that public virtue is only an aggregate of private. But, the distinctions established in society undermine both, by beating out the solid gold of virtue, till it becomes only the tinsel-covering of vice; for, while wealth renders a man more respectable than virtue, wealth will be sought before virtue; and, while women's persons are caressed, when a childish simper shows an absence of mind—the mind will lie fallow. Yet, true voluptuousness must proceed from the mind—for what can equal the sensations produced by mutual affection, supported by mutual respect? What are the cold or feverish caresses of appetite, but sin embracing death, compared with the modest overflowings of a pure heart and exalted imagination? Yes, let me tell the libertine of fancy when he despises understanding in woman—that the mind, which he disregards, gives life to the enthusiastic affection from which rapture, short-lived as it is, alone can flow! And, that, without virtue, a sexual attachment must expire, like a tallow candle in the socket, creating intolerable disgust. To prove this, I need only observe, that men who have wasted great part of their lives with women, and with whom they have sought for pleasure with eager thirst, entertain the meanest opinion of the sex. Virtue, true refiner of joy! if foolish men were to fright thee from earth, in order to give loose to all their appetites without a check—some sensual wight of taste would scale the heavens to invite thee back, to give a zest to pleasure!

That women at present are by ignorance rendered foolish or vicious, is, I think, not to be disputed; and, that the most salutary effects tending to improve mankind, might be expected from a revolution in female manners, appears at least, with a face of probability, to rise out of the observation. For as marriage has been termed the parent of those endearing charities, which draw man from the brutal herd, the corrupting intercourse that wealth, idleness, and folly produce between the sexes, is more universally injurious to morality, than all the other vices of mankind collectively considered. To adulterous lust the most sacred duties are sacrificed, because, before marriage, men, by a promiscuous intimacy with women, learned to consider love as a selfish gratification—learned to separate it not only from esteem, but from the affection merely built on habit, which mixes a little humanity with it. Justice and friendship are also set at defiance, and that purity of taste is vitiated, which would naturally lead a man to relish an artless display of affection,

Edited from *A Vindication of the Rights of Woman,* 1792, Chapter 13, which is now in the public domain.

rather than affected airs. But that noble simplicity of affection, which dares to appear unadorned, has few attractions for the libertine, though it be the charm, which, by cementing the matrimonial tie, secures to the pledges of a warmer passion the necessary parental attention; for children will never be properly educated till friendship subsists between parents. Virtue flies from a house divided against itself—and a whole legion of devils take up their residence there.

The affection of husbands and wives cannot be pure when they have so few sentiments in common, and when so little confidence is established at home, as must be the case when their pursuits are so different. That intimacy from which tenderness should flow, will not, cannot subsist between the vicious.

Contending, therefore, that the sexual distinction, which men have so warmly insisted upon, is arbitrary, I have dwelt on an observation, that several sensible men, with whom I have conversed on the subject, allowed to be well founded; and it is simply this, that the little chastity to be found amongst men, and consequent disregard of modesty, tend to degrade both sexes; and further, that the modesty of women, characterized as such, will often be only the artful veil of wantonness, instead of being the natural reflection of purity, till modesty be universally respected.

From the tyranny of man, I firmly believe, the greater number of female follies proceed; and the cunning, which I allow, makes at present a part of their character, I likewise have repeatedly endeavored to prove, is produced by oppression. Were not dissenters, for instance, a class of people, with strict truth characterized as cunning? And may I not lay some stress on this fact to prove, that when any power but reason curbs the free spirit of man, dissimulation is practiced, and the various shifts of art are naturally called forth? Great attention to decorum, which was carried to a degree of scrupulosity, and all that puerile bustle about trifles and consequential solemnity, which Butler's caricature of a dissenter brings before the imagination, shaped their persons as well as their minds in the mold of prim littleness. I speak collectively, for I know how many ornaments to human nature have been enrolled amongst sectaries; yet, I assert, that the same narrow prejudice for their sect, which women have for their families, prevailed in the dissenting part of the community, however worthy in other respects; and also that the same timid prudence, or headstrong efforts, often disgraced the exertions of both. Oppression thus formed many of the features of their character perfectly to coincide with that of the oppressed half of mankind; for is it not notorious, that dissenters were like women, fond of deliberating together, and asking advice of each other, till by a complication of little contrivances, some little end was brought about? A similar attention to preserve their reputation was conspicuous in the dissenting and female world, and was produced by a similar cause.

Asserting the rights which women in common with men ought to contend for, I have not attempted to extenuate their faults; but to prove them to be the natural consequence of their education and station in society. If so, it is reasonable to suppose, that they will change their character, and correct their vices and follies, when they are allowed to be free in a physical, moral, and civil sense.

Let woman share the rights, and she will emulate the virtues of man; for she must grow more perfect when emancipated, or justify the authority that chains such a weak being to her duty. If the latter, it will be expedient to open a fresh trade with Russia for whips; a present which a father should always make to his son-in-law on his wedding day, that a husband may keep his whole family in order by the same means; and without any violation of justice reign, wielding this scepter, sole master of his house, because he is the only being in it who has reason; the divine, indefeasible, earthly sovereignty breathed into man by the Master of the universe. Allowing this position, women have not any inherent rights to claim; and, by the same rule their duties vanish, for rights and duties are inseparable.

Be just then, Oh you men of understanding! and mark not more severely what women do amiss, than the vicious tricks of the horse or the ass for whom you provide provender, and allow her the privileges of ignorance, to whom you deny the rights of reason, or you will be worse than Egyptian task-masters, expecting virtue where nature has not given understanding!

Part Ten: Art and Aesthetics

Introduction

To get started, we can say that *art* includes physical objects such as paintings and sculpture, performances such as live music and dancing, and other mediums such as film, among other things. Again, to get started, we can say that *aesthetics* is our various responses (emotional or intellectual) to art. In its simplest sense then, we can say that art is the object, while aesthetics is the appreciation.

It is quite common to see lists of the "best" movies, actors, songs, singers, novels, paintings, sculpture, and commercials, to mention only a few categories. You might agree with those who created the list, or you might disagree. When disagreements arise, we can ask whether or not disputes over "aesthetic taste" can be rationally debated. Are aesthetic judgments simply matters of personal taste, or are there objective standards by which we can judge artistic creations or performances?

Some argue that an objective standard for art is not possible because all artistic judgments are merely expressions of personal taste, or are determined by one's culture or even the era in which one happens to live. (We are using the term "art" in a general sense, to include the categories listed above such as music, paintings, and film.) In other words, some argue that all personal tastes are relative. This kind of argument considers artistic judgments to be similar to personal preferences about food. For example, when someone says, "I think pepperoni pizza is the best kind of pizza," what she is really saying is, "Pepperoni pizza is my favorite," which is a subjective claim.

However, for other people, the debate should concentrate on the *function* of art. The reading by Henri Bergson focuses on aspects of "the comical" which, Bergson argues, is a strictly human condition that relies on our intelligence. One of the outcomes of comedy is laughter, which can be understood when it is placed in a social context. In other words, the *function* of the comical and laughter is a social one, or as Bergson puts it, a "sort of social gesture." For comedy to function properly, it must have a social signification.

We can also ask this question: If two people can both provide *reasons* for why each prefers one piece of art to another, then can those reasons constitute a rational debate? In other words, if the two people can agree on some working definition of the *function of art*, then perhaps they can move the discussion forward.

Some people have argued that art has an essential *political function*; thus, they judge the "value" of a piece of art by whether or not it serves to promote group solidarity. There are even some cultures or religious belief systems that hold that art is evil; therefore, they feel justified in destroying certain images or prohibiting the playing of music.

If art does have a function—or functions—then perhaps we can inquire whether one of the functions of art is to express, or to represent, some universal human emotion or condition, thereby allowing individuals to *connect* to others, to have *interpersonal experiences*. If so, then can we use that to discuss the *effectiveness* of a given piece of art?

One attempt to discuss the effectiveness of a specific kind of art—tragedy—is found in Aristotle's work on the subject. For Aristotle, each tragic situation is a specific set of events that inspires a sense of fear or pity. Aristotle explains how and why a tragic story or play, to be effective, must be an *imitation* of an action that is serious. The tragedy must have two essential parts: a *plot*, which is the specific arrangement of incidents; and it must show human *character*, specific qualities of people. For Aristotle, the glue that holds the parts together is the *structure* of the incidents. In other words, tragedy is not merely an imitation of people, but "of an action and of life, and life consists in action."

Is art supposed to create something *beautiful*, or does it only need to move us emotionally? For George Santayana, it is quite natural to try to understand our *sense of beauty* by looking at a work of art as a *physical object*, to think about its *abstract form*, and also to analyze it through a set of *aesthetic values*. However, Santayana argues that an *individual aesthetic feeling* cannot be taken apart and analyzed as separate parts; it is simply *an experience*. In addition, when we call something "beautiful," we have the distinct sense that it is something indescribable; that whatever it is or means "can never be said."

Arthur Schopenhauer argues that in order to be a genuine work of art it must answer the question, "What is life?" A genuine work of art will answer that question in its own way with perfect correctness. According to Schopenhauer, each piece of art provides us with at most a fleeting and incomplete satisfaction: "Every work of art accordingly really aims at showing us life and things as they are in truth, but cannot be directly discerned by every one through the mist of objective and subjective contingencies." However, the greatest aspect of art cannot be given directly to the senses; it must be born in the imagination of the beholder.

Aristotle

TRAGEDY

Tragedy is an imitation of an action that is serious, complete, and of a certain magnitude; in language embellished with each kind of artistic ornament, the several kinds being found in separate parts of the play; in the form of action, not of narrative; through pity and fear effecting the proper purgation of these emotions.

Tragedy is the imitation of an action; and an action implies personal agents, who necessarily possess certain distinctive qualities both of character and thought; for it is by these that we qualify actions themselves, and these—thought and character—are the two natural causes from which actions spring, and on actions again all success or failure depends. Hence, the plot is the imitation of the action—by "plot," I here mean the arrangement of the incidents. By "character," I mean that in virtue of which we ascribe certain qualities to the agents. Thought is required wherever a statement is proved, or, it may be, a general truth enunciated.

But most important of all is the structure of the incidents. For tragedy is an imitation, not of men, but of an action and of life, and life consists in action, and its end is a mode of action, not a quality. Now character determines men's qualities, but it is by their actions that they are happy or the reverse. Dramatic action, therefore, is not with a view to the representation of character: character comes in as subsidiary to the actions. Hence the incidents and the plot are the end of a tragedy; and the end is the chief thing of all. Again, without action there cannot be a tragedy; there may be without character. If you string together a set of speeches expressive of character, and well finished in point of diction and thought, you will not produce the essential tragic effect nearly so well as with a play which, however deficient in these respects, yet has a plot and artistically constructed incidents. Besides which, the most powerful elements of emotional interest in Tragedy are parts of the plot. A further proof is that novices in the art attain to finish of diction and precision of portraiture before they can construct the plot.

The plot, then, is the first principle, and, as it were, the soul of a tragedy; character holds the second place. A similar fact is seen in painting. The most beautiful colors, laid on confusedly, will not give as much pleasure as the chalk outline of a portrait. Thus tragedy is the imitation of an action, and of the agents mainly with a view to the action.

Next in order is thought—that is, the faculty of saying what is possible and pertinent in given circumstances. Character is that which reveals moral purpose, showing what kind of things a man chooses or avoids. Speeches, therefore, which do not make this manifest, or in which the speaker does not choose or avoid anything whatever, are not expressive of character. Thought, on the other hand, is found where something is proved to be or not to be, or a general maxim is enunciated. The power of Tragedy, we may be sure, is felt even apart from representation and actors. Besides, the production of spectacular effects depends more on the art of the stage machinist than on that of the poet.

These principles being established, let us now discuss the proper structure of the Plot, since this is the first and most important thing in tragedy. According to our definition, tragedy is an imitation of an action that is complete, and whole, and of a certain magnitude. A whole is that which has a beginning, a middle, and an end. A beginning is that which does not itself follow anything by causal necessity, but after which something naturally is or comes to be. An end, on

Edited from *Poetics,* Section 1, Parts VI-IX, and XXIV-XXV. Translated by S. H. Butcher, 1895, which is now in the public domain.

the contrary, is that which itself naturally follows some other thing, either by necessity, or as a rule, but has nothing following it. A middle is that which follows something as some other thing follows it. A well constructed plot, therefore, must neither begin nor end haphazardly, but conform to these principles.

A beautiful object, whether it is a living organism or any whole composed of parts, must not only have an orderly arrangement of parts, but must also be of a certain magnitude; for beauty depends on magnitude and order. Therefore, in the plot, a certain length is necessary, and a length which can be easily embraced by the memory. And to define the matter roughly, we may say that the proper magnitude is comprised within such limits, that the sequence of events, according to the law of probability or necessity, will admit of a change from bad fortune to good, or from good fortune to bad.

Unity of plot does not, as some persons think, consist in the unity of the hero. For infinitely various are the incidents in one man's life which cannot be reduced to unity; and so, too, there are many actions of one man out of which we cannot make one action.

As therefore, in the other imitative arts, the imitation is one when the object imitated is one, so the plot, being an imitation of an action, must imitate one action and that a whole, the structural union of the parts being such that, if any one of them is displaced or removed, the whole will be disjointed and disturbed. For a thing whose presence or absence makes no visible difference, is not an organic part of the whole.

It is, moreover, evident from what has been said, that it is *not* the function of the poet to relate *what has happened*, but *what may happen*—what is possible according to the law of probability or necessity. The poet and the historian differ not by writing in verse or in prose. The true difference is that one relates what *has* happened, the other what *may* happen. Poetry, therefore, is a more philosophical and a higher thing than history: for poetry tends to express the universal, history the particular. By the universal, I mean how a person of a certain type on occasion speaks or acts, according to the law of probability or necessity; and it is this universality at which poetry aims in the names she attaches to the personages.

But again, tragedy is an imitation not only of a complete action, but of events inspiring fear or pity. Such an effect is best produced when the events come on us by surprise; and the effect is heightened when, at the same time, they follows as cause and effect. The tragic wonder will then be greater than if they happened of themselves or by accident; for even coincidences are most striking when they have an air of design. Such events seem not to be due to mere chance. Plots, therefore, constructed on these principles are necessarily the best.

A perfect tragedy should be arranged not on a simple but on a complex plan. It should, moreover, imitate actions which excite pity and fear, this being the distinctive mark of tragic imitation. It follows that the change of fortune presented must not be the spectacle of a virtuous man brought from prosperity to adversity: for this moves neither pity nor fear; it merely shocks us. Nor, again, that of a bad man passing from adversity to prosperity: for nothing can be more alien to the spirit of tragedy; it possesses no single tragic quality; it neither satisfies the moral sense nor calls forth pity or fear. Nor, again, should the downfall of the utter villain be exhibited. A plot of this kind would, doubtless, satisfy the moral sense, but it would inspire neither pity nor fear; for pity is aroused by *unmerited misfortune*, fear by the misfortune of a man like ourselves. Such an event, therefore, will be neither pitiful nor terrible. There remains, then, the character between these two extremes—that of a man who is not eminently good and just, yet whose misfortune is brought about not by vice or depravity, but by some error or frailty. He must be one who is highly renowned and prosperous.

A well-constructed plot should, therefore, be single in its issue. The change of fortune should be not from bad to good, but, reversely, from good to bad. It should come about as the result not of vice, but of some great error or frailty, in a character either such as we have described, or better rather than worse. A tragedy, then, to be perfect according to the rules of art should be of this construction.

Fear and pity may be aroused by spectacular means; but they may also result from the inner structure of the piece, which is the better way. For the plot ought to be so constructed that, even without the aid of the eye, he who hears the tale told will thrill with horror and melt to pity at what takes place. But to produce this effect by the mere spectacle is a less artistic method, and dependent on extraneous aids. Those who employ spectacular means to create a sense not of the terrible but only of the monstrous, are strangers to the purpose of tragedy; for we must not demand of tragedy any and every kind of pleasure, but only that which is proper to it. And since the pleasure which the poet should afford is that which comes from pity and fear through imitation, it is evident that this quality must be impressed upon the incidents.

Let us then determine what are the circumstances which strike us as terrible or pitiful. Actions capable of this effect must happen between persons who are either friends or enemies or indifferent to one another. If an enemy kills an enemy, there is nothing to excite pity either in the act or the intention—except so far as the suffering in itself is pitiful. So again with indifferent persons. But when the tragic incident occurs between those who are near or dear to one another—if, for example, a brother kills, or intends to kill, a brother, a son his father, a mother her son, a son his mother, or any other deed of the kind is done—these are the situations to be looked for by the poet.

The poet should prefer probable impossibilities to improbable possibilities. The tragic plot must not be composed of irrational parts. Everything irrational should, if possible, be excluded; or, at all events, it should lie outside the action of the play. But once the irrational has been introduced and an air of likelihood imparted to it, we must accept it in spite of the absurdity.

The poet being an imitator, like a painter or any other artist, must of necessity imitate one of three objects—things as they were or are, things as they are said or thought to be, or things as they ought to be. The vehicle of expression is language—either current terms or, it may be, rare words or metaphors. There are also many modifications of language, which we concede to the poets.

Henri Bergson

AN ANIMAL WHICH LAUGHS, AND IS LAUGHED AT

What does laughter mean? What common ground can we find between the grimace of a merry-andrew, a play upon words, an equivocal situation in a burlesque, and a scene of high comedy? What method of distillation will yield us invariably the same essence from which so many different products borrow either their obtrusive odor or their delicate perfume? The greatest of thinkers, from Aristotle downwards, have tackled this little problem, which has a knack of baffling every effort, of slipping away and escaping only to bob up again, a pert challenge flung at philosophic speculation.

Our excuse for attacking the problem in our turn must lie in the fact that we shall not aim at imprisoning the comic spirit within a definition. We regard it, above all, as a living thing. However trivial it may be, we shall treat it with the respect due to life. We shall confine ourselves to watching it grow and expand. Passing by imperceptible gradations from one form to another, it will be seen to achieve the strangest metamorphoses. We shall disdain nothing we have seen. Maybe we may gain from this prolonged contact, for the matter of that, something more flexible than an abstract definition—a practical, intimate acquaintance, such as springs from a long companionship. And maybe we may also find that, unintentionally, we have made an acquaintance that is useful. For comic spirit has a logic of its own, even in its wildest eccentricities. It has a method in its madness. It dreams, I admit, but it conjures up in its dreams visions that are at once accepted and understood by the whole of a social group. Can it then fail to throw light for us on the way that human imagination works, and particularly social, collective, and popular imagination? Begotten of real life and akin to art, should it not also have something of its own to tell us about art and life?

At the outset we shall put forward three observations which we look upon as fundamental. They have less bearing on the actually comic than on the field within which it must be sought. The first point to which attention should be called is that the comic does *not* exist outside the pale of what is strictly *human*. A landscape may be beautiful, charming and sublime, or insignificant and ugly; it will never be laughable. You may laugh at an animal, but only because you have detected in it some human attitude or expression. You may laugh at a hat, but what you are making fun of, in this case, is not the piece of felt or straw, but the shape that men have given it—the human caprice whose mold it has assumed. It is strange that so important a fact, and such a simple one too, has not attracted to a greater degree the attention of philosophers. Several have defined man as "an animal which laughs." They might equally well have defined him as an animal which is laughed at; for if any other animal, or some lifeless object, produces the same effect, it is always because of some resemblance to man, of the stamp he gives it or the use he puts it to.

Here I would point out, as a symptom equally worthy of notice, the *absence of feeling* which usually accompanies laughter. It seems as though the comic could not produce its disturbing effect unless it fell, so to say, on the surface of a soul that is thoroughly calm and unruffled. Indifference is its natural environment, for laughter has no greater foe than emotion. I do not mean that we could not laugh at a person who inspires us with pity, for instance, or even with affection, but in such a case we must, for the moment, put our affection out of court and impose silence upon our pity. In a society composed of pure intelligences there would probably be no more tears, though perhaps there would still be laughter; whereas highly emotional souls, in tune and unison with life,

Edited from *Laughter,* Chapter I. Translated by Cloudesley Brereton and Fred Rothwell, 1914, which is now in the public domain.

in whom every event would be sentimentally prolonged and reechoed, would neither know nor understand laughter. Try, for a moment, to become interested in everything that is being said and done; act, in imagination, with those who act, and feel with those who feel; in a word, give your sympathy its widest expansion: as though at the touch of a fairy wand you will see the flimsiest of objects assume importance, and a gloomy hue spread over everything. Now step aside, look upon life as a disinterested spectator: many a drama will turn into a comedy. It is enough for us to stop our ears to the sound of music in a room, where dancing is going on, for the dancers at once to appear ridiculous. How many human actions would stand a similar test? Should we not see many of them suddenly pass from grave to gay, on isolating them from the accompanying music of sentiment? To produce the whole of its effect, then, the comical demands something like a momentary anesthesia of the heart. Its appeal is to intelligence, pure and simple.

This intelligence, however, must always remain in touch with other intelligences. And here is the third fact to which attention should be drawn. You would hardly appreciate the comical if you felt yourself isolated from others. Laughter appears to stand in need of an echo. Listen to it carefully: it is not an articulate, clear, well-defined sound; it is something which would fain be prolonged by reverberating from one to another, something beginning with a crash, to continue in successive rumblings, like thunder in a mountain. Still, this reverberation cannot go on for ever. It can travel within as wide a circle as you please: the circle remains, none the less, a closed one. Our laughter is always the laughter of a group. It may, perchance, have happened to you, when seated in a railway carriage or at *table d'hote* [a meal served at a stated hour and fixed price], to hear travelers relating to one another stories which must have been comical to them, for they laughed heartily. Had you been one of their company, you would have laughed like them, but, as you were not, you had no desire whatever to do so. A man who was once asked why he did not weep at a sermon when everybody else was shedding tears replied: "I don't belong to the parish." What that man thought of tears would be still more true of laughter. However spontaneous it seems, laughter always implies a kind of secret freemasonry, or even complicity, with other laughers, real or imaginary. How often has it been said that the fuller the theatre, the more uncontrolled the laughter of the audience? On the other hand, how often has the remark been made that many comic effects are incapable of translation from one language to another, because they refer to the customs and ideas of a particular social group? It is through not understanding the importance of this double fact that the comical has been looked upon as a mere curiosity in which the mind finds amusement, and laughter itself as a strange, isolated phenomenon, without any bearing on the rest of human activity. Hence those definitions which tend to make the comic into an abstract relation between ideas: "an intellectual contrast," "a patent absurdity," etc., definitions which, even were they really suitable to every form of the comic, would not in the least explain why the comical makes us laugh.

How, indeed, should it come about that this particular logical relation, as soon as it is perceived, contracts, expands and shakes our limbs, while all other relations leave the body unaffected? It is not from this point of view that we shall approach the problem. To understand laughter, we must put it back into its natural environment, which is society, and above all must we determine the utility of its function, which is a social one. Such, let us say at once, will be the leading idea of all our investigations. Laughter must answer to certain requirements of life in common. It must have a *social* signification.

Let us clearly mark the point towards which our preliminary observations are converging. The comical will come into being, it appears, whenever a group of men concentrate their attention on one of their number, imposing silence on their emotions and calling into play nothing but their intelligence. What, now, is the particular point on which their attention will have to be concentrated, and what will here be the function of intelligence? To reply to these questions will be at once to come to closer grips with the problem. Consider this example: *A man, running along the street, stumbles and falls; the passers-by burst out laughing.* They would not laugh at him, I imagine, could they suppose that the whim had suddenly seized him to sit down on the ground. They laugh because his sitting down is involuntary. Consequently, it is not his sudden change of attitude that raises a laugh, but rather the involuntary element in this change—his clumsiness, in fact. Perhaps there was a stone on the road. He should have altered his pace or avoided the obstacle. Instead of that, through lack of elasticity, through absentmindedness and a kind of physical obstinacy, *as a result, in fact, of rigidity or of momentum*, the muscles continued to perform the same movement when the circumstances of the case called for something else. That is the reason of the man's fall, and also of the people's laughter.

Now, take the case of a person who attends to the petty occupations of his everyday life with mathematical precision. The objects around him, however, have all been tampered with by a mischievous wag, the result being that when he dips his pen into the inkstand he draws it out all covered with mud; when he fancies he is sitting down on a solid chair he finds himself sprawling on the floor; in a word, his actions are all topsy-turvy or mere beating the air, while in every case the effect is invariably one of momentum. Habit has given the impulse: what was wanted was to check the movement or deflect it. He did nothing of the sort, but continued like a machine in the same straight line. The victim, then, of a practical joke is in a position similar to that of a runner who falls—he is comical for the same reason. The laughable element in both cases consists of a certain *mechanical inelasticity*, just where one would expect to find the wide awake adaptability and the living pliableness of a human being. The only difference in the two cases is that the former happened of itself, whilst the latter was obtained artificially. In the first instance, the passer-by does nothing but look on, but in the second the mischievous wag intervenes.

All the same, in both cases the result has been brought about by an external circumstance. The comical is therefore accidental: it remains, so to speak, in superficial contact with the person. How is it to penetrate within? The necessary conditions will be fulfilled when mechanical rigidity no longer requires for its manifestation a stumbling-block which either the hazard of circumstance or human knavery has set in its way, but extracts by natural processes, from its own store, an inexhaustible series of opportunities for externally revealing its presence.

Suppose, then, we imagine a mind always thinking of what it has just done and never of what it is doing, like a song which lags behind its accompaniment. Let us try to picture to ourselves a certain inborn lack of elasticity of both senses and intelligence, which brings it to pass that we continue to see what is no longer visible, to hear what is no longer audible, to say what is no longer to the point: in short, to adapt ourselves to a past and therefore imaginary situation, when we ought to be shaping our conduct in accordance with the reality which is present. This time the comic will take up its abode in the person himself; it is the person who will supply it with everything—matter and form, cause and opportunity. Is it then surprising that the absent-minded individual—for this is the character we have just been describing—has usually fired the imagination of authors of comedy? Absentmindedness, indeed, is not perhaps the actual fountain-head of the comical, but surely it is contiguous to a certain stream of facts and fancies which flows straight from the fountain-head. It is situated, so to say, on one of the great natural watersheds of laughter.

Now, the effect of absentmindedness may gather strength in its turn. There is a general law, the first example of which we have just encountered, and which we will formulate in the following terms: when a certain comic effect has its origin in a certain cause, the more natural we regard the cause to be, the more comical shall we find the effect. Even now we laugh at absentmindedness when presented to us as a simple fact. Still more laughable will be the absentmindedness we have seen springing up and growing before our very eyes, with whose origin we are acquainted and whose life-history we can reconstruct. To choose a definite example: suppose a man has taken to reading nothing but romances of love and chivalry. Attracted and fascinated by his heroes, his thoughts and intentions gradually turn more and more towards them, till one fine day we find him walking among us like a somnambulist. His actions are distractions. But then his distractions can be traced back to a definite, positive cause. They are no longer cases of *absence* of mind, pure and simple; they find their explanation in the *presence* of the individual in quite definite, though imaginary, surroundings. Doubtless a fall is always a fall, but it is one thing to tumble into a well because you were looking anywhere but in front of you, it is quite another thing to fall into it because you were intent upon a star. It was certainly a star at which Don Quixote was gazing. How profound is the comic element in the over-romantic, Utopian bent of mind! And yet, if you reintroduce the idea of absentmindedness, which acts as a go-between, you will see this profound comic element uniting with the most superficial type. Yes, indeed, these whimsical wild enthusiasts, these madmen who are yet so strangely reasonable, excite us to laughter by playing on the same chords within ourselves, by setting in motion the same inner mechanism, as does the victim of a practical joke or the passerby who slips down in the street. They, too, are runners who fall and simple souls who are being hoaxed—runners after the ideal who stumble over realities, child-like dreamers for whom life delights to lie in wait. But, above all, they are past-masters in absentmindedness, with this superiority over their fellows that their absentmindedness is systematic and organized around one central idea, and that their mishaps are also quite coherent, thanks to the inexorable logic which reality applies to the correction of dreams, so that they kindle in those around them, by a series of cumulative effects, a hilarity capable of unlimited expansion.

Now, let us go a little further. Might not certain vices have the same relation to character that the rigidity of a fixed idea has to intellect? Whether as a moral kink or a crooked twist given to the will, vice has often the appearance of a curvature of the soul. Doubtless there are vices into which the soul plunges deeply with all its pregnant potency, which it rejuvenates and drags along with it into a moving circle of reincarnations. Those are tragic vices. But the vice capable of making us comical is, on the contrary, that which is brought from without, like a ready-made frame into which we are to step. It lends us its own rigidity instead of borrowing from us our flexibility. We do not render it more complicated; on the contrary, it simplifies us.

Here lies the essential difference between comedy and drama. A drama, even when portraying passions or vices that bear a name, so completely incorporates them in the person that their names are forgotten, their general characteristics effaced, and we no longer think of them at all, but rather of the person in whom they are assimilated; hence, the title of a drama can seldom be anything else than a proper noun. The reason is that, however intimately vice, when comical, is associated with persons, it nonetheless retains its simple, independent existence, it remains the central character, present though invisible, to which the characters in flesh and blood on the stage are attached. At times it delights in dragging them down with its own weight and making them share in its tumbles. More frequently, however, it plays on them as on an instrument or pulls the strings as though they were puppets. Look closely: you will find that the art of the comic poet consists in making us so well acquainted with the particular vice, in introducing us, the spectators, to such a degree of intimacy with it, that in the end we get hold of some of the strings of the marionette with which he is playing, and actually work them ourselves; this it is that explains part of the pleasure we feel. Here, too, it is really a kind of automatism that makes us laugh—an automatism, as we have already remarked, closely akin to mere absentmindedness. To realize this more fully, it need only be noted that a comic character is generally comical in proportion to his ignorance of himself. The comical person is unconscious. As though wearing the Ring of Gyges with reverse effect, he becomes invisible to himself while remaining visible to all the world.

A character in a tragedy will make no change in his conduct because he will know how it is judged by us; he may continue therein even though fully conscious of what he is and feeling keenly the horror he inspires in us. But a defect that is ridiculous, as soon as it feels itself to be so, endeavors to modify itself or at least to appear as though it did. Indeed, it is in this sense only that laughter "corrects men's manners." It makes us at once endeavor to appear what we ought to be, what some day we shall perhaps end in being.

It is unnecessary to carry this analysis any further. From the runner who falls to the simpleton who is hoaxed, from a state of being hoaxed to one of absentmindedness, from absentmindedness to wild enthusiasm, from wild enthusiasm to various distortions of character and will, we have followed the line of progress along which the comic becomes more and more deeply imbedded in the person, yet without ceasing, in its subtler manifestations, to recall to us some trace of what we noticed in its grosser forms, an effect of automatism and of inelasticity. Now we can obtain a first glimpse—a distant one, it is true, and still hazy and confused—of the laughable side of human nature and of the ordinary function of laughter.

What life and society require of each of us is a constantly alert attention that discerns the outlines of the present situation, together with a certain elasticity of mind and body to enable us to adapt ourselves in consequence. *Tension* and *elasticity* are two forces, mutually complementary, which life brings into play. If these two forces are lacking in the body to any considerable extent, we have sickness and infirmity and accidents of every kind. If they are lacking in the mind, we find every degree of mental deficiency, every variety of insanity.

Finally, if they are lacking in the character, we have cases of the gravest inadaptability to social life, which are the sources of misery and at times the causes of crime. Once these elements of inferiority that affect the serious side of existence are removed—and they tend to eliminate themselves in what has been called the struggle for life—the person can live, and that in common with other persons. But society asks for something more; it is not satisfied with simply living, it insists on living well. What it now has to dread is that each one of us, content with paying attention to what affects the essentials of life, will, so far as the rest is concerned, give way to the easy automatism of acquired habits. Another thing it must fear is that the members of whom it is made up, instead of aiming after an increasingly delicate adjustment of wills which will fit more and more perfectly into one another, will confine themselves to respecting simply the fundamental conditions of this adjustment: a cut-and-dried agreement among the persons will not satisfy it, it insists on a constant striving after reciprocal adaptation. Society will therefore be suspicious of all *inelasticity* of character, of mind and even of body, because it is the possible sign of a slumbering activity as well as of an activity with separatist tendencies, that inclines to swerve from the common center round which society gravitates: in short, because it is the sign of an eccentricity. And yet, society cannot intervene at this stage by material repression, since it is not affected in a material fashion. It is confronted with something that makes it uneasy, but only as a symptom—scarcely a threat, at the very most a gesture. A gesture, therefore, will be its reply. Laughter must be something of this kind, a sort of *social gesture*. By the fear which it inspires, it restrains eccentricity, keeps constantly awake and in mutual contact certain activities of a secondary order which might retire into their shell and go to sleep, and in short, softens down whatever the surface of the social body may retain of mechanical inelasticity. Laughter, then, does not belong to the province of aesthetics alone, since unconsciously (and even immorally in many particular instances) it pursues a utilitarian aim of general improvement. And yet there is something aesthetic about it, since the comical comes into being just when society and the individual, freed from the worry of self-preservation, begin to regard themselves as works of art. In a word, if a circle is drawn around those actions and dispositions—implied in individual or social life—to which their natural consequences bring their own penalties, there remains outside this sphere of emotion and struggle—and within a neutral zone in which man simply exposes himself to man's curiosity—a certain rigidity of body, mind and character that society would still like to get rid of in order to obtain from its members the greatest possible degree of elasticity and sociability. This rigidity is the comical, and laughter is its corrective.

Still, we must not accept this formula as a definition of the comical. It is suitable only for cases that are elementary, theoretical and perfect, in which the comical is free from all adulteration. Nor do we offer it, either, as an explanation. We prefer to make it, if you will, the *leitmotiv* [a recurrent theme] which is to accompany all our explanations. We must ever keep it in mind, though without dwelling on it too much, somewhat as a skillful fencer must think of the discontinuous movements of the lesson while his body is given up to the continuity of the fencing-match.

George Santayana

A PLEDGE OF THE POSSIBLE

In surveying so broad a field we stand in need of some classification and subdivision; and we have chosen the familiar one of *matter*, *form*, and *expression*, as least likely to lead us into needless artificiality. But artificiality there must always be in the discursive description of anything given in consciousness. Psychology attempts what is perhaps impossible, namely, the anatomy of life. Mind is a fluid; the lights and shadows that flicker through it have no real boundaries, and no possibility of permanence. Our whole classification of mental facts is borrowed from the physical conditions or expressions of them. The very senses are distinguished because of the readiness with which we can isolate their outer organs. Ideas can be identified only by identifying their objects. Feelings are recognized by their outer expression, and when we try to recall an emotion, we must do so by recalling the circumstances in which it occurred.

In distinguishing, then, in our *sense of beauty*, an appreciation of sensible material, one of abstract form, and another of associated values, we have been merely following the established method of psychology, the only one by which it is possible to analyze the mind. We have distinguished the elements of the object, and treated the feeling as if it were composed of corresponding parts. The worlds of nature and fancy, which are the object of aesthetic feeling, can be divided into parts in space and time. We can then distinguish the material of things from the various forms it may successively assume; we can distinguish, also, the earlier and the later impressions made by the same object; and we can ascertain the coexistence of one impression with another, or with the memory of others. But aesthetic feeling itself has no parts, and this physiology of its causes is not a description of its proper nature.

Beauty as we feel it is something indescribable: what it is or what it means can never be said. By appealing to experiment and memory we can show that this feeling varies as certain things vary in the objective conditions; that it varies with the frequency, for instance, with which a form has been presented, or with the associates which that form has had in the past. This will justify a description of the feeling as composed of the various contributions of these objects. But the feeling itself knows nothing of composition nor contributions. It is an affection of the soul, a consciousness of joy and security, a pang, a dream, a pure pleasure. It suffuses an object without telling why; nor has it any need to ask the question. It justifies itself and the vision it gilds; nor is there any meaning in seeking for a cause of it, in this inward sense. Beauty exists for the same reason that the object which is beautiful exists, or the world in which that object lies, or we that look upon both. It is an experience: there is nothing more to say about it. Indeed, if we look at things teleologically, and as they ultimately justify themselves to the heart, beauty is of all things what least calls for explanation. For matter and space and time and principles of reason and of evolution, all are ultimately brute, unaccountable data. We may describe what actually is, but it might have been otherwise, and the mystery of its being is as baffling and dark as ever.

But we—the minds that ask all questions and judge of the validity of all answers—we are not ourselves independent of this world in which we live. We sprang from it, and our relations in it determine all our instincts and satisfactions. This final questioning and sense of mystery is an unsatisfied craving which nature has her way of stilling. Now we only ask for reasons when we are surprised. If we had no expectations we should have no surprises. And what gives us expectation is the spontaneous direction of our thought, determined by the structure of our brain and the effects of our experience. If our spontaneous thoughts came to run in harmony with the course of nature, if our expectations were then continually fulfilled, the sense of mystery would vanish. We should be incapable of asking why the world existed or had such a nature, just as we are now little inclined to ask why anything is right, but mightily disinclined to give up asking why anything is wrong.

This satisfaction of our reason, due to the harmony between our nature and our experience, is partially realized already. The sense of beauty is its realization. When our senses and imagination find what they crave, when the world so shapes itself or so molds the mind that the correspondence between them is perfect, then perception is pleasure, and existence needs no apology. The duality which is the condition of conflict disappears. There is no inward standard different from the outward fact with which that outward fact may be compared. A unification of this kind is the goal of our intelligence and of our affection, quite as much as of our aesthetic sense; but we have in those departments fewer examples of success. In the heat of speculation or of love there may come moments of equal perfection, but they are unstable. The reason and the heart remain deeply unsatisfied. But the eye finds in nature, and in some supreme achievements of art, constant and fuller satisfaction. For the eye is quick, and seems to have been more docile to the education of life than the heart or the reason of man, and able sooner to adapt itself to the reality. Beauty therefore seems to be the clearest manifestation of perfection, and the best evidence of its possibility. If perfection is, as it should be, the ultimate justification of being, we may understand the ground of the moral dignity of beauty. Beauty is a pledge of the possible conformity between the soul and nature, and consequently a ground of faith in the supremacy of the good.

Arthur Schopenhauer

ART TAKES AWAY THE MIST

Not merely philosophy but also the fine arts work at bottom towards the solution of the problem of existence. For in every mind that once gives itself up to the purely objective contemplation of nature a desire has been excited, however concealed and unconscious it may be, to comprehend the true nature of things, of life and existence. For this alone has interest for the intellect as such, i.e., for the pure subject of knowledge which has become free from the aims of the will; as for the subject which knows as a mere individual the aims of the will alone have interest.

On this account the result of the purely objective apprehension of things is an expression more of the nature of life and existence, more an answer to the question, "What is life?" Every genuine and successful work of art answers this question in its own way with perfect correctness. But all the arts speak only the naive and childish language of perception, not the abstract and serious language of *reflection*; their answer is therefore a fleeting image: not permanent and general knowledge. Thus for *perception* every work of art answers that question, every painting, every statue, every poem, every scene upon the stage: music also answers it; and indeed more profoundly than all the rest, for in its language, which is understood with absolute directness, but which is yet untranslatable into that of the reason, the inner nature of all life and existence expresses itself. Thus all the other arts hold up to the questioner a perceptible image, and say, "Look here, this is life." Their answer, however correct it may be, will yet always afford merely a temporary, not a complete and final, satisfaction. For they always give merely a fragment, an example instead of the rule, not the whole, which can only be given in the universality of the *conception*. Therefore, for reflection and abstraction to give an answer which just on that account shall be permanent is the task of philosophy. However, we see here on what the relationship of philosophy to the fine arts rests, and can conclude from that to what extent the capacity of both, although in its direction and in secondary matters very different, is yet in its root the same.

Every work of art accordingly really aims at showing us life and things as they are in truth, but cannot be directly discerned by every one through the mist of objective and subjective contingencies. Art takes away this mist.

The works of the poets, sculptors, and representative artists in general contain an unacknowledged treasure of profound wisdom; just because out of them the wisdom of the nature of things itself speaks, whose utterances they merely interpret by illustrations and purer repetitions. On this account, however, everyone who reads the poem or looks at the picture must certainly contribute out of his own means to bring that wisdom to light; accordingly he comprehends only so much of it as his capacity and culture admit of; as in the deep sea each sailor only lets down the lead as far as the length of the line will allow. Before a picture, as before a prince, every one must stand, waiting to see whether and what it will speak to him; and, as in the case of a prince, so here he must not himself address it, for then he would only hear himself.

It follows from all this that in the works of the representative arts all truth is certainly contained, yet only virtually or implicitly; philosophy, on the other hand, endeavors to supply the same truth actually and explicitly, and therefore, in this sense, is related to art as wine to grapes. What it promises to supply would be, as it were, an already realized and clear gain, a firm and abiding possession; while that which proceeds from the achievements and works of art is one

Edited From *The World as Will and Idea,* Vol. III, Chapter XXXIV. Translated by R. B. Haldane, and J. Kemp, 1909, which is now in the public domain.

which has constantly to be reproduced anew. Therefore, however, it makes demands, not only upon those who produce its works, but also upon those who are to enjoy them which are discouraging and hard to comply with. Therefore, its public remains small, while that of art is large.

The cooperation of the beholder, which is referred to above, as demanded for the enjoyment of a work of art, depends partly upon the fact that every work of art can only produce its effect through the medium of the fancy; therefore it must excite this, and can never allow it to be left out of the play and remain inactive. This is a condition of the aesthetic effect, and therefore a fundamental law of all fine arts. But it follows from this that, through the work of art, everything must not be directly given to the senses, but rather only so much as is demanded to lead the fancy on to the right path; something, and indeed the ultimate thing, must always be left over for the fancy to do. Even the author must always leave something over for the reader to think; for Voltaire has very rightly said, "The secret of being a bore is to tell everything." But besides this, in art the best of all is too spiritual to be given directly to the senses; it must be born in the imagination of the beholder, although caused by the work of art. It depends upon this that the sketches of great masters often effect more than their finished pictures; although another advantage certainly contributes to this, namely, that they are completed offhand in the moment of conception; while the perfected painting is only produced through continued effort, by means of skillful deliberation and persistent intention, for the inspiration cannot last till it is completed.

From the fundamental aesthetical law we are speaking of, it is further to be explained why wax figures never produce an aesthetic effect, and therefore are not properly works of fine art, although it is just in them that the imitation of nature is able to reach its highest grade. For they leave nothing for the imagination to do. Sculpture gives merely the form without the color; painting gives the color, but the mere appearance of the form; thus both appeal to the imagination of the beholder. The wax figure, on the other hand, gives all, form and color at once; from which arises the appearance of reality, and the imagination is left out of account. Poetry, on the contrary, appeals indeed to the imagination alone, which it sets in action by means of mere words.

An arbitrary playing with the means of art without a proper knowledge of the end is, in every art, the fundamental characteristic of the dabbler. Such a man shows himself in the pillars that support nothing, aimless volutes [spiral, scroll-like ornaments often affixed to pillars], juttings and projections of bad architecture, in the meaningless runs and figures, together with the aimless noise of bad music, in the jingling of the rhymes of senseless poetry, etc.

It follows from my whole view of art, that its aim is the facilitating of the knowledge of the Ideas of the world (in the Platonic sense, the only one which I recognize for the word "Idea"). The Ideas, however, are essentially something perceptible, which, therefore, in its fuller determinations, is inexhaustible. The communication of such an Idea can therefore only take place on the path of perception, which is that of art. Whoever, therefore, is filled with the comprehension of an Idea is justified if he chooses art as the medium of its communication. The mere conception, on the other hand, is something completely determinable, therefore exhaustible, and distinctly thought, the whole content of which can be coldly and dryly expressed in words.

Now to desire to communicate such a conception by means of a work of art is a very useless circumlocution, indeed belongs to that playing with the means of art without knowledge of its end which has just been condemned. Therefore a work of art which has proceeded from mere distinct conceptions is always ungenuine. If now, in considering a work of plastic art, or in reading a poem, or in hearing a piece of music (which aims at describing something definite), we see, through all the rich materials of art, the distinct, limited, cold, dry conception shine out, and at last come to the front, the conception which was the kernel of this work, the whole notion of which consequently consisted in the distinct thinking of it, and accordingly is absolutely exhausted by its communication, we feel disgusted and indignant, for we see ourselves deceived and cheated out of our interest and attention.

We are only perfectly satisfied by the impression of a work of art when it leaves something which, with all our thinking about it, we cannot bring down to the distinctness of a conception. The mark of that hybrid origin from mere conceptions is that the author of a work of art could, before he set about it, give in distinct words what he intended to present; for then it would have been possible to attain his whole end through these words. Therefore it is an undertaking as unworthy as it is absurd if, as has often been tried at the present day, one seeks to reduce a poem of Shakespeare's or Goethe's to the abstract truth which it was its aim to communicate.

Certainly the artist ought to think in the arranging of his work; but only that thought which was *perceived* before it was thought has afterwards, in its communication, the power of animating or rousing, and thereby becomes imperishable. We shall not refrain from observing here that certainly the work which is done at a stroke, like the sketches of painters already referred to, the work which is completed in the inspiration of its first conception, and as it were unconsciously dashed off, like the melody which comes entirely without reflection, and quite as if by inspiration. And finally, also the lyrical poem proper, the mere song, in which the deeply felt mood of the present, and the impression of the surroundings, as if involuntarily, pours itself forth in words, whose meter and rhyme come about of their own accord—that all these, I say, have the great advantage of being purely the work of the ecstasy of the moment, the inspiration, the free movement of genius, without any mixture of intention and reflection; hence they are through and through delightful and enjoyable, without shell and kernel, and their effect is much more inevitable than that of the greatest works of art, of slower and more deliberate execution. In all the latter, thus in great historical paintings, in long epic poems, great operas, etc., reflection, intention, and deliberate selection has had an important part. Understanding, technical skill, and routine must here fill up the gaps which the conception and inspiration of genius has left, and must mix with these all kinds of necessary supplementary work as cement of the only really genuinely brilliant parts.

This explains why all such works, except the perfect masterpieces of the very greatest masters (as, for example, "Hamlet," "Faust," the opera of "Don Juan"), inevitably contain a mixture of something insipid and wearisome, which in some measure hinders the enjoyment of them. Proofs of this are the "Messiah," "Paradise Lost," and the "Aeneid." But that this is the case is the consequence of the limitation of human powers in general.

Part Eleven: Does Life Have Meaning?

Introduction

Does your life have meaning whether or not you accomplish anything during your lifetime? Does it have meaning as soon as you are born, or does it acquire meaning in the course of your life? Is life *intrinsically* meaningful (by its very nature)? Does a long life ensure that your life has meaning? Can a life lived in isolation from others have meaning, or does a meaningful life require interaction with others? Are evil lives meaningful? Are short and painful lives meaningful? Can an unpleasant or unhappy life be meaningful?

There are other phrases that capture the intent of these questions: *the significance of life*; *an important life; a valuable life; a worthwhile life*. Can we determine whether one person's life is more (or less) meaningful than another person's life? And even if we can somehow claim that one person's life is more meaningful than another's life, can we still hold that both persons lives have equal *value*? Is a meaningful existence relative to a person, a society, a time, or are there universal objective standards?

In the first reading of this section, Epicurus offers a universal prescription: our lives should be directed to the pursuit of happiness. We can achieve happiness by pleasure but, as Epicurus explains, pleasure is simply the "absence of pain in the body and of trouble in the soul." Being aware that we are mortal allows us to enjoy life as long as we have it, without worrying about death or desiring immortality. In fact, some have argued that life can have meaning solely within the physical world in which we live, regardless of whether God exists.

We often judge an action or behavior by its consequences. We can often separate short- and long-term consequences of an action. For example, there is a scene in the novel *The Razor's Edge* where someone lies about an invitation to a costume ball in order for a dying man to have one last pleasant moment immediately before he dies. This act of kindness has no long-term effect on the universe—it will be completely forgotten sooner or later—but it had an important meaning to the few people who witnessed it.

Along these lines, we can ask whether being a creative person—e.g., an artist, scientist, philosopher, teacher—guarantees a meaningful life. Yet we can again ask, "Is it necessary that you accomplish something, or help others, or create something, or build something, in order for your life to have meaning?" Is watching TV a meaningful activity? Is passively watching anything meaningful? What if someone observes birds all their adult life but never writes anything or shares the observations with anyone else—is that life meaningful? If you give a large amount of your money to charities, but your motive is simply to avoid paying high taxes, then what meaning should we assign to your actions? The relevance of short- and long-term consequences of actions can itself be challenged. For example, what if someone asked the following questions: "Would life have no meaning if it arose by chance? Does life have meaning only if it was intended?"

Does Life Have Meaning?

At the end of their search to find out whether or not life has meaning, some have concluded that life is meaningless. This philosophical belief is illustrated in the reading by Arthur Schopenhauer, in which he argues that our lives lack meaning because we can never be satisfied. On the one hand, if we have not yet satisfied our desires, then we are unhappy; on the other hand, if we have satisfied our desires, then we are bored and unhappy. According to Schopenhauer, "This is direct proof that existence has no real value in itself; for what is boredom but the feeling of the emptiness of life?"

If it is possible to view our lives from an external viewpoint—looking at the universe as a whole—then everything we do appears insignificant. Moreover, if humans eventually cease to exist in the universe, then the meaning of any act, life, or even humanity would seem to disappear. If life is absurd, then what should be our response? Despair, anger, apathy, and resignation are possibilities, but so too are defiance and a sense of irony.

Epicurus

IN WAKING OR IN DREAM

Let no one be slow to seek wisdom when he is young nor weary in the search thereof when he is grown old. For no age is too early or too late for the health of the soul. And to say that the season for studying philosophy has not yet come, or that it is past and gone, is like saying that the season for happiness is not yet or that it is now no more. Therefore, both old and young ought to seek wisdom, the former in order that, as age comes over him, he may be young in good things because of the grace of what has been, and the latter in order that, while he is young, he may at the same time be old, because he has no fear of the things which are to come. So we must exercise ourselves in the things which bring happiness, since, if that be present, we have everything, and, if that be absent, all our actions are directed toward attaining it.

Accustom yourself to believe that death is nothing to us, for good and evil imply awareness, and death is the privation of all awareness; therefore a right understanding that death is nothing to us makes the mortality of life enjoyable, not by adding to life an unlimited time, but by taking away the yearning after immortality. Life has no terror for those who apprehend that there is no terror in ceasing to live. Foolish, therefore, is the person who says that he fears death, not because it will pain when it comes, but because it pains in the prospect. Whatever causes no annoyance when it is present, causes only a groundless pain in the expectation. Death, therefore, the most awful of evils, is nothing to us, seeing that when we are alive, death has not come, and, when death has come, we are not alive. It is nothing, then, either to the living or to the dead; for with the living it is not, and the dead no longer exist. But in the world, at one time people shun death as the greatest of all evils, and at another time choose it as a respite from the evils in life. The wise person does not deprecate life nor does he fear the cessation of life. The thought of life is no offense to him, nor is the cessation of life regarded as an evil. And even as people choose of food not merely and simply the larger portion, but the more pleasant, so the wise seek to enjoy the time which is most pleasant and not merely that which is longest. And he who admonishes the young to live well and the old to make a good end speaks foolishly, not merely because of the desirability of life, but because the same exercise at once teaches to live well and to die well. Much worse is he who says that it were good not to be born, but when once one is born to pass with all speed through the gates of Hades. For if he truly believes this, why does he not depart from life? It were easy for him to do so, if once he were firmly convinced. If he speaks only in mockery, his words are foolishness, for those who hear him do not believe him.

We must remember that the future is neither wholly ours nor wholly not ours, so that neither must we count upon it as quite certain to come, nor despair of it as quite certain not to come.

We must also reflect that some desires are natural, others are groundless; and that of the natural, some are necessary as well as natural, and some natural only. And of the necessary desires some are necessary if we are to be happy, some if the body is to be rid of uneasiness, some if we are even to live. He who has a clear and certain understanding of these things will direct every preference and aversion toward securing health of body and tranquility of mind, seeing that this is the sum and end of a happy life. For the end of all our actions is to be free from pain and fear, and, when once we have attained all this, the tempest of the soul is laid; seeing that the living creature has no need to go in search of something that is lacking, nor to look for anything else by which the good of the soul and of the body will be fulfilled. When we are pained, then, and then only, do we feel the need of pleasure. For this reason we call pleasure the alpha and omega of a happy life. Pleasure is our first and kindred good. It is the starting-point of every choice and of every aversion, and to it we come back, inasmuch as we make feeling the rule by which to judge of every good thing. And since pleasure is our first and native good, for that reason we do not choose every pleasure whatever, but often pass over many pleasures when a greater annoyance ensues from them. And often we consider pains superior to pleasures when submission to the pains for a long time brings us as a consequence a greater pleasure. While therefore all pleasure, because it is naturally akin to us is good, not all pleasure is worthy of choice, just as all pain is an evil and yet not all pain is to be shunned. It is, however, by measuring one against another, and by looking at the conveniences and inconveniences, that all these matters must be judged. Sometimes we treat the good as an evil, and the evil, on the contrary, as a good. We regard independence of outward things as a great good, not so as in all cases to use little, but so as to be contented with little if we have not much, being honestly persuaded that they have the sweetest enjoyment of luxury who stand least in need of it, and that whatever is natural is easily procured, and only the vain and worthless hard to win. Plain fare gives as much pleasure as an expensive diet, when the pain of want has been removed, while bread and water confer the highest possible pleasure when they are brought to hungry lips. To habituate one's self, therefore, to a simple and inexpensive diet, supplies all that is needed for health, and enables a person to meet the necessary requirements of life without shrinking, and it places us in a better condition when we approach at intervals a costly fare and renders us fearless of fortune.

When we say, then, that pleasure is the end and aim, we do not mean the pleasures of the prodigal or the pleasures of sensuality, as is understood by some through ignorance, prejudice, or willful misrepresentation. By pleasure we mean the absence of pain in the body and of trouble in the soul. It is not an unbroken succession of drinking-bouts and of merrymaking, not sexual love, not the enjoyment of the fish and other delicacies of a luxurious table, which produce a pleasant life; it is sober reasoning, searching out the grounds of every choice and avoidance, and banishing those beliefs through which the greatest disturbances take possession of the soul. Of all this the greatest good is prudence. For this reason prudence is a more precious thing even than the other virtues, for it is not possible to lead a life of pleasure which is not also a life of prudence, honor, and justice; nor lead a life of prudence, honor, and justice, which is not also a life of pleasure. For the virtues have grown into one with a pleasant life, and a pleasant life is inseparable from them.

Who, then, is superior in your judgment to such a person? He holds a holy belief concerning the gods, and is altogether free from the fear of death. He has diligently considered the end fixed by nature, and understands how easily the limit of good things can be reached and attained, and how either the duration or the intensity of evils is but slight. Destiny, which some introduce as sovereign over all things, he laughs at and scorns, affirming rather that some things happen of necessity, others by chance, others through our own agency. For he sees that necessity destroys responsibility and that chance or fortune is inconstant; whereas our own actions are free, and it is to them that praise and blame naturally attach. It were better, indeed, to accept the legends of the gods than to bow beneath destiny which the natural philosophers have imposed. The one holds out some faint hope that we may escape if we honor the gods, while the necessity of the naturalists is deaf to all entreaties. Nor does he hold chance to be a god, as the world in general does, for in the acts of a god there is no disorder; nor to be a cause, though an uncertain one, for he believes that no good or evil is dispensed by chance to people so as to make life happy, though it supplies the starting-point of great good and great evil. He believes that the misfortune of the wise is better than the prosperity of the fool. It is better, in short, that what is well judged in action should not owe its successful issue to the aid of chance.

If you reflect on these ideas day and night, both by yourself and with those who are like you, then you will not be disturbed—either in waking or in dream—but you will live as a god among people. For people lose all appearance of mortality by living in the midst of immortal blessings.

Arthur Schopenhauer

THE VANITY OF EXISTENCE

This vanity finds expression in the whole way in which things exist; in the infinite nature of Time and Space, as opposed to the finite nature of the individual in both; in the ever-passing present moment as the only mode of actual existence; in the interdependence and relativity of all things; in continual Becoming without ever Being; in constant wishing and never being satisfied; in the long battle which forms the history of life, where every effort is checked by difficulties, and stopped until they are overcome. *Time* is that in which all things pass away; it is merely the form under which the *will to live*—the thing-in-itself and therefore imperishable—has revealed to it that its efforts are in vain; it is that agent by which at every moment all things in our hands become as nothing, and lose any real value they possess.

That which *has been* exists no more; it exists as little as that which has *never* been. But of everything that exists you must say, in the next moment, that it has been. Hence something of great importance now past is inferior to something of little importance now present, in that the latter is a *reality* and related to the former as something to nothing.

A man finds himself, to his great astonishment, suddenly existing, after thousands and thousands of years of non-existence: he lives for a little while; and then, again, comes an equally long period when he must exist no more. The heart rebels against this, and feels that it cannot be true.

Of every event in our life we can say only for one moment that it *is*; for ever after, that it *was*. Every evening we are poorer by a day. It might, perhaps, make us mad to see how rapidly our short span of time ebbs away; if it were not that in the furthest depths of our being we are secretly conscious of our share in the exhaustible spring of eternity, so that we can always hope to find life in it again.

Consideration of the kind, touched on above, might, indeed, lead us to embrace the belief that the greatest *wisdom* is to make the enjoyment of the present the supreme object of life; because that is the only reality, all else being merely the play of thought. On the other hand, such a course might just as well be called the greatest *folly*: for that which in the next moment exists no more, and vanishes utterly, like a dream, can never be worth a serious effort.

The whole foundation on which our existence rests is the present—the ever-fleeting present. It lies, then, in the very nature of our existence to take the form of constant motion, and to offer no possibility of our ever attaining the rest for which we are always striving. We are like a man running downhill, who cannot keep on his legs unless he runs on, and will inevitably fall if he stops; or, again, like a pole balanced on the tip of one's finger; or like a planet, which would fall into its sun the moment it ceased to hurry forward on its way. Unrest is the mark of existence.

In a world where all is unstable, and nothing can endure, but is swept onwards at once in the hurrying whirlpool of change; where a man, if he is to keep erect at all, must always be advancing and moving, like an acrobat on a rope—in such a world, happiness in inconceivable.

How can it dwell where, as Plato says, *continual Becoming and never Being* is the sole form of existence? In the first place, no man is ever happy; he spends his entire life striving after something which he thinks will make him happy; he seldom attains his goal, and when he does, it is only to be disappointed; he is mostly shipwrecked in the end, and comes into harbor with masts and

Edited from *Essays of Schopenhauer*, Translated by Sara Hay Dircks, 1880, which is now in the public domain.

rigging gone. And then, it doesn't matter whether he has been happy or miserable, because his life was never anything more than a present moment always vanishing; and now it is over.

At the same time, it is a wonderful thing that, in the world of human beings as in that of animals in general, this manifold restless motion is produced and kept up by the agency of two simple impulses—hunger, and the sexual instinct; aided a little, perhaps, by the influence of boredom, but by nothing else; and that, in the theatre of life, these suffice to form the *prime mover* of how complicated a machinery, setting in motion the strange and varied show!

On looking a little closer, we find that inorganic matter presents a constant conflict between chemical forces, which eventually annihilates it; and on the other hand, that organic life is impossible without continual change of matter, and cannot exist if it does not receive perpetual help from without. This is the realm of *finite existence*, and its opposite would be an *infinite existence,* exposed to no attack from without, and needing nothing to support it; the realm of eternal peace; some timeless, changeless state, one and undiversified; the negative knowledge of which forms the dominant note of the Platonic philosophy. It is to some such state as this that the denial of the will to live opens up the way.

The scenes of our life are like pictures done in rough mosaic. Looked at closely, they produce no effect. There is nothing beautiful to be found in them, unless you stand some distance off. So, to gain anything we have longed for is only to discover how vain and empty it is; and even though we are always living in expectation of better things, at the same time we often repent and long to have the past back again. We look upon the present as something to be put up with while it lasts, and serving only as the way towards our goal. Hence most people, if they glance back when they come to the end of life, will find that all along they have been living *temporarily*: they will be surprised to find that the very thing they disregarded and let slip by unenjoyed, was just the life in the expectation of which they passed all their time. Of how many a man may it not be said that hope made a fool of him until he danced into the arms of death!

Then again, how insatiable a creature is man! Every satisfaction he attains lays the seeds of some new desire, so that there is no end to the wishes of each individual will. And why is this? The real reason is simply that, taken in itself, *Will* is the lord of all worlds: everything belongs to it, and therefore no one single thing can ever give it satisfaction, but only the whole, which is endless. For all that, it must rouse our sympathy to think how very little the *Will*, this lord of the world, really gets when it takes the form of an individual; usually only just enough to keep the body together. This is why man is so very miserable.

Life presents itself chiefly as a task—the task, I mean, of subsisting at all. If this is accomplished, life is a burden, and then there comes the second task of doing something with that which has been won—of warding off boredom, which, like a bird of prey, hovers over us, ready to fall wherever it sees a life secure from need. The first task is to win something; the second, to banish the feeling that it has been won; otherwise it is a burden.

Human life must be some kind of mistake. The truth of this will be sufficiently obvious if we only remember that man is a compound of needs and necessities hard to satisfy; and that even when they are satisfied, all he obtains is a state of painlessness, where nothing remains to him but abandonment to boredom. This is direct proof that existence has no real value in itself; for what is boredom but the feeling of the emptiness of life? If life—the craving for which is the very essence of our being—were possessed of any positive intrinsic value, there would be no such thing as boredom at all: mere existence would satisfy us in itself, and we should want for nothing.

But as it is, we take no delight in existence except when we are struggling for something; and then distance and difficulties to be overcome make our goal look as though it would satisfy us—an illusion which vanishes when we reach it; or else when we are occupied with some purely intellectual interest—when in reality we have stepped forth from life to look upon it from the outside, much after the manner of spectators at a play. And even sensual pleasure itself means nothing but a struggle and aspiration, ceasing the moment its aim is attained. Whenever we are not occupied in one of these ways, but cast upon existence itself, its vain and worthless nature is brought home to us; and this is what we mean by boredom. The longing after what is strange and uncommon—an innate and ineradicable tendency of human nature—shows how glad we are at any interruption of that natural course of affairs which is so very tedious.

That this most perfect manifestation of the will to live, the human organism, with the cunning and complex working of its machinery, must fall to dust and yield up itself and all its strivings to extinction—this is the naive way in which Nature, who is always so true and sincere in what she says, proclaims the whole struggle of this will as in its very essence barren and unprofitable. Were it of any value in itself, anything unconditioned and absolute, it could not thus end in mere nothing.

If we turn from contemplating the world as a whole, and, in particular, the generations of men as they live their little hour of mock-existence and then are swept away in rapid succession; if we turn from this, and look at life in its small details, as presented, say, in a comedy, how ridiculous it all seems! It is like a drop of water seen through a microscope, a single drop teeming with *infusoria* [single-celled organisms]; or a speck of cheese full of mites invisible to the naked eye. How we laugh as they bustle about so eagerly, and struggle with one another in so tiny a space! And whether here, or in the little span of human life, this terrible activity produces a comic effect.

It is only in the microscope that our life looks so big. It is an indivisible point, drawn out and magnified by the powerful lenses of Time and Space. No one has ever felt perfectly happy in the present moment; if he had it would have intoxicated him.

William James

IS LIFE WORTH LIVING?

When Mr. Mallock's book with this title appeared some fifteen years ago, the jocose answer that "it depends on the *liver*" had great currency in the newspapers. The answer that I propose to give tonight cannot be jocose. In the words of one of Shakespeare's prologues,

> I come no more to make you laugh; things now,
> That bear a weighty and a serious brow,
> Sad, high, and working, full of state and woe,

must be my theme. In the deepest heart of all of us there is a corner in which the ultimate mystery of things works sadly, and I know not what such an Association as yours intends nor what you ask of those whom you invite to address you, unless it be to lead you from the surface-glamour of existence and for an hour at least to make you heedless to the buzzing and jigging and vibration of small interests and excitements that form the tissue of our ordinary consciousness. Without further explanation or apology, then, I ask you to join me in turning an attention, commonly too unwilling, to the profounder bass-note of life. Let us search the lonely depths for an hour together and see what answers in the last folds and recesses of things our question may find.

With many men the question of life's worth is answered by a temperamental optimism that makes them Incapable of believing that anything seriously evil can exist. Our dear old Walt Whitman's works are the standing textbook of this kind of optimism; the mere joy of living is so immense in Walt Whitman's veins that it abolishes the possibility of any other kind of feeling:

> To breathe the air, how delicious!
> To speak, to walk, to seize something by the hand!
> To be this incredible God I am!
> I praise with electric voice.
> For I do not see one imperfection in the universe.
> And I do not see one cause or result lamentable at last.

So Rousseau, writing of the nine years he spent at Annecy, with nothing but his happiness to tell:

> How tell what was neither said nor done nor even thought, but tasted only and felt, with no object of my felicity but the emotion of felicity itself. I rose with the sun and I was happy; I went to walk and I was happy; I saw Maman and I was happy; I left her and I was happy. I rambled through the woods and over the vine-slopes, I wandered in the valleys, I read, I lounged, I worked in the garden, I gathered the fruits, I helped at the indoor work, and happiness followed me everywhere; it was in no one assignable thing; it was all within myself; it could not leave me for a single instant.

If moods like this could be made permanent and constitutions like these universal, there would never be any occasion for such discourses as the present one. No philosopher would seek to prove articulately that life is worth living, for the fact that it absolutely is so would vouch for itself and the problem disappear in the vanishing of the question rather than in the coming of anything like a reply. But we are not magicians to make the optimistic temperament universal; and alongside of the deliverances of temperamental optimism concerning life, those of temperamental pessimism always exist and oppose to them a standing refutation. In what is called circular insanity, phases of melancholy succeed phases of mania, with no outward cause that we can discover, and often enough to one and the same well person life will offer incarnate radiance today and incarnate dreariness tomorrow, according to the fluctuations of what the older medical books used to call the concoction of the humors. In the words of the newspaper joke, "it depends on the liver." Rousseau's ill-balanced constitution undergoes a change, and behold him in his latter evil days a prey to melancholy and black delusions of suspicion and fear. And some men seem launched upon the world even from their birth with souls as incapable of happiness as Walt Whitman's was of gloom.

That life is not worth living the whole army of suicides declare an army whose rollcall, like the famous evening drum-beat of the British army, follows the sun round the world and never terminates. We, too, as we sit here in our comfort, must "ponder these things," for we are of one substance with these suicides, and their life is the life we share. The plainest intellectual integrity, nay, more, the simplest manliness and honor, forbid us to forget their case.

To come immediately to the heart of my theme, then, what I propose is to imagine ourselves reasoning with a fellow-mortal who is on such terms with life that the only comfort left him is to brood on the assurance "you may end it when you will." What reasons can we plead that may render such a brother (or sister) willing to take up the burden again ? Ordinary Christians, reasoning with would-be suicides, have little to offer them beyond the usual negative "thou shalt not." God alone is master of life and death, they say, and it is a blasphemous act to anticipate his absolving hand. But can we find nothing richer or more positive than this, no reflections to urge whereby the suicide may actually see, and in all sad seriousness feel, that in spite of adverse appearances even for him life is worth living still? There are suicides, and suicides in the United States about three thousand of them every year, and I must frankly confess that with perhaps the majority of these my suggestions are impotent to deal. Where suicide is the result of insanity or sudden frenzied impulse, reflection is impotent to arrest its headway; and cases like these belong to the ultimate mystery of evil concerning which I can only offer considerations tending towards religious patience at the end of this hour.

Most of you are devoted for good or ill to the reflective life. Many of you are students of philosophy, and have already felt in your own persons the skepticism and unreality that too much grubbing in the abstract roots of things will breed. This is, indeed, one of the regular fruits of the over-studious career. Too much questioning and too little active responsibility lead, almost as often as too much sensualism does, to the edge of the slope, at the bottom of which lie pessimism and the nightmare or suicidal view of life. But to the diseases which reflection breeds, still further reflection can oppose effective remedies; and it is of the melancholy and Weltschmerz [a feeling of melancholy and pessimism] bred of reflection that I now proceed to speak.

Let me say immediately that my final appeal is to nothing more recondite than religious faith. So far as my argument is to be destructive, it will consist in nothing more than the sweeping away of certain views that often keep the springs of religious faith compressed; and so far as it is to be constructive it will consist in holding up to the light of day certain considerations calculated to let loose these springs in a normal, natural way. Pessimism is essentially a religious disease. In the form of it to which you are most liable it consists in nothing but a religious demand to which there comes no normal religious reply. Now there are two stages of recovery from this disease, two different levels upon which one may emerge from the midnight view to the daylight view of things, and I must treat of them in turn. The second stage is the more complete and joyous, and it corresponds to the freer exercise of religious trust and fancy. There are, as is well known, persons who are naturally very free in this regard, others who are not at all so. There are persons, for instance, whom we find indulging to their heart's content in prospects of immortality, and there are others who experience the greatest difficulty in making such a notion seem real to themselves at all. These latter persons are tied to their senses, restricted to their natural experience; and many of them moreover feel a sort of intellectual loyalty to what they call hard facts which is positively shocked by the easy excursions into the unseen that they witness other people make at the bare call of sentiment. Minds of either class may, however, be intensely religious. They may equally desire atonement, harmony, reconciliation, and crave acquiescence and communion with the total Soul of Things. But the craving, when the mind is pent in to the hard facts, especially as "Science" now reveals them, can breed pessimism, quite as easily as it breeds optimism when it inspires religious trust and fancy to wing their way to an other and a better world.

That is why I call pessimism an essentially religious disease. The nightmare view of life has plenty of organic sources, but its great reflective source in these days, and at all times, has been the contradiction between the phenomena of Nature and the craving of the heart to believe that behind Nature there is a spirit whose expression Nature is. What philosophers call natural theology has been one way of appeasing this craving. That poetry of nature in which our English literature is so rich has been another way. Now suppose a mind of the latter of our two classes, whose imagination is pent in consequently, and who takes its facts "hard"; suppose it, moreover, to feel strongly the craving for communion, and yet to realize how desperately difficult it is to construe the scientific order of Nature either theologically or poetically, and what result can there be but inner discord and contradiction? Now this inner discord (merely as discord) can be relieved in either of two ways. The longing to read the facts religiously may cease, and leave the bare facts by themselves. Or supplementary facts may be discovered or believed in, which permit the religious reading to go on. And these two ways of relief are the two stages of recovery, the two levels of escape from pessimism, to which I made allusion a moment ago, and which what follows will, I trust, make more clear.

Starting then with Nature, we naturally tend, if we have the religious craving, to say with Marcus Aurelius, "O Universe, what thou wishest I wish." Our sacred books and traditions tell us of one God who made heaven and earth, and looking on them saw that they were good. Yet, on more intimate acquaintance, the visible surfaces of heaven and earth refuse to be brought by us into any intelligible unity at all. Every phenomena that we would praise there exists cheek by jowl with some contrary phenomenon that cancels all its religious effect upon the mind. Beauty and hideousness, love and cruelty, life and death keep house together in indissoluble partnership; and there gradually steals over us, instead of the old warm notion of a man-loving Deity, that of an awful Power that neither hates nor loves, but rolls all things together meaninglessly to a common doom. This is an uncanny, a sinister, a nightmare view of life, and its peculiar eeriness or poisonousness lies expressly in our holding two things together which cannot possibly agree, in our clinging on the one hand to the demand that there shall be a living spirit of the whole, and, on the other, to the belief that the course of nature must be such a spirit's adequate manifestation and expression. It is in the contradiction between the supposed being of a spirit that encompasses and owns us and with which we ought to have some communion, and the character of such a spirit as revealed by the visible world's course, that this particular death-in-life paradox and this melancholy-breeding puzzle reside.

This is the first stage of speculative melancholy. No brute can have this sort of melancholy, no man that is irreligious can become its prey. It is the sick shudder of the frustrated religious demand, and not the mere necessary outcome of animal experience. The mood of levity, of "I don't care," is for this world's ills a sovereign and practical anesthetic. But no! Something deep down tells us that there is a spirit in things to which we owe allegiance and for whose sake we must keep up the serious mood, and so the inner fever and discord also are kept up for Nature taken on her visible surface reveals no such spirit, and beyond the facts of Nature we are at the present stage of our inquiry not supposing ourselves to look.

Now, I do not hesitate frankly and sincerely to confess to you that this real and genuine discord seems to me to carry with it the inevitable bankruptcy of natural religion naively and simply taken. There were times when Leibnitzes with their heads buried in monstrous wigs could compose Theodicies, and when stall-fed officials of an established church could prove by the valves in the heart and the round ligament of the hip-joint the existence of a "Moral and Intelligent Contriver of the World." But those times are past; and we of the nineteenth century, with our evolutionary theories and our mechanical philosophies, already know nature too impartially and too well to worship unreservedly any god of whose character she can be an adequate expression. Truly all we know of good and beauty proceeds from nature, but nonetheless so all we know of evil. Visible nature is all plasticity and indifference, a moral multiverse, as one might call it, and not a moral universe. If there be a divine Spirit of the universe, Nature, such as we know her, cannot possibly be its *ultimate word* to man. Either there is no spirit revealed in nature, or else it is inadequately revealed there; and (as all the higher religions have assumed) what we call visible nature, or *this* world, must be but a veil and surface-show whose full meaning resides in a supplementary unseen or *other* world.

I cannot help, therefore, accounting it on the whole a gain (though it may seem for certain poetic constitutions a very sad loss) that the naturalistic superstition, the worship of the god of nature simply taken as such should have begun to loosen its hold upon the educated mind. In fact, if I am to express my personal opinion unreservedly, I should say (in spite of its sounding blasphemous at first to certain ears) that the initial step towards getting into healthy ultimate relations with the universe is the act of rebellion against the idea that such a God exists.

We are familiar enough in this community with the spectacle of persons exulting in their emancipation from belief in the God of their ancestral Calvinism, him who made the garden and the serpent and pre-appointed the eternal fires of hell. Some of them have found more humane Gods to worship, others are simply converts from all theology; but both alike they assure us that to have got rid of the sophistication of thinking they could feel any reverence or duty towards that impossible idol gave a tremendous happiness to their souls. Now, the idol of a worshipful spirit of Nature also leads to sophistication; and in souls that are religious and would also be scientific, the sophistication breeds a philosophical melancholy from which the first natural step of escape is the denial of the idol; and with the downfall of the idol, whatever lack of positive joyousness may remain, there comes also the downfall of the whimpering and cowering mood. With evil simply taken as such, men can make short work, for their relations with it then are only practical. It looms up no longer so spectrally, it loses all its haunting and perplexing significance as soon as the mind attacks the instances of it singly and ceases to worry about their derivation from the "one and only Power."

Here, then, on this stage of mere emancipation from monistic superstition, the would-be suicide may already get encouraging answers to his question about the worth of life. There are in most men instinctive springs of vitality that respond healthily when the burden of metaphysical and infinite responsibility rolls off. The certainty that you now *may* step out of life whenever you please, and that to do so is not blasphemous or monstrous, is itself an immense relief. The thought of suicide is now no longer a guilty challenge and obsession.

Meanwhile we can always stand it for twenty-four hours longer, if only to see what tomorrow's newspaper will contain or what the next postman will bring. But far deeper forces than this mere vital curiosity are arousable, even in the pessimistically-tending mind; for where the loving and admiring impulses are dead, the hating and fighting impulses will still respond to fit appeals. This evil which we feel so deeply is something which we can also help to overthrow, for its sources, now that no "Substance" or "Spirit" is behind them, are finite, and we can deal with each of them in turn. It is, indeed, a remarkable fact that sufferings and hardships do not, as a rule, abate the love of life; they seem, on the contrary, usually to give it a keener zest. The sovereign source of melancholy is repletion. Need and struggle are what excite and inspire us; our hour of triumph is what brings the void.

The sentiment of honor is a very penetrating thing. When you and I, for instance, realize how many innocent beasts have had to suffer in cattle-cars and slaughter-pens and lay down their lives that we might grow up, all fattened and clad, to sit together here in comfort and carry on this discourse, it does, indeed, put our relation to the Universe in a more solemn light. Are we not bound to do some self-denying service with our lives in return for all those lives upon which ours are built? To hear this question is to answer it in only one possible way, if one have a normally constituted heart!

Thus, then, we see that mere instinctive curiosity, pugnacity, and honor may make life on a purely naturalistic basis seem worth living from day to day to men who have cast away all metaphysics in order to get rid of hypochondria, but who are resolved to owe nothing as yet to religion and its more positive gifts. A poor halfway stage, some of you may be inclined to say; but at least you must grant it to be an honest stage; and no man should dare to speak meanly of these instincts which are our nature's best equipment, and to which religion herself must in the last resort address her own peculiar appeals.

Now I wish to make you feel that we have a right to believe that the physical order is only a partial order; we have a right to supplement it by an unseen spiritual order which we assume on trust, if only thereby life may seem to us better worth living again. But as such a trust will seem to some of you sadly mystical and execrably unscientific, I must first say a word or two to weaken the veto which you may consider that Science opposes to our act.

There is included in human nature an ingrained naturalism and materialism of mind which can only admit facts that are actually tangible. Of this sort of mind the entity called "Science" is the idol. Fondness for the word "scientist" is one of the notes by which you may know its votaries; and its short way of killing any opinion that it disbelieves in is to call it "unscientific." It must be granted that there is no slight excuse for this. Science has made such glorious leaps in the last three hundred years, and extended our knowledge of Nature so enormously both in general and in detail; men of science, moreover, have as a class displayed such admirable virtues, that it is no wonder if the worshippers of Science lose their head. In this very University, accordingly, I have heard more than one teacher say that all the fundamental conceptions of truth have already been found by Science, and that the future has only the details of the picture to fill in. But the slightest reflection on the real conditions will suffice to show how barbaric such notions are. They show such a lack of scientific imagination, that it is hard to see how one who is actively advancing any part of Science can make a mistake so crude. Think how many absolutely new scientific conceptions have arisen in our own generation, how many new problems have been formulated that were never thought of before, and then cast an eye upon the brevity of Science's career. It began with Galileo just three hundred years ago. For thinkers since Galileo, each informing his successor of what discoveries his own lifetime had seen achieved, might have passed the torch of Science into our hands as we sit here in this room. Indeed, for the matter of that, an audience much smaller than the present one, an audience of some five or six score people, if each person in it could speak for his own generation, would carry us away to the black unknown of the human species, to days without a document or monument to tell their tale. Is it credible that such a mushroom knowledge, such a growth overnight as this, can represent more than the minutest glimpse of what the Universe will really prove to be when adequately understood? No! Our Science is a drop, our ignorance a sea. Whatever else be certain, this at least is certain: that the world of our present natural knowledge is enveloped in a larger world of some sort of whose residual properties we at present can frame no positive idea.

Agnostic positivism, of course, admits this principle theoretically in the most cordial terms, but insists that we must not turn it to any practical use. We have no right, this doctrine tells us, to dream dreams, or suppose anything about the unseen part of the universe, merely because to do so may be for what we are pleased to call our highest interests. We must always wait for sensible evidence for our beliefs; and where such evidence is inaccessible we must frame no hypotheses whatever. Of course this is a safe enough position in abstraction. If a thinker had no stake in the unknown, no vital needs, to live or languish according to what the unseen world contained, a philosophic neutrality and refusal to believe either one way or the other would be his wisest cue. But, unfortunately, neutrality is not only inwardly difficult, it is also outwardly unrealizable, where our relations to an alternative are practical and vital. This is because, as the psychologists tell us, belief and doubt are living attitudes, and involve conduct on our part. Our only way, for example, of doubting, or refusing to believe, that a certain thing is, is continuing to act as if it were not. If, for instance, we refuse to believe that the room is getting cold, we must leave the windows open and light no fire just as if it still were warm. If I refuse to believe that you are worthy of my confidence, I must keep you uninformed of all my secrets just as if you were unworthy of the same. And similarly if, as the agnostics tell me, I must not believe that the world is divine, I can only express that refusal by declining ever to act distinctively as if it were so, which can only mean acting on certain critical occasions as if it were not so, or in an unmoral and irreligious way. There are, you see, inevitable occasions in life when inaction is a kind of action and must count as action, and when not to be *for* is to be practically *against.* And in all such cases strict and consistent neutrality is an unattainable thing.

And after all, isn't this duty of neutrality where only our inner interests would lead us to believe, the most ridiculous of commands? Isn't it sheer dogmatic folly to say that our inner interests *can* have no real connection with the forces that the hidden world *may* contain? In other cases, divinations based on inner interests have proved prophetic enough. Take Science herself! Without an imperious inner demand on our part for ideal, logical, and mathematical harmonies, we should never have attained to proving that such harmonies lie hidden between all the chinks and interstices of the crude natural world. Hardly a law has been established in Science, hardly a fact ascertained, that was not first sought after, often with sweat and blood, to gratify an inner need. Whence such needs come from we do not know; we find them in us, and biological psychology so far only classes them with Darwin's "accidental variations." But the inner need of believing that this world of nature is a sign of something more spiritual and eternal than itself is just as strong and authoritative in those who feel it, as the inner need of uniform laws of causation ever can be in a professionally scientific head. The toil of many generations has proved the latter need prophetic. Why *may* not the former one be prophetic, too? And if needs of ours outrun the visible universe, why may not that be a sign that an invisible universe is there? What, in short, has authority to *debar* us from trusting our religious demands? Science as such assuredly has no authority, for she can only say what is, not what is not; and the agnostic "thou shalt not believe without coercive sensible evidence" is simply an expression (free to any one to make) of private personal appetite for evidence of a certain peculiar kind.

Now, when I speak of trusting our religious demands, just what do I mean by "trusting"? Is the word to carry with it license to define in detail an invisible world and to anathematize and excommunicate those whose trust is different? Certainly not! Our faculties of belief were not primarily given us to make orthodoxies and heresies withal; they were given us to live by. And to trust our religious demands means first of all to live in the light of them, and to act as if the invisible world which they suggest were real. It is a fact of human nature that men can live and die by the help of a sort of faith that goes without a single dogma or definition. The bare assurance that this natural order is not ultimate but a mere sign or vision, the external staging of a many-storied universe, in which spiritual forces have the last word and are eternal; this bare assurance is to such men enough to make life seem worth living in spite of every contrary presumption suggested by its circumstances on the natural plane. Destroy this inner assurance, vague as it is, however, and all the light and radiance of existence is extinguished for these persons at a stroke. Often enough the wild-eyed look at life, the suicidal mood will then set in.

And now the application comes directly home to you and me. Probably to almost every one of us here the most adverse life would seem well worth living, if we only could be *certain* that our bravery and patience with it were terminating and eventuating and bearing fruit somewhere in an unseen spiritual world. But granting we are not certain, does it then follow that a bare trust in such a world is a fool's paradise and lubberland, or rather that it is a living attitude in which we are free to indulge? Well, we are free to trust at our own risks anything that is not impossible and that can bring analogies to bear in its behalf. That the world of physics is probably not absolute, all the converging multitude of arguments that make in favor of idealism tend to prove. And that our whole physical life may lie soaking in a spiritual atmosphere, a dimension of Being that we at present have no organ for apprehending, is vividly suggested to us by the analogy of the life of our domestic animals. Our dogs, for example, are *in* our human life but not *of* it. They witness hourly the outward body of events whose inner meaning cannot, by any possible operation, be revealed to their intelligence, events in which they themselves often play the cardinal part. My terrier bites a teasing boy, for example, and the father demands damages. The dog may be present at every step of the negotiations, and see the money paid without an inkling of what it all means, without a suspicion that it has anything to do with *him*. And he never *can* know in his natural dog's life. Or take another case which used greatly to impress me in my medical-student days. Consider a poor dog whom they are vivisecting in a laboratory. He lies strapped on a board and shrieking at his executioners, and to his own dark consciousness is literally in a sort of hell. He cannot see a single redeeming ray in the whole business; and yet all these diabolical-seeming events are usually controlled by human intentions with which, if his poor benighted mind could only be made to catch a glimpse of them, all that is heroic in him would religiously acquiesce. Healing truth, relief to future sufferings of beast and man are to be bought by them. It is genuinely a process of redemption. Lying on his back on the board there he is performing a function incalculably higher than any prosperous canine life admits of; and yet, of the whole performance, this function is the one portion that must remain absolutely beyond his ken. Now turn from this to the life of man. In the dog's life we see the world invisible to him because we live in both worlds. In human life, although we only see our world, and his within it, yet encompassing both these worlds a still wider world may be there as unseen by us as our world is by him; and to believe in that world *may* be the most essential function that our lives in this world have to perform. But "*may* be! *may* be!" one now hears the positivist contemptuously exclaim; "what use can a scientific life have for maybes?" Well, I reply, the "scientific" life itself has much to do with maybes, and human life at large has everything to do with them. So far as man stands for anything, and is productive or originative at all, his entire vital function may be said to be to deal with maybes. Not a victory is gained, not a deed of faithfulness or courage is done, except upon a maybe; not a service, not a sally of generosity, not a scientific exploration or experiment or text-book, that *may* not be a mistake. It is only by risking our persons from one hour to another that we live at all. And often enough our faith beforehand in an uncertified result *is the only thing that makes the result come true.* Suppose, for instance, that you are climbing a mountain and have worked yourself into a position from which the only escape is by a terrible leap. Have faith that you can successfully make it, and your feet are nerved to its accomplishment. But mistrust yourself, and think of all the sweet things you have heard the scientists say of *maybes*, and you will hesitate so long that, at last, all unstrung and trembling, and launching yourself in a moment of despair, you roll in the abyss. In such a case (and it belongs to an enormous class), the part of wisdom as well as of courage is to *believe what is in the line of your needs*, for only by the belief is the need fulfilled. Refuse to believe, and you shall indeed be right, for you shall irretrievably perish. But believe, and again you shall be right, for you shall save yourself. You *make* one or the other of two possible universes true by your trust or mistrust, both universes having been only *maybes,* in this particular, before you contributed your act.

Now, it appears to me that the question whether life is worth living is subject to conditions logically much like these. It does, indeed, depend on you the liver. If you surrender to the nightmare view and crown the evil edifice by your own suicide, you have indeed made a picture totally black. Pessimism, completed by your act, is true beyond a doubt, so far as your world goes. Your mistrust of life has removed whatever worth your own enduring existence might have given to it; and now, throughout the whole sphere of possible influence of that existence, the mistrust has proved itself to have had divining power. But suppose, on the other hand, that instead of giving way to the nightmare view you cling to it that this world is not the *ultimatum.*

Suppose, however thickly evils crowd upon you, that your unconquerable subjectivity proves to be their match, and that you find a more wonderful joy than any passive pleasure can bring in trusting ever in the larger whole. Have you not now *made* life worth living on *these* terms? What sort of a thing would life really be, with *your* qualities ready for a tussle with it, if it only brought fair weather and gave these higher faculties of yours no scope? Please remember that optimism and pessimism are definitions of the world, and that our own reactions on the world, small as they are in bulk, are integral parts of the whole thing, and necessarily help to determine the definition. They may even be the decisive elements in determining the definition. A large mass can have its unstable equilibrium overturned by the addition of a feather's weight. A long phrase may have its sense reversed by the addition of the three letters, *n, o, t.* This life *is* worth living, we can say, *since it is what we make it, from the moral point of view*, and we are determined to make it from that point of view, so far as we have anything to do with it, a success.

Now, in this description of faiths that verify themselves I have assumed that our faith in an invisible order is what inspires those efforts and that patience of ours that make this visible order good for moral men. Our faith in the seen world's goodness (goodness now meaning fitness for successful moral and religious life) has verified itself by leaning on our faith in the unseen world. But will our faith in the unseen world similarly verify itself? Who knows?

Once more it is a case of *maybe.* And once more *maybes* are the essence of the situation. I confess that I do not see why the very existence of an invisible world *may* not in part depend on the personal response which any one of us may make to the religious appeal. God himself, in short, *may* draw vital strength and increase of very being from our fidelity. For my own part, I do not know what the sweat and blood and tragedy of this life mean, if they mean anything short of this. If this life be not a real fight, in which something is eternally gained for the Universe by success, it is no better than a game of private theatricals from which one may withdraw at will. But it *feels* like a real fight; as if there were something really wild in the Universe which we, with all our idealities and faithfulnesses, are needed to redeem. And first of all to redeem our own hearts from atheisms and fears. For such a half-wild, half-saved universe our nature is adapted. The deepest thing in our nature in this Binnenleben (buried life of human beings), this dumb region of the heart in which we dwell alone with our willingnesses and unwillingnesses, our faiths and fears. As through the cracks and crannies of subterranean caverns the earth's bosom exudes its waters, which then form the fountain-heads of springs, so in these crepuscular depths of personality the sources of all our outer deeds and decisions take their rise. Here is our deepest organ of communication with the nature of things; and compared with these concrete movements of our soul all abstract statements and scientific arguments, the veto, for example, which the strict positivist pronounces upon our faith, sound to us like mere chatterings of the teeth. For here possibilities, not finished facts, are the realities with which we have actively to deal; and to quote my friend William Salter, of the Philadelphia Ethical Society, "the essence of courage is to stake one's life on a possibility, so the essence of faith is to believe that the possibility exists."

These, then, are my last words to you: Be not afraid of life. Believe that life is worth living, and your belief will help create the fact. The "scientific proof" that you are right may not be clear before the day of judgment (or some stage of Being which that expression may serve to symbolize) is reached. But the faithful fighters of this hour, or the beings that then and there will represent them, may then turn to the faint-hearted, who here decline to go on, with words like those with which Henry IV greeted the tardy Crillon after a great victory had been gained: "Hang yourself, brave Crillon! We fought at Arques, and you were not there."

Bertrand Russell

FATE IS SUBDUED BY THE MIND

To Dr. Faustus in his study, Mephistopheles told the history of the Creation, saying:

> "The endless praises of the choirs of angels had begun to grow wearisome; for, after all, did he not deserve their praise? Had he not given them endless joy? Would it not be more amusing to obtain undeserved praise, to be worshipped by beings whom he tortured?" He smiled inwardly, and resolved that the great drama should be performed.
>
> "For countless ages the hot nebula whirled aimlessly through space. At length it began to take shape, the central mass threw off planets, the planets cooled, boiling seas and burning mountains heaved and tossed, from black masses of cloud hot sheets of rain deluged the barely solid crust. And now the first germ of life grew in the depths of the ocean, and developed rapidly in the fructifying warmth into vast forest trees, huge ferns springing from the damp mould, sea monsters breeding, fighting, devouring, and passing away. And from the monsters, as the play unfolded itself, Man was born, with the power of thought, the knowledge of good and evil, and the cruel thirst for worship. And Man saw that all is passing in this mad, monstrous world, that all is struggling to snatch, at any cost, a few brief moments of life before Death's inexorable decree. And Man said: 'There is a hidden purpose, could we but fathom it, and the purpose is good; for we must reverence something, and in the visible world there is nothing worthy of reverence.' And Man stood aside from the struggle, resolving that God intended harmony to come out of chaos by human efforts. And when he followed the instincts which God had transmitted to him from his ancestry of beasts of prey, he called it Sin, and asked God to forgive him. But he doubted whether he could be justly forgiven, until he invented a divine Plan by which God's wrath was to have been appeased. And seeing the present was bad, he made it yet worse, that thereby the future might be better. And he gave God thanks for the strength that enabled him to forgo even the joys that were possible. And God smiled; and when he saw that Man had become perfect in renunciation and worship, he sent another sun through the sky, which crashed into Man's sun; and all returned again to nebula.
>
> "'Yes,' he murmured, 'it was a good play; I will have it performed again.'"

Such, in outline, but even more purposeless, more void of meaning, is the world which Science presents for our belief. Amid such a world, if anywhere, our ideals henceforward must find a home. That Man is the product of causes which had no prevision of the end they were achieving; that his origin, his growth, his hopes and fears, his loves and his beliefs, are but the outcome of accidental collocations of atoms; that no fire, no heroism, no intensity of thought and feeling, can preserve an individual life beyond the grave; that all the labors of the ages, all the devotion, all the inspiration, all the noonday brightness of human genius, are destined to extinction in the vast death of the solar system, and that the whole temple of Man's achievement must inevitably be buried beneath the debris of a universe in ruins—all these things, if not quite beyond dispute, are yet so nearly certain, that no philosophy which rejects them can hope to stand. Only within the scaffolding of these truths, only on the firm foundation of unyielding despair, can the soul's habitation henceforth be safely built.

How, in such an alien and inhuman world, can so powerless a creature as Man preserve his aspirations untarnished? A strange mystery it is that Nature, omnipotent but blind, in the revolutions of her secular hurryings through the abysses of space, has brought forth at last a child, subject still to her power, but gifted with sight, with knowledge of good and evil, with the capacity of judging all the works of his unthinking Mother. In spite of Death, the mark and seal of the parental control, Man is yet free, during his brief years, to examine, to criticize, to know, and in imagination to create. To him alone, in the world with which he is acquainted, this freedom belongs; and in this lies his superiority to the resistless forces that control his outward life.

The savage, like ourselves, feels the oppression of his impotence before the powers of Nature; but having in himself nothing that he respects more than Power, he is willing to prostrate himself before his gods, without inquiring whether they are worthy of his worship. Pathetic and very terrible is the long history of cruelty and torture, of degradation and human sacrifice, endured in the hope of placating the jealous gods: surely, the trembling believer thinks, when what is most precious has been freely given, their lust for blood must be appeased, and more will not be required. Since the independence of ideals is not yet acknowledged, Power may be freely worshipped, and receive an unlimited respect, despite its wanton infliction of pain.

But gradually, as morality grows bolder, the claim of the ideal world begins to be felt; and worship, if it is not to cease, must be given to gods of another kind than those created by the savage. Some, though they feel the demands of the ideal, will still consciously reject them, still urging that naked Power is worthy of worship. Such also is the attitude of those who, in our own day, base their morality upon the struggle for survival, maintaining that the survivors are necessarily the fittest. But others, not content with an answer so repugnant to the moral sense, will adopt the position which we have become accustomed to regard as specially religious, maintaining that, in some hidden manner, the world of fact is really harmonious with the world of ideals. Thus Man creates God, all-powerful and all-good, the mystic unity of what is and what should be.

But the world of fact, after all, is not good; and, in submitting our judgment to it, there is an element of slavishness from which our thoughts must be purged. For in all things it is well to exalt the dignity of Man, by freeing him as far as possible from the tyranny of non-human Power. When we have realized that Power is largely bad, that man, with his knowledge of good and evil, is but a helpless atom in a world which has no such knowledge, the choice is again presented to us: Shall we worship Force, or shall we worship Goodness? Shall our God exist and be evil, or shall he be recognized as the creation of our own conscience?

The answer to this question is very momentous, and affects profoundly our whole morality. The worship of Force, to which Carlyle and Nietzsche and the creed of Militarism have accustomed us, is the result of failure to maintain our own ideals against a hostile universe: it is itself a prostrate submission to evil. If strength indeed is to be respected, let us respect rather the strength of those who refuse that false "recognition of facts" which fails to recognize that facts are often bad. Let us admit that, in the world we know, there are many things that would be better otherwise, and that the ideals to which we do and must adhere are not realized in the realm of matter. Let us preserve our respect for truth, for beauty, for the ideal of perfection which life does not permit us to attain, though none of these things meet with the approval of the unconscious universe. If Power is bad, as it seems to be, let us reject it from our hearts. In this lies Man's true freedom: in determination to worship only the god created by our own love of the good, to respect only the heaven which inspires the insight of our best moments. In action, in desire, we must submit perpetually to the tyranny of outside forces; but in thought, in aspiration, we are free, free from our fellow-men, free from the petty planet on which our bodies impotently crawl, free even, while we live, from the tyranny of death. Let us learn, then, that energy of faith which enables us to live constantly in the vision of the good; and let us descend, in action, into the world of fact, with that vision always before us.

When first the opposition of fact and ideal grows fully visible, a spirit of fiery revolt, of fierce hatred of the gods, seems necessary to the assertion of freedom. To defy with Promethean constancy a hostile universe, to keep its evil always in view, always actively hated, to refuse no pain that the malice of Power can invent, appears to be the duty of all who will not bow before the inevitable. But indignation is still a bondage, for it compels our thoughts to be occupied with an evil world; and in the fierceness of desire from which rebellion springs there is a kind of self-assertion which it is necessary for the wise to overcome. Indignation is a submission of our thoughts, but not of our desires; the Stoic freedom in which wisdom consists is found in the submission of our desires, but not of our thoughts. From the submission of our desires springs the virtue of resignation; from the freedom of our thoughts springs the whole world of art and philosophy, and the vision of beauty by which, at last, we half reconquer the reluctant world. But the vision of beauty is possible only to unfettered contemplation, to thoughts not weighted by the load of eager wishes; and thus Freedom comes only to those who no longer ask of life that it shall yield them any of those personal goods that are subject to the mutations of Time.

But there is in resignation a further good element: even real goods, when they are unattainable, ought not to be fretfully desired. To every man comes, sooner or later, the great renunciation. For the young, there is nothing unattainable; a good thing desired with the whole force of a passionate will, and yet impossible, is to them not credible. Yet, by death, by illness, by poverty, or by the voice of duty, we must learn, each one of us, that the world was not made for us, and that, however beautiful may be the things we crave, Fate may nevertheless forbid them. It is the part of courage, when misfortune comes, to bear without repining the ruin of our hopes, to turn away our thoughts from vain regrets. This degree of submission to Power is not only just and right: it is the very gate of wisdom.

But passive renunciation is not the whole of wisdom; for not by renunciation alone can we build a temple for the worship of our own ideals. Haunting foreshadowings of the temple appear in the realm of imagination, in music, in architecture, in the untroubled kingdom of reason, and in the golden sunset magic of lyrics, where beauty shines and glows, remote from the touch of sorrow, remote from the fear of change, remote from the failures and disenchantments of the world of fact. In the contemplation of these things the vision of heaven will shape itself in our hearts, giving at once a touchstone to judge the world about us, and an inspiration by which to fashion to our needs whatever is not incapable of serving as a stone in the sacred temple.

Except for those rare spirits that are born without sin, there is a cavern of darkness to be traversed before that temple can be entered. The gate of the cavern is despair, and its floor is paved with the gravestones of abandoned hopes. There Self must die; there the eagerness, the greed of untamed desire must be slain, for only so can the soul be freed from the empire of Fate. But out of the cavern the Gate of Renunciation leads again to the daylight of wisdom, by whose radiance a new insight, a new joy, a new tenderness, shine forth to gladden the pilgrim's heart.

When, without the bitterness of impotent rebellion, we have learnt both to resign ourselves to the outward rules of Fate and to recognize that the non-human world is unworthy of our worship, it becomes possible at last so to transform and refashion the unconscious universe, so to transmute it in the crucible of imagination, that a new image of shining gold replaces the old idol of clay. In all the multiform facts of the world—in the visual shapes of trees and mountains and clouds, in the events of the life of man, even in the very omnipotence of Death—the insight of creative idealism can find the reflection of a beauty which its own thoughts first made. In this way mind asserts its subtle mastery over the thoughtless forces of Nature. The more evil the material with which it deals, the more thwarting to untrained desire, the greater is its achievement in inducing the reluctant rock to yield up its hidden treasures, the prouder its victory in compelling the opposing forces to swell the pageant of its triumph. Of all the arts, Tragedy is the proudest, the most triumphant; for it builds its shining citadel in the very center of the enemy's country, on the very summit of his highest mountain; from its impregnable watchtowers, his camps and arsenals, his columns and forts, are all revealed; within its walls the free life continues, while the legions of Death and Pain and Despair, and all the servile captains of tyrant Fate, afford the burghers of that dauntless city new spectacles of beauty. Happy those sacred ramparts, thrice happy the dwellers on that all-seeing eminence. Honor to those brave warriors who, through countless ages of warfare, have preserved for us the priceless heritage of liberty, and have kept undefiled by sacrilegious invaders the home of the unsubdued.

But the beauty of Tragedy does but make visible a quality which, in more or less obvious shapes, is present always and everywhere in life. In the spectacle of Death, in the endurance of intolerable pain, and in the irrevocableness of a vanished past, there is a sacredness, an overpowering awe, a feeling of the vastness, the depth, the inexhaustible mystery of existence, in which, as by some strange marriage of pain, the sufferer is bound to the world by bonds of sorrow. In these moments of insight, we lose all eagerness of temporary desire, all struggling and striving for petty ends, all care for the little trivial things that, to a superficial view, make up the common life of day by day; we see, surrounding the narrow raft illumined by the flickering light of human comradeship, the dark ocean on whose rolling waves we toss for a brief hour; from the great night without, a chill blast breaks in upon our refuge; all the loneliness of humanity amid hostile forces is concentrated upon the individual soul, which must struggle alone, with what of courage it can command, against the whole weight of a universe that cares nothing for its hopes and fears. Victory, in this struggle with the powers of darkness, is the true baptism into the glorious company of heroes, the true initiation into the overmastering beauty of human existence. From that awful encounter of the soul with the outer world, enunciation, wisdom, and charity are born; and with their birth a new life begins. To take into the inmost shrine of the soul the irresistible forces whose puppets we seem to be—Death and change, the irrevocableness of the past, and the powerlessness of Man before the blind hurry of the universe from vanity to vanity—to feel these things and know them is to conquer them.

This is the reason why the Past has such magical power. The beauty of its motionless and silent pictures is like the enchanted purity of late autumn, when the leaves, though one breath would make them fall, still glow against the sky in golden glory. The Past does not change or strive; like Duncan, after life's fitful fever it sleeps well; what was eager and grasping, what was petty and transitory, has faded away, the things that were beautiful and eternal shine out of it like stars in the night. Its beauty, to a soul not worthy of it, is unendurable; but to a soul which has conquered Fate it is the key of religion.

The life of Man, viewed outwardly, is but a small thing in comparison with the forces of Nature. The slave is doomed to worship Time and Fate and Death, because they are greater than anything he finds in himself, and because all his thoughts are of things which they devour. To abandon the struggle for private happiness, to expel all eagerness of temporary desire, to burn with passion for eternal things—this is emancipation, and this is the free man's worship. And this liberation is effected by a contemplation of Fate; for Fate itself is subdued by the mind which leaves nothing to be purged by the purifying fire of Time.

United with his fellow-men by the strongest of all ties, the tie of a common doom, the free man finds that a new vision is with him always, shedding over every daily task the light of love. The life of Man is a long march through the night, surrounded by invisible foes, tortured by weariness and pain, towards a goal that few can hope to reach, and where none may tarry long. One by one, as they march, our comrades vanish from our sight, seized by the silent orders of omnipotent Death. Very brief is the time in which we can help them, in which their happiness or misery is decided. Be it ours to shed sunshine on their path, to lighten their sorrows by the balm of sympathy, to give them the pure joy of a never-tiring affection, to strengthen failing courage, to instill faith in hours of despair. Let us not weigh in grudging scales their merits and demerits, but let us think only of their need—of the sorrows, the difficulties, perhaps the blindnesses, that make the misery of their lives; let us remember that they are fellow-sufferers in the same darkness, actors in the same tragedy as ourselves. And so, when their day is over, when their good and their evil have become eternal by the immortality of the past, be it ours to feel that, where they suffered, where they failed, no deed of ours was the cause; but wherever a spark of the divine fire kindled in their hearts, we were ready with encouragement, with sympathy, with brave words in which high courage glowed.

Brief and powerless is Man's life; on him and all his race the slow, sure doom falls pitiless and dark. Blind to good and evil, reckless of destruction, omnipotent matter rolls on its relentless way; for Man, condemned today to lose his dearest, tomorrow himself to pass through the gate of darkness, it remains only to cherish, ere yet the blow falls, the lofty thoughts that ennoble his little day; disdaining the coward terrors of the slave of Fate, to worship at the shrine that his own hands have built; undismayed by the empire of chance, to preserve a mind free from the wanton tyranny that rules his outward life; proudly defiant of the irresistible forces that tolerate, for a moment, his knowledge and his condemnation, to sustain alone, a weary but unyielding Atlas, the world that his own ideals have fashioned despite the trampling march of unconscious power.